Making Media

D1291244

Making Media

Production, Practices, and Professions

Edited by
Mark Deuze and Mirjam Prenger

Amsterdam University Press

Cover illustration: Artwork by Wineke Gartz

Cover design: Gijs Mathijs Ontwepers, Amsterdam
Lay-out: Crius Group, Hulshout

ISBN   978 94 6298 811 8
e-ISBN   978 90 4854 015 0
DOI   10.5117/9789462988118
NUR   810

Table of Contents

Introduction

1. Making Media: Production, Practices, and Professions   13
   Mark Deuze and Mirjam Prenger

Production

Research

2. Media Industries: A Decade in Review   31
   Jennifer Holt and Alisa Perren

3. Media Production Research and the Challenge of Normativity   45
   David Lee and Anna Zoellner

4. Access and Mistrust in Media Industries Research   61
   Patrick Vonderau

5. Cultural and Creative Industries and the Political Economy of Communication   73
   Bernard Miège

6. The Platformization of Making Media   85
   David Nieborg and Thomas Poell (with Mark Deuze)

Economics and Management

7. The Disappearing Product and the New Intermediaries   99
   Chris Bilton

8. Value Production in Media Industries and Everyday Life   111
   Göran Bolin

9. Transformation and Innovation of Media Business Models   121
   Mikko Villi and Robert G. Picard

10. Shifts in Consumer Engagement and Media Business Models   133
      Sylvia Chan-Olmsted and Rang Wang

11. Media Industries' Management Characteristics and Challenges in a Converging Digital World   147
      Paolo Faustino and Eli Noam

Policy

12. Global Media Industries and Media Policy   163
      Terry Flew and Nicolas Suzor

13. Media Concentration in the Age of the Internet and Mobile Phones   175
      Dwayne Winseck

Practices

Innovation

14. Making (Sense of) Media Innovations   193
      Arne H. Krumsvik, Stefania Milan, Niamh Ní Bhroin, and Tanja Storsul

15. Start-up Ecosystems Between Affordance Networks, Symbolic Form, and Cultural Practice   207
      Stefan Werning

Work Conditions

16. Precarity in Media Work   223
      Penny O'Donnell and Lawrie Zion

17. Making It in a Freelance World   235
      Nicole S. Cohen

18. Diversity and Opportunity in the Media Industries   247
      Doris Ruth Eikhof and Stevie Marsden

19. Labour and the Next Internet   259
    Vincent Mosco

Affective Labour

20. Affective Labour and Media Work   275
    Eugenia Siapera

21. Affective Qualities of Creative Labour   287
    Zelmarie Cantillon and Sarah Baker

22. A Business of One or Nurturing the Craft: Who are You?   297
    Ilana Gershon and Mark Deuze

Professions

Music

23. Music in Times of Streaming: Transformation and Debate   309
    Sofia Johansson

24. Popular Music, Streaming, and Promotional Media: Enduring and
    Emerging Industrial Logics   321
    Leslie M. Meier

Television

25. Show Me the Money: How Revenue Strategies Change the Creative
    Possibilities of Internet-Distributed Television   337
    Amanda D. Lotz

26. Flexibility, Innovation, and Precarity in the Television Industry   347
    Paul Dwyer

Social Media

27. Creator Management in the Social Media Entertainment Industry   363
    David Craig

28. #Dreamjob: The Promises and Perils of a Creative Career in Social Media   375
    Brooke Erin Duffy

Public Relations and Advertising

29. Redefining Advertising in a Changing Media Landscape   389
    Sara Rosengren

30. Perceptions and Realities of the Integration of Advertising and Public
    Relations   399
    Dustin Supa

Digital Games

31. Game Production Logics at Work: Convergence and Divergence   413
    Aphra Kerr

32. Reflections on the Shifts and Swerves of the Global Games Industry   427
    Casey O'Donnell

Journalism

33. 'It Never Stops': The Implicit Norm of Working Long Hours in
    Entrepreneurial Journalism   441
    Amanda Brouwers and Tamara Witschge

34. Transmedia Production: Key Steps in Creating a Storyworld   453
    Ana Serrano Tellería (with Mirjam Prenger)

Conclusion

35. Making Media: Observations and Futures   465
    Henry Jenkins, Elizabeth Saad Corrêa, Anthony Fung, and Tanja Bosch

Author Biographies   481

Introduction

1. Making Media: Production, Practices, and Professions

Mark Deuze and Mirjam Prenger

Introduction

What does it mean to make media professionally? To be a journalist, a marketing communicator, advertising creative, or public relations practitioner? What is it like to work in film or television, to develop games, to be a musician, or manage a record label for a living? It is safe to say that the answers to these questions vary greatly. Whereas the various fields of cultural work used to be considered in terms of their specifics, contemporary scholarship acknowledges the great diversity and hybridization of practices and careers that make up formerly distinct professions in the media industries. Profound transformations are afoot in the areas of technology and digitalization, management and economics, culture and audience preferences, as well as in the role politics and policymaking plays in both enabling and constraining the ways in which media industries and professionals can do their work and earn a living.

This book aims to investigate, illustrate, and critically analyse how the various technological, political, economic, and social transformations are affecting the media industries as well as the people professionally making media. The goal is to provide those interested in studying media industries and production, and those considering a career in the media a clear grasp of the relevant topics and themes, as well as an understanding of what shapes media work. The authors gathered in this volume provide a comprehensive review of the scholarly research on making media, delving specifically into emerging themes such as the emotional quality of media work, the radical changes affecting the business operations of media firms, and ways in which precarity determines the lived experience of media professionals across a variety of media industries. In doing so, we endeavour to bring into conversation different domains of theory and practice in media industries: political economy and cultural studies; the sociology of work and psychology of professional decision-making; production and management studies.

In order to grasp the many developments shaping the creative work media professionals do, we have structured this book in three sections: production, practices, and professions. Media *production* considers issues at play within, across, and around the institutions and forces that create our media, our information, and our culture: management and economics, media policy, markets, consumers (Hesmondhalgh,

2006; Paterson, Lee, Saha, & Zoellner, 2015). Media *practices* involve the various ways in which media professionals make media (and, importantly, how they 'make it work' in the media industries): innovation, working conditions, affective labour. Media *professions* are those more or less demarcated fields of work that make up professional life in the media industries, including (but not limited to): journalism, advertising, marketing communications, public relations, digital games, television, music and recording, and social media entertainment.

Media production

Technology has always been an amplifier and accelerator of media industry trends, just as developments in media making have inspired and supercharged the development of technology. However, in recent decades there has been a marked shift from consumer electronics to information technology as the most powerful sectoral force shaping how media content gets produced, distributed, and experienced. At the heart of the changes within and across the media industries is the role of the internet, platforms, and connected devices such as smartphones. In only a short time these technologies and the businesses that thrive within these infrastructures – the so-called new intermediaries, from hardware manufacturers (Samsung, Apple) and software developers (Microsoft, Alphabet, Tencent) to platforms (Facebook, Google, YouTube) and online marketplaces and services (Netflix, Amazon, Spotify) – have uprooted and disrupted the ways in which legacy media operate. Generally, it is safe to say that these technologies and corporations have nestled themselves firmly in-between media users and producers, making each of them co-dependent on their products and platforms for formatting, distributing, accessing, and sharing media content.

As media institutions (and the people working across the media industries) adapt to this new reality, the values, expectations, and structures of the digital economy come to co-determine creative decisions and processes. Automation, data, and algorithms play an increasing role in all forms of media work, acting as demand predictors as well as content creators (Napoli, 2014). The digital technological context of media work means that more focus is placed on user-generated content and consumer engagement, as well as on generating (and using) data about users and consumers of products and services online.

As institutions across the media industries respond to (and, in part, join forces with) the new cultural intermediaries, they continue to computerize and digitalize all elements of the production cycle of making media. Sometimes, this means that entire divisions, departments or standalone companies are formed, and new professional roles emerge – such as content manager, engagement editor, data analyst, and digital editor. In other instances, the emerging technological context is implemented to primarily facilitate existing work and production processes – generally leading to job cuts and other 'doing more work with fewer workers' deleterious managerial interventions. To some extent, all of this means that the standard ways of doing things can change quite substantially in the industry, while, at the same time, some companies use newer technologies primarily to maintain and streamline existing structures and production cycles.

Key is that processes of disruption and consolidation co-exist, in essence liquefying and solidifying media production at the same time.

Media practices

In terms of the actual work of making media, the emerging technological context of media work diminishes the cost of the production of media. Media companies large and small struggle to adapt, as they tend to be stuck in 'heavy' material contexts consisting of expensive studio complexes and associated equipment, dedicated newsrooms, content management systems, and other proprietary software packages and hardware configurations designed for particular uses within specific companies and industries.

The immaterial context of media organization and management similarly comes under pressure from technological changes. Legacy media are historically oriented toward specific schedules associated with platform-specific production processes benchmarked by deadlines, around which other societal systems – such as companies, government institutions, and political parties – traditionally organize their operations (as expressed through press conferences, national and global release schedules of films and games, and routinized cycles in advertising determined by events and seasons). However, the digital realm introduces a new media logic, one that seems oblivious to industrial-age schedules or more or less predictable production cycles, forcing organizations to aggressively replace 'analogue' production practices with 'digital' ones. The digital economy tends to be sold as one that is 'always on' and therefore managing a permanent publication presence is of the essence to any media firm or professional wishing to stand out. In the process, new technologies (and associated values and practices) are introduced to manage an organization of work that is supposedly more flexible, nimble, and (most importantly) always ready to go.

In manufacturing, the process of acceleration (while cost-cutting) is known as the managerial philosophy of 'just-in-time' production: the production of goods to meet customer demand exactly in time, quality, and quantity. This approach is also part and parcel of much media work, where continuous deadlines have become the norm. Furthermore, media practices are disjointed because of the increasingly networked nature of the production cycle – where you can be part of a product, process, or professional peer group without necessarily being in the same building, city, or even country. As media industries diversify their activities across multiple media and markets, media professionals are expected to cultivate cross-media proficiencies and multi-skill (rather than honing their craft in one specific area of expertise).

Key is that media practices are both accelerating and being supplemented by a wide array of new roles, skills, and competences, contributing to an ongoing destabilization process both felt and experienced by practitioners.

Media professions

What all of this worldwide shuffling of the cards with which media makers have to play means for media professions, is that the boundaries between formerly distinct peer-based communities of practice are blurring. Media work, once located in institutions where contracted labourers would produce content under informal, yet highly structured working conditions, today is best typified by a lived experience of precarity and fragmentation. As freelancing, part-timing, temping, or otherwise contingent work becomes the norm across journalism, film and television, games, music and recording, advertising, and social (entertainment) media, practitioners increasingly move within and between professions. Journalists cross-subsidize their work with copywriting for commercial purposes, marketing agencies set up fully fledged newsrooms to provide quality content to clients, musicians earn a living by partnering with brands, film and television makers cross industry lines left and right, and those most versatile in computer skills can be found anywhere in the industry – not just in digital studios.

At the same time, a media professionals' primary way of making sense of him or herself is through recursive self-reference, particularly when it comes to those professionals working inside more or less established companies. More often than not, this means that the various developments affecting the industry – such as emerging technologies, new business models, national and international media policies, and changing audience tastes, habits, and influences – are perceived as coming from the outside, and the digital future is therefore seen as something happening to media industries and professionals (rather than, for example, also occurring because of the way they function and work). For media practitioners whose identities are tied to the specific way they perform (or used to perform) their work, these changes can be experienced as a profound threat to their profession. As a consequence, there can be a hesitation in embracing the many new opportunities, affordances, and convergences that the disruption and transformation of the media industries offer.

There is no formal entry requirement to any kind of media work – although students around the world flock to media degrees like bees to honey, expecting a perfect gateway to what seems like a highly attractive industry. Simultaneously, institutions for higher education worldwide provide a wide range of (skills-based) media production tracks and degrees, offering the promise of employment in an exciting, dynamic, and high-profile field. Media industries are overpopulated with young, passionate and hard-working men and women, usually living and working in the heart of the city in close proximity to each other, their work, and sources of entertainment. However, what often remains unseen is the ambiguous reality behind the glossy, attractive image of media work: the enormous amount of emotional labour that is required to 'stay in' the industry, the ability to handle rejection, stress, and permanent impermanence, the need to constantly perform and present yourself in the best possible light in order to succeed, and having to financially and emotionally cope with being un(der)paid while trying to 'make it work' in an unforgiving climate.

The informal nature and relative ease of getting into the industry furthermore belie its highly complex, bureaucratic, computerized, and formulaic nature. Often the lofty ideal of self-actualization through meaningful creative work suffers as media professionals experience boredom, frustrated development, and feelings of powerlessness (Hesmondhalgh & Baker, 2011, p. 39). The informality of media work is a structural feature, championed by both employees and employers as a liberating element privileging creativity and innovation, while simultaneously functioning as a highly effective de-politicizing device, as few media workers find time, motivation, or social support to mobilize against exploitative labour arrangements (McRobbie, 2016).

Key is that the work of making media belongs at once to a clearly recognizable set of distinct industries, practices, and professions, while, at the same time, it can be considered to be transforming, destabilizing, and even de-professionalizing (Witschge & Nygren, 2009) in the process.

Main trends in making media

Surveying the fast-growing literature on what making media professionally is like, interviewing and observing media workers, and teaching media production offers excellent data to synthesize the consequences of the aforementioned changes in media making. This corpus has been subjected to a principal component analysis (PCA), a technique used in statistics to recognize patterns in a dataset by organizing the variance hierarchically, thereby only selecting those components that display the greatest variance for further analysis. In social theory – particularly in the work of Luhmann (1990) – principal components are seen as essential constituents of social systems that 'transform themselves into themselves' (Mingers, 2003, p. 404). In other words: a principal component is something – a trend, a concept, or a specific set of circumstances – that all practitioners who make media professionally experience in one way or another, whether in journalism, advertising, marketing communications, public relations, digital game development, film and television, music and recording, or social media work.

In operationalizing the concept of principal components, the distinctive role that specific trends, concepts, or circumstances play in making media is the key to identifying them. We identified nine principal components: collapse, hybridity, affordance, power, flexibility, precarity, entrepreneurship, agency, and affect. We will briefly discuss each concept, recognizing how these developments, at times, conjure contradictory experiences for media professionals.

Collapse

There is an overall sense of collapse across the media industries: a collapse of parts, units, functions, roles, business and revenue models, for example. Whether real or perceived, there is a prevailing sense and discourse that traditional ways of doing things do not work (anymore) in the digital age. Particularly when it comes to business models, the relative stability of advertising and sales has collapsed into online (and offline) business models that combine revenue streams from multiple sources, cultivate and commodify relations with consumers, and bypass media producers altogether in order to co-create with media users (as citizen journalists, influencers, and productive fans). At the same time, the rapid adoption of digital devices and platforms as the go-to technologies for accessing and experiencing media fundamentally altered the habits of audiences, collapsing the categories of consuming and producing media. Collapse is also present in the distinctly 'making' aspects of media making, as genres, storytelling formats, and creative practices collapse in favour of hybrid or hybridized media products and production processes. Everywhere we see an ongoing convergence of different domains, sectors, and disciplines within and across the media industries, bringing new challenges for managing media firms and production processes.

Hybridity

Media products become increasingly hybridized under conditions of collapse, and are difficult to place into categories that can be effectively isolated and subsequently micro-managed. Combined with the increasingly promotional role of media content, this has caused boundaries between professions and practices to blur. The rise of branded content and native advertising (i.e. advertising in the form of editorial content) in journalistic media, for instance, has blurred the distinction between journalism and advertising, just as the distinction between authentic content and paid-for experiences and opinions can be hard to make in social media entertainment (cf. YouTubers), and a musician's live performance can simultaneously be a promotion of a product or a brand.

Hybridization has implications for media makers, who must be simultaneously generalists and specialists, combining the command of one profession with knowledge of a host of others. Media makers face pressures to combine particular activities associated with making – such as gathering, selecting, curating, producing, editing, writing, filming, designing, coding, so on and so forth – with work to do in the areas of the promotion and distribution of media content. For many, if not most media workers, making media increasingly coincides with distributing, promoting, and selling media, partly because their livelihood depends on it, in part because this is something employers expect, and also because the aforementioned collapse of distinct departments and roles within the media industries shifts the responsibility for managing every aspect of making media from the firm to the individual professional.

Affordance

Although technological developments can most certainly be described in terms of the rise of new digital intermediaries, platformization, datafication, and algorithms, we should not ignore the tremendous affordances new media also offer to makers. The underdetermined nature of digital media enable practitioners to experiment with telling stories in all kinds of ways. Opportunities arise in the fields of extended reality (XR) and transmedia storytelling, where media makers are challenged to use multiple media channels, formats, and interfaces. Through new (and often relatively cheap and easy to use) technologies, more people can participate in making media than ever before, stimulating both the emergence of a truly global market for media makers, as well as local playgrounds for the inclusion of many different voices and communities. The possibilities to interact with audiences have increased significantly, paving the way for various forms of co-creation. Although traditional (advertising and sales-based) business models of media organizations are under pressure, the opportunities to monetize media content and products expand, just as the platforms on which content can be shared multiply, potentially providing media makers with more autonomy and creative freedom.

Power

Given the profound transformations across the media industries and the corresponding destabilization of media professions and practices, questions of power become highly relevant. There is a general shift in power being whisked away from professional content creators to media users and owners – and, specifically, the new digital intermediaries. As a result, most professional practitioners experience media work as precarious. They are being underpaid and undervalued for their contributions, and are expected to do more than before (often with fewer resources at their disposal or colleagues to collaborate with). Although unions are active to some extent in the media industries, media makers tend not to become members of such formal organizations. Precarious working conditions and networked production processes furthermore tend to handicap efforts to mobilize otherwise fragmented media professionals.

On the other hand, the number of professional associations is rising across the various industries. Media professionals do find new ways to organize themselves, both online (through closed Facebook and LinkedIn groups, for example) as well as offline (especially in the context of distinctly local communities and place-based social support structures). By developing infrastructures to support independent work, these types of formal and informal alliances help to counteract the various forms of power imbalance that are visible within the media industries.

Flexibility

Flexibility (whether numerical, functional, temporal, or financial) is a key governing principle in media work, and runs through all accounts of what it is like to make it work as a professional media maker. Numerical flexibility refers to the creative use of workforce numbers to manage a media organization. This means, for example, that even a full-time salaried and contracted position can disappear in an instant, work potentially moves overseas overnight, and your team may dissipate at any moment due to suddenly changing working arrangements. Functional flexibility describes the division of the media workforce in a multi-skilled core of employees and a periphery of freelance professionals. The overall trend is that this 'core' is not only diminishing, but also does not offer many guarantees in terms of job security. At the same time, freelancers generally report not seeking the relative safety of a full-time contract with an established media company, even though many freelance media workers struggle to make a living (Deuze & Witschge, 2018). The overall lack of dependable, well-organized (such as '9-to-5' type) working schedules is known as temporal flexibility, whereas financial flexibility refers to the generally uneven, individualized, and performance-based systems of rewards and remunerations (instead of uniform salaries) in place across the media industries.

To be flexible – as a media firm or professional – thus means many things at the same time. Flexibility both disrupts established practices of making media as well as consolidates (and, perhaps more importantly, naturalizes) specific ways of organizing the work. What flexibility particularly brings to making media, is *presentism*: a form of limiting and defusing concern for one's work and career prospects by focusing on the present (Goyanes & Rodríguez-Gómez, 2018) to the detriment of historical understanding and rational anticipation of possible futures (Bourdieu, 1998).

Precarity

Media work is a lesson in precarity, meaning: coming to terms with having little or no control over 'what happens next' in your professional career. Although this is not necessarily a new situation for many media professionals, precariousness is evident in constantly changing labour conditions, in particular the rise of the so-called gig economy with its emphasis on short-term project labour, often organized through online platforms. Such a way of living and working – of having a workstyle rather than a lifestyle (Deuze, 2007) – among other things necessitates the maintenance of a permanent self-promotional profile across various social networks.

This is not to say that the 'happy few' who have indeed secured stable, steady jobs supported by contracts and excellent labour conditions (such as a pension plan and medical insurance policies) do not experience precariousness. This is quite possibly the most important insight regarding this principal component of professional media makers: regardless of your formal status as a worker in the media industries, you always work from project to project, from one story to the next, from task to assignment – all the while governed by the informal rule that you are only as good as your last production.

One way to master the art of living with precarity is finding a way to cross-subsidize the work: doing what you have to do in order to do what you want to do. This model is quite common in regions where a lot of high profile media companies are based, such as Soho in London, Hollywood in Los Angeles, and Madison Avenue in New York. Beyond film, advertising, and television, this way of working increasingly applies elsewhere in the media industries as well, especially in journalism. As mixing news work with other communication-related jobs such as public relations tends to be perceived as rather problematic when it comes to the editorial autonomy of reporters, these forms of cross-subsidy are not without complications. Since precarity has become a permanent component of making media professionally, practitioners will have to figure out how to deal with (potential) professional frictions resulting from cross-subsidizing their work.

Entrepreneurship

The rise of entrepreneurship, framed as an individual solution to systemic problems, is clearly visible within media industries. It is a dominant frame in contemporary policy and management discourse. One's ability to take risks, find new business opportunities, and being a successful self-promoter tends to be heralded as an appropriate response to a contingent and altogether precarious industry context. However, an alternative conceptualization of being entrepreneurial can be identified as well: not as a 'business saviour' (Sørensen, 2008), but as the building block of a social support system – as a skillset contributing to sustainable community-formation and the design of creative solutions for urgent problems in everyday life and society at large.

The rhetoric and logic of start-up culture and entrepreneurialism can be perceived all around us. It propagates a playful mindset, sees disruption as a force for good, and equates work with passion, thereby celebrating and naturalizing the overwork through which the 'passion project' of making media is pursued professionally. The entrepreneurial mindset reinforces the idea that making media is not just a way to make a living – it becomes your identity. Making media – being a journalist, a recording artist, a game developer, an Instagram influencer – is not something you do, it's something you are. And, we should add, rebelling against who you are is something most of us would understandably hesitate to do.

Agency

Making media professionally puts practitioners in a field of sometimes complimentary, and often competing pressures and forces. In essence, these elements comprise content, connectivity, creativity, and commerce. Media industries produce content, but also invest in platforms for connectivity – where fans and audiences provide the free labour of sharing, commenting, and co-creating content. Media work is based on the creative desire to tell stories – a feeling common among practitioners across the various media industries, generally associated with a wish to do so autonomously – yet tends to take place within a distinctly commercial context. Within the broader context of the principal components that make up media work, it is up to each professional to find agency by negotiating and balancing these four core pressures.

Agency for professional media makers can be expressed on different levels. On the individual level, practitioners build networks – not just as a way to find and get new jobs, assignments, and clients, but also to build a social support structure. Peer communities are a crucial part of the job, and are often distinctly local – as in the media industries all production is global but all work is local. This international division of cultural labour means that each individual media worker is responsible for preparing, finding, and keeping employment in the context of a truly global industry. Particularly freelancers have to find creative and experimental ways to address work-related challenges outside official legal regimes – including visibility projects, organized campaigns, and collective organizations. The media tend to cluster in specific (urban) areas, within which an ongoing exchange of labour, talent, and skills takes place between people and organizations. This creates a sense of community that can help practitioners to collectively find some agency vis-à-vis an otherwise uncontrollable international division of labour.

On the macro level, agency can be found through a keen understanding of the global production networks of the media industries and the way markets function. This for example means that, while overall the various industries prefer to invest in proven formats and predictable products (such as movie, television and game franchises, established beats in news media, genre conventions in music), every company needs to engage in exploratory innovation as well in order not to fall behind, as well as to secure the 'next big thing'.

Affect

Above all, media work is a form of affective labour: work that elicits an affective investment from its practitioners exceeding conscious deliberation, and that is intended to elicit a similarly pre-cognitive response in people. In the contemporary attention economy, engagement is a key aspect of making media: not just getting people to notice and pay attention to your product or service – which is difficult enough – but even more so, to get people engaged, to suspend their disbelief, to keep them coming back for more. Insights from consumer psychology and behavioral design are becoming quite popular in the media industries, propelled by the enormous amount of data that media users generate online, and propped up by companies such as Facebook and Google. At the same time, media professionals are also, to some extent, expected to surrender completely to their work, in part encouraged by comfortable, and at times even playful working environments – which, in the case of freelancers, also include the private home, or any one of the countless cozy coffee shops and cafés serving as informal office spaces.

What is key here, is the fundamental role feelings and emotions play in making media, and making it work as a media professional. Not only is the labour affective, it is immaterial: a category of work where people turn the whole self into work. Where material labour refers to learned skills in industrial settings – like operating machinery –immaterial labour includes social and communication skills. Affective and cognitive activities – the way we feel about ourselves, things, and each other, and how we make sense of these aspects of our lives – become commodified in media work. They are part of 'what it takes' to be a professional media maker: to develop a sense of taste, to empathize with the desires and needs of others, to translate all of this in products and services that appeal to people.

Media work is furthermore a form of emotional labour, denoting the process by which workers are expected to manage their feelings in accordance with organizationally defined rules and guidelines. Managing (and more often than not repressing) one's emotions is key to survival and success in media work. Negative emotions such as hate, anger, jealousy, and sadness are usually not tolerated – especially among newcomers. Although conflict is an often cherished aspect of media work – generally considered to be conducive to creativity and innovation – the level of friction allowed in media work should not be overestimated. This requires constant, careful calibration by each and every media professional.

Finally, media work as a form of affective labour is passionate: extreme emotions are part of making the work meaningful. Although one could argue that, according to objective standards, many (if not most) media workers suffer from all kinds of labour exploitation – doing underpaid or unpaid work, experiencing dismissal or rejection for no apparent reason – still, many express that they 'cannot believe I'm getting paid to do this!' Passion is the extreme emotional energy that keeps the engine running, both in terms of how workers make sense of themselves and their role in the 'creativity machine' of the media industries, and how the work gets 'sold' to newcomers and outsiders: as something you have to be passionate about.

(How to use) this book

Structuring the dynamic world of making media in production, practices, and professions allows us to focus on the different ways these principal components impact (and are shaped by) the way professionals work. In each section, the various authors address several (if not all) of these components in terms of their specific research topic. We endeavoured to include a wide array of researchers – 53 authors from fourteen different countries – who provide different theoretical perspectives as well as insights into internationally varying experiences. Chapters within each section are divided by theme, and relate to each other as some focus on general, overarching developments, while others offer detailed case studies in specific national or industrial contexts. At the end of each chapter we offer a reading guide with three suggested connections to other chapters, organized around a taxonomy of *cases* – referring to another chapter where a specific case or example of the argument is elaborated in more detail; *contexts* – linking to work in the book that provides the bigger picture of the phenomenon under investigation; and *contrasts* – thought-provoking additional reading offering alternate or critical perspectives.

It is our intention that this book serves as a gateway to the scholarly study of (professional) media making, as well as a way to prepare for (and make sense of) a career in the media industries. To that effect, there is no single pathway through the book. We advise the reader to pick a first chapter to read (after this one) based on a specific question or concern he or she may have, and take it from there – either by subsequently reading the other chapters within that particular section or by following the taxonomy of recommendations we have included. The works cited in the reference section at the end of each chapter may serve as further suggestions for study beyond this book.

By way of introduction, we conclude this chapter with a short summary of the how the three sections of this book are organized.

The first section of this book, on media *production*, kicks off with a series of essays on the history, traditions, and contemporary challenges of media industries and production scholarship. The study of media production and work knows a rich history, coming from a variety of disciplines and coalescing around a couple of fundamental approaches, generally divided into: sociological approaches to the organization of media work; political economy approaches to the media; management, business and organizational studies; and media and cultural policy studies. Recurring questions inspiring such research focus on the various ways in which the creative and production processes in media industries are organized, coordinated, and managed, what role and influence media ownership, size, and strategy have (specifically regarding the autonomy of media workers and the diversity of media), and what the nature and experience of work is in the media industries.

The section on media production starts off with chapters by Jennifer Holt and Alisa Perren, David Lee and Anna Zoellner, and Patrick Vonderau in which they take stock of the research on media industries and highlight several issues that researchers face. Providing a conceptual framework, Bernhard Miège revisits and updates his earlier foundational work, while David Nieborg and Thomas Poell give insight in the process of platformization. Similarly, Dwayne Winseck, Terry Flew, and Nicolas Suzor offer reviews of important developments in media policy and how this affects the organization of work in the industry. Tackling fundamental issues regarding the business of media industries, the contributions by Chris Bilton, Paolo Faustino and Eli Noam, and Mikko Villi and Robert Picard address what the transformation of business models means for media managers. Amidst analyses about how media audiences' needs are shifting and consumers are even turning into producers themselves, Göran Bolin, Sylvia Chan-Olmsted, and Rang Wang offer important perspectives on the changing nature of value as well as markets for media production.

In the second section of the book – on the *practices* of making media – Arne Krumsvik, Stefania Milan, Niamh Ní Bhroin, and Tanja Storsul unpack the dominant rhetoric of innovation in making media, Stefan Werning unravels the discourse on startups and entrepreneurship, and Vincent Mosco calls attention to the profound role automation, robotization, and data analytics have come to play. Beyond these broad perspectives we look at the concrete experiences of (different categories of) media professionals in a changing industry, whereby Penny O'Donnell and

Lawrie Zion, Doris Ruth Eikhof and Stevie Marsden, and Nicole Cohen offer cases in Australia, the United Kingdom, and Canada. Recognizing that what gives making media meaning is often determined by its potential for self-fulfillment, Eugenia Siapera, Zelmarie Cantillon, and Sarah Baker examine the pitfalls of media making as a form of affective labour and Ilana Gershon and Mark Deuze offer alternative perspectives on how to 'make it work' in the media.

In the concluding section of the book – on media *professions* – we take all the important work on media industries and production on the road through a variety of case studies of specific industries and accompanying professions, ranging from music and recording (Sofia Johansson and Leslie Meier), television (Amanda Lotz and Paul Dwyer), social media entertainment (Brooke Erin Duffy and David Craig), advertising and public relations (Sara Rosengren and Dustin Supa), digital games (Aphra Kerr and Casey O'Donnell), and journalism (Ana Serrano Tellería, Amanda Brouwers, and Tamara Witschge).

We wrap up the book with a discussion with Henry Jenkins, whose publications on textual poaching, convergence culture, and spreadable media have been so influential. He is arguably one of the few scholars in the field of media industries and production whose work speaks to both the industry and the academy. Responding to his observations are colleagues from around the world: Tanja Bosch, Anthony Fung, and Elizabeth Saad Corrêa. We conducted interviews with these keen observers of the media on the basis of key insights we gained from assembling this book.

There is a lively debate among those studying media industries and production whether the kind of scholarship as represented in this book can, or even should, serve the interests of the industry and those vying a career in the media. Some advocate direct engagement with the industry, seeking a dialogue with hopes of improving the plight of media workers, identifying creative and innovative potential, hoping that scholarship can contribute to making better media (Jenkins, 2006; Jenkins, Ford & Green, 2013). Others remain sceptical about such alliances, instead arguing for sustained critique regarding the ways in which the media are particularly good at exploiting the emotional investment and passion of (especially younger) media makers, how commercial pressures serve to frustrate and distort the creative autonomy and range of voices possible in mainstream media production, and how schools and universities become complicit in maintaining often poor working conditions across the cultural, creative, and media industries (Mayer, 2011, 2017; McRobbie, 2016; Banks, 2017). In general, it is important to note that most, if not all scholars in this area are deeply invested in improving the working lives of media professionals, in promoting a rich diversity in media making practices across the various industries, and in further professionalizing the emerging discipline of media production studies (including, but not limited to Deuze, 2007, 2011; Holt & Perren, 2009; Paterson, Lee, Saha & Zoellner, 2015).

The idea for this book was born when developing the outline for a brand new course for (advanced) undergraduate students who are considering careers in the media. Instead of offering them skills training or internship preparation, the goal was to give them a critical sense of the key forces, dynamics, and trends shaping the work of those who make media professionally. The learning goal was to prepare them for a job and, at the same time, help them critically reflect on what it is like to make media. The hope is that the approach and range of perspectives outlined here inspire students to do research and develop theory, as well as analyse and debate the role production practices play in the creation of media.

Making media is exciting, frustrating, inspiring, bewildering, problematic, complicated, and fun – and this book endeavours to be all of that, too.

References

Banks, M. (2017). *Creative Justice: Cultural Industries, Work and Inequality.* London: Rowman & Littlefield.

Bourdieu, P. (1998). *Acts of Resistance: Against the New Myths of Our Time.* Cambridge: Polity Press.

Deuze, M. (2007). *Media Work.* Cambridge: Polity Press.

Deuze, M. (ed.). (2011). *Managing Media Work.* London: SAGE Publications.

Deuze, M. & Witschge, T. (2018). 'Beyond Journalism: Theorising the Transformation of Journalism', *Journalism, 19*(2), 165-181.

Goyanes, M. & Rodríguez-Gómez, E.F. (2018). 'Presentism in the Newsroom: How Uncertainty Redefines Journalists' Career Expectations', *Journalism*, 1-17. https://doi.org/10.1177/1464884918767585.

Hesmondhalgh, D. (ed.). (2006). *Media Production.* Maidenhead and Milton Keynes: Open University Press.

Hesmondhalgh, D. & Baker, S. (2011). *Creative Labour: Media Work in Three Cultural Industries.* London: Routledge.

Perren, A. & Holt, J. (eds). (2009). *Media Industries: History, Method, and Theory.* Malden, MA: Blackwell.

Jenkins, H. (2006). *Convergence Culture. Where Old and New Media Collide.* New York: New York University Press.

Jenkins, H., Ford, S. & Green, J. (2013). *Spreadable Media.* New York: New York University Press.

Luhmann, N. (1990). 'The Autopoiesis of Social Systems', in N. Luhmann, *Essays on Self-reference* (1-20). New York: Columbia University Press.

Mayer, V. (2011). *Below the Line: Television Producers and Production Studies in the New Economy*. Durham, NC: Duke University Press.

Mayer, V. (2017). *Almost Hollywood, nearly New Orleans: A Film Economy Romance*. Berkeley, CA: University of California Press.

McRobbie, A. (2016). *Be Creative*. Cambridge: Polity Press.

Mingers, J. (2003). 'Can Social Systems be Autopoietic? Bhaskar and Giddens' Social Theories', *Journal for the Theory of Social Behaviour, 34*(4), 403-428.

Napoli, P. (2014). 'On Automation in Media Industries: Integrating Algorithmic Media Production into Media Industries Scholarship', *Media Industries Journal, 1*(1), 33-38.

Sørensen, B.M. (2008). '"Behold, I am Making all Things New": The Entrepreneur as Savior in the Age of Creativity', *Scandinavian Journal of Management, 24*(2), 85-93.

Paterson, C., Lee, D., Saha, A. & Zoellner, A. (eds). (2015). *Advancing Media Production Research*. Basingstoke: Palgrave MacMillan.

Witschge, T. & Nygren, G. (2009). 'Journalism: A Profession under Pressure?', *Journal of Media Business Studies, 6*(1), 37-59.

Production

Research

2.   Media Industries: A Decade in Review

Jennifer Holt and Alisa Perren

Since 2008, there has been a stunning expansion in research, teaching, and collective conversation on the media industries. This chapter highlights some of the most compelling, inspiring, and provocative scholarship in the field to be published in the past decade, focusing on four areas: creative labour and media work, digital distribution, platforms and algorithmic culture, and infrastructure.

Introduction

In March 2008 – roughly ten years prior to the writing of this chapter – we composed the introduction to our twenty-article edited volume, *Media Industries: History, Theory, and Method*. The process of drafting the book's introduction marked the final step in a roughly three-year editorial process, driven by our desire to initiate a dynamic conversation amongst scholars working in such fields as film and media studies, sociology, anthropology, journalism, communication, economics, and more.

Two key forces motivated us to publish *Media Industries*. First, we believed the dramatic industrial transformations of the time merited heightened attention from qualitatively oriented, critically minded scholars working in humanistic traditions. Notable developments circa 2007-2008 included the continued diffusion of broadband and mobile devices; the ever-increasing dominance of cable and satellite television accompanied by the growing commercial viability of niche-oriented content; the heightened market power and cultural influence of regional media corporations in countries including Brazil, India, and China; the accelerated privatization and deregulation of media across the globe; the ongoing ascent of a new wave of search engines including Yahoo! and Google; the rapid growth of brand-new social media platforms such as Twitter and Facebook plus the expansion of just-launched online video services including YouTube and Hulu; the progressive reorientation of the screen industries in the wake of the boom-and-bust cycle of DVD as well as growing competition posed by then-largely-DVD-by-mail service, Netflix; and the political and economic turmoil accompanying the final years of the Presidency of George W. Bush.

Second, we sought to use our collection as a means of uniting what we perceived to be existent, but frequently disconnected conversations about the media industries. We were inspired by the rich body of existing scholarship – in fact, many of our contributors had played a part in generating that work. But we also felt the frustration of operating within disciplinary silos, and the lack of precise terminology within which to engage with the industrial developments then taking place. In the heyday of the rhetoric about media convergence, we aspired for greater scholarly convergence, moving once and for all beyond the long-standing 'political economy vs. cultural studies' (or political economy *and* cultural studies) debates to instead pursue an 'open conceptual discussion about the many ways that media industry research has been undertaken in the past and [imagine] what interdisciplinary models, methods, and visions it might embrace in the future' (Holt & Perren, 2009, p. 2).

Our primary directive to our contributors, based on their own distinctive, diverse disciplinary perspectives and research orientations, was that they describe what they perceived 'media industry studies' might look like moving forward. Our main objective at that point was simply to 'articulate the diverse academic traditions and common threads defining media industry studies while also illustrating how integrated analyses of media texts, audiences, histories, and culture could enable more productive scholarship' (*Ibid.*). We scarcely could have imagined the degree of scholarly productivity soon to take place within media industry studies. (Notably, in the same year *Media Industries* was published, Havens, Lotz, and Tinic published their conceptual framework for industry studies in their influential paper "Critical Media Industry Studies: A Research Approach," and Caldwell, Mayer, and Banks published their landmark anthology *Production Studies: Cultural Studies of the Media Industries.*)

From the time of our book's publication in 2009 to the present moment, we have witnessed a stunning expansion in research, teaching, and collective conversation on the media industries. There are now media industries scholarly interest groups within a wide range of professional organizations, including the European Communication Research and Education Organization (ECREA), the International Communication Association (ICA), the International Association of Mass Communication Research (IAMCR), the Society for Cinema and Media Studies (SCMS), and more. Issues of *Cinema Journal* (2013) and *Creative Industries* (2014) have featured dedicated sections on media industry studies; university departments and centres have developed long-standing initiatives focused on topics pertaining to issues such as creative labour and distribution; and conferences specifically dedicated to engaging the breadth of industry oriented scholarship take place all over the world. In addition, we have both been part of a team of scholars from universities around the globe involved in launching the first open-access, peer-reviewed journal dedicated to critical, qualitatively oriented scholarship, creatively titled *Media Industries*.

It is safe to say that media industry studies is now a mature field. At this moment, it is worth stepping back to consider both what has transpired in the media industries during the past decade as well as what we perceive to be especially vibrant areas of media industries scholarship.

Developments in the global media industries

No doubt we could dedicate an entire chapter just to surveying the notable developments in the global media industries over the last ten years. That said, digitization has been among the most significant forces at work, shaping everything from industrial structures to business models, distribution strategies to marketing activities, and labour conditions to production practices. Among the most prominent developments we have witnessed connected to processes of digitization include:

– the increasing threats posed by technology companies such as Amazon, Apple, Facebook, Google/YouTube, and Netflix to the traditional operations of legacy media companies such as Time Warner, Disney, Viacom/Paramount, and NewsCorp/Fox;
– the media industries' increasing surveillance of the online activities and personal data of internet users (and media audiences), thereby eroding our individual rights to privacy in the digital space;
– the related acceleration in targeting and personalizing media, facilitating the expansion of cultural silos in online platforms;
– the ongoing expansion of the 'gig economy' and reliance on free labour cultivated via internships, fan engagement, crowdsourcing, and more;
– the decline of physical media sales (and in particular, DVD), and the concurrent rise of streaming services;
– the emergence of 'digital native' media forms such as web series and podcasts;
– the lag between media policy and technological developments, impacting everything from free speech to internet access to environmental conditions;
– the heightened monitoring and control by governments and corporations over material infrastructures in both autocratic and democratic regimes;
– ongoing waves of acquisitions and mergers by upstart technology operations as well as incumbent media companies seeking the 'appropriate' structure, scale, and scope;
– the collapse of the business model for (print) journalism, and the subsequent restructuring and reorientation of that industry and its professional practices in the digital realm;
– the launch and circulation of #blacklivesmatter, #metoo, and #timesup (among other cyberactivism campaigns) following a wave of news stories about sexual and racial abuse rapidly diffused via social media.

In light of these developments, we have chosen to highlight below what we find to be some of the most compelling, inspiring, challenging, and provocative scholarship in the field to be published since *Media Industries: History, Theory, and Method.*

With our earlier volume, we mainly focused on laying out macro-level stakes for researchers and students alike in the interest of encouraging wide-ranging discussion. This conversation persists, and indeed, there continues to be ongoing debate about what constitutes media industry studies – what its politics and desired outcomes should be, how social scientific (and more quantitatively oriented) research might be incorporated, and so on.

Such macro-level conversations are valuable. But given the ever-expanding body of work that might be situated within media industry studies at this juncture, we find it beneficial to take a somewhat more micro-level approach here. We will focus on just four sub-areas: creative labour and media work, digital distribution, platforms and algorithmic culture, and infrastructure. Scholars conducting research in these areas have creatively traced historical patterns, formulated conceptual frameworks, and practiced innovative methodologies, all-the-while engaging with the moving target of study that is the contemporary digital media industries.

Creative labour and media work

As the media and technology industries have expanded and diversified during the past decade, scholarship on these industries has similarly proliferated and actively engaged with the evolving economic, social, and cultural conditions of media work. Many scholars have revisited Karl Marx, reassessing his foundational ideas about topics such as exploitation, necessary labour time, and surplus labour time in light of the expansion of social media platforms, digitally networked technologies, and new professional identities (Dyer-Witheford & de Peuter, 2009; Fuchs, 2014; Maxwell, 2017; Scholz, 2013). Debate initiated prior to the mid-2000s regarding how to conceptualize the nature of creative work has shifted alongside the changing roles and contributions of those variably described as audiences, users, amateurs, prosumers, and fans in the digital media landscape (see foundational work by Smythe, 1981; Terranova, 2000; Bruns, 2008; and Jenkins, 2006, as well as more recent work by Arvidsson & Bonini, 2015; Pérez-González, 2012; De Kosnick, 2016; Stanfill & Condis, 2014). In an effort to more precisely capture the affective, subjective (and often gendered, raced, and classed) dimensions of contemporary digital media work, scholars also have advanced terminology such as 'hope labour' (Kuehn & Corrigan, 2013; Fast et al., 2016), 'aspirational labour' (Duffy, 2015), and 'good work' (Hesmondhalgh & Baker, 2011).

Such scholarship has been accompanied by a growing body of case studies of the particular conditions experienced by creative workers 'on the ground' in specific local, regional, national, and transnational industrial contexts (see, for example,

Ganti, 2012; Kokas, 2017; Marwick, 2013; Mayer, 2011). Earlier political economic analyses such as those provided by Susan Christopherson (2006) and the authors of *Global Hollywood* (Miller *et al.*, 2001) illustrated, at a more macro-level, the far-reaching impact of digitization, globalization, conglomeration, and deregulation on creative workers. In more recent years, collections such as Curtin and Sanson's *Precarious Creativity* (2017) have sought to reveal on a more micro-level the 'multiple and specific ways that local labour practices engage with and contest processes of media globalization' by 'transgressing disciplinary, methodological, and geographic boundaries' (*Ibid.*, p. 10).

Concurrently, scholars situating themselves within the growing body of work in the cultural studies of production have employed more 'bottom-up' methods including interviews, observation, archival research, and discourse analysis to examine the raced, classed, gendered, and sexualized nature of creative work past and present. These scholars have charted the politics and practices involved in varied work roles and professional identities, including executive assistants, camera operators, and casting agents (see Hill, 2016; Sinkiewicz, 2016; Warner, 2015, as well as edited collections by Szczepanik & Vonderau, 2013; Banks, Conor, & Mayer, 2016). Complementing these perspectives on above- and below-the-line labourers are projects addressing the nature of managerial work and cultural intermediaries (Deuze, 2011; Smith Maguire & Matthews, 2014; Johnson, Kompare, & Santo, 2014). Such research underscores the value of perceiving network executives, talent scouts, market researchers, and brand managers (among others) 'not merely as a work category responsible for overseeing labour, but as a kind of labour' (Johnson, Kompare, & Santo, 2014, p. 19).

Digital distribution

Even as more attention has been directed towards media workers occupying managerial positions, so too have scholars been increasingly mindful of how distribution itself functions as the locus for a great deal of cultural and political power. As defined by Sean Cubitt (2005), 'distribution is responsible not only for intervening between but also for managing the relationships of consumers and producers: the acceleration and delay, promotion and restriction, the spatiotemporal orchestration of flows' (*Ibid.*, p. 195). The activities in which distributors engage include assembling financing, procuring and/or licencing rights for various platforms or markets, managing the inflow and outflow of income from corporate partners, designing release schedules and marketing strategies to establish and sustain audience awareness, and building and maintaining libraries (Perren, 2013, p. 166).

Scholars have sought to understand both the historical precedents (Hoyt & Govil, 2014; Kidman, 2015) as well as changes in stakeholder relations and business models related to the shift to digital distribution (Curtin, Holt, & Sanson, 2014). Of special interest have been the ways that new markets have been formed – and also, frequently circumvented via piracy – with the expansion of the sharing economy (Elkins, 2016; Lobato & Thomas, 2015; Steemers, 2016). Also of growing concern have been the spatial dimensions of digital distribution – 'the physical, place-specific geographies, infrastructures, and material conditions' tied to the circulation of media (Hessler & Rodriguez, 2015).

Platforms and algorithmic culture

Connected to much of the work in distribution studies, data and platform studies also have grown dramatically in scope and substance in the last decade (see for example the very useful Critical Algorithm Studies reading list created by the Social Media Collective scholars at Microsoft Research (URL: tinyurl.com/smclist). Indeed, the role of personal data, algorithms, and streaming media platforms have come to define much of the industry's digital distribution strategies during this time. This area of scholarship has illuminated the degree to which 'big data' and corporate surveillance of our online activities have tailored our choices, dictated our preferences, and shaped our everyday lives (see, for example, Van Dijk, 2013; Arsenault, 2017; Willson, 2016; Schneier, 2015). Ted Striphas (2015) has explored the 'algorithmic culture' that has emerged as the decision-making force in our public and private lives (also see Galloway, 2007). Gillespie (2014) has characterized the power of algorithms as 'a means to know what there is to know and how to know it, to participate in social and political discourse and to familiarize ourselves with the publics in which we participate' (*Ibid.*, p. 167).

Data and algorithms generated on social media platforms have granted advertisers unprecedented access and automated insights into audience activities. These analytics have allowed marketers to refine advertising strategies and audience measurement, and have transformed the nature of audience engagement with content (Turow, 2013; Kosterich & Napoli, 2015; Moe *et al.*, 2016). 'Big data' employed by content creators like Netflix and Amazon has been increasingly used in the development of programming and in television culture itself (Havens, 2014; Kelly, 2017). Through processes such as the cultural curation and moderation function of platforms, this data and the algorithms it generates have also been instrumental in delineating the limits of expression in media culture (Gillespie, 2018).

Scholars in this area have also used their work to interrogate the sovereignty, values, and source of control and power in our digital culture represented by big data, search engines, and their algorithms. In their formative essay, boyd and Crawford (2011) offered six provocations for big data:

1. Automating research changes the definition of knowledge
2. Bigger data are not always better data
3. Limited access to Big Data creates new digital divides
4. Not all data are equivalent
5. Claims to objectivity and accuracy are misleading
6. Just because it is accessible doesn't make it ethical

Others have followed up in this spirit of critical media literacy to further expose the values inherent in search engine culture and biometric information technologies, especially those reinforcing the long histories of bias and discrimination along the lines of race and gender (Browne, 2015; Noble, 2018).

The work in this area of industry studies also has ramifications for governments and their citizens, and offers insight into protest movements and abuses of political power (see Tufekci, 2017; Lee and Chan, 2018 for excellent examples). Ongoing revelations regarding social media platforms (particularly Facebook) exploiting and selling user data without their knowledge have lent a new gravity to the calls to civic action found in journalistic and scholarly work. Gillespie (2018), for example, has urged that we 'be the custodians of the custodians', as he connects participatory culture to a lack of accountability eroding our public sphere: 'Participation comes with its own form of responsibility. We must demand that [platforms] take on an expanded sense of responsibility, and that they share the tools to govern collectively' (*Ibid.*, p. 226). This call for greater platform transparency and the danger our culture faces without it (see Annany & Crawford, 2018) were visible in media industry scholarship long before many of the most dramatic scandals involving social media manipulation of data ever broke in the press.

Infrastructure

Infrastructure studies has a substantive historical and disciplinary relationship to platform studies, as Plantin *et al.* (2016) have eloquently articulated. It has also been an area of great energy and expansion for industry studies and a site for productive interdisciplinarity in the last ten years. An essential component of infrastructure is the study of technological systems, and the study of media technologies has its own long tradition in the social sciences as well as in the humanities. Such work has only grown more critical for media industry scholars in the era of digital distribution.

Influential formative studies such as those by Innis (1972), McLuhan (1964), Eisenstein (1979), and Carey (1983) demonstrated the vast networks and mutually constitutive influences between technology and culture, communication, and ideology. Scholars such as Marvin (1988), Gitelman (2006), and Sterne (2012) have continued this tradition with complex histories of media technologies and forms, often revealing the long arcs of dynamic relationships in the development of print, electronic, and digital media. We see this work as fundamental to the analyses of digital media and materiality, informing a growing trend in relating media technologies and practices to the study of media infrastructures – the 'situated sociotechnical systems that are designed and configured to support the distribution of audiovisual signal traffic' (Parks & Starosielski, 2015, p. 4).

As Lisa Parks (2015) has articulated, the concept of 'infrastructural imaginaries – ways of thinking about what infrastructures are, where they are located, who controls them, and what they do' (*Ibid.*, p. 355) has enriched media industry studies in myriad ways over the last decade. It has informed research on media industries and environmental issues (Maxwell & Miller, 2012), the networks and data centres of 'the cloud' (Hu, 2016), and the intermediaries directing much of the activity in the digital media ecosystem (Braun, 2013; Lobato, 2016). This orientation also has helped inform scholarship on the politicization of distribution pipelines such as broadband networks (Crawford, 2013; Holt, 2014; Kimball, 2015) and undersea cables (Starosielski, 2015), as well as related infrastructures such as streaming platforms (Erikson et al., 2018) and data centres (Hogan, 2015). Additionally, internet architecture and policy (Van Schewick, 2010; De Nardis, 2014) has been the focus of significant literature coming from legal and internet governance studies, connecting network design and economics to issues of access, privacy, and digital citizenry. This infrastructural turn has allowed media industry scholars in the humanities to benefit from research being done in law, policy, communication, and beyond, as we all work toward a common, interdisciplinary goal of advancing this burgeoning field.

Conclusion

All the sub-areas described in this chapter are united by a broader focus on issues of access, publics, and networks, and ultimately drive the field of media industry studies into a new era of scholarly activism. There is a common theme connected to the tone of the industry scholarship produced in the last ten years: the prior optimism regarding the possibilities of digital distribution and participatory culture has largely been replaced by a far more sombre recognition of the harsh realities of the contemporary digital ecosystem. At the same time, the scholarly work has become increasingly sophisticated, incisive, and ambitious. We have been impressed by the impact of our colleagues' contributions all over the world, and amazed by the reach and expanse of this evolving field.

Space constraints prevent us from delving into many of the other vibrant areas explored by media industry studies scholars, including: privacy and surveillance studies; cultural economy of finance; media and cultural policy; cultural intermediaries and gatekeepers; retailing, exhibition, and experiential entertainment; festivals, awards, and cultures of prestige; and advertising and promotional culture, to name just a few. Although we are unable to address discussions of specific industry sectors such as music, gaming, and publishing, along with accounts of work on geographical regions such as Latin America, Africa, and Asia at length here, work in these areas continues to grow. (Those seeking accessible surveys of particular national and regional industries, as well as distinct industrial sectors, are encouraged to turn to the *International Screen Industries* book series edited by Michael Curtin and Paul McDonald.) Our hope is that by pointing to select highlights of scholarly work, we can facilitate further dialogue regarding future directions for media industry studies and contribute to the growing global conversation about how we might all develop original historical analyses, innovative methodologies, and imaginative theoretical frameworks in the digital era.

Further reading

- Case: The working conditions and labour requirements for 'making it' as an online content creator – Duffy (p. 375)
- Context: Five current issues and trends relating to the media industries as a result of digitization and the rise of the global communication giants – Miège (p. 73)
- Contrast: On the value and challenges of media industries research, focusing on the question of (digital) access – Vonderau (p. 61)

References

Ananny, M. & Crawford, K. (2018). 'Seeing Without Knowing: Limitations of the Transparency Ideal and Its Application to Algorithmic Accountability', *New Media & Society*, 20 (3), 973-989.

Arsenault, A. H. (2017). 'The Datafication of Media: Big Data and the Media Industries', *International Journal of Media & Cultural Politics*, 13(1-2), 7-24.

Arvidsson, A. & Bonini T. (2015). 'Valuing Audience Passions: From Smythe to Tarde', *European Journal of Cultural Studies*, 18(2),158-173.

Banks, M., Conor, B. & Mayer, V. (eds) (2016). *Production Studies, The Sequel! Cultural Studies of the Global Media Industries*. New York: Routledge.

boyd, d. & Crawford, K. (2011). 'Six Provocations for Big Data. Social Science Research Network'. Retrieved from: http://papers.ssrn.com/sol3/papers.cfm?abstract_id=1926431

Brannon Donoghue, C. & Warner, K. (2014). 'Introduction', *Creative Industries Journal*, *7*(1), 1-2.

Braun, J. (2013). 'Transparent Intermediaries: Building the Infrastructures of Connected Viewing', in J. Holt & K. Sanson (eds). *Connected Viewing: Selling, Sharing, and Streaming Media in the Digital Era* (124-143). New York: Routledge.

Browne, S. (2015). *Dark Matters: On the Surveillance of Blackness*. Durham, NC: Duke University Press.

Bruns, A. (2008). *Blogs, Wikipedia, Second Life, and Beyond: From Production to Produsage*. New York: Peter Lang.

Caldwell, J., Mayer, V. & Banks, M. (eds). (2009). *Production Studies: Cultural Studies of Media Industries*. New York: Routledge.

Carey, J.W. (1983). 'Technology and Ideology: The Case of the Telegraph', *Prospects*, *8*, 303-325.

Christopherson, S. (2006). 'Behind the Scenes: How Transnational Firms Are Constructing a New International Division of Labor in Media Work', *Geoforum*, *37*, 739-751.

Crawford, S. (2013). *Captive Audience: The Telecom Industry and Monopoly in the New Gilded Age*. New Haven, CT: Yale University Press.

Cubitt, S. (2005). 'Distribution and Media Flows', *Cultural Politics*, *1*(2), 193-214.

Curtin, M. & Sanson, K. (eds). (2016). *Precarious Creativity: Global Media, Local Labor*. Oakland, CA: University of California Press.

Curtin, M., Holt, J. & Sanson, K. (eds). (2014). *Distribution Revolution: Conversations about the Digital Future of Film and Television*. Oakland, CA: University of California Press.

Davis, D.W. & Yueh-yu Ye, E. (2008). *East Asian Screen Industries*. London: BFI Palgrave.

De Kosnick, A. (2016). *Rogue Archives: Digital Cultural Memory and Media Fandom*. Cambridge, MA: MIT Press.

De Nardis, L. (2014). *The Global War for Internet Governance*. New Haven, CT: Yale University Press.

Deuze, M. (ed.). (2011). *Managing Media Work*. Thousand Oaks, CA: SAGE Publications.

Duffy, B. (2015). 'The Romance of Work: Gender and Aspirational Labor in the Digital Culture Industries', *International Journal of Cultural Studies*, *19*(4), 441-457.

Dyer-Witheford, N. & de Peuter, G. (2009). *Games of Empire: Global Capitalism and Video Games*. Minneapolis, MN: University of Minnesota Press.

Eisenstein, E. (1979). *The Printing Press as an Agent of Change: Communications and Cultural Transformations in Early Modern Europe*. Cambridge: Cambridge University Press.

Elkins, E. (2016). 'The DVD Region Code System: Standardizing Home Video's Disjunctive Global Flows', *International Journal of Cultural Studies*, *19*(2), 225-240.

Erikson M., Fleischer, R., Johanson, A., Snickars, P. and Vonderau, P. (2018). *Spotify Teardown: Inside the Black Box of Music Streaming*. Cambridge, MA: MIT Press.

Fast, K., Örnebring, H. & Karlsson, M. (2016). 'Metaphors of Free Labor: A Typology of Unpaid Work in the Media Sector', *Media, Culture & Society*, *38*(7), 963-978.

Fuchs, C. (2014). *Digital Labor and Karl Marx*. New York: Routledge.

Galloway, A. R. (2007). *Gaming: Essays on Algorithmic Culture*. Minneapolis, MN: University of Minnesota Press.

Ganti, T. (2012). *Producing Bollywood: Inside the Contemporary Hindi Film Industry*. Durham, NC: Duke University Press.

Gillespie, T. (2010). 'The Politics of Platforms', *New Media & Society, 12*(3), 347-364.

Gillespie, T. (2014). 'The Relevance of Algorithms', in T. Gillespie, P.J. Boczkowski, & K.A. Foot (eds), *Media Technologies: Essays on Communication, Materiality, and* Society (167-193). Cambridge, MA: MIT Press.

Gillespie, T. (2018). *Custodians of the Internet*. New Haven, CT: Yale University Press.

Gitleman, L. (2006). *Always Already New*. Cambridge, MA: MIT Press.

Havens, T. (2014). 'Media Programming in an Era of Big Data', *Media Industries, 1*(2). http://dx.doi.org/10.3998/mij.15031809.0001.202.

Havens, T., Lotz, A.D. & Tinic, S. (2009). 'Critical Media Industry Studies: A Research Approach', *Communication, Culture & Critique, 2*(2), 234-253.

Hessler, J. & Rodriguez, J.L. (2015). 'Introduction: Digital Distribution and Cultural Power', *Media Fields Journal, 10*. Retrieved from http://mediafieldsjournal.squarespace.com/digital-distribution-intro/.

Hesmondhalgh, D. & Baker, S. (2011). *Creative Labour: Media Work in Three Cultural Industries*. New York: Routledge.

Hill, E. (2016). *Never Done: A History of Women's Work in Media Production*. New Brunswick, NJ: Rutgers University Press.

Hogan, M. (2015). 'The Archive's Underbelly: Facebook's Data Storage Centers', *Television New Media 16*(1), 3-18.

Holt, J. (2014). 'Regulating Connected Viewing: Media Pipelines and Cloud Policy', in J. Holt & K. Sanson (eds), *Connected Viewing: Selling, Streaming, and Sharing Media in the Digital Age* (19-39). New York: Routledge.

Holt, J. & Perren, A. (2009). 'Introduction: Does the World Really Need One More Field of Study?', in J. Holt & A. Perren (eds), *Media Industries: History, Theory, and Method* (1-16). Malden, MA: Wiley-Blackwell.

Hoyt, E. & Govil, N. (2014). 'Thieves of Bombay: United Artists, Colonial Copyright, and Film Piracy in the 1920s', *Bioscope: South Asian Screen Studies, 5*(1), 5-27.

Hu, T.H. (2016). *A Prehistory of the Cloud*. Cambridge, MA: MIT Press.

Innis, H.A. & Innis, M.Q. (1972). *Empire and Communications*. Toronto: University of Toronto Press.

Jenkins, H. (2006). *Convergence Culture: Where Old and New Media Collide*. New York: New York University Press.

Johnson, D., Kompare, D. & Santo, A. (eds). (2014). *Making Media Work: Cultures of Management in the Entertainment Industries*. New York: New York University Press.

Kelly, J.P. (2017). 'Television by the Numbers: The Challenges of Audience Measurement in the Age of Big Data', *Convergence, 1.* https://doi.org/10.1177/1354856517700854.

Kidman, S. (2015). 'Self-Regulation through Distribution: Censorship and the Comic Book Industry in 1954', *Velvet Light Trap, 75,* 21-37.

Kimball, D. (2015). 'Sponsored Data and Net Neutrality: Exemption and Discrimination in the Mobile Broadband Industry', *Media Industries, 2*(1). http://dx.doi.org/10.3998/mij.15031809.0002.103.

Kokas, A. (2017). *Hollywood Made in China.* Oakland, CA: University of California Press.

Kosterich, A. & Napoli, P.M. (2015). 'Reconfiguring the Audience Commodity: The Institutionalization of Social TV Analytics as Market Information Regime', *Television & New Media, 17*(3), 254-271.

Kraidy, M.M. & Khalil, J.F. (2009). *Arab Television Industries.* London: BFI Palgrave.

Kuehn, K. & Corrigan, T.F. (2013). 'Hope Labor: The Role of Employment Prospects in Online Social Production', *The Political Economy of Communication, 1*(1). Retrieved from http://www.polecom.org/index.php/polecom/article/view/9/64.

Lee, F.L.F. & Chan, J.M. (2018). *Media and Protest Logics in the Digital Era: The Umbrella Movement in Hong Kong.* New York: Oxford University Press.

Lobato, R. (2016). 'The Cultural Logic of Digital Intermediaries: YouTube Multichannel Networks', *Convergence, 22*(4), 348-360.

Lobato, R. & Thomas, J. (2015). *The Informal Media Economy.* Malden, MA: Polity Press.

Marvin, C. (1988). *When Old Technologies Were New.* New York: Oxford University Press.

Marwick, A. (2013). *Status Update: Celebrity, Publicity, and Branding in the Social Media Age.* New Haven, CT: Yale University Press.

Maxwell, R. (ed.) (2017). *The Routledge Companion to Labor and Media.* New York: Routledge.

Maxwell, R. & Miller, T. (2012). *Greening the Media.* Oxford: Oxford University Press.

Mayer, V. (2011). *Below the Line: Producers and Production Studies in the New Television Economy.* Durham, NC: Duke University Press.

McDonald, P. (2013). 'In Focus: Media Industries Studies', *Cinema Journal, 52*(3), 145-188.

McLuhan, M. (1964). *Understanding Media: Extensions of Man.* New York: McGraw-Hill.

Miller, J. (2016). *Nollywood Central: The Nigerian Videofilm Industry.* London: BFI Palgrave.

Miller, T., Govil, N., McMurria, J. & Maxwell, R. (2001). *Global Hollywood,* London: British Film Institute.

Moe, H., Poell, T. & Van Dijck, J. (2016). 'Rearticulating Audience Engagement', *Television & New Media, 17*(2), 99-107.

Noble, S.U. (2018). *Algorithms of Oppression: How Search Engines Reinforce Racism.* New York: NYU Press.

Parks, L. (2015). '"Stuff You Can Kick": Toward a Theory of Media Infrastructure', in P. Svensson & D.T. Goldberg (eds), *Between Humanities and the Digital* (355-373). Cambridge, MA: MIT Press.

Parks, L. & Starosielski, N. (eds) (2015). *Signal Traffic: Critical Studies of Media Infrastructures*. Urbana, IL: University of Illinois Press.

Pérez-González, L. (2012). 'Amateur Subtitling as Immaterial Labour in Digital Media Culture: An Emerging Paradigm of Civic Engagement', *Convergence, 19*(2), 157-175.

Perren, A. (2013). 'Rethinking Distribution Studies for the Future of Media Industry Studies', *Cinema Journal, 52*(3), 165-171.

Plantin J.C., Lagoze, C., Edwards, P.N. & Sandvig, C. (2018). 'Infrastructure Studies Meet Platform Studies in the Age of Google and Facebook', *New Media & Society, 20*(1), 293- 310.

Schneier, B. (2015). *Data and Goliath*, New York: W.W. Norton & Company.

Scholtz, T. (ed.). (2013). *Digital Labor: The Internet as Playground and Factory*. New York: Routledge.

Sinkiewicz, M. (2016). *The Other Air Force: U.S. Efforts to Reshape Middle East Media Since 9/11*. New Brunswick, NJ: Rutgers University Press.

Smith Maguire, J. & Matthews, J. (eds) (2014). *The Cultural Intermediaries Reader*. Thousand Oaks, CA: SAGE Publications.

Smythe, D.W. (2006), 'On the Audience Commodity and Its Work', in Meenakshi G.D. & D.M. Kellner (eds), *Media and Cultural Studies* (230-256). Malden, MA: Wiley-Blackwell. (Original work published 1981).

Stanfill, M. & Condis, M. (2014). 'Fandom and/as Labor', in Stanfill, M., & Condis, M. (eds), 'Fandom and/as Labor. [Special issue]', *Transformative Works and Cultures, 15*. http://dx.doi.org/10.3983/twc.2014.0593.

Starosielski, N. (2015). *The Undersea Network*. Durham, NC: Duke University Press.

Steemers, J. (2016). 'International Sales of U.K. Television Content', *Television & New Media, 17* (8), 734-753.

Sterne, J. (2012). *MP3: The Meaning of a Format*. Durham, NC: Duke University Press.

Striphas, T. (2015). 'Algorithmic Culture', *European Journal of Cultural Studies, 18*(4-5), 395-412.

Szczepanek, P. & Vonderau, P. (eds) (2013). *Behind the Screen: Inside European Production Cultures*. New York: Palgrave Macmillan.

Terranova, T. (2000). 'Free Labor: Producing Culture for the Digital Economy', *Social Text, 18*(2), 33-58.

Tufekci, Z. (2017). *Twitter and Tear Gas: The Power and Fragility of Networked Protest*. New Haven, CT: Yale University Press.

Turow, J. (2013). *The Daily You: How the New Advertising Industry is Defining Your Identity and Your Worth*. New Haven, CT: Yale University Press.

Van Dijk, J. (2013). *The Culture of Connectivity*. Oxford: Oxford University Press.

Van Schewick, B. (2010). *Internet Architecture and Innovation*. Cambridge, MA: MIT Press.

Warner, K. (2015).*The Cultural Politics of Colorblind TV Casting*. New York: Routledge.

Willson, M. (2017). 'Algorithms (and the) Everyday', *Information, Communication & Society, 20*(1), 137-150.

3. Media Production Research and the Challenge of Normativity

David Lee and Anna Zoellner

Critical media production research is much needed and can benefit society as well as the media industries themselves. But critical production researchers face many barriers and constraints. This chapter discusses practical concerns for undertaking media production research, focusing on the most problematic areas: resources, access, and field relations.

Introduction

Media production research investigates how the organizations and individuals who create our media content operate. It explores the everyday conditions and processes of how media texts come into being and aims to understand how and why media texts take their particular form. This is a notoriously opaque, not to say secretive, subject creating specific challenges for researchers studying media production. Most of the publicly available knowledge about how media are made, stems from information that media institutions publish themselves. In his investigation of the American film and television industry, Caldwell (2008) draws attention to the self-reflexive nature of these industries and the way they expose their production processes. Yet, in most cases, this builds a carefully constructed promotional image rather than exposing problems that could explain critical issues in media representation.

Academically, media production research is now an established field of research, with its own conferences, anthologies, and institutional research groups (Paterson *et al.*, 2016a), alongside numerous methodological reflections on doing research (e.g. Havens *et al.*, 2009; Paterson *et al.*, 2016b). Rather than revisiting this ground, our focus in this chapter is on the challenge of normativity in media research: considering this issue from a historical, political, and methodological perspective. By this, we mean approaches to media production that have a distinctive ethical and moral orientation towards the object of study, rather than neutral, descriptive, or administrative approaches. We focus on the normative in media production studies because not only is the challenge of taking such an approach a relatively undiscussed issue, but also because of the growing political and social necessity for theoretically rigorous, normative approaches to social research.

As such, we see an apparent need to address media power across multiple terrains and distinct but interrelated issues, from global macro-scale challenges of environmental crisis, inequality, and capitalism, to localized media crises including abuses of patriarchal power and the gender pay gap issue (Lee & Allen, 2017). The need for a normative, ethical approach to media research is clear, but, as we will discuss below, the challenges to taking this approach are also growing, particularly in the current research funding climate with its focus on impact and administrative 'usability' (Schlesinger, 2016a).

Studying media production through a normative lens has implications for research design and fieldwork. In order to understand how media institutions work behind closed doors, we need direct access to media producers – that is: all media workers involved in the creation and dissemination of media texts – and production processes, as well as a certain degree of collaboration. This, however, can prove quite difficult to achieve, and research from a critical perspective raises concerns and consequently resistance among the media producers we aim to study.

In this chapter, we unpack such challenges and tensions. Following an overview of key normative positions in production studies, we discuss practical concerns for undertaking media production research, focusing on the most problematic areas of research design and conduct: resources, access, and field relations. In this discussion, we reflect on the impact recent developments in media practice and environment as well as in academia have had on production research. In other words, this chapter focuses on the barriers and constraints for critical media production researchers, whilst emphasizing the vital need to maintain and strengthen political normativity.

The challenge of normativity

Much critically informed research of media production is, by its nature, predominantly normative, if we define normative as that which is informed by moral and ethical concerns, and which has a clear moral position. Ultimately, the researchers undertaking this work ask: how can media best serve the people? Such research tends to come from within media and communication studies. However, the normative focus of this mode of production research has altered significantly since the foundational concerns of the early production studies scholars (the so-called first wave) (Cottle, 2000), through to contemporary moral economy concerns with social justice and human flourishing (Banks, 2017; Hesmondhalgh & Baker, 2011; Wright, 2015).

Meanwhile, parallel strands of research on production are distinctly non-normative, including research from within management and organizational studies focused on economic growth, business strategy, or how the media can best serve business interests (Davis & Scase, 2000; Tschmuck, 2003), as well as some strands of sociological research that aims for a relatively neutral position to describe reality (Peterson & Berger, 1975; Peterson, 1985). Connected to this is the growing reach and priority given to 'administrative' research, often funded by government agencies, which is tied to government agendas around 'impact', 'creative economy', and 'skills' (Schlesinger, 2016a).

In this section, we outline shifts and continuities in normative approaches to media production in recent decades, followed by a reflection on the ongoing challenge and importance of moral, ethical, and political motivations in such research. This allows us to identify the variegated concern with the normative in production research, illustrating how such concerns (and the lack of them) are rooted in broader historical and cultural trends, as well as the changing political economy of the media. For the sake of argument, therefore, we have chosen to identify three separate categories of production research that tackle normativity (or choose not to) in distinctive ways. It is important to note that such a categorization does not aim to represent the breadth and diversity of media production research, which would be impossible within the limits of this short chapter.

First, there is the 'first wave' of production studies, largely emerging from the US and the UK in the 1970s and early 1980s – best illustrated by the work of media sociologists such as Altheide (1976), Alvarado and Stewart (1985), Schlesinger (1987), and Elliot (1972). These formative production studies were often concerned with the influence of capitalist ideology on individual cultural producers and the relationship between structure – the oftn routinized and formulaic ways in which media work was organized – and 'superstructure' – how media productions were supposed to turn a profit. The question of agency and autonomy were explicitly emphasized. The quality of the media text produced (be it a documentary, news, journalism) and its ideological function within society were foregrounded as a major concern of such research.

Second, there is the category of research emerging from within cultural studies from the late 1990s onwards, focused on precarious work, governmentality (as in the organized practices through which media workers are governed), individualization, self-exploitation, and risk. Responding to the increasing precarity of cultural work, as well as its proliferation as a dominant mode of employment, the focus of this scholarly work is explicitly political, opposed to the valorization of 'creativity' within policy discourse, and is less concerned with the media content being produced than with the experiences of individual cultural producers. Concerns around governmentality and the internalization of power are pivotal to this work, although some critics have argued that little space is left for individual agency or the possibility of social change (see Hesmondhalgh, 2009). Key writers involved in this work include McRobbie (2002), Ross (2004), Ursell (2000), and Gill (2002).

Third, there is a relatively recent and still-evolving body of work (sometimes, but not always) influenced by moral philosophy and 'moral economy' approaches to media production, which is explicitly concerned with moral normativity and focused on questions of 'good work', 'justice', inequality, and the media texts produced in contemporary production contexts. Such work fits into a more general critique of capitalism (and therefore media production under capitalism) and seeks to consider media production within the context of wider social concerns such as inequality (Oakley & O'Brien, 2016; Banks, 2017), human flourishing (Hesmondhalgh, 2017), and environmental crisis (Pettinger, 2015).

Patterns of continuity can be identified across these bodies of research: for example, the question how powerful interests and concerns shape texts are central and ongoing, but changes are apparent. We can see how the focus of contemporary researchers' interests have extended to include policymakers, management, and audiences (Schlesinger, 2016a). A clear shift in the political economic structure of the media industries is also apparent as this work is surveyed historically, from the relatively stable workplace foci of the early production researchers, to the fragmented and networked precarity studied by writers such as De Peuter *et al.* (2017). An interest in below-the-line workers and supporting industries can also be noted as a more recent trend (Mayer, 2011). While the rise of apolitical, economistic research has come to dominate certain sub-fields of production studies, ethical and political concerns with media and power have certainly gained ground in the wake of the financial crisis and the rise of authoritarian, right-wing populism. Below, we consider some of the methodological challenges that are posed to those undertaking critical research.

Methodological implications

As explained above, media production research is concerned with the activities and opinions of media producers and what influences them, prompting researchers to adopt what Sayer calls an 'intensive' research design (1992, 2000). Intensive research aims to explore causal processes in a limited number of cases, it investigates how processes work and what agents actually do. Whilst extensive research is concerned with identifying 'common properties and general patterns of a population as a whole' (Sayer, 1992, p. 242), intensive research provides a 'causal explanation of the production of certain objects or events' by studying the actual connections between actors (*Ibid.*, p. 243). Its methodology is consequently qualitative in nature and often ethnographic, using forms of observation and in-depth interviewing as its two primary methods (Newcomb, 1991). They provide the opportunity to observe social practices, explore the mindset of media producers, and reveal constraints, complexities, and discourses at play in the process (Cottle, 2007).

Whilst these methods permit researchers to gather the thick, in-depth data needed to describe, explain, and evaluate media production practices, they also depend greatly on the cooperation of media producers. And critical production research often invites resistance from the very institutions it aims to investigate, precisely because of its emphasis on political normativity. This has implications for the design and conduct of such research and direct consequences for data quality. Of course, all media research and research methods suffer certain limitations; we focus here on challenges that are particularly pronounced when researching sites of media production. The most significant hurdles to successful undertaking production research are connected to the hidden nature and commercial objectives of the processes it aims to reveal. They lead to access restrictions, create tensions in the field, and call for resource-intensive methods.

Funding

Ethnographic research provides rich data for media production researchers but, compared to other research methods, it involves a long and intensive fieldwork process that commands extensive institutional and personal resources. Researchers have spent months, even years, as observers or participant observers in media institutions, requiring them to be relieved from regular teaching and administrative duties (Ryfe, 2016). Consequently, to obtain sufficient funding to cover this labour-intensive process can be challenging. The affordability of extended ethnographic research in an academic context is relatively low and today predominantly tends to be undertaken as part of doctoral research projects.

Obtaining research funding is a general challenge that can be further pronounced depending on fashions and priorities of research funding bodies. For example, research funding around the world increasingly focuses on impact-led data collection, which favours more predictable and less explorative work. As Schlesinger (2016a) has recently argued, the focus on impact and 'knowledge exchange' means that media production research 'has to negotiate with a creative economy discourse that has a global purchase' (*Ibid.*, p. 32). This situation does not favour more critical approaches to media production, for those 'dissenters' from the creativity script, 'the price is to be largely ignored outside academic debate and sometimes within it' (*Ibid.*). Funding is, of course, a major part of this – who gets funded and for what in many ways predetermines the changing nature of the field. For example, getting access to do market research for a company may be relatively unproblematic; equally, administrative research within the industry opens up many more sources of potential funding.

However, finding funding for normative, critical research is a different thing altogether. Ethnographic production research with unpredictable and ungeneralizable outcomes, tends not to be a priority for funding bodies. Strictly administrative research aiming for an increase of industry efficiency, profitability, or sustainability is more likely to meet current funding criteria compared to political and normative research that explores complex questions about commercial constraints, unequal labour markets, and sources of exploitation.

This situation challenges critical researchers to come up with alternative solutions in order to limit the drain on financial resources and research duration. For example, this may include shorter but repeated visits to field sites over a longer period, rather than being continuously embedded in a media institution. Choosing local research sites and subjects makes this easier to achieve and allows for ad hoc visits. Another strategy is to carry out interviews, rather than extended ethnographic observation in the field. Interviews can be scheduled more flexibly and require less time in comparison, but they are still fairly labour-intensive and incur additional costs through travel and transcription. Yet, even provided resources for production research are available, researchers need to overcome a second barrier to making media production research happen: obtaining access to the field of production.

Access

Access to the object of their investigation is an essential condition for any researcher. For researchers studying media production, this can prove to be an extraordinary challenge, especially compared to textual or audience research. The hidden nature of production requires direct access to media producers and production processes to collect data. If access is not granted, research sites for production research are often difficult to replace as research interests tend to focus on the operation of particular institutions or gatekeepers. Difficulties gaining access are a common grievance shared by production researchers and a typical subject of reflection in their publications (e.g. Born, 2004; Dornfeld, 1998; Silverstone, 1985). A small-scale survey among media ethnographers by Paterson and Zoellner (2010) explored their experience concerning access to media production sites. It showed that the most common reasons to refuse researchers access to production companies are, firstly, time and therefore economic concerns for media producers who need to invest part of their personal and professional time to participate in the research process, and secondly, concerns about potential negative publicity and the disclosure of confidential information with consequent risks for intellectual property. As our own research experience has shown, concerns over the implications of disclosure do not necessarily imply a general disinterest towards production research. Rather, most people like to talk about what they do, but many prefer to do so off-record.

The growth of media institutions across various media platforms in recent decades has done little to reduce the struggle over access. Rather than alleviating the problem, since there are more production sites to approach for research, the fierce competition in a predominantly commercial environment heightens producers' concerns and secrecy remains a key business principle. Furthermore, organizations that are frequently the subject of critical academic research are particularly wary about submitting to independent scrutiny. The expansion of production studies as a field has led to greater visibility of production researchers and their work, and therefore increased media producers concerns about publicity. It also means more people are trying to get access, whilst the number of media organizations – especially the most influential ones – is limited, despite the recent growth of the sector.

Public service media organizations, on the other hand, have an obligation to public accountability that should make them more open to production researchers (Lindlof, 1995) and institutions like the BBC have met this expectation, although hesitantly (e.g. Born, 2004; Schlesinger, 1987). However, these organizations are small in number and, in Western societies, mostly positioned in the broadcasting sector with few cases in other media industries such as publishing, music, or video games. And, being subjected increasingly to public scrutiny and internal reorganization, even these organizations may refuse access (e.g. Munnik, 2016).

Researchers have adopted various strategies to overcome this resistance. They include, firstly, compromises with regard to the publication of research findings. For example, researchers may offer media institutions and producers anonymity, exclude certain aspects or delay publication to protect commercial confidentiality (Freeman, 2016). However, this may not always be possible or impact on research validity, especially if the people or organizations involved are easily identifiable due to their position in their respective industry or the texts they create (Bruun, 2016).

Secondly, researchers have drawn on their own industry experience, i.e. previous professional experience as media workers, in access negotiations. According to Paterson and Zoellner (2010, 98-99), professional experience can offer 'insider' access and increase the level of trust between media producer and researcher as 'one of us' encouraging greater levels of disclosure from the former. Of course, such familiarity with the studied field may risk a certain lack of distance and openness that could lead to a kind of professional blindness (Burgess, 1984). On the other hand, it assists researchers in better understanding the practices they observe in a busy workplace that leaves little time for basic explanations (Newcomb, 1991).

Thirdly, in ethnographic research, researchers may become active participants in the research site rather than just being observers. Active participation can make the researcher presence less obtrusive in the field and offer organizations free labour as a trade-off for access. It also facilitates greater access within the field, as a participant-researcher needs to have access to specific processes, communication, and documentation in order to successfully fulfil his or her contribution to the production (e.g. Dornfeld, 1998; Zoellner, 2010; Ryfe, 2016). On the downside, this approach carries the risk of 'going native', influences observed reality, and creates challenges for balancing the time spent in the field between media work and academic research.

Finally, production research may focus on activities that are openly observable either in person (for example, attending a talk show as a member of the studio audience), or online (for example, following the progress of a crowdfunding project). Or, rather than investigating specific individuals and institutions, research may be based on interviews with certain types of media workers, which may allow for anonymization and easier contributor replacements. For example, the majority of the recent work on media labour is based on interview data. This approach offers easier access and requires less resources, but it also intensifies challenges for the interaction with media producers in the field.

Field relations

Related to the problems researchers experience over access are challenges they encounter during fieldwork. These challenges are rooted in the particular nature of media producers as research subjects. Although it can be supplemented with document analysis, for example in form of historical archive-based research (e.g. Lee & Corner, 2017), the empirical study of media production always depends on the cooperation of media producers in the field. Often it is hard to achieve this cooperation, even if general access to a production site has been granted. Researchers might experience a sceptical or hostile attitude to their work and consequently meet resistance in the field. This may include refusing access to meetings and documentation, postponing conversations and interviews, and withholding or concealing information.

There are several factors that contribute to hesitation and opposition among media producers. Historically, the relationship between the media and media scholarship has been full of tensions, with frequent critical and dismissive reference to media studies in media representations (Curran, 2013). Based on interviews with media industry scholars, Freeman (2016) reports a sense of distance and distrust towards academia linked to a perceived lack of relevance and understanding in media studies, on the one hand, and concerns about being the subject of critical scrutiny that may challenge industry accounts, on the other hand.

In addition to this rather general attitude, challenges in the field are rooted in the specific professional characteristics of media producers and the relative position of power they hold in society. Media producers are powerful gatekeepers and creators of information with expert knowledge who, in a methodological context, need to be understood and studied as an elite (see Radway, 1989; Moyser & Wagstaffe, 1987). Bruun (2016) suggests that they are furthermore exclusive informants, who are investigated not as representatives of an elite, but as means to gain insight into the production of media texts. Media producers often have exclusive knowledge, making them irreplaceable as research participants. This creates an asymmetry in the power relationship between media producer and researcher which influences the research process and can lead to a 'patronizing and impatient attitude towards the researcher' (*Ibid.*, p. 139).

Besides, media producers are highly self-reflexive in their professional practice (Caldwell, 2008). The fact that media producers themselves are in the business of studying, interpreting, and representing reality in one form or other – often through a critical lens – can make them particularly cautious towards being the subject of research and concerned about the research outcome and consequences (e.g. Deacon *et al.*, 1999). This can encourage producers to repeat information that has already been publicized – and thus sanctioned by the media institution in question – about the media text, organization, or practice under investigation. Although this in itself can be considered a research finding, it makes it difficult for researchers to gather new insights.

A critical research approach, as we suggest here, tends to aggravate these tensions and concerns. Bruun (2016) suggests counterbalancing the effects of the asymmetric power between media producer and researcher by regarding their relationship as a 'meeting between professionals from different fields', with academics sharing access to the public sphere and therefore being a contributor to media content and the public cultural debate (*Ibid.*, 139-140). Such framing can aid negotiations over access and facilitate a more equal footing in the research field.

Other factors to reduce barriers and resistance in the field are participation in the field and professional familiarity with industry conditions, processes, and developments, as they can help to build trust between researcher and media producers (Bruun, 2016; Munnik, 2016). Getting to know the research subjects over time can further help to enhance trust, for example through a longer fieldwork period or repeat visits. As a participant in the field, the position within the organizational hierarchy also matters. The higher up, the more respect and access a researcher may be granted. On the other hand, participating in a position with low hierarchical status can make a researcher less visible and obtrusive in the field and thus reduce awareness and increase openness among the studied media producers (Grindstaff, 2002).

Approaching and engaging with media producers across different levels of power and drawing on their own networks through snowballing techniques are further helpful strategies (Bruun, 2016, p. 141). Finally, a multi-method approach and data triangulation combining information gathered through observation, interviews, and document study for example, help to overcome problems of authenticity and promotional discourses in media producers' responses as well as to verify research data.

Conclusion

The challenges for normative, critically informed media production research in the twenty-first century are manifold, as outlined above. Undertaking production research has never been methodologically, financially, and theoretically straightforward, and researchers have always had to grapple with the multiple challenges of access, funding, and distrust. However, the nature of the contemporary challenges is distinctive.

In the UK, for example, transformations in the political economy of the funding environment, closely connected to the rise of 'creative economy' orthodoxy and impact case studies that are deemed 'useful' to policymakers and industry bodies, have reduced the scope for production researchers to carry out in-depth, critical, and immersive research. Such dynamics are not unique to the UK, and evidence of similar policy orientations and funding requirements are in evidence globally, although the language and tropes used may be different (Schlesinger, 2016b).

Changes in media industries and production also create challenges – researchers must respond to digitalization, convergence, new platforms, corporate conglomeration, transnational production and distribution, and changing labour structures. Struggles in gaining access and negotiating gatekeepers are not new, but the obstacles posed by regimes of reputation management and public relations to researchers seeking access are of a new intensity.

Nevertheless, new challenges present new opportunities. Politically and ethically, studies of media production have never seemed more vital. In an age of 'fake news', increasing social and political polarization, not to mention global crises of capitalism and the environment, studying the role that the media play in defining and shaping our public sphere is a matter of political urgency. To name just one example, the recent surge of so-called poverty porn programming on television screens has not only responded to a political climate of anti-welfare austerity, but also helped define the toxic nature of that discourse. As Benedictis *et al.* (2017) have shown, understanding the production processes and the moral economy involved in the creation of such content is a critical intellectual task. Such a case study illustrates the broader requirements for intensive, critical media production studies to help inform our understanding of media power.

The political economic and creative transformations within media industries and production also suggest new research foci and call for methodological expansion. With few exceptions, existing media production research tends to focus on individual sites of production within a single national context. We argue that, in order to understand contemporary media production in its international, digital, and corporate setting, we need to broaden our research approach. We need more comparative multi-sited, multi-national production research to learn more about the interconnected and transnational nature of media production. We need more longitudinal studies to assess change and continuity in an ever-changing industrial context. And we need more research that combines the study of production processes and practices with an analysis of content and form of media texts that considers genre and industry specifics to further our critical investigation not only of how media are made, but also what is good and bad about it.

Such an expansion of media production research does not reduce the methodological and normative challenges we have described above. Rather, it increases the need for funding as well as the dependency on access and media producer cooperation in most cases. However, a politically pro-active approach supported by digital technology may counteract some of these limitations. For example, lobbying for greater transparency and accountability of media organizations could provide arguments for academic access to production sites and encourage these organizations to enable production research. Developing large-scale, cross-disciplinary research projects, on the other hand, would enable researchers to approach various diverse funding opportunities, spreading the challenge of obtaining resources across team members from different research groups. Similarly, production research could form just one part of a larger project that applies multiple methods and thus might overcome funding bodies' concerns over resources and impact.

Finally, we should explore the opportunities digital and online technology offer for accessing and investigating production processes and practices. This may, for example, include remote-recording of meetings, access to producers' digital devices or obtaining copies of their work through automated back-ups, screen capture or cloud storage. It may, moreover, prove fruitful to further develop online ethnography (collecting data from sources online with specific reference to media professionals and/or the media production process).

To facilitate future production research in order to broaden our understanding of media production matters, especially considering the growth and diversity of the media industries and ongoing transformations in organizational form, economic structure, and everyday practices. The largely invisible nature of production helps to perpetuate problematic practices and structures within the media industries including, for example, gender inequality, abuses of power, and creative constraints. Media production research can reveal such conditions and contribute to industrial change. Critical media production studies provide a rare countervailing current against the logics of commercialization within the media industries, providing a space to reflect on the potential public value of cultural production. As such, critical production research can benefit not only society but the media industries themselves.

As Freeman (2016) highlights, media producers rarely have the opportunity to critically evaluate their practice in a work environment marked by time and commercial pressure. Critical academic research is dedicated specifically to such evaluation. It offers different perspectives and values for the consideration of creative practice, provides insights about the future of media production based on a consideration of change and continuity, and offers the rare opportunity to reflect on 'good work' and a better media system.

Further reading
- Case: Three case studies on the working conditions within the cultural and creative industries and how they are affectively experienced – Cantillon & Baker (p. 287)
- Context: An overview of the most compelling, inspiring, and provocative scholarship in the field of media industry studies to be published in the past decade – Holt & Perren (p. 31)
- Contrast: How the question of (digital) access forms a challenge for media industries research – Vonderau (p. 61)

References

Altheide, D. (1976). *Creating Reality: How Television News Distorts Events*. Los Angeles, CA: SAGE Publications.

Alvarado, M. & Stewart, J. (1985). *Made for Television: Euston Films Limited*. London: BFI Publishing.

Banks, M. (2017). *Creative Justice: Cultural Industries, Work and Inequality*. London: Pickering & Chatto Publishers.

BBC (2017). 'Harvey Weinstein Timeline: How the Scandal Unfolded', BBC News (24 November). Retrieved from http://www.bbc.co.uk/news/entertainment-arts-41594672.

Born, G. (2004). *Uncertain Vision: Birt, Dyke and the Reinvention of the BBC*. London: Secker & Warburg.

Burgess, R. G. (1984). *In the Field: An Introduction to Field Research*. London: George Allen and Unwin.

Bruun, H. (2016). 'The Qualitative Interview in Media Production Studies', in C. Paterson, D. Lee, A. Saha & A. Zoellner (eds). *Advancing Media Production Research* (131-146). London: Palgrave Macmillan.

Caldwell, J. (2008). *Production Culture: Industrial Reflexivity and Critical Practice in Film and Television*. Durham, NC, and London: Duke University Press.

Cottle, S. (2000). 'New(s) Times: Towards a 'Second Wave' of News Ethnography', *Communications*, 25(1), 19-42.

Cottle, S. (2007). 'Ethnography and News Production: New(s) Developments in the Field', *Sociology Compass*, 1(1), 1-16.

Curran, J. (2013). 'Mickey Mouse Squeaks Back: Defending Media Studies', in *Keynote Address to MECCSA Conference*. University of Derry. Retrieved from http://www.meccsa.org.uk/news/mickey-mouse-squeaks-back-defending-media-studies/.

Davis, H. & Scase, R. (2000). *Managing Creativity*. Philadelphia, PA: Open University Press.

De Benedictis, S., Allen, K. & Jensen, T. (2017). 'Portraying Poverty: The Economics and Ethics of Factual Welfare Television', *Cultural Sociology, 11*(3), 337-358.

De Peuter, G., Cohen, N.S. & Saraco, F. (2017). 'The Ambivalence of Coworking: On the Politics of an Emerging Work Practice', *European Journal of Cultural Studies*, 20(6), 687-706.

Deacon, D., Murdock, G., Pickering, M. & Golding, P. (1999). *Researching Communications: A Practical Guide to Methods in Media and Cultural Analysis*. London: Arnold.

Dornfeld, B. (1998). *Producing Public Television, Producing Public Culture*. Princeton, NJ: Princeton University Press.

Elliot, P. (1972). *The Making of a Television Series: A Case Study in the Sociology of Culture*. London: Constable.

Freeman, M. (2016). *Industrial Approaches to Media: A Methodological Gateway to Industry Studies*. London: Palgrave.

Gill, R. (2002). 'Cool, Creative and Egalitarian? Exploring Gender in Project-Based New Media Work in Euro', *Information, Communication & Society*, 5(1), 70-89.

Grindstaff, L. (2002). *The Money Shot: Trash, Class, and the Making of TV Talk Shows*. Chicago, IL: University of Chicago Press.

Havens, T., Lotz, A.D. & Tinic, S. (2009) 'Critical Media Industry Studies: A Research Approach', *Communication, Culture & Critique*. 2(2), 234-253.

Hesmondhalgh, D. (2009). 'Politics, Theory and Method in Media Industries Research', in J. Holt & A. Perren (eds), *Media Industries: History, Theory, Method* (245-255). Malden, MA and Oxford: Blackwell Publishing.

Hesmondhalgh, D. (2010). 'Normativity and Social Justice in the Analysis of Creative Labour', *Journal for Cultural Research*, 14(3), 231-249.

Hesmondhalgh, D. (2017). 'Capitalism and the Media: Moral Economy, Well-Being and Capabilities', *Media, Culture & Society*, 39(2), 202-218.

Hesmondhalgh, D. & Baker, S. (2011). *Creative Labour: Media Work in Three Cultural Industries*. London: Routledge.

Hutton, J. G., Goodman, M. B., Alexander, J. B. & Genest, C. M. (2001). 'Reputation Management: The New Face of Corporate Public Relations?', *Public Relations Review*, 27(3), 247-261.

Lee, D. & Allen, K. (2017). 'Government Media Policy Means BBC Pay Inequality is Likely to Grow Worse', *The Conversation* (24 July). Retrieved from https://theconversation.com/government-media-policy-means-bbc-pay-inequality-is-likely-to-grow-worse-81411.

Lee, D. & Corner, J. (2017). 'After Dark: Channel 4's Innovation in Television Talk', *Journal of British Cinema and Television, 14*(4), 445-463.

Lindlof, T. (1995). *Qualitative Communication Research Methods*. Thousand Oaks, CA: SAGE Publications.

Mayer, V. (2011). *Below the Line: Producers and Production Studies in the New Television Economy*. Durham, NC: Duke University Press.

McRobbie, A. (2002). 'Clubs to Companies: Notes on the Decline of Political Culture in Speeded up Creative Worlds', *Cultural Studies*, 16(4), 516-531.

Moyser, G. & Wagstaffe, M. (eds). (1987). *Research Methods for Elite Studies*. London: Allen and Unwin.

Munnik, M. (2016). 'When You Can't Rely on Public or Private: Using the Ethnographic Self as Resource', in C. Paterson, D. Lee, A. Saha & A. Zoellner (eds), *Advancing Media Production Research* (147-160). London: Palgrave Macmillan.

Newcomb, H. (1991). 'The Creation of Television Drama', in N. Jankowski & K. Jensen (eds), *A Handbook of Qualitative Methodologies for Mass Communication Research* (93-107). London: Routledge.

Oakley, K. & O'Brien, D. (2016). 'Learning to Labour Unequally: Understanding the Relationship between Cultural Production, Cultural Consumption and Inequality', *Social Identities*, 22(5), 471-486.

Paterson, C. & Zoellner, A. (2010). 'The Efficacy of Professional Experience', *Journal of Media Practice,* 11(2), 97-109.

Paterson, C., Lee, D., Saha, A. & Zoellner, A. (2016a). 'Production Research: Continuity and Transformation', in C. Paterson, D. Lee, A. Saha & A. Zoellner (eds), *Advancing Media Production Research: Shifting Sites, Methods, and Politics* (3-19). London: Palgrave Macmillan.

Paterson, C., Lee, D., Saha, A. & Zoellner, A. (eds) (2016b). *Advancing Media Production Research: Shifting Sites, Methods, and Politics*. London: Palgrave Macmillan.

Peterson, R.A. (1985). 'Six Constraints on the Production of Literary Works', *Poetics*, 14, 45-67.

Peterson, R.A. & Berger, D.G. (1975). 'Cycles in Symbol Production: The Case of Popular Music', *American Sociological Review*, 40, 158-73.

Pettinger, L. (2015). *Work, Consumption and Capitalism*. London: Palgrave Macmillan.

Radway, J. (1989). 'Ethnographies among Elites: Comparing Discourses of Power', *Journal of Communication Inquiry*, 13(2), 3-11.

Ross, A. (2004). *No-Collar: The Humane Workplace and Its Hidden Costs*. Philadelphia, PA: Temple University Press.

Ryfe, D. (2016). 'The Importance of Time in Media Production Research', in C. Paterson, D. Lee, A. Saha & A. Zoellner (eds), *Advancing Media Production Research* (38-50). London: Palgrave Macmillan.

Sayer, A. (1992). *Method in Social Science: A Realist Approach*. 2nd ed. London: Routledge.

Sayer, A. (2000). *Realism and Social Science*. Thousand Oaks, CA and London: SAGE Publications.

Schlesinger, P. (1987). *Putting 'Reality' Together: BBC News*. London: Taylor & Francis.

Schlesinger, P. (2016a). 'On the Vagaries of Production Research', in C. Paterson, D. Lee, A. Saha & A. Zoellner (eds), *Advancing Media Production Research*, (20-37). London: Palgrave Macmillan.

Schlesinger, P. (2016b). 'The Creative Economy: Invention of a Global Orthodoxy', *Les Enjeux de l'information et de la communication*, 2, 187-205.

Silverstone, R. (1985). *Framing Science: The Making of a Television Documentary*. London: British Film Institute.

Tschmuck, P. (2003). 'How Creative are the Creative Industries? A Case of the Music Industry', *The Journal of Arts Management, Law, and Society*, 33(2), 127-41.

Ursell, G. (2000). 'Television Production: Issues of Exploitation, Commodification and Subjectivity in UK Television Labour Markets', *Media, Culture & Society*, 22(6), 805-825.

Wright, K. (2015). 'A Quiet Revolution: The Moral Economies Shaping Journalists' Use of NGO-Provided Multimedia in Mainstream News about Africa' (PhD thesis). Goldsmiths, University of London, London.

Zoellner, A. (2010). 'Creativity and Commerce in Independent Television Production: Developing Documentaries in the UK and Germany' (PhD thesis). University of Leeds, Leeds.

4.   Access and Mistrust in Media Industries Research

Patrick Vonderau

Studying the media industries means dealing with all kinds of tensions. This chapter discusses the value and challenges of media industries research, focusing on the question of (digital) access. Access is a complex problem that touches upon political, strategical, ethical, and methodological choices to be made by the researcher.

Introduction

In the context of the study of media production and industries and the making of media, I think of 'theory' and 'practice', or media studies and media work, as unlike cultures that interact on many levels. While differing in many ways, and perhaps even disagreeing on their exchange itself, these groups can still 'hammer out a local coordination despite vast global differences'. Peter Galison, a historian of science, has described such coordination between dissimilar groups as a 'trading zone' in his account of modern physics (Galison, 1997, p. 783).

We can think of media industries research as one such contact zone where exchange happens between different groups – academics, industry professionals, policymakers, journalists, and consumers. Doing research in this area requires crossing two boundaries simultaneously: the boundary in-between academic disciplines, on the one hand, and the boundary between academia and the world it observes, on the other. It requires engaging in intra-group contact between various disciplines as well as in inter-group encounters between media studies and media work.

Media industries research often goes along with an experience of tensions that result from such encounters. Proponents of the field describe its mission as a 'transdisciplinary conversation about the converging global media landscape' (Holt & Perren, 2009, p. 14). It is an integrative approach to studying cultural production bottom-up, focusing on the role of individual agents within larger media structures. This means importing participant observation, ethnography, shadowing, interviewing, and other social science methods into humanities-based research traditionally premised on analysing and interpreting texts (Caldwell, 1993). It also means engaging in a direct conversation with those involved in producing and distributing texts.

To study the media industries thus has become a way of critical social thinking, and has established a trading zone between the humanities and social sciences, and between media and communication studies. It is also one of the few areas of academic work that not only encourages, but requires direct engagement with media work. Landmark studies such as Grindstaff's *The Money Shot: Trash, Class, and the Making of TV Talk Shows* (2002), Born's *Uncertain Vision: Birt, Dyke and the Reinvention of the BBC* (2005), or Caldwell's *Production Culture: Industrial Reflexivity and Critical Practice in Film and Television* (2008) have all grown out of industry-academic interaction that included both critical theorizing and direct workplace observation. Some scholars have turned from academics to media practitioners, others from professional insiders to academic observers (e.g. Hill, 2016).

Establishing such contact zones between theory and practice, and in-between disciplines that are sometimes seen as antagonistic, also comes with tensions or unwanted results. On an inter-group level, the relation between researcher and researched is marked by asymmetries and often quickly changing imbalances of power that are difficult to control for both sides. Industry-academic encounters include complex negotiations of disclosure, tacit expectations regarding trade-offs or gift-giving, and a game of partly covert intentions. Mutual trust and empathy factor in the ways the relation is set up and affect the quality of the data it may generate.

Intra-group encounters between scholars in the humanities and the social sciences are equally troubled, as text- and reception-oriented thought does not necessarily harmonize with social interests and an empiricist toolkit. Production Studies, for instance, a particularly successful subfield of academic exchange, has been hastily labelled without a proper contact language in place. Production scholars often engage in 'foreigner talk' (Galison, 1997, p. 770), borrowing methods from the social sciences. While it has become fashionable to do 'participant observation' in a media company, key concepts such as 'industry' or 'production' tend to remain undefined (Hesmondhalgh, 2010, p. 4).

This chapter addresses these problems through the lens of access. 'Access', here, is not confined to the issue of making first contact or establishing rapport with an industry insider. Rather, I understand access in the sense first proposed by anthropologist Laura Nader, as a form of 'studying up in our own society' (1972, p. 5). I will first discuss Nader's well-known position and that of her critics before briefly specifying an actual problem area and concrete ways to overcome the difficulties to be encountered there.

Studying up, down, sideways, or not at all

Writing in 1972, Nader was under the impression of Vietnam and the ongoing public protests when calling for the study of 'the colonizers rather than the colonized, the culture of power rather than the culture of the powerless' (*Ibid.*, p. 289). At her moment of writing, to study 'ourselves' and society at home, rather than original peoples on faraway islands was an obvious choice for anthropology, which had, as Nader noted, somewhat lost social relevance. In building on this prevailing 'normative impulse', Nader suggested 'studying up' to 'communication industries', banks, insurance companies, and major state institutions, rather than merely 'down' to the victims of the system. In doing so, she hoped to translate the political concern of her students into a form of research engagement with organizations and institutions that was both scientifically adequate and democratically relevant. To get 'at the mechanisms whereby far away corporations and large scale industries are directing the everyday aspects of our lives' (*Ibid.*, p. 19) meant that scholars would create transparency, and thus allow others to hold the powerful accountable. It meant a change in perspective as well as in the relation between researcher and researched. In short, Nader called for research as a form of engagement that would establish 'public access to information affecting the public interest' by linking the perspective of studying down to that of studying up (*Ibid.*).

How does this idea of access to power systems resonate with today's media industries research? In recent decades, such research has grown into one of the largest and most vibrant areas of media and communication studies, with multiple scholarly associations, specialized journals, conferences, and a steady annual output of book publications. The majority of this work takes a critical stance on the industries. Scholars have studied various consequences of digital disruption, such as the market power of tech companies, financial speculation, algorithmic biases and discrimination, user surveillance, misinformation, automation, precarious labour, or lack of regulatory oversight. Many of these researchers are quoted in the news, team up with journalists, or engage with the public via newspapers and trade magazines, academic news organizations such as *The Conversation*, and social media. Others provide information or advice to policymakers. To claim that this work is largely 'celebratory' is therefore misleading (cf. Wasko & Meehan, 2013). On the contrary, it seems fair to say that the general public today has much better access to critical information and differentiated debates about media industries than fifty years ago. Given that this is also the result of disciplinary border-crossing in the trading zone (Cottle, 2003, p. 5), it likewise misses the point to insist on clearly separated disciplinary silos and 'traditions' (Wasko & Meehan, 2013).

The question is, however, how deep that access goes, how it may be established and maintained, and what kind of methodological and ethical considerations it may require. Anthropologists who have studied the media industries are usually more wary of 'studying up' than non-anthropologists. Hortense Powdermaker, for instance, the social anthropologist often referred to as the first to do participant observation inside a Hollywood film studio in 1946-47, later acknowledged her dislike of this fieldwork, 'more so than of any of my other field experiences' (1966,

p. 211). She related this discontent with her book to both the research situation and her own disposition. Participant observation in the sense once proposed by Bronisław Malinowksi (1922), as a form of objectivity reached through immersion, by 'grasping the natives point of view, his relation to life, and to realize his vision of his world' (*Ibid.*, p. 25), was hardly possible:

> Data from interviews and filing cabinets were supplemented by a limited and rather superficial observation and participation. Occasionally, I went on a set and watched the director, actors, camera man, script-girl, and the many technicians involved in the shooting of a small scene. But repetition of this kind of observation neither gave me new data nor deepened my understanding. [...] The observer's role, as well as the participant's, was lacking in my Hollywood study. I did not *see* and *hear* people in actual work and life situations (Powdermaker, 1966, p. 222).

Powdermaker tried to balance the lack of data with archival work and interviews, but only managed to score very few interviews with 'the powerful men at the top', and these interviews 'resulted in only superficial data and impressions. Many would not consent to be interviewed at all and others agreed only if their public relations aide was present – not an interview in my estimation' (1966, p. 216). Apart from social issues, she also confessed to a psychological problem: normative bias and a craving for popularity. Somewhat embarrassed, Powdermaker later wondered 'what the book might have been if some of my involvements had not been hidden' and 'if my value system had not so aggressively dominated the whole study' (*Ibid.*, p. 231). She also disclosed that the structuring analogy of her book – to compare Hollywood to a primitive society marked by a habitat, myths, taboos, gods, and so on – was merely 'a gimmick, designed to make the book more popular rather than meaningful' (p. 231; cf. Powdermaker, 1950).

As a consequence, later anthropological work has largely given up on the idea of classic participant observation 'inside' the industry and on the notion of 'the industry' as a clearly demarcated field (Gusterson, 1997, p. 115). Sherry Ortner, for instance, suggests studying the 'inside/outside binary' instead – or what she describes as Hollywood's 'elementary structure' – that is, cultural practices to install and maintain boundaries between who is inside and who is not. Accordingly, Ortner devised a new method, 'interface ethnography', as a form of participant observation in the very border areas where a given community of cultural producers constitutes itself (2010, p. 213). Production scholars within media and communication studies have similarly suggested focusing on 'para-industries', in the sense of all those 'industrial, cultural and corporate fields that surround, buffer and complicate any access to what we traditionally regard as our primary objects of media research' (Caldwell, 2014, p. 721). Yet, such precautions have not made the industries more accessible or researchers less attention-seeking, nor have they helped them to overcome normative bias; rather, the opposite.

Ortner, assessing the difficulties she faced in gaining access to Hollywood interviewees, noted with surprise that they were 'working in the same general cultural zone as ourselves', but that belonging to this same 'class fraction', or what she called 'the PMC, the professional managerial class', did not ease the task of establishing rapport (Ortner, 2010, p. 223). She also admitted that her personal dislike of Hollywood mainstream production hampered her research capabilities, and she documents how an interviewee confronted her directly about her ignorance of the field. He 'clearly had no respect for academics', Ortner laments (*Ibid.*, p. 225), but one wonders what she might have expected: a 'studying up' on the practitioner's part? Thinking of the research relation in terms of class is little helpful. To enter a contact zone or sharing a similar social and educational background does not mean that researcher and researched are on par, or that the relation would be symmetrical. You can belong to the same social class, yet still to different cultures – and to acknowledge difference may be a precondition for discovering something new.

While Ortner struggled with her own situatedness in the field, others struggle with the fact that access to industries has to be constantly renegotiated. Since the 1950s, most media industries are not only dispersed spatially in a way that makes it difficult to construct a physical field site, they are also more used to researchers. Sensationalist disclosures by academics and journalists have contributed to today's culture of background- and agenda-checking and are one among several reasons that institutions of power often become 'impenetrable bastions of enclosure' (*Ibid.*, p. 221). For researchers, getting access at times amounts to a 'military campaign': it is 'partly legalistic, partly about sheer determination, partly about luck, and partly about going to key gatekeepers' (Szczepanik, 2013, p. 113). Once established, the relation between researcher and researched still is marked by imperfect reciprocity, role play, and 'bizarre forms of complicity' (Mayer, 2008, p. 145), with the scholar having to place herself variably at the low or high end of the control chain she aims to observe. It therefore is not always useful to follow the commonplace advice of establishing trust first in a research relationship, and to be open and transparent about one's aims. For trust may be unforgiving if you breach it (Carey, 2018).

As a consequence of these problems, a large part of media industries research today sits uncomfortably between 'up' and 'down' perspectives. Some media scholars proclaim to study 'sideways', but implicitly treat their subjects as something to study up to, raising questions about hidden complicity or ideologies. Others prefer to study at a distance, based on limited direct contact and on what social scientists have derogatively described as 'parachute' ethnographies, briefly jumping into this or that field from above for illustrative data.

Most media scholars still study down, however, following the predilection for the underdog that Nader tried to steer away from. Given the difficulty of talking to executives, isn't it better to just speak with those affected by their doing? Yet, such positioning also risks establishing a fixed system of normative reasoning around our relation to the researched. While normativity has been institutionalized in research areas such as political economy, it has limited acceptance in the social sciences. Do media workers suffer more than, say, teachers? Has the flurry of research on precarious media work contributed to changing labour conditions? Is this research always original and socially relevant for others, or is it sometimes engaging in 'pseudo-problematization' that 'reproduces the researcher's own assumptions' and merely follows a dynamic of 'adding-to-the-literature' (Alvesson *et al.*, 2017, p. 94)?

The tensions thus are considerable for media industry researchers, boxed in as they are between triumphalists and sceptics, public interest and corporate secrecy. Universities expect them to deliver on 'impact', humanists expect criticism, social scientists to move beyond normativity, and research subjects expect to be respected. Such are the odds in a trading zone, reminding us that trade always is inherently about conflict and competing expectations. The notion of a trading zone indeed 'highlights the multiple areas of conflict, miscomprehension, or incommensurability' that can arise between those engaging in exchange (Finch & Geiger, 2010, p. 119). To complain about this situation is as pointless for a media scholar as it is for a marine biologist to complain about the wetness of sea water. Especially since it is entirely possible to hammer out some local coordination despite all the vast global differences.

The real question to tackle, I argue, is how to develop a self-reflexive methodology and ethical judgement that responds to the ways these zones or sites of encounter are changing after the turn to the digital. Or, to again paraphrase Nader, how to create public access to information affecting the public interest in an era where 'information' and 'public interest' are redefined by engineers, internet entrepreneurs, and algorithms?

From access to digital access

Media companies whose main outputs are defined as information goods protected by intellectual property standards understandably prefer secrecy over public scrutiny, especially when heavily investing up front in the development of such property, as in the film industry. In order to avoid potential harm to their products and brands, these companies regularly use gatekeeping arrangements when interacting with scholars. Research interest is sometimes ignored, but it is also often welcomed, provided that it can be vetted, filtered, and guided in order to impose symmetry or at least balance between the legal and ethical interests of both the researcher and the researched. Sometimes, this balance of interest is secured in strictly formal ways and includes non-disclosure agreements, endorsements, or method sanctioning. Often, however, it develops more informally, built on mutual respect and the fact that many, if not most, media executives have both an academic background and a vested interest in studies of their operations that differ from business consultancy.

While digital industries are not necessarily an exception to this rule, it is hard to overlook the fact that the dynamics surrounding the issue of access have developed on somewhat different terms. Platforms such as Spotify, the music streaming service, for instance, obtain existing copyrighted content from sources they do not directly control, distribute this content, and produce customer data based on the interest the content generates. Various types of users are implicated in their product, or even *are* the product. Posing as open, accessible, and on par with their users in order to build these communities, digital media companies also create a legal frame around this arrangement that is both more restrictive and intrusive than earlier licence agreements. Spotify's Terms of Service, for instance, grant users a 'limited, non-exclusive, revocable' licence to use Spotify's content, while requiring users to grant Spotify a perpetual, irrevocable, worldwide licence of 'your User Content in connection with the Service through any medium' (Spotify, 2017). Users are also required to allow the service to use the processor, bandwidth, and storage hardware on their devices, to 'provide advertising and other information', and 'to allow our business partners to do the same'. Spotify even planned to access user contacts, photos, and GPS location before being stopped by the users and the press (Hern & Rankin, 2015).

Media scholars planning to research these services are part of an asymmetrical arrangement before even having begun their research. Nothing prevents them, of course, from extending their empirical work beyond the online presence of a given business. Thanks to such work, there is rich ethnographic documentation of developer communities, organizational cultures, and work practices (Kunda, 2006; Marwick, 2013; Gregg, 2015). On a data level, however, where corporations interface with their customers, access is framed in a way that prevents such in-depth scrutiny. Digital companies have gradually turned away from earlier 'soft power' arrangements with researchers, systematically channeling and formalizing this relationship. The most obvious example is, again, a given platform's Terms of Service; in Spotify's case, user guidelines do not permit, 'for any reason whatsoever', the research of Spotify with digital methods, and the relation is non-negotiable in situ (Spotify, 2017).

Channelling and formalizing goes beyond contractual frameworks, however. It concerns 'informed consent' more generally, a legal requirement and ethical imperative adopted from clinical research that has long guided scholars in conceiving their relation to the researched. In analogue environments, informed consent is what researchers get from their research subjects. In the digital sphere, it is the researchers who have to consent first in order to access a given service. Consent here is 'thin and fictional', according to legal experts, with current consent rules often 'disregarding the bilateral nature of consent transactions' (Grimmelmann, 2015, p. 246; Schermer *et al.*, 2014, p. 178). Digital services constantly do research on their users. Facebook, for instance, employs hundreds of social scientists. In 2012, Facebook tried to manipulate 689,003 users' feelings by altering their news feed (Grimmelmann, 2015). The company did not notify (let alone seek consent from) its research subjects.

Digital media companies also strategically manage their relationship with academia. Like any other major industry, media industries seek to assuage concerns by co-opting the discourse of their critics; they promote themselves as responsible, enhance their reputation through forging strategic partnerships, and occasionally spread uncertainty and doubt (Kirsch, 2014, p. 3). Research divisions at Microsoft, Facebook, Spotify, or Intel pay respected academics to set the agenda of public debate. Concepts launched from within the industry, such as 'platform', have become epistemic frames for critical research and policymaking. Scholars using metrics or tools for data collection found on platforms 'enter into highly troubling relations of dependency with the infrastructures and organizations that make them available' (Marres, 2017, p. 182). In 2018, Facebook increased this dependence by introducing 'a new model for industry-academic partnerships' designed to 'help' academics using their data (Gluckman, 2018), effectively restricting rather than enabling access to scholars.

As a consequence, researchers may be enticed or coerced into adopting the gatekeeper's perspective. Although this does not devalue future research accomplishments, it raises the question why research can or should not be imagined outside such symbiotic relationships between industries and their observers, and about the value and ethics of media industries research as such. Sociologist Niklas Luhmann (1994) once argued that all forms of science, including use-oriented research, are operating as 'distinction-generating programs' (*Ibid.*, p. 645), and thus crucially depend on establishing a difference between their observations and their objects. Where such distinctions are eliminated, we cannot speak of science, according to Luhmann. Does this mean that media industries research is no longer possible, now that the industries have moved online?

Conclusion

Looking back at the controversies within the modern physics community, Peter Galison observed that despite disagreeing on the meaning of the exchange itself, various subcultures with distinct identities still managed to coordinate and even to develop a useful contact language. As we have seen, 'access' is a complex problem that touches upon political, strategical, ethical, and methodological choices to be made by the researcher. It is not despite, but *because* of difference that exchange is possible, as I would like to argue in conclusion. Researchers do not need to insist on studying 'sideways', 'up', or 'down', because there is no need whatsoever to bring yourself into an immersive relationship of any kind with your subject, by making the other more important, comparing her to yourself, or by bringing her down to size. Rather, scholars studying media industries may want to adopt an 'attitude of outsidedness' that not only recognizes difference, but explores it. As organizational sociologist Barbara Czarniawska notes, 'an observer can never know *better* than an actor; a stranger cannot say *more* about any culture than a native, but observers and strangers can see *different* things than actors and natives can' (2014, p. 45).

It is only through such mutual respect between strangers that symmetry may occur, according to Czarniawska. This also means giving up an ideal of trust inherited from earlier field and clinical research; for strangers may respect each other without fully trusting each other. Trust, in fact, 'always implies a degree of dependency' and also a 'redistribution of control', as we 'relinquish control over our environment and attempt to extend control over others' (Carey, 2017, p. 7). To 'mistrust' means, in methodological terms, to use forms of non-participant observation, such as shadowing, when empirically being inside the field (Czarniawska, 2007). It means to carefully juxtapose data gathered 'inside' with those gathered 'outside', and to critically think through the boundary established between the two. Doing so also means to question – and occasionally break out of – epistemic frames that are taken for granted and suggested as the one and only way of doing the work. Scholars often will need to engage in covert research, rather than merely following a gatekeeper (Calvey, 2017), and this even may include violating a platform's Terms of Services. As a research ethics committee stated, 'If we only work with permission of Large Corporation, can we ever be critical of Large Corporation?' (SIGCHI Research Ethics, 2017).

Researchers do not have to study large corporations, of course, or to enter these companies on data level, as 'industries' is a flexible term that may variously comprise markets, networks or entrepreneurs as much as creative workarounds where data gathering may be objectionable. Where major digital companies are studied, however, 'symmetric fieldwork' is a best practice in media industries research in regard to strategy, methods, and politics. It does not strive to be 'nice to the natives' and is both fairer and more adequate in an industry context, because it 'allows one-self to be problematized in turn – at a certain cost to the researcher, of course' (Czarniawska, 2007, p. 12). To limit the costs, researchers then need to engage in a thorough risk assessment before starting their projects, and to explain their choices in ethical terms. This includes avoiding collecting any user data or sensitive company data, and to engage in context-sensitive, practical ethical judgement on a case-by-case level (Salganik, 2018). Importantly, it also includes matching approaches and methods to a given company's own informational norms.

Here, we finally return to the engagement Laura Nader was trying to inspire in her students; for the study of digital media industries and their role in disinformation is needed more than ever before.

Further reading
- Case: An ethnographic study of game developers and the changes in the game industry – O'Donnell (p. 427)
- Context: An overview of the most compelling, inspiring, and provocative scholarship in the field of media industry studies to be published in the past decade – Holt & Perren (p. 31)
- Contrast: Practical concerns for undertaking media production research, with a focus on the areas of access, resources, and field relations – Lee & Zoellner (p. 45)

References

Alvesson, M. *et al.* (2017). *Return to Meaning: A Social Science with Something to Say.* Oxford: Oxford University Press.

Finch G. (2010). 'Markets are Trading Zones: On the Material, Cultural, and Interpretative Dimensions of Market Encounters', in L. Araujo *et al.* (eds), *Reconnecting Marketing to Markets* (117-137). Oxford: Oxford University Press.

Caldwell, J.T. (1993). 'Televisuality as a Semiotic Machine: Emerging Paradigms in Low Theory', *Cinema Journal, 32*(4), 24-48.

Caldwell, J.T. (2008). *Production Culture: Industrial Reflexivity and Critical Practice in Film and Television.* Durham, NC and London: Duke University Press.

Caldwell, J.T. (2014). 'Para-Industry, Shadow Academy', *Cultural Studies, 28*(4), 720-740.

Calvey, D. (2017). *Covert Research: The Art, Politics and Ethics of Undercover Fieldwork.* London: SAGE Publications.

Carey, M. (2018). *Mistrust: An Ethnographic Theory.* Chicago, IL: HAU Books.

Cottle, S. (2003). *Media Organization and Production.* London: SAGE Publications.

Czarniawska, B. (2007). *Shadowing: And Other Techniques for Doing Fieldwork in Modern Societies.* Malmö: Liber.

Czarniawska, B. (2014). *Social Science Research: From Field to Desk.* London: SAGE Publications.

Galison, P. (1997). *Image and Logic: A Material Culture of Microphysics.* Chicago, IL: University of Chicago Press.

Ganti, T. (2012). *Producing Bollywood: Inside the Contemporary Hindi Film Industry.* Durham, NC: Duke University Press.

Gluckman, N. (2018). 'Facebook Says It Will Help Academics Use Its Data', *The Chronicle of Higher Education* (13 April).

Gregg, M. (2015). 'Hack for Good: Speculative Labour, App Development and the Burden of Austerity', *Fibreculture Journal, 25.* doi: 10.15307/fcj.25.186.2015.

Grimmelmann, J. (2015). 'Law and Ethics of Experiments on Social Media Users', *Colorado Technology Law Journal, 219*(13), 221-270.

Gusterson, H. (1997). 'Studying Up Revisited', *Political and Legal Anthropology Review, 20*(1), 114-119.

Hern, A. & Rankin, J. (2015). 'Spotify's Chief Executive Apologises after User Backlash over New Privacy Policy, *The Guardian* (21 August). Retrieved from www.theguardian.com/technology/2015/aug/21/spotify-faces-user-backlash-over-new-privacy-policy.

Hesmondhalgh, D. (2010). 'Media Industry Studies, Media Production Studies', in J. Curran (ed.), *Media and Society* (145-163). London: Bloomsbury.

Hill, E. (2016). *Never Done: A History of Women's Work in Media Production.* New Brunswick, NJ: Rutgers University Press.

Holt, J. & Perren, A. (eds). (2009). *Media Industries: History, Theory, and Method.* Chichester: Wiley-Blackwell.

Kirsch, S. (2014). *Mining Capitalism: The Relationship between Corporations and their Critics.* Berkeley, CA: University of California Press.

Kunda, G. (2006). *Engineering Culture: Control and Commitment in a High-Tech Corporation.* Philadelphia, PA: Temple University Press.

Luhmann, N. (1994). *Die Wissenschaft der Gesellschaft.* Frankfurt am Main: Suhrkamp.

Malinowski, B. (1922). *Argonauts of the Western Pacific: An Account of Native Enterprise and Adventure in the Archipelagos of Melanesian New Guinea.* London: Routledge & Kegan Paul.

Marres, N. (2017). *Digital Sociology: The Reinvention of Social Research.* Cambridge: Polity Press.

Marwick, A. (2013). *Status Update: Celebrity, Publicity, and Branding in the Social Media Age.* New Haven, CT: Yale University Press.

Mayer, V. (2008). 'Studying Up and F**cking up: Ethnographic Interviewing in Production Studies', *Cinema Journal, 47*(2), 141-148.

Nader, L. (1972). 'Up the Anthropologist: Perspectives Gained from Studying Up', in D.H. Hymes (ed.), *Reinventing Anthropology* (284-311). New York: Random House.

Ortner, S. (2010). 'Access: Reflections on Studying Up in Hollywood', *Ethnography, 11*(2), 211-233.

Pandian, A. (2015). *Reel World: An Anthropology of Creation.* Durham, NJ and London: Duke University Press.

Powdermaker, H. (1950). *Hollywood. The Dream Factory.* New York: Little, Brown & Co.

Powdermaker, H. (1966). *Stranger and Friend: The Way of An Anthropologist.* New York: Norten & Company.

Salganik, M. (2018). *Bit by Bit: Social Research in the Digital Age.* Princeton, NJ: Princeton University Press.

Schermer, B.W. *et al.* (2014). 'The Crisis of Consent: How Stronger Legal Protection may Lead to Weaker Consent in Data Protection', *Ethics and Information Technology, 16*(2), 171-182.

SIGCHI Research Ethics (2017). 'Do Researchers Need to Follow TOS?', *Medium* (30 November). Retrieved from https://medium.com/sigchi-ethics-committee/do-researchers-need-to-follow-tos-f3bde1950d3c.

Spotify (2017). 'Terms and Conditions of Use' (6 July). Retrieved from www.spotify.com/us/legal/end-user-agreement/#s4.

Szczepanik, P. (2013). 'On the Ethnography of Media Production: An Interview with Georgina Born', *Illuminace, 25*(3), 99-119.

Wasko, J. & Meehan, E. (2013). 'Critical Crossroads or Parallel Routes? Political Economy and Approaches to Studying Media Industries and Cultural Products', *Cinema Journal, 52*(3), 150-156.

5. Cultural and Creative Industries and the Political Economy of Communication

Bernard Miège

Media are part of the cultural industries. But what are the cultural industries, how do they differ from the creative industries, and how can we study the changes they are undergoing as a result of digitalization and the rise of the global communication giants? Using the lens of the political economy of communication, this chapter maps and discusses five current issues and trends relating to both industries.

Introduction

Economics is still far from being a significant part of humanities and social science work on media and communication. More often than not, economics is called upon to support reasoning and as an illustration or justification for changes and evolutions that are considered indisputable. In these situations, the economy generally resembles technology: it cannot be called into question. It illuminates the course of events. And in the last few decades it was essentially liberal, or more precisely neo-liberal thinking that inspired the approaches of economists.

It is the merit of a few pioneers (Dallas Smythe, Herbert Schiller, Thomas Guback, and Nicholas Garnham, among others) to have laid the foundations for a new and different approach that places economic logic in its increasingly internationalized historical and cultural context, and links it with social logic, thereby explaining the development of media and cultural industries. As Vincent Mosco rightly stated in a book that was published more than twenty years ago, but that is still relevant today: what defines the political economy of communication is the focus 'on the relation between the production, distribution and consumption of communication in historical and cultural context. This comprehensive analysis of the commodity form in communication includes an examination of print, broadcast and new electronic media, the role and the function of the audience, and the problem of social control' (Mosco, 1996).

The authors mentioned above proposed political economy as an analytical orientation due to transformations that were beginning to assert themselves in the function and role of media in various societies. These transformations have steadily increased, ultimately generating profound mutations characteristic of a (globalized) order of information and communication. More and more researchers are trying to study, specify in-depth, and confront these mutations.

If we were to synthesize the main proposals of the political economy of communication (PEC) today, we would focus on the following aspects:

- in general, the work developed under its label brings together several disciplines (especially economics, sociology, and political science, as well as cultural studies);
- as far as possible, observations should not be limited to a short time span (and to the foreseeable future), but they must articulate this dimension of time within a longer time frame; it is, for instance, a frequent mistake to think that that current informational and communicational phenomena emerged only with digital techniques;
- increasingly, studies are attempting to take into account the whole 'product cycle' of communication, not only from the point of view of the production process and the strategies of the producers, but also by integrating the strategies of the broadcasters, the sustainability of practices, the changes in technical innovations, and the reception by audiences;
- as regards the cultures at the heart of the activities made possible by the consumption of media products, we are equally interested in the phenomena of domination (in a globalized world), in the complexity of practices and their great differentiation (by ages, genders, social categories, cultures), and in the emphasis placed on the activity of consumers in an environment marked by commodification;
- finally, while information and communication play an increasing role in world trade to the benefit of mainly American companies and firms (notably the Big Five: Facebook, Apple, Alphabet, Microsoft, and Amazon), this tendency, incontestably, is accompanied by what must be regarded as a marked evolution towards a multi-polarization of the world, initiated especially by the BRIC countries (Brazil, Russia, India, and China).

This chapter presents five current issues and trends relating to the study of cultural and creative industries in the context of the PEC. Before doing so, it will first provide some methodological considerations, explain the difference between cultural and creative industries, and give a synthetic presentation of the diverse contributions of researchers to the field.

Methodological considerations

From a methodological point of view, it must be stressed that the studies under the PEC umbrella combine theoretical elaboration and empirical observation. The two components are indispensable, and theoretical reflexivity is regularly accompanied by field surveys, which explains the importance afforded to the social sciences. It is now accepted that it is not enough simply to have conceptual discussions or to just analyse global data. Such a broad perspective clearly distinguishes PEC from many other academic approaches and particularly from the work of media professionals or publicists.

However, it must be recognized that this perspective sometimes presents difficulties, for example when one is interested, as indicated above, in the whole cycle of a product or in the evolution of a sector or a chain (for example: book publishing). In these cases, it is difficult to simultaneously grasp parameters such as changes in industrial strategies and changes in consumption, as well as changes in the use of technical tools. How, then, should one proceed?

On the one hand, most of the time, one should not consider phenomena in their entirety or globality (for example, the evolution of the listening practices of all recorded music), nor limit oneself to microeconomic or micro-sociological investigations (investigating how someone listens to one particular music product). The best strategy is to choose a position that can be qualified as medium-range, neither macro, nor micro.

On the other hand, modelling on a more comprehensive scale can be used from the moment when the analysis has revealed a certain number of recurrent features that are relatively stable, at least in the middle term. The notion of a model is at the very least ambiguous, as well as scientifically criticized, because it is frequently associated with generalizations and forecasting. Another approach must be used, which considers the models as simplified representations of a process or system in order to highlight recurring and repeatable operating rules. One can thus observe similarities, oppositions and differences, and outline theoretical proposals likely to help understand the issues.

Cultural and creative industries

But what are the cultural industries? What is their originality, their real singularity? What explains their constant development for over a century, and the fact that this development has accelerated in the recent period?

Many authors do not address these questions, or are content with considerations of common sense, as if it were self-evident to treat publishing books, producing and streaming films, broadcasting programmes, producing recorded music, making video games, as well as spreading professional and scientific information and all the practices made possible by the use of information and communication technologies in an equivalent way. To point out that all these activities are made up of multiple socio-symbolic productions, which are regularly renewed and recognized more or less universally, is by no means sufficient. For it is also possible to indicate that there are many other productions of this type, equally commercial, which are not organized according to industrial modalities: for example, live shows, the arts, and so on. Together with other authors, I have endeavoured to clarify the specificities of the cultural industries beyond their various channels (Miège, 2011a,b, 2017); here I can only provide the essential points.

The main features of the cultural (and informational) industries can be summarized in five characteristics. Firstly, there is *a remarkable diversity of cultural products*. The world of the cultural industries is very diverse and includes a multitude of products. How can cultural commodities produced according to artisanal and small-scale methods coexist with a conception of production on an industrial scale? This coexistence – of the work of a struggling singer-songwriter right next to the management of recording artists with a global audience – is essential, and at the heart of the enormous variety of types of products observable. Either way, a process of reproduction is at work, hence a central position must be granted to the notion of reproducibility – of production processes and practices, of genres, formats and conventions, of ways of managing and promoting the work, of patterns of distribution and consumption of goods and services.

A second feature of the cultural (and informational) industries is *the unpredictable character of cultural (or informational) values* generated by industrialized cultural products. A significant proportion of cultural and informational products never, or rarely make it to the market, and that proportion is bigger than in other categories of industrialized day-to-day products (be it shampoo or car tyres). To attempt to control the effects of the uncertain character of product value, the cultural industries have devised a series of strategies to counter the enormous uncertainty and risk involved in producing their goods and services, such as: calculating cost per series or catalogue rather than per product; price fixing with wide margins beyond usual norms; not paying wages to staff (instead relying on per-project contracts and various forms of unpaid labour); the distribution of economic risks to smaller subcontractors called on to take artistic risks and innovate. These methods are somewhat structural and justify a separate treatment for the cultural and informational industries amongst other industrial fields.

A third feature forms *the specific working conditions*, characterized by an appeal to artistic and intellectual workers for product conception that operates mainly according to artisan modalities that are supposed to guarantee creative autonomy. It is important to note the recurring particularities of payment terms for most of those involved in product design – artists, creators and makers, freelance, occasional and atypically employed workers, technicians, etc. Payment for the majority of them falls outside the scope of the traditional wage system and they are often forced to accept being paid after the moment of conception via systems such as copyright enforcement and freelance remuneration. There are some permanent workers (statutory) in the media, but in every company, the employment of statutory workers is doubled by the employment of workers without any formal status, who do precarious and intermittent work. This is an established way of doing things that helps to provide fluid management of strong artistic and intellectual workforces that need to be able to adapt at any time to any number of fresh demands: genres, forms, standards, technologies, markets. This system creates permanent insecurity and leads to the existence of a reservoir of workers always ready to work under conditions of minimal job or wage security.

The fourth important characteristic of the cultural (and informational) industries is the existence of *two fundamental* (*generic*) *models* that form the basis of the exploitation of industrialized cultural merchandise from creation to consumption: the editorial model and the flow model. The world of cultural and informational products is extremely diverse. In these conditions, it is not surprising that the encounter between producers, artistic and intellectual workers, managers, directors, and technicians on the one hand, and consumers, readers, listeners, viewers, and internet users on the other, occurs in very diverse ways. These considerations lead to a fundamental distinction between an editorial model (originally book-, disc-, and film editing) and a flow model (originally mass radio and television). The distinction between the editorial model and the flow model has nothing to do with the material or immaterial character of programmes or cultural products. What distinguishes them is the possibility of accessing a unique and individualized programme, on the one hand, and a continually accessible set of programmes on the other hand; in the first case (the editorial model) with payment of the consumer, in the second (the flow model) by appealing to advertising resources.

These two models could be considered as ideal types. Digital technology at the moment favours the flow model and intervenes in the editorial model. The conditions have become very variable and, in fact, we find durable situations functioning partly according to one model and partly according to the other. There are currently six variations (Miège, 2017): 'Print News' with an almost complete series of situations moving between both editorial and flow models; 'Online documentary products'; 'Club logic' that allows subscribers to access a certain number of services, specially TV programmes, for the duration of the subscription; 'Brokerage', for which an intermediary, a broker or some kind of representative negotiates with distributors which products may be of interest to the consumer; 'Online special portal provider' with variable payment options; and, since the development of online social networks; and 'Platforms' that can be used to manage audiences.

The fifth and last feature of the cultural (and informational) industries is *a moderate internationalization* partially respecting national cultures as well as the private interests of firms. One may be surprised by this proposition; indeed, for a long time, American content firms (e.g. majors in the cinema, recorded music, or broadcasting) as well as Asian conglomerates have led aggressive strategies to conquer world markets, and this trend has undoubtedly increased with the advent of digital technologies. But even though these movements can hardly be contested, one should not forget the resulting opposition and even resistance. It is well known that the negotiations for the liberalization of world trade have met with disagreements about the products of the cultural industries, whether in the framework of the WTO or in concerns voiced at the UNESCO about diversity of cultural expressions. Furthermore, internationally operating cultural industries are often forced to localize their products and services to accommodate local tastes and market sensitivities.

With regard to the creative industries (architecture, fashion, design, performing and visual arts, etc.), there are some clear differences in comparison to the cultural industries (Bouquillion, Miège & Moeglin, 2013). While similarities and trends towards cooperation can be observed between both industries, these findings ignore a whole series of dissimilarities that are all the more evident (Bouquillion, Miège & Moeglin, 2015).

Firstly, the creative dimension of economic activities within the creative industries (and even more so for those that are specifically linked to the creative economy) cannot be placed on the same level as the social, symbolic, and imaginary dimension that is at the foundation of the cultural industries. In any case, the social recognition and, therefore, legitimacy of this creative dimension is less assured and more diffuse than those associated with cultural industries, even if this varies from one culture to another. Simply put, creativity is a value that is essentially attached to all production and economic activity.

There is also considerable heterogeneity between the various productive activities that authors classify as creative industries. Most of the time, these activities are not individualized and are combined with others. It has been pointed out that this is the case with design and architecture, but it is necessary to add creative work in advertising and, to some extent, the fashion industry and the clothing industry. What is identified as the creative industries is therefore either inseparable from mass industrial activities, in which they are the design phase, or it is removed from activity in the industrial sphere, as, for example, visual arts.

Product consistency seems to be similar if not analogous in the cultural as well as creative industries, but in both categories of industries analogies mainly concern semi-reproducible products (which remains a minority type within the cultural industries) and quite rarely concern reproducible (mass)products. And a significant difference emerges as to the very nature of these products: if both use creativity in the design phase, the products of the creative industries are also backed by the heritage they reproduce and extend by being exchanged and resold (as is the case with luxury goods and in the fashion industry). This is rarely the case for cultural products, only some of which have secondary markets for passionate collectors.

The phenomenon of the star system (or starization) is apparently common in both industries, but there are notable dissimilarities. In the creative industries it concerns the creators, whereas in the cultural industries it is the leading interpreters who become stars.

With regard to the entrepreneurial form within the creative industries, creation is done largely in-house. This is different from cultural industries, where the conception phase continues to be – usually – outsourced (writing books, recording music, making films), except in those industries that are organized as media industries (press, radio, and television) and in the 'new' industries (such as video games and app development).

Finally, if we look at the distribution of products, we note that the distribution of products from the creative socioeconomic sectors seems to obey the very specific rules that differentiate them from the cultural industries. All these creative companies are obliged to reserve a large part of their resources for fixed assets, such as a theatre, a rehearsal studio, office spaces, and retail real estate. On the other hand, within the cultural industries, only cinematographic exploitation presupposes such major fixed assets. News organizations generally have abandoned ownership of printing presses, film and television production is often outsourced or takes place in rented studios (with rented equipment), and all products are increasingly sold and distributed online.

Between the two categories of industries there thus remain significant differences. The products of the creative industries are backed by patrimonies and are often acquired for resale. The design of creative products is largely internalized (done in-house), whereas the reverse is true for cultural products. Brands and trust in brands is essential in the formation of use values within the creative industries. Finally, the distribution of products from the creative industries still requires the implementation of physical distribution, and remote access to products remains marginal.

However, as digitalization increasingly affects all industries (but with significant differences), there is some convergence between the cultural and creative industries taking place. At the same time, the position of the cultural socioeconomic sectors is still (very) dominant, according to macroeconomic indicators such as employment, turnover, and capitalization (Miège, 2018).

Five keys issues and trends

Social science research is very reserved in predicting future societal developments, but researchers must aim to identify the main issues and clarify situations that experts and publicists tend to make opaque or unnecessarily complex. We will limit ourselves here to five of these issues and trends relating to the study of cultural and creative industries, inspired by a PEC perspective.

1. *Towards maintaining significant distinctions between cultural industries and creative industries*

Above, we have shown that there are common traits, but also profound dissimilarities between these two industries. Despite this, experts and especially political or economic decision makers are convinced that their fusion is on its way and some even predict a wholesale collapse of the cultural industries in favour of the creative industries. However, this prospect does not seem likely. After the creative industries became in vogue in the late 1990s as a policy instrument, some of that initial enthusiasm seems to have waned as managing and steering the creative industries (and collapsing the cultural industries – including the media – into this category) has proven to be complicated and expensive.

2. *The domination of informational-communicational capitalism and the platform economy*

Since the beginning of the twenty-first century, the most decisive phenomenon has been the rapid rise of technology and telecommunication industries. Worldwide groups (the Big Five as well as Twitter and Netflix) have now become dominant in many sectors of the global economy, and particularly in relation to industrial cultural production. The power of these platforms does not come from their intervention in production itself, but from their continuous and unrestrained action in the measurement of audiences, ranking of preferences, construction of reputations, and predictive analytics. The management of data of all kinds has become central to the cultural industries, yet less so for the creative industries. Through their platforms, at the level of intermediation and the management of advertising, the strong influence of these new world giants is affirmed. Will they restructure the cultural sectors? Most of the activities that were already in decline (for example, newspapers) have been affected. Others (e.g. cinema and recorded music) have reorganized and adapted. We must be attentive to the evolution of the platforms as well as the overall platform economy that is emerging online. In response to the data-driven global strategies of these information and communication giants – a process considered to be part of informational-communicational capitalism – we can expect profound changes in the capitalization of culture and media.

3. *Blockbusters vs. Niches vs. Production of amateurs*

One can observe the rise of a kind of double movement depending on the particular sector of media production. On the one hand, there is a concentration of means (as much financial as artistic, technical, and promotional) on a small number of blockbuster titles through the organization of distribution – through advanced sales, allocation of production and promotion budgets, and franchising investments. On the other hand, more niches are created through limited editions and with carefully targeted potential audiences. Such productions tend to have low profit margins, are difficult to finance and concurrently take recourse to other compensating revenue streams, including requests for crowdfunding, sponsorships, minimal sales guarantees by sellers, and so on. This kind of media production is reinforced by the possibilities of the digital realm, where production and distribution costs have dropped significantly.

In the end, making media is not actually restricted by this double movement, but reinforced. In book publishing, music, and even film production, the annual number of titles is growing, as well as reaching a now-global audience. But there is no longer any compensation between one movement and the other. Traditionally, many media firms would recoup the costs of niche productions with the revenue generated by blockbuster titles. As both production, promotion, and consumption goes global, the risk and uncertainty involved makes major firms hesitant to continue such a dual structure.

At the same time, attention should also be paid to the production of amateurs (e.g. user-generated content), which is often celebrated by the optimistic thinkers of technological modernity (such as Henry Jenkins), and actually encouraged and even driven by the digital technologies and techniques now widely available. To date, it is difficult to evaluate the long-term effects of this modality.

4.   *Towards creation without recognized legal protections?*
The issue of intellectual property rights is very topical, especially because the Big Five are trying, by all means possible, to avoid paying the fees that authors and performers are entitled to, and often prefer to negotiate very low-wage packages (such as Apple), or wait for states or authors' societies to demand, expressly or through the courts, payments that are generally very inadequate. In reality, the demands and expectations of those who make media and those involved in the production cycle (technicians, designers, publishers, etc.) remain largely unknown. On the one hand, because the rights of creators are not yet sufficiently recognized throughout the world. On the other hand, the specificity of these remunerations is not really accepted. Payment tends not to be related to what the makers' contributions are to the creation and intermittence of work, and it can be justly criticized when it leads to considerable differences in pay between 'stars' (and other 'above the line' workers) and others. It is therefore to be expected that there will be considerable confusion in this area, as well as difficult international negotiations, legal proceedings, and the continuation of avoidance strategies by the media industries.

5.   *Inability to adapt public policies to the new industrial framework*
In democratic regimes, such as in Europe, the development of cultural industries has taken place with the support of states and the use of numerous means, financial as well as regulatory. This was also the case for the launch of most creative industries. At

present, however, public policies are mainly oriented towards adaptation to the so-called digital economy and have provided support to the powerful firms that dominate world markets by offering a largely deregulated space. This is now changing, with new tax policies in the United States, and new policies regarding individual data protections and maybe a more appropriate payment of taxes in the European Union, but these advances are very modest.

A remaining problem is that policies tend to be partitioned according to industry sectors, with different rules and frameworks for film, television, journalism, music, games, and so on. Thus, media industries run the risk of becoming poorly paid providers of the technology and telecommunication industries, with the latter being less powerful than the first ones, who are the leaders in contemporary capitalism. In the absence of regulatory measures, economic liberalism becomes increasingly unchallenged and does not provide cultural and creative production the share that it is due.

Conclusion

Media, as formative elements of what makes up the cultural industries, are unique because of the way their production process is organized, how they provide people with culture and information both within and outside of the private sphere, and how the specific way their production processes work tends to be increasingly universal and truly global. Using a political economy of communication framework, we can study and understand the media industries in an interdisciplinary manner, bringing together insights from economics, sociology, and political science, as well as cultural studies.

Considering the development of the media over time, we can gain an appreciation of what makes them possible, understanding how they work the way they do, and how their entire product cycle functions – taking into account the roles played by creators, makers, funders, businesses, technologies, as well as audiences. What the political economy of communication framework does is draw our attention to the way in which the multi-polarized world is being shaped by the media and cultural industries on a global scale.

Further reading
- Case: An exploration of the powerful role platforms have in shaping professional media production – Nieborg & Poell (p. 85)
- Context: An overview of the most compelling, inspiring, and provocative scholarship in the field of media industry studies to be published in the past decade – Holt & Perren (p. 31)
- Contrast: How the new intermediaries such as Facebook and Google facilitate and profit from new forms of consumption without creating or producing content – Bilton (p. 99)

References

Bouquillion, P. & Combès Y. (eds) (2012). *Creative Economy, Creative Industries*. Paris: PUV.

Bouquillion, P., Miège B. & Moeglin P. (2013). *L'industrialisation des biens symboliques – Les industries créatives en regard des industries culturelles*. Grenoble: PUG.

Bouquillon P., Miège B. & Moeglin P. (2015). 'Industries du contenu et industries de la communication. Contribution à une déconstruction de la notion de créativité', *Les Enjeux de l'Information et de la Communication*, *16*(3B), 17-26.

De Bustos, J. (2016). 'Los grupos mundiales de comunicación y de entretenimiento, en el camino hacia la digitalización', *Les Enjeux de l'information et de la communication*, *18*(2), 127-144.

Garnham, N. (1990). *Capitalism and Communication: Global Culture and the Economics of Information*. London: SAGE Publications.

Guback, T. (1969). *The International Film Industry*. Bloomington, IN: Indiana University Press.

Herman, E.S. & McChesney, R.W. (2001). *The Global Media: The New Missionaries of Corporate Capitalism*. London: Cassel.

Lacroix, J.G. & Tremblay, G. (1997). *The 'Information Society' and Cultural Industries Theory*. London: SAGE Publications.

Miège, B. (1989).*The Capitalization of Cultural Production*, New York/Bagnolet: International General.

Miège, B. (2011). 'Theorizing the Cultural Industries: Persistent Specificities and Reconsiderations', in J. Wasko, G. Murdock & H. Sousa (eds), *The Handbook of Political Economy of Communication* (83-108). Chichester: Wiley- Blackwell.

Miège, B. (2017). *Les industries culturelles et créatives face à l'Ordre de l'Information et de la Communication,* Grenoble: PUG, collection communication en plus.

Miège, B. (2018). 'There are still many Dissimilarities between Creative Industries and Cultural Industries', *Les Enjeux de l'Information et de la Communication*, n°18/3A, 2017, p.77 à 87, consulté le mercredi 22 août 2018, [en ligne] URL: https://lesenjeux.univ-grenoble-alpes.fr/2017-supplementA/06-Miege/'

Mosco, V. (1996).*The Political Economy of Communication*. London: SAGE Publications.

Murdock, G. & Golding P. (1977). *Cultural Capitalism: The Political Economy of Mass Communications*. London: Routledge

Schiller, H. (1976). *Communication and Cultural Domination*. White Plains, NY: International Arts and Sciences Press.

Smythe, D.W. (1980). *Communication, Capitalism, Consciousness in Canada*. Norwood, NJ: Ablex.

Wasko, J., Graham, M. & Sousa, H. (eds) (2011). *The Handbook of Political Economy of Communication*. Chichester: Wiley-Blackwell.

Winseck, D.R. & Jin, D.J. (eds) (2011).*The Political Economies of Media: The Transformation of the Global Media Industries*. London and New York: Bloomsbury Academic.

6.   The Platformization of Making Media

David Nieborg and Thomas Poell (with Mark Deuze)

As media makers, companies, and industries are increasingly dependent on digital platforms to publish and promote their work, media content becomes a contingent commodity. This chapter discusses how to research the process of platformization and explores the powerful role platforms have in shaping professional media production, thereby affecting the autonomy of media makers.

Introduction

Over the past decade, media makers such as news organizations and game developers have explored a new mode of production, distribution, and monetization. Typically, developers and publishers start the content production cycle by identifying trending social media topics or popular genres, as well as by calculating production costs and advertising revenue potential. After content has been produced, users are 'aggregated' via a wide range of social platforms. These social media circulation efforts, in turn, generate relevant data on user engagement and retention, which are subsequently employed to calculate whether it is profitable to further optimize content and invest in paid-for promotion, or halt the engagement-optimization-retention-acquisition cycle (Van Dijck, Poell, & De Waal, 2018).

These emerging practices render cultural production and cultural commodities 'contingent'. In previous work on digital platforms, contingency is understood in two distinct, but closely interrelated ways (Morris, 2015). First, it is argued that cultural production is progressively 'contingent on', that is, dependent on a select group of powerful digital platforms. In the West, these are Google, Apple, Facebook, Amazon, and Microsoft (GAFAM), which allow content developers to systematically track and profile the activities and preferences of billions of users. This increasingly close relation between cultural producers and platforms is a form of platform dependence, affecting all forms of media making. Another way in which media products and services accessible via digital platforms are contingent is that they become contingent commodities: malleable, modular in design, and informed by datafied user feedback, open to constant revision and recirculation.

Platformization can be defined as the penetration of economic, governmental, and infrastructural extensions of digital platforms into the web and app ecosystems, fundamentally affecting the operations of media industries and production practices. Critically exploring these shifts is particularly important because the 'platform' metaphor, as Gillespie (2010) argues, obfuscates as much as it reveals. It obscures how social media and other digital services, labeled as platforms, not just facilitate socioeconomic, cultural, and political interaction, but very much organize and steer this interaction. In other words: platforms are anything but neutral. As cultural production in general and media work in particular is becoming increasingly platform dependent, the autonomy and economic sustainability of particular forms of production is increasingly compromised.

In this chapter, we discuss how business studies, political economy, and software studies have contributed to the study of the platformization, which blind spots characterize each perspective, and then proceed to bring the three theoretical perspectives traditionally associated with platform research into dialogue. Explicating our approach, we specifically draw from examples in the news and games industries, as these appear to follow distinctly different trajectories of platformization.

Starting with the latter, digital games, arguably more so than many other types of cultural commodities, have been platform dependent from their inception. Because games are component-based software, their malleability and modularity allows for easy upgrading, extension, and recirculation, all of which play into the contingent nature of the cultural commodity (Nieborg, 2015). News production, by contrast, has historically been platform independent. It is only with the growing importance of online publishing that news production is progressively dependent on the tools, advertising revenue, and data and governance standards of the GAFAM platforms, resulting in content becoming increasingly contingent as well.

In our analysis, we primarily focus on Facebook and Apple, which occupy a central role in the news and games sectors. By contrasting these two cultural commodity types, we show that each instance of media making, while both drawn into the economies and material infrastructures of platforms, follows a distinct trajectory in how production and circulation processes are reorganized.

Theorizing platformization

The first important body of research on platformization is generated by a prolific and diverse collective of business scholars, who primarily focus on for-profit companies operating as intermediaries in platform markets. Business scholars understand platforms as 'matchmakers' (Evans & Schmalensee, 2016) or 'platform-mediated networks' (McIntyre and Srinivasan, 2017), who interface among different sides. This can mean various kinds of institutional actors (or 'complementors'), as well as 'end-users' (i.e. consumers), thereby constituting multisided markets, whereby digital platforms insert themselves as new cultural intermediaries (Negus, 2002) between media makers and media users, at times bypassing or replacing existing businesses such as film and music publishers, record labels, and broadcast organizations. For the study of the platformization of cultural production, the business literature is particularly relevant, because it provides insight in the economic mechanisms and managerial strategies underlying platform markets. These mechanisms and strategies help to explain the increasingly dominant position of platform companies, which, by virtue of their roles as aggregators and mediators, are able to exert significant control over the institutional relationships with end-users and complementors.

In terms of economic mechanisms, business scholars demonstrate that multisided markets are subject to network effects: the costs of the production and consumption of goods and services that affect third parties. For example, one can speak of positive network effects when more end-users join Facebook, making the platform more valuable for other end-users. This, in turn, increases value for a wide range of complementors, such as cultural content producers, advertisers, and many other third parties.

The business literature also discusses managerial strategies particular to multisided markets. For example, how network effects allow platform holders to set pricing structures where one side of the market, the 'money side', covers the costs of the other side, the 'subsidy side' (Evans & Schmalensee, 2016). For example, end-user access to Facebook is free and subsidized by the money generated by businesses that are charged a fee when end-users click on an ad. To facilitate platform entry, subsidies can be used to offer an accessible computational infrastructure to complementors so they can develop and distribute 'complements', such as apps (Tiwana, 2014). The business literature shows that if a platform holder manages to launch at the right time, adopt an optimal pricing structure, and provide an accessible infrastructure, strong winner-take-all effects can come into play, ultimately allowing a platform to aggregate a disproportionate amount of users, revenue, and/or profit.

A problematic aspect of this literature is that business scholars tend to treat platforms as relatively static objects (Tiwana, 2014). Expediting the contingency of cultural commodities (such as all media products and services), digital platforms themselves are continuously in flux as well (Morris, 2015). Their holding companies constantly adjust platform technologies, business models, and governance structures. Therefore, a more historically informed perspective that accounts for the evolving nature of platforms is warranted.

Moreover, there is a noticeable lack of scholarly analysis of the platform-complementor relationship in its different facets. Consequently, there is little guidance on the nature and composition of complementor communities: what motivates media makers to contribute to platforms, what strategies do they develop, and how do platforms support, ignore, or bar them (McIntyre & Srinivasan, 2017). If one wants to really understand how professional media making is evolving, it is crucial to address these questions, as platformization fundamentally changes the economic and institutional configuration in which cultural production takes shape as content producers are always in a position of dependency.

This is where the work of political economic researchers comes in, as these scholars are specifically concerned with platform power and politics. Critical political economists have taken a historical, normative, and critical approach towards theorizing the platformization of cultural production (Mosco, 2009). They do so by emphasizing the inherent accumulative tendency of capital and corporate ownership and its subsequent effects on the distribution of power, and the precarious and exploitative nature of cultural and (immaterial) labour of both producers and end-users. User-driven cultural production is clearly thriving, but it is subsumed under a wider economic regime of 'platform capitalism' (Srnicek, 2016). As the GAFAM platforms represent a centralized, proprietary mode of cultural production, they effectively advance what Benkler (2006) calls 'the project of control' and its two pillars of commercialization and corporate concentration (*Ibid.*, p. 32).

The broader issue of commercialization is theorized in-depth by a group of critical political economists who build on Marx's labour theory of value and Smythe's (1981) notion of the 'audience commodity'. They draw attention to the ongoing commodification of content, the exploitation of cultural labour, and the (immaterial) labour of users (McGuigan & Manzerolle, 2014). Along similar lines, critical scholars have been pointing towards the ongoing trend of corporate concentration (Winseck & Jin, 2011). Political economic research helps us to critically consider how platformization affects media plurality, the independence of cultural producers, access to media, and the influence of owners.

Yet, while political economists are acutely aware of the labour issues that arise from platform-dependent cultural production, less attention is paid to how this translates into the transformation of cultural commodities. Similar to business scholars, political economists rarely take the contingent nature of commodities into consideration. Moreover, scholars in this critical tradition do not systematically engage with one of the roots of the unprecedented concentration of media ownership and control in the hands of a few major platforms: the evolution of multisided markets.

Next to business studies and political economy, the emerging and overlapping fields of software, platform and app studies supplement our understanding of platformization by focusing on the material, computational and infrastructural dimension of platforms (Montfort & Bogost, 2009; Helmond, 2015; Plantin *et al.*, 2016). The starting point for much of this research concerns the end-user/platform relationship and comprises detailed explorations of how the socio-technical features of platforms allow and prompt both cultural producers and end-users particular types of activities, connections, and knowledge, while excluding other things one could possibly do with and on these platforms.

Considering how digital platforms work, in the words of Gillespie (2014), we can see an emerging knowledge logic, which 'depends on the proceduralized choices of a machine, designed by human operators to automate some proxy of human judgment or unearth patterns across collected social traces' (*Ibid.*, p. 192). This emerging platform logic can be contrasted with the traditional 'editorial logic', which more explicitly relies on the 'choices of experts' for the sake of a professional ideal. Alternatively, media production tends to be governed by a market logic, as the products of services of media industries tend to survive solely if these succeed in attracting the attention of (paying) audiences (Deuze, 2007, p. 98). Professional media making tends to be increasingly influenced, if not governed by a platform logic, acting as a necessary precondition for market and editorial logics to function. As a result, media makers are progressively orienting their production and circulation strategies towards the recommendation, ranking, and other kinds of end-user facing algorithms of major platforms.

To more fully understand this platform logic, software studies offers explorations of the computational back-end of platforms. As digital platforms become central actors in all realms of cultural production, it becomes a crucial question under what conditions platforms allow complementors access to the means of production and circulation. Infrastructural access to Application Programming Interfaces (APIs) and Software Development Kits (SDKs) is among the primary ways in which platforms control the professionals and businesses that seek to reach audiences through their sites, applications and interfaces. Similarly, it should be observed that data infrastructures, such as APIs, not only preformat, process, and articulate end-user activities (Kitchin, 2014), they also push media makers to align and subsequently integrate their own data infrastructures and strategies with those of the platforms. Consequently, content developers have to align their own business models and production and circulation philosophies with those of leading platforms (Nieborg, 2015).

While software studies scholars devote ample attention to the intricate connections between platform business models and technologies, less attention is paid to how the economic strategies of platforms and complementors become entangled and what the political economic implications of these relationships are. Lastly, work in software studies acknowledges both platform integration and dependency, as well as the evolving nature of platform design, but is less concerned with questions pertaining to cultural production, let alone cultural commodities. As the discussion of the three scholarly approaches suggests, to understand how the platformization of media work unfolds we need to untangle the mutual articulation of changing market arrangements, governance frameworks, and infrastructures of content production, distribution, and commercial imperatives.

Shifting markets

The global market for media products and services entails two major shifts amplified and accelerated by the rise of platforms: a shift from one- or two-sided markets to intricate multisided platform configurations, and strong winner-take-all effects affecting all sides in platform markets. Vital to observe is that before digital platforms became ubiquitous, media industries operated as prototypical two-sided markets. Consider, for example, the print segment of the news industry and the console segment in the games industry. News organizations and media publishers were matchmakers between readers or viewers and advertisers, and game consoles brought together game publishers and players. These two-sided configurations allowed content developers not only to exert control over the means of production and distribution, in the news industry large media publishers occupied a top position in the advertising food chain because of their ability to attract and retain large audiences (Turow, 2011).

In the emerging platform ecosystem, a small number of transnational corporations is able to aggregate unprecedented numbers of end-users (and thus attention), and then, by ways of indirect network effects, advertisers. Next to these two sides, digital platforms have been proactive in adding other sides to their businesses, most notably advertising intermediaries, societal institutions, and cultural content producers. Facebook, for example, has become a dominant data-intermediary, sporting millions of connections with companies, institutions, and content developers, each of which operate in different regions and have different histories, incentives, and business models. In Facebook's ecosystem, content producers are on the subsidy side and occupy a precarious position.

What distinguishes multisided platform markets from past market configurations is that for platform holders, content developers can become dispensable. For Facebook, content developers are not a crucial part of the chicken-and-egg equation. That is, when it came to launching the platform and kick starting positive direct and indirect network effects, the most critical sides for the platform were users and advertisers. Content developers are just another side, and individual games, magazines, and newspapers are increasingly interchangeable and abundantly available cultural commodities. Compare this to the aforementioned two-sided nature of print news, in which the news publisher controlled the relationship between readers and advertisers (around a scarce commodity: quality news). Or, compare this to the two-sided game console configuration, where game publishers are the money side and revenue is generated via the sale of premium-priced software, thus incentivizing more sustainable platform-complementor relationships. Conversely, social media and mobile media are general-purpose platforms. Even though news and game offerings do hold value for users, and thus for platform holders, they are not the primary money side for Facebook or Apple and thus less important when platform managers consider pricing, governance, and platform data strategies.

The impact of platform dependency is particularly clear in the news industry, which over the last two decades has come under increasing economic pressure. In their attempts to adapt to the new economic reality, news organizations have been forced to fundamentally reinvent how they monetize editorial expertise and content. Spurred by digital publishers, such as *BuzzFeed* and the *Huffington Post*, news organizations have developed networked strategies to profit from platform network effects. These organizations optimized news production and circulation for multisided digital platforms to maximize user traffic and advertising revenue. While for some this strategy has been effective in generating significant user traffic, in economic terms it has not necessarily made these organizations more sustainable businesses.

It is crucial to observe that platformization makes publishers increasingly dependent on platforms (Nielsen & Ganter, 2017) and thus subject to the political economy of multisided markets. Publishers pursuing platform-oriented distribution strategies are subject to strong direct network effects, as platform sharing practices and algorithmic curation tend to favour viral content. Moreover, these strategies lead to a shift in control and oversight. The direct relationship news organizations enjoyed with their audiences is increasingly intermediated by platforms, which are known to be reluctant to share valuable data and make constant changes to their algorithms determining how and which users get exposed to content.

Although the games industry has undergone similar effects of platformization, it has been much more successful in developing new revenue streams. The rise of major digital platforms in the mid-2000s, launching social network services, smartphones and tablets, radically transformed the games industry (Kerr, 2017). Game developers gained access to much wider and diverse audiences as these new platforms offered games that were more accessible both to players and developers. As a result, game apps emerged as a vibrant new sub-segment in the wider games industry, which continues to see double-digit revenue growth on a global basis.

Coinciding with the launch of new game platforms has been the widespread adoption of the freemium or 'free-to-play' business model, in which revenue is generated via a mix of optional in-game purchases and advertising (Nieborg, 2015). The freemium development aligns directly with the particular technological and economic affordances of platforms. For game developers looking for sustainable revenues, the low barrier to market entry these platforms offer demands a different strategic approach to content development, which necessitates heavy investments in player acquisition and retention. Similar to the news industry, game developers must adjust their business models to an ecosystem flushed with content.

This new era of abundance favours data-driven game design strategies intensifying the contingent nature of cultural commodities. Game developers leverage the contingent nature of games as software by continuously altering, extending, and upgrading game content and functionalities, while simultaneously optimizing its monetization model. For example, games in the popular *Candy Crush Saga* franchise leverage the connective affordances of Facebook by suggesting players to directly contact their Facebook Friends to ask for bonuses or to unlock additional game content.

Next to directly integrating platform functionalities in a game's design, developers are increasingly reliant on the platform's data-driven advertising ecosystems (Nieborg, 2017). Expectedly, this techno-economic alignment has profound political economic implications. Mobile multiplayer games such as *Clash Royale* and *Mobile Strike*, each of which generate hundreds of thousands of dollars in global revenue on a daily basis, are subject to strong direct network effects that increase player retention. This makes it difficult for new market entrants to gain market share. While platform owners have a number of curatorial and algorithmic tools at their disposal to (re)direct players or readers away from incumbents and towards novel content, as we will argue below, their current platform politics and governance policies belie such approaches.

Changing governance

To develop a comprehensive understanding of how platformization shapes cultural production and distribution, we cannot restrict the analysis to shifting market structures, but we also need to account for how digital platforms affect power relations in the media industries and the autonomy of media makers. Transnational platform companies tend to set global, rather than local standards regarding content. The dominance of the US-owned and operated GAFAM platforms effectively entails a globalization of US cultural standards concerning what is and what is not permitted (Jin, 2015). Such standards are operationalized through platform policies, codified in Terms of Service, Terms of Use, and developer guidelines, such as Apple's App Store Review Guidelines. On the basis of such policies, platforms filter and remove content and block users from platforms and app stores. Typically, these regulations prohibit violence, nudity, and discrimination, which can scare away advertisers and end-users or become a source of legal issues. How such rules are interpreted and acted upon is, however, opaque and frequently causes controversy, as platforms intervene deeply in the curation of culture and the organization of public communication.

Exploring how platform governance influences particular industries, it is important to consider the histories of specific fields of cultural production. The issue of accountability concerns content moderation, but also algorithmic content curation, which has a large impact but is much harder to observe, let alone audit. Algorithmic curation affects the visibility of individual content items, but also of entire news outlets. Every major change in Facebook's News Feed algorithms tends to have a dramatic impact on the traffic volumes of particular news outlets (Nielsen & Ganter, 2017). Furthermore, the impact of platform sorting practices is exceptionally strong because many news organizations are incentivized to align their content strategies with platform-defined markers of popularity, rather than traditional quality indicators. By doing so, news organizations are effectively reifying dominant platform governance strategies.

Situated at the opposite end of the spectrum in terms of platform dependence, the impact of platform governance on the games industry has been less controversial than in the news industry. Game developers are accustomed to grapple with the hardware, software, and platform governance frameworks of consoles that are relatively standardized across regions and hardware generations. Nevertheless, the growing importance of online platforms that are not specifically designed for gaming has complicated the governance of game production, circulation, and monetization. Nowhere is this more visible than in the mobile game segment, in which Apple's App Store plays an important role. App developers are faced with a constantly shifting, intricate, and often opaque set of developer guidelines.

Whereas suppressing news content has clear moral and ethical implications, the non-trivial costs of developing an individual game app, only to see it rejected after submission, increases the precarity of this particular mode of game development. Game developers are at a platform's full mercy, which not just affects the economic sustainability of game production, but also its viability as a form of artistic expression. Platform provisions have a clear chilling effect on developers, who want to make artistic or political statements about, gender (in)equality, labour exploitation, organized violence, or repressive governments.

These examples suggest that to understand how platformization shapes cultural expression, it is crucial to carefully examine the seemingly serendipitous and minor changes in platform governance. While these changes affect all cultural industries, we simultaneously should be attentive to the variations between industries. Given different traditions of governance and platform dependency, each industry is characterized by its own set of power relations and questions and concerns regarding the autonomy of cultural producers.

Over the past decade, digital platforms have initiated a range of services, enticing producers to host, distribute and monetize their content via their platforms. By offering ready access to APIs, SDKs, and developer documentation, platforms offer news publishers and game developers a seemingly attractive alternative to physical distribution infrastructures, or self-operated digital properties. Next to hosting content, platforms also provide a variety of integrated services to complementors, all of which leverage the infrastructural features – ubiquity, accessibility, reliability, invisibility – of platform technologies (Plantin *et al.*, 2016).

In the news industry, platform-integration has led to large-scale content unbundling. Instead of focusing on highly curated content packages (i.e. newspapers), news organizations are increasingly investing in the platformed distribution of individual stories, which are contingent in their structure and content. The ubiquitous use of data analytics enables precise user targeting, the ability to respond to real-time trends, 'A/B' or split testing content such as headlines and formats, as well as the development of long-term strategies on how to continue drawing platform users. Most legacy news media have adopted such strategies, datafying their operations to more adequately respond to evolving interests of platform users. Thus, similar to music and games, news content becomes 'permanently impermanent' as it gets modularized, revised and recirculated, transforming it into a contingent cultural commodity.

Conclusion

To develop a more comprehensive understanding of the platformization of cultural production, we have staged a dialogue between three disparate bodies of scholarly work: business studies, critical political economy, and software studies. Each research tradition offers a valuable avenue to analyse the multidimensional playing field in which platformization takes place, focusing on related changes in market structures, governance frameworks, and infrastructures. Although there are differences between media industries in trajectories of platformization, this process is decidedly a global phenomenon, affecting all industries and every (professional) media maker one way or another. The potent combination of ballooning market capitalization, ready access to (venture) capital, and positive network effects have resulted in an unprecedented accumulation of economic resources by platform behemoths in a constantly evolving ecosystem that, for those producing content and services in the media industries is fraught with a loss of autonomy, risk, and uncertainty.

Further reading
- Case: How the rise of mobile and free-to-play games has changed the digital games industry in the past ten years – Kerr (p. 413)
- Context: How the new platforms facilitate and profit from new forms of consumption without creating or producing content – Bilton (p. 99)
- Contrast: How national governments are seeking to assert control over platforms such as Facebook and Google – Flew & Suzor (p. 163)

Acknowledgements: A version of this chapter originally appeared as an article in *New Media & Society*: D.B. Nieborg & T. Poell (2018). 'The Platformization of Cultural Production: Theorizing the Contingent Cultural Commodity', *New Media & Society*. Advance online publication. https://doi.org/10.1177/1461444818769694.

References

Benkler, Y. (2006). *The Wealth of Networks. How Social Production Transforms Markets and Freedom.* New Haven, CT: Yale University Press.

Deuze, M. (2007). *Media Work.* Cambridge: Polity.

Evans, D.S. & Schmalensee, R. (2016). *Matchmakers. The New Economics of Multisided Platforms.* Cambridge, MA: Harvard Business Review Press.

Gillespie, T. (2010). 'The Politics of "Platforms"', *New Media & Society*, 12(3), 347-364.

Gillespie, T. (2014). 'The Relevance of Algorithms', in T. Gillespie, P.J. Boczkowski & K.A. Foot (eds), *Media Technologies. Essays on Communication, Materiality, and Society* (167-194). Cambridge, MA: The MIT Press.

Helmond, A. (2015). 'The Platformization of the Web: Making Web Data Platform Ready', *Social Media + Society*, 1(2), 1-11.

Jin, D.Y. (2015). *Digital Platforms, Imperialism and Political Culture.* New York: Routledge.

Kerr, A. (2017). *Global Games: Production, Circulation and Policy in the Networked Era.* London: Routledge.

Kitchin, R. (2014). *The Data Revolution. Big Data, Open Data, Data Infrastructures and Their Consequences.* London: SAGE Publications.

McGuigan, L. & Manzerolle, V. (eds) (2014). *The Audience Commodity in a Digital Age. Revisiting a Critical Theory of Commercial Media.* New York: Peter Lang.

McIntyre, D.P. & Srinivasan, A. (2017). 'Networks, Platforms, and Strategy: Emerging Views and Next Steps', *Strategic Management Journal*, 38(1), 141-160.

Montfort, N. & Bogost, I. (2009). *Racing the Beam. The Atari Video Computer System.* Cambridge, MA: The MIT Press.

Morris, J.W. (2015). *Selling Digital Music, Formatting Culture.* Oakland, CA: University of California Press.

Mosco, V. (2009). *The Political Economy of Communication* (2nd ed.). London: SAGE Publications.

Negus, K. (2002). 'The Work of Cultural Intermediaries and the Enduring Distance Between Production and Consumption', *Cultural Studies*, 16(4), 501-515.

Nieborg, D.B. (2015). 'Crushing Candy: The Free-to-Play Game in its Connective Commodity Form', *Social Media + Society*, 1(2), 1-12.

Nieborg, D.B. (2017). 'App Advertising: The Rise of the Player Commodity', in J.F. Hamilton, R. Bodle & E. Korin (eds), *Explorations in Critical Studies of Advertising* (28-41). New York: Routledge.

Nielsen, R.K. & Ganter, S.A. (2017). 'Dealing with Digital Intermediaries: A Case Study of the Relations between Publishers and Platforms', *New Media & Society*. Advance online publication. DOI: 10.1177/1461444817701318.

Plantin, J.C., Lagoze, C., Edwards, P.N. *et al.* (2016). 'Infrastructure Studies Meet Platform Studies in the Age of Google and Facebook', *New Media & Society*. Advance online publication. DOI: 10.1177/1461444816661553.

Smythe, D. (1981). 'On the Audience Commodity and Its Work', in D. Smythe, *Dependency Road: Communications, Capitalism, Consciousness, and Canada* (22-51). Norwood: Ablex.

Srnicek, N. (2016). *Platform Capitalism*. Cambridge: Polity Press.

Tiwana, A. (2014). *Platform Ecosystems. Aligning Architecture, Governance, and Strategy*. Amsterdam: Morgan Kaufmann.

Turow, J. (2011). *The Daily You: How the New Advertising Industry is Defining Your Identity and Your Worth*. New Haven, CT: Yale University Press.

Van Dijck, J., Poell, T. & De Waal, M. (2018). *The Platform Society. Public Values in a Connective World*. Oxford: Oxford University Press.

Winseck, D.R. & Jin, D.Y. (eds) (2011). *The Political Economies of Media. The Transformation of The Global Media Industries*. London: Bloomsbury.

Production

Economics and Management

7. The Disappearing Product and the New Intermediaries

Chris Bilton

Media products are no longer the primary source of value in the creative and media industries. The new intermediaries – search engines, social media platforms, hardware and software providers, and online marketplaces such as Amazon, Facebook, Google, and Apple – facilitate and profit from new forms of consumption without creating or producing content. This chapter explores the consequences of this changing media ecosystem.

Introduction

Media products are symbolic goods whose value and meaning are only revealed at the point of consumption. The 'what' of media content is mediated by the 'how', 'where', and 'who' of media consumption. This makes media content an unstable, unpredictable commodity. It also raises the stakes around the consumer experience as the site where value and meaning are realized.

The experiential value of media content – a commonplace of media theory – has gained fresh impetus as a result of changes in media technology, economics, industry structure, and consumption. The most successful media businesses today are increasingly detached from the business of media production. Instead, they are capitalizing on these social, technological, and economic changes to exploit a dominant position as trusted intermediaries who monopolize consumer attention, particularly online.

This chapter uses the concept of the 'disappearing product' (Bilton, 2017) to consider the rise of a new type of intermediary, whose business depends on the commodification of consumer attention rather than the dissemination of media content. The business model of these intermediaries devalues media content and marginalizes media producers. The threat to the survival of media producers, especially smaller enterprises, extends to the sustainability of the wider media ecology. The chapter concludes by considering some implications for media production, marketing, and education.

From content to context

Given the speed of technological change, today's prophecies are tomorrow's banalities and yesterday's realities are soon forgotten. Younger readers will have to imagine a time around 1999 (a time when people still rented DVDs and bought newspapers), when a combination of technological, economic, and social changes ushered in what we then called 'new media' and what we today call 'media'.

In the last century, media were considered as separate industries – broadcasting or audiovisual, film, books, newspapers. Digital formats collapsed these distinctions (Pool, 1984). Content has become infinitely malleable, shareable, and 'spreadable' (Jenkins *et al.*, 2013). One casualty of the new media reality was intellectual property rights. A system designed to attribute and reward content creators was stretched by online platforms that made no distinction between publishing, copying, and sharing. Content and authorship were destabilized by interactivity and participation, by other producers, and by consumers, making it hard to pin down any single authoritative version of a media text. Piracy had previously referred to something like an illegal copy of a DVD or a bootleg record. Now, it seemed to engulf the entire Web 2.0 culture of participation and sharing, making pirates of us all.

The threat to copyright was compounded by the new economics of cultural production and consumption. Previously, media businesses had relied on mass reproduction of a few successful hit products to cross-subsidize a long tail of failures. As consumers learned to make their own copies – and also to recognise the zero-marginal cost of doing so – it became practically and morally difficult to sustain the old business model. With the growing availability of free content, consumers found that they could make and distribute content of their own, while producers found that high consumer value (and in some cases high production cost) did not translate into high prices.

Convergent technologies and emerging business models were reflected by industry restructuring. Firstly, new technologies and business models reduced the cost of production and distribution, cutting out some of the 'gatekeeper' businesses that had previously occupied the profitable centre of the media value chain. Now, producers could communicate directly with consumers. This disintermediation, promising a democratization and diversification of the old monopolies, was rapidly succeeded by a process of reintermediation as a new generation of intermediaries responded to a new set of consumer needs. It turned out that consumers were not satisfied by an endless stream of cheap and free content; they wanted content to be filtered, aggregated, personalized, bundled, unbundled, curated, accelerated, repackaged. And whilst the old gatekeepers were still attempting to close the gates on this new age of plenty, threatening legal action against copyright infringement, seeking to monetize new patterns of consumption, the new intermediaries were ready to step into the gap. Instead of controlling the means of production, these new intermediaries understood how to manage the means of consumption.

The fourth element of media transformation, along with the technological, economic, and structural changes outlined above, was more cultural. The generation who grew up with the new age of digital plenty are actively participating in the media they consume. Digital tools have narrowed the gap between consumers and producers. User-generated content and user-distributed content have led to an expectation that content should be inclusive, participatory, and interactive.

As with the other changes outlined here, this was not so much a new development as an intensification and acceleration of existing consumer behaviour. Media consumption has never been an entirely passive activity. Interpretation, choice, self-projection, and collective re-imagining of meanings have been the subject of media studies since the late 1970s, notably in the field of cultural studies (Fiske, 1989; Hall, 1980; Radway, 1984). But the new co-creation in the digital media context was more accessible and more all-embracing. Instant online connection and the proliferation of individualised personal devices (mobile media) led to a new wave of 'we-media' and 'self-media', respectively. Consumers were part of the product as never before. For many commentators (Leadbeater, 2008; Tapscott & Williams, 2006; Shirky, 2010) these new patterns of consumption and exchange represent a new opportunity. Others worry that the quality and value of content is undermined by a pervasive narcissism, where the quality of information has become less important than the identities and relationships we construct around it (Keen, 2007; Carr, 2011).

The 'disappearing product' is an attempt to reflect on this changed media landscape. Crucially, we have moved from 'content is king' to 'context is king'; content and content creators are no longer the primary source of value in the creative and media industries. Of course, consumption has always been an important site of value creation in these industries, and theories of co-creation or creative consumption are not in themselves new. What is different in our new media ecosystem is the changing role of the new intermediaries, which facilitate and profit from these new forms of consumption.

The new intermediaries

The new intermediaries are those businesses, primarily technology companies, which have become the primary gateways to information for many consumers, not by controlling content, but by managing consumption. Search engines, social media, and broadband providers are not in the business of creating or producing content. Certainly, they provide access to content, either for a modest subscription, or for free, gaining their revenues by selling advertising or consumer data. This shift in the business model, from production to consumption, is the key to their success. The largest of the new intermediaries, the Big Four of Apple, Amazon, Facebook, and Google, currently represent a total market value of over $2 trillion – comparable to the entire GDP of a sizeable economy such as France. Apple alone is the most valuable company on the planet in terms of equity currently valued at over $750 billion, with the other three not far behind.

Whereas the old intermediaries (publishers, broadcasters, record labels, film studios), acted as gatekeepers by controlling and filtering content, the new intermediaries have thrown the gates wide open. Anything goes, so long as there is a public appetite for what is being offered. Indeed, part of the democratic appeal of the new intermediaries is their non-judgemental or agnostic attitude to content quality or value. Ordinary consumers can generate and distribute their own work alongside the professionals. Because the business model no longer depends on content sales, there are no barriers and no restrictions, no discriminatory pricing. As noted in the previous section, much of the available content is free. Consequently, profits depend not on what we are consuming, but how we are consuming it – in particular, how long we spend on a site, how likely we are to click on the next link, how many times we view, like or share the same story.

In the last century, critics were concerned that the intermediaries were turning cultural and media products into mere commodities; by giving the product away, the new intermediaries signal a more ambitious attempt to turn consumption and consumers themselves into the commodity. In an attention economy, where time spent is the main metric of value, every click and every second is valuable, accumulating into advertising revenues, consumer profiling data, subscription charges or some combination of all three.

The business model of the new intermediaries does not require investment in the creation of content, particularly if content can be sourced from users themselves or else acquired for minimal cost (Hesmondhalgh, 2010; Keen, 2007, pp. 135-136). Publishers or broadcasters of the last century, however much they were in the business of exploiting their monopoly power in the value chain, still had a direct interest in acquiring compelling, innovative, and diverse content; at the very minimum, they could not afford to drive producers out of business. Consequently, traditional publishers formed strategic alliances with smaller production enterprises, often to their mutual benefit. Both sides of the partnership also had a mutual interest in upholding copyright.

The new intermediaries have facilitated the availability of free content, to the point where, even when a price tag is attached, many consumers will attempt to obtain the content for free, whether legally or illegally. On the other hand, this free content can generate advertising revenues, consumer data capture and analysis, predictive customer profiling, all of which are immensely profitable. Just as British pubs make more of their money from food than selling beer, today's media industries make more from monetizing media consumption (through advertising and consumer data) than from selling media content.

Rather than investing in content, the new intermediaries have preferred to invest in delivery and distribution – for instance, acquiring rival platforms like WhatsApp and YouTube, or investing in smarter technology to track consumer behaviour and target advertising more effectively.

More recently, however, the content agnostic new intermediaries have begun to take a greater interest in production. In 2017, Apple hired Jay Hunt, former controller of BBC1 and chief creative officer of Channel 4, together with two senior executives from Sony Pictures Television. Amazon has moved from distribution into publishing original content with its television streaming service on Amazon Prime. Despite Facebook's unsuccessful bid for Indian Premier League cricket in 2017, and a perhaps surprising decision by both Facebook and Amazon not to bid for English Premier League rights in 2018, the company is already exploring live streaming of sports, especially in the United States. Netflix, sometimes bracketed alongside the Big Four as FAANG (Facebook, Apple, Amazon, Netflix, Google – comprising five of the fastest growing companies on the US stock market), has led the way in developing original content (see Monster Movies box).

Monster Movies

Netflix Originals and Amazon Prime both demonstrate the emerging media production capacity of what had previously been exclusively retail/distribution businesses. To what extent are these moves strategic or merely tactical? Amazon's TV streaming and self-publishing platforms are perhaps driven not so much by a desire to produce content for its own sake, but rather to reinforce and demonstrate their strong bargaining position to other providers, notably broadcasters and publishers. Both Netflix Originals and Amazon Prime also take advantage of the intermediary's sophisticated mapping of consumer preferences to match supply with demand; neglecting this opportunity would be a failure to leverage their primary assets. Consumer insight, consumer trust, and synergies with other parts of their existing business give Amazon Prime and Netflix a distinctive commercial advantage when designing media content.

Netflix prides itself on the accuracy and detail of its algorithms that allow it to track consumer preferences and tailor content accordingly. Netflix has used this insight to first acquire, then commission and produce original programming under the Netflix Originals brand. In turn, this has allowed Netflix to develop niche content, identifying underlying preferences for genres, artists, or themes to inform creative decisions, reducing risks, and connecting diverse content with diverse audiences. In 2015, Netflix moved from original television into original film, initially streaming movies to its subscribers, but also partnering with established producers and directors, and gaining some limited release in cinemas. In 2017, the company entered an original Korean film, *Okja*, at the Cannes Film Festival.

The reaction to this unexpected intervention, at the world's best-known film festival in a country with a proud cinematic tradition, was initially hostile. French and Korean distributors refused to show the film. Festival organizers were accused of breaching protocol by including a film that had not been previously screened in cinemas. The president of the Cannes jury, film director Pedro Almodovar, confirmed that such a move would not be tolerated at next year's festival.

Yet *Okja* still performed well at the box office. Boos for the Netflix company logo in Cannes gave way to a four-minute ovation for the film itself. One could argue that this alternative, quirky film (an eco-comedy about a giant pig) with its young, critically acclaimed Korean director and an international cast and crew was precisely the kind of distinctive, independent-minded content that might not have gained a commercial release from more conservative film distributors.

Just as Netflix's algorithms have allowed it to develop niche programming for precisely targeted audiences in the form of Netflix Originals TV programming, perhaps the new intermediaries are challenging old monopolies and opening up new channels of communication. Of course, it is impossible to know whether Netflix sees programming content as a means for deepening its customer relationship algorithms and consumer data, or vice versa. But it does raise the question as to what impact the new intermediaries might have upon our media ecology, culturally as well as economically.

These moves follow a strategy of backwards integration, taking advantage of the weak bargaining position of suppliers in the value chain to compete with and ultimately bypass the established providers of media content. In the United Kingdom, based on figures in their annual reports, annual revenues for BBC, ITV, and Sky for 2015/16 were, respectively, £4.8 billion, £3 billion, and £12 billion; the corresponding figures for Apple, Google, Amazon, and Facebook were, respectively, £166.3 billion, £50.5 billion, £72.5 billion, and £12.5 billion.

Sports rights, especially football, have been the key to unlocking market share in the UK broadcast market; the commercial opportunity for Facebook, in terms of access to users and consequent possibilities for targeted advertising, would appear irresistible. Facebook and Google, having together absorbed most of the global media spend on advertising, now threaten to backwards integrate the advertising industry value chain by setting up their own creative departments, which will collaborate with (and eventually bypass) the creative agencies currently supplying advertiser content.

What will be the consequences of the move by today's content agnostic intermediaries into tomorrow's content production? The new intermediaries have successfully presented themselves as plucky outsiders, challenging established media interests and championing consumers through the provision of more or less free content, whilst at the same time establishing a monopolistic control over media distribution. This has inevitably marginalized and undermined not only content creators, but also many traditional publishers of media content. The move into media content consolidates the competitive position.

It is possible that the new intermediaries, by opening up new channels of distribution, might enhance media diversity; this is the argument presented by Chris Anderson and his theory of the Long Tail (2006). Anderson argued that technologies had reduced the costs of production and distribution, making it more possible and more profitable to sustain a longer inventory of products. Where traditional publishers banked on a handful of hit products to bankroll a roster of misses, the new intermediaries could cultivate a much wider range of content. They were less reliant on product sales; diversity of content allowed them to deliver a more customized product to their users or subscribers, capitalizing on their precisely tailored algorithms and trusted customer relationships. Against this, the tendency towards monopoly among the Big Four may gradually reduce any incentive to innovate as market competition declines.

Amazon, Facebook, Google, and Apple may be acquiring or even producing some original content, but their business model remains focused on media consumption. Legally, too, it is in their interests to continue to be labelled as platforms rather than publishers; this semantic confusion clears them of legal liability and regulation over the third-party content they continue to distribute, avoiding responsibility when accused of displaying inappropriate content or fake news. For these reasons, it seems unlikely that original content will become central to the business models of Apple, Amazon, Facebook, and Google. Simply put, this is not how they make their money.

On the other hand, even if only a fraction of their budgets is diverted into media content, this will allow them to continue dominating the market. This raises the possibility that our future media industries will be controlled by a handful of non-media businesses with no vested interest in the cultural quality or commercial value of the media they produce or distribute. History shows that when media become dependent on advertising rather than audiences, there is a tendency towards media monopoly, loss of autonomy, and loss of diversity (Bagdikian, 1990, pp. 120-133).

Our changing media ecosystem

The shift from content to consumption as the core of value creation in the media industries has both an economic and cultural dimension. Economically, the change in business models has led to a reconfiguring of the value chain in favour of those involved in designing and packaging the consumer experience, rather than building and creating cultural content. At the same time, these new media monopolies are reinforcing their market position by backwards integrating content production, film and TV production (Amazon), advertising content (Facebook and Google), and music and TV services (Apple) into a new generation of vertically integrated global companies. Even setting aside concerns over deliberate manipulation or political interference, the proliferation and popularity of sensational and trivial material on these platforms inevitably squeezes out more rational debate. Culturally, the emphasis on consumption as the site where meaning is not only realized, but also amplified and redirected has an impact on cultural expression and authorship. This is the new reality of the disappearing product.

The emergence of fake news in 2016 provides one example of what this new media landscape might look like. Once the cultural relevance and commercial value of information is measured according to patterns of consumption, rather than any intrinsic value, media producers become marginalized, and their media content becomes a commodity designed to attract consumer attention and advertiser revenues. The term 'fake news' was initially popularized by incoming US President Donald Trump to denigrate established media organisations like CNN and *The New York Times*, which created coverage critical of his policies and personality. However, the term was rapidly turned back the other way to describe the spread of disinformation on social media, often manipulated to support political interests, including Trump's election campaign. Because social media value news according to its exchange value (the number of times a piece of news is shared or liked), rather than its use value (its authentic truth and meaning), the provenance or credibility of the source becomes negligible and in many cases untraceable.

Andrew Keen's critique of online culture – 'shattering the world into a billion personalized truths' (Keen, 2007, p. 17) – highlights the relativism and indeterminacy of the news reports shared through social media. The quality of our public sphere is corroded by confirmation biases and self-interest, but for the new intermediaries the panic over fake news only increases their share of consumer attention. By undermining trust in established quality media and encouraging people to spend time sharing and interacting with each other about news rather than reading it, fake news becomes a self-fulfilling prophecy, as well as a commercial opportunity.

The new media ecology does open up new channels for communication. Dis-intermediation of the value chain allows news providers to build more direct connections with audiences. In 2016, Peter Jukes, a British journalist and writer who had crowdfunded his own coverage of the UK phone-hacking trial in 2014, joined forces with crowdfunded journalism organization Byline (URL: byline.com). Byline promises a model of journalism 'by the people, for the people', bypassing traditional news outlets and allowing journalists to speak directly to readers, some of whom pay to sponsor particular lines of investigation or regular columnists.

The relationship with its readers means it remains genuinely independent, unlike other online news platforms which have had to seek investment from larger media companies (for example AoL's 2011 acquisition of *The Huffington Post*).

Like musicians interacting with fans, journalists and newspapers are finding new ways to connect to their readers, especially online. There are some similarities here with the secondary revenue streams beyond the product, which are exploited by the new intermediaries. The difference is that musicians and journalists, together with their supporters, are able to develop what marketers refer to as 'the extended product' – the associations and potential uses of the product reimagined by users – whereas new intermediaries are promoting 'the product surround' – a set of value-added services that surround the product, but are disconnected from its inherent meaning and value (Bilton, 2017, pp. 81-91).

Whereas the product surround distracts from content, focusing instead on value-added services used to deliver content, the extended product reconnects content with its potential value for users, through customization, community building, and interactive relationships. To some extent, the extended product can thereby rescue the disappearing product of media content from imminent obscurity and trivialisation. In this business model, content producers remain committed to the underlying value of the music or the journalist content, and engaging with the business of media consumption becomes a matter of economic necessity, rather than a free choice (Oakley, 2014). At the same time, this entrepreneurial hustling also buys them some degree of autonomy.

Conclusion

For media producers, whether journalists, television producers, or film-makers, the new challenge is to take ownership of the way their work is mediated and marketed. The relationship with audiences is too valuable to surrender to the new intermediaries, who have monopolized consumer attention through a promise of choice, free access, convenience, and always on connectivity. Organizations like Byline are unlikely to replace Facebook or even traditional news organizations, but they offer something like Facebook's sense of community and like-minded connection, funnelling the value back to the content creators instead of to a third party. And provided enough users of the service care enough about that difference to pay for it, Byline (and a host of other entrepreneurial new media ventures emerging worldwide) will survive.

Surviving in the new media landscape will require a change of mindset, recognizing that media production is no longer simply a matter of producing great content. Media producers must take in the whole value chain and reclaim their relationship with media consumers. This will be no easy task given the monopoly power and sophisticated targeting of the new intermediaries, but it seems possible that at least some users will prefer to connect with a real journalist/film-maker/musician than with a plausible algorithm. New technologies make it possible for producers to gain greater control over how their work is perceived, packaged, and consumed, and to gain more direct access to their users.

A related challenge in the new media economy will be equipping the next generation of media practitioners for a changing media landscape. In universities, media production, media sociology and cultural studies, and media management and media business have often been taught as separate modules, sometimes as separate courses in separate departments. In common with other contributors to this volume, this chapter advocates an interdisciplinary approach to media education, aligned with the experience of our students rather than the expertise of our teachers. In particular, there is a need to bridge between the processes of media production (creative practice, writing, technical and editing skills, journalism) and an understanding of media consumption (marketing and management, audience studies, fandom).

Between production and consumption, students also need some understanding of the structure of the media industries in terms of the value chains and networks that join them together, the political economy of media, and the policy mechanisms that might be applied to govern them. In working across these disciplines, there is a tension between a cultural and managerial approach, but this is something that our students will have experienced as media consumers and will have to negotiate as media workers. Extending definitions of content to encompass the way media content is consumed and understood also entails a reframing of what we mean by creativity. Creativity theory emphasizes the value and perception of value, not just the generation of novel ideas; mere novelty does not satisfy the definition of creativity (Boden, 1994; Bilton, 2015), any more than media content describes the range of practices and disciplines comprising contemporary media as it is experienced by the end user.

The disappearing product describes an emerging set of processes in the media and creative industries, neither a static state, nor an inevitable destination. It will be up to the next generation to integrate their media production experience with an understanding of user experiences – to combine media production with media marketing and management. If we can cultivate a more holistic understanding of both media and creativity among our students, the disappearing product might gradually come back into focus as a reimagined version of our future media.

Further reading

- Case: How revenue models and financing strategies of companies such as Netflix have influenced the content of internet-distributed television – Lotz (p. 337)
- Context: The various new forms of value which circulate in digital markets, resulting from different ways in which media makers and users value media – Bolin (p. 111)
- Contrast: How national governments are seeking to assert control over internet intermediaries such as Facebook and Google – Flew & Suzor (p. 163)

References

Anderson, C. (2006). *The Long Tail*. New York: Hyperion.

Bagdikian, B. (1990). *The Media Monopoly* (3rd ed.). Boston, MA: Beacon Press.

Bilton, C. (2015). 'Uncreativity: The Shadow Side of Creativity', *International Journal of Cultural Policy, 21*(2), 153-167.

Bilton, C. (2017). *The Disappearing Product: Marketing and Markets in the Creative Industries*. Cheltenham: Edward Elgar.

Boden, M. (1994). 'What is Creativity?', in M. Boden (ed.), *Dimensions of Creativity* (75-117). London: Bradford Books.

Carr, N. (2011). *The Shallows: How the Internet is Changing the Way We Think, Read and Remember*. London: Atlantic Books.

Fiske, J. (1989). *Television Culture*. London: Routledge.

Hall, S. (1980). 'Encoding/Decoding', in S. Hall, D. Hobson, A. Love & P. Willis (eds), *Culture, Media Language: Working Papers in Cultural Studies 1972–1979* (128-138). London: Hutchinson.

Hesmondhalgh, D. (2010). 'User-Generated Content, Free Labour and the Cultural Industries', *Ephemera, 10*(3/4), 267-284.

Jenkins, H., Ford, S. & Green, J. (2013). *Spreadable Media: Creating Value and Meaning in a Networked Culture*. New York: New York University Press.

Keen, A. (2007). *The Cult of the Amateur: How Today's Internet is Killing our Culture*. New York: Doubleday.

Leadbeater, C. (2008). *We-Think*. London: Profile.

Oakley, K. (2014). 'Good Work? Rethinking Cultural Entrepreneurship', in C. Bilton & S. Cummings (eds), *Handbook of Management and Creativity* (145-159). Cheltenham: Edward Elgar.

Pool, I. de Sola (1983). *Technologies of Freedom*. Cambridge, MA: Harvard University Press.

Radway, J. (1984). *Reading the Romance: Women, Patriarchy and Popular Literature*. Chapel Hill, NC: University of North Carolina Press.

Shirky, C. (2010). *Cognitive Surplus: Creativity and Generosity in a Connected Age*. London: Allen Lane.

Tapscott, D. & Williams, A.D. (2006). *Wikinomics: How Mass Collaboration Changes Everything*. London: Atlantic Books.

8. Value Production in Media Industries and Everyday Life

Göran Bolin

With the digitalization of the media, many of the business models of media companies have become obsolete and had to be adapted. Various new forms of value circulate in digital markets, resulting from the different ways in which professional media makers and everyday media users value media. This chapter discusses these different forms of value and the relations between them.

Introduction

The making of media has historically moved through a number of distinct phases, each of which can be related to the forms of production and reproduction of communication in society. From the earliest forms of writing, through typographic culture in the wake of the printing press, and then electronic culture from the telegraph and onwards to the present digital era, reproduction technologies and the cultures that have been formed around them have impacted our abilities to communicate with one another, and to produce and consume media. Each phase has introduced shifts in the nature of communication and cultural production, as well as in the way cultural works have been appreciated during production and in reception.

Appreciation is arguably a form of valuation, that is, an assignment of value to an object or a practice. Media have been appreciated, or valued, for their functionality, effectivity, for their aesthetic qualities, or for their abilities to produce economic wealth. We can think of these valuation practices as a basic motivation for engaging with media, irrespective of whether we are producing or consuming media. In fact, the relation between production and consumption has altered with the technological shift of digitalization, as the means of making media have become increasingly widespread among media users.

If mechanical reproduction introduced a change to art and cultural objects, as Walter Benjamin (1936/1977) once famously argued, the age of digital reproduction has introduced yet another shift in this relation (Bolin, 2011, p. 67). Mechanical reproduction – the printing press, photography, cinema – made exact copies of original art and media texts possible. With digital reproduction, texts not only became reproducible without loss of quality, they also became freed from their tangible carriers: the book, the printed photography, the celluloid film, the shellac record, the video tape, etc. However, while digitalization means that the media texts have become freed from their carriers, they also require technological means of consumption in order for media users to be able to decode the digits in which the texts are constructed. These means of consumption are, at the same time, the main means of production on part of everyday media users: the laptop, tablet computer, or smartphone. Thus, with digitalization and the increased spread of mobile and cheap technologies, more people get access to the means of media production and also the tools for distribution of content. Ordinary media users can now not only take photos in the same way as in pre-digital times, but also manipulate them in editing programs, and upload them on, for example, social networking sites for distant others to consume.

Digitalization was accompanied by a restructuring of many of the business models of the old media industries, as well as the birth of entirely new models related to media that are born into the digital world. The music industry, for one, has gone from a primarily records-based industry (that is, earning their main revenues from record sales), to a concert-based model (Spilker, 2017). Many of these business models are based on the collection and analysis of user data for their production of economic value. Value, however, is a concept that extends beyond economic value, and means different things for different agents involved in the productions-consumption circuit of the media. While economic value is at the heart of the commercial parts of the media industries, for other types of media production it might mean other things. For the public service media, for example, who are not run for profit, value means public value. And for individual media users it can mean a range of other things, for example social, cultural, aesthetic, or political value.

In this chapter, first, these different forms of value will be discussed; how and under which conditions they are produced, who are the agents involved in this production, and what are the social and cultural consequences of this. Next, the very concept of value will be elaborated on in more detail, tracing the roots of the concept and discussing how value is produced, what its role is in the general production and consumption processes of the media, and how value forms part of two distinct and separate fields of cultural production. Finally, the argument will be summarized and some conclusions will be drawn.

Value and media production

The concept of value was thoroughly discussed 'in the eighteenth-century discourse of political economy' (Guillory, 1993, p. xiii), not least by Scottish philosopher Adam Smith (1776/1991), who, in *The Wealth of Nations,* elaborated on the distinction between use value and exchange value (a distinction already introduced in ancient philosophy by Aristotle). Smith pointed out that most things that are useful, that is, have 'value in use', cannot be sold, which means that they do not have 'value in exchange' (*Ibid.*, p. 24f). Smith, and later other economic philosophers such as David Ricardo and especially Karl Marx (1867/1976), developed these ideas into the labour theory of value. This theory holds that value has its root in human activity – labour. In Marx's formulation of the value of commodities, these are based in the combination of labour and raw material. The worker tools the raw material into a commodity, and it is the amount of work laid down in production that impacts the value of the commodity.

It has often been pointed out that Marx's theory of value is insufficient for understanding the workings of the media – and understandably so, since the media were not as an important part of public life in the mid-nineteenth century when Marx was active (e.g. Murdock, 2000). Twentieth-century economists such as John Kenneth Galbraith (1958/1964) have, for example, pointed out that symbolic dimensions of capitalist commodity production in the form of advertising and branding problematized economic theory. We might therefore need to integrate the labour theory of value with other accounts of how value is produced.

Philosopher Douglas Magendanz (2003) holds the concept of value as indefinable. Nonetheless, it can be understood through a range of ramifying concepts such as 'belief'. When we value a thing, we make 'a reflective judgment of worth', says Magendanz (2003, p. 444). Value is thus the result of the activity of valuation. We *give* value to something, and determine its worth against an 'agreed or assumed standard, criterion, or measure' (*Ibid.*, p. 443f). This means that value is socially constructed, using measures that are commonly agreed on, or, using the words of French sociologist Pierre Bourdieu (1993), produced within a specific *field of cultural production*. Such a field is, according to Bourdieu, centred on a value that all involved in the field agree is worth struggling or competing for. This value can be economic, but it can also be cultural, aesthetic, political, and affective. The field further consists of collective or individual agents who compete for and believe in this value. Belief, then, is also central to Bourdieu's field theory (Bourdieu, 1977/1993). The founding belief in any value system or field is that values can be hierarchically ordered in terms of quantity (more or less), or quality (good or bad), as David Graeber (2001, p. 16) has pointed out.

A field, then, is a system of relations between agents competing for a common value. Some of the institutional agents in the field have consecrating power, that is, the power to judge what are high and low or good and bad assets of the value in question. A field is structured according to the relations between the competing agents. The literary field, which is one of Bourdieu's (1992/1996) main examples, consists of authors, critics, academics, and others who wish to voice their opinion in matters concerning the field's specific value. Some institutional agents have strong consecrating power, for example the Nobel committee, which hands out Nobel prizes and thus bestow the prize winner with legitimacy, prestige, and acknowledged positions within the field. A field needs to have a certain amount of relative autonomy, in the sense that the value that the field is centred on is judged by members of the field, and is not dependent on 'outer demand', that is, forces outside of the field. A field of cultural production that is weak in autonomy might be more dependent on other fields, for example the economic, or the political field.

When we speak about value in relation to commodities, we often do that within the framework of market economy. Markets are arenas for the circulation of commodities. This circulation presupposes both production and consumption of commodities, and in political economy this production-consumption circuit (or product cycle) is at the centre. For the discussion of value, however, it is important to extend this discussion beyond the commercial market economy, and also include the cultural economy, where production is somewhat different. The relations between these two fields of media production is the focus of the next section.

The two fields of media production

Everyday media users are equipped with the means of cultural production in the form of computers, laptops, and smartphones. This means that all media users are also, at least to some extent and in some specific situations, media producers. Some theorists have argued that the distinctions between being a consumer and producer have collapsed, but in everyday practice it is more accurate to regard this as an ongoing oscillation between the roles of producer and consumer. However, it is also important to distinguish between different types of media production, since production in everyday contexts – uploading a photo to Instagram, leaving a comment under a YouTube video – differs significantly from the type of production that occurs by professional makers in the media industries – not only in scale, but also in kind. The differences are outlined in Table 1 below.

Table 1   Two fields of cultural production/consumption

Everyday media production	Industrial media production
Non-profit motivation	Profit motivation
Social and cultural economy	Market economy
Production of difference	Commodity production
Sign value	Exchange value

Firstly, industrialized media production is, with a few notable exceptions such as public service media, profit motivated. This is seldom the driving force behind everyday media production. Economic value is simply not the motor of amateur music production, nor is it the motive for uploading pictures on social networking media such as Instagram or Facebook. This means that where industrialized media production occurs within the framework of a market economy, everyday media production is situated in a social and cultural economy, where production results in identity, social difference, and cultural value rather than in economic profits. So, rather than exchange value, everyday media production is centred on sign value.

What makes making media in the context of an industrialized setting particularly interesting is the tension between its for-profit motive and the motivation of its professional practitioners, who tend to share with everyday ('amateur') media producers a desire to make media for non-profit, aesthetic, and affective reasons. This, in turn, explains professional media makers' orientation towards each other when looking for validation and value in their work; journalists care more about whether their colleagues say they have done a good job than the number of clicks their story got on the news organization website. Whereas the media industry tends to be driven by exchange value, the culture of production within media firms tends to be governed by sign value.

If use value concerns the utility of the good or the commodity, and exchange value is related to the price on the market, sign value is that value which gives status when it is spent or consumed. If we exemplify this with a car, we could say that all cars will take us from home to work – they are functional in use, and in that respect different cars do not differ very much from each other. Some cars, however, will cost us more than others to buy: their exchange value differs because they are made of a certain kind of material, and have required more working hours to produce. Some cars will also have sign value, which means that they have been equipped with (de)sign features that add to their exchange value. Sign value, then, has very little to do with the functionality of the thing, but more with the semiotic appearance of it – the impression it will make on others depending on if we drive a Volvo or a Rolls Royce. It is thus a marker of distinction, and it is produced through signifying practices.

In that sense, sign value is, on the one hand, contributing to the exchange value of commodities, but it can also be extracted as a value of its own. In fact, some commodities in the age of digital reproduction are entirely made up of signs. Take the audience commodity, for example. The audience commodity is constructed from calculations based on statistical samples. It supposedly reflects those who engage with a specific medium or media content, but the statistical figures *are* not the audience. These figures are a representation of the audience that is calculated on the bases of samples and probability theory, and we can never be sure of their accuracy.

In fact, the audience commodity as a statistical sample is entirely dependent on the belief, or trust, that the buyer has in the accuracy of the sample. This is why the sellers of the audience commodity are so eager to convince their customers (advertising agencies, media buyers, planners) that they can trust in their figures.

The type of figures that those who are engaged in web analytics present, and the difficulties in the customer's ability to decode them, have increased tremendously with online marketing on social networking media and other sites in the platform economy. While decreasing attention is paid to the traditional sociological descriptors of the audience commodity (e.g. age, sex, education), more emphasis is put on behaviour: *what you do* in digital space is more important than *who you are*. Content recommendation systems are a good example of this. There are several principles for such systems, from the more basic types where you are suggested content based on previous choices on a specific site (e.g. Amazon), to more advanced systems that base content recommendations and search engine rankings on types of collected behaviour across platforms and services.

However, such advanced systems for 'capturing the digital consumer' also poses a potential problem for the audience industry, since few people have the technological skills to understand just how the commodity is made. Actors within this economy often need to have the data translated into meaningful categories, that is, traditional sociological variables such as age, sex, income, education, geographical location, etc. (Bolin & Andersson Schwarz, 2015). Everyday media users have even more difficulties; they often have very vague ideas on how their data is treated, who has access to it, who owns what has been uploaded on the web, and how their actions are converted into the 'currency' that is the audience commodity (Kennedy *et al.*, 2015; Turow *et al.*, 2015).

The sign commodity

The sign structure of the audience commodity is indicative of the way in which sign commodities are constructed in the platform economy. Pure sign commodities have an intangible quality that makes them difficult to understand for most lay people, they are entirely dependent on belief. Being constructed in the digital domain, they lack a material base in raw material, since their worth is dependent on belief alone.

The specificities of cultural objects are thus radicalized in the digital era, as many of them have no tangible base but are pure sign structures. This also provokes a distinction between tangible and intangible cultural objects and commodities, which I call sign commodities here. Admittedly, many cultural objects have always had an intangible character. A piece of music, for example, is hard to put in your pocket or hold in your hand, as is a performance at the theatre, a recited poem, an enlightening lecture, a radio play – at least when it comes to the *performance* of all of these examples.

If laid down on tangible carriers – the printed scores of a symphony, the videotaped version of a theatre performance, a recording of the recital of a poem – they naturally can be held in our hands, which, up to the point of digitalization, was the most common way for us to experience these works. With digitalization, however, we no longer need these tangible carriers as we can all have access to these works on the web. This is the radical difference between analogue and digital circulation of cultural objects.

A consequence of this is that the political economy of the intangible cultural commodity differs from that of the tangible cultural commodity. With the rise of modern mass media and the 'information society', manifest and tangible commodities have increasingly been replaced by intangible commodities.

In the platform economy of today, focused as it is on intangible, pure sign commodities, raw material is of an entirely different kind compared to what it was in the pre-digital era. In those times, raw material could be touched, held in the hand, and when it was tooled into a new commodity, the raw material was gone, realized in productive consumption. This is not the case with the intangible commodity. When everyday media users engage in non-profit motivated media production within the framework of the cultural economy, they not only produce pictures, texts, videos, etc., which are then uploaded on websites and social networking media, they are in that process also producing social, aesthetic, and cultural value. In addition, they also produce a string of digital remains for the industrial media industries to take advantage of and appropriate as raw material in the field of industrialized media production. This practice is common in advertising and marketing, where campaigns are geared toward getting 'influencers' to promote and circulate brand messages for the advertisers, or in journalism where news organizations hope that audience members will share and forward their reports. The fruits of media user labour, then, get drawn from its original field of everyday production into the field of industrialized media production, where it is then further tooled into an audience commodity that can circulate on that commercial market.

Conclusion

Value, as has been shown in this chapter, appears in many forms. It is both a practice of measuring, and a thing. It can be a quantity as well as a quality, and it can be tied to either tangible or intangible commodities. Media production in the pre-digital world differed significantly from how media commodities are produced today. With the digitalization of the media, many of the old business models have become obsolete, since their ability to produce economic value have become undermined in the wake of the increased fluidity of the digital commodities. Knowledge of how value is produced can help explain these changes.

Knowledge of the plurality of value forms that circulate in both everyday media production and industrialized media production can also help explain why many of us ordinary users and producers of non-economic value forms freely contribute to the large profits of transnational media corporations, and have them collect vast amounts of data on our behaviour, social networks, movements in space, and many other kinds of information that form the basis for the audience commodity.

The production of value is at the centre of most, if not all, activities that we engage with in relation to the media. We cannot really escape value and the moral, aesthetic, and other valuation processes that surround media. It is, of course, not the only reason why we engage with media, but it is indeed the main answer to why we find engaging with them worthwhile.

Further reading
- Case: How creators – influencers, YouTubers, vloggers, game players – use platforms to engage with global fan communities for commercial and cultural value – Craig (p. 363)
- Context: Five current issues and trends relating to the media industries as a result of digitalization and the rise of the global communication giants – Miège (p. 73)
- Contrast: How the new platforms facilitate and profit from new forms of consumption without creating or producing content – Bilton (p. 99)

References

Andersson, H.C. (1980). *The Emperor's New Clothes*. London: Hodder and Stoughton.

Baudrillard, J. (1981). *For a Critique of the Political Economy of the Sign*. St. Louis, MI: Telos (Original work published 1972).

Baudrillard, J. (1975). *The Mirror of Production*. St. Louis, MI: Telos (original work published 1973).

Benjamin, W. (1977). 'The Work of Art in the Age of Mechanical Reproduction', in J. Curran, M. Gurevitch & J. Wollacott (eds), *Mass Communication and Society* (384-408). London: Edward Arnold (original work published 1936).

Bjur, J. (2009). *Transforming Audiences: Patterns of Individualization in Television Viewing*. Göteborg: JMG.

Bolin, G. (2011). *Value and the Media. Cultural Production and Consumption in Digital Markets*. Farnham: Ashgate.

Bolin, G. & Andersson Schwarz, J. (2015). "Heuristics of the Algorithm. Big Data, User Interpretation and Institutional Translation", *Big Data & Society*, 2(2), 1-12.

Bourdieu, P. (1993). 'The Production of Belief: Contribution to an Economy of Symbolic Goods', in P. Bourdieu, *The Field of Cultural Production. Essays on Art and Literature* (74-111). Cambridge: Polity (original work published 1977).

Bourdieu, P. (1996). *The Rules of Art. Genesis and Structure of the Literary Field.* Cambridge: Polity (original work published 1992)

Bourdieu, P. (1993). *The Field of Cultural Production. Essays on Art and Literature.* Cambridge: Polity.

Castells, M. (1996). *The Information Age: Economy, Society and Culture. Part 1: The Rise of the Network Society.* Malden, MA: Blackwell.

Dewey, J. (1939). *Theory of Valuation.* Chicago, IL: Chicago University Press.

Dumont, L. (1980). *Homo Hierarchicus: The Caste System and its Implications.* Chicago, IL: Chicago University Press (original work published 1966).

Dumont, L. (2013). 'On Value. The Radcliffe-Brown Lecture in Social Anthropology, 1980', *HAU: Journal of Ethnographic Theory, 3*(1), 287-315 (original work published 1980).

Galbraith, J.K. (1958). *The Affluent Society.* London: Hamish Hamilton.

Galbraith, J.K. (1970). 'Economics as a System of Belief', *American Economic Review, 60*(2), 469-478.

Graeber, D. (2001). *Toward and Anthropological Theory of Value. The False Coin in Our Own Dreams.* New York: Palgrave.

Guillory, J. (1993). *Cultural Capital. The Problem of Literary Canon Formation.* Chicago, IL: The University of Chicago Press.

Hall, S. (1973). *Encoding/Decoding in the Television Discourse.* Stencilled occasional paper from CCCS no. 7. Birmingham: Birmingham University/CCCS.

Kennedy, H., Elgesem, D. & Miguel, C. (2015). 'On Fairness: User Perspectives on Social Media Data Mining', *Convergence, 21*(4), 1-19.

Magendanz, D. (2003). 'Conflict and Complexity in Value Theory', *The Journal of Value Inquiry, 37,* 443-453.

Marx, K. (1976). *Capital. A Critique of Political Economy. Volume One.* London: Penguin Books (original work published 1867).

Murdock, G. (2000). 'Peculiar Commodities: Audiences at Large in the World of Goods', in I. Hagen & J. Wasko (eds), *Consuming Audiences? Production and Reception in Media Research* (47-70). Cresskill, NJ: Hampton Press.

Spilker, H.S. (2017). *Digital Music Distribution: The Sociology of Online Music Streams.* London: Routledge.

Smith, A. (1991) *The Wealth of Nations.* New York: Alfred A. Knopf (original work published 1776).

Turow, J., Hennessy, M. & Draper, N. (2015). *The Trade-Off Fallacy. How Marketers are Misrepresenting American Consumers and Opening Them up to Exploitation.* Philadelphia, PA: Annenberg School of Communication.

Van Couvering, E. (2008). 'The History of the Internet Search Engine: Navigational Media and the Traffic Commodity', *Information Science and Knowledge Management, 14,* 177-206.

9. Transformation and Innovation of Media Business Models

Mikko Villi and Robert G. Picard

Transformations in the media environment and media consumption have created the need for new business models and the reconceptualization of media business-es. This chapter discusses the problem with the traditional business models and how the digital transition has made it necessary to embrace and explore audience-first business models.

Introduction

In the past two decades, the foundations of doing business in the media industry have been changing rapidly. Many of the media industry's most long-standing practices and business models have been losing ground, and media companies have needed to develop new organizational practices and procedures, new business concepts, and new strategies (Malmelin & Villi, 2017a). Business models explain the business logic of specific enterprises and the products, services, and relationships upon which the business and activities are based. They identify the consumer needs to be met, provide insight into where and how value is created, reveal how its value constellations will operate, identify dependencies and interdependences, and explain how the company and its offerings differ from competitors. In doing so, business models show how enterprises will overcome the most common reasons for failure: lack of market need, poor products and services, lack of attention to customers, inability to organize business relationships effectively, and losing out to more effective competitors.

The contemporary business model perspective for all media enterprises involves creating new processes, products, and ways of presenting content, and changing the relationships between consumers and the enterprise. Thus, the focus is not only on the revenue streams. It is crucial to embrace this larger perspective. However, for many legacy media organizations such transformation is not always easy, as most legacy media have grown up in a 'steady state' environment, where change has been rather gradual and well signposted (Küng, 2017). Now, their business models need to be adapted to the digital media environment that is influenced by rapid advances in media technology and the emergence of new platforms and new media consumption habits.

This chapter focuses on how transformations in the media environment and among media consumers have created the need for new business models and the reconceptualization of media businesses. The goal of the chapter is to provide an understanding of media business models and especially the challenges in innovating and creating new business models that can 'make it work'.

Outdated media business models

Media companies following a traditional business model are no longer as profitable as they used to be. For instance, the decline of advertising in printed magazines and newspapers and the growth of online advertising (that is skewed to a few platforms), the distribution of free online content, and changes in consumers' media behaviour have combined to undermine the print industry's traditional business model. The basic print business model was based on creating mass audiences by keeping content prices low and then selling the audiences to advertisers who wish to reach them. That model was facilitated by publishers enjoying near monopolies on production and distribution in specific geographic areas, which limited competition for both audiences and advertising. In the digital age, such monopolies are extremely difficult to uphold.

Although it is important to maintain advertising as a source of revenue, its significance is declining – in many print operations, subscriptions already provide most of the revenue. Because only a few leading digital operations generate sufficiently large audiences to rely on digital advertising, most news providers need to pursue revenue growth through subscriptions and other forms of consumer income. Media executives in print publishing stress the need to make a swift transition towards a business based on the digital subscriptions of paying customers and predict that publishers with models relying solely or even mainly on advertising will either have to find other sources of revenue, eke out a marginal economic future with very low levels of content investment, or go bust (Thompson, 2016). This is not a universal trend, however, as in Asia, Latin America, and Southern Europe the focus on advertising income continues, while the willingness or ability of readers to pay for content is more limited (Newman, 2017).

Because of the general shift to subscription revenue, news providers are relating to consumers differently than in the past and employing pricing models that differ from those of the original print and broadcast products. Many offer varying prices for access from different bundles of devices and platforms, and for different levels of access to premium and specialized news content. No longer is all content provided to all consumers at the same price. News organizations are refocusing on quality and unique journalism that people hopefully are prepared to pay for – they aim for 'quality reach', rather than just big numbers (Newman, 2017). New media business models do not diminish content quality, but they rather *demand* it – this is actually a positive development when considering the future of journalism.

What is also clear is that content providers are becoming less dependent on any one form of funding than they have been for about 150 years. As the dual model in print media of combining earnings from both readers and advertisers is outdated in many respects, media businesses depend increasingly on pulling in money from more diverse revenue sources. Multiple revenue streams from readers and advertisers, from events and e-commerce, from foundations and sponsors, and from related commercial services such as Web hosting and advertising services are all contributing income (Picard, 2014). Pursuing such revenue requires organizational changes and incurs costs not previously common in media. However, although e-commerce and events can be helpful, the bottom line for content publishers is whether the content they produce is worth paying for (Thompson, 2016).

Print publishers must engage in broader thinking about business models that demonstrates a focus on value, services, and relationships. Traditional print businesses are evolving into diversified media corporations with extensive product, service, and brand portfolios (Malmelin & Villi, 2017b). Business model innovation is focused on building and nurturing value-creating relationships with readers, advertisers, partners, and intermediaries (Picard, 2011). When those relationships are effective, they become the bases for revenue-producing activities.

The focus on consumer income is not common only to print media. As television is evolving from linear broadcasting towards on-demand models, the ad-supported television business is also partly transforming into a subscription business. This is evident in how an increasing number of television viewers subscribe to such online providers as *Netflix*. The on-demand television business is built around satisfying consumers, and, consequently, advertisers have far less influence than before.

Although all segments of the media industry are being affected by contemporary changes in technology, competition, and consumer choice, the extent and rate of change vary significantly. Media companies rethinking their business models and adapting them for the digital world must evaluate their current models honestly, identify what must change, and alter their business models, products, and processes to accomplish those changes. Importantly, it is essential for them to adjust their business models in ways that are appropriate for their individual markets and customers, not merely to copy what others are doing. Because multiple revenue streams are being pursued, organizations need multiple business models for different aspects of their operations. The need for multiple business models for different media products and other revenue producing activities has, thus, done away with the idea of a single business model for media firms.

The effect of digital transition on media business models

A major factor affecting the transformation of media business models is digital transition. Digital transition refers to the shift to distributing media content on online platforms, where the content is consumed by using digital devices such as laptops, mobile phones, and tablet computers (Villi & Hayashi, 2017). This gradual transition can be compared to a journey (Schlesinger & Doyle, 2015). The endpoint of digital transition is a digital-only media outlet, the content of which is no longer available on the traditional platforms (print, broadcast television channels). Digital transition affects the whole chain of industry operations from content production to content distribution and consumption.

In the digital media space, legacy media compete for both the time and money of media consumers with an array of new digital-only players. Many net native companies (e.g. *HuffPost*, *Vox*, and *Buzzfeed*) tend to evidence higher entrepreneurial attitudes and more flexibility in their business models (Ruotsalainen & Villi). They often work in the craft mode, focusing on special topics, employing specialized techniques such as investigative or data journalism, or serving smaller localities as news providers (Picard, 2014). They also tend to have a wider range of revenue sources than larger firms – perhaps out of necessity.

The small journalistic enterprises are more likely to seek supporting memberships and offer member events that produce higher engagement with audiences. In contrast, many established media organizations evidence an unwillingness or inability to consider value creation and business relationships in the broader way that digital competitors and emerging content providers are embracing (Lehtisaari *et al.*).

As for television companies, they must figure out how to confront such new content producers and intermediaries as *Netflix, Hulu, Amazon*, and *YouTube*. However, these new digital players cannot be called 'small' in any sense, as they often have resources that are vastly larger than those of the legacy television companies.

Digital products are not merely extending the distribution of content, but require companies to understand that their nature and consumption patterns differ significantly. This means that digital products face entirely different issues that require different strategies, content, presentation, business models, and operating structures. Operating in the digital environment is forcing companies to make significant investments in technology, software, and systems, as well as in the personnel to manage and operate them. Newspaper organizations such as the *New York Times, The Washington Post, The Wall Street Journal*, and *The Guardian*, which have led these developments, perceive those investments as central to their strategies and future growth.

Many smaller media organizations seem to think that they must follow the bigger players without developing their own business models and strategy or without regard to whether they will be equally useful. The use of technology is then the goal rather than the means to a goal. In many enterprises, digital operations and new revenue initiatives are being pursued without creating comprehensive strategies, without fully considering their requirements, and without establishing new business models or providing adequate and appropriate resources.

Platformization

In the midst of the digital transition, the main challenge for media companies is not always the production of media content, but rather the distribution and monetization of that content (Picard, 2011). Particularly critical is gaining awareness and obtaining audiences for media products among the younger generations (Chyi & Lee, 2013). In this, the social media platforms, such as *Instagram*, *Facebook* and *Twitter*, are a focal bridge to audiences, as they play an important role in extending the reach and acquiring potential new customers for media companies. The online platforms are in a key position in a situation where the dual business model of media companies – combining earnings from both consumers and advertisers – is challenged by changes in advertising and media consumption habits. The platform companies become (often unwelcome) partners in some business models of media firms and the relationship with these online platforms must be managed for optimal value contribution and to reduce value diversion and capture on their part.

The term 'platformization' refers to the extension of social media platforms, the drive to make online content 'platform ready', and the rise of the platform as the dominant infrastructural and economic model of the social web (Gillespie, 2010; Helmond, 2015). Platformization is not an uncomplicated development trend for media companies. When they build new relations with social media companies, the latter can control the arrangement and reap most of the financial benefit (Mitchell, 2015). Media companies lose control over distribution and thereby also control over the connection with their audience and the access to the data the audience provides. When content is accessed through third parties such as Facebook, getting useful data is difficult because it is in the interest of Facebook to keep much of that data in-house for their own use. In addition, most media firms – if not all – are disadvantaged in comparison to the platform companies when it comes to size and resources.

The social media platforms represent the biggest shift in the strategic environment for many media companies: while they bring access to potentially huge audiences, they also compromise revenues, control over the context in which content is consumed, contact with audiences, and quality of data (Küng, 2017). Platformization is also a problem for media brands since much of the recognition credit may be inherited by the platform – some users do not even notice where the content originally came from when they read a news story on social media (Newman, 2016).

Audience-first business models and consumer engagement

As noted, many media business models relate to generating income and data from the consumers. The changing media consumption patterns, shifting revenue streams and platformization require media companies to think more strategically and flexibly about their relationships with multiple consumer groups and to implement changes to better link with consumers. Many new ideas around media innovation focus on gaining and retaining loyal paying consumers, in a sense applying an audience-first strategy (Lehtisaari *et al.*).

Consumers can be extremely valuable to media companies in at least three additional areas: in content production and the provision of networks, in development and innovation, and as a source of information and data (Bechmann & Lomborg, 2013; Malmelin & Villi, 2017a). Traditionally, media consumers have been regarded as relatively passive objects of business marketing and sales efforts. In so doing, the companies have failed to take advantage of the opportunity to involve consumers in the processes of designing, marketing, and developing products and services (Malmelin & Villi, 2017b).

Media companies are increasingly using the data obtained from digital and mobile interactions to understand media consumers and their consumption patterns. The data provides evidence about consumer relationships and how they can be nurtured more suitably. As data can help media companies serve consumers better, great thought must be put into how to use the data strategically. It is important, however, to remember that improving relationships and the value delivered to consumers is the goal of the activity, not merely the gathering and analysis of data.

Hand in hand with collecting media consumer data goes the understanding that media companies need to develop new models for consumer engagement (Lehtisaari *et al.*). Of essence is the creation of a personal relationship between consumers and the media brand. Engagement is based on feelings of affinity and attachment, not merely on exchange and consumption. Relationships based on transactions and functional usefulness produce relatively low-level connections and do not create much value for the consumer or the company. Building higher-level relationships requires mutual respect and the pursuit of joint benefit. Higher-level relationships evoke emotions, senses of belonging, involvement, and perhaps also a sense of 'ownership' of the media brand.

There are many ways to measure the strength of relationships with media consumers. At the low level, they tend to be assessed through engagement measures such as clicks, time spent reading, and commenting. Higher-level relationships tend to be indicated by factors such as membership, participation in events, providing suggestions and advice, and co-creating content. Establishing productive relationships is easier said than done. It is not enough for the company to want a relationship; they must persuade consumers and others that there is benefit for them in the relationship. Relationships cannot just be a way for the company to market to targeted consumers; they must deliver value for consumers as well.

At the centre of many media business models concentrated on developing consumer relationships is the service-dominant media logic. This service logic builds on the service-dominant logic of marketing (Vargo & Lusch, 2004). According to the service-dominant logic, value is increasingly co-created with the consumer rather than embedded in an output. At the core of the service-dominant media logic is, thus, an interactive consumption process between the media company and the media consumer. From the point of view of the service-dominant logic the audience can be an operant resource and co-actor, rather than an operand resource, a 'target' of content production (Vargo & Lusch, 2004). The value is created not by the producer alone in the production process, but in the interactive consumption process between the producer and consumer (Prahalad & Ramaswamy, 2004). The value is then not in the media product but in the process, the *service*.

The service logic differs from the goods-dominant logic, which is the production-oriented and company-centric logic that has been the driving logic of the media business for more than two centuries. The traditional goods-dominant logic considers the value to be created when a product is made – the product has a value in itself – and the consumers are outside of this process.

In the traditional model of mass communication, a newspaper or a television company created the value of the media product without consumer involvement. Following the service-dominant logic, the value is now increasingly created as a consequence of nurturing the activities of media consumers. Service logic is based on establishing and maintaining individual relationships, anticipating and solving consumers' needs, creating simplicity and ease of use, and focusing on interactions with consumers. Consumer satisfaction is central in the service logic. As in many other industries, media industry business models that do not start with effective value propositions on how they will serve consumers' needs will not succeed over time. Pursuing audience-first business models requires changes in organizational culture and structure in order to provide the required interactions necessary to make it successful.

The need for organizational change

Innovation is key when facing the challenges of changing social, economic and technological environments for media companies, and surviving in highly competitive markets (see Küng, 2013). Although many media enterprises are attempting to develop innovative business models, innovation is a problematic concept as it involves products, technologies, and processes. Much of what is called innovation is often not innovation, but rather adaptation. Changing to adopt new possibilities and pursue new opportunities is important, but does not represent innovation. Firms are not innovative because they decide, for example, to use social networks to increase contact with readers and potential readers, or because they optimize their content for mobile use.

The innovation of new media business models also requires organisational transformation and a change of mindsets, often unlearning the trade and its institutional truths (Lehtisaari *et al.*). The brakes on media innovation are mostly cultural, in the news industry frequently residing within the newsroom where systemic, well-rooted practices and preferred work patterns dominate (Ess, 2014) – a result of the ideology of journalistic practice embedded in a particular form of production (Deuze, 2005). Other legacy media industries – such as advertising and television production – have similar cultural problems.

It can be argued that in addition to shifting the mindset, people working in the media industry need a broader range of skills and knowledge. Contemporary media business models and activities require knowledge and skills sets often absent within the traditional staff. These include digital content production, web design, digital marketing and sales, social media content coordination, digital account management, and web analytics, as well as relationship management and engagement facilitation for readers, advertisers, and other stakeholders. Expanding a business model to include new activities and revenue through content syndication, specialized newsletters, event production and management, branded content and merchandise, and creative services also requires the business to acquire personnel with skills and abilities not present in most legacy media businesses today. The skills especially needed are an entrepreneurial attitude, a competitive drive, a service mentality, and the ability to create individual business models and value-creating strategies for each activity.

Conclusion

A fundamental problem of many media organizations is that they are so busy with the operational aspects of digital products that they devote little time to deep strategic thinking, especially in organizations without personnel specifically assigned to strategy and business development. Most media companies that approach digital products without more sophisticated perspectives in their business models will be disappointed in the financial results, because their products will not effectively serve audiences, advertisers or themselves.

Despite a great deal of organizational change since the millennium, the organizational arrangements necessary to fully exploit digital operations and to succeed in the digital space are not yet fully in place in most media companies. There is no single correct organizational solution to deal with the increasing number of products and varying business models in media organizations today. The organizations need to be ambidextrous, exploiting existing products to enable incremental innovation and, at the same time, are adaptive to changes in the environment and explore new opportunities to foster more radical innovation (Andriopoulos & Lewis, 2009). In newspaper organizations this means that, on the one hand, the print business requires nurturing, and on the other, new digital offerings need to be developed. The danger in this can be that a 'playing it safe' attitude might be brought in from the print business to the digital publishing context (Lehtisaari *et al.*).

The key point about contemporary media business models is that they are not just about revenue, but increasingly about relationships with consumers, value creation, and continual product and service improvement. Establishing a new business model or models is not as simple as deciding to change the model. It requires a new strategy and resources that make the strategy feasible. New business models, products, and services also require a change in organizational thinking to become more entrepreneurial and willing to accept failure and outcomes different from what has been anticipated. Media organizations might need to some degree to adopt the 'fail forward' or 'fail fast, fail often' styles of thinking that are familiar from Silicon Valley.

Accepting failure is a huge challenge for most media organizations because they have not needed to take risks in their business models for generations. Today, as legacy media products decline and change, not taking risks is dangerous in itself because it leads to lost opportunities and inability to grow and develop in new ways, forcing the firm to live on existing, weakening business models. They might seem to be doing well enough for the time being, but are actually 'failing slowly', which in the end leads to a final 'death spiral' from which there probably is no return.

Further reading
- Case: What the transformation of the media industry and its business models means from the perspective of managing media firms – Faustino & Noam (p. 147)
- Context: How media consumer engagement has become the fundamental driver of value creation in media companies' business strategies – Chan-Olmsted & Wang (p. 133)
- Contrast: How the new platforms facilitate and profit from new forms of consumption without creating or producing content – Bilton (p. 99)

Acknowledgements: A portion of this chapter appeared in Lehtisaari, K., Grönlund, M., Lindén, C-G., Villi, M., Picard, R.G., Mierzejewska, B.I. & Ropnack, A. (2017). *Uutismedian uudet liiketoimintamallit Yhdysvalloissa* [New Business Models of News Media in the US]. Aleksanteri Papers 1/2017. Helsinki: University of Helsinki. The report was funded by The Media Industry Research Foundation of Finland. It is used with permission.

References

Andriopoulos, C. & Lewis, M.W. (2009). 'Exploitation-Exploration Tensions and Organizational Ambidexterity: Managing Paradoxes of Innovation', *Organization Science, 20*(4), 696-717. https://doi.org/10.1287/orsc.1080.0406.

Bechmann, A. & Lomborg, S. (2013). 'Mapping Actor Roles in Social Media: Different Perspectives on Value Creation in Theories of User Participation', *New Media & Society, 15*(5), 765-781. https://doi.org/10.1177/1461444812462853.

Chyi, H. I. & Lee, A. M. (2013). 'Online News Consumption: A Structural Model Linking Preference, Use, and Paying Intent', *Digital Journalism, 1*(2), 194-211. https://doi.org/10.1080/21670811.2012.753299.

Deuze, M. (2005). 'What is Journalism? Professional Identity and Ideology of Journalists Reconsidered', *Journalism, 6*(4), 442-464. https://doi.org/10.1177/1464884905056815.

Ess, Charles M. (2014). 'Editor's Introduction: Innovations in the Newsroom – and Beyond', *Journal of Media Innovations, 1*(2), 1-9.

Gillespie, T. (2010). 'The Politics of "Platforms"', *New Media & Society, 12*(3), 347-364. https://doi.org/10.1177/1461444809342738.

Helmond, A. (2015). 'The Platformization of the Web: Making Web Data Platform Ready', *Social Media + Society, 1*(2). https://doi.org/10.1177/2056305115603080.

Küng, L. (2013). 'Innovation, Technology and Organisational Change. Legacy Media's Big Challenges', in T. Storsul & A.H. Krumsvik (eds), *Media innovations: A multidisciplinary study of change* (9-12). Gothenburg: Nordicom.

Küng, L. (2017). *Going Digital: A Roadmap for Organisational Transformation*. Oxford: Reuters Institute for the Study of Journalism.

Lehtisaari, K., Villi, M., Grönlund, M., Lindén, C.-G., Mierzejewska, B. I., Picard, R. G. & Röpnack, A. (forthcoming). 'Comparing Innovation and Social Media Strategies in Scandinavian and US Newspapers', *Digital Journalism*.

Malmelin, N., & Villi, M. (2017a). 'Co-creation of What? Modes of Audience Community Collaboration in Media Work', *Convergence: The International Journal of Research into New Media Technologies*, *23*(2), 182-196. https://doi.org/10.1177/1354856515592511.

Malmelin, N. & Villi, M. (2017b). 'Media Work in Change: Understanding the Role of Media Professionals in Times of Digital Transformation and Convergence', *Sociology Compass*, *11*(7). https://doi.org/10.1111/soc4.12494.

Mitchell, A. (2015). 'State of the News Media 2015 Overview', in *State of the News Media 2015* (4-9). Location?: Pew Research Center.

Newman, N. (2016). 'Overview and Key Findings', in N. Newman, R. Fletcher, Levy, D.A.L. & Kleis Nielsen, R. (eds), *Reuters Institute Digital News Report 2016* (). Oxford: Reuters Institute for the Study of Journalism.

Newman, N. (2017). 'Executive Summary and Key Findings', in N. Newman, R. Fletcher, A. Kalogeropoulos, Levy, D.A.L. & Kleis Nielsen, R. (eds), *Reuters Institute Digital News Report 2017* (9-27). Oxford: Oxford University.

Picard, R.G. (2011). *The Economics and Financing of Media Companies* (2nd ed.). New York: Fordham University Press.

Picard, R.G. (2014). 'Twilight or New Dawn of Journalism? Evidence from the Changing News Ecosystem', *Journalism Studies*, *15*(5), 500-510. https://doi.org/10.1080/146167 0X.2014.895530.

Prahalad, C. K. & Ramaswamy, V. (2004). 'Co-creation Experiences: The Next Practice in Value Creation', *Journal of Interactive Marketing*, *18*(3), 5-14. https://doi.org/10.1002/dir.20015.

Ruotsalainen, J. & Villi, M. (forthcoming). 'Hybrid Engagement: Discourses and Scenarios of Entrepreneurial Journalism', *Media and Communication*.

Schlesinger, P. & Doyle, G. (2015). 'From Organizational Crisis to Multi-Platform Salvation? Creative Destruction and the Recomposition of News Media', *Journalism*, *16*(3), 305-323. https://doi.org/10.1177/1464884914530223.

Thompson, M. (2016). 'The Challenging New Economics of Journalism', in N. Newman, R. Fletcher, Levy, D.A.L. & Kleis Nielsen, R. (eds), *Reuters Institute Digital News Report 2016* (107-108). Oxford: Reuters Institute for the Study of Journalism.

Vargo, S. L. & Lusch, R. F. (2004). 'Evolving to a New Dominant Logic for Marketing', *Journal of Marketing*, *68*(1), 1-17. https://doi.org/10.1509/jmkg.68.1.1.24036.

Villi, M. & Hayashi, K. (2017). '"The Mission is to Keep this Industry Intact": Digital Transition in the Japanese Newspaper Industry', *Journalism Studies*, *18*(8), 960-977. https://doi.org/10.1080/1461670X.2015.1110499.

10. Shifts in Consumer Engagement and Media Business Models

Sylvia Chan-Olmsted and Rang Wang

The media industry is changing to adapt to an environment that is characterized by the fragmentation of media options, competition for attention, and empowered audiences. Consumer engagement has become the key to success for many media companies. This chapter reviews the shifts of business models in the media industry and discusses how media consumer engagement is becoming the fundamental driver of value creation in media companies' business strategies.

Introduction

In most market-driven countries that allow for private enterprises and/or commercial activities, the media industry, like all other consumer goods or service industries, has certain business characteristics that drive its operations. In other words, for media companies that do not exist solely by public mandates, a primary goal would be to make money. In its simplest definition, a business model describes what a company plans to do to make money (Ovans, 2015). What is of central importance for media companies to achieve this goal is to attract and retain audiences. If there is no audience, media content is of no commercial value. To attract and retain audiences, media companies need to create value for them at the right time and in the right context.

The global media market is in a challenging, but also exciting time. Constant technological changes fuel competition, fragmentation, and uncertainty. At the same time, there are new opportunities to interact with audiences, cultivate communities, and even source interesting content from audiences. Indeed, the most significant implication of communication technology advances in the last decade is the empowerment of consumers. Today's audiences are no longer passive recipients of content, but empowered media consumers who can co-create value in the new media ecosystem. Therefore, in this time of change, the best way to understand how the media industry is shifting its operations to adapt to the environment is to learn how it plans to make money by creating value for and harvesting the value co-created by its audiences.

This chapter reviews the shifts of business models in the media industry and discusses how media consumer engagement is becoming the fundamental driver

Figure 1   Content, data, and engagement in value co-creation

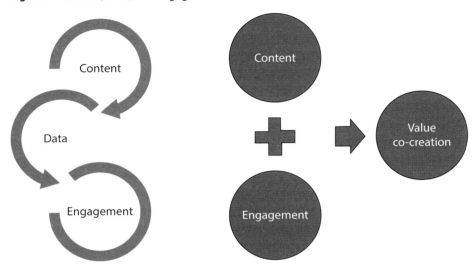

of value creation in media companies' business strategies. The core proposition here is that the consumption of media content can be enhanced by data-based audience intelligence and engagement, thus creating value for both the audience and media (see Figure 1).

The challenge now is how the value can be monetized sustainably when technology continues to evolve and audiences continue to demand more.

Media business models

The definition of business model varies across disciplines. As mentioned earlier, it is fundamentally what Lewis stated, 'how you planned to make money' (Lewis, 1999, p. 256). Diving deeper into the concept to address business processes and systems, Magretta (2002) argued that business models can be defined in terms of a value chain. A business model should describe activities associated with making products/services (e.g. designing, purchasing raw materials, and manufacturing) and selling them (e.g. finding and reaching customers, identifying values customers want, and delivering values).

Osterwalder (2013) insisted that a business model is a set of assumptions regarding not only the value chain, but also value proposition, customer relationships, channels, customer segments, cost structures, and revenue streams. With a focus on customer value proposition – how companies help customers to solve their problems and fulfil their needs – Johnson, Christensen, and Kagermann (2008) presented a four-element framework of successful business models. In addition to customer value proposition, the framework includes profit formula, resources needed to deliver the customer value proposition profitably, and processes that make the profitable delivery of customer value proposition repeatable and scalable.

In essence, business models are about the value creation system, namely how companies create value for consumers and themselves. In the media sector, there are three main business models that have been adopted over the years in various forms, namely, advertising-based, subscription-based, and transaction-based.

1. Advertising-based models. Media companies with advertising-based models usually offer content to audiences at no or little cost. The content is, in a sense, used as an exchange for audience attention, which is, in theory, sold to advertisers at a price dictated by the supply and demand of ad inventories. With this approach, media content providers are motivated to attract the largest possible audience with mass appeal content or target attractive audience segments desired by advertisers with niche content. The model works well in creating value when there are limited alternatives and the audience themselves relinquish the control and choice to others because they do not, in a sense, directly pay for the content they consume. With the trend towards audience empowerment and the challenge of getting audience's 'attention' in a media environment full of options, advertising-based models are losing their steam.

There has also been a reallocation of advertising spending from legacy media to online and mobile media. Worldwide, though most advertising money is still spent on television, mobile platform has come in a close second, with desktop internet following it. Other media, such as print, out-of-home, cinema, and radio have fallen far behind (but hold steady). In addition, there are new, powerful players competing for the advertising dollars traditionally went to print and TV media. Technology companies and digital platforms like Google and Facebook, with their advanced targeting ability and access to extensive audience data, have grown to be formidable advertising platforms for marketers.

The value proposition of an advertising-based business model has changed. It is likely to remain viable only when audience insights and engagement are taken into consideration in the process, or when rare, irreplaceable, and inimitable content is offered by media companies that provide advertising options (e.g. prominent unfolding live events such as the FIFA World Cup, the Olympics, and national elections).

2. Subscription-based models. In contrast with an advertiser-control system, some media companies charge audiences a recurring subscription fee for accessing media content or premium services (e.g. no advertising) periodically. Media companies with subscription-based models are in a better position to design and control the audience consumption experience and gather audience insights directly. Under this revenue model, media companies need to have the ability to continuously offer content/services that have ongoing consumption values. That is, they not only have to invest in access to exclusive content and new content creation, but also pay close attention to maintaining relationships with their customers. A great example of companies in this category is Netflix.

Many media companies, whether traditional or digital, are transforming their business models to subscription-based ones or a hybrid model of subscription and advertising. In an economic sense, the success of such subscription-based models signals the rise of consumer sovereignty in the media sector. The empowerment of media consumers here translates to advertising avoidance and consumer willingness to pay for high-quality content and good consumption experience. In other words, subscription-based media services are becoming very popular as they give audience more control of their experience, selection, and personalization.

3. Transaction-based models. Instead of paying a subscription for bundled products periodically, some media companies charge audience a one-time fee to access media content. This method works well for individual media items that offer clear, exclusive, or time-limited value. Good examples are books and pay-per-view sports events. While a transaction-based model gives media consumers the freedom to choose and control cost, it may not offer the best consumption experience because of the complexity in payment and access in a multiplatform environment full of media options from offline to online, from PC to mobile devices, and so on.

Besides advertising, transaction, and subscription models, there are other innovative approaches to make money from the exchange of media content and revenues in the digital environment. Focusing on the notion of audience value, we will discuss how audience insights and actions can be monetized as a form of business model.

Audience insights monetization. Today's media companies can derive value from their audiences more than just selling them to advertisers. With thoughtful data collection, audience analysis, and engagement programmes, media companies can harvest the value of aggregated audience insights as a marketing partner to advertisers. The truth is, the traditional segmentation of target audiences is no longer sufficient in today's fragmented attention economy. In the digital environment, media companies need deep audience insights to improve and market their products, and become the knowledge partner to advertisers. Audience value can also be created from carefully managed audience communities, social media connections, and content co-creation. There are abundant opportunities to grow this triangular relationship into potential e-commerce type of interactions, benefiting both the media and marketers, as well as satisfying engaged audience communities.

Crowdfunding. The value of audience is most evident in the case of direct funding of media content. Crowdfunding has been used in movie production for years, but now has expanded to even the production of news content. For example, *The Guardian* Australia received $150,000 in its first local crowdfunding campaign that initially targeted $50,000 only (Bennett, 2018). *The Guardian*'s success is not an isolated incident as crowdfunding has become an effective business model for many media content producers around the world. It offers media consumers a direct means of impacting the direction of content production. For instance, news media adopting this business model emphasize the values of journalistic independence and editorial freedom, and their commitment to offering paywall-free, ad-free, and high-quality content. Consumer interest in the specific content, appeals, and/or causes are prerequisites for the application of this business model. In addition, the maintenance of good producer-consumer relationships is critical for the sustainability of media companies relying on the crowdfunding model.

In most cases, media companies use a hybrid business model to make money. For example, YouTube offers free content with ads and a subscription service (i.e. YouTube Red) that removes all ads. US broadcast networks invest in subscription streaming services like Hulu and CBS All Access in addition to maintaining their advertising-based business models. Even CBS All Access uses tiered pricing systems with different levels of commercials. In addition, the choice of business models is dynamic. For example, in search of sustainable business models in the digital economy, *The Wall Street Journal* introduced a paywall and gradually increased the volume of content behind the paywall while lowering the content that is available for free. Recently, the paywall has become smart: it bends to individual readers, tightening or loosening according to a reader's consumption habits and likelihood to pay (Wang, 2018). Another example is Netflix, which switched from a transaction model to a subscription model, and strategically from offline rental to online streaming, and from content distribution to original content production.

Drivers of change: Shifts in audience and market players

The discussion of business models shows how the media industry has to adjust in response to environmental changes. This section of the chapter addresses the two biggest changes in recent years concerning the media market, namely, the empowerment of the audience and the entry of tech companies into the media market. Specifically, we will present the key drivers that have contributed to the development of audience sovereignty and growth of tech media players.

The increase in the number of platforms and devices. Today's audiences routinely integrate TV, computer, and mobile devices in the consumption of media content. In addition, there is an oversupply of content products. The average media consumer watches multiple television channels, visits numerous websites, and uses many different smartphone apps every day. Gaming consoles and handhelds are added to the mix for young consumers. When supply is abundant, value would tip towards demand.

The culture of multiscreen and multitasking. Today's consumers tend to do multiple things at the same time. Overall, the majority of media consumers are multitasking – as people are concurrently exposed to different media at the same time. They can surf the web, use social media, read emails, message, watch videos, and browse for products/services online more or less simultaneously. Younger consumers are even more likely to multitask while watching TV. The multitasking tendency elevates the relative importance of 'attention' over usage. That is, the significance of media engagement over simple media usage and the need to go beyond counting audience ratings and reach with other metrics.

The preference for streaming media, especially video streaming. Consumers want to have the autonomy of choosing what, how, when, and where they consume media content, and the mechanism of streaming satisfies these needs. Among all types of streaming services, video streaming grows the most rapidly. Video streaming is driving the decline in pay TV subscription (Deloitte, 2018). For video streaming services, original content is becoming a major driver of growth, for example inspiring platforms like Netflix to invest in local content production around the world. Digital platforms such as Google's YouTube offer an audience-centric content creation and distribution system with the ability to collect data from all interactions.

The world of constant social media interactions. Consumers are now much more connected by social media. Social media apps remain the top mobile apps in terms of usage, followed by weather, browser, games, and streaming music (Deloitte, 2016). Checking social networks is a daily habit for most internet and mobile users. Social media has become a top source of news, brand information, brand interaction, and interpersonal interaction. The extensive and constant use of social media magnifies the power of the audience through network effects.

The growth of mobile-centric lifestyles. Smartphones have become the hub of daily activities for today's media consumers. In fact, heavy mobile consumption has expanded from younger consumers to more age groups. The mobile-centric lifestyle places tech companies at an advantage over traditional media companies that are more used to provide home-based content, which explains the rapid growth of advertising expenditure in the mobile environment as well as the rise of app developers and publishers (such as Supercell, Niantic, King Digital, NetMarble, Peak Games, and Miniclip). The mobile games production network is a truly global market, with companies from countries in North America, Asia, the Middle East, and Europe all counting as global stars.

The integration of media and life. One of the biggest media consumption changes in the past decade is the demise of content dayparting (i.e. schedule content delivery based on the typical activity patterns of the audience). Increasingly, there is a sort of media-life integration as new communication technologies make it possible to access media content at any time and any place. In the old days, there was specific 'media time' – a relatively large chunk of time devoted to media consumption – such as the time for newspapers before breakfast, for television shows after dinner, and for books at bed. Nowadays, there is diminishing distinct 'media time' because media content is consumed by consumers in-between their other daily tasks in everyday lives, across platforms and devices. Media is also more about problem solving than in the past. For instance, consumers use their smartphones to get news updates, play games, check social media, and watch short videos whenever they have a break or notifications pop up. The media-life integration trend leads to a closer connection between media and consumers and the need for media to understand how and in what contexts consumers use their products throughout the day.

Tech-media content creation, aggregation, and distribution. Started as digital platforms, tech giants such as Google, Facebook, Apple, and Amazon are now entering the mainstream media space. In fact, many consumers consider them as media companies rather than platforms. The tech-media convergence has a considerable impact on the media industry and caused several substantial shifts in media content creation/aggregation/distribution and revenue generation.

The arrival of tech giants largely changed how media content is created, aggregated, and distributed. First of all, tech giants empowered non-professional content creators and fostered more demand for content creation. An example is YouTube personalities. Globally, the majority of YouTube users visit YouTube at least daily and they prefer videos uploaded by people than by companies or institutions (ComScore & YouTube, 2016; Statista, 2016). Non-professional creators offer consumers more choices that are of high relevance and engagement. Media consumers now demand both mass appeal and niche content. Second, tech giants led to more reliance on audience insights, changing how media products are produced and evaluated.

Third, tech giants changed how content is aggregated and distributed as consumers may not receive the same bundle of content. What is delivered to them is highly personalized based on a variety of factors such as their interests, review history, social networks, and other users' choices. Finally, tech companies are built to enable a closer connection between media and consumers, as they enable consumers to develop direct relationships with content creators and provide them with more access points to media content in consumer journeys through multimedia devices, social media, and online communities. For example, consumers can interact with content creators on Facebook and YouTube, and can access media content through various Google products (e.g. Google Play Music and Search) from multiple Google devices (e.g. Pixel 2, VR headset, and Google Home).

Media consumer engagement

As mentioned earlier, we are now in an era of audience fragmentation and media competition for attention and deep involvement. To succeed in such an environment, media managers need to pay attention to the assessment of 'quality' in addition to 'quantity' when interacting with audiences. High-quality interactions that enable consumers to co-create unique experiences with the media are means to develop sources of competitive advantage (Prahalad & Ramaswamy, 2004). It is our proposition that consumer engagement has become the key to success in today's media industry. Only through engagement, media companies can reach consumers, strengthen connections, and leverage value co-creation.

The term 'engagement' has been interpreted as connection, attachment, emotional involvement, and/or participation (Brodie, Hollebeek, Jurić & Ilić, 2011), and has been used in connection with customer, consumer, and brand. Engagement occurs by virtue of interactive, co-creative experiences with a focal agent/object in relationships (Brodie *et al.*, 2011). Therefore, it is different from traditional media 'involvement', which lacks the interactivity aspect of media consumption experience. Scholars have proposed several dimensions of consumer engagement, such as cognitive engagement, emotional engagement, behavioral engagement, social engagement, and experiential engagement (Gambetti, Graffigna & Biraghi, 2012; Hollebeek, Glynn, & Brodie, 2014).

In spite of the dimensionality, the emphasis of the concept is on the quality of media-audience relationships – media should offer audiences high-quality interactions that enable them to co-create unique experiences with the media. By acting on audience insights, creating attractive and relevant content, providing consistent and optimized experiences across platforms and devices, empowering consumers, and utilizing social media, media companies can engage their customers.

Acting on consumer insights. Data helps the improvement of products/services (Lacy, 2018). Obtaining consumer insights is the first step to engage consumers. For example, after figuring out that consumers would rather immerse into one show and binge-watch it than juggle multiple shows, Netflix decided to release all the new episodes of a season at once (Epstein, 2016). This seemingly simple decision contributed to Netflix's growth into a leading global brand in the video streaming sector. In addition to traditional ways to gather consumer insights (e.g. market research), big data now offers a chance to probe richer consumer information in terms of both breadth and depth, which helps to improve media outlets' content and engagement. For example, Spotify uses big data to curate playlists for users and predict Grammy Awards winners each year, which adds one more way for consumers to engage with the brand in addition to using the service.

Creating attractive, relevant content. Content is the core product of media companies; consumers engage with media content before engaging with the media companies behind the content. Having realized the importance of content, many tech giants (such as Apple and Facebook) are now investing heavily in original content. Not just good content, but good contextualized content might be the key to success in today's media market, as personal and contextual relevance of content to consumers is also an important strategy to win over the attention of the audience in a fragmented environment.

Providing consistent and optimized cross-platform and cross-device experience. Experience across platforms and devices should be not only consistent, but also optimized based on the unique characteristics of each platform and device. For example, for consumers subscribing to a news service, a consistent experience may include the ability to continue reading a news story on a mobile phone from where they left on a laptop. An optimized experience may consist of content and mechanism adjusted based on platforms and devices such as brief breaking news in the notification center on smartphones, high-definition videos on devices with bigger screens, short video clips on social media for quick viewing and sharing, and so on. Although the trend of multi-platform and multi-device brings more challenges to media companies in terms of platform building, content production, and management strategy, it can be rewarding because a relationship with consumers across platforms/devices is stronger than that on a single platform/device.

Empowering consumers. To leverage the value of co-creation, media companies need to empower consumers. Strategies to achieve the goal include enabling two-way communications, incorporating user generated content (UGC), initiating crowd-funding and crowdsourcing, involving peer influencers, building peer evaluation systems, and developing consumer communities. For example, Amazon allows consumers to submit stories to its in-house production studio and crowdsources feedback from consumers on stories that have been selected.

Utilizing social media. A tool that presents an incredible opportunity for engagement is social media. Wikström and Ellonen (2012) discussed the characteristics of social media in three aspects: interactivity, UGC, and community. They studied how these media impacted legacy media's business models and found that social media features have enhanced and complemented the value propositions of these companies. Social media was used to develop more active relationships with consumers. In addition, consumers now act as co-creators of content through social media. For example, popular video game titles *Fallout 3* and *Mass Effect 3* both offered fans new downloadable content that effectively changed the endings to each game, after fans outcry on social media that the original endings did not justify the time investment made by the players (Clarkson, 2013). This was a mutually beneficial solution that successfully extracted value from audience engagement on social media to both increase revenue through the sale of 'extended cut' versions of the games, while simultaneously addressing the content needs of audiences.

In essence, social media offers the core value of engagement and, developed from there, the supplemental value of content and community building. From this perspective, media companies need new competencies in creating meaningful interactions with consumers, cultivating media-consumer relationships in a co-creation situation, and developing communities that resonate with consumers. While social media has not directly affected media companies' revenue models, it has had significant impacts on value creation from other indirect aspects, such as brand equity. Kumar and George (2007) demonstrate that the value of a customer should not be measured by a single transaction, but by the total value generated by their cumulative relationship with a brand.

Conclusion: The new value creation system

As indicated at the beginning, the core proposition of this chapter is that the consumption of media content can be enhanced by data-based audience intelligence and engagement, thus creating value for both the audience and media. So what does this new value creation system look like?

The changes in audience behaviours and market players discussed above have led to a shift in the value creation system. Traditionally, in the company-centric view of value creation, consumers and media companies had distinct roles. In media value chain, products and services that contain value are created, aggregated, and distributed by media companies, and then consumed by audiences. The value is exchanged from companies to consumers through this process (Karlseng & Ingholm, 2016).

However, the situation has been changed. On the one hand, consumers are no longer satisfied with their traditional end-user role. They want to be involved in creating and developing media products and services, and they are eager to share their thoughts and experiences with other consumers (Ramaswamy & Gouillart, 2010). On the other hand, the development of technology and the proliferation of interaction channels enable consumers to do so. As a result, the line between consumers and producers is blurring. Through UGC, crowdsourcing, and crowd-funding, consumers become contributors and creators. The media value chain is evolving into a multi-directional system. Value is no longer created by companies alone, but co-created by companies and consumers.

The change from value creation to co-creation fundamentally altered the relationship between audiences and media. The new value co-creation system produces content and experiences that are meaningful to individuals and can generate value for businesses (Prahalad & Ramaswamy, 2004). The implication here is that there are now new requirements for media companies to develop competencies in cultivating and managing the co-creation process with audiences. While business models might be about how to make money, competitive strategies are about how to do it better than others. And today's media companies need to pay attention to five areas of strategies, namely consumer, content, context, connection, and contrast of privacy-value, to do better than others in this new value creation system.

Consumer. Again, the consumer is the foundation. Consumer insights, as garnered from the analytics of behavioral data and other tools assessing consumers' cognitive and emotional interactions with media, and consumer empowerment, namely embracing consumers into the value creation system, are of central importance to leverage co-creation. Direct revenues generated from this aspect for media companies include crowdfunding and consumer insight monetization. It also contributes to advertising, subscription, and potential transaction.

Content. Content is the king. The key consumer value propositions here include the provision of engaging and relevant content and the on-demand delivery of the content. Revenues can be generated through advertising, subscription, or ad-subscription combinations. The key is to find a sustainable content creation and distribution system that evolves around the audience.

Context. Context and content are symbiotic in a digital world. Given the growing media fragmentation and competition for audience attention, content alone can hardly break through the clutter. The contextualization of content consumption experiences becomes critical. The key consumer value proposition here is the provision of content in an easy-to-use, aggregated, personalized, fluidly integrated, interactive, and relevant way.

Connection. Connection is the differentiator. When consumer, content, and context are set, connection is what makes a difference. Here, the focus is on connecting consumers to the media networks both physically and mentally. The key consumer value propositions in this area include the provision of stable connections with media products across devices, assistance in interpersonal connections between consumers, and access to communities of shared interests.

Contrast of privacy-value. Some call this the 'privacy paradox', where tech companies make better products and improve their services because they can utilize the data they gathered, thus increasing the value delivered to consumers (Lacy, 2018). The power of data in value creation is evident as tech companies like Amazon, Netflix, and Google have higher customer satisfaction index in general. However, at the same time, there are unintended consequences because of the extensive collection and use of user data (*Ibid.*). The Cambridge Analytics incident in 2018 concerning Facebook's dealing of user privacy illustrates the importance of balancing this privacy-personalization dilemma if a company wants to sustain its relationship with the audience.

We would like to conclude this chapter with the argument that the media industry is shifting its operations to adapt to an environment that is characterized by the fragmentation of media options, competition for attention, and empowered audiences. Its path to success is the adoption of business models and strategies that utilize data, engage audiences, and co-create value through content.

Further reading
- Case: How changes in business models of companies such as HBO and Netflix have influenced the content of internet-distributed television – Lotz (p. 337)
- Context: Why the digital transformation has made it necessary to embrace and explore audience-first business models – Villi & Picard (p. 121)
- Contrast: How influencers, YouTubers, vloggers and game players use platforms to engage with global fan communities for commercial value – Craig (p. 363)

References

Bennett, L. (2018). 'Guardian Smashes $150k Crowdfunding Goal', *AdNews* (14 February). Retrieved from http://www.adnews.com.au/news/guardian-smashes-150k-crowdfunding-goal.

Brodie, R. J., Hollebeek, L. D., Jurić, B. & Ilić, A. (2011). 'Customer Engagement: Conceptual Domain, Fundamental Propositions, and Implications for Research', *Journal of Service Research*, *14*(3), 252-271.

Clarkson, S. (2013). 'Mass Effect 3's Ending Disrespects Its Most Invested Players', (12 April). Retrieved from https://kotaku.com/5898743/mass-effect-3s-ending-disrespects-its-most-invested-players.

ComScore, & YouTube. (2016). *Preferred Types of Video Content Accessed via YouTube According to Weekly Online Video Viewers in the United States as of January 2016, by Age Group.* Retrieved from https://www.statista.com/statistics/688576/youtube-video-content-preference-age-usa/.

Deloitte. (2016). *Digital Democracy Survey: A Multi-Generational View of Consumer Technology, Media and Telecom Trends.* Retrieved from http://www2.deloitte.com/us/en/pages/technology-media-and-telecommunications/articles/digital-democracy-survey-generational-media-consumption-trends.html.

Deloitte (2018). *Digital Media Trends Survey.* Retrieved from https://www2.deloitte.com/content/dam/insights/us/articles/4479_Digital-media-trends/4479_Digital_media%20trends_Exec%20Sum_vFINAL.pdf.

Epstein, Z. (2016). 'Netflix Exec Explains 2 Reasons Why the Company Won't Release Shows on a Weekly Schedule' (5 February). Retrieved 28 May 2018, from http://bgr.com/2016/02/05/netflix-shows-release-schedule-exec/.

Gambetti, R. C., Graffigna, G. & Biraghi, S. (2012). 'The Grounded Theory Approach to Consumer-Brand Engagement: The Practitioner's Standpoint', *International Journal of Market Research*, *54*(5), 659-687.

Hollebeek, L. D., Glynn, M. S. & Brodie, R. J. (2014). 'Consumer Brand Engagement in Social Media: Conceptualization, Scale Development and Validation', *Journal of Interactive Marketing*, *28*(2), 149-165.

Johnson, M. W., Christensen, C. M. & Kagermann, H. (2008). 'Reinventing Your Business Model', *Harvard Business Review*, (December), 59-68.

Karlseng, E. & Ingholm, H. O. (2016). 'Co-creation in the Media Industry',. Retrieved from https://brage.bibsys.no/xmlui/handle/11250/2404278.

Kumar, V. & George, M. (2007). 'Measuring and Maximizing Customer Equity: A Critical Analysis', *Journal of the Academy of Marketing Science*, *35*(2), 157-171.

Lacy, L. (2018). '20 Takeaways from Mary Meeker's 2018 Internet Trends Report', *Adweek* (31 May). Retrieved from https://www.adweek.com/digital/20-takeaways-from-mary-meekers-2018-internet-trends-report/.

Lewis, M. (1999). *The New New Thing: A Silicon Valley Story*. New York: W. W. Norton & Company.

Magretta, J. (2002). 'Why Business Models Matter', *Harvard Business Review*, 80 (5), 86-92.

Osterwalder, A. (2013). 'A Better Way to Think about Your Business Model' (6 May). Retrieved from https://hbr.org/2013/05/a-better-way-to-think-about-yo.

Ovans, A. (2015). 'What is a Business Model? ' (23 January). Retrieved from https://hbr.org/2015/01/what-is-a-business-model.

Prahalad, C. K. & Ramaswamy, V. (2004). *The Future of Competition: Co-creating Unique Value with Customers*. Boston, MA: Harvard Business Press.

Ramaswamy, V. & Gouillart, F. J. (2010). *The Power of Co-creation: Build It with Them to Boost Growth, Productivity, and Profits*. New York: Simon and Schuster.

Statista. (2016). *YouTube Usage Frequency of Active Users Worldwide as of 3rd Quarter 2016*. Retrieved from https://www.statista.com/statistics/421973/frequency-youtube-use/.

Wang, S. (2018). 'After Years of Testing, The Wall Street Journal has Built a Paywall that Bends to the Individual Reader' (22 February). Retrieved from http://www.niemanlab.org/2018/02/after-years-of-testing-the-wall-street-journal-has-built-a-paywall-that-bends-to-the-individual-reader/.

Wikström, P. & Ellonen, H.-K. (2012). 'The Impact of Social Media Features on Print Media Firms' Online Business Models', *Journal of Media Business Studies*, 9(3), 63-80.

11. Media Industries' Management Characteristics and Challenges in a Converging Digital World

Paolo Faustino and Eli Noam

The ongoing convergence of technology, media, and telecommunications has not only transformed the media industry, but also the management practices. This chapter outlines specific challenges for the management of media companies and discusses what convergence means from the perspective of managing media firms.

Introduction

In the last twenty years, there has been considerable discussion about the transformation of the media industry and its relation with telecommunications, bringing these industries closer and making them more convergent – mostly in terms of content management and distribution. Thus, convergence (especially driven by digitalization and deregulation) can be seen as a characteristic trend. This allows for and encourages a confluence between platforms that used to be treated as separate entities in policy issues and which did not often compete directly.

Due in large part to the severe economic recession, media companies in many information markets are not as profitable as they were in the past (especially in Europe and the United States), and traditional business models are no longer as valid as they used to be in the twentieth century. Also, the competition with digital and internet-based firms and online streaming services is growing. This has changed the competitive situation for traditional media companies.

The media industry is characterized by radical disruption and is going through a period of accelerated transformation. This has deep effects on management strategies and practices within and across media companies and industries. It is equally clear, however, that we find divergent characteristics among media industries that recommend distinct practices and strategies for responding to the specificities of diverse media companies and products. Demands on management competencies regarding key media-related practices and strategies are different depending on whether we are referring to a regional newspaper, a national telecommunications company or a transnational television company.

Nonetheless, many media industries are converging and companies are increasingly conglomerated. According to Gershon (2009, p. 269), 'the clear lines and historical boundaries that once separated the fields of broadcasting, cable and telephony are becoming less distinct. A natural convergence of industries and information technologies is blurring those distinctions'. Thus, today's media managers face new industry players and more diverse issues compared with years past. As Borders (2006, p. 118) noted, 'convergence does not operate in a vacuum of the print, broadcast and online newsroom, marketing and promotion; convergence to the audience and advertisers is essential'.

Although one can identify differentiating features of media industries compared to other industries, at the level of business management there are analogies. These include, according to Deuze (2007, p. 63), 'global and local ('glocal') competition, and corporate concerns over sales, advertising revenue, and profits'. Albarran (2002) observed that media management requires a combination of competencies, some general, some characteristic of media as a whole, and some specific to particular media industries, requiring particular individual and unique talents. Clearly, there is great need to develop a more comprehensive and comparative understanding of what is perhaps too simplistically described as 'media management' in the context of transforming and converging industry disciplines and sectors.

According to several authors (Towse, 2008; Picard, 2002), media differ from other products and services due to differences in the mechanics of supply and demand. On the one hand, media products are the result of creative, informative, and artistic work. Therefore, their products receive copyrights, which does not happen with most other types of products and industries. Also, media companies are more visible to consumers because they are an integral part of everyday life. Because of their cultural, political, and social goals, media are more influenced by public policies and regulations than many other industries, and often operate in publicly sanctioned and 'owned' spaces (such as the broadcasting spectrum and wireless frequencies).

Another key distinguishing aspect of media industries from other industries is that content creators and media business managers work in independent ways and are often deliberately separated. This has long been made clear in the separation of editorial and business management in news organizations. However, this idea – that advertising and news (or, more generally, business and creative practices) are separated domains – has changed significantly due to increasing competition, higher uncertainty, and declining margins. Overall, we see an ongoing convergence of different domains, sectors, and disciplines within and across the media industries, bringing new challenges for managing media firms, business models, and production processes.

In this chapter, we outline the specific challenges, opportunities, strategies, and tactics in the management of media companies, with specific reference to businesses that operate on an international or even global scale. As even smaller and local media firms tend to be linked up in larger, global production networks, these managerial issues increasingly affect all professional media makers. Second, we map ways of understanding convergence from the perspective of managing media firms. We conclude by identifying key themes in media management theory, research, and practice resulting from our own research (for greater detail, see Faustino & Ribeiro, 2016; Noam, 2016, 2018).

Media management: Competencies and challenges

There are two classic economic 'public good' characteristics of information:
1. it is difficult to control the access to information because it is not physical ('non-excludability');
2. it is easy to share the product ('joint consumption').

Many media products are distributed for free rather than sold. Information is also publicly generated and distributed widely in a subsidized manner. However, media products are increasingly sold to regular customers by way of subscriptions or pay-services, be it online newspapers, movies, TV series, videogames, and live TV channels.

   As suggested by Gershon (2009), media managers must be able to cultivate tone and setting, promoting a positive and creative environment where content makers feel free to produce the best work within resource limitations. Being a successful media manager involves six fundamental competencies:
1. planning;
2. organization;
3. leadership;
4. staff management;
5. control;
6. communication.

It has to be noted that these are not unique to media firms. The distinction lies in the types of workers the media boss is managing. In many cases, it is not easy to manage creative talent. This means that the six competencies, and their particular features, will be applied somewhat differently than in other industries.

   Planning, for example, is essential but challenging when so much related to the media enterprise is not stable. Planning in a newspaper company, for example, must be done on a daily basis, since each newspaper issued is a micro-project with a life-span of 24 hours. Organizing is complex in big companies, often with sharp differences between content makers in various professions and managers at diverse levels. Leadership is vital, yet media workers are typically sceptical by nature and not easy to lead or persuade. The staff is diverse with a broad range of skill sets and personality types, which can make it difficult to work in required team-based contexts. While control is important, success often depends on relatively high degrees of autonomy among workers. Furthermore, as much of the work is based on temporary alliances, impermanent affiliations, and fuelled by a range of subcontracted and outsourced labour, overseeing and managing media makers is particularly complex.

According to Herrick (2003, p. 57), the three most critical skills for running a media company are: cash flow management through accounting and marketing, people management through interpersonal skills, and time management of executives and staff. Additionally, the need for training is intensely felt by media companies and linked to the levels of required practical knowledge and adaption to the use of new technologies and converging industries (Faustino, 2009). The necessary skills and needs for training are listed in Table 1.

Table 1   Main needs for training in media companies

Managers	Management skills	Insight in anticipating the environment of future businesses
		Support innovative ideas and putting them into practice
		Provide adequate training and motivation
	Behaviour skills	Negotiation skills
		Networking skills
		Demonstrate flexibility
	Personal skills	Problem solving skills
		Constant updating towards the industry novelties
		Innovation and creativity skills
Editorial offices	Technical skills	Knowledge of new digital technologies
		Capacity to develop content on multiple platforms
		Knowledge of the propositions of the new media
	Behaviour skills	Demonstrate flexibility
		Professional empowering and continuous training
		Capacity to respect the ethical and deontological principles of the job
	Personal skills	Professional integrity
		Adaptation capacity
		Capacity to remain up-to-date

Source: Faustino (2009)

Technology inspires changes not only in terms of content production, but also in content distribution. This offers managers and investors the possibility to expand and diversify across a range of media platforms. In this context, platform convergence – especially the interlinkage between traditional media and telecommunications – can also be seen, on one hand, as an aspect that influences professional profiles and the skills of employees, and, on the other hand, as a generator of new challenges to management strategies and the development of business models for media products, particularly in distribution and payment for content. A range of characteristic dimensions that are important to business approaches is illustrated in Table 2.

Table 2   Business approaches in the media and strategic and operational management

Types of platform/ business management	Newspapers	Magazines	Television	Radio	Online	Cinema
Profile and dimension of the companies	A few large ones and several small ones	A few large ones and several small ones	A few large ones and some medium ones	A few large ones and several small ones	A few large ones and several small ones	A few large ones and several small ones
Stage of the product's lifecycle	Decline trend	End of maturity	End of maturity	End of maturity	Moderate growth	Moderate growth
Management of distribution and logistics	High complexity	High complexity	Low complexity	Low complexity	Low complexity	High complexity
Market and competitive level	Oligopolistic structure	Oligopolistic structure	Oligopolistic structure	Duopolistic structure	Competitive structure	Oligopolistic structure
Target customers and markets	Readers and advertisers	Readers and advertisers	Viewers and advertisers	Listeners and advertisers	Users and advertisers	Mainly viewers
Business turnover	Tends to be low	Tends to be high	Tends to be stable	Tends to be stable	Tends to be moderate	Tends to be high
Investment on human capital	Frequently high	Frequently high	Frequently high	Frequently low	Frequently low	Frequently high
Business relation with the local culture	High dependence	Low dependence	Moderate dependence	Moderate dependence	Moderate dependence	Low dependence
Cost and investment structure	Tends to be high	Tends to be low	Tends to be high	Tends to be low	Tends to be low	Tends to be high
Activity and production seasonality	Tends to be continuous	Tends to be continuous				Tends to be unique
Scope of geographical coverage	Moderate	Moderate	Moderate	High	High	High

Source: Faustino & Ribeiro (2016)

The table illustrates many aspects of business approaches that may influence media management practices and strategies, and which should be taken into account when studying and understanding managing and making media. It is also important to remember that senior managers and employees of media companies have usually been trained to work on a particular platform (radio, television, magazines, or newspapers) and rarely have (or can be expected to come in with) an integrated view of the complementarities of different media.

Such a singular platform approach is no longer compatible with the current competitive context. Today, media management requires broader skills as well as nuanced understandings of diverse platforms, flexibility and adaptability to accommodate different work processes and contexts, and training initiatives that promote these skills. This professional and competitive demand for a multimedia perspective not only requires new training; it also calls for the increased introduction of related theories and practices, such as management models, business models, and production and distribution models that are influenced by the convergence of the Technology, Media, and Telecommunications (TMT) sectors.

Table 3 organizes the differences and similarities between companies in the TMT sectors, and notes characteristics that influence management and business models of each subsector. Notwithstanding specific characteristics, the main functions traditionally associated with business management have a common application.

In order to identify the similarities and differences between media companies, including their relation with telecommunication companies, it is relevant to know the features of the different types of media companies with regard to their market, financial, operational, and business dynamics. It therefore becomes increasingly important to analyse media products' interactions, to identify the various aspects of their creation and distribution, and to comprehend their dependencies and vulnerabilities.

Companies focused on unique creative products – such as books, computer games, music, and movies – implement strategies where the profit from one product is used to cover the expenses of another product. According to the 'hit' model, successful products compensate for investments in unsuccessful products, and generate all the profits. Managers focus on marketing to fight the high risk of failure, which Picard (2002) calls 'management of failure'. Companies focused on continuous creative products – newspapers, magazines, and television series – can concentrate on improving the content over time through research on audience's preferences, renovating the creative staff, and through the replacement of products as some go stale and others pop up. In this situation, concentrating on branding strategies is especially important. Competition in both types (single and serial) concerns the scope of the contents' selection and processing, and their longevity expectation.

Table 3   Similarities and differences between the media, telecommunications and other industries

Sectors/characteristics	Media	Telecommunications	Technology
Public visibility	High	Moderate	Low
Regulatory policies	High	Moderate	Low
Funding model	Dual*	Hybrid	Unique
Creativity and knowledge	Very intensive	Moderately intensive	Shortly intensive
Intellectual property	Very important	Very important	Important
Profit orientation	Low	High	Moderate
Social and public status	High	Moderate	Low
Influence on society	High	Moderate	Low
Work precariousness	High	Low	Moderate
Impact of the digital	High	High	Moderate
Product perishability	High	Low	Low
State as owner	High (on public broadcasters)	Low and decreasing	Low
Competition level	Moderate	High	High
Work organization	High autonomy	Moderate autonomy	Low autonomy
Product and marketing	Conflicting	Consensual	Consensual

* The main exceptions to this dual funding model are the book and the film segments. However, we can identify increasingly frequent situations of dual funding in the movie business, mostly via advertising, including product placements. In the case of the book segment, sales remain almost the only source of funding, although there are situations of sponsorships.
Source: Faustino & Ribeiro (2016)

Differences in media environments and the surrounding economic forces account for differences in production characteristics. The media differ when acting in production environments that rely on economies of *unit costs* and *fixed costs*. According to Towse (2008) and Throsby (2001), those that operate in economies of unit costs (books, magazines, newspapers, games, CDs, and DVDs) feature activities based on an economy of scale: there is a decrease in the cost as consumption increases. In these industries, products depend on a physical process of production. The process involves high logistics that entail additional costs for storage, transportation, and distribution. In fixed costs economies, additional production costs are not significant. The production costs of media such as cinema, television channels, and the internet tend to be based on product quality and branding. These industries rely especially on economies of scale and all the cost is in the first copy. In the case of TV series, for each episode there is a first copy, whose quality affects the main product (the series) as whole. Differences produced by these factors account for variation in the structure of costs and in the pressures experienced by business.

Since the late twentieth century, the differentiation of media support has increased significantly. The fundamental factors are the rapid expansion of personal computing, the increase in broadband, the exponential increase in computing power, and the progressive growth rate of the telecommunications industry. This has had drastic consequences for traditional media industries as a disruptive and destabilizing effect, but it also opened new areas of business opportunity.

Management practices and business strategies in converging media industries

There is little evidence that company size and platform type create substantial differences in terms of management practices applied to different media companies. Much of the general principles in business management and strategy work are applied regardless of the platform, type of company, or media product. However, we must consider that a company with activities in several types of media requires a greater effort in managing its portfolio, particularly in its attempt to maximize possible synergies between several businesses in its operations. It would also need to clearly distinguish the forms of content distribution according to platform-specific characteristics.

The business dimension can generate a greater concern with the product's risk management, to the extent that it is necessary to mitigate the risks associated with projects that require large investments. Larger media companies tend to dispose of smaller assets (media products) that do not generate significant business volumes and margins, because they sometimes require a level of business management work that is as demanding as with the larger assets.

There are distinct levels and characteristics in management approaches for the media. It is predictable that a larger company with more resources will have more sophisticated politics in terms of talent management, business organization, marketing management, and other operational domains. It is equally clear that smaller companies tend to have more fluid business structures and organizational models, not only because they privilege functional versatility but because they rely on more subcontracted work and have less internal moving parts. They do not necessarily lack strategy or knowledge, but have less resources and opportunity risks are higher.

In spite of differences specific to various media industries, media firms are increasingly adopting management practices fundamental to market logic. This circumstance also reflects the tendency of media products to be increasingly perceived as a commodity rather than a primarily symbolic good or outcome of a creative process with intrinsic value. Thus, the management practices adopted by media companies increasingly bring other industries' practices closer. For its part, technology has contributed to the standardization of management processes and operations by creating software and other models of business management support that are generally applicable.

The combination of increasing convergence, automation and standardization of business and creative processes on the one hand, and radical disruption, market fragmentation, and the entry of new companies from non-traditional media sectors into the field on the other hand, has forced management approaches to adopt new methods. None of these new methods come easy: they challenge the established cultures of media firms, and pose significant challenges for the industry. In Table 4, by way of general classification, we can observe some aspects that reflect characteristics associated with traditional media management versus a contemporary media management approach.

Table 4   Aspects associated with traditional and modern management of media

Traditional management approach	Contemporary management approach
Cultural products	Economic products
Monomedia products	Multimedia products
Lower technology-based products	Higher technology-based products
Products with a limited portfolio	Products with large portfolios
Products with clear barriers or boundaries	Products without clear barriers or boundaries
Single-use products	Reusable products
Journalistic products	Journalistic and marketing products
Monomedia management	Multimedia management
Limited areas of required knowledge	Expansive areas of required knowledge

Source: Faustino & Ribeiro (2016)

The industries that lead digital convergence include computing (both hardware and software), telecommunications, and content production. With the advent of the internet, the proliferation of computers and globalization, the telecommunications sector has been challenged to solve infrastructure problems and propose new solutions. New features of the devices allow access to content, and also allow users to create, publish and share content, whether through computers, tablets, or smartphones. The content industry has also modified its production, communication, marketing, and distribution processes.

In other words, media companies are increasingly co-developing with the information and communications technologies sector, resulting in the new designation of a macro-sector: TMT. Convergence in technology, media, and telecommunications contributes to the standardization of management practices and business strategies.

In many media companies, one finds a convergence of business models, distribution platforms, means of production, marketing tools, and types of interactivity with the consumer. Regardless of the type, size or geography of the firm or production network, they are confronted, to a greater or lesser extent, with similar challenges in terms of management strategies and practices in the following areas: the creation of new products, innovation of production, promotion and publication practices, diversification of revenues, reorganization of work, brand management, investment in technology, cooperation with companies, cost reduction, project management, portfolio management, talent management, multiplatform content, continuing training, audience engagement, and productive synergies (such as branded content and native advertising).

The convergence of media industries coincides with an increasing role for audience measurement in real time, which leads to a profound change in how to manage, produce, distribute, and create advertising. Changes in converged and digital business models have also forced organisations into new human resources policies regarding qualifications and talent profiles – where technology companies now for example hire social scientists and anthropologists, and media firms recruit data analysts and computer programmers.

Convergence also impacts the structure of the media industry, offering opportunities for consolidation into multinational corporations as much as opening up spaces for new types of nimble companies and production networks. As Noam (2018) suggests, digital technology advancements combined with lower prices makes music, video, and text items cheaper to produce; this allows the entry of many small producers. Anderson (2006) called this phenomenon the 'long tail', when the content may be produced and distributed profitably to millions of niche markets, instead of firms focusing on producing a single product with broad appeal. The long tail phenomenon contrasts with the concept of scale economies. These opposing tendencies create new pressures and alignments.

In the past, economic sectors in the media had limited relation to each other and operated in what amounted to separate markets. Newspaper companies, for example, did not compete directly with broadcasting, and telecommunications had nothing to do with content. But the current trend is quite the opposite and emphasizes convergent businesses. With the advent of the internet and the globalization it has engendered, the media industry (broadly construed here) has been challenged to solve complex problems related to changes in infrastructure. Solutions have increasingly focused on the need to dematerialize content. The physical book, newspaper, and music CD become less viable as all types of content and services are offered in digital form online, by a growing variety of players. Media companies are increasingly developing their capabilities for articulation with information technologies and across communication sectors.

To understand convergence from the perspective of managing media firms, it is necessary to comprehend the interdependence between actors in TMT and the three platforms crucial to the process of making and distributing media goods: print media (newspapers and magazines), electronic media (television and radio channels, satellite and cable broadcasting), and telecommunications – mainly internet. As Killebrew (2005) suggests, from a technological perspective, the goal of convergence is to allow for a combination of different platforms in order to provide information and entertainment to the public by sharing numerous technical resources. The goal is also to guarantee a relatively equal distribution to each available platform.

Despite this, in practical terms the results can be the opposite, with big operators using economies of scale to fight and eliminate smaller, less popular players. Therefore, infrastructure networks – consisting of the companies providing access to content online – impose themselves as an increasingly dominant factor. The fight over 'Net neutrality' is a key outcome of this struggle between the companies that 'control the pipes' versus those that produce, publish, and publicize media content and services. The media industry is going through a complicated and sweeping process of change in which doubts and uncertainties about traditional business models and management practices are multiplied.

Conclusion

The sustainability of business models and financing is at the forefront of concerns about the future of the media industries and making media, particularly with regard to the role of news and information that is essential to ideals of public access, shared narratives, and democratic principles of quality, diversity, and plurality in content and services offered. It is difficult to support good journalism without adequate resources; the same goes for an independent cultural sector in national economies (such as a national film and documentary filmmaking industry, public service broadcasting, and a music and recording sector supporting local and regional talent). These concerns should concern society. Democracy, even in politically stable countries, is not a definitive achievement but an ongoing struggle. This calls for a pluralistic and independent media system.

Media companies will require managers to have experience in multiple types of media product segments, and makers from a variety of backgrounds who can (and are motivated to) collaborate and co-create. In practice, this challenge is more complex to materialize as the media ecosystem continues to undergo profound changes – technologically, entrepreneurially, financially, and globally. The question is: how can a media professional be effectively trained to work successfully in a sector that undergoes permanent change? If one makes a comparison with other industries, such as banks, car manufacturers or airlines, one may observe that these companies resort to more scientific approaches applied to corporate management and frequently the managers of these companies are real 'superstars'. In media companies, managers are usually unpopular, they tend to operate in the shadow of the 'creatives', who have prestige and public visibility. In show business, there is no show without business, and no business without show. However, this may be the only industry in which the board and/or shareholders need to apologize for doing what managers do: raise funds, select projects, control costs. and market products.

In summary, the media industry has undergone significant changes since the end of the twentieth century, more than in any other period of media history. This highlights the need for new knowledge and the need to raise professional profiles in media organisations, regardless of type or sector. The answer to these challenges is not easy to implement. There is a need for media companies as well as for academia to develop new media management and production research approaches, tools, and knowledge for a better understanding of the emerging environment.

Further reading

- Case: How national telecommunications, internet, and media markets converge and are becoming more concentrated in Canada – Winseck (p. 175)
- Context: The transformation and innovation of media business models and shifts in business strategies – Villi & Picard (p. 121)
- Contrast: How the new platforms facilitate and profit from new forms of consumption without creating or producing content – Bilton (p. 99)

References

Albarran, A. (2002). *Management of Electronic Media*. Boston, MA: Wadsworth.

Anderson, C. (2006). *The Long Tail: Why the Future of Business Is Selling Less of More.* New York: Disney Hyperion.

Borders, G.L. (2006). *Media Organizations and Convergence*. Mahwah, NJ: Lawrence Erlbaum Associates.

Deuze, M. (2007). *Media Work*. Cambridge: Polity.

Drucker, P. (1986). *Innovation and Entrepreneurship – Practice and Principles*. New York: Harper and Row.

Faustino, P. (2009). *Análise e Prospectiva dos Media em Portugal: Tendências, Mercado e Emprego*. Lisbon: MediaXXI.

Faustino, P. (2015), *Concentration, Diversity of Voices and Competition in the Media Market*. Lisbon: MediaXXI.

Faustino, P. & Ribeiro, L. (2016). 'Characteristics, Similarities and Distinctions in Management across Media Industries', in G.F. Lowe & C. Brown (eds), *The Management of Media Firms and Industries: What's So Special About Media Management?* Berlin: Springer Scientific.

Gershon, R. (2009). *Telecommunications and Business Strategy.* New York: Routledge, Taylor & Francis Group.

Herrick, D.F (2003). *Media Management in the Age of Giants: Business Dynamics of Journalism.* Oxford: Blackwell Publishing.

Killebrew, K. (2005). *Managing Media Convergence: Pathways to Journalistic Cooperation.* Oxford: Blackwell Publishing.

Lowe, G.F. & Martin, F. (2014). *The Value of Public Service Media.* Göteborg: Nordicom

Noam, E. (1991). *Television in Europe.* New York/Oxford: Oxford University Press.

Noam, E. (2015). 'Does Media Management Exist?', in P. Faustino *et al.* (eds), *Media Industry Dynamics – Management, Concentration, Policies, Convergence and Competition.* Lisbon: MediaXXI.

Noam, E. (2016). *Who Owns the World's Media? Media Concentration and Ownership around the World.* New York: Oxford University Press.

Noam, E. (2018, in press). *Managing Media and Digital Organizations.* New York: Palgrave MacMillan.

Picard, R.G. (2002). *The Economics and Financing Media Companies.* New York: Fordham University.

Sohn, A., Wicks, J, Lacy, S. & Sylvie, G. (1999). *Media Management: A Casebook Approach* (2nd ed.). Mahwah, NJ: Lawrence Erlbaum Associates.

Tassel, J. & Poe-Howfield, L. (2010). *Managing Electronic Media: Making, Marketing, and Moving Digital Content.* Oxford: Focal Press.

Throsby, D. (2001). *Economics of Culture.* Cambridge: Cambridge University Press.

Towse, R. (2008). *A Textbook of Cultural Economics.* Cambridge: Cambridge University Press.

Vizjak, A. & Ringlstetter, M. (eds) (2003). *Media Management – Leveraging Content for Profitable Growth.* Munich: Springer.

Wossner, M. (2003). 'The Media: An Industry with Tradition at the Crossroads', in A. Vizjak & M. Ringlstetter (eds), *Media Management – Leveraging Content for Profitable.* Munich: Springer.

Production

Policy

12. Global Media Industries and Media Policy

Terry Flew and Nicolas Suzor

Media regulation in the digital age poses distinct challenges. Many national governments are seeking to assert control over what their citizens can access online, whereas intermediaries such as Facebook and Google strive to turn the internet into a global platform. This chapter discusses how national and global forces intersect in distributing media across territorial boundaries.

Introduction

It has long been a truism of communication and media studies that the media are global. The Canadian communications theorist Marshall McLuhan spoke of a 'global village' that was increasingly unified through broadcast technologies, and a variety of media events have sought to enact this globality, including the Olympics and the FIFA World Cup sporting events, concert events such as Live Aid (1985) and Live Earth (2007), and charity singles such as 1984's famous 'We Are the World'. Chris Rojek has described the global media event as 'the most heart-warming goodwill newsletter of modern times', where 'we are conscious of being part of an international community in which pre-ordained divisions of race, class, religion, sexual orientation, politics and the vulture logic of capitalism appear to magically vanish' (Rojek, 2012, p. vi).

The spirit of the global *ecumene* invoked by global media has carried over into the digital space. Founder and CEO Mark Zuckerberg termed his 2017 mission statement on how Facebook can be a force for good in the world 'Building Global Community' (Zuckerberg, 2017). Addressing his statement to 'our community', Zuckerberg describes Facebook's mission as being on 'a journey to connect the world', as a company that 'stands for bringing us closer together and building a global community'. Understanding Facebook as a company that 'can [...] develop the social infrastructure to give people the power to build a global community that works for all of us', he proposed that:

> Progress now requires humanity coming together not just as cities or nations, but also as a global community. [...] My hope is that more of us will commit our energy to building the long term social infrastructure to bring humanity together. The answers to these questions won't all come from Facebook, but I believe we can play a role (*Ibid.*).

A recurring feature of the media is that its production and distribution centres are far more geographically concentrated than its global reception, or perhaps rather the perception of its global nature. The geographer Paul Adams has made the point that studies of the global distribution of communications infrastructure consistently show that:

> We have a wealthy connected world, and a poor disconnected world [...] we see a digital continuum, and along this continuum many countries occupy a rather predictable place as their level of national wealth conditions their level of media access [...] 'global' does not mean homogeneous; instead the geography of flows is highly uneven (Adams, 2009, p. 67).

This spatial concentration of media manifests itself within as well as between nation states. Highly successful media clusters develop in global cities such as New York, Los Angeles, London, Paris, Tokyo, and Beijing, while the global distribution of the ICT industry has proven to be no less concentrated, in city-regions such as San Francisco/Silicon Valley, Cambridge, and Boston, as well as the other major global media cities (Karlsson & Picard, 2011).

For those working in the media, media globalization has ambivalent consequences. On the one hand, it marks out opportunities to work across many parts of the world, on location, secondment, or on an ongoing basis, and to gain a genuinely international perspective on people, cultures, and events. At the same time, it often means that media work is highly concentrated, and very often in high cost locations. The requirement to be based in London, Washington, New York, Los Angeles or another expensive global metropolis in order to advance one's career can come at a personal and financial cost. Moreover, it runs the risk that under-reported parts of the world – which may be the so-called fly over states of the US Midwest or the post-industrial regions of Western Europe as much as African countries or Eastern Europe – continue to be neglected in international media coverage, and are subjected to often superficial or inaccurate analysis. As the global rise of populism has reminded us, a common mindset shaped by global liberal cosmopolitanism can mean missing important developments happening outside of major urban centres.

We therefore need to consider how media making on a global scale is framed by the geographies of uneven development. Contrary to Zuckerberg's speculations, this does not mean an inexorable spatial shift from the national to the global. Media laws and policies continue to be predominantly framed at the national level, and city and national governments play a central role in enabling – and in some contexts blocking – the flows of global media content.

Indeed, one reason for Zuckerberg's 2017 mission statement was the concern that there is a retreat from globalization taking place, with the rise of nationalist movements in various countries, and growing populist skepticism towards global free trade, multilateral institutions, and cultural cosmopolitanism, towards what has been termed post-globalization (Flew, 2018). Many of the nations with the highest internet user populations, including China, Russia, Turkey, Pakistan, Iran, Egypt, Venezuela, and Saudi Arabia, do not have a globally open internet, and it has been argued that internet freedom has been declining in the 2010s (Freedom House, 2017). This chapter will consider how local, national, and global forces intersect in making media – in both its traditional and digitally networked forms – and distributing it across territorial boundaries.

The rise and fall of the libertarian internet

When the internet was young, it seemed as if it would be unregulatable. In 1996, John Perry Barlow proclaimed the internet to be 'naturally independent' of the rule of territorial states, as global Cyberspace became 'the new home of Mind' (Barlow, 1996). It seemed impossible to enforce laws that were based around top-down distribution of media content by centralized and territorially-based companies against the anonymous masses of internet users distributed around the world. John Gilmore, one of the founders of the Electronic Frontiers Foundation, famously observed that '[t]he internet treats censorship as damage, and routes around it' (Elmer-Dewitt, 1993).

Some territorial states seemed to agree, at least rhetorically. The 1997 White Paper of the National Telecommunications and Infrastructure Administration (NTIA), which framed US policy towards internet governance under the Clinton Administration and beyond, identified as one of its core principles that:

> The internet succeeds in great measure because it is a decentralized system that encourages innovation and maximizes individual freedom. Where possible, market mechanisms that support competition and consumer choice should drive the management of the internet because they will lower costs, promote innovation, encourage diversity, and enhance user choice and satisfaction (quoted in Mathiason, 2009, p. 56).

For the early years of development of the internet, the concept of it being a global platform that evolved independently of nation states had considerable traction, and both the emergent ICT giants and civil society organizations favoured bottom-up, decentralized governance over government legislation and controls, which were generally seen as constituting censorship.

The notion of the internet as a 'wild frontier' gradually subsided, as it became an increasingly mainstream, commercial, and mass media series of websites, apps and platforms. National governments were not content to cede sovereignty over the internet, and by-and-large, courts and legislatures around the world found ways to enforce their laws. Of particular importance in this respect were questions of national security: as global conflicts intensified in the 2000s in the wake of the 9-11 attacks on US cities, the wars in Iraq and Afghanistan, and other regional conflicts, imperatives to control information flows and protect commercially and militarily sensitive infrastructure saw greater cooperation between the major technology companies and national governments. This was revealed in the United States by the Edward Snowden revelations about the National Security Agency (NSA) and the PRISM project, and had long been the norm in countries such as China, Iran, and Russia.

It was also apparent that the internet was not a wholly separate place; it was made up of real people communicating through physical infrastructure, often within the reach of the law enforcement and judicial arms of territorial states (Goldsmith & Wu, 2006). Incitement to terrorism or violence, access to pornography, and the protection of children from potentially harmful content remained priorities of national governments towards their citizens, and as it became more apparent that online content was a growing element of media consumption, the internet came to be more subject to media laws, policies, and regulations. Referring to the – ultimately unsuccessful – attempts by the Australian government in the late 2000s to introduce mandatory internet filtering of content that would be 'refused classification' under the national classification laws, Lilian Edwards made the observation that:

> By the 2000s, the cyber-libertarian tendency had retreated and it had become well established that nation states had both the right to regulate, and an interest in regulating, the internet, and in particular, an interest in protecting children – as the internet ceased to be the plaything of only academics, researchers and geeks, and became part of daily social and family life (Edwards, 2009, p. 626).

Challenges of internet governance

Regulating the internet poses distinct challenges, and no regulatory regime will ever be completely effective. The decentralized nature of online networks, the bottom-up nature of content creation and distribution, and the challenges of determining territorial jurisdiction with regards to a global network render the internet environment very different to mass communications media. Moreover, it remains possible for people to evade law enforcement online, particularly by turning to encrypted, hidden virtual networks ('darknets') and registering in physical jurisdictions where extradition is difficult.

It would be a mistake, however, to think that the internet is therefore inherently ungovernable. If we interpret governance in a broader sense than simply government regulation, incorporating 'the totality of institutions and instruments that shape and organize a policy system – formal and informal, national and supranational, public and private, large-scale and smaller-scale' (Freedman, 2008, p. 14), then we can identify that the internet is regulated and managed at several levels.

Internet governance operates in both a narrow and a broad sense. In the narrow sense, internet governance is 'about the ordering of whatever technical systems enable the operation of the global network of networks as a platform for applications' (Solum, 2009, p. 49). But the technical infrastructure of the internet 'interacts with the ability of governments to regulate applications, content and human activities that are enabled and facilitated by use of the internet' (Solum, 2009, p. 50), meaning that the scope of internet governance is potentially far wider.

The major work of regulating the internet today is undertaken by large technology and telecommunications companies, who are subject to the laws not just of their home countries, but also of the other countries where they have substantial business interests and assets. If the influence of mass media publishers diminished, they were replaced with new, even larger and more powerful publishers of the internet age. These intermediaries play a critical role in governing the internet by developing and managing its infrastructure (OECD, 2010). Intermediaries of all types – the owners of physical pipes, the providers of core routing services, the search engines that make content visible, the content hosts, and the social media platforms – all shape how people communicate in important but different ways. All these organizations make decisions that have a real impact on public culture and the social and political lives of their users (DeNardis, 2014).

The technical choices that internet intermediaries make have consequences for how people communicate, meaning that these decisions, whether explicit or hidden, are embedded in the very architecture of the infrastructure and services that make up the internet (Lessig, 2006). These intermediaries govern their networks in ways that further their own economic interests, but they are also the focal points of control, where pressure can be most effectively deployed to influence user behaviour. These pressures increase every day, as various groups of governments, users, private interests, and civil society learn how to more effectively regulate the behaviour of users indirectly by making demands of intermediaries.

The key outstanding challenges of media regulation in the digital age arise from the complexity of regulating in a contested global arena where national policies are often in conflict and laws are not always enforceable in a straightforward way. There is a great deal of work to be done to recast the tools of media regulation that work in a broadcast and mass media environment to effectively operate in a digital media environment, particularly given the speed with which content is uploaded and circulated, and the question of whether technical adherence to laws is best undertaken by the intermediaries themselves rather than by government (Flew, 2016). While the latter has the advantage of enabling greater effectiveness, it also has the potential to mean that decisions are being made about public speech and freedom of expression with little or no accountability or transparency. There is a 'difficult balance to be struck between allowing these private companies the right to run their own business affairs and remain profitable, and the almost-public function that [digital platform companies] now perform' (Edwards, 2009, p. 669).

The first major challenge is one of scale. Historically, media policy has worked on the assumption that publishers and broadcasters know about and control the material they are distributing, and can therefore be held responsible for its contents. The massive User-Generated Content (UGC) and social media platforms we know today, however, are built on the fundamental principle that they do not screen content in advance. The scale at which UGC sites operate means that it is impossible to screen in advance. On YouTube, for example, it is generally estimated that users uploaded more than 400 hours of video content to YouTube every minute of every day. Like most other social media platforms, YouTube relies on complaints mechanisms that enlists users to do the bulk of the work involved in finding offensive videos. The flagging system is an ingenious invention: rather than moderate all content in advance, flagging lets YouTube wait and see which of the millions of videos on its network other users think are inappropriate (Crawford & Gillespie, 2014). Only once a video has received enough complaints does it go into a queue where a human moderator might look at it.

Many of the major Western platforms operate from the legal safety of US law, which provides them with almost complete autonomy to make and enforce their own rules. Except in a few specific cases – primarily child pornography and copyright infringement – US platforms are never liable for what people post or do on their networks. The key provision that immunizes US platforms is Section 230 of the Communications Decency Act 1996, and it has become a fundamentally important shield for digital media platforms, providing immunity from legal requests to remove content, and allowing for contractual Terms of Service that users agree to when joining, which gives them absolute discretion over what they choose to remove.

The protection that Section 230 provides is, however, almost unique to the United States. For the last two decades, it has shaped the law and debates over how the world regulates internet content. For the massive service providers that are based primarily in the US, it is seen as absolutely vital. But around the world, the protection it provides often seems to go too far. The protection it gives to providers that host user reviews is the same protection that immunizes hosts of the most vile and repulsive content on the open web. For victims of image-based abuse (sometimes known as 'revenge porn'), for example, Section 230 can seem to provide far too much immunity for the operators of websites dedicated to hosting abusive images (Suzor, Seignior, & Singleton, 2017).

Other countries have much stricter rules than the US does about defamation, privacy, and offensive content. Courts and legislatures in these countries have frequently held service providers responsible for material on their networks posted by their users. Some providers can afford to be completely based within the US and mostly ignore requests from other countries, but most large commercial providers have business interests in other countries, and they therefore have to work out how to deal with legal standards that differ from place to place. Geolocation technology has also improved, and it is now common for platforms to block content in various jurisdictions. YouTube, for example, blocks videos that criticize the King of Thailand, which is a criminal offence under Thailand's *lèse-majesté* rules. Turkey routinely requires Twitter to block access to tweets that are critical of Turkish President Erdogan or advance pro-Kurdish political views (Zittrain *et al.*, 2017). In most cases, providers choose only to enforce these rules in a way that affects people within those countries. Users with IP addresses that look like they are based in one of these countries will see an error message, but the content will still be visible to viewers from other countries (or people who can use a VPN or other tool to mask their location).

Many governments are now seeking, with renewed vigour, to assert control over what their citizens can access online. Domestic media policy has always been concerned with the regulation of immoral and indecent content. Many countries have classification schemes and standards about what content is acceptable to distribute, in what forms, at what times, and to which audiences. In the mass media age, media regulation was targeted primarily by imposing obligations on publishers, retailers, and broadcasters. Now, national governments are exerting increasing pressure to find tools to apply these rules to internet content.

There is also the emergence of an unequal global distribution of labour associated with content moderation. While much of the internet traffic is generated in higher-income parts of the world, the management of illegal or problematic content is being increasingly outsourced to lower-wage workers in the developing world. Roberts (2016) has made the point that global commercial content moderation (CCM) is a largely invisible activity to platform users, and that 'companies' desire to keep CCM work in the shadows therefore gives the impression that such content is just what is out there in the culture [...] and hides the human decision-making processes and curation work form the view of their user-participants' (Roberts, 2016, p. 157). This has the side effect of rendering not only CCM work, but CCM workers, invisible, 'spending a work life in the squalid sections of the internet, sifting through its detritus and its most disturbing content (*Ibid.*). The outsourcing of such work to the developing world is a marker of the extent to which the internet has not levelled opportunities to participate in global digital culture.

As governments continue to pressure tech companies to regulate the content they carry, we continue to see major conflicts of rights and liberties. This is particularly visible when content regulation is used anti-democratically to silence particular people or political points of view, or is carried out in a way that is arbitrary or capricious. This happens, for example, when governments lean on internet intermediaries to remove or block content without a valid court order. In these circumstances, global media platforms face real difficulties in deciding whether to comply with legal orders that have a negative impact on human rights or run the risk of being blocked entirely by a national government.

Conclusion

There is a general consensus that many of the major contemporary media policy issues require responses that go beyond the level of nation states and national regulations. In their overview of contemporary challenges of media and communications policy, Picard and Pickard (2017, p. 35) observe that 'the global nature of communications has somewhat reduced the ability of nation states to significantly control and direct media and communications internally'.

Media globalization is particularly challenging to policymakers as it intersects with a transformation of media itself, due to media convergence and the rise of global digital platforms such as Google, Amazon, Netflix, and Facebook, meaning that 'highly concentrated global digital intermediaries in content agglomeration, search, and social media increasingly play significant roles in content access and provision' (Picard & Pickard, 2017, p. 23). As a result:

> Policies pursued in the past for broadcasting, telecommunications, and media are often inadequate for contemporary media and communications. The complexities of contemporary digital systems and networks, cable and satellite operations, internet-distributed content, social media, and cross-platform activities necessitate different methods to address the issues and challenges they pose. Domestic policies can address some issues, but global policy is progressively more germane to address communication challenges (*Ibid.*, p. 1).

Policymakers internationally have acknowledged the challenge, even if they struggle to adapt the platform-specific regulations of the twentieth century to the convergent media environment of the twenty-first century (Flew, 2016).

The question of whether the digital platform companies are media businesses, and hence can be appropriately regulated in order to achieve desirable communication policy outcomes, is hotly debated (Napoli & Caplan, 2017; Gillespie, 2018).

A plethora of controversies around digital and social media, ranging from 'fake news' and its political impact to revenge porn, extremist content, cyberbullying, gender-based online harassment, and hate speech, have triggered a growing public expectation that digital platforms need to be held accountable to the public interest, particularly as 'these firms are increasingly monitoring, regulating, and deleting content, and restricting and blocking some users, functions that are very akin to editorial choices' (Picard & Pickard, 2017, p. 6). Not surprisingly, traditional media companies are often at the forefront of such demands, pointing to what they see as an unacceptable regulatory asymmetry between public interest criteria applied to publishing and broadcasting that is evaded in the online arena, as digital platforms present themselves as simply the conduits for the communication activities of others, rather than as media companies in their own right (Felle, 2017).

While there are arguments that a move from national media policies towards global media policy would be desirable (e.g. Mansell & Raboy, 2011), the likelihood of regulatory harmonization on a global scale is currently low. While there may be agreement that 'Internet governance requires institutional structures that cross national boundaries' (Solum, 2009, p. 59), there is no comparable agreement about who is best placed to undertake such roles. The proposal that governance of domain name registration should shift from international non-government organizations such as ICANN to more representative international organizations such as the International Telecommunications Union (ITU), as was recommended at the ITU's World Conference on International Telecommunications in Doha in 2012, was strongly rejected by both the US government and the leading US-based digital platform companies, notably Google (Schemeil, 2012). China's proposals for a global internet governance framework that enshrines 'national cyber-sovereignty' as a core principle are likely to meet a similarly frosty reception in the US context (Shen, 2016). At the same time, other global powers, most notably the European Union, are articulating a more interventionist approach to their relations with the digital platform companies than the 'hands-off' approach that has prevailed in the US, and in dominant debates over internet governance.

National media policies also cause difficulties as states again seek to impose their content regulation rules globally. The major fear at the dawn of the commercial internet was that nations with wildly different standards about what content was acceptable would each try to impose those standards on the entire world. In these circumstances, internet intermediaries are often caught between conflicting legal systems, with no easy way out. Some people worry about the increasing fragmentation of the global internet – as different countries continue to impose different standards, we may see major fault lines in the services that are available in different regions. This generates the prospect of a global 'Splinternet', where users have profoundly different experiences of internet use based on the territory in which they are accessing platforms and content.

This would undercut the economic benefits in terms of reduced transaction costs of cross-border communication and information flows that have been central to the 'digital dividend' of the period since the mid-1990s, as well as the political opportunities for more open and democratic societies associated with greater freedom of expression. The latter is a particular concern if intermediaries respond to the pressure of competing national media policies and simultaneously obey the law of multiple jurisdictions, by imposing a lowest-common denominator standard of acceptable speech, to the great detriment of many.

Further reading
- Case: How media regulators in Canada have influenced the development of the Canadian media landscape – Winseck (p. 175)
- Context: Five current issues and trends relating to the media industries as a result of digitalization and the rise of the global communication giants – Miège (p. 73)
- Contrast: How the internet intermediaries facilitate and profit from new forms of consumption without creating or producing content – Bilton (p. 99)

References

Barlow, J. (2017). *A Declaration of the Independence of Cyberspace*. Retrieved from http://homes.eff.org/~barlow/Declaration-Final.html.

Crawford, K. & Gillespie, T. (2014). 'What is a Flag for? Social Media Reporting Tools and the Vocabulary of Complaint', *New Media & Society*, *18*(3), 410-428.

DeNardis, L. (2014). *The Global War for Internet Governance*. New Haven, CT: Yale University Press.

Edwards, L. (2009). 'Pornography, Censorship and the Internet', in L. Edwards & C. Waedle (eds), *Law and the Internet* (3rd ed.) (623-669). Portland, OR: Hart Publishing.

Elmer-Dewitt, P. (2017). *First Nation in Cyberspace*. Retrieved from http://kirste.userpage.fu-berlin.de/outerspace/internet-article.html.

Felle, T. (2017). 'Facebook's 'Fake News' Plan is Doomed to Failure – Social Media Must Do More to Counter Disinformation'. Retrieved from https://www.city.ac.uk/news/2017/april/facebooks-fake-news-plan-is-doomed-to-failure-social-media-must-do-more-to-counter-disinformation.

Flew, T. (2016). 'Convergent Media Policy: Reflections on the Australian Case', in S. Simpson, H. van den Bulck & M. Puppis (eds), *European Media Policy for the Twenty-First Century: Assessing the Past, Setting Agendas for the Future* (219-237). London: Routledge.

Terry Flew (2018). 'Post-Globalisation', *Javnost – The Public*, 25(1-2), 102-109. DOI: 10.1080/13183222.2018.1418958.

Freedman, D. (2008). *The Politics of Media Policy*. Cambridge, UK: Polity Press.

Freedom House (2017). *Freedom on the Net 2017: Manipulating Social Media to Undermine Democracy*. Washington DC: Freedom House.

Gillespie, T. (2018). 'Governance of and by Platforms', in J. Burgess, T. Poell & A. Marwick (eds), *SAGE Handbook of Social Media* (254-278). London: SAGE Publications.

Goldsmith, J. & Wu, T. (2006). *Who Controls the Internet? Illusions of a Borderless World*. New York: Oxford University Press.

Karlsson, C. & Picard, R. (2011). *Media Clusters: Spatial Agglomeration and Content Capabilities*. Cheltenham: Edward Elgar.

Lessig, L. (2008). *Code (Version 2.0)*. New York: Basic Books.

Mansell, R. & Raboy, M. (2011). 'Foundations of the Theory and Practice of Global Media and Communication Policy', in: M. Raboy & R. Mansell (eds), *Handbook of Global Media and Communication Policy* (1-20). Malden, MA: Wiley-Blackwell.

Mathiason, J. (2009). *Internet Governance: The New Frontier of Global Institutions*. London: Routledge.

Napoli, P. & Caplan, R. (2017). 'Why Media Companies Insist They're Not Media Companies, Why They're Wrong, and Why It Matters', *First Monday, 22*(5). https://doi.org/10.5210/fm.v22i5.7051.

OECD (2010). *The Economic and Social Role of Internet Intermediaries*. Retrieved from https://www.oecd.org/internet/ieconomy/44949023.pdf.

Picard, R. & Pickard, V. (2017). *Essential Principles for Contemporary Media and Communications Policymaking*. Oxford: Reuters Institute for the Study of Journalism.

Roberts, S. (2016). 'Commercial Content Moderation: Digital Labourers' Dirty Work', in S.U. Noble & B. M. Tynes (eds), *The Intersectional Internet: Race, Sex, Class and Culture Online* (147-160). New York: Peter Lang.

Rojek, C. (2013). *Event Power: How Global Events Manage and Manipulate*. London: SAGE Publications.

Schemeil, Y. (2012). 'Global Governance: Evolution and Innovation in International Relations', in E. Brousseau, M. Merzouki & C. Meadel (eds), *Governance, Regulations and Powers on the Internet* (186-208). Cambridge: Cambridge University Press.

Shen, H. (2016). 'China and Global Internet Governance: Toward an Alternative Analytical Framework', *Chinese Journal of Communication*, 9(3), 304-324.

Solum, L. (2009). 'Models of Internet Governance', in L. Bygrave and M. Bing (eds), *Internet Governance: Infrastructure and Institutions* (48-91). Oxford: Oxford University Press.

Statistic Brain (2016). *YouTube Company Statistics – Statistic Brain*. Retrieved from http://www.statisticbrain.com/youtube-statistics/.

Suzor, N., Seignior, B. & Singleton, J. (2017). 'Non-Consensual Porn and the Responsibilities of Online Intermediaries', *Melbourne University Law Review, 40*(3), 1057-1097.

Van den Bulck, H. & Donders, K. (2014). 'Analysing European Media Policy: Stakeholders and Advocacy Coalitions', in K. Donders, J. Loisen & C. Pauwels (eds), *The Palgrave Handbook of European Media Policy* (19-35). Basingstoke: Palgrave Macmillan.

Zittrain, J., Faris, R., Noman, H., Clark, J., Tilton, C. & Morrison-Westphal, R. (2017). *The Shifting Landscape of Global Internet Censorship*. Retrieved from https://cyber.harvard.edu/publications/2017/06/GlobalInternetCensorship.

Zuckerberg, M. (2017). *Building Global Community*. Retrieved from https://www.facebook.com/notes/mark-zuckerberg/building-global-community/10103508221158471/?pnref=story.

13. Media Concentration in the Age of the Internet and Mobile Phones

Dwayne Winseck

Media concentration is more important than ever in an age of mobile phones, the internet, and information abundance. Taking Canada as an example, this chapter investigates how telecommunications, internet and media industries are becoming more concentrated, and whether the fear of domination by internet giants like Google and Facebook is justified.

Introduction

This chapter offers a guide on how to study the media industries in the age of the internet and mobile phones, using Canada as a case study. It is based on research done as part of the Canadian Media Concentration Research (CMCR) Project and reflections on how to recast how our field thinks about the political economies of communication. It draws on lessons learned from work done as part of the International Media Concentration Research Project, a project spearheaded by Eli Noam that resulted in the publication of *Who Owns the World's Media* (2017) – an authoritative and detailed review of the telecommunications, internet, and media industries in thirty countries. It also relies on experience gained from participating in several contentious policy and regulatory proceedings that have shaped the internet, mobile wireless, and media in Canada in recent years.

The starting premise of this chapter is that we must take the media industries as serious objects of analysis, and clearly define what we mean by 'the media'. Media concentration is more important than ever in an age of mobile phones, the internet, and information abundance. This chapter will introduce some of the essential sources, tools, and challenges that are present in this sort of research. The aim is to encourage engaged, independent, and critical scholarship that is reliable, reasonably easy to use, and open to others to verify and use for their own research.

Like everybody, media researchers have limited time, resources, and knowledge and, consequently, they must set a hierarchy of research priorities. This means putting the structure, dynamics, economics, evolution, and forces that shape the media industries at the top of the list (Garnham, 1990). This focus is crucial because we live at a critical juncture in time when decisions made in the near future will shape the media landscape for decades – if lessons from the 'industrial media' set down in the nineteenth and twentieth centuries are any guide.

Media concentration: What to study, why, and how

The CMCR project's approach begins by charting the development of the Canadian network media economy from 1984 until the present, and with a deceptively simple yet profoundly important question as its guiding light: have telecommunications, internet, and media markets in Canada become more concentrated over time, or less?

Our approach to answering this question, and to understanding the implications of the trends it reveals, involves collecting, organizing, and analysing data for eighteen sectors of the telecoms, internet, and media industries. We refer to them collectively as the network media economy. In carrying these activities out, we follow a scaffolding approach – first, revenue and market share data is collected on a company-by-company and sector-by-sector basis. We then group each of the sectors covered into three relevant categories – network infrastructure, content industries, and online media – which form the basis for comparative analysis. From there, we scaffold upwards to give a portrait of the network media economy as a whole. We then use standard measures for assessing the industry. Additional comparisons are made across time, media, and in relation to trends in other countries around the world that are reasonably comparable to Canada.

In *Who Owns the World's Media*, Eli Noam laments the prior absence of a systematic body of evidence that would allow researchers to create a coherent portrait of the state of media concentration in most countries around the world. He points to two culprits behind this reality: one, gathering such information is not easy; and two, the issue is highly politicized. In Canada, Philip Savage argues much the same when he observes that 'the media ownership debate [...] tends to occur in a vacuum, lacking evidence to ground arguments or potential policy creation either way' (Savage & Gasher, 2008, p. 295). Concerns with media concentration also tend to be episodic and hinge on the events of the moment. The lack of common research methods adds to the problem too. Without clearly defining 'the media', some researchers see them as forever becoming more concentrated (Bagdikian, 2004). Others cast the net widely to include traditional media, data-driven platforms, ICTs, mobile phones, internet access, the internet-of-things, and others – creating a vast 'digital ecosystem' where even the biggest digital media goliaths appear as tiny specks (Skorup & Adam, 2013; Eisenach & Soria, 2016).

Given these challenges, it is essential to clearly delineate the scope of the terrain from the outset. As indicated above, our research focuses on the study of long-term trends in media concentration for eighteen key sectors that are based, for the most part, on the North American Industrial Classification System (NAICS), which is used by both Statistics Canada and US sources in their publication of industry data. This step allows us to establish the revenue for each sector before tallying up the market share of each player within them. The data gathered covers the period from 1984 to 2016 so that developments and trends can be assessed over time.

The next step is to identify and gather data for each ownership group in each sector with more than a one per cent share of the market. In this regard, past studies, trade association reports, historical accounts, and newspaper reports are useful tools for identifying the key players. Revenue is used as the base unit of analysis instead of audience share or circulation because it is a consistent measure that can be used across all media.

Annual reports are also an obligatory source of information from publicly traded companies who are legally obligated to disclose certain kinds of audited information to investors. Poring over such documents generates rich insights into the dynamics of the contentious issues and context that surrounds the media industries. Yet, there are limits to these sources too. For one, disclosure requirements vary by country. Second, companies present data in wildly different ways that often veer far from the standard NAICS classifications. Researchers often have to prise apart large and fungible categories that may make sense for companies, but which may group newspapers, books, and magazines all under the 'publishing' label. At other times, partial bits of information are given that require the unknown bits to be filled in from other sources.

Matters are tough when it comes to publicly traded and regulated companies but tougher yet when they are neither. In Canada, this problem bedevils the book, film, and music industries, and we have not been able to complete the analysis of these sectors because of it. Furthermore, many media companies are not publicly traded, and thus available information is scarce and not easily verified. It is another irony that while the media hold themselves up as guardians of transparency and public disclosure for government, businesses, and the economy and society at large, they are neither when it comes to their own affairs.

Finally, consultants' reports, the business press and online sources such as Alexa. com, Comscore, and Internet World Stats are valuable sources, but they can be extremely expensive, inconsistent, and tied too closely to clients' needs. Cultivating relationships with government agencies, consultancies, and regulated companies can also be helpful in prising loose valuable data on the industries.

Recall that to organize and analyse the collected data, we follow three steps in a scaffolding approach. At each step, we use concentration ratios (CR) and the Herfindahl-Hirschman Index (HHI) to depict levels of concentration over time. The CR method adds the shares of each firm in a market and makes judgements based on a widely accepted standard, with four firms (CR4) having more than half of the market share being considered to indicate high levels of concentration.

The HHI method squares and sums the market share of each firm in a market to arrive at a total. If there are 100 firms in a market with a one per cent market share each (HHI=100) then markets are considered highly competitive, while a monopoly exists when a single firm has a 100 per cent market share (HHI=10,000). The US Department of Justice embraced revised HHI guidelines in 2010 for categorizing the intensity of concentration. The new thresholds are:

–   HHI < 1500   Competitive and Diverse
–   HHI > 1500 but < 2,500   Moderately Concentrated
–   HHI > 2,500   Highly Concentrated

Many observers dismiss concerns with media concentration in the age of the internet. To them, the internet renders such concerns obsolete. And indeed, that this is an age of information abundance is clear. Both established media companies and new media (and journalistic) ventures produce more content and services than ever before, and people upload and share their own media online at ever-increasing numbers.

This said, research on media concentration is as important as ever. It is worth noting as well that Canada, while dwarfed by the United States, has the ninth largest media economy in the world, after France and Spain but before Italy and Australia (Noam, 2016, p. 1264). This casts doubt on the article of faith in certain circles that Canada's small market requires big domestic media conglomerates to compete on a global scale. Moreover, the Canadian network media economy has quadrupled in size between 1984 and 2016.

As part and parcel of the growth of the network media economy, many wholly new segments have been added to it or expanded immensely over the past several decades (i.e. mobile phones, internet access, IPTV, internet streaming TV, pay TV, internet news, internet advertising). Many of these segments rely solely, or at least heavily, on subscriber fees rather than advertising. These are the 'pay-per' media and their revenue now far outstrips advertising-supported content media, while online advertising still holds a more modest place in the overall scheme of things.

Growth and concentration trends in the content media industries

While trends in Canada have slightly lagged those in Europe and the US, newspaper revenue peaked in 2008 period, since then steadily falling. At the time of writing, digital revenues constituted just 8.4 per cent of all newspaper revenue – a far cry from the revenue lost. Since 2008, eleven paid dailies and thirteen free dailies have closed, while a dozen-and-a-half have cut their publishing schedule from six days a week to four. While this chapter was being written in November 2017, at least 30 more newspapers were shut and 290 jobs cut by Postmedia and Torstar (Watson, 2017). Concentration in the Canadian newspaper industry rose steadily from 1984 until 2000, peaking in 2011. Since then, the HHI dropped to 1608 – the lower end of the 'moderately concentrated' end of the scale. However, rather than reflecting a gain for diversity, the decline came about as struggling newspaper groups spun off some papers and closed others.

The trends and dynamics for broadcast television in Canada are similar but not quite as severe. Broadcast television ownership became more widely dispersed from the late 1980s until 1996, but the trend reversed in the late-1990s as the two English-language networks – CTV and Global – consolidated the ownership groups behind them, and as the French-language TVA network in Quebec was consolidated under the control of Quebecor. In line with a history of high levels of concentration in broadcast TV, last year saw the top four groups take 86.4 per cent of all revenue. Still, broadcast TV revenues slid down fast from an all-time high in 2011. Eight local TV stations have closed since 2009 and local broadcast TV news staff were cut by four per cent between 2012 and 2014 (Newman *et al.*, 2016, p. 80) and at least another 1,540 television and radio jobs cut in the two years since. 'In the last seven or eight years, we've lost more than 10,000 journalism jobs', according to media researcher Romayne Smith Fullerton (CBC, 2016). Similar statistics have been reported in the United States, Australia, and elsewhere. These concerns have spawned reviews of the state of local news by the Canadian Heritage Parliamentary Committee and the CRTC, each of which struggled to offer solutions to the problems at hand (Standing Committee on Canadian Heritage, 2017; CRTC, 2016). Despite an increase in investments and subsidies from the government into local and community news, concern is widespread that too little is being done to staunch the bleeding.

While the above paints a grim picture, such accounts are not without problems. For one, tallying up the jobs lost does not count for jobs gained. Statistics Canada data in Figure 1 paints a different picture, with the number of journalists *rising* over the last 30 years and hitting an all-time high in 2013 before slipping since.

As Figure 1 shows, the number of full-time journalists increased from 10,000 in 1987 to 11,631 last year. Also consider that, after years of slow growth, consolidation, and cut backs, the number of journalists had fallen to a little over 6,000 in 1998. If we take that as our base, the number of journalists has nearly doubled since then. Yet, at the same time, the network media economy has quadrupled in size, meaning that the number of journalists has declined in relative terms. Strikingly, whatever growth in the number of journalists has taken place has been outpaced by the number of people working in the publicity industries: advertising, marketing communications, and public relations.

Unlike advertising-dependent newspapers and broadcast TV, pay TV services have expanded by leaps and bounds prompting the broadcast industry to concentrate

Figure 1   Journalists vs PR, advertising, and marketing professions, 1987-2016

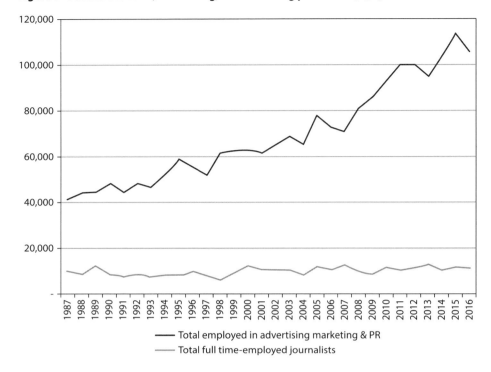

in response. The steep rise in TV concentration between 2010 and 2014 was due to four major transactions, while the downward trend in the last two years reflects the steady decline of the CBC and the rise of internet streaming services, notably Netflix. Moreover, the spin-off of a few pay TV services by big players like Bell and Shaw (Corus) has breathed new life into smaller ones like Blue Ant, Channel Zero, DHX, Stingray, APN, V, and CHEK. While this has added some diversity to the field, the latter's combined market share is less than that of the biggest independent, Astral Media, on the eve of its takeover by Bell in 2013.

Growth and concentration trends in the network infrastructure industries

Unlike newspapers and broadcast television and, to a lesser degree, magazines and radio, the bandwidth business has soared. Revenue for wireless and internet access services has been rising steadily. Revenue for cable, IPTV, and satellite TV services drifted downwards slightly as cord-cutting started to chip into subscriber levels and revenue. At the same time, and consistent with international trends, concentration in wireless, internet access, and cable TV have fallen, albeit from extremely high levels to ones that are still at the very high end of the scale.

The mobile wireless market is highly concentrated with three national carriers – Rogers, Telus, and Bell – accounting for 91.2 per cent of the sector's revenue in 2016, down a per cent from a year earlier but still firmly at the 'highly concentrated' end of the scale. A similar story applies to residential internet access and cable TV services. Last year, the incumbent cable and telephone companies accounted for 88 per cent of the residential retail internet access market, while independent internet service providers like Teksavvy and Distributel accounted for the rest. Retail internet access is a duopoly in Canada, with some competition on the margins.

The relatively quick pace of the telephone companies' IPTV over the past half-decade has steadily chipped away at the cable monopoly. In 2016, the incumbent cable companies held just over 60 per cent of the market share, while telephone companies picked up the rest. Local broadcast distribution markets are still extremely concentrated by the standards of the HHI, with a score of 5309 – over twice the threshold for the 'highly concentrated' designation.

Core elements of the internet

While many observers believe that the internet kills concerns with concentration, concentration levels for many core elements of the 'desktop internet' (wireline access) and 'mobile internet' (wireless access) range from very high to sky-high. This said, we start the discussion with one area that is remarkably and increasingly diverse: internet news sources.

Canadians get their news from a wide plurality of internet news sources: old (CBC, Postmedia, *Toronto Star*, CTV) and new (*Huffington Post*, *Buzzfeed*), domestic and foreign (BBC, Yahoo!-ABC, *Guardian*, *New York Times*). Online news is one of the most diverse media sectors covered by the CMCR Project and it has become more so over time. The top four internet news sources – the CBC, Weather Network, Postmedia, and Yahoo!-ABC – accounted for a little less than a quarter of average monthly traffic to online news sites last year and the HHI score was at the very low end of the scale (333).

Look elsewhere, however, and the opposite trend is clear. Google dominates the search engine market, and its grip is growing. Google accounted for 91.4 per cent of searches in 2016, while Microsoft (5.2%), Yahoo! (2.9%) and DuckDuckGo (0.3%) trailed far behind. The HHI score was sky-high at 8383. Social network sites display a similar but not as pronounced trend. The data is limited and dries up after 2013 but is still useful. In 2013, Facebook accounted for 46 per cent of unique visitors to social media sites in Canada, followed by Twitter (15%), LinkedIn (12%), Tumblr (12%), Instagram (9%), and Pinterest (6%) (Duong & Adamo, 2013). With a HHI score of 2762, social network sites were highly concentrated.

Levels of concentration are also sky-high for desktop web browsers. The top four companies – Google Chrome (56.4%), Microsoft's Explorer (26.1%), Firefox (12.2%), and Apple's Safari (3.5%) – had an HHI of 4023 last year. Similar characteristics hold for mobile browsers, with Google's Android or Chrome browser at 61 per cent and Apple's Safari at 29.9 per cent in 2016 (HHI: 4649) (Net Marketshare, 2017).

The same applies to desktop operating systems where three entities account for 100 per cent of the installed base and an HHI score of 8415: Microsoft Windows (91.1%), Apple OS X (6%), and Linux (2.5%). For smartphone operating systems, the top four players accounted for 99 per cent of the market: Google's Android OS (64.4%), Apple's iOS (33.1%), Microsoft (0.9%) and Symbian (0.7%). The HHI score was 5245.

Similar patterns stand out in internet streaming television services, as well as with respect to internet advertising. There has been a massive transfer of ad dollars from 'traditional media' to 'the internet'. To be sure, at the time of writing, internet advertising is worth more than total advertising for television and newspapers *combined*, and it is clear Facebook and Google have been the primary beneficiaries of that growth. Such realities bolster critics' claims that they are siphoning off revenue from broadcast television, newspapers, and other ad-supported media, and basically killing journalism and democracy. The Public Policy Forum conjured up just such an image in a report earlier this year with its lurid references to 'the vampire squids of Silicon Valley' (Public Policy Forum, 2017). But, while superficially attractive, this diagnosis ignores the fact that while internet advertising continues to soar, advertising spending across *all media* has been in slow decline in 'real dollar' terms, on a per capita basis, and relative to the size of the network media economy.

Blaming 'the internet' also ignores the fact that advertising was never allied with newspapers or broadcasters out of a sense of loyalty, but because they were the best means for assembling and delivering audiences. Internet giants like Google and Facebook have now stepped into their place. Facebook delivers audiences to advertisers for a fraction of the cost compared to print and broadcast media, and with far more sophisticated knowledge of those audiences – for better or worse, given the huge privacy issues implicated. These accounts also sidestep questions about the self-inflicted damage of two decades of flipping and consolidating newspaper and television properties at precisely the moment these companies needed all the resources they could muster to address the changes heralded in by the transition to the internet age.

The 'Battle of the Stacks' and diagonal and vertical integration

Yet, to stop the analysis at this point offers only a partial picture. Open the lens further, and we can see that the processes of consolidation have yielded two major groups at the core of the internet- and mobile wireless-centric communications universe. On one side, there is the half-dozen global internet giants with significant operations in Canada: Google, Facebook, Apple, Microsoft, Netflix, and Twitter. While massive in terms of global reach and market capitalization, they play a more limited role *within* Canada, as evidenced by the fact that they account for just under six per cent of all revenue across the network media economy.

Over-and-against them is handful of media and communications conglomerates of domestic origins – Bell, Rogers, Telus, Shaw, and Quebecor. These 'big five' accounted for 71.1 per cent of the nearly CAD$80 billion network media economy last year, down from 74.4 per cent two years earlier. They are diagonally- and vertically-integrated and, based on revenue earned in Canada, they are many times larger than Google, Facebook, Netflix, and Twitter.

To be sure, these two groups of companies engage in something of a 'battle of the stacks'. The communications-centric global giants seek to leverage their control over carriage and content across an expanding media universe. At the same time, the 'platform stack' conglomerates seek to control the key interfaces across the fields where they are active and which structure people's attention, time, money, and interactions with others. The thread tying both together appears to be their efforts to carve up the common internet into semi-feudal sovereign spaces (Chandler, 2012; Pasquale, 2017).

The 'battle of the stacks', however, is rather limited given the scale of their respective footprints within Canada and because of the internet giants' lack of control over the networks used to access their services. While the internet giants are increasingly building their own planetary-scale networks to bring their content closer to their users' doorsteps, the chance of them building out the last mile links that the broadband and mobile wireless operators control is slight. Consider, as well, that while Facebook's average revenue per user (ARPU) was an estimated CAD$63.50 last year, mobile operators in Canada obtained that amount in a month per subscriber (CRTC,2017).

This next and crucial point draws our attention to a unique feature that sets Canada apart from most other countries: its sky high levels of *diagonal* and *vertical* integration, given that the big five communications operators control all the access networks while also owning most of the main television services. In terms of diagonal integration, Canada is unique in the extent to which mobile wireless and wireline infrastructures are integrated into single companies, with the last stand-alone mobile network operator (MNO) – Wind Mobile – acquired by Shaw in 2016. In the US, T-Mobile and Sprint are stand-alone MNOs, and Vodafone serves as a good proxy for this in the many countries that it operates in around the world. Stand-alone MNOs are important even in highly concentrated markets, because they challenge diagonally integrated companies that tend to manage (and limit) rivalry and price competition across each of their platforms and services. The result is, typically, better affordability, more generous data allowances, and the greater availability of services (Rewheel/research, 2017).

Consistent with these typical expectations, study after study suggests that while the uptake of wireline internet access fares reasonably well in Canada relative to most OECD and EU countries, it ranks very poorly when it comes to mobile wireless adoption (Berkman Centre for Internet & Society, 210X; OECD, 2016; FCC, 2016a). Wireless prices are high, the price of data exorbitant, and data allowances low. This, in turn, impinges on how people use the internet and mobile phones to communicate with one another and to consume and share entertainment, news, and everything else that they do with the general-purpose internet infrastructure and connected devices (FCC 2016b, para. 265).

The extent of vertical-integration in Canada is also exceptionally high. While not new, the sheer magnitude of vertical integration in Canada, and how fast things came to be so, is worth noting. The scale of vertical integration more than doubled between 2010 and 2013, and by last year the 'big four' – i.e. Bell, Rogers, Shaw (Corus), and Quebecor – accounted for 55.6 per cent of all revenue across the network media economy, compared to 13.6 per cent in the United States for example. The big four vertically integrated conglomerates are the centrepieces of the network media economy in Canada. However, such companies are rare in the US. The only US company that comes close to the model embodied by the 'big four' is Comcast NBCUniversal – but unlike its northern counterparts, it does not own a stand-alone mobile wireless service. The vertically-integrated companies' share of the network media economy in Canada is four times such companies' share in the US.

Look across the border and around the world, and the structural integration of telecoms and TV is rare. These differences matter because stand-alone cable companies, broadcast TV and pay TV services tend to compete more aggressively with one another. With less concern about cord-cutting, stand-alone broadcasters and pay television groups, for instance, have been quicker to launch streaming TV services to meet audiences where they are at. Entities that don't simultaneously own broadband infrastructure and media content have also launched more stand-alone internet streaming services. In the US, Comcast is the only major player that has *not* developed its own streaming services other than its joint interest in the ad-based Hulu with Time Warner, Disney, and News Corporation (FCC, 2016b, paras. 116-119; FCC, 2017, paras. 116-119).

Conclusion

The broad message of this chapter has been that we live in an age of information abundance, but that it is unevenly distributed, for reasons that we can go a long way towards explaining. Using Canada as a case study, we observe that most sectors of the network media economy are highly concentrated by empirical and historical standards, but the knife is not all to one side. The content media are becoming less concentrated, sometimes for better and sometimes with outcomes that are ambivalent or for the worse. These trends are consistent with trends across the 30 countries studied and reported on in *Who Owns the World's Media*.

But so, too, are the other trends that we have outlined, namely that when it comes to the centre of gravity in the media today, it is *bandwidth* and *connectivity* that rule the roost – not *content*. And to the extent that there is another dimension to this, it is that the centre of the network media economy rests with the 'pay-per' media, which outstrip advertising-based media by a rate of 5:1. Another thing is also true: bandwidth, at least when you buy it at the retail level, and in Canada, is still expensive. And a thing that is similar to what we find around the world, is the sky-high concentration in each of the network media industries and the core elements of the internet. But Canada is unique in the extent to which diagonal and vertical integration set it apart from the rest of the world.

These trends gives rise to the 'battle of the stacks', wherein the internet giants of planetary scale and top-of-the-charts market capitalization confront a handful of domestic communications conglomerates with a reach and scale that dwarf the operations of the giants in Canada. That is not to say that Google, Apple, Facebook, Amazon, and Microsoft should be beyond scrutiny – far from it. But we must have a proper sense of scale for each of these groups, and act accordingly.

The idea that media concentration is high, and vertical and diagonal integration extremely high, has been found to be factually-based by administrative tribunals such as the CRTC and the courts. Consequently, regulators have stiffened their spines and acted in a manner in recent years that marks a clear break from the regulatory hesitation that has defined so much of the regulatory culture in Canada in the past. They have done so by adopting wholesale access frameworks for fibre-to-the-doorstep and mobile wireless networks, while fortifying common carrier principles (or 'net neutrality'), including a de facto ban on 'zero-rated' and 'pay-to-play' schemes (CRTC, 2015, para. 123).

These issues have involved adjudicating between different claims: about power, control and freedom of expression, about whose interests are to prevail when there is a clash between these considerations, and about where such things reside in the internets – at the ends of the networks, and in the hands of people to the maximum extent possible, or at the core of the network under the control of those who own the internets? On such questions, the CRTC has been clear: people's freedom of expression rights and control over communications have priority.

The CRTC has been especially blunt with respect to wireless services, stating that whatever 'competition that does exist today is largely, if not entirely, a result of regulatory intervention' (CRTC, 2015, para. 123). In addition, a trilogy of decisions required companies to adopt skinny basic cable TV packages and to offer subscribers fully unbundled TV services on an a-la-carte basis. The vertically-integrated companies have also been prodded to offer stand-alone streaming TV services to better compete with the American digital media giants (CRTC, 2015b). The incumbent industry players have fought these developments tooth-and-nail, but without much to show for all their fury, and things have changed favourably as a result.

The unfinished business arises out of the question of whether regulators will continue to hold the line, and if scholars will continue to do the research that we need to do for both critical media industries studies, as well as to weigh in on issues from the point of view of independent scholarship and the public interest. The unfinished business is also what to do about the global internet giants? Calling them 'vampire squids' and pleading for lost advertising dollars to be 'repatriated' just won't cut it. And, in any case, little would change as advertising spending in Canada appears to be on the decline as it is.

Still, their domination of internet advertising and reliance on data extraction does reveal a need to deal with these firms in ways that address, among other things, antitrust, and the privacy implications of 'surveillance capitalism' (Pasquale, 2015). That they have inserted themselves into the political process as well as outlets for campaign advertising messaging and spending, as well as hunkering down with the major political parties as advisors and operatives, also means that their influence on politics, speech, and the rules that govern elections in democratic societies must be dealt with (Nanji, 2017; Owen, 2017). In sum, we need critical media industries studies, but we must also have critical political economies of communication in the age of the internet, mobile phones, internet giants, and the 'battle of the stacks'.

Further reading
- Case: How the rise of internet-distributed television produced by companies such as Netflix has influenced the media content – Lotz (p. 337)
- Context: Five current issues and trends relating to the creative and cultural industries as a result of digitalization and the rise of the global communication giants – Miège (p. 73)
- Contrast: What concentration and convergence means from the perspective of managing media firms – Faustino & Noam (p. 147)

References

Bagdikian, B. H. (2004). *The New Media Monopoly* (7th ed.). Boston, MA: Beacon Press.

Berkman Centre for Internet & Society (2010). 'Next Generation Connectivity'. Retrieved from http://cyber.harvard.edu/sites/cyber.harvard.edu/files/Berkman_Center_Broadband_Final_Report_15Feb2010.pdf.

CMCRP (2017a). 'Media & Internet Concentration, 1984-2016'. Retrieved from http://www.cmcrp.org/wp-content/uploads/2017/11/CMCR_Media__Internet_Concentration_27112017_Final.pdf.

CMCRP (2017b). 'Media & Internet Concentration, 1984-2016'. Retrieved from http://www.cmcrp.org/wp-content/uploads/2017/11/CMCR_Media__Internet_Concentration_27112017_Final.pdf.

CMCRP (2017c). 'Workbook'. Retrieved from http://www.cmcrp.org/wp-content/uploads/2017/11/CMCRP_workbook_2016_for_the_web.xlsx.

CRTC (2015a). 'Telecom Regulatory Policy 2015-326'. Retrieved from http://www.crtc.gc.ca/eng/archive/2015/2015-326.pdf.

CRTC (2015b). 'The Way Forward: Broadcasting Regulatory Policy CRTC 2015-86'. Retrieved from http://crtc.gc.ca/eng/archive/2015/2015-86.pdf.

CRTC (2016). 'Broadcasting Regulatory Policy CRTC 2016-224'. Retrieved from http://www.crtc.gc.ca/eng/archive/2016/2016-224.pdf.

CBC (2016, January 28) 'Episode Transcript'. Retrieved from http://www.cbc.ca/radio/thecurrent/the-current-for-january-28-2016-1.3423319/january-28-2016-episode-transcript-1.3424300#segment2.

Chandler, A. (2012). 'Facebookistan', *North Carolina Law Review*, 90(5), 1807-1842.

Chung, E. (2016). 'Google, Canadian Media Outlets Launch AMP Websites'. Retrieved from http://www.cbc.ca/news/technology/google-amp-1.3611399.

Cisco (n.d.) 'Visual Networking Index (VNI) Forecast Highlights Tool'. Retrieved from https://www.cisco.com/c/m/en_us/solutions/service-provider/vniforecast-highlights.html

Crawford, S. (2011). Say You Were Canadian. Retrieved from http://scrawford.net/say-you-were-canadian/.

Duong, K. & Adamo, S. (2013). '2013 Canada Digital Future in Focus', *ComScore*. Retrieved from http://www.comscore.com/Insights/Presentations-and-Whitepapers/2013/2013-Canada-Digital-Future-in-Focus?cs_edgescape_cc=GB.

Eisenach, J. & Soria, B. (2016). 'A New Regulatory Framework for the Digital Ecosystem'. Retrieved from https://www.gsma.com/publicpolicy/wp-content/uploads/2016/09/GSMA2016_Report_NewRegulatoryFrameworkForTheDigitalEcosystem_English.pdf.

Ernst & Young (2017). 'IAB Canada 2016 Actual + 2017 Estimated Canadian Internet Advertising Revenue Survey'. Retrieved from https://iabcanada.com/content/uploads/2017/07/IABCanadaRevenueSurveyFinal2017.pdf.

FCC (2016a). Fifth Report DA 16-97.

FCC (2016b). Seventeenth Report DA 16-510.

FCC (2017). Eighteenth Report DA 17-71.

Garnham, N. (1990). *Capitalism and Communication*. London: SAGE Publications.

IHS Markit (2016). 'Canadian SVoD Service Shomi to Close November 2016'. Retrieved from https://technology.ihs.com/584102/canadian-svod-service-shomi-to-close-november-2016

International Telecommunication Union (n.d.). World Telecommunication/ICT Indicators Database. Retrieved from http://www.itu.int/en/ITU-D/Statistics/Pages/publications/wtid.aspx.

Internet World Stats (2017). 'North America'. Retrieved from http://www.Internetworldstats.com/america.htm#ca.

Miege, B. (1989). *The Capitalization of Cultural Production*. Amsterdam: International General.

Nanji, S. (2017, October 21). 'Experts Say Facebook's 'Election Integrity' Plan Misses the Mark', *Toronto Star*. Retrieved from https://www.thestar.com/news/gta/2017/10/21/experts-say-facebooks-election-integrity-plan-misses-the-mark.html.

Net Marketshare (2017). 'Browser Market Share'. Retrieved from https://netmarketshare.com/.

Newman, N., Fletcher, R., Levy, D.A.L. & Kleis Nielsen, R. (2016). 'Digital News Report 2016'. Retrieved from http://reutersinstitute.politics.ox.ac.uk/sites/default/files/research/files/Digital%2520News%2520Report%25202016.pdf.

Noam, E.M. & The International Media Concentration Collaboration (2016). *Who Owns the World's Media?* New York: Oxford University Press.

Nordicity & Miller, P. (2015). 'Near Term Prospects for Local TV in Canada'. Retrieved from https://www.friends.ca/files/PDF/nordicity-miller-report-on-future-of-local-tv-final.pdf.

OECD (2016). 'OECD Broadband Statistics'. Retrieved from https://www.oecd.org/sti/broadband/1.3-SubsByTech-2016-12.xls.

Owen, T. (2017, October 19). 'Is Facebook a Threat to Democracy?', *The Globe and Mail,* Retrieved from https://www.theglobeandmail.com/opinion/is-facebook-a-threat-to-democracy/article36661905/.

Pasquale, F. (2015). *The Black Box Society*. Cambridge, MA: Harvard University Press.

Pasquale, F. (2017). 'From Territorial to Functional Sovereignty: The Case of Amazon'. Retrieved from https://lpeblog.org/2017/12/06/from-territorial-to-functional-sovereignty-the-case-of-amazon/.

Pew Research Center (2013). 'Respect for Journalists' Contributions Has Fallen Significantly in Recent Years'. Retrieved from http://www.pewresearch.org/fact-tank/2013/07/25/respect-for-journalists-contributions-has-fallen-significantly-in-recent-years/.

Picard, R. G. (2011). *The Economics and Financing of Media Companies* (2nd ed.). Fordham, NY: Fordham University.

Public Policy Forum (2017). 'The Shattered Mirror'. Retrieved from https://shatteredmirror.ca/wp-content/uploads/theShatteredMirror.pdf.

Rewheel/research (2017). 'Tight Oligopoly Mobile Markets in EU28 in 2015'. Retrieved from http://research.rewheel.fi/insights/2016_jan_premium_tightoligopoly_eu28/.

Savage, P. & Gasher, M. (2008). 'Gaps in Canadian Media Research', *Canadian Journal of Communication, 33*(2), 291-301.

Skorup, B. & Thierer A. (2013). 'Uncreative Destruction', *Federal Communications Law Journal, 65*(2), 157-201.

Standing Committee on Canadian Heritage (2017). 'Meeting No. 5 CHPC – Standing Committee on Canadian Heritage'. Retrieved from http://parlvu.parl.gc.ca/XRender/en/PowerBrowser/PowerBrowserV2/20160225/-1/24623?useragent=Mozilla/5.0 (Macintosh; Intel Mac OS X 10_8_5) AppleWebKit/537.36 (KHTML, like Gecko) Chrome/48.0.2564.116 Safari/537.36.

Statcounter GlobalStats (2017). 'Search Engine Market Share in Canada – November 2017'. Retrieved from http://gs.statcounter.com/search-engine-market-share/all/canada/.

Statistics Canada (2016a). 'LFS Public Relations and Journalism Occupations'. Retrieved from https://drive.google.com/file/d/0B3WCF51KmyImd0o4SVpNczQ1dkU/view

Statistics Canada (2016b). Life in the Fast Lane: How Are Canadians Managing? Retrieved from http://www.statcan.gc.ca/daily-quotidien/171114/dq171114a-eng.htm?HPA=1.

US DOJ & the FTC (2010). 'Horizontal Merger Guidelines'. Retrieved from https://www.justice.gov/sites/default/files/atr/legacy/2010/08/19/hmg-2010.pdf.

Vogel, H.L. (2011a). *Entertainment Industry Economics* (8th ed.). Cambridge: Cambridge University Press.

Watson, H.G. (2017). 'Torstar and Postmedia Swapped 41 Newspapers and Are Closing Most of Them'. Retrieved from http://j-source.ca/article/torstar-postmedia-swapped-41-newspapers-closing/.

Winseck, D. (2012). 'Critical Media Research Methods: Media Ownership and Concentration', in I. Wagman & P. Urquhart (eds), *Cultural Industries.Ca*. Toronto: Lorimer.

Practices

Innovation

14.   Making (Sense of) Media Innovations

Arne H. Krumsvik, Stefania Milan, Niamh Ní Bhroin,
and Tanja Storsul

Media innovation is all around us in the form of new genres, new products, and new platforms. But how can we understand these innovations? This chapter provides a theoretical exploration of the concept of media innovation and presents three steps to analyse them. It helps us understand what media innovations are, what is new about them, and what makes them possible.

Introduction

Innovation is about change. Media products and services are changing. The processes of production and distribution of media are changing. The ownership and financing of media are changing. The roles of users are changing. And our ideas of media are changing. This chapter introduces media innovation as a research area, and provides a three-step model for analysing and developing media innovations.

In order to understand and explain current developments in the media landscape, we first have to ask 'what is changing?'. We propose that media innovations are related to (1) product innovation, (2) process innovation, (3) position innovation, (4) paradigmatic innovation, (5) genre innovation, and (6) social innovation. The second step is to ask 'what is the degree of novelty?'. Finally, the third step is to identify and understand key influences on innovation in the media. This three-step approach will be useful for scholars as well as practitioners, in analysing and developing media innovations.

Media researchers have always been concerned with media change – with new media, new genres, and new ways of using media. Researching new media developments, their political, cultural, and economic contexts, new formats and new forms of user involvement are important issues in media research. This concern with new media has, to a great extent, not been grounded in explicit theoretical considerations about innovation. The field of media studies has been dominated by the overarching traditions of political economy and cultural studies, and this has prompted a heated debate as to whether 'the economic determinants at work' or 'the cultural discourses at play' should be given the explanatory emphasis (Cottle, 2003; Ytreberg, 1999).

A key contribution from the emerging research arena of media innovation studies is to offer a broader perspective, and provide new insights into and greater knowledge about what characterizes media innovation, how media innovation develops, what structural conditions facilitate and shape innovation, and what the current trends in product development and user involvement are (Storsul & Krumsvik, 2013; Sylvie, 2014). The lens of innovation theory is a valuable tool for understanding current developments in the media landscape, the sociocultural conditions of the innovations, the role of technology, and power relations in media making.

Approaches to innovation

Innovation is a concept with multiple meanings. In everyday language, innovation is often used as a synonym of invention. In innovation literature, however, innovation and invention are typically separated as different concepts. An invention is a new idea or a new theoretical model, while an innovation is the implementation of this invention in a market or a social setting. There is often a long time-span between an invention and an innovation. Although Leonardo da Vinci invented and made drawings of the helicopter in the 1400s, it was not until almost 500 years later that this invention was developed into a helicopter that actually flew with people inside (Godø, 2008).

Thus, innovation implies introducing (and implementing) something new into the socioeconomic system. Furthermore, what is new is not necessarily an invention, but more typically involves new combinations of existing ideas, competences, and resources (Schumpeter, 1934/1943; Shtern *et al.*, 2013). An innovation can be based on existing technologies and off-the-shelf products. A key to understanding innovation is that existing knowledge is implemented in new contexts and that this opens up new possibilities.

There have been several different approaches to understanding and explaining innovation. One of the first major contributors of theoretical insight into innovation was Joseph Schumpeter. Inspired by Karl Marx, Schumpeter was concerned with explaining what caused long-term economic change. He contradicted established theory of the early 1900s and argued that the key driver to economic change was not primarily competition between companies in a market, but innovation and new technologies that enabled new forms of competition, and thereby caused more fundamental changes in the economy (Godø, 2008; Fagerberg, 2005).

Schumpeter maintained that the economy developed in cycles, since competition through innovations like new commodities, technologies or types of organization would annihilate established companies and destroy the old established economic order. He called this process of creativity and innovation leading to destruction of the established order 'creative destruction'.

Another important approach to innovation is economic. Economic innovation models are concerned with who gains from innovation, what interests are involved, how they are organized, and who succeeds and who fails in the market (Godø, 2008). The role of disruptive innovations (Christensen, 1997) in redefining media markets and business models, and the role of users in driving innovation (Hippel, 2005; Tapscot & Williams, 2006), are important contributions for those who seek to understand and explain new developments in media markets.

Constructivist models emphasize the innovation process itself. The focus is then shifted towards investigating what happens in the innovation processes, what the role of technology is, and what the power relations are between established and new actors (Godø, 2008). A leading approach among these is actor-network theory (Latour & Wolgaar, 1979; Callon, 1986), which considers the relationships between everything involved in the process of innovation – including the roles of humans and technologies. It has, for example, been used in studies of innovation in the newsroom (Domingo *et al.*, 2012).

All these approaches to innovation are relevant in studying media-related change. But what is media innovation?

What is media innovation?

Media innovation can include change in several aspects of the media landscape – from the development of new media platforms, to new business models, to new ways of producing media texts or genres. We propose that media innovations involve changes in product, process, position, paradigm, genre, and society (see also Francis & Bessant, 2005; Shtern *et al.*, 2013). We apply these elements to analyse both commercial and not-for-profit innovations.

Product innovation relates to changes in the products/services offered by an organization. This may imply the innovation of new media platforms, such as the smartphone, or of new media services, such as content streaming services, Wikipedia or media apps for tablets (Krumsvik *et al.*, 2013). Furthermore, it could also imply the innovation of communication patterns, for example encouraging audience interaction with TV programmes through the use of second screens (cf. De Meulenaere *et al.*, 2015).

Process innovation refers to changes in the ways in which products/services are created and delivered. This includes how media businesses organize their activities (Bauman, 2013). It also includes processes outside established institutions, for example, where users are involved in collaborative innovation (cf. Lüders, 2016; see also Hippel, 2005; Tapscott & Williams, 2006). Collaborative initiatives, such as Linux or Wikipedia, are examples of product innovations developed through process innovation.

Position innovation involves changes in how products and services are positioned or framed. Media companies who reposition their brands, products, or services are engaging in position innovation. Innovative product positioning involves 'advertising, marketing, media, packaging and the manipulation of various signals' (Francis & Bessant, 2005). Typical examples would be a magazine repositioning itself for a new target audience. For example, between 2012 and 2015, the lifestyle magazine *Elle* repositioned itself as *Elle 360*, a multiplatform company (Champion, 2015). Another example would be how the BBC in the 1990s repositioned itself as a global media corporation (Francis & Bessant, 2005).

Paradigmatic innovation includes changes in mindset, values, and business models. When the music industry shifted from CD sales to streaming services, this represented a paradigmatic innovation. The newspaper industry is in a similar process, where the focus is no longer primarily on print, but rather on online services. Media companies are increasingly more committed in their search for sustainable business models for online services (cf. Barland, 2015). In general, the process of datafication, where user interactions with media content and services are aggregated and analysed for commercial purposes, is a paradigmatic innovation. Datafication follows from other broad processes of change, such as digitalization and mediatization (cf. Schäfer & Van Es, 2017).

Genre innovation is a fifth kind of media innovation that is particularly relevant to the media and communication industries. Media products and services can be categorized and developed according to genres. A genre innovation can consist of combining or using elements from existing genres, or developing and introducing new genre elements into a familiar one. Ultimately, genre innovation aims at establishing successful imitations, or iterations, of itself (see also Grøgaard, 2016).

Finally, *social innovation* involves the innovative use of media and communication services for social purposes (Ní Bhroin, 2015). Here, social change is introduced through blending new and/or existing combinations of media products and/or services, for example to produce media that cater to the needs of a linguistic minority. Social innovation meets social needs and improves people's lives (Mulgan *et al.*, 2007). We therefore add society as a sixth element that can be changed through media.

Degree of novelty

We also need to consider how new something must be in order to be an innovation. The media industries are characterized by a constant search for new content, markets, and business models (cf. Løvlie, 2016). So what should we characterize as simply product development or reorganization, and when can these kinds of changes be characterized as innovations? This problem is discussed by Dogruel (2013), who proposes that a useful starting point would be to say that an innovation is more than a new film or another magazine. It must have some kind of additional impact, economically or socially, to be called an innovation.

These innovations can represent a gradual improvement, or they can embed more fundamental upgrades. Many terms have been used to describe this dimension. In the Schumpeterian tradition, incremental versus radical innovation is often presented as a main dichotomy. Incremental innovation refers to gradual improvements where one innovation builds on another. Radical innovation, on the other hand, includes innovations with far-reaching consequences that may change the economy through creative destruction (Schumpeter, 1943). Similarly, but with a different emphasis, Clayton Christensen (1997) has coined the concepts 'sustaining and disruptive innovations', in which disruptive innovation is one particular kind of radical innovation. Even if disruptive technologies initially underperform compared to established products in the mainstream market, they may end up actually becoming the mainstream market.

Research relating to genre innovation makes interesting contributions with regard to conceptualizing degrees of novelty. Miller (2016) explores how genre innovation is often explained through the frameworks of evolution or emergence. She compares these frameworks to the concepts of incremental and radical change, and finds that the evolution of a new genre is more analogous to incremental change, while the emergence of genre involves more radical change. Using the example of blogs, she argues that this genre built on a series of evolutionary changes – such adapting the personal diary to an online format – however, the emergence of blogs as a genre, synthesizing a range of incremental changes, and the rapid diffusion of this genre among users, was a more disruptive process.

In media industries, as in other settings, most innovations are incremental or sustaining. They involve small changes of products or processes that do not challenge the economy or the logic of the media market. These innovations are initiated and managed in order to secure the economic survival of legacy media businesses.

Some innovations, however, have more far-reaching consequences. The internet, and ways in which the internet has been used, are good examples of disruptive or potentially disruptive innovations. Music streaming has changed music markets. Google and Facebook challenge media advertising income with particular consequences for the news industry. Television is increasingly moving in the direction of niche products, non-linear scheduling, and streaming services. This is an important part of the contemporary context, where the existing media industry knows that the rules of the game are changing, and in order to survive they must innovate.

Influences on media innovations

So far, this chapter has presented a theoretical exploration of the concept of media innovation. It has also explored the degree of novelty of media innovations. We submit that media innovations can be product, process, position, paradigm, genre or social innovations. In the context of legacy media and established firms, most innovations are sustaining in nature, concerned with supporting economic survival.

To date, scholars of media innovation have not significantly explored new genres of innovation in legacy media products and services initiated outside of existing media organizations. Regarding journalism, examples include citizen journalism such as Znet, or journalism that arises in more amorphous structures and informal contexts, such as social movements (Milan, 2013). At the same time, we know that disruptive innovations are most likely to be introduced by players outside of traditional media industries. This points towards a knowledge gap with regards to understanding how new users, new players in the media landscape, and new practices may influence media innovations.

This leads us to the third step of our approach. Here, we discuss the factors that drive (or hinder) media innovations. Arising from our research to date, we group these factors according to (1) media institutional factors; (2) technological developments; (3) sociocultural conditions and power relations.

Media institutional factors

Media institutional factors include both exogenous and internal influences. Exogenous influences include market opportunities, user, and competitor behaviour. Storsul and Krumsvik (2013) outline how technological advances tend to be resisted or ignored by the traditional media industry, resulting in disruptive innovations from outsiders.

Regulation is another important exogenous factor and includes subsidies, ownership limitations, licensing, and direct state involvement in the form of public service broadcasting ownership. In Europe, newspapers receive indirect state support through reduced or zero value added tax (VAT) on subscriptions, while the full rate is added to the sale of digital media. This legal framework constitutes a major barrier for innovation of paper/digital bundled revenue models (Sjøvaag & Krumsvik, 2017). Doyle (2013) asks whether the policy environment in broadcasting industries is fully attuned to facilitating the innovative use of digital infrastructures. Media policy typically attempts 'to solve yesterday's problems' (Lund, 2016).

Internal factors such as company strategy, leadership and vision, capacity and resources, and culture and creativity also influence media innovation. *Company strategy* reflects the media organizations' approach towards innovation. Global social media have disrupted both user behaviour and advertising revenue for legacy media. Legacy media have been found to be significantly less innovative in product, service, and process innovation than other service firms (Krumsvik *et al.*, 2017; see also Bleyen *et al.*, 2014). At the same time, media industries are driven by a norm of newness. There is a constant need for new content, ideas, products, and services, which has a related impact on the pace at which media innovations are developed and need to be diffused (Løvlie, 2016).

Leadership and vision involves the strength of the top executive and his or her vision for the company, which may extend beyond the official strategy approved by the board. While executives in newspapers owned by media groups score systematically higher on innovation indicators than their colleagues in independent newspapers (Krumsvik *et al.*, 2013), the latter are more focused on product innovations enabled by the unique features of each platform, whereas corporate media executives are more interested in efficiency through process innovations (Krumsvik, 2014).

Organizational structure relates to how the media company is organized, and whether it operates as an integrated company or with separate independent business units. In this regard, Christensen (1997) argues that incumbents will in most cases fail when attempting to capitalize on a disruptive technology, unless the new initiative is granted autonomy. This can be done in three ways: (1) spinning off an independent company – a model used by major newspapers; (2) creating a new organizational structure with teams physically located together and with personal responsibility for the success of the new project – an option used by BBC Online (Küng, 2007); or (3) acquiring an organization that meets the requirements of the new task. Gilbert (2002), Domingo *et al.* (2012), Boczkowski (2004) and several other researchers have found autonomy in new media development key to the success of an innovation project. A key issue for media firms is to avoid internal pressures created by social inertia and obduracy: a general reluctance to change among those working within established companies usually due to tradition and habit, but also caused because innovations are not properly embedded in the specific context of the company involved.

The *capacity and resources* of the editorial, production and distribution competences of a media organization affect its ability to innovate. For example, historically many newspapers were developed by book publishers that had excess printing capacity and needed the presses to keep rolling. In recent years, the increasingly digital distribution of television has enabled the development of streaming services such as Netflix (Zboralska & Davis, 2017).

Industry norms may define the scope of innovations in the media industries. Journalistic norms imply a 'church and state' separation between commerce and journalism, with implications for the influence of commercial considerations in operations as well as in the development of new products and services. These kinds of organizational walls may also define the competences of personnel involved in innovation processes, as editorial departments tend to lead product development. To safeguard the norms of journalism, the ownership of media companies is sometimes organized as a trust. Research has found these kinds of media organizations, with their defensive measures against market influence, to be less innovative than other types of media companies (Sjøvaag & Krumsvik, 2017).

Culture and creativity represent a change-oriented perspective in media production studies, inspired by the idea that people work within all kinds of structures that both enable and constrain what they do, while the way people do things also changes the structures within which they work (Nygren, 2008). Studies of major broadcasting organizations, i.e. CNN and BBC, demonstrated how company culture plays an important role, as their core products and competitive strengths are deeply rooted in the inner beliefs common to those working there (Küng, 2000, 2007; Krumsvik, 2013). The shared assumptions of members of an organization can result in inertia and can represent a hindrance to change, yet at the same time the culture of a company or network can also facilitate creativity and innovation.

Technological developments

Technology and innovation are inextricably linked. Küng (2013) has pointed out how innovation is the motor of technological advancement and draws attention to the need for media organizations to innovate in order to respond to technological advancement. On the other hand, Dogruel (2013) show how technological developments can also be considered to be threatening for existing media structures.

Technological change, and in particular digitalization, opens new opportunities in media industries, and can lead to the development of new products and services. At the same time, it might also disrupt existing business models. Related to this, media corporations are experimenting with new business models, based on datafication, i.e. the aggregation of data about user interactions with new media.

Research relating to media innovations acknowledges the importance of technological change as a contextual factor in media innovation. A number of contributions distinguish between innovations in technological infrastructure and innovations in media practice (cf. Bruns, 2014; Bleyen *et al.*, 2014). Bruns (2014) argues that media innovation is about media practice at least as much as it is about technology. He maintains that the continuing mediatization of society, and the shift towards a more widespread participation of ordinary users as active content creators and media innovators, creates a need to investigate media innovations as interlinked with everyday practices of media, technological, and societal change.

Sociocultural factors and power relations

Media users, or 'the people formerly known as the audience' (Rosen, 2006), are, as a consequence of digitalization, mediatization, and datafication, increasingly involved in processes of media innovation, both within and beyond legacy media institutions. Westlund and Lewis (2015) highlight audiences as important agents of media innovations in news media. Using actor-network theory, they have devised a typology of interactions between audiences, actors, and actants which play a role in media innovations.

Because of the involvement of users, the innovation and diffusion of media innovations are more interconnected (Dogruel, 2014). The networked structure of initiatives such as Wikipedia and Linux and of social innovation processes, facilitate both collaborative and autonomous innovation by users (Storsul & Krumsvik, 2013; Ní Bhroin, 2013). Media usage and user experience must therefore be taken into consideration when analysing media and communication innovations (see also Trappel, 2015). At the same time, a more critical analysis is required with regard to how the processes and logics of datafication influence user autonomy.

Bruns (2014) proposes that the media ecology is a constitutive element of societal structure, and that by consequence media innovations both reflect and bring about social change. We therefore need to understand the relationship between media innovations and established media industries with respect to the potential to affect societal change. Trappel (2015) proposes that scholars should explore the structural conditions that foster media innovations. In particular, he notes that a failure to analyse power relations 'would mean to dismiss the most promising explanatory factor from the analysis. Power makes or breaks innovation' (*Ibid.*, p. 19).

Conclusion

Innovations in media occur for a variety of reasons, take place within a variety of conditions, and take shape in different ways inside and outside of media firms. Depending on your perspective, innovation can be understood as the outcome of creative destruction, economic shifts, or as a more gradual process.

In the innovation process it is important to consider the roles and relations between all the people, organizations, and technologies involved. Within existing and established media companies and conglomerates, innovation tends to follow a more incremental path, whereas external groups (such as start-ups and other industry newcomers, and generally small to medium-sized companies) tend to move more quickly. This explains the distinction between sustaining and disruptive innovations.

In terms of what exactly is being innovated within media industries, we draw distinctions between product innovation, process innovation, position innovation, paradigmatic innovation, genre innovation, and social innovation. The third step of our approach involves the grouping of the factors that drive (or hinder) media innovations. These factors or elements influencing how innovations take shape are media institutional factors, technological developments, and sociocultural conditions and power relations.

With our three-step approach, one can gain a greater knowledge about what characterizes media innovation, how media innovation develops, and under what structural conditions innovation takes place. The lens of innovation theory helps us to understand complex current developments in the media landscape, and provides an invaluable tool for media scholars and professionals alike.

Further reading
- Case: How digitalization has driven the innovation and transformation of the music industry – Johansson (p. 309)
- Context: What the rise of new intermediaries such as Amazon, Facebook, Google, and Apple has meant for the changing media ecosystem – Bilton (p. 99)
- Contrast: How outsourcing and flexible specialization failed to promote innovation in TV production in the UK – Dwyer (p. 347)

Acknowledgements: This chapter builds in part on Storsul, T. & Krumsvik A.H. (2013). 'What is Media Innovations?' in T. Storsul & A.H. Krumsvik (Eds.), *Media Innovations: A Multidisciplinary Study of Change* (13-26). Gothenburg: Nordicom.

References

Barland, J. (2015). 'Research Brief: Innovation for New Revenue Streams from Digital Readers: The Case of VG+', *Journal of Media Innovations, 2*(1), 123-130.

Bleyen, V.A., Lindmark, S., Ranaivoson, H. & Ballon, P. (2014). 'A Typology of Media Innovations: Insights from an Exploratory Study', *Journal of Media Innovations, 1*(1), 28-51.

Boczkowski, P. J. (2004). *Digitizing the News: Innovation in Online Newspapers*. Cambridge, MA: The MIT Press.

Bruns, A. (2014). 'Media Innovations, User Innovations, Societal Innovations', *Journal of Media Innovations, 1*(1), 13-27.

Callon, M. (1986). 'Some Elements of a Sociology of Translations: Domestication of the Scallops and the Fishermen of St Brieuc Bay', in J. Law (ed.) *Power, Action and Belief: A New Sociology of Knowledge?* (196-223). London: Routledge.

Castells, M. (1996). *The Rise of the Network Society*. Oxford: Blackwell.

Christensen, C.M. (1997). *The innovator's Dilemma: When New Technologies Cause Great Firms to Fail*. Boston, MA: Harvard Business School Press.

Champion, K.M. (2015). 'Experimentation and Imitation: The Journey to Elle 360', *The Journal of Media Innovations*, 2(1), 23-40.

Cottle, S. (ed.) (2003). *Media Organization and Production*. London: SAGE Publications.

De Meulenaere, J., Bleumers, L. & Van den Broeck, W. (2015). 'An Audience Perspective on the 2nd Screen Phenomenon', *Journal of Media Innovations*, 2(2), 6-22.

Dogruel, L. (2013). 'Opening the Black Box. The Conceptualising of Media Innovation', in T. Storsul & A.H. Krumsvik (eds), *Media Innovations: A Multidisciplinary Study of Change* (29-43). Gøteborg: Nordicom.

Dogruel, L. (2014). 'What is so Special about Media Innovations? A Characterization of the Field', *Journal of Media Innovations*, 1(1), 52-69.

Domingo, D., Micó, J.L. & Masip. P. (2012). 'Convergence Hit the Wall: Reassessing Theoretical Approaches to Explain Innovation Failure in Newsrooms', presented at The International Symposium on Media Innovations, Oslo, 2012.

Fagerberg, J. (2006). 'Innovation: A Guide to the Literature', in J. Fagerberg, D. Mowery & R. Nelson (eds), *The Oxford Handbook of Innovation* (11-28). New York: Oxford University Press.

Francis, D. & Bessant, J. (2005). 'Targeting Innovation and Implications for Capability Development', *Technovation, 25*(3), 171-183.

Gilbert, C. (2002). 'Can Competing Frames Co-exist? The Paradox of Threatened Response', in *Working Paper 02-056*. Boston, MA: Harvard Business School.

Godø, H. (2008). *Innovasjonsledelse: Teknologiutvikling fra idé til forretningsplanlegging*. Trondheim: Tapir.

Grøgaard, S. (2016). 'Three Incidents at the Border of Genre', *Journal of Media Innovations*, 3(2), 20-29.

Ihlebæk, K.A, Krumsvik, A.H. & Storsul, T. (2014). 'En kamp om makt og mening: Casestudie av Nordlys på iPad', in L. Morlandstø & A.H. Krumsvik (eds), *Innovasjon og verdiskaping i lokale medier* (127-142). Oslo: Cappelen Damm Akademisk.

Krumsvik, A.H., Kvale, K. & Pedersen, P.E. (2017). 'Market Structure and Innovation Policies in Norway', in H. van Kranenburg (ed.). *Innovation Policies in the European News Media Industry: A Comparative Study* (149-160). Berlin: Springer.

Krumsvik, A.H. (2014). 'Newspaper Ownership and the Prioritization of Digital Competences', *Digital Journalism, 3*(5), 777-790. doi: 10.1080/21670811.2014.941234.

Krumsvik, A.H. (2013). 'From Creator of Change to Supporter of the Traditional: The Changing Role of CNN.com', *Journal of Applied Journalism & Media Studies, 2*(3), 397-415. DOI: 10.1386/ajms.2.3.397_1.

Kung, L. (2013). 'Innovation, Technology and Organisational Change. Legacy Media's Big Challenges. An Introduction', in T. Storsul & A. H. Krumsvik (eds), *Media Innovations: A Multidisciplinary Study of Change* (9-12).Gøteborg: Nordicom.

Kung, L. (2007). *When Innovation Fails to Disrupt: A Multi-Lens Investigation of Successful Incumbent Response to Technological Discontinuity: The Launch of BBC News Online.* Jönköping: MMTC.

Küng, L. (2008). *Strategic Management in the Media: Theory to Practice.* London: SAGE Publications.

Küng-Shankleman, L. (2000). *Inside the BBC and CNN: Managing Media Organizations.* London, New York: Routledge.

Latour, B. & Woolgar, S. (1986). *Laboratory Life: The Social Construction of Scientific Facts.* Princeton, NJ: Princeton University Press (Original work published 1979).

Lüders, M. (2016). 'Innovating with Users Online? How Network Characteristics Affect Collaboration for Innovation', *Journal of Media Innovations, 3*(1), 4-22.

Lund, A. B. (2016). 'A Stakeholder Approach to Media Governance', in G.F. Lowe & C. Brown (eds), *Managing Media Firms and Industries: What's So Special about Media Management?* (103120). Heidelberg: Springer.

Lund, M.T.K. & Puijk, R. (2012). 'Rolling News as Disruptive Change. A Managerial Perspective on TV 2 and VG in Norway', *Nordicom Review, 33*(1), 67-81.

Løvlie, A. (2016). 'Designing Communication Design', *Journal of Media Innovations, 3*(2), 72-87.

Mainsah, H., Brandzæg, P.B. & Følstad, A. (2016). 'Bridging the Generational Culture Gap in Youth Civic Engagement through Social Media: Lessons Learnt from Young Designers in Three Civic Organisations', *Journal of Media Innovations, 3*(1), 23-40.

Milan, S. (2013). *Social Movements and their Technologies: Wiring Social Change.* London: Palgrave Macmillan.

Miller, C.R. (2016). 'Genre Innovation: Evolution, Emergence or Something Else?', *Journal of Media Innovations, 3*(2), 4-19.

Ní Bhroin, N. (2013). 'Small Pieces in a Social Innovation Puzzle? Exploring the Motivations of Minority Language Users in Social Media', in T. Storsul & A.H. Krumsvik (eds), *Media Innovations: A Multidisciplinary Study of Change* (219-238). Gøteborg: Nordicom.

Ní Bhroin, N. (2015). 'Social Media-Innovation: The Case of Indigenous Tweets', *Journal of Media Innovations, 2*(1), 89-106.

Nygren, G. (2008). *Nyhetsfabriken: Journalistiske yrkesroller i en förändrad medievärld.* Lund: Studentlitteratur AB.

Nyre, L. (2014). 'Media Design Research', *Journal of Media Innovations, 1*(1) 86-109.

Roginsky, S. (2014). 'Social Network Sites: An Innovative Form of Political Communication? A Socio-Technical Approach to Media Innovation', *Journal of Media Innovations, 1*(2), 97-125.

Rosen, J. (2006). 'The People Formerly Known as the Audience', *PressThink: Ghost of Democracy in the Media Machine.* Retrieved from http://archive.pressthink.org/2006/06/27/ppl_frmr.html.

Schäfer, M.S. & Van Es, K. (eds) (2017). *The Datafied Society: Studying Culture through Data.* Amsterdam: Amsterdam University Press.

Schumpeter, J. (1934). *The Theory of Economic Development.* London: Transaction Publishers.

Schumpeter, J. (1943). *Capitalism, Socialism and Democracy*. London: Routledge.

Shtern, J., Paré, D.J., Ross, P. & Dick, M. (2013). 'Historiographic Innovation. How the Past Explains the Future of Social Media Services', in T. Storsul & A.H. Krumsvik (eds), *Media Innovations: A Multidisciplinary Study of Change* (239-253). Gøteborg: Nordicom.

Sjøvaag, H. & Krumsvik, A.H. (2017), 'In Search of Journalism Funding. Scenarios for Future Media Policy in Norway', *Journalism Practice*. doi: 10.1080/17512786.2017.1370972.

Storsul, T. & Krumsvik A.H. (2013). 'What is Media Innovations?', in T. Storsul & A.H. Krumsvik (eds), *Media Innovations: A Multidisciplinary Study of Change* (13-26). Gøteborg: Nordicom.

Sylvie, G. (2014). 'Establishing Media Innovations as a Research Arena', *Journal of Media Innovations, 1*(1), 131-133.

Tapscott, D. & A.D. Williams (2006). *Wikinomics. How Mass Collaboration Changes Everything*. London: Atlantic Books.

Trappel, J. (2015). 'What to Study When Studying Media and Communication Innovation? Research Design for the Digital Age', *Journal of Media Innovation*, *2*(1), 7-22.

Von Hippel, E. (2005). *Democratizing Innovation*. Cambridge, MA: The MIT Press.

Webster, F. (1995). *Theories of the Information Society*. London and New York: Routledge.

Westlund, O. & Lewis, S (2014). 'Agents of Media Innovations: Actors, Actants and Audiences', *The Journal of Media Innovations* 1(2), 10-35.

Ytreberg, E. (1999). *Allmennkringkastingens autoritet: Endringer i NRK Fjernsynets tekstproduksjon, 1987-1994*. Oslo: University of Oslo.

Zboralska, E. & Davis, C.H. (2017). 'Transnational Over-the-Top Video Distribution as a Business and Policy Disruptor: The Case of Netflix in Canada', *Journal of Media Innovations*, *4*(1), 4-25.

15. Start-up Ecosystems Between Affordance Networks, Symbolic Form, and Cultural Practice

Stefan Werning

Start-ups have become highly influential, with start-up logic permeating increasing aspects of private and social life. But how can we study and understand them? This chapter outlines possible media and culture studies perspectives on start-ups and entrepreneurship. It conceptualizes start-ups as a 'new medium' and situates them within contemporary (media) culture, viewing start-up ecosystems respectively as affordance networks, a symbolic form, and a cultural practice.

Introduction

Across the media industries, entrepreneurship has come to be regarded as a key variable determining one's success as a firm or professional. In recent decades, the ability and willingness to strike out on your own to create a new business – a start-up – has become a particular, and often cherished, manifestation of such talent. Today, start-ups in the media industry are common, contributing to a 'start-up culture' embraced by many.

In doing so, media follow a broader trend popularized by the tech industry, but also applicable in many other domains. The notion of start-ups and the corresponding focus on small businesses has gradually permeated economic thought since the late 1950s, but its relevance rapidly increased in the 1980s and quickly spread into other social discourses after the dot-com bubble in the late 1990s and especially the beginning of the global financial crisis in 2007/2008.

The social impact of embracing start-ups and the values they propagate must be considered ambivalent. For instance, the so-called appification of immigration, i.e. the creation of start-ups to alleviate the problems of people fleeing from the Syrian civil war, has helped many refugees locate family members or find a place to stay with host families. Yet, scholars like Brabham (2017) indicate that start-up rhetoric institutionalized by crowdfunding platforms (foregrounding flexible business models and bottom-up financing) can be socially harmful in the long run if applied indiscriminately to domains such as art or education. Indeed, recent controversies surrounding companies like Uber and Airbnb suggest that many technology start-ups become increasingly disassociated from the societies they originate from.

Critical issues start with the lack of a consensual transdisciplinary definition of start-ups. In academic literature, this question is not frequently asked, which leads to multiple competing discipline-specific ontologies. Depending on the purpose of the respective study, start-ups are e.g. understood as a new type of company, a technological innovation, environments shaped by a particular archetype of business leader (the 'entrepreneur'), or as a facet of contemporary urban culture, since more and more metropoles across the world aspire to become start-up hubs (Fratzscher *et al.*, 2016).

The definition of start-ups has been closely linked to the notion of entrepreneurship, which, according to Joseph Schumpeter, ensures economic innovation and growth through an ongoing process of 'creative destruction', i.e. of destroying established industry sectors to create ever new markets. Still, as Shane and Venkataraman (2000) point out, a conceptual framework for defining entrepreneurship is similarly lacking and should not, as in previous research, focus entirely on the 'enterprising individuals', but also on the 'presence of lucrative opportunities' (*Ibid.*, p. 218).

Definitions by founders and venture capitalists are more specific, and accentuate different aspects (e.g. Robehmed, 2013). For instance, Neil Blumenthal, the founder of Warby Parker, posits that start-ups are 'working to solve a problem where the solution is not obvious and success is not guaranteed', thus emphasizing the element of risk-taking. Adora Cheung, the co-founder of Homejoy, instead argues that 'start-up is a state of mind', thus pointing to cultural or even psychological aspects that make people 'forgo stability' and seek 'the excitement of making immediate impact'.

Since even industry professionals use these categories ambiguously, it appears most useful to interpret them as frames (Werner & Cornelissen, 2014), that is as competing discursive constructions that serve the purpose of the person employing them. For example, the head of Y Combinator accelerator, the most prominent global start-up incubator to date, claims that 'a company five years old can still be a start-up' but that 'ten [years] would start to be a stretch', without substantiating his rather arbitrary distinction. While all these definitions make plausible points, the very ambiguity itself might be one of the defining characteristics of start-ups and their contentious role in contemporary society and culture, similar to how Sutton-Smith (1997) posits ambiguity as one of the defining elements of play, after comparing its multifarious competing rhetorics.

The novelty of contemporary start-up culture compared to earlier uses of the term is arguably predicated on changes in three key domains: the formation of highly networked start-up ecosystems through application programming interfaces (APIs), profound changes in the 'investment landscape' (Prive, 2014), and changes in the performativity of founders and the mediatization of start-ups within mainstream media culture. These factors suggest a combination of 1) technological, 2) economic, and 3) cultural developments that mutually influence each other. Relevant existing research on start-ups has similarly focused on technological, socioeconomic, and – to a much lesser degree – cultural topics.

In the first category, common software development practices (Giardino *et al.*, 2014) and app development (Mosemghvdlishvili & Jansz, 2013) have been investigated from an ethnographic perspective. With reference to social aspects of start-ups, Brereton and Jones (2006) studied the social media use of entrepreneurs, while Lugovic and Ahmed (2015) specifically investigated patterns of Twitter use among European start-up founders. More broadly, in the second category, with a focus on economic aspects, Ouimet and Zarutskie (2014) compared demographic characteristics of start-up employees. Organizational aspects play an important role as well, as e.g. in a foundational early study by Van de Ven, Hudson, and Schroeder (1984) on 'designing' business start-ups, or more recent comparative work on situational factors and their impact on early organizational activities (e.g. Naldi & Picard, 2012). Finally, in the third category, with a focus on cultural developments, several studies provide overviews of regional specificities in start-up hubs across the world, which usually focus on quantifiable factors, but – through critical comparison – can lead towards a systematic culturally comparative view on start-ups. Motohashi (2012) identified important discrepancies between biotechnology firms in Japan and the US, e.g. regarding size, growth, and disposition towards risk, but primarily explains them in terms of differences in the respective venture capital markets. Focusing on individual regions, Ghosh, Bhowmick, and Guin (2014) analyse the notion of perceived uncertainty in the Indian start-up ecosystem and Kon *et al.* (2014) provide a conceptual framework of the Israeli start-up ecosystem that may be generalizable for future research along these lines.

Adding to these primarily sociological perspectives, this chapter aims to conceptualize start-ups as a 'new medium' and to situate them more broadly within contemporary (media) culture, i.e. to outline several potential trajectories for a media and culture studies perspective on start-up ecosystems. For that purpose, the following sections will briefly characterize start-up ecosystems as affordance networks, a symbolic form, and a cultural practice.

Understanding start-up ecosystems as affordance networks

Start-up ecosystems can be investigated using different methodologies common within media and culture studies, including software studies (Fuller, 2008), platform studies (Gillespie, 2017), code studies (Marino, 2006), web studies (Gauntlett, 2000), gadget analysis (Verhoeff, 2009), and digital methods (Rieder & Röhle, 2012). Yet, to study processes of meaning-making within the start-up ecosystem, the most immediately applicable approach appears to be a comparative affordance analysis of the apps they create.

The notion of affordances as used in this context refers to design choices and functionalities that encourage particular forms of use and interpretation without imposing them. The term originated in the psychology of perception, but was later appropriated for the critical study of software (cf. e.g. Curinga, 2014; Light, Burgess, & Duguay, 2016). While all aspects of software design enable some form of user interaction, this definition of affordances particularly refers to interface elements that produce norms (Stanfill, 2015) or otherwise make meaningful distinctions. The iconic 'swipe logic' (David & Cambre, 2016) implemented by dating start-up Tinder to browse user profiles serves to illustrate the point. Swiping not only allows for users to quickly access profile data, but also imbues the left and right swipe with normative connotations and remediates not only the gesture of turning the pages of a book, but also of skimming through a product catalogue.

Yet, as the technical value propositions of start-ups are both rapidly changing and deeply interconnected, it does not make sense to focus on individual applications – as in traditional affordance analyses. Therefore, they can be more appropriately defined as 'affordance networks' (Rasi, Hautakangas, & Väyrynen, 2015). To outline these affordance networks, it is necessary to map patterns of affordance change within start-up ecosystems over time, for example to show how iconic features like Snapchat's AR lenses or Tinder's aforementioned swipe gesture produce 'ripple effects' within the respective ecosystem through imitation and variation. For instance, Werning (2017a) points out how affordance changes across social media start-ups gradually frame economic practices like shopping or stock market investment into forms of para-social online interaction. It is important to note that the notion of 'affordances' in this context does not only include user interface conventions or technical properties that are invisible to the regular user (such as the weighting of factors in a recommendation algorithm), but also economic design choices (for example using a (reverse) auction model over a more traditional pricing mechanism). Thus, if we are to consider start-ups as a 'new medium' rather than simply a business innovation, the company itself and its basic economic properties are integral to how it creates meaning.

Start-ups as a symbolic form

Shortly after his election as president of France, Emmanuel Macron declared that he 'want[s] France to be a start-up nation[...] a nation that thinks and moves like a start-up' (Agnew, 2017, p. 4). With that slogan, Macron, who has himself been described as a 'start-up politician' (*Ibid.*, p. 5) since he had launched his political party En Marche! only one year before his successful election, characteristically chose start-ups as a metaphor for his proposed system of governance that contemporary nation states should adopt to be able to act flexibly and efficiently in the face of political, economic and social instability. According to a venture capital investor, Macron is allegedly 'disrupting politics in the same way that start-ups are seeking to disrupt their own sectors' (*Ibid.*, p. 14). This quote indicates that the logic of start-ups appears to gradually trickle down into other societal domains like politics or education and to become accepted as a broader cultural principle. Apart from the notion of disruption, this particularly includes practices like 'tweaking' (Bogost, 2016), which lead to a cycle of conceptualization, prototyping, testing, launching, constant updating, and eventually pivoting or discontinuing.

In that sense, start-ups currently fulfil a similar purpose and have similar social significance as databases in the 1990s and early 2000s, which Manovich (1999) and Paul (2007) have described using the terms 'symbolic form' and 'cultural form' respectively. Originally, art historian Erwin Panofsky employed the concept of symbolic form to describe how the construction of central perspective in Western art history developed from a purely aesthetic device into a 'schema linking the social, cognitive, psychological, and especially technical practices of a given culture' (as cited in Jeong, 2013, p. 5). That is, by institutionalizing and gradually refining its underlying techniques, the representation of central perspective in art became a way of perceiving and interpreting the world. Lev Manovich adapted the concept to analyse the formative influence that databases as a technical protocol exert on the organization of cultural information. Thus, instead of as a visual 'form', Manovich interprets Panofsky's concept as a purely symbolic structure. Writing in the late 1990s, Manovich originally considered the multimedia CD-ROM to be a paradigmatic example of this database structure, but as the creation, sharing, and manipulation of web-based datasets has continually gained traction, Manovich's claim that we perceive real-world issues (and potential ways to solve them) through the 'lens' of databases is becoming all the more plausible.

Coming back to the initial example, start-ups as a techno-economic 'form' arguably develop a similarly formative influence on contemporary patterns of thought. That is, due to their ubiquity and the allure of a few extremely successful examples, start-ups are increasingly perceived and deployed as 'ready-made' solutions for all kinds of problems and become black-boxed 'filters', through which we perceive and interpret social issues.

Eric Ries' book *The Lean Start-up* (Ries, 2011) is regarded by many as the 'bible' of this contemporary start-up rationality, and introduced or at least popularized several of its key concepts, including the minimum viable product (i.e. the smallest possible prototype that still affords obtaining real-world user feedback), split-testing (i.e. simultaneously rolling out and comparing slightly different versions of an app or website), and pivoting (i.e. the structured change of key elements of a start-up's value proposition). Taken together, these principles lead to a form of hypothesis-driven entrepreneurship, i.e. they require the entrepreneur to continually formulate, test, and update hypotheses about the company's design as well as users' behaviour and demands.

Considering start-ups as a symbolic form, it appears plausible that iconic aspects of start-up logic such as Ries' notion of the minimum viable product not only characterize companies, but are also applied on different levels, e.g. more specifically as a framework for product design (Hokkanen, Kuusinen, & Väänänen, 2016) or, as proposed in many online discussions, even as an everyday life principle. A similar transfer of start-up thinking is illustrated by Bruun-Jensen and Hagel (2015), who argue that start-ups increasingly pursue a similar 'design' approach to their business models – recombining basic elements into 'barely working prototype models, specifically designed to test key risks' (*Ibid.*, p. 2) – that they apply to their actual products.

A suitable framework to further contextualize start-ups as a symbolic form can be media ecology, specifically Douglas Rushkoff's view on corporatism as a media environment (2012). Rushkoff argues that 'the corporate sphere has become for many an imperceptible medium in which human affairs just occur' (*Ibid.*, p. 22), i.e. its specific mechanisms of representation become naturalized over time. The logic of start-ups as a media environment manifests itself in at least two ways, within physical environments such as office spaces, and within narrative environments, i.e. the growing body of start-up stories becoming cultural narratives. Both types of environments are amply documented online. For instance, start-up offices have been documented episodically and on dedicated websites.

The increasing pervasiveness of start-up stories in mainstream media discourse similarly contributes to the naturalization of start-up logic. Technology blogs regularly profile start-up founders, and websites like Medium.com publish founder biographies to make start-ups more relatable on a personal level. Many of these stories closely follow Joseph Campbell's archetype of the Hero's Journey and stylize the founders' personal experiences as quasi-mythological narratives about overcoming hardships and realizing one's true potential. Finally, web platforms like Quora and Reddit afford discussions between aspiring founders and those already established in the business and bridge the epistemic gap between both spheres. Accordingly, Haegens (2014) argues that start-ups are gradually replacing traditional corporations as models and metaphors of neoliberal self-description, and increasingly shape everyday-life rhetoric. This, in turn, propels larger media firms and conglomerates to promote 'start-up-thinking' within their companies, for example by stimulating 'intrapreneurship' (Boyles, 2016) in order to infuse experimentation and creativity – an increasingly common practice in news organizations and publishing houses around the world.

Start-ups as a cultural practice

Not all start-up founders fit the description of saviour or hero, though. In November 2010, Lynn Perkins wondered why she could easily book a restaurant reservation online, yet had to spend hours calling and e-mailing to find a babysitter for her twin boys. To understand and address the problem, Perkins founded UrbanSitter together with three friends, using Facebook Connect to access the networks of parents and sitters and bring the two together. The service was initially created without a business model, as a response to a personal lived experience, and Perkins used 'genre elements' from a different start-up, the restaurant reservation service OpenTable, to 'express her view' on the subject matter. The example of UrbanSitter substantiates the notion of start-ups as a symbolic form but, even more, suggests to alternatively conceive start-ups, with Couldry (2004), as practice or, with Krämer and Bredekamp (2013), as cultural technique, where the founding of a start-up can be a way of thinking about and engaging with a real-world situation or problem rather than being primarily driven by a techno-economic or business rationale.

The common but often marginalized practice of entrepreneurial restarts launching another business after a failed venture illustrates the relevance of a focus on start-ups as cultural practice. The ambiguity of re-starting, which can both benefit and hamper subsequent founding endeavours, is often regarded as an internally homogenous aspect of entrepreneurial experience (Metzger, 2006). But re-starting comprises a broad spectrum of possible practices, each of which produces slightly different discourses and value negotiations. Consider for example the different ways of thinking about the valorisation of risk-taking and failure in the US versus Europe.

A central and otherwise often ignored characteristic of start-up founding as cultural practice is the underlying playful mindset. Sicart (2014) defines playfulness as a resistive attitude that allows for 'appropriat[ing] a context that is not created or intended for play' (p. 27), but which 'respects the purposes and goals of that object or context' (*Ibid.*, p. 21). This definition very adequately describes the role of technology start-ups within contemporary industries, especially considering that Sicart expressly defines play as 'creative' (*Ibid.*, p. 17) and 'disruptive' (p. 14). One common site for playful start-up practices are hackathons and start-up jams (Leckart, 2012); short-term competitions, in which founders impose arbitrary constraints such as unfamiliar tools and new team members on themselves to master the skills they need as an entrepreneur. Start-up jams essentially constitute a design strategy, closely resembling the notion of 'exploratory design games' (Brandt, 2006, p. 57), where games are used to organize participatory product design processes. This underlying design rationality is applied both to the 'product' (the app, the company itself, and the business model, including aspects like value proposition, market segment, value chain, and network), as well as 'revenue generation mechanism(s)' (Chesbrough, 2007, p. 13).

Conclusion: Opportunities for further research

This chapter has outlined three distinct ways of conceptualizing the cultural relevance of start-ups and aims to show how the increasing naturalization of start-up logic in contemporary societies makes it plausible to understand them as a 'new medium' rather than simply as an economic form. Due to the limited scope of this chapter, several important aspects had to be set aside but shall at least be pointed out as opportunities for further research to conclude this argument.

First, the mediatization of entrepreneurship plays an important, but still understudied role in cementing start-ups as a symbolic form. For example, TV shows – both fictional (like HBO's *Silicon Valley*) and non-fictional (like ABC's *Shark Tank* or CNBC's *Billion Dollar Buyer*) – embed start-ups and the people behind them firmly within popular discourse. In 2007, the EU even commissioned an expert report titled *Promoting entrepreneurship on TV and in other audio-visual media*, which was aimed at 'improving the image of entrepreneurship in Europe' (*Ibid.*, p. 4) and promoting the creation of small and medium enterprises (SMEs).

Second, start-up development is slowly taking hold in very different areas of the world, even in war zones like Gaza City (Cordoba, 2014), where – unlike in functioning post-industrial economies – it arguably starts as a social movement and only later may gain economic traction. Cordoba argues that start-ups 'provided an outlet for ideas already percolating in the city's cafes and coffee shops', and have become one of the driving forces behind the economic reconstruction, as internet businesses mostly transcend geographic boundaries and require comparatively little material infrastructure. Despite drastically different sociocultural circumstances, start-ups emerging in this context like Wasselni, a social networking tool that hails taxis and private cars, can appear surprisingly familiar, which suggests an increasing hybridization between regional cultural influences and a broader, seemingly transcultural 'language' of start-up development and technological affordances (such as presented through the ubiquity of smartphones). Moreover, studies on start-up ecosystems in the Middle East (Schroeder, 2013) indicate that entrepreneurship can constitute a unifying trait regardless of 'mother tongues, religions, and colours' (*Ibid.*, p. 11), even though several Middle Eastern start-ups specifically build their value proposition on making religious participation as a cultural technique easier and more comfortable to reconcile with the users' daily schedules (*Ibid.*, p. 179).

The fact that start-ups – similar to other creative and cultural industries (Wilson & Dissanayake, 1996) – operate within a state of tension between regionally specific production cultures and potentially global audiences suggests taking a broader cultural convergence perspective on start-up ecosystems. For instance, the crystallization of start-up hubs is heavily dependent on the surrounding urban and popular culture. Los Angeles in particular has become attractive for start-ups like The Honest Company as they start 'tapping into cultural phenomena, trends and fundamental lifestyle changes' (Yanover, 2016). This applies not only on an urban, but also on a national level. For instance, the Dutch start-up ecosystem is characterized by environmental factors such as the appointment of Prince Constantijn as start-up ambassador in 2016, the specificity of Amsterdam and its local incubator policy, the widespread use of Dutch start-ups like WeTransfer and Piggy.nl in everyday life, and even the localization of start-ups for the Dutch market, as in the case of Uber Bike.

Finally, it is important to at least briefly acknowledge a few critical social aspects, that warrant further research. Chief among them is the lack of ethnic, gender and overall demographic diversity, both within start-ups and investor firms (Raina, 2017), which has been pointed out as a major reason for the increasing disconnect between start-ups and the societies they are supposed to serve. While in many current debates this problem is framed as a 'new' phenomenon, 'gender effect[s]' in entrepreneurship have already been documented in the 1990s (Verheul & Thurik, 2001) and earlier. Thus, rather than focusing on the alleged novelty of start-ups and on short-term actionable insights, a media and culture studies perspective can help situate them within broader historical and cultural contexts.

Further reading
- Case: How start-up culture is experienced in the everyday practice of entrepreneurial journalism – Brouwers & Witschge (p. 441)
- Context: Five current issues and trends relating to the creative and cultural industries as a result of digitalization and the rise of the global communication giants – Miège (p. 73)
- Contrast: The lack of diversity in the creative media industries in the UK – Eikhof & Marsden (p. 247)

References

Agnew, H. (2017). 'Emmanuel Macron Inspires Entrepreneurs with Start-up Nation Vision', *Financial Times* (17 June). Retrieved from https://www.ft.com/content/9dee1ca6-5270-11e7-a1f2-db19572361bb.

Bogost, I. (2016). 'Go Tweak Yourself, Facebook', *The Atlantic* (28 April). Retrieved from http://www.theatlantic.com/technology/archive/2016/04/go-tweak-yourself-facebook/480258/.

Brabham, D.C. (2017). 'How Crowdfunding Discourse Threatens Public Arts', *New Media & Society, 19*(7), 983-99. https://doi.org/10.1177/1461444815625946.

Brandt, E. (2006). 'Designing Exploratory Design Games', in *Proceedings of the Ninth Conference on Participatory Design: Expanding Boundaries in Design – PDC '06, 1* (57-66). New York: ACM Press. https://doi.org/10.1145/1147261.1147271.

Brereton, D. & Jones, O. (2006). 'Social Networks and Business Start-ups: A First-Hand Account of Entrepreneurship', *Manchester Metropolitan University Business School Working Paper Series, 1*(21). Manchester: Manchester Metropolitan University.

Bruun-Jensen, J. & Hage, J. (2015). 'Minimum Viable Transformation', Business Trends Series. Retrieved from https://dupress.deloitte.com/dup-us-en/focus/business-trends/2015/minimum-viable-business-model-transformation-business-trends.html.

Chesbrough, H. (2007). 'Business Model Innovation: It's Not Just about Technology Anymore', *Strategy & Leadership, 35*(6). https://doi.org/10.1108/10878570710833714.

Cordoba, A. (2014). 'What It's Like to Build a Start-up in Gaza as the Bombs Drop', *Wired Magazine* (February). Retrieved from https://www.wired.com/2014/10/like-build-start-up-gaza-strip-bombs-drop/.

Couldry, N. (2004). 'Theorising Media as Practice', *Social Semiotics, 14*(2), 115-32. https://doi.org/10.1080/1035033042000238295.

Curinga, M.X. (2014). 'Critical Analysis of Interactive Media with Software Affordances', *First Monday, 19*(9). Retrieved from http://firstmonday.org/ojs/index.php/fm/article/view/4757/4116.

David, G. & Cambre, C. (2016). 'Screened Intimacies: Tinder and the Swipe Logic', *Social Media + Society, 2*(2), 1-11. https://doi.org/10.1177/2056305116641976.

Fratzscher, M., Gornig, M., Freier, R. & Kritikos, A.S. (2016). 'Transforming Berlin from a Start-up Hub into an Economically Thriving Metropolis', *DIW Economic Bulletin, 6*(29/30),321-25.

Fuller, M. (2008). *Software Studies: A Lexicon*. Cambridge, MA: MIT Press.

Gauntlett, D. & Horsley, R. (eds) (2000). *Web Studies: Rewiring Media Studies for the Digital Age* (2nd ed.). London: Bloomsbury Academic.

Ghosh, S., Bhowmick,B. & Guin, K.K. (2014). 'Perceived Environmental Uncertainty for Start-ups: A Note on Entrepreneurship Research from an Indian Perspective', *Technology Innovation Management Review, 4*(8), 27-35.

Giardino, C., Unterkalmsteiner, M., Paternoster, N., Gorschek, T. & Abrahamsson, P. (2014). 'What Do We Know about Software Development in Start-ups?', *IEEE Software, 31*(5), 28-32. https://doi.org/10.1109/MS.2014.129.

Gillespie, T. (2017). 'The Platform Metaphor, Revisited', *HIIG Science Blog.* Retrieved from https://www.hiig.de/en/blog/the-platform-metaphor-revisited/.

Haegens, K. (2014). 'Het Zelf Als Onderneming: Ik Is Een Start-Up', *De Groene Amsterdammer, 138*(27/29). Retrieved from https://www.groene.nl/artikel/ik-is-een-start-up.

Hokkanen, L., Kuusinen, K. & Väänänen, K. (2016). 'Minimum Viable User Experience: A Framework for Supporting Product Design in Start-ups', *Lecture Notes in Business Information Processing, 251*, 66-78. https://doi.org/10.1007/978-3-319-33515-5_6.

Jeong, S. (2013). *Cinematic Interfaces: Film Theory After New Media.* New York: Routledge.

Kon, F., Cukier, D., Hazzan, O. & Yuklea, H. (2014). 'A Panorama of the Israeli Software Start-up Ecosystem', *SSRN Electronic Journal.* https://doi.org/10.2139/ssrn.2441157.

Krämer, S. & Bredekamp, H. (2013). 'Culture, Technology, Cultural Techniques – Moving Beyond Text', *Theory, Culture & Society, 30*(6), 20-29.

Leckart, S. (2012). 'The 48-Hour Start-up', *Wired Magazine, 20*(3), 106-111, 124.

Light, B., Burgess, J. & Duguay, S. (2016). 'The Walkthrough Method: An Approach to the Study of Apps', *New Media and Society, 20*(3), 881-900. https://doi.org/10.1177/1461444816675438.

Lugovic, S. & Ahmed, W. (2015). 'An Analysis of Twitter Usage Among Start-ups in Europe', in *5th International Conference 'The Future of Information Sciences, INFuture2015: E-Institutions – Openness, Accessibility, and Preservation'.* Zagreb. Retrieved from http://darhiv.ffzg.unizg.hr/8479/.

Manovich, L. (1999). 'Database as Symbolic Form', *Millenium Film Journal, 34*. Retrieved from http://www.mfj-online.org/journalPages/MFJ34/Manovich_Database_FrameSet.html.

Marino, M.C. (2006). 'Critical Code Studies', *Electronic Book Review.* Retrieved from http://www.electronicbookreview.com/thread/electropoetics/codology.

McNely, B.J., Gestwicki, P., Gelms, B. & Burke, A. (2013). 'Spaces and Surfaces of Invention: A Visual Ethnography of Game Development', *Enculturation, 15*. Retrieved from http://enculturation.net/visual-ethnography.

Metzger, G. (2006). 'Once Bitten, Twice Shy? The Performance of Entrepreneurial Restarts', *SSRN Electronic Journal.* https://doi.org/10.2139/ssrn.955756.

Mosemghvdlishvili, L. & Jansz, J. (2013). 'Negotiability of Technology and Its Limitations: The Politics of App Development', *Information, Communication & Society, 16*(10), 1596-1618. https://doi.org/10.1080/1369118X.2012.735252.

Motohashi, K. (2012). 'A Comparative Analysis of Biotechnology Start-ups between Japan and the US', *Social Science Japan Journal, 15*(2), 219-37. https://doi.org/10.1093/ssjj/jys007.

Naldi, L. & Picard, R.G. (2012). '"Let's Start an Online News Site": Opportunities, Resources, Strategy, and Formational Myopia in Start-ups', *Journal of Media Business Studies, 9*(4), 69-97. https://doi.org/10.1080/16522354.2012.11073556.

Ouimet, P. & Zarutskie, R. (2014). 'Who Works for Start-ups? The Relation between Firm Age, Employee Age, and Growth', *Journal of Financial Economics, 112*(3), 386-407. https://doi.org/10.1016/j.jfineco.2014.03.003.

Paul, C. (2007). 'The Database as System and Cultural Form: Anatomies of Cultural Narratives', in V. Vesna (ed.), *Database Aesthetics: Art in the Age of Information Overflow* (95-109). Minneapolis, MN: University of Minnesota Press.

Prive, T. (2014). 'What Investors Are Thinking About Today – Versus 10 Years Ago', *Forbes Magazine* (19 February). Retrieved from https://www.forbes.com/sites/tanyaprive/2014/02/19/what-investors-are-thinking-about-today-versus-10-years-ago/.

Raina, S. (2017). 'VC Financing and the Entrepreneurship Gender Gap', *SSRN Electronic Journal*. https://doi.org/10.2139/ssrn.2846047.

Rasi, P., Hautakangas, M. & Väyrynen, S. (2015). 'Designing Culturally Inclusive Affordance Networks into the Curriculum', *Teaching in Higher Education, 20*(2), 131-142. https://doi.org/10.1080/13562517.2014.957268.

Rieder, B. & Röhle, T. (2012). 'Digital Methods: Five Challenges', in D.M. Berry (ed.), *Understanding Digital Humanities* (67-84). Basingstoke & New York: Palgrave Macmillan.

Ries, E. (2011). *The Lean Start-up. How Today's Entrepreneurs Use Continuous Innovation to Create Radically Successful Businesses*. New York: Crown Business.

Robehmed, N. (2013). 'What Is A Start-up?', *Forbes Magazine* (16 December). Retrieved from https://www.forbes.com/sites/natalierobehmed/2013/12/16/what-is-a-startup/#2f251b6d4044.

Rushkoff, D. (2012). 'Monopoly Moneys: The Media Environment of Corporatism and the Player's Way out'. Utrecht University Repository. Retrieved from http://dspace.library.uu.nl/handle/1874/250622.

Shane, S. & Venkataraman, S. (2000). 'The Promise of Enterpreneurship as a Field of Research', *The Academy of Management Review, 25*(1), 217-26. https://doi.org/10.2307/259271.

Sicart, M. (2014). *Play Matters*. Cambridge, MA: The MIT Press.

Stanfill, M. (2015). 'The Interface as Discourse: The Production of Norms through Web Design', *New Media & Society, 17*(7), 1059-74. https://doi.org/10.1177/146144481452087.

Sutton-Smith, B. (1997). *The Ambiguity of Play*. Cambridge, MA: Harvard University Press.

Van de Ven, A.H., Hudson, R. & Schroeder, D.M. (1984). 'Designing New Business Start-ups: Entrepreneurial, Organizational, and Ecological Considerations', *Journal of Management, 10*(1), 87-108. https://doi.org/10.1177/014920638401000108.

Verheul, I. & Thurik, R. (2001). 'Start-Up Capital: Does Gender Matter?', *Small Business Economics, 16*(4), 329-46. https://doi.org/10.1023/A:1011178629240.

Verhoeff, N. (2009). 'Theoretical Consoles: Concepts for Gadget Analysis', *Journal of Visual Culture, 8*(3), 279-98. https://doi.org/10.1177/1470412909105693.

Werner, M.D. & Cornelissen, J.P. (2014). 'Framing the Change: Switching and Blending Frames and Their Role in Instigating Institutional Change', *Organization Studies, 35*(10), 1449-1472. https://doi.org/10.1177/0170840614539314.

Werning, S. (2017a) (in press). 'Ethical Implications of Affordance Change in Contemporary Social Media Platforms', *Communication and Culture Review*, *1*(1).

Werning, S. (2017b). '"Re-Appropriating' Facebook. The Use of Web APIs as Collective Cultural Practice', *Digital Culture & Society*, *3*(2), 183-206.

Wilson, R. & Dissanayake, W. (eds) (1996). *Global/Local: Cultural Production and the Transnational Imaginary*. Durham, NC and London: Duke University Press.

Yanover, M. (2016). 'Pop Culture Stimulates the Evolution of the LA Tech Scene', *TechCrunch*. Retrieved from https://techcrunch.com/2016/07/23/pop-culture-stimulates-the-evolution-of-the-la-tech-scene/?guccounter=1.

Practices

Work Conditions

16. Precarity in Media Work

Penny O'Donnell and Lawrie Zion

Media work is more precarious now than at any time in recent history. This means next-generation media professionals need to prepare themselves for challenging working lives. Taking the Australian job market as an example, this chapter points out three important developments regarding media work and elaborates on the new skills needed to find employment in the dynamic field of media.

Introduction

Media work is changing and, in the process, media professionals are being forced to wise up to new labour market realities and adjust their career expectations accordingly. We have done longitudinal research on Australian media professionals caught up in significant digital industry restructuring and job cuts that have unhinged many careers. The *New Beats Project* has tracked the experiences of some of the more than 2,500 journalists estimated to have been laid-off from newsrooms since 2012 (see newbeatsblog.com). The following snapshot of one younger Australian journalist's responses to job loss and re-employment illustrates exactly what learning to live with the precarity of media work means in practice:

> 'Lily' was laid-off after her media company centralized news operations and cut staff. The dismissal notice stung her pride. She had not anticipated her busy job reporting daily breaking news for the online desk was at risk. It also broke her confidence. She had landed the work after graduating from her journalism degree, only to find herself back in the labour market within two years. 'You do have the view that you are disposable', she says, 'no matter how good or bad or how you are at your job'. Despite her youth and digital know-how, she found it hard to restart her career. There were many, many more PR and corporate communication jobs on offer than newsroom work, but Lily hesitated. She had watched her classmates take jobs in teaching and fashion design rather than cross-over to what they all jokingly referred to as the 'dark side'. Eventually, Lily got full-time work in an insurance company media unit, as the social media editor. She believes many next generation media professionals will end up creating content for corporate newsrooms. 'I used to do a lot of stories on fires, crashes, that sort of stuff', she says. 'Now, I do stories on how to prevent fires and crashes, which is quite funny!'

As Lily's story indicates, media workers have had to adjust their expectations. For a start, Lily has abandoned any hope of a working life spent in newsrooms chasing daily news stories. Instead, she has embraced two new trends in journalism: job growth in non-traditional organizations (e.g. corporations, banks, sporting bodies), and market demand for hybrid forms of editorial content (e.g. corporate journalism, native advertising) (O'Donnell, 2017, p. 163). Yet, she chose not to relinquish her journalistic professional identity (Sherwood & O'Donnell, 2016), instead embracing the job of writing branded content as a 'next-generation' media career. In this chapter, we argue that those who understand labour market dynamics, and know how to live with the precarity of media work, are the most likely to continue finding employment in the field.

Media work in fractured job market

Media work attracts younger Australians because it appears more creative, interesting, and long-lasting than many other jobs on offer. Employment as a multimedia specialist, web designer, social media journalist, or television presenter is highly prized, but so-called fantasy media careers, such as YouTubers or bloggers, are popular too (Australian Institute of Family Studies, 2017, p. 14).

The good news is there are many media career options. The tough news is that employers spend an average of six seconds reading a résumé, expect a lot from new recruits, and rarely offer a 'job for life'. In fact, the gig economy is on the rise, one in three working Australians is now employed part-time (McCrindle Research, 2017), and only six per cent of adult Australians end up in the careers they wanted when they were younger (Foundation for Young Australians, 2016, p. 6).

In Australia, as elsewhere, the twenty-first century has seen unprecedented growth in employment arrangements that create precarious work and cause worker insecurity (Kalleberg, 2009, p. 1; Healy & Nicholson, 2017). Today's teenagers must prepare for challenging working lives. The 2016 census figures show workers aged fifteen to 34 concentrated in low-skilled jobs, such as hospitality, food preparation or sales. This work is relatively easy to get but often monotonous and unsatisfying, leaving many younger Australians keen to move into professional jobs, such as media work. Yet, job tenure is increasingly elusive across all types of employment. Australian job analysts forecast that teenagers should be prepared for as many as seventeen changes in employer across five different occupations (McCrindle Research, 2014). This suggests aspiring media professionals need to add job switching skills (e.g. career management, networking) to their media toolkits, alongside digital literacy, critical thinking, creativity, and other essentials.

In Australia, which has a workforce of around 12.3 million, most entry-level jobs in the media typically require tertiary qualifications and wide-ranging skill-sets that support a range of career options. The top career category is advertising, marketing, public relations, and sales – a very large occupational cluster that, at the time of writing, employs over 200,000 professionals, and continues to create job openings. Graphic artists, illustrators, multimedia specialists, and web designers make up the next biggest occupational group. Three other clusters of traditional media occupations have notably fewer workers: journalists and other writers; artistic directors, media producers, and presenters; and film, television, radio, and stage directors. In 2017, the average age of media professionals was 37 years.

Media careers have long been differentiated by industry sector as well as occupational roles. Newspaper journalism is high-profile due to its long-standing connection to democratic politics, and, until recently, it was seen as a model career because it offered relatively stable, well-paid work in newsrooms. By contrast, media professionals in other creative industries – such as advertising, film, television, radio, design, or music – typically do more episodic, project-based work, often under precarious work arrangements. Independent contracting, freelancing, and unpaid internships are common. Nonetheless, the national media workers' union in Australia, the Media, Entertainment and Arts Alliance (MEAA), describes employment in these careers as 'atypical' (Walters, Warren, & Dobbie, 2006) rather than insecure. This is the union's way of acknowledging that many creative professionals prefer flexible work styles, even when they result in unpredictable pay and working conditions. It is also true that workforce reduction and staff job cuts have increased 'atypical' work across all media sectors. For example, while perhaps one in four laid-off journalists we surveyed were re-employed in some kind of journalism work, (Zion et al., 2016, p. 121) only one in ten of them were in full-time journalism roles.

Gender inequality in media careers is also widespread. Journalism is the only gender-balanced media occupation in Australia (50.8 per cent males, 49.2 per cent females). Conversely, gender imbalance in advertising, marketing, public relations, and sales work is linked to a significant gender pay gap: almost two thirds of managers in this occupation are males (62.3 per cent), working full-time, while over two thirds of public relations professionals are females (72.8 per cent) on modest, part-time wages (Australian Government, 2017). The gender equity activist group *Women in Media* blames Australia's 'blokey' culture for this kind of workforce discrimination. National convener Tracey Spicer says: 'progress towards equality for women in media is disappointingly slow. While there are more women than ever before working in the industry, they still dominate the lower paid, less powerful positions' (see www.womeninmedia.net/).

New realities

In what ways, then, is media work changing? The most far-reaching shift has been growing commercialization as a result of rapid change in the ways media industries do business in the post-industrial era. Back in the twentieth century, advertising was a major revenue source for media industries, and it paid for the content produced and distributed to mass audiences. Today, global tech giants Facebook and Google hardly produce any content themselves, but take most of online advertising revenue worldwide. They can do this because they have mastered the art of digital data collection and analysis, and have unprecedented audience reach. This highly profitable new business model is crushing national publishing and broadcasting industries by diverting advertising dollars offshore and, thus, stripping away their audiences, revenue streams, and viability.

In Australia, as elsewhere, the impact of Facebook and Google on local media markets, including the spread of fake news and other forms of disinformation, has provoked political furore. Government regulators in several countries investigate the tech giants for potential anti-competitive practices and misuse of market power, although, if the claims are proved, it remains unclear how seemingly irreversible global market trends might be remedied. Meanwhile, all commercial major media companies have restructured, downsized, and pursued drastic cost-cutting strategies. They have also introduced new digital content production models that put pressure on media professionals to boost profitability by producing and marketing commercially successful content.

There is much debate about the rise of commercial thinking as an integral part of media work (Malmelin & Villi, 2017, p. 5). Those in favour claim media success properly depends on audience focus, and media workers need to know how to market content, generate online traffic, and develop digital influence. Alternatively, critics worry that commercialization downgrades media professionals' expertise, challenges their creative autonomy, and threatens the quality and social value of media content. The broader concern, as Graeme Turner argues, is that the media's changing commercial structures – from marketization of the internet, to monetization of audience online activity, and largely invisible forms of dataveillance (monitoring digital data relating to personal details or online activities) – rearrange media power dynamics in ways we are yet to fully understand (Turner, 2016, p. 128). Media students are therefore encouraged to analyse the growing prominence of commercial thinking across the media in relation to the political economy of global ownership, control, and use of media resources.

Another significant, if understated, shift in media work is driven by growing research interest in the labour context of digital media production. An expanding literature on how media work is now organized, paid for, and experienced gives media students prior warning of challenging workforce trends. Mark Deuze's innovative theoretical and empirical research on media work provides great momentum to this area of study (Deuze, 2007). It invites media academics to research the mundane practicalities of media work if they want to create greater understanding of its huge appeal and multifaceted challenges. At the same time, it encourages media practitioners to use the insights gleaned from this research as a practical tool for navigating changing industry conditions (Elefante & Deuze, 2012, p. 11). These include increasing employment precarity in a global market saturated with media (Deuze, 2014, p. 1), jobs that promise creative opportunities but are often mired in overwork and disorganization, the similarity of workstyles found across the distinct media occupations, and, amidst perennial industry volatility, a worrying shortage of leadership and change management skills (Bartosova, 2011, p. 198). Also of interest is the wider issue of user work or audience labour associated with the rise of networked participatory culture, because it recasts media work to include paid and unpaid communicative activities (e.g. engagement, interaction) as well as content production (Malmelin & Villi, 2017, p. 9).

The main benefit of access to this research is that it demystifies media employment practices that are both rewarding *and* exploitative. This means media students can develop a strong understanding of media work before they sign on. Beyond the commercialization of media work, we discuss workforce flexibility and the increasing differentiation between stable and contingent media careers as two other topics of critical importance to professional media making.

Workforce flexibility

The gig economy is now a worldwide phenomenon, known for its task-based, short-term employment contracts, or gigs, which take many forms. Dream gigs are flexible, allow people to schedule work around personal and family commitments, and lead to other jobs. Flexible work arrangements can be really beneficial, particularly for teenagers looking to get a foot into the labour market, or those who want more control over their work-life balance. Moreover, in countries with high-speed internet, working from home has become a viable and desirable work option for highly-skilled professionals in the media industries (e.g. designers, creatives, and content writers). All this leads some economists to argue the gig economy is a sharing economy that fosters productivity and income growth. Online talent platforms – think Freelancer, Uber, Deliveroo, or Airtasker – have now streamlined the process of finding, managing, and getting paid for many types of freelance work, and they enable people otherwise marginalized from the job market, as well as professionals, to engage in peer-to-peer labour transactions (Minifie & Wilshire, 2016, p. 33).

Yet, others question the exploitative nature of gigonomics. Crappy gigs are all too common, and see people doing stressful, poorly paid, dead-end work, while, at same time, they are constantly hustling for the next job. The gig economy is spreading worldwide because employers are intent on phasing out full-time jobs, deregulating labour relations, and cutting wage costs (Kalleberg, 2009). Most short-term employment contracts now on offer include few, if any, benefits (i.e. no overtime, holiday pay, healthcare, or pension plans).

In everyday street talk, to be 'gig'd' means to be cheated out of something crucial. The simple truth is that the gig economy turns workers with legislated employment rights into independent contractors who individually must fend for themselves. Under Australian law, they are denied the right to collectively bargain with employers. Nonetheless, more than 1,400 freelance journalists are currently paid up members of the MEAA, which continues to demand that big media publishers provide them with fairer contracts, pay rates, copyright, defamation protection, and other terms of engagement. Unions have a long and successful history of advocating for decent employment and living standards across Australia's relatively small labour market. The 2017 'Digital Rights in Australia Report' confirmed public support for their approach. It found Australians expect to see the gig economy's flexible forms of work better regulated via targeted employment policies. They want government to reduce the financial insecurity of precarious work (Goggin *et al.*, 2017, p. 37). Unions and other professional associations internationally are lobbying for similar protections and arrangements for media workers, signalling a growing awareness about the rights (or lack thereof) of those working in the gig economy.

Stable and contingent media careers

Recent research on changes in journalism careers provides detailed analysis of the variable labour structures of media work within an occupational group and, thus, greater insight into the differences between stable and contingent media careers. In one study, Roei Davidson and Oren Meyers conceptualize journalistic careers as occupational paths or trajectories that may combine different types of employment practices, resources, and identities across any individual working life. They identify five types of journalism careers: professional, bureaucratic, entrepreneurial, unwillingly entrepreneurial, and non-employed (Davidson & Meyers, 2016).

Professionalism is identified as the 'ideal' journalistic career type, for its emphasis on autonomy, shared expertise, and a strong public interest ethos. Yet, the study finds this career path only exists in stable, bureaucratic newsroom settings (e.g. large media companies, public service media) or via access to the flexible and plentiful entrepreneurial work opportunities found elsewhere in the labour market (e.g.

self-employment, portfolio workstyles). The bureaucratic career variant provides job security, organizational resources, and shared professional identity, but it is also associated with hierarchical decision-making, managerialism, and conformity. In any case, it is available only to a shrinking minority of journalists.

Alternatively, there are growing numbers of self-employed journalists marketing their professional expertise beyond newsrooms, and it is within this 'entrepreneur' career variant that the study finds evidence of increasing differentiation between stable and contingent career paths. The gap is expressed in two ways: career options and professional identities.

In the first instance, entrepreneur journalists who opt to create their own business ventures are seen to enjoy more stable career paths because they are self-directed and purposive. Conversely, those forced into the gig economy, and continuous job searching, are deemed to be 'unwillingly entrepreneurial' as their careers futures depend on labour market trends beyond their control. Many laid-off Australian journalists are now in the 'unwilling' category, and report problems of employment uncertainty, income loss, and, in the case of older journalists, ageism (see also Zion *et al.*, 2016). When it comes to identities, their study finds entrepreneur journalists are not tied to traditional notions of professionalism. Instead, some re-centre their identities on work skills that can be adapted to suit available work opportunities. In these cases, adaptability can mean career longevity. As one Australian ex-journalist now doing public relations work explains: 'I feel that I've gained new skills in a professional sense and added to an extensive range of contacts. These will stand me in good stead as I prepare for the next stage of my career' (Sherwood & O'Donnell, 2016, p. 13). At the same time, identity loss is common amongst ex-journalists who find themselves forced to work in non-journalistic media roles.

Finally, the non-employed career type acknowledges the voluntary labour of citizen journalists, social media users, and others who practice journalism without getting paid for their work. It is a curious, outlier category, linked to recent critical work on labour exploitation (Hesmondhalgh, 2016; Perlin, 2012). However, unlike interns, who also work long hours for little or no pay, the non-employed do not seem to expect future employment or career progression. They are post-industrial media's labile labourers (Morgan & Nelligan, 2017). Yet, their presence alongside other media workers reminds us that career types not only shape individual working lives, but also the range and diversity of media practices. For example, at a time when commercial thinking and entrepreneurialism increasingly dominate media work, it is worth considering how voluntary journalistic labour may have contributed to 'the opening up of the public sphere' (Davidson & Meyers, 2016, p. 208). In this way, as Davidson and Meyers indicate, career pluralism can be seen as a more socially consequential goal than career stability because it potentially supports a more dynamic and interesting media landscape.

Job switching skills

What does it take, then, to switch jobs? Of course, there is no one answer to this deceptively simple question. The point is to consider the possibility before it becomes a reality. In the following case study, a veteran journalist shows how job switching can be made easier by recognizing your strengths and building on your track record:

> Wendy Hargreaves launched an online guide to food/fun/travel, called 'Five of the Best' (see fiveofthebest.com), within days of losing her job at a major metropolitan daily newspaper. It was a calculated risk. As the paper's former Food Editor, she was aware of a gap in local food reporting following her media company's decision at the time to centralize coverage from head office in another city. Added to that, she had good contacts and a loyal audience of 10,000 social media followers from her time on the food round. Creating a new start-up gave Wendy the opportunity to snatch back her audience. Over five years, she has developed the digital magazine into a successful, fully-funded venture with a monthly readership of 60,000. Her portfolio workstyle mixes editorial work with gigs as a media commentator, food reviewer, event host, keynote speaker, freelance writer for Australian Gourmet Traveller's website, and ambassador for Australia's biggest charity kitchen FareShare. It is over 30 years since Wendy started as a cadet journalist on a regional newspaper. She still has a lot to look forward to.

Wendy does not list work as a media career manager in her portfolio, but she should because she has clearly found a productive way to translate a good journalistic idea into sustainable self-employment. In today's fractured media employment landscape, this is a significant achievement.

Multidisciplinary or 'convergent' skills are seen as key resources for all types of media managers working in post-industrial media. These skills are numerous (e.g. project management, leadership for innovation, data analytics, business acumen). Some appear overly complex and time-consuming, as Daniela Bartosova notes: 'managers should be able to create bridges between creative workers, technology software and platforms, and device developers, telecommunications executives, and amateur media players. This requires an understanding [...] of the very different mindsets party to this new emergent style of collaboration' (Bartosova, 2011, p. 198). Yet, there is also straightforward advice: 'The key to managing one's career in the media [...] is not to work alone and to build networks as social support structures rather than opportunities for finding work' (Elefante & Deuze, 2012, p. 20).

Feeling precarious, finding a way forward

Precarity in media work is commonly associated with non-permanent or flexible types of employment, and related practical problems such as fear of job cuts, financial worries or concern about upskilling as technology advances. Less is known about the emotional impact of precariousness, but George Morgan argues it damages younger workers trying to get into the labour market by undermining their capacity to plan for the future or develop a coherent self-identity. He says: 'If the cornerstones of life — place of residence, source of employment and social networks — are completely unstable, there is little chance to speak with any confidence and certainty'(Morgan, 2015, pp. 3-4). The following case study of a working-class young man from Sydney's western suburbs seeking work experience in the local film and television industry illustrates how rejection can silence ambition and hope:

> 'Joe' is 27 years old, unemployed and keen to work as a film or television cameraman, editor or sound and lighting technician. After completing a film and television course at a local technical college, he contacted a number of production houses in search of work experience. Despite his willingness to work for free doing basic 'odd jobs', he got nowhere. 'They're not interested', he said, 'or if they were going to let me in, they'd want me to bring more to the table, I guess, more experience and other contacts, just more to the table.' In other words, to be considered for work experience, he had to deliver something of real value to those he wished to network with (e.g. new contacts or skills). The experience left Joe feeling hopeless and unfairly excluded from his desired occupational community by gate-keepers intent on protecting their own work opportunities (Nelligan, 2015, pp. 23-24).

Loss of individual voice is linked to another aspect of precarity, that is, the loss of collective voice associated with trade unions, professional associations, and other forms of worker advocacy. Before the rise of the gig economy, 40 per cent of Australian workers were trade union members compared to just fifteen per cent of today's workforce.

Into this gap, young entrepreneurs have moved to create online resources to help themselves and others find decent work, and maintain well-being, in challenging times. Impressive Australian examples include Media Diversity Australia, a new not-for-profit venture promoting media jobs for professionals from culturally diverse backgrounds, JobHack, a free online course on how to create your own start-up or freelance job, and Found Careers, a Sydney-based mobile hiring platform known as 'Tinder for jobs', which launched in 2016 and now processes 200,000 jobs per month. Alternatively, ReachOut Australia leads the field in advocacy on youth mental health and hosts an online toolbox of more than 50 well-being apps. Of course, not everyone is in a position to create initiatives of this kind, yet these four examples suggest one productive means of learning to live with work precarity is to find shared solutions to problems that are too often characterized as the personal failings of individuals.

Conclusion

Employment arrangements that create precarious media work and cause worker insecurity are on the rise in Australia, as elsewhere. As we have identified in our research on the careers of laid off journalists in Australia, this can have an impact on everything from professional identity to a sense of well-being. Our main contention is that finding ongoing employment in the field requires an understanding of the current labour market dynamics and a capacity to live with uncertainty. We hope to have offered some timely and detailed discussion of major developments in media work in the post-industrial era, ranging from the commercialization of media work, the repercussions of Facebook and Google's business model, and global media power dynamics, to the changes in the way media work is organized, paid for, and experienced.

The *News Beats Project* findings highlight the growing diversity of professional pathways in media. As well as tracking industry trends, further research might explore in more detail the key themes of flexible employment, media career management, job switching skills, and shared solutions to living with precarity. Research of this kind will contribute to broader understandings of career fluidity, and the impact it has, in turn, on professional identities in the age of precarities.

Further reading

- Case: What it's like to work as an entrepreneur journalist – Brouwers & Witschge (p. 441)
- Context: The technological foundations, labour implications, and social-economic consequences of the Next Internet – Mosco (p. 259)
- Contrast: How being a 'business of one' – always managing and promoting yourself – could be replaced by craftsmanship – Gershon & Deuze (p. 297)

References

Australian Government (2017). 'Job Outlook', *Department of Employment*. Retrieved from https://joboutlook.gov.au/.

Australian Institute of Family Studies (2017). *The Longitudinal Study of Australian Children Annual Statistical Report 2016*. Melbourne: AIFS.

Bartosova, D. (2011). 'The Future of the Media Professions: Current Issues in Media Management Practice', *International Journal on Media Management*, *13*(3), 195-203.

Davidson, R. & Meyers, O. (2016). 'Toward a Typology of Journalism Careers: Conceptualizing Israeli Journalists' Occupational Trajectories', *Communication, Culture & Critique*, *9*(2), 193-211.

Deuze, M. (2007). *Media Work*. Cambridge: Polity Press.

Deuze, M. (2014). 'Work in the Media', *Media Industries Journal*, *1*(2). http://dx.doi.org/10.3998/mij.15031809.0001.201.

Elefante, P.H. & Deuze, M. (2012). 'Media Work, Career Management, and Professional Identity: Living Labour Precarity', *Northern Lights: Film & Media Studies Yearbook*, *10*(1), 9-24.

Foundation for Young Australians (2016). *The New Work Mindset*. Retrieved from http://www.fya.org.au/wp-content/uploads/2016/11/The-New-Work-Mindset.pdf.

Goggin, G., Vromen, A., Weatherall, K., Martin, F., Webb, A., Sunman, L. & Bailo, F. (2017). *Digital Rights Report*. Sydney: University of Sydney.

Healy, J. & Nicholson, D. (2017). 'The Costs of a Casual Job are Now Outweighing any Pay Benefits', *The Conversation* (3 September). Retrieved from https://theconversation.com/the-costs-of-a-casual-job-are-now-outweighing-any-pay-benefits-82207.

Hesmondhalgh, D. (2015). 'Exploitation and Media Labor', in R. Maxwell (ed.). *The Routledge Companion to Labor and Media* (30-39). New York: Routledge.

Kalleberg, A.L. (2009). 'Precarious Work, Insecure Workers: Employment Relations in Transition', *American Sociological Review*, *74*(1), 1-22.

Malmelin, N. & Villi, M. (2017). 'Media Work in Change: Understanding the Role of Media Professionals in Times of Digital Transformation and Convergence', *Sociology Compass*, *11*(7). DOI: 10.1111/soc4.12494.

McCrindle Research (2014). 'Job Mobility in Australia', *The McCrindle Blog* (18 June). Retrieved from http://mccrindle.com.au/.

McCrindle Research (2017). 'Latest Census Data: How Australians Learn, Work & Commute', *The McCrindle Blog* (23 October). Retrieved from http://mccrindle.com.au/.

Minifie, J. & Wiltshire, T. (2016) *Peer to Peer Pressure: Policy for the Sharing Economy*. Melbourne: Grattan Institute.

Morgan, G. (2015). 'Youth and Precarious Work', *Social Alternatives*, *34*(4), 3-4.

Morgan, G., & Nelligan, P. (2017). *The Creativity Hoax. Precarious Work in the Gig Economy*. London: Anthem Press.

Nelligan, P. (2015). 'No Guarantees: Preparing for Long-Term Precarious Employment in the Australian Film and Television Industry', *Social Alternatives*, *34*(4), 22-27.

O'Donnell, P. (2017). 'Beyond Newsrooms: Younger Journalists Talk about Job Loss and Re-employment in Australian Journalism', *Australian Journalism Review*, *39*(2), 157-169.

Perlin, R. (2012). *Intern Nation: How to Earn Nothing and Learn Little in the Brave New Economy*. London: Verso Books.

Sherwood, M. & O'Donnell, P. (2016). 'Once a Journalist, Always a Journalist? Industry Restructure, Job Loss, and Professional Identity', *Journalism Studies*. DOI: 10.1080/1461670X.2016.1249007.

Turner, G. (2015). *Re-inventing the Media*. London: Routledge.

Walters, E., Warren, C. & Dobbie, M. (2006). *The Changing Nature of Work. A Global Survey and Case Study of Atypical Work in the Media Industry*. Geneva: International Federation of Journalists.

Zion, L., Dodd, A., Sherwood, M., O'Donnell, P., Marjoribanks, T. & Ricketson, M. (2016). 'Working for Less: The Aftermath for Journalists Made Redundant in Australia between 2012 and 2014', *Communication Research and Practice*, 2(2), 117-136.

17. Making It in a Freelance World

Nicole S. Cohen

The numbers of self-employed workers in media are growing globally. While digital technologies have made it easier to work as a freelancer, it has become more difficult to earn a decent living. This chapter surveys the range of ways that freelancers in media and cultural sectors are collectively working to protect their rights and improve their conditions.

Introduction

In October 2017, 48 American freelancers who contribute to *Ebony* and *Jet*, a pair of lifestyle magazines for African-American readers, filed a lawsuit against Ebony Media and the private equity group that owns the magazines, claiming that together freelancers were owed US$80,000 in unpaid fees. The group of freelancers included writers, photographers, graphic designers, and videographers who were each owed hundreds or thousands of dollars; money offered in exchange for articles and images but never paid (Channick, 2017). In the months leading up to the lawsuit, freelancers took their complaints to social media, using the Twitter hashtag #EbonyOwes to drum up public support, alerting many to a not-so-secret reality of freelance life: that when companies struggle financially, or when editors forget to file invoices, or when payroll departments are slow to process payments, it is individual freelancers who pay. In the Netherlands, similar action was prompted in 2015 with the Twitter hashtag #tegendebakker, and freelancers worldwide often share experiences of not being paid adequately using #freelance.

Waiting weeks, months, and even years to be paid for articles, photographs, and other pieces of work is a persistent reality for freelance media and cultural workers. 'When you are a freelancer, getting paid for the work you do becomes a second job in and of itself', writes an American freelance journalist. 'You're sending countless emails to dozens of people over weeks, months, and (in some cases…) years just to get paid for the labour you did' (Chamseddine, 2017). Such firsthand accounts from freelancers working in media and cultural industries trouble the notion that freelancing means an easy life of sleeping in, working from home in your pajamas, going for a jog in the middle of the day, and plugging in to work only if and when one wants. While most freelancers do have freedom from the constraints of a nine-to-five life in the sense that they do not go to the same office each day, and many are able to pick and choose the projects they take on, for the vast majority of media freelancers, life is characterized by hustle: long hours, constantly pitching ideas and perpetually seeking future work, producing work as quickly as one can to make low pay per project worth it, juggling multiple projects, chasing late payments, self-promoting, and negotiating what one freelancer calls 'the dual pressure to appear productive and successful while also available for hire' (Cagle, 2014; Vallas & Christin, 2017). As many aspiring and emerging media workers are learning, while digital technologies have made it easier for almost anyone to work as a freelancer, it has become more difficult than ever to earn a decent living.

This chapter discusses freelancers' conditions and surveys the range of ways that individual freelancers in media and cultural sectors are collectively working to call attention to power dynamics and social relations of labour in media and cultural work. As media work becomes increasingly fragmented, technologically mediated, and precarious, freelance media workers are proving that the most effective way to protect their rights is by acting together for change.

The realities of freelance work

While commentators and pundits still embrace the notion that 'everybody's going freelance' (Baer, 2013) and celebrate terms such as 'independent worker', 'micro-entrepreneur', and 'free agent', freelance media workers are drawing attention to the complex and often contradictory material realities of freelance work. Through articles, blog posts, and social media posts, freelancers outline the precarious nature of their employment status and the effects precarity has on their work and lives (for an in-depth review, see Cohen, 2016). Precarious employment is defined as 'work for remuneration characterized by uncertainty, low income, and limited social benefits and statutory entitlements' (Vosko, 2010, p. 2). As self-employed workers, freelancers do not legally have access to unions that could collectively bargain on their behalf (for minimum wage scales, for example) or to protections under labour law, nor can they access social benefits such as healthcare, employment insurance, or parental leave – typically, such access is provided through an employment relationship.

Because freelancers are paid per piece of work they successfully produce – or, in the case of writers, per word published – they generally earn much lower income than employed workers doing similar work (McKercher, 2009) and work long hours. As independent contractors, freelancers do not work for a single company, but rather sell discrete pieces of work to a range of companies: an article, an image, a design, or a website, for example. They negotiate their own fees per project, if they can negotiate at all – only twenty per cent of the 200 freelance writers I have surveyed are able to set their own rates of pay most of the time; generally, fees and rates for work are set by the company (Cohen, 2016, p. 94). This means freelancers themselves are responsible for finding and securing work, never knowing where their next project or pay cheque will come from. For many, the persistent and underlying precarity of self-employment manifests as a sense of anxiety or insecurity about uncertain futures, social isolation, income instability, and a lack of access to mentorship or training, which can inhibit career development (Lewchuk *et al.*, 2014).

Despite such conditions, numbers of self-employed workers globally are growing. In Canada, 2.9 million people are self-employed, with growth each year (Statistics Canada, 2017). In the United States, 15 million people were self-employed in 2015 – 10.1 per cent of the workforce (Hipple & Hammond, 2016). In Europe, 30.6 million were self-employed in 2016, 14 per cent of the workforce (Eurostat, n.d.). These numbers tend to be higher in the media, cultural and creative industries, which are known for project-based work and historical reliance on freelance, contract, and part-time workers (Murdock, 2003).

Although working freelance can be a deliberate choice as well as something one is forced to do due to lack of employment opportunities, a freelance life does not offer everyone equal opportunities. As Melissa Gregg (2008) argues, under neo-liberalism, women in the US are frequently given the 'choice' to work freelance as a way to balance work and family in lieu of states developing social solutions to gendered divisions of social reproductive labour, such as childcare policies. Studies have also found that female media freelancers are paid less than men, per project, but also overall (HoneyBook, 2017). Some people embrace the 'independence, flexibility, self-direction, and agency' that one can potentially access as a freelancer (Perlin, 2012). Others freelance because it is the only form of employment available to them in the industry in which they've trained to work. As a freelance journalist told me, 'After graduating from university and then a college course, I thought I would freelance "until something else came along", but there has been more and more freelance work and fewer other options' (Cohen, 2016, p. 84).

It is impossible, however, to assess people's motivations to work freelance without understanding the broader context that shapes people's abilities to decide what form their employment will take. The confluence of neo-liberal globalization, accelerating speed of production and expansion in digitally networked media industries, volatile markets for advertising and traditional revenue streams in media, unprecedented amounts of content created daily on a global scale, and a desire by media corporations to remain agile and flexible, have resulted in a shrinking core of permanent staff and an expanding periphery of freelancers, part-time workers, interns, and temporary employees globally (Deuze, 2007; Winseck, 2010). Media firms in particular are able to outsource work to freelancers and contractors, as there is a surplus of highly skilled, trained professionals ready to work for often low pay, what Graham Murdock (2003, p. 22) calls the 'reserve army' of cultural labour. Precarious forms of employment such as freelance have obvious benefits for companies, including lower labour costs, no responsibility for training, overhead or benefits, and offloaded risk to a legion of skilled workers hustling to sell their works. Overall, what has historically been a way for media and cultural workers to gain autonomy over their craft and control over their working conditions has become a way for companies to lower the costs of media and cultural production and transfer the risk and insecurity of production onto individual workers.

To counter such pressures, freelance media and cultural workers are increasingly speaking out about their working conditions and experimenting with collective and collaborative methods to address challenges they face. They are presenting ways to make freelance work more equitable and fair. Twitter hashtag campaigns are just one example of how individual freelancers and collective organizations such as unions and professional associations are using a variety of strategies to publicize, organize, and ultimately transform their working conditions.

Collective response

Freelance cultural workers such as actors, directors, and screenwriters have been unionized for decades under a system of voluntary recognition, where employer associations have agreed to collectively bargain for minimum wage scales and other worker protections (Gray & Seeber, 1996). Key to these arrangements is that freelancers for film and television, for example, work collaboratively on set and therefore could, if needed, shut down production by collectively walking off the job (Haiven, 2006). An individual media freelancer, working from home or a coworking space, does not have such leverage. Freelancers work alone, often do not know other freelancers, and, especially those at the beginning of their careers, do not know how much they should be paid for their work.

Freelancers exist in what organizer Joel Dullroy (2013, p. 3) calls 'a grey zone of employment activity, outside the protections of long-established labour regulations' in most Western states. Legally classified as self-employed workers or independent contractors (despite the fact that many are economically dependent on one organization and therefore misclassified as freelancers), freelancers exist 'outside the ambit of labour protection and collective bargaining' and are positioned as entrepreneurs or small business owners who do not require legal protection (Fudge, 2003, pp. 36-37). So, freelancers have had to find creative and experimental ways to address work-related challenges outside official legal regimes, including visibility projects, organized campaigns, and collective organizations.

Visibility projects

Online visibility projects are advocacy campaigns and collective efforts to improve freelancers' conditions. Freelance journalists, for example, have created websites and digital lists to publicize information on how much publications pay. Media outlets never advertise their pay rates publicly, and freelancers often have no idea how much they should be paid for their work. The website *Who Pays Writers?* calls itself 'an anonymous, crowdsourced list of which publications pay freelance writers, and how much'. It launched in 2012 as a Tumblr, born from freelancer Manjula Martin's discussion with friends about why writers don't know how much other writers are paid. Martin realized that secrecy about pay only benefits those who sign the cheques, and *Who Pays Writers?* was born (Cohen, 2016, p. 163).

Other visibility projects offer collective moral support for refusing low-paid gigs. Freelancers use the popular Twitter hashtag #dontworkforfree to publicize and deride postings for unpaid work, to express anger at being repeatedly asked to work for no pay, and to encourage other cultural workers to refuse unpaid work. A US-based freelancer anonymously tweets from the handle @crapwritinggigs, broadcasting snarky jabs at online freelance ads. Other cultural workers have written attention-grabbing blog posts decrying the incessant request to work for free, including journalists, actors, bloggers, and visual artists.

A particularly bold tactic has been to name-and-shame companies and individuals requesting unpaid work. Groups like the Musicians Union and the Canadian Intern Association create 'walls of shame' to publicly (and anonymously) call-out companies and engagers asking professionals to work for free, bringing negative publicity to their business. Many times, the tactic works: the Canadian Intern Association reports a 50 per cent success rate; half the postings on its Wall of Shame end up converted to paid internships (Brophy, Cohen, & de Peuter, 2015).

Visibility projects are cathartic, but they are also examples of counter-publicity, whereby media makers create media texts and appropriate communicative technologies as tools to publicize their labour conditions. Counter-publicity serves to undercut freelancers' sense of individual frustration and isolation and plays a vital role in developing a collective response to labour pressures. Visibility projects are also acts of solidarity that can counter the competitiveness and individualization fostered among freelancers competing for work, a dynamic that often lowers wages.

Organized campaigns

Many individuals fear putting their names on blogs and social media posts or other public complaints about their industry, as most media freelancers rely on their reputation to secure future work. No one wants to be marked as 'difficult to work with' in tight-knit, competitive industries built on reputation and social ties. And so, vital to the improvement of freelancers' working conditions are campaigns organized by collectives, professional associations, and unions, in which freelancers can participate anonymously. Much like counter-publicity, campaigns draw attention to work-related challenges, but they also advocate for specific changes in policy or behaviour, from companies or governments, to improve security and benefits for freelancers.

The Musician's Union, a global organization of working musicians, for instance, runs the Work Not Play campaign to draw attention to the precarious conditions most of its 30,000 members navigate. Most musicians have to work non-music-related jobs to pay their bills, and musicians face intensifying pressure to work for free, from charity gigs to spectacular and well-financed events like the Olympics. The campaign aims to educate people who hire musicians as well as fans about the fact that playing music is work, not just a hobby, and should be paid as such. Similarly, the Writers' Guild of Great Britain (WGGB), which represents writers in TV, film, books, radio, theatre, comedy, animation, and video games, is running its Free is NOT an Option campaign, also to tackle the incessant request that writers work for free. In a membership survey, the WGGB (2015) found that 87 per cent of respondents working in film and TV report an increase in requests to work for no pay. The campaign includes guidelines for freelance writers on what is reasonable to do for no pay, and involves lobbying the government to generate support. The Dutch Association for Journalists and the freelancers' collective De Coöperatie started similar campaigns in 2017. These campaigns are vital for challenging the 'do-what-you-love' mentality often used to convince freelance media and cultural workers that if they truly care (or are 'passionate') about the work they do, then they should not expect payment (Tokumitsu, 2015).

Despite its towering title, the Freelancers' Rights Movement, launched in 2014, was, in effect, a public online campaign aimed at illuminating the growing freelance workforce in Europe (in media work and beyond) and raising awareness about challenges these workers face. The campaign has several demands, expressed emphatically on its website: 'recognise freelancers! give us access! count us! give us a voice! treat us fairly!'. The goal of the campaign was to draw attention to the fact that freelancers and self-employed workers are left out of policy, social security, and government representation in the European Union, and to lobby governments to expand policies and social protections to cover freelancers.

More specific campaigns have targeted companies on particular issues and prove that when acting together, freelancers are able to improve their conditions. Contracts for copyright in particular have spurred initiatives by photographers, visual artists (CARFAC, 2016), and writers. In the digital era, publishers are issuing contracts that demand for escalating rights to freelancers' work in a range of digital formats for a one-time, small, bundled, upfront payment, rather than paying them for each discreet use of their work over time. This is how media companies exploit workers (Cohen, 2016), and individuals often have no leverage when negotiating contracts. Organized campaigns have been a vital way freelancers can resist. In 2013, for example, Canadian freelance journalists were angry about a restrictive copyright contract presented by magazine publishing giant tc Media. The new contract would require freelancers to sign away their moral rights (or, the right to be recognized as the author of an article) and 'grant tc Media full copyright across all of its brands, in all languages, on all platforms, for eternity […] applied to all current and yet to-be invented media forms where writers' works appeared' (Salamon, 2016). The campaign was initiated by L'Association des journalistes indépendants du Québec and was run in coalition with four journalist and writers' associations. The groups used social media to mobilize freelancers and concerned Canadians, using the hashtag #nesignezpas (don't sign) to publicize the bad contract. The pressure worked: tc Media amended the contract, demonstrating that online tools can be used in conjunction with organization to mobilize a disparate group (Salamon, 2016).

Collective organizations

Many campaigns are successful because they have been organized and run by collective organizations representing freelancers. Although freelance media and cultural workers are often assumed to be 'lone wolves' and highly individualistic, freelance media and cultural workers of all stripes have long histories of forming and joining collective organizations, from professional associations to more labour-oriented organizations such as guilds. Freelancers join groups for many reasons: to access health benefits, to temper endemic isolation, to develop skills and receive training, to meet others, and to find work. Many organizations will track down engagers that do not pay (a form of wage theft) and can advise on worrisome contracts and pay rates. While most freelancer organizations are unable to collectively bargain, which would go the furthest to standardize and make equitable fees, contracts, and working conditions, they are experimenting with a range of ways to represent freelancers.

The Brooklyn-based Freelancers Union has been the most visible in advocating for freelancers. The union began as a way to provide American freelancers with health insurance in the form of affordable group benefits, offering members advice, supports, and services, such as a tool for generating a contract, forums for freelancers to connect, corporate discounts, health clinics, and yoga classes. The Freelancers Union has lobbied policymakers for laws to better protect freelancers in New York State, including getting tax reform passed so that those who earn under

US$100,000 do not have to pay business and personal revenue tax (Abrahamian, 2012). The organization led the passage of the 2017 *Freelance Isn't Free Act* in the City of New York, which now requires engagers to provide signed contracts to all freelancers and specify deadlines for payment. The bill ensures that the Department of Consumer Affairs can now enforce the provision and use of contracts and can penalize companies that break the rules with fines or jail – guarantees that have until now only been available to employees.

The National Writers Union (NWU), which supported *Ebony* freelancers with their lawsuit, is a local of the United Autoworkers Union, and is rooted in a tradition of solidarity with the labour movement. The union has negotiated contracts with several media outlets to protect freelance journalists' rights, provides grievance services, and contract advice, and has led lawsuits against the *New York Times* to defend freelancers' copyrights to electronic rights and against Google over Google Books. The NWU offers group benefits, engages in advocacy, and has won some important victories for its members.

Less formally, groups like the Internet Creators Guild are developing tools for advocating on behalf of 'online creators', mostly those who create content for YouTube, including basic information sharing and guidance on how to get paid for online work. Models, visual artists, and graphic designers have established organizations with similar goals.

Canada has long history of active professional associations that represent media and cultural freelancers, including poets, editors, playwrights, and journalists, but over the past decade more union-oriented organizations have emerged to better protect freelancers by fostering a worker-based – rather than an entrepreneurial or professional-based – identity. The Canadian Freelance Union, founded in 2009, is local of Unifor, Canada's largest private sector union. It recently launched its first-ever freelance organizing drive and is gaining momentum among young freelance media workers. The Canadian Media Guild launched a Freelance Branch and its parent union, the Communication Workers of America-Canada, runs an Associate Member's Program, which offers training in skills and labour rights to emerging media workers, freelancers, and interns – membership totals 1,000 across the country (membership is free). While relatively new experiments, these collective efforts hold great promise in enabling freelancers to access benefits, share information, receive legal counsel, and fight bad contracts.

In Europe, the European Freelancers Movement is connected to organizations that represent freelancers in eleven countries, including France, Germany, Italy, Belgium, Croatia, the Netherlands, Poland, Romania, Spain, and the United Kingdom, linked under the banner of the European Forum of Independent Professionals, a not-for-profit organization (founded in 2010) that does research and engages in advocacy in at the European Union level. Other emergent experiments include cooperative cultural collectives and web-based organizations that produce and help freelancers sell their works for fair pay.

Supporting freelance work

The collective initiatives outlined in this chapter are just some examples of how freelance media and cultural workers are coming together to develop infrastructures to support independent work. Because freelancers generally have no single employer to which they can direct demands for better payment or improved treatment, they are organizing to combine resources to support each other. The most concrete of these efforts, collective organizations, are places freelancers can access services they lack, including health insurance and benefits. In fact, gaining access to services such as health benefits has been a main driver of the development of freelance organizations. Most freelance professional associations are attractive to freelancers because of access to group benefits. In this way, many organizations are effectively service organizations, offering freelancers services in exchange for fees. This can be limiting, as a more solidaristic identity and politicized understanding of the labour politics of freelance work is needed among freelancers to achieve more lasting change to many of the challenges freelancers face (see Cohen, 2016).

Some organizations go beyond a service mentality: the Netherlands' Broodfonds (bread fund) consists of small groups of people who pay into a 'mutual sickness fund […] based on how much they would like to receive if they fall ill' (Dullroy, 2015; see broodfonds.nl). In 2017, the Broodfonds had 13,266 participants organized into 304 small groups to reinforce a sense of community, and payments are referred to as 'gifts'. This is an example of a bottom-up safety net vital to surviving in a freelance world.

What freelancers' groups and campaigns have made clear is that the legal and policy regimes underpinning labour law in most Western states needs to be transformed in an era of precarious employment, where growing numbers of people work outside of regulated employment relationships, including workers in media and cultural industries. Leah Vosko (2010) has argued that the new world of work needs to adopt a 'beyond employment' model of social protection that would provide every person, 'regardless of their labour force status', with labour and social protections 'from birth to death, in periods of training, employment, self-employment, and work outside the labour force, including voluntary work and unpaid caregiving' (*Ibid.*, p. 219). Such a broad vision makes clear the big-picture thinking needed to improve the working lives of freelance media and cultural workers, and meaningfully goes beyond arguments that individuals must simply be better entrepreneurs and hustlers.

Conclusion

Organizing freelancers collectively is challenging. Most are contracted under highly individual terms, work in physical isolation from one another, and generally have different mindsets about how to address work-related challenges. Yet, collective organizing is vital. Increased competition globally pushes wages down and draws individuals into highly exploitative working relationships. Companies have much greater power than individual freelancers and are able to impose unfair contracts without much pushback. Faced with a complex, opaque contracts for assignments, most freelancers would prefer just to sign than ask questions and risk losing work. Low wages, a lack of security, and extended periods of unpaid work mean that freelancing as a form of employment is unaffordable to many, especially those who do not have a financially supportive spouse or family. If freelancing is the only entry point to many media and cultural sectors, labour dynamics limit who is able to work in media and culture, creating divisions based on gender, race, and class, and risking the creation of homogenous media content.

Overall, it is vital to ask who benefits from a growth in freelance work. Freelancing has a contradictory nature: it can be simultaneously risky and rewarding, precarious and satisfying. For companies, relinquishing immediate control over employees – transforming full-time work into self-employment, freelance, casual, or temporary work – can be both profitable as well as increase logistical and managerial complexity. A more fundamental critique would point to the exploitative potential freelance labour has for capital to increase the extraction of surplus value from workers. Deepening precarity is experienced as highly individualized, and so freelancers are told that solutions are individual, too: work harder, take on more clients, or sleep less. But as the growing number of collective organizations, campaigns, and visibility projects show, the best way to make it in a freelance world is together, not alone.

Further reading

- Case: The working conditions and labour requirements for 'making it' as a freelance online content creator – Duffy (p. 375)
- Context: Three important developments regarding media work and the skills needed to find employment in the dynamic field of media – O'Donnell & Zion (p. 223)
- Contrast: How social inequalities in media work arise and what might be done to tackle them – Eikhof & Marsden (p. 247)

References

Abrahamian, A.A. (2012). 'The 'I' in Union', *Dissent*. Retrieved from http://www.dissent-magazine.org/article/the-i-in-union.

Baer, D. (2013). 'Why Everybody's Going Freelance', *Fast Company* (12 September). Retrieved from http://www.fastcompany.com/3017222/leadership-ow/whyeverybodys-going-freelance.

Brophy, E., Cohen, N.S. & De Peuter, G. (2015). 'Labour Messaging: Practices of Autonomous Communication', in R. Maxwell (ed.), *The Routledge Companion to Media and Labour* (315-326). London: Routledge.

Cagle, S. (2014). 'Eight Years of Solitude: On Freelance Labour, Journalism, and Survival', *Medium* (15 March). Retrieved from https://medium.com/@susie_c/eight-years-of-solitude-110ee3276edf.

Channick, R. (2017). 'Freelancers Sue Ebony Magazine, Claiming $70,000 in Unpaid Work', *Chicago Tribune* (6 September). Retrieved from http://www.chicagotribune.com/business/ct-ebony-freelance-lawsuit-0907-biz-20170906-story.html.

CARFAC [Canadian Artists Representation] (2016). *CARFAC'S UN WIPO Intervention* (29 November). Retrieved from http://www.carfac.ca/news/2016/11/29/carfacs-un-wipo-intervention/.

Chamseddine, R. (2017). 'Pay Your Goddam Writers', *Southlawn* (10 November). Retrieved from https://thesouthlawn.org/2017/11/10/pay-your-goddamn-writers/.

Cohen, N.S. (2016). *Writers' Rights: Freelance Journalists in a Digital Age*. Montreal and Kingston: McGill-Queen's University Press.

Deuze, M. (2007). *Media Work*. Cambridge, UK: Polity.

Dullroy, J. (2013). 'Introducing the Freelancers' Rights Movement', in J. Dullroy & A. Cashman, *Independents Unite! Inside the Freelancers' Rights Movement* (1-6). Berlin: Freelancers Movement.

Dullroy, J. (2015). 'Freelancers Unite to Get Sickness and Other Employment Benefits'', *The Guardian* (14 January). Retrieved from http://www.theguardian.com/money/2015/jan/14/freelance-payment-sickness-leave.

Eurostat (n.d.). *Taking a Look at Self-Employed in the EU*. Retrieved from http://ec.europa.eu/eurostat/web/products-eurostat-news/-/DDN-20170906-1.

Fudge, J. (2003). 'Labour Protection for Self-employed Workers', *Just Labour, 3*(Fall), 36-45.

Gray, L.S. & Seeber, R.L. (1996). *Under the Stars: Essays on Labour Relations in Arts and Entertainment*. Ithaca, NY: ILR Press.

Gregg, M. (2008). 'The Normalization of Flexible Female Labour in the Information Economy', *Feminist Media Studies, 8*(3), 285-99.

Haiven, L. (2006). 'Expanding the Union Zone: Union Renewal through Alternative Worker Organizations', *Labour Studies Journal, 31*(3), 85-116.

Hipple, S.F. & Hammond, L.A. (2016). *Self-Employment in the United States*. Retrieved from https://www.bls.gov/spotlight/2016/self-employment-in-the-united-states/home.htm.

HoneyBook (2017). *2017 Gender Pay Gap: Creative Economy Report* (11 October). Retrieved from https://www.honeybook.com/gender-pay-gap.

Lewchuk, W. *et al.* (2014).'"Is Precarious Employment Low Income Employment?" The Changing Labour Market in Southern Ontario', *Just Labour, 22*, 51-73. Retrieved from http://www.justlabour.yorku.ca/volume22/pdfs/05_lewchuk_et_al_press.pdf.

McKercher, C. (2009). 'Writing on the Margins: Precarity and the Freelance Journalist', *Feminist Media Studies, 9*(3), 370-374.

Murdock, G. (2003). 'Back to Work: Cultural Labour in Altered Times', in A. Beck (ed.), *Cultural Work* (15-36). London: Routledge.

Perlin, R. (2012). 'The Graduate with a Precarious Future', *New Left Project* (22 March). Retrieved from http://www.newleftproject.org/index.php/site/article_comments/the_graduate_with_a_precarious_future.

Ross, A. (2013). 'In Search of the Lost Paycheck', in T. Scholz (ed.), *Digital Labour: The Internet as Playground and Factory* (13-32). New York: Routledge.

Salamon, E. (2016). 'E-Lancer Resistance', *Digital Journalism, 4*(8), 980-1000.

Statistics Canada (2017). *Self-Employment, Historical Summary* (6 January). Retrieved from http://www.statcan.gc.ca/tables-tableaux/sum-som/l01/cst01/labour64-eng.htm.

Tokumitsu, M. (2015). *Do What You Love: And Other Lies About Success and Happiness*. New York: Regan Arts.

Vallas, S. & Christin, A. (2017). 'Work and Identity in an Era of Precarious Employment: How Workers Respond to "Personal Branding" Discourse', *Work and Occupations*. https://doi.org/10.1177/0730888417735662.

Vosko, L.F. (2010). *Managing the Margins: Gender, Citizenship, and the International Regulation of Precarious Employment*. New York: Oxford University Press.

Winseck, D. (2010). 'Financialization and the "Crisis of the Media": The Rise and Fall of (Some) Media Conglomerates in Canada', *Canadian Journal of Communication, 35*(3), 365-393.

WGGB [Writers' Guild of Great Britain] (2015). *Free is NOT An Option* (3 March). Retrieved from https://writersguild.org.uk/wggb_campaigns/free-is-not-an-option/.

18. Diversity and Opportunity in the Media Industries

Doris Ruth Eikhof and Stevie Marsden

The creative media industries are incredibly influential in shaping twenty-first-century lives, but their workforce fails to reflect the diversity of societies overall. Using the creative media industries in the United Kingdom as an example, this chapter examines the ambiguous reality behind the glossy, attractive image of media work. It discusses how social inequalities in media work arise and what might be done to tackle them.

Introduction

In the second half of 2017, work and careers in the creative media industries attracted a lot of media attention. The revelations about Harvey Weinstein's misconduct towards women workers initiated a broader discussion about sexual harassment and misogynist industry culture (e.g. Dean, 2017). In the UK, the lack of workforce diversity also continues to attract general attention, with film and TV celebrities like Idris Elba, David Oyelowo, and Julie Walters speaking out about the under-representation of women, disabled workers, and workers from ethnic minority and working-class backgrounds. Cracks have started to appear in the image of media work as desirable or glamorous. This image had, for two decades, dominated on screen – think *Sex and the City*, *Bridget Jones' Diaries* – as well as in policy documents heralding the media industries as employing a 'creative class' of diverse workers and driving economic prosperity for all (Florida, 2004).

Researchers of work and employment in the creative media industries have studied the ambiguous reality behind the glossy, attractive image of media work for a while. This chapter brings together key arguments and evidence from that research to discuss media work, diversity, and opportunity. In doing so, this chapter mainly draws on evidence from the UK's creative media industries. This selection is deliberate. The UK has been a policy leader in promoting the creative industries and has thus attracted early attention of critical scholars of media work as well. Its creative media industries, i.e. TV, film, radio, interactive media, animation, computer games, facilities, photo imaging, and publishing, employ up to 80 per cent of workers in the creative industries as defined by the UK government (DCMS,

2001; Creative Skillset, 2010), generate two thirds of the creative industries' revenue, and often feature as 'target' industries for policymakers.

The creative media industries are incredibly influential in twenty-first-century lives: they shape what we see and talk about, what we regard as important, how we perceive ourselves and others, and the conversations we want to contribute to, face-to-face or on social media. Yet, a look at employment statistics quickly shows that the creative media workforce is anything but representative of the UK's society: in 2012, 36 per cent of the creative media industries workforce were women, 5.4 per cent were from ethnic minority backgrounds (Creative Skillset, 2012, p. 4), and 18 per cent came from working-class backgrounds – as opposed to a national average of 34.7 per cent of those aged 23-69 (O'Brien *et al.*, 2016, p. 123). And while the mean annual gross income of creative media workers is comparatively high (£33,900 compared to UK average of £27,271), women earn less than men (£32,400 p.a. vs £33,900 p.a.), and ethnic minorities earn less than their white colleagues (£32,950 p.a. vs £33,900 p.a.). Previous analysis of Creative Skillset data showed that pay gaps by gender and ethnicity remain when age and occupation are controlled for (Creative Skillset, 2005), indicating the existence of gendered and racial pay discrimination. Also, average annual earnings were substantially lower for disabled workers (£25,450) and higher for workers who had attended private schools, i.e. came from privileged social backgrounds (£39,850). These trends are similar worldwide, as evidenced, for example, by studies on women in the media by the European Institute for Gender Equality (EIGE, 2013), the Inclusion Initiative at the University of Southern California (USC Annenberg, 2017), the International Women's Media Foundation, the 2015 Global Media Monitoring Project report (Macharia, 2015), and the Global Gender Gap Report by the World Economic Forum (WEF, 2017).

The statistics strongly suggest that both opportunities to work in the creative media industries and the compensation earned from media work are unequally allocated and that there are barriers to 'getting in and getting on' for certain groups of workers (Randle & Culkin, 2009). To better understand how social inequalities in media work arise and what might be done to tackle them, we need to understand the individual experience of media work as well as the industry context in which that individual work takes place. This chapter explores both in turn.

Charlotte's story

To understand individual experiences of media work, we turn to the story of Charlotte York, a British broadcaster and writer, who we interviewed for a previous project and who, under a pseudonym, talked candidly about her career (read York's full account in Eikhof & York (2016), the source of all verbatim quotes in this section).

We have chosen York's story because it demonstrates how individual careers in media are shaped by a complex interplay of work and employment circumstances. While her account is, to some degree, women-specific, it also echoes accounts of media workers from other under-represented groups (e.g. Grugulis & Stoyanova, 2012; Randle *et al.*, 2015; Randle & Hardy, 2016; Thanki & Jefferys, 2006-2007).

Charlotte York had always wanted to work in TV. Coming from a family without any connections to media or broadcasting, it took a bit of luck to get in. But once she had landed a job as a researcher on a quiz show, she soon moved on, and worked as a presenter in children's TV and then current affairs with big broadcasters. At the height of her TV career, York was the youngest presenter on the flagship current affairs show of one of the UK's biggest broadcasters. Right from the start, York noticed the gendered aspects of TV careers:

> It was obvious that almost no women at producer level had children. That struck me as extremely curious and also really troubling. [...] And despite the department being full of brilliant women at producer level, the one male in the department was the boss – a pattern repeated in many of the departments in which I would work. [...] By the time I had moved into presenting for the big current affairs shows on national TV, anyone who wanted a family dropped out of production and few ever came back (Eikhof & York, 2016, p. 156).

York worked hard at establishing her career, from one project to another: 'Once I was in the system and making contacts, it was much easier to get re-hired on other jobs through word of mouth, or to follow a producer to their next job' (*Ibid.*, p.4).

She soon learned that 'you need to be more than just great at your job and a "good" person – you need to be more focused [and] better networked' (*Ibid.*, p. 7). York quickly realized that the decision makers were often 'people with better political or survival skills than programme-making skills' (*Ibid.*, p. 10) from a white, male and middle-class background and that women in particular were faced with a 'very obvious glass ceiling' (*Ibid.*). To quell the 'typical freelance neurosis that the job offers would dry up' (*Ibid.*), York supplemented her broadcasting work with writing for national newspapers and magazines, and eventually published popular history books. Helpfully, the books established her as an expert rather than a 'show-and-tell presenter' who, as one (female) commissioner told York, was '"too young and pretty to have any authority as an expert"' (*Ibid.*, p. 7). Such sexism, York recalls, was casual and frequent, as was 'men try[ing] it on' (*Ibid.*, p. 156).

Working in TV was thrilling but 'working hours were long [...] working 51 days, having one day off then working 49 days. And these were flat-out – working 18 hour days then jumping on a plane to get the red-eye flight back to the UK so I could edit a story for that evening's transmission. Yes, it was exciting, but it was also knackering. And it was hard enough to maintain a partner let alone a family' (*Ibid.*, p. 157). When York finally fell pregnant, she didn't tell anyone: 'I lined my handbag with a sick-bag so I could vomit as discretely as possible. The film crew just assumed I had bulimia so I got away with it for months. [...] I was terrified that it would be the end of my career' (*Ibid.*).

Determined to combine career and caring, she took her toddler, baby, and a travelling nanny with her for a year-long overseas shoot in New Zealand. 'I'd be doing a 13 hour day, coming home to take over the childcare, cook supper, feed and then settle a toddler and a baby. [...] On my one 'day off' a week, I was doing full-on single parenting, trying to give my children a nice, 'normal' experience of a day-out' (*Ibid.*). It was important to her to maintain her identity as a TV presenter and that her – eventually four – boys saw her being successful beyond her domestic role. 'But', York acknowledges, 'the reality [...] is that you have to compromise every step of the way once you have a family.' (*Ibid.*, p. 9).

In her mid-40s, York encountered another, again clearly gendered, obstacle to working in the media: ageism. She saw almost all her female presenter friends leave the industry and a very famous woman broadcaster warned her '"You fall off a cliff once you hit 50"' (*Ibid.*, p. 158). Looking back on her career, York says she has had 'mind-blowing opportunities' and, mostly, does not regret choosing media as her career. However:

> [...] when I hear young women saying how they want to get into the media, I always tell them, "Don't!" – choose a job that is in the creative industries but one that offers more of a career structure that gives you a longer working life. I love working in the media, that is, actually making TV and radio programmes. It's the best job in the world. But I don't love all the guff that goes along with that industry, and I hate what it's done to many of the brilliant and talented women I know (*Ibid.*, p. 159).

It is, though, 'a tough drug to kick', says York: 'My female colleagues and I were talking about it only a few days ago – it makes us so angry but we can't give up' (*Ibid.*).

The industry context of media work

Charlotte York's account gives rich insight into the conflicting experience of working in the media. As we argued in the beginning, this individual experience needs to be understood in the broader industry context in which it is situated. Two closely entwined aspects are relevant in this regard: the creative media industries' model of production and its industry culture.

Production in the creative media industries revolves around projects that bring together teams to produce a specific output. Once that output is achieved – a film has been shot, for instance, or a reality TV show produced over a pre-set number of weeks – the teams disband. From a business point of view, project-based production can be advantageous: it reduces costly commitments, for instance to permanently employed staff or production premises, which, in the face of unpredictable product markers, makes production less risky (Caves, 2000; Hesmondhalgh, 2013). Importantly for media workers, project-based production translates into work and employment conditions typically characterized by the following:

– *High employment insecurity.* A large share of employment contracts in the creative media industries are temporary and only last for the duration of the project, and 24 per cent of the creative industries workforce in the UK are freelancers (Creative Skillset, 2012, p. 5). Employment on projects alternates with long periods spent looking for work (Euston & Caldwell-French, 2017; Eikhof & Warhust, 2013). While a few superstars can rely on a continuous stream of high wages, for the majority of media workers project-based employment means income insecurity and having to bear the costs and risks of insurance, social security, sick pay, maternity leave, etc. (Gill, 2002).

– *Low/unpaid entry-level jobs.* Because projects are only temporary, there is little incentive for employers to train workers, for instance through apprenticeships. Instead, industry entrants work as runners and assistants and acquire the necessary skills and capabilities through 'learning by watching' (DeFillippi & Arthur, 1998, p. 132). Positions in which workers learn on the job are poorly paid, or even undertaken as unpaid internships, rewarded only by 'copy and credit' (BECTU, 2009; Randle & Culkin, 2009). Although many industry entrants are graduates, starting salaries tend to be much lower than the average graduate entry salary (Eikhof & Warhurst, 2013). Entry-level workers effectively pay for their own training through forfeited earnings.

– *Recruitment through networks.* Tight production and project schedules make recruitment mistakes costly – producers cannot afford to replace team members who turn out to be not right for the job (Caves, 2000). To reduce the risk of hiring the wrong person, recruiters often rely on their own networks of contacts and previous collaborators, or on recommendations from trusted colleagues. A Creative Skillset (2010) survey found that more than three quarters of participants had been recruited into their current job informally, i.e. they had been contacted directly by their employer or by someone with whom they had previously worked.

– *Long and unsocial working hours.* Long working days and working unsocial hours, including evenings and weekends is the norm rather than the exception in the creative media industries. In 2014, the UK's creative media workers

worked on average 9.1 hours per day and 44.6 hours per week, with even higher weekly totals in specific industries, e.g. 52.6 hours/week in cable & satellite TV (Creative Skillset, 2014, p. 17).
– *Working away from home.* Media work is often geographically dispersed – on location for a shoot or at a client's office, for instance – and requires frequent and long travel. In combination with long working days, this geographical dispersion means that workers have to work away from home a lot (Euston & Caldwell-French, 2017).

These characteristics of work and employment make participation and advancement in media work less likely for some groups of workers than for others. Widespread employment insecurity and low or no wages at entry level make maintaining a career in media significantly more difficult for workers from socio-economically disadvantaged backgrounds and those who have to provide for dependants. Media workers who cannot draw on familial capital or the support of spouses to buffer periods of unemployment have to branch out, like Charlotte York did, into other work, typically teaching or hospitality. But while working outside media may pay the rent, it also takes away time from establishing one's career in the media (Randle *et al.*, 2007).

The importance of personal networks for getting jobs and maintaining one's professional profile also poses substantial challenges. Individuals from working-class and ethnic minority backgrounds are much less likely to have access to the proverbial 'old boys networks' that build on connections made at university or through parents' networks (Grugulis & Stoyanova, 2012; Thanki & Jefferys, 2006-2007). Networking typically takes place outside the office, after work, and often in bars or restaurants, which excludes individuals who are physically unable to access such spaces, whose religion prevents them from frequenting venues that sell alcohol or whose caring responsibilities restrict their after-hours availability (Randle & Hardy, 2016). For women, the semi-private setting of networking raises further issues, as in such contexts they tend to be judged as females rather than professionals (Gill, 2002).

Finally, long and unsocial working hours, and the need for media workers to be geographically mobile make establishing and maintaining a career in media particularly challenging for workers with caring responsibilities, with limited economic resource or with physical disabilities. As women are still more likely to be primary carers than men, the need to be temporally and geographically flexible is particularly problematic for female workers, for most of whom Charlotte York's solution of a travelling nanny is not an option. In a 2007 study, female interviewees stated that particularly the mobility and flexibility requirements of media work meant having a successful career required them to put their personal lives on hold (Creative Skillset, 2009; see also, O'Brien, 2014). These flexibility requirements have a financial dimension as well: having to meet expenses for extra childcare, travel to locations and accommodation is disproportionately more difficult for media workers from disadvantaged backgrounds and those who need to provide for others (Euston & Caldwell-French, 2017). Disabled workers face both practical and financial obstacles to meeting the mobility demands of media work and often find themselves quite literally barred from 'getting in and getting on' (Randle & Hardy, 2016).

The impacts of the creative media industries' work and employment conditions on workforce diversity and opportunity are well evidenced. Far less academic research exists that explores the media's industry culture and how it influences perceptions of what talent and skill look like. But while evidence may be limited in scope and breadth, some clear themes are emerging. Firstly, women – in particular in front of the camera, but also generally – are expected to conform to beauty ideals of youthfulness and sexiness. On-screen work gets substantively more difficult to obtain as women enter their 40s and 50s (Eikhof & York, 2016) and women were found to engage in 'beauty work' to maintain their appearances, and thus their careers (Spedale & Coupland, 2014). Secondly, ideas of performance and presence feature strongly in the creative media industries, described by a news reporter as 'the "got to be there, got to do it"-atmosphere in the newsroom' (House of Lords Select Committee, 2015). Thirdly, sexual harassment and assault appear to be widespread. Again, systematic and large-scale evidence on this issue is outstanding, but emerging studies and anecdotal evidence published in general media point to a widespread and structural problem (e.g. Hennekam & Bennett, 2017). Fourthly, as with the cultural industries generally, the creative media industries' perception of talent appears to centre on 'Euro-centric, male, white and middle-class standards of [...] talent and creativity' (Eikhof, 2017, p. 301). Female, non-white, disabled, or working-class workers are still perceived as a deviation from that informal, but powerful blueprint of what a creative media worker does or should look like.

Both work and employment conditions, on the one hand, and industry culture, on the other, thus result in obstacles to workforce participation and advancement that certain groups of workers find disproportionately more difficult to overcome. Moreover, many workers, of course, face more than one such obstacle, as illustrated in our example of Charlotte York, whose media career was challenged by caring responsibilities, sexist and ageist perceptions of talent, and limited finances for buffering unemployment. Systematic research into the impact of such intersectionalities is only just beginning to emerge (CAMEo, 2018). What is clear though is that work and employment conditions on the hand and industry culture on the other combine into a complex web of obstacles as a result of which opportunities to get in and on in media work are unequally distributed in favour of white, male, middle-class, and able-bodied workers.

Increasing workforce diversity in the creative media industries

Workforce diversity in the creative media industries has become recognized as an issue to be addressed. In line with UK cultural industries more broadly, media industry organizations such as the British Film Institute, Women in Film and Television, Creative Skillset, or the union BECTU have called for initiatives that make media work more accessible to a broader range of workers. Typical interventions to improve workforce diversity have included mentoring programmes or training programmes specifically for women, working-class or ethnic minority workers (e.g. CAMEo, 2018; Maxwell, 2013).

Underlying such initiatives is an approach seeking to 'make good' the 'deficiencies' of individual workers – their lack of social or economic capital, industry knowledge or skills, most commonly. Such 'enabling initiatives' (CAMEo, 2018), however, are unlikely to bring about significant and immediate change because they work within the current system and reinforce rather than challenge it. Providing better access to networks for workers who do not command enough social capital themselves may be helpful for the individual worker but does not lower the barriers for other non-networked individuals. Similarly, providing bursaries for trainees who cannot afford to work for free or for low wages helps on a case-by-case basis but does not challenge the assumption that industry entrants should be able to provide for themselves while learning on the job.

What is required to really improve workforce diversity in the creative media industries and to challenge existing inequalities in media work are changes to industry practices and perceptions (Banks, 2017; Eikhof & Warhurst, 2013). Recognition of this need for systemic change is slowly starting to emerge and to be translated into practice, both in the UK and internationally. Critics might argue that increasing workforce diversity should be pursued out of conviction rather than to achieve monetary aims. However, experience from other sectors suggests that such incentives can help mainstream better practice and implement a sense of institutional or organizational responsibility and accountability. That sense of responsibility and accountability on the part of someone other than the individual in question is an important aspect of facilitating change, and one that the more traditional, enabling initiatives fail to incorporate. Economic indicators worldwide additionally show a strong correlation between a country's gender gap and its economic performance.

Another approach to facilitating systematic change is to focus on crucial decision makers – those in powerful positions who decide on individuals' opportunities to participate and advance in media work (Eikhof, 2017). Currently, these decision-makers disproportionately allocate opportunity to white, middle-class, and able-bodied males. That is partly so because decision-makers appear to appoint in their own image (Eikhof, 2017; Wreyford, 2015): women producers, for instance, are substantially more likely to work with female directors and scriptwriters than their male counterparts. Perceptions of individuals from certain groups also play a role. In film commissioning, for instance, women producers are perceived as a 'riskier investment' than their male counterparts (European Women's Audiovisual Network, 2016), not least because they are seen as more likely to have their work compromised by caring commitments (Creative Skillset, 2009). Ethnic minority actors are perceived through the lens of ethnicity-related role types (the Islamic terrorist, the Hispanic maid) rather than individual talent (Saha, 2012).

Overall though, how the decisions are made that allocate opportunity for workforce participation and advancement in media work is still poorly understood. More research is needed to disentangle the different influences such as unconscious bias from industry-specific constructions of talent and – real or imagined – business pressures that constrain unconventional or riskier recruitment choices. Promising industry initiatives focused on decision makers are beginning to emerge, e.g. by Canada-based campaigners Women in View, but more empirical insight is needed to make industry action more effective and widespread.

Conclusion

The lack of workforce diversity in the creative media industries has become increasingly well documented. Workforce statistics evidence the disproportionately low participation and pay for women, disabled workers, and workers from ethnic minority backgrounds, and better data on socio-economic background is also emerging. Encouragingly, there is now increasing recognition both in the industries and in the general public that this lack of diversity in media work is problematic, for a whole range of reasons, and needs to be addressed.

Workers' stories such as that of Charlotte York powerfully illustrate both the commitment and motivations individuals bring to the industry, and the obstacles they face in realising their ambitions and contributing to the industry. Such accounts are personally touching and an understandable reaction is to try to help the individual workers in question and improve their opportunities and experiences in the media industries. But however well-intended such support might be, supporting individual workers ultimately supports a system that is deeply flawed in the way it allocates opportunity. What is needed is systematic change, brought about through political campaigning and cross-industry alliances, and supplemented by solid empirical insight and evidence. Promising signs are emerging, but the media industries have a long way to go yet.

Further reading

- Case: How gender and class divisions play a role in social media work – Duffy (p. 375)
- Context: Three important developments regarding media work and the skills needed to find employment in the dynamic field of media – O'Donnell & Zion (p. 223)
- Contrast: How freelancers in the media industry are collectively working to protect their rights and improve their position – Cohen (p. 235)

References

Banks, M. (2017). *Creative Justice: Cultural Industries, Work and Inequality.* London: Rowman & Littlefield.

BECTU (2009). 'Expenses-Only Engagements are Illegal, Say Employment Tribunals', Retrieved from https://www.bectu.org.uk/news/548.

CAMEo (2018). *Workforce Diversity in the UK Screen Sector. Evidence Review.* Leicester: CAMEo Research Institute.

Caves, R.E. (2000). *Creative Industries.* Cambridge, MA: Harvard University Press.

Creative Skillset (2005). *Survey of the Audio Visual Industries' Workforce 2005.* London: Creative Skillset.

Creative Skillset (2008). *Feature Film Production: Workforce Survey Report 2008.* London: Creative Skillset.

Creative Skillset (2009). *Why Her? Factors that Have Influenced the Careers of Successful Women in Film and Television.* London: Creative Skillset.

Creative Skillset (2010). *2010 Creative Media Workforce Survey.* London: Creative Skillset.

Creative Skillset (2012). *Employment Census of the Creative Media Industries.* London: Creative Skillset.

Creative Skillset (2014).*The Creative Media Workforce Survey 2014: Summary Report.* London: Creative Skillset.

Dean, D. (2017). 'Harvey Weinstein: Showbusiness Voices Signal the Sad Ubiquity of Sexual Abuse in Industry', *The Conversation.* Retrieved from https://theconversation.com/harvey-weinstein-showbusiness-voices-signal-the-sad-ubiquity-of-sexual-abuse-in-industry-85693.

DeFillippi, R.J. & Arthur, M.D. (1998). 'Paradox in Project-Based Enterprise: The Case of Film Making', *California Management Review, 40*(2), 125-139.

Department for Culture, Media and Sport (DCMS) (2001). *Creative Industries Mapping Document.* London: DCMS.

Eikhof, D.R. (2017). 'Analysing Decisions on Diversity and Opportunity in the Cultural and Creative Industries: A New Framework', *Organization, 24*(3), 289-307.

Eikhof, D.R. & York, C. (2016). '"It's a Tough Drug to Kick": A Woman's Career in Broadcasting', *Work, Employment & Society, 30*(1), 152-161.

Eikhof, D.R. & Warhurst, C. (2013). 'The Promised Land? Why Social Inequalities are Systemic in the Creative Industries', *Employee Relations*, 35(5), 495-508.

European Institute for Gender Equality (2017). *Review of the implementation of the Beiling Platform for Action in the EU Member States: Women and the Media – Advancing Gender Equality in Decision-making in Media Organisations*. Retrieved from file:///Z:/Downloads/MH3113742ENC-Women-and-Media-Report-EIGE.pdf.

European Women's Audiovisual Network (2016). *Where are the Women Directors? Report on Gender Equality for Directors in the European Film Industry, 2006-2013*. Retrieved from http://www.ewawomen.com/uploads/files/MERGED_Press-2016.pdf.

Euston, E. & Caldwell-French, E. (2017). *Creative Freelancers*. London: Creative Industries Federation.

Florida, R. (2004).*The Rise of the Creative Class*. New York: Basic Books.

Gill, R. (2002). 'Cool, Creative and Egalitarian? Exploring Gender in Project-Based New Media Work in Europe', *Information, Communication and Society*, 5(1), 70-89.

Grugulis, I. & Stoyanova, D. (2009). '"I Don't Know Where You Learn Them": Skills in Film and TV', in A. McKinlay & C. Smith (eds), *Creative Labour* (135-155). London: Palgrave.

Grugulis, I. & Stoyanova, D. (2012). 'Social Capital and Networks in Film and TV: Jobs for the Boys?', *Organization Studies*, 33(10), 1311-31.

Hennekam, S. & Bennett, D. (2017). 'Sexual Harassment in the Creative Industries: Tolerance, Culture and the Need for Change', *Gender, Work & Organization*, 24(4), 417-434.

Hesmondhalgh, D. (2013). *The Cultural Industries* (3rd edition). London: SAGE Publications.

House of Lords (2015). 'Women in News and Current Affairs Broadcasting', Select Committee on Communications. Retrieved from http://www.publications.parliament.uk/pa/ld201415/ldselect/ldcomuni/91/91.pdf.

Macharia, S. (2015). *Global Media Monitoring Project Report 2015*. Retrieved from http://cdn.agilitycms.com/who-makes-the-news/Imported/reports_2015/global/gmmp_global_report_en.pdf.

Maxwell, G.A. (2004). 'Minority Report: Taking the Initiative in Managing Diversity at BBC Scotland', *Employee Relations*, 26(2), 182-202.

O'Brien, A. (2014). '"Men Own Television": Why Women Leave Media Work', *Media, Culture & Society*, 36(8), 1207-1218.

O'Brien, D., Laurison, D., Miles, A. & Friedman, S. (2016). 'Are the Creative Industries Meritocratic? An Analysis of the 2014 British Labour Force Survey', *Cultural Trends*, 25(2), 116-131.

Randle, K. & Culkin, N. (2009). 'Getting In and Getting On in Hollywood: Freelance Careers in an Uncertain Industry', in A. McKinlay & C. Smith (eds), *Creative Labour* (93-115). London: Palgrave.

Randle, K. & Hardy, K. (2017). 'Macho, Mobile and Resilient? How Workers with Impairments are Doubly Disabled in Project-Based Film and Television Work', *Work, Employment and Society*, 31(3), 447-464.

Randle, K., Leung, W.F. & Kurian, J. (2007). *Creating Difference, Creative Industries Research and Consultancy Unit.* Hatfield: University of Hertfordshire.

Randle, K., Forson, C. & Calveley, M. (2015). 'Towards a Bourdieusian Analysis of the Social Composition of the UK Film and Television Workforce', *Work, Employment & Society*, *29*(4), 590-606.

Saha, A. (2012). '"Beards, Scarves, Halal Meat, Terrorists, Forced Marriage": Television Industries and the Production of "Race"'. *Media, Culture & Society*, *34*(4), 424-438.

Spedale, S., Coupland, C. & Tempest, S. (2014). 'Gendered Ageism and Organizational Routines at Work: The Case of Day-Parting in Television Broadcasting', *Organization Studies*, *35*(11), 1585-1604.

Thanki, A. & Jefferys, S. (2006-2007). 'Who are the Fairest? Ethnic Segmentation in London's Media Production', *Work Organisation, Labour & Globalisation*, *1*(1), 108-118.

USC Annenberg School for Communication and Journalism (2017). 'USC Annenberg Launches "Annenberg Inclusion Initiative"'. Retrieved from https://annenberg.usc.edu/research/annenberg-inclusion-initiative/usc-annenberg-launches-annenberg-inclusion-initiative.

World Economic Forum (2017). *The Global Gender Gap Report 2017*. Retrieved from http://www3.weforum.org/docs/WEF_GGGR_2017.pdf

Wreyford, N. (2015). 'Birds of a Feather: Informal Recruitment Practices and Gendered Outcomes for Screenwriting Work in the UK Film Industry', *Sociological Review*, *63*(1), 84-96.

19. Labour and the Next Internet

Vincent Mosco

The Next Internet, bringing together cloud computing, big data analytics, and the Internet of Things, is just around the corner. It will profoundly influence not only our daily lives, but our jobs and working conditions as well. This chapter discusses the technological foundations, labour implications, and socio-economic consequences of the Next Internet.

Introduction

The internet, as we have known it for almost three decades, is changing and the Next Internet may do more to disrupt the world than its older sibling. The Next Internet is far from fully formed and still bears some of the characteristics of the original. But it is growing rapidly and is already challenging the vision of a democratic, decentralized, and pluralistic digital world.

The Next Internet brings together three interconnected systems: cloud computing, big data analytics, and the Internet of Things. It promises centralized data storage and services in vast digital factories that process and build algorithms from the massive streams of information gathered by networked sensors stored in every possible consumer, industrial, and office device, as well as in living bodies. In doing so, it is creating major social challenges, including for the workplace. This chapter explores the technological foundations, labour implications, and socio-economic consequences of the Next Internet.

Technology

The brilliance of the original internet was figuring out how to get a decentralized, distributed world of servers to talk to one another and thereby connect users through simple, universal software standards. This began to change with the growth of cloud computing, symbolized best by the enormous data centres that have sprung up, seemingly overnight, all over the world. The cloud is a system for storing, processing, and distributing data, applications, and software using remote computers that provide IT services on demand for a fee. Familiar examples include Google's Cloud Platform, Apple's iCloud, Microsoft's Office 365, and the largest cloud computing company in the world, Amazon Web Services.

The cloud enables businesses, government agencies, and individuals to move their data from onsite IT departments and personal computers to large data centres located all over the world. What is saved in storage space also opens a rapidly growing business for companies that profit from storage fees, from services provided online, and from the sale of customer data to firms interested in marketing products and services. Government surveillance authorities (including the intelligence agencies) also work closely with cloud companies to meet their security and intelligence needs. The diverse collection of computer servers providing the foundation for the original Internet has evolved into a centralized, global system of data centres, each containing tens to hundreds of thousands of linked servers, connected to the world through telecommunications systems.

Big data analytics makes up the second leg of the Next Internet. In spite of the proliferation of fancy new job titles – like data scientist – that fuel enthusiasm, there is very little that a social scientist or digital humanities scholar would find novel in the big data approach. It generally involves taking a large, often massive, and, almost always, quantitative data set, and examining the specific ways the data do or do not cohere or correlate. The purpose of data science is to draw conclusions – when the data refers to human activities – about current behaviour and attitudes and to make predictions. The aim is to produce algorithms or a set of rules that specify conclusions to be drawn or actions to be taken under specific conditions.

Facebook, for example, takes the data generated by its two billion or so users and relates the 'likes' associated with posts about everything from friends and family members, celebrities, companies, and politicians to views about society, products, and, of course, cats. These enable the company to develop profiles on groups and subsets of its subscribers which Facebook sells to marketers who target users with customized ads sent to their Facebook pages – a practice that years ago, in the pre-social media age, Oscar Gandy called the panoptic sort (Gandy, 1993). Google does the same for search topics as well as for the content of Gmail (and all its other services), and Amazon creates profiles of its users based on searches and purchases on its site. Given the limitations of quantitative correlational analysis, especially the absence of historical context, theory, and subjectivity (qualitative data is ignored or poorly translated into numbers), such analysis is not always accurate. Incidents of big data failures, on such projects as seasonal flu forecasting and building models for economic development, are mounting, as are the opportunities to make mischief with data for profit (Mosco, 2014).

One has to look no further than the 2016 US presidential election when big data analysis not only failed to forecast the outcome, it may also have shaped the result. That is because it produced flawed algorithms that led the Hillary Clinton camp to take an overly cautious approach because it believed in the data suggesting she was the clear leader and likely winner. This amounted to a massive case of what Gandy would appreciate as a panoptic missort.

Nevertheless, for simple questions such as what are the likes and dislikes of every conceivable demographic cohort or for drawing conclusions about users based on their friendship and follower networks, the massively large stores of data available for analysis in the digital factories that make up the cloud offer major incentives for companies and governments to invest in data centres and in big data analysis. It is reasonable to be concerned that singular reliance on big data in research is paving the way for what might best be called *digital positivism*, a methodological essentialism that ignores history, theory, and subjectivity.

The cloud and big data are enhanced substantially by the growth of the Internet of Things. From watches that monitor blood pressure to refrigerators that order fresh milk, from assembly lines 'manned' by robots to drones that deliver weapons, it promises a profound impact on individuals and society. The Internet of Things refers to a system that installs sensors and processing devices into everyday objects (watches), production tools (robotic arms), and armaments (weaponized drones), and connects them in networks that gather and use data on their performance. The sensors in a refrigerator form a network of things that report on what's inside and how it is used. The Internet of Things is made possible by advances in the ability to miniaturize scanning devices and provide them with sufficient processing power to monitor activity, analyze usage, and deliver results over electronic networks (Greengard, 2015).

A 2015 report from the private think tank McKinsey concluded that by 2025 the Internet of Things will have an economic impact of between $3.9 and $11.1 trillion (US) which, at the high end, is over 10 per cent of the world economy (Manyika *et al.*, 2015). Significantly, it is the manufacturing sector, and especially General Electric, that leads the way as machine production and opportunities for operational surveillance enable more tightly managed and efficient factories and global supply chains. But these will also extend, McKinsey maintains, to offices, retail operations, the management of cities, and overall transportation, as automated vehicles take to the streets and highways made 'smart' by sensors embedded everywhere. Heightened monitoring will also extend to the home, promising greater control over heating and cooling, and ordering food and supplies, as well as to the body, where sensors will continuously monitor fitness, blood pressure, heart rate, and the performance of vital organs.

Work

What are the labour implications of the Next Internet? When thoughts turn to employment in the tech industry, especially for the top companies, they are filled with visions of opulent workplaces with plenty of games, good food, freedom, and a casual atmosphere. Google, which sits atop *Fortune* magazine's list of the top 100 companies in the United States to work for, has become the model for this dream. The company is well known for its luxury extras like free chef-prepared food, laundry and personal grooming services. It set the industry standard for parental leave, supports transgender rights, holds serious workshops on race and gender bias, and generally promotes an inclusive and safe workplace. Engineers design their own workspaces, choose their preferred ergonomic furniture, and use just the right workout equipment. As long as they satisfy the requirements of their work group, they can come and go as they please. Given all the perks, most remain.

Not all companies, not even other elite Next Internet firms, are as generous as Google. Nevertheless, most share in what is rightly called the 'tech aristocracy', whose commodified work selves are richly rewarded. However, this is only a thin sliver of the labour force in these industries. The Next Internet is built on a global division of labour whose human cost is rarely captured in the logistics charts that map the world economy. Much attention is paid to the lavish working conditions enjoyed in Silicon Valley and Seattle where most research, design and engineering work takes place. However, these workers comprise a small fraction of those directly involved in the production process. Work actually begins in places like the coltan mines of the Democratic Republic of the Congo where workers using their own hands and primitive tools suffer some of the most hideous working conditions. They earn a pittance to dig for the mineral that Apple uses in the iPhone and Samsung in its Galaxy, and which is essential to many other devices and systems that power the Next Internet. Moreover, the fight to control revenue from the mines has fuelled a twenty-year war.

Most of the Next Internet's hardware is actually built in East Asia, South Korea, and China where the Taiwanese company Foxconn and other contractors and sub-contractors for the major consumer electronics companies operate large factory complexes that resemble the company towns of the early industrial era. Employees live in crowded dormitories and are required to eat at company cafeterias. They toil for long hours at low pay and encounter hazardous working conditions that contain numerous toxic substances to manufacture devices, including cloud data centre servers, the many devices that communicate with them, and now the sensors embedded in objects and people. Suffering from the exhaustion that would understandably accompany a 70-hour or longer workweek, many employees must deal with neurological and respiratory disorders emanating from the dangerous chemicals they are exposed to all day (Linchuan Qiu, 2016).

What has been called the 'Iron Triangle' rules high-tech production: ever-higher product value, ever-accelerating production speeds, and ever-cheaper production costs. Record-breaking market capitalizations for tech firms do not come without a price that, in addition to affecting workers mining essential rare metals in Africa and making iPhones in the sweatshops of China, also affects those labouring in warehouses where employees of online stores such as Amazon and Bol fill orders that the company promises its best customers will be delivered the next day.

Other forms of onerous work that facilitates a digital economy include online content moderators, workers whose job it is to scrub social media sites, mobile apps, and cloud services of highly offensive, often violent and sexual content, before it reaches users. This is not the hateful bigotry that has led advertisers to flee Google and YouTube. It is far worse. These employees protect users by sifting through the toxic waste of social media to identify posts that are so offensive they must be rejected even before appearing on social media sites.

Most content moderators work in Asia, primarily in the Philippines, for low wages, filling their day with long hours spent staring into an ugly sea of depravity. Things got so bad for content moderators at Microsoft that they sued the company, claiming that exposure to images of 'indescribable sexual assaults' and 'horrible brutality' led to severe post-traumatic stress disorder (PTSD). Microsoft did nothing to dispute the claims. This also appears to be the case at Facebook where, according to Sarah T. Roberts, a leading academic expert in the field, 'People can be highly affected and desensitized. It's not clear that Facebook is even aware of the long-term outcomes, never mind tracking the mental health of the workers' (Solon, 2017). As a result, many leave after a short time because the work is difficult to bear. Their labouring selves are not only commodified, they are thoroughly degraded.

Another example typical of the future of work in a digital age is a growing category known as 'gig' workers: people who sell their labour one assignment, project or deliverable at a time. Although the media industries in particular rely overwhelmingly on all kinds of so-called atypical workers – including freelance, temporary, and gig workers – this category of labour is so large that those toiling in the 'gig economy' have become iconic for the fate of employment in the Next Internet era. In the online context, gig work is an industry with many one-off or on-demand jobs, where workers are hired in a digital marketplace mainly for companies with a strong tech presence. Common characteristics now include low-wages, precarious work, and no benefits other than a wage that might be based on a specific task or hours worked. Many millions worldwide are active in this gig economy – including those who drive their cars around for companies like Uber and Lyft.

Amazon is a leader in the field with its Mechanical Turks: workers who are hired on a piecework basis carrying out one job at a time, usually involving tasks that computers alone cannot carry out. A company or person who might need someone to find objects in photographs, write comments for a website or participate in a social science experiment, will post the job on Amazon's site and set a payment price. These Requesters then choose among the applicants who are called Providers or Turkers. With low piece-rate payments and little protection for Turkers, exploitation has been rampant and some workers have banded together to organize online. Nevertheless, given the growing number of people who need extra cash or who want the freedom to work only on short-term projects, the service remains popular. With Mechanical Turk as a platform, Amazon built the foundation for jobs that require little investment in workers who use their own tools to complete a task, are paid little, and receive no company perks, certainly a far cry from playing foosball at Google's headquarters (Harris, 2014).

The icon for gig economy labour is the ride-sharing firm Uber, which has combined technological prowess with precarious labour to shakeup the taxi industry in much of the world. Using digital technology to match drivers with riders and to measure, monitor, and quantify, with the help of riders, the precise value of driver labour, Uber has become a multi-billion dollar company. The company employs hundreds of data scientists to manage and manipulate the behaviour of drivers to obtain the maximum amount of work for the lowest possible wage with the least disruption and resistance. Given its ability to measure and monitor the precise details of driver behavior, such as breaking and acceleration speed, and the precise details of traffic flows, Uber management can exercise extraordinary control over its workforce.

Nowhere is the fully commodified gig economy worker better captured than in a 2016 incident involving Uber's main competitor Lyft, which portrays itself as the more warm-hearted of the two industry disrupters. That image took a revealing turn when its public relations department decided to publicize the remarkable dedication of one of its drivers who, although nine-months pregnant and experiencing the onset of labour contractions, kept picking up fares. Thankfully, her final ride request was a short one that, as the contractions deepened, gave her barely enough time to give birth without incident. To Lyft, the driver is a worker hero, so devoted to her job that she worked until the baby arrived. The driver is celebrated in a post, complete with a photo of her new daughter pictured wearing a 'Little Miss Lyft' onesie, as if to announce that the company was not only slapping its brand on her mom, but on the baby as well. The post concluded by calling on Lyft workers to share similar 'exciting Lyft stories'. However, the company did not offer to provide her with health insurance, maternity leave, or any benefits at all. Companies like Uber and Lyft view these as drags on the digital gig economy. Perhaps these are the reasons why she drove to the end of her pregnancy. She had no choice (Menegus, 2016).

It may be horrifying, but there is nothing exceptional in Lyft's response. Consider the company Fiverr, which has raised over $110 million in venture capital funds to support a business that matches buyers and sellers of digital services, including people who charge as little as $5, hence the name, to carry out a service like making a creative birthday video. Fiverr not only celebrates quantified and commodified workers, it delivers its vision with a slick aesthetic. 'In Doers We Trust' is an advertising campaign that, in stark black, white, and grey images, profiles people who give up everything, endure every hardship, to succeed as 'doers'. Insisting in its ads that these are not thinkers, dreamers, or planners, Fiverr just wants doers. As one puts it: 'You eat your coffee for lunch. You follow through on your follow through. Sleep deprivation is your drug of choice. You might be a doer' (Tolentino, 2017). The company that identifies itself as the world's largest marketplace for digital services presents its icon of the gig economy as someone who gives up food and sleep to work as a low-wage freelancer.

Automation

Jobs in the merchandise industry are disappearing at a rapid pace, both at large companies with many franchises, and at small, often local, stores. Led by Amazon, e-commerce has expanded rapidly since 2014, leading experts to conclude that in-store shopping has reached a tipping point and is headed for a sharp decline. Retail chains are declaring bankruptcy and thousands upon thousands of shops have been shuttered around the world. Visits to shopping malls have plummeted and investors have pretty well given up the ghost. Restaurants and entertainment venues once picked up the slack, but observers do not expect this to continue. As a result, the retail collapse has surpassed even the Great Recession of 2008 (Thompson, 2017).

Hollowing out large malls and small shopping centres, this transformation is having a profound impact on a society where many workers are employed in retail. It is becoming increasingly clear that one consequence of the Next Internet and its reliance on online shopping is an upheaval in one of the major providers of full-time work in the global economy, especially for women. For them, it is a cruel irony that Amazon, which is one of the primary causes of retail's demise, is building a handful of brick and mortar shops, as if to mock a bygone era, museums to a past that will not likely be recovered. But, some experts argue, it is more complicated. Some of these jobs will be replaced by warehouse work needed to serve the growing hordes of online shoppers. Sceptics about job loss maintain that automation is all part of the natural process of creative destruction that, since the time economist Joseph Schumpeter described the concept, has led to the recognition that this is simply part of a healthy economic system. Nevertheless, such assessments provide cold comfort to those who are actually losing their jobs, including many warehouse and retail workers whose jobs have gone to robots.

It is tempting to assume that the media industry, with its reliance on creativity and artistic design, has less to fear from the prospect of automation. However, this is not the case. Companies such as NAMEN provide automated writing services for news organizations, replacing certain basic news genres – such as sports coverage and financial reporting – with 'robot journalism' (Carlson, 2015). Digital ads can be generated on demand more or less automatically and advertising space is traded online by bots in real-time while users click on links and surf the web. Computer hardware and software plays an increasingly dominant role in the film, broadcast and music industries, shaping and influencing all elements of the production and recording process. Game engines – complex pieces of software that function as the foundation upon which developers can run the games they make – are a key ingredient of the digital game industry, to some extent taking over creative control from developers (especially those without resources to develop their own engine). Similarly, content management systems that govern what can (and cannot) be published in print media are an unavoidable part of the work of journalists.

The impact of the Next Internet on jobs and the labour process is an important policy issue. At first glance, it is tempting to think 'here we go again', because the impact of technology on jobs has been discussed for many decades, especially since the end of World War II when computer scientist Norbert Wiener generated considerable public debate by raising the specter of massive job loss due to automation. At the same time, the Next Internet is creating, and will likely continue to create, employment, including traditional construction jobs in the build out of global networks of cloud data centres, in the new profession of data science, and in the control, maintenance, and monitoring of networked things, including robots. But it is important to approach the impact of computer technology on jobs and the economy with caution. As research documents show, overall employment has been much more closely tied to a nation's GDP than to computerization and, except for the late 1990s when there was massive investment in hardware, the long-promised productivity gains from IT have failed to materialize, creating a so-called productivity paradox as more investments in IT do not lead to more work or increase the productivity of workers (Gordon, 2016).

Today, there are far more opportunities for the new technology to eliminate human labour, including media work. This is in keeping with a general tendency that a researcher for the private think tank Gartner Associates summarizes succinctly: 'The long run value proposition of IT is not to support the human workforce – it is to replace it' (Dignan, 2011b). The Next Internet creates immediate opportunities for companies to rationalize their operations via information technology. Next Internet companies maintain that their systems can break a pattern in business organizations that began when the first mainframe computers entered the workplace. Back then, all business and government agencies insisted that it was essential to operate their own information technology departments and, especially for larger organizations, their own data centres. Next Internet supporters insist that it is no longer essential to build and run thousands of organization-specific facilities when a few large data centres can meet the demand at lower cost with fewer professional personnel. The savings in labour costs, they maintain, pay for the transition. This process has already begun, and early studies demonstrate that, even with limited downsizing of IT departments, companies are saving between fifteen and twenty per cent of their IT budgets (Howlett, 2014).

The Next Internet also makes possible the widespread rationalization of most creative and information-based labour because the work of these occupations increasingly involves the production, processing, and distribution of data. According to one observer, '[i]n the next 40 years analytics systems will replace much of what the knowledge worker does today' (Dignan, 2011a). Whatever the precise share of the workforce directly threatened and in the high-risk category for job loss, there is no doubt that the current trend is to use software to shift knowledge worker labour over to machine systems. We are now beginning to see the impacts on education, healthcare, the law, accounting, finance, sales, and the media.

Private and public sector organizations are encouraged to outsource all but their core business processes to companies like Salesforce.com, which specializes in managing vast databases of customer information, a job that marketing and client service departments contained inside companies once typically performed. We are also seeing this take place at the pinnacle of financial services where the world's largest investment fund company BlackRock began restructuring and eliminating the jobs of some of its top traders in 2017 because many investment decisions are now being made by algorithms. At the other end of the Next Internet occupational structure, driverless trucks are expected to decimate what was once a staple of good, full-time, unionized jobs. Other predictions foresee the gradual disappearance of the majority of jobs in medical records maintenance and analysis, air traffic control, surgeries at hospitals, and most management tasks at the majority of big companies.

Within media industries, as most of its business shifts to online, there have been profound job losses across all disciplines as media professionals are expected to do more work with fewer colleagues. Especially the larger media firms tend to be managed with the expectation that digitalization offers a more efficient way of working – an approach that is also forced upon the industry as it struggles to maintain its analogue business model in the online market. Even leaving room for the hyperbole that enthusiastic artificial intelligence, machine learning, robot and other forms of automation experts often bring to their predictions, it is reasonable to conclude that we are in the midst of a massive transformation in labour (Dreyfuss, 2017).

Conclusion: A call for action

It is far from certain what the precise impact of the Next Internet will be for jobs and the quality of work. Mass unemployment is one possibility. So, too, is a world where those with jobs will have to learn how to work with robots and other forms of intelligent machines. Living labour, as Karl Marx called it, is rapidly being overtaken by the dead labour of machines. As a result, governments, which will pay the price for negative outcomes, are trying to find solutions to what most agree will be one crisis or another that is soon to hit workers throughout the world.

Over the forty years that I have been writing about communication technology, each wave of new technologies brought predictions about job loss that were not realized. As it turns out, the primary shift in global labour over the past 50 years has been the massive movement of industrial jobs from the West to China, some of which have been replaced with lower paying service and retail work. As a result, the West has experienced pockets of decline in its industrial heartland alongside the equally significant growth of service occupations.

The transformation has been undoubtedly significant, not the least because it contributed to political upheavals such as Brexit, the election of Donald Trump, and the growing worldwide popularity of populist political movements and authoritarian regimes. The primary reasons for the transformation are social, political, and economic – not technological. They arise from trade agreements that offered the West low wage industrial labour from less developed countries and, in return, provided China, India, and other Asian nations with a path to rapid development. However, with the growth of the Next Internet, forecasts of automation-induced unemployment may finally be realized.

The replacement of living with dead labour has always promised significant cost savings, but these could not be easily realized until dead labour was given enough artificial intelligence or decision-making capabilities to carry out the jobs of skilled and semi-skilled labour, not just the work performed by unskilled labourers. The convergence of the cloud with big data and the Internet of Things means that the time has arrived when executives in the financial services industry are joining telephone operators and factory workers in the ranks of the unemployed. Moreover, many skilled and unskilled workers are right now in the process of training their automated replacements.

The declining cost and miniaturization of the sensors and processors that comprise artificial intelligence devices make them increasingly cost-effective, even for the lowest-wage countries. As a result, even China, where the world's factories once found seemingly unlimited cheap labour, is deploying robotics throughout the workforce. This results from labour shortages in China owing to its one-child policy, the lack of interest in factory labour among China's increasingly prosperous population, and the growing ability of China's blue-collar workforce to command higher wages (Bloomberg News, 2017).

There are increasing calls for action across the political spectrum to address this likely structural shift in the production and distribution of goods and services. These typically start with proposals for more education and training with specific attention to those skills that are unlikely to be automated or at least those jobs for which human labour is likely to retain the upper hand over machines. In a nod to the need for training in analog skills, jobs requiring strong face-to-face communication skills, whether with customers, fellow workers, suppliers, or investors, are attracting special attention. There is also a great need for training in human-machine interaction, an area that has been understandably ignored because there were few machines that required more than occasional programming, maintenance, and upgrading. Intelligent machines are increasingly the workmates of human employees who will have to learn unique interactive skills to maintain a reasonably harmonious relationship. In the past, when machines broke down, we used to joke that they had minds of their own. They now do.

Because neo-liberalism stripped most of the power that trade unions once wielded, workers have little recourse and practically no say in the radical transformation underway. There have been some legislative attempts to provide a basic package of benefits to the millions of gig economy workers who lack the ability to take sick days, protect themselves from the economic impact of a sudden disability, or make even the most minimal investment toward their retirement. However, unions and professional associations representing creative employees have made it easier for workers to deal with inevitable ups and downs of the industry. For example, when the online news platform *Huffington Post* laid off scores of workers in the United States in 2017, 39 were represented by the Writers Guild of America East and were protected by a union contract that provided severance pay and ongoing health benefits. Moreover, there are grounds for hope in the European Union, and especially in Germany, where unions retain enough power to threaten even dominant Big Tech firms such as Amazon whose attempts to apply American-style management, with its bare bones pay packages and no benefits, have been rebuffed by organized labour (Wingfield & Eddy, 2013).

Absent a major reversal in labour-management relations, the primary policy response that might prove beneficial for the mass of citizens is a guaranteed basic income provided to all as a right of citizenship. There are many different plans and a variety of names given to the concept. Universal basic income proposals derive from the recognition that the onrush of automation will leave many without the likelihood of finding a job that pays a living wage. Such a situation will not only increase poverty, it also has the potential to diminish demand significantly enough to put economies in a constant state of stagnation that risks regular downward spirals into recession and depression.

The idea of a universal basic income has attracted considerable international attention, with Finland, Canada, the Netherlands, and Italy all involved in a range of national and local trials. Traditional promoters of free market capitalism provide formidable opposition, but many business leaders are backing the idea.

These includes leaders in the tech community, such as Facebook founder Mark Zuckerberg and Sam Altman, president of the powerful venture capital firm Y Combinator. Moreover, the growing recognition that accelerating inequality is an urgent problem has mobilized social movements that view universal income proposals as the leading edge of a progressive offensive in a post-Internet world (Sodha, 2017). The pressure of social movements will be particularly important when the idea reaches the point of producing detailed policies, because the actual significance of a universal basic income will be determined by the amounts of funding and the eligibility requirements. How universal? How basic? What, if any, are the employment requirements? These are likely to be central policy questions as the Next Internet rolls out.

Further reading
- Case: How the gig economy is growing and media work in Australia is becoming more precarious – O'Donnell & Zion (p. 223)
- Context: An exploration of the rise of the platforms and the powerful role they have in shaping professional media production – Nieborg & Poell (p. 85)
- Contrast: How freelancers in the media industry are collectively working to protect their rights and improve their position – Cohen (p. 235)

References

Bloomberg News (2017). 'Inside China's Plans for World Robot Domination', *Bloomberg Technology* (24 April). Retrieved from https://www.bloomberg.com/news/articles/2017-04-24/resistance-is-futile-china-s-conquest-plan-for-robot-industry.

Carlson, M. (2015). 'The Robotic Reporter', *Digital Journalism*, *3*(3), 416-431, DOI: 10.1080/21670811.2014.976412.

Dignan, L. (2011a). 'Analytics in 40 years: Machines will Kick Human Managers to the Curb', *ZDNet* (18 October). Retrieved from http://www.zdnet.com/article/analytics-in-40-years-machines-will-kick-human-managers-to-the-curb/.

Dignan, L. (2011b). 'Cloud Computing's Real Creative Destruction may be the IT Workforce', *ZDNet* (24 October). Retrieved from http://www.zdnet.com/article/cloud-computings-real-creative-destruction-may-be-the-it-workforce/.

Dreyfuss, E. (2017). 'Hate to Break it to Steve Mnuchin but AI's Already Taking Jobs", *Wired* (24 March). Retrieved from https://www.wired.com/2017/03/hate-break-steve-mnuchin-ais-already-taking-jobs/.

Gandy, O. (1993). *The Panoptic Sort*. New York: Westview Press.

Gordon, R.J. (2016). *The Rise and Fall of American Growth*. Princeton, NJ: Princeton University Press.

Greengard, S. (2015). *The Internet of Things*. Cambridge, MA: MIT Press.

Harris, M. (2014). 'Amazon's Mechanical Turk Workers Protest: "I Am a Human Being, Not an Algorithm"', *The Guardian* (3 December). Retrieved from https://www.theguardian.com/technology/2014/dec/03/amazon-mechanical-turk-workers-protest-jeff-bezos.

Howlett, D. (2014). 'Exclusive: Computer economics study – Cloud Saves 15 Percent', *Diginomica* (13 February). Retrieved from http://diginomica.com/2014/02/13/exclusive-computer-economics-study-cloud-saves/.

Linchuan Qiu, J. (2016). *Good-bye iSlave*. Urbana, IL: University of Illinois Press.

Manyika, J. *et al.* (2015). *Unlocking the Potential of the Internet of Things*. Retrieved from http://www.mckinsey.com/business-functions/business-technology/our-insights/the-Internet-of-things-the-value-of-digitizing-the-physical-world.

Menegus, B. (2016). 'Lyft Thinks It's "Exciting" That a Driver Was Working While Giving Birth', *Gizmodo* (22 September). Retrieved from https://gizmodo.com/lyft-thinks-its-exciting-that-a-driver-was-working-whil-1786970298.

Mosco, V. (2014). *To the Cloud*. New York: Routledge.

Sodha, S. (2017). 'Is Finland's Basic Universal Income a Solution to Automation, Fewer Jobs and Lower Wages?', *The Guardian* (19 February). Retrieved from https://www.theguardian.com/society/2017/feb/19/basic-income-finland-low-wages-fewer-jobs.

Solon, O. (2017). 'Facebook is Hiring Moderators: But is the Job Too Difficult for Humans?', *The Guardian* (4 May). Retrieved from www.theguardian.com/technology/2017/may/04/facebook-content-moderators-ptsd-psychological-dangers.

Thompson, D. (2017). 'The Silent Crisis of Retail Employment', *The Atlantic* (18 April). Retrieved from https://www.theatlantic.com/business/archive/2017/04/the-silent-crisis-of-retail-employment/523428/.

Tolentino, J. (2017). 'The Gig Economy Celebrates Working Yourself to Death', *The New Yorker* (22 March). Retrieved from www.newyorker.com/culture/jia-tolentino/the-gig-economy-celebrates-working-yourself-to-death.

Wingfield, N. & Eddy, M. (2013). 'In Germany, Union Culture Clashes with Amazon's Labor Practices', *New York Times* (4 August). Retrieved from http://www.nytimes.com/2013/08/05/business/workers-of-amazon-divergent.html.

Practices

Affective Labour

20. Affective Labour and Media Work

Eugenia Siapera

Part of the job of media workers is to use their own emotions in order to produce emotions in the public. But what does this mean for the workers and for the media themselves? This chapter presents research on affective and emotional labour in media and journalism, and discusses the potential as well as the dangers involved in affective labour, especially for media workers in the digital era.

Introduction

In 1946, Hortense Powdermaker, an anthropologist whose previous fieldwork had been among the headhunting tribes in New Guinea, found herself researching Hollywood. She considered Hollywood as a particular kind of social system, with its own habitat, taboos, gods, and even magic. She saw Hollywood as part of a key tension: that of the mass production of dreams. Or, as a critic put it, 'an industry churning out mass-produced dreams with all the cold efficiency of a Detroit auto plant' (James, 1989). Powdermaker herself wrote:

> Hollywod is engaged in the mass production of prefabricated daydreams. [...] The question is therefore asked, Is the Hollywood system the most appropriate one for the making of movies-one form of an ancient and popular art, storytelling, in which the storyteller's imagination and understanding of his fellow men have always been a necessary ingredient? (Powdermaker, 1951, p. 39)

What happens when storytelling, at once individual and social, creative, imaginative, and emotive, becomes part of a factory-style production process? While this question is primarily oriented to the macro-sociological level of the media industry, our examination here is more closely focused on a crucial aspect: media workers themselves and their labour.

As with the industry as a whole, media labour operates on a similar premise: workers' knowledge, creativity, and their emotional world, in short, their whole subjectivity, is mobilized as an economic resource. Unlike, for example, workers in a factory who sell their time and manual skills and then go home and forget about it, media workers (and in general cognitive, non-manual workers) engage their whole self in their work, and part of their job is to use emotions in order to produce emotions in others. But what are the implications of this for the workers and for the media themselves? In addressing this question, this chapter will begin with a discussion of the main theoretical positions on immaterial, affective, and emotional labour, before moving on to look more closely at research on media workers. The final part will outline the potential as well as the dangers involved in affective labour, especially for media workers in the digital era.

Immaterial, affective, and emotional labour: Key terms and debates

In an intriguing part of the *Grundrisse* (1858) – Karl Marx's unpublished notes that fed into and clarified *Das Kapital* – Marx makes the following point: when technology evolves, when machines take over much of human labour, then workers' labour itself will change. The worker, argues Marx,

> steps to the side of the production process instead of being its chief actor. In this transformation, it is neither the direct human labour he himself performs, nor the time during which he works, but rather the appropriation of his own general productive power, his understanding of nature and his mastery over it by virtue of his presence as a social body – it is, in a word, the development of the social individual which appears as the great foundation-stone of production and of wealth (Marx, 1858/1993, p. 705).

What Marx is saying here is that if machines take over the menial and repetitive tasks, then human labour will consist of using and applying knowledge. This kind of labour does not involve strength or technical skills, but rather the application of knowledge accumulated through people being part of society and through formal education at schools and universities.

Although immaterial labour has certain defining characteristics, it takes different forms. Hardt and Negri (2000) distinguish between three main types. The first is attached to the industrial production, incorporating communication technologies to the extent that the whole production process is wholly transformed: the design, manufacture, marketing, distribution, and sale of goods all require a communication component and are blending material and immaterial forms of labour. The second type of immaterial labour is that performed by, for example, computer programmers and communication technology experts at the top end of the scale, but also by those involved in more routine tasks, for example outsourced data workers, on the bottom end. The third type of immaterial labour is affective labour, involving 'the creation and manipulation of affects', and whose 'products' include 'a feeling of ease, well-being, satisfaction, excitement, passion-even a sense of connected-ness or community' (Hardt, 1999, p. 96).

The term emotional labour is more often encountered in sociological works and it has been defined as 'the process by which workers are expected to manage their feelings in accordance with organizationally defined rules and guidelines' (Wharton, 2009, p. 147). Affective labour is therefore broader and encompasses emotional labour. Rather than being mutually exclusive, material labour and the various forms of immaterial labour are blended, with most types of work requiring a mixture of skills. For example, nurses perform both the menial tasks of changing bedsheets and the affective tasks of looking after patients' well-being. Similarly, a worker in film production may perform a variety of tasks, for example camera work that requires the use of the body, and more intellectual ones, such as editing.

Discussions of immaterial labour have given rise to three sets of debates: one concerning the gendered nature of much of this kind of labour, secondly the question of value and compensation for this kind of labour, and thirdly the political potential of the shift towards immaterial and affective labour. The basis and impetus for discussions on immaterial labour emerged out of feminist theory and debates of the early 1970s: feminists explicitly thematized the kind of domestic labour performed by women, including child-bearing, child-rearing, and most care tasks in addition to the more menial tasks of cleaning, cooking and so on, whose value had been ignored by Marxist theory.

Leopoldina Fortunati (1981/1995), one of the main participants in these debates, argued that women's reproductive labour has to be seen as part of capitalist relations of production and therefore should be compensated for in a manner equivalent to other labour. But how can we calculate the value added by reproductive labour and how can we think about compensating workers involved in this kind of labour? However, feminists did not raise the issue of compensation in order to get money for unpaid work; they did so because they wanted first and foremost to revolutionize social relations. As Federici (2012, p. 15) argued, in demanding wages, the feminist activists knew that their demands could not be met 'without at the same time revolutionizing – in the process of struggling for [the wage] – all our family and social relations'. Thinking about value therefore represents a call to go beyond the question of monetary compensation and to re-think how society is organized.

These discussions have directly influenced debates on the role and value of affective labour within the broader context of the socioeconomic shift towards immaterial labour. An important part of the arguments on the value of affective labour concern its commodification. For the value of something to be calculated, it must be commodified, or in other words, it must enter the market and be sold and bought for a price. But this is not something that can always be done with affective labour. By introducing the issue of wages for women's work, the feminist movement in effect raised the question of how to think of non-commodified forms of labour, such as those that involve care and affect – or in Marxist terms, more use-value than exchange value. They are therefore valuable for their own sake rather than because they can be exchanged for profit. But this also implies that affective labour both is and isn't part of capitalist social relations. And this is precisely where some of its political potential lies: in representing a kind of labour than is not subsumed by the market.

High-end immaterial labour and affective work are pleasurable: they cannot be compared to the alienated work of the assembly line. The creativity involved in designing new objects, in writing a script, in photographing; the pleasures to be gotten out of singing or performing; the satisfaction obtained through a journalistic investigation that exposed wrongdoings or that facilitated the voices of those in the margins: all these imply that the kind of one-sided exploitative relationship between employers (capital) and employees (labour) is much more complex in immaterial and affective labour. Moreover, as Hardt and Negri (2000) argue, immaterial labour always requires social interaction and cooperation, but this is something that occurs organically, from within, and is not imposed on or orchestrated by capital – labour does not any longer need someone with capital to come and put it into work, but it can get together and apply its own labour power.

> Today productivity, wealth, and the creation of social surpluses take the form of cooperative interactivity through linguistic, communicational, and affective networks. In the expression of its own creative energies, immaterial labor thus seems to provide the potential for a kind of spontaneous and elementary communism (Hardt & Negri, 2000, p. 294).

In effect, affective labour can produce positive externalities, such as communities and social networks, which can on the one hand lead to alternative forms of production and life, but on the other can be appropriated and commodified by capital. This ambiguity is found at the heart of sociological research on this area, and it is clearly evidenced in research on affect and emotion in media work.

Affective labour and media work: Key findings

While the conceptualizations of affective labour rely on macro-sociological analyses of shifting trends in employment, to understand what goes on at the level of the actual labour process we need research at the meso and micro level, looking at the actual practices involved in immaterial and affective labour. In terms of media and journalistic work, there is a dearth of studies that understand the specificity of this kind of labour. Studies of journalistic and media work, for example, Lewis, Holton and Coddington (2013) on reciprocal journalism, have looked on the social aspects of journalistic work but have not contextualised these in terms of the current debates on affective labour and did not consider the implications for journalistic labour and the tensions and ambiguities involved. Other work has focused on the immaterial and self-organizing components but positioned these in terms of entrepreneurialism, often overlooking the affective labour on which entrepreneurialism relies. On the other hand, when the affective component of journalistic and media work has been considered, this has been within the framework of emotional labour, which tends to focus very critically on the commodification aspects of this kind of work, but overlooks its potential.

So, while the work of media and journalism has always been intellectual and hence immaterial, its affective dimension has not been closely studied. At the same time, there is increasing recognition that this element is becoming more and more necessary for journalism and media work. For example, recent handbooks and textbooks show that affective components have become part of the skillset that journalists and other media workers need to learn: Hill and Lashmar (2014) have a section on 'Building Online Communities' (*Ibid.*, p. 141) and 'Encouraging Users to Share News Content' (*Ibid.*, p. 154); in Tony Harcup's textbook on journalism, there is a chapter on 'Engaging with the audience' (2015, p. 219). These, and other similar works, offer tips on how to connect with readers, how to keep them interested, how to blend personal and professional tone in writing, and so on. In more theoretical terms, research has highlighted the shift towards 'affective news' (Papacharissi, 2015), and the increasingly important role of emotion in the current media environment (Beckett & Deuze, 2016; Wahl-Jorgensen, 2016). However, the work that goes into the production and circulation of affect, and the ongoing work of creating and managing relationships with others (co-workers/sources/readers/audiences) needs a closer look, as it may be changing the very character of media work.

When it comes to looking for changes in journalistic and media labour, discussion typically revolves around the role of digital technology and the rise of entrepreneurialism. There is a long list of authors who have traced the changes that digital technology has brought to journalistic and media practices (among others, Bardoel, 1996; Pavlik, 2000; Deuze, 2007; Witschge & Nygren 2009; Hermida, 2010). Their work has shown some of the effects of the introduction of digital technology into the newsroom and in the media production process. On the other hand, research has also shown that some of these effects may be more directly linked to broader shifts in management strategies than technology per se. For example, Ornebring (2010) showed that historically technology has been used as an efficiency mechanism leading to redundancies and this process has continued with journalism and media work. Similar arguments are made by Paulussen (2012) who points to shifts towards flexible and individualized labour in journalism discussed in terms of digital innovation and disruption. Both Ornebring and Paulussen, as well as Deuze

(2007) consider that the flexibilization of labour, i.e. the loss of permanent, salaried posts, and the resulting shift towards the precarious model of the freelancer, or the individuated worker, is characteristic of media and journalistic work.

While this shift is widely recognized, it is often couched in the positive and overly optimistic tone of entrepreneurialism (Vos & Singer, 2016). In entrepreneurial media work, the entrepreneur is typically involved in both the creative and the business side of things. An influential strand of relevant literature, represented most notably by Jeff Jarvis (2009), believes that entrepreneurialism is the key to the future of journalistic and media work. However, the focus is more on the market and profit side of things rather than on the public mission of journalism and the social benefits of media outputs. Furthermore, there is a tendency to emulate the Silicon Valley start-up model, with an emphasis on large profits and quick exits (Pein, 2014). Entrepreneurs are understood as unique, gifted individuals. But the reality is very different: apart from the fact that most start-ups end in failure (Statistic Brain, 2017), the view that success is the result of individual effort and drive is wrong. As Yann Moulier-Boutang (2012) argues, in informational or cognitive capitalism, innovation emerges out of knowledge, which, in turn, relies on social relationships, cooperation, and social exchange. This social element and the need for cooperation points to the importance of the affective component involved in all this.

On the other hand, research on the affective dimension of media and journalism tends to focus on the output and the consumption/use side. Papacharissi (2015), whose work has been pivotal in highlighting the role of affect, refers to the rise of affective news: a hybrid blending information, personal experience, opinion, and emotion. The emerging affective publics are collaboratively involved in the production and circulation of such news. Wahl-Jorgensen (2016) points to how the epistemology of journalism is currently undergoing a shift from objectivity towards emotional engagement and to more 'personalized, subjective and emotional forms of narrative' (*Ibid.*, p. 132). Beckett and Deuze (2016) call for a better understanding of how emotions can contribute to improving and enriching journalism without compromising its ethical and social value. Linking journalistic storytelling with emotions and affect has helped dissolve unhelpful and gendered dichotomies between rationality and emotion. However, the work that is involved in producing these emotions requires further unpacking.

This is precisely where we can locate research on affective and emotional labour in media and journalism: as a bridge between research on changes in media and journalistic labour and research on the shift towards emotion and affect. The pivotal work here is Arnie Hochschild's research on the so-called pink collar work of flight attendants. Hochschild defines emotional labour as 'the management of feeling to create a publicly observable facial and bodily display', which then has the effect of creating a particular emotional state in other people (1983/2012,

p. 7). Hochschild found that flight attendants were regulating their emotions in ways required by their job: they used smiles, extreme politeness, controlled body movements, and so on, in order to elicit cooperation. Her work shows that emotional labour requires that workers strategically manage their emotions at the behest of their employers, pointing to the expansion of work into the domain of feelings and affect. No longer are emotions the truthful expressions of innermost feelings, but they are manipulated and used at will to generate profits for others. This points to the alienating effects of this kind of labour: not only are workers separated from the fruits of their labour, as in classic Marxism, they are also separated from their feelings. On the other hand, Hochschild recognizes that emotions are inevitably 'managed' and subjected to rules in all contexts. However, the main point of departure is that in emotional labour emotions are taken from the private sphere and imported into the sphere of work, 'where they are processed, standardized, and subjected to hierarchical control' (*Ibid.*, p. 153).

Hesmondalgh and Baker's (2013) work on the cultural industries has taken these concepts to the media and more specifically to how creative workers in television are negotiating and managing their emotions vis-à-vis their co-workers and managers, as well as vis-à-vis their audiences and fans. To study these, they focused on a specific format, that of the TV talent show, in which young, mostly precarious, media workers had to coach and elicit cooperation from ordinary people looking to participate in the show. As Grindstaff (2002), has shown, a key part of such TV shows involves eliciting emotional responses from participants, and in doing so media workers must manage their emotions accordingly; this is achieved by 'either pretending to care about guests or trying not to care too much' (*Ibid.*, p. 132). In Hesmondalgh and Baker's study, members of the show production team, found themselves really emotionally invested in some contestants, often finding it hard to dissociate themselves, despite trying to keep an emotional distance.

One can easily imagine a similar dynamic at play when journalists report on tragic events, conflict and war – for example, in 2016, the CNN newscaster Kate Bolduan cried as she presented a news item featuring a five-year-old boy rescued in Syria (Nagesh, 2016). An additional finding by Hesmondalgh and Baker (2013) concerns the role of precarity: aware of the precariousness of media work, young workers managed their emotions in ways that avoided falling out with people holding key positions, but also more broadly in ways that avoided conflict and confrontation. In this way, Hesmondalgh and Baker's work concurs with Hochschild's findings of emotional labour as including both the evocation and the suppression of emotion.

Similar findings are reported by Soronen (2017) in her work on women's magazines. Workers there, including editors, art directors and photographers, have to manage their emotions vis-à-vis their projected audiences, but also towards one another. In the case of the former, they seek to evoke a specific emotional state in readers, associated with being cool. In case of the latter, workers feel the need to supress feelings of stress and anxiety. More broadly, Soronen (2017) understands the emotional state of the precarious project workers through Berlant's (2011) concept of 'cruel optimism'. Berlant (2011) uses this term to refer to the continuous attachment to unachievable ideals, such as job security and progressive political and social equality, despite evidence that these are no longer possible in conditions of neoliberal capitalism.

This management of emotions within a context of cruel optimism – that has workers speak of their passion for their job even at the face of low-paid, low-opportunity precarious work – might operate as a coping mechanism. Notwithstanding all this, Soronen, as well as Hesmondalgh and Baker, report that their research participants still experience positive emotional states associated with the creative and social aspects of their job, pointing to the complex ways in which positive and negative emotions are blended, creating mixed experiences for media workers.

But this management of emotions is only one part of affective labour. As a result of a complex set of factors – including widespread precarity in the field, the emergence of a hybrid media system (Chadwick, 2013), which alters the conditions of public visibility, and the shift towards entrepreneurship – media workers have found themselves in a position where creating and managing networks of, and direct relationships with readers/audiences is an increasingly necessary part of their job. For example, the US-based trade magazine *Backstage* has recently published a guide titled 'What social media does an actor need' (24 July, 2017).

Media work is increasingly incorporating an affective element over and above the actual job description. We can refer to this as an affective rather than an emotional kind of labour because it involves not only the immediate management of emotions at the level of individuals, but more broadly the creation of networks and communities, which, in turn, (re)produce society in specific ways. Following Hardt (1999), we move beyond the immediate products of emotional labour (for example, compliance, cooperation, customer satisfaction, etc.) towards the broader social products of affective labour: the creation and management of social relationships, or what may be referred to as social reproduction – the reproduction of society.

Siapera and Iliadi (2015) focused on freelance journalists who created and maintained social networks of readers/followers through Twitter. For the participants in the study, the creation and maintenance of such networks requires the investment of one's 'authentic' self, the investment of personal time, and the investment of care. These aspects of affective labour are ambiguous.

On the one hand, mobilizing an authentic and complete self (as opposed to, for example, the manipulation and suppression of emotions in instances of emotional labour) appears to form the basis of more genuine relationships. There is less alienation or separation of the self from its labour. Taking into account that the self does not pre-exist the social world, but it is co-produced within it, this investment of the 'authentic' self, as expressed by respondents, is taken to mean the production of a self that is experienced as less alienating – a point also found in work on immaterial labour (Berardi, 2009).

On the other hand, success hinges on the extent to which the projected self is acceptable to others, pointing to the need to not only have the skills required of media work, but also to produce a personality and self that are palatable to readers/audiences. Moreover, the self is removed from its immediate context of social relations and placed in the context of the market: workers are literally selling themselves. The investment of time is equally ambiguous: in building and maintaining networks, workers need extra time, above and beyond their actual work, and this is a standard expectation. However, there is neither acknowledgement, nor compensation for this extra time. In Marxist terms, workers add value to their labour by being on social media, but this is not explicitly measured or included in the value calculations: in this respect, it is pure surplus, or profit that goes to those who will eventually employ the worker. Nevertheless, both the investment of one's self and the investment of time and care, feed into to the development of an organic relationship between media workers and their followers, as well as to the emergence of stronger bonds between core groups or networks that may evolve into communities.

Conclusion

Affective labour, insofar as it (re)produces less alienated, more autonomous selves and relationships, can be seen as having an important political potential for emancipation. In these terms, affective labour is involved in the (re)production of selves as well as important social bonds that may help mitigate the individuation imposed by the neo-liberal turn – or at least provide better coping mechanisms for dealing with the culture of individuation. Moreover, to the extent that this labour leads to reciprocal relationships, media workers are placing themselves more firmly in the social domain in ways that were not possible in earlier media epochs. This can feed into their media work. We are no longer in the dream factory but in a new phase which entails an important promise for more control and autonomy over one's work and one's self and creativity too.

What cannot be denied however, is that this kind of labour is directly exploited and used to generate surplus value for others – the workers' employers. This work is expected but never compensated for, as workers' affective labour is not really what they are hired for. Moreover, subsuming affective labour within the domain of the market subjects it to a market logic of capital accumulation, exchange, profit, and loss, none of which are compatible with human affects, desires, and emotions.

Jarrett (2015), writing on the labour of digital users, refutes the binary between either a wholly radical and autonomous agency or a wholly subsumed and exploited activity. Rather, she argues, we must see this kind of labour in terms of a continuum across which some moments are subsumed and exploited while others remain inalienable 'living, concrete labour, escaping capture, measure and categorization within economic categories' (*Ibid.*, p. 215). Applying Jarrett's arguments to affective labour in media work, we can see how some moments may be liberating and emancipating, while others may be exploitative and alienating. For media workers, it means paying attention to the nuances of interacting with the subjects and the receivers of their work beyond the strict requirements of the job description. Identifying the various moments and seeking to find the conditions that are more satisfactory may be more fruitful than denying wholesale the potential of affective labour to (re)socialize all of us in more thoughtful and caring ways.

Further reading

- Case: Affective labour in entrepreneurial journalism – Brouwers & Witschge (p. 441)
- Context: How the media industry is changing and becoming more focused on media consumer engagement – Chan-Olmsted & Wang (p. 133)
- Contrast: How the working conditions within the cultural and creative industries are affectively experienced – Cantillon & Baker (p. 287)

References

Bardoel, J. (1996). 'Beyond Journalism: A Profession between Information Society and Civil Society', *European journal of communication*, 11(3), 283-302.

Beckett, C. & Deuze, M. (2016). 'On the Role of Emotion in the Future of Journalism', *Social Media+ Society*, 2(3).

Berardi, F. (2009). *The Soul at Work: From Alienation to Autonomy*. Los Angeles, CA: Semiotext(e).

Berlant, L.G. (2011). *Cruel Optimism*. Durham, NC: Duke University Press.

Chadwick, A. (2013). *The Hybrid Media System: Politics and Power*. Oxford: Oxford University Press.

Deuze, M. (2007). *Media Work*. Cambridge: Polity.

Federici, S. (2012). *Revolution at Point Zero: Housework, Reproduction, and Feminist Struggle*. Oakland, CA: PM Press.

Fortunati, L. (1995). *The Arcane of Reproduction: Housework, Prostitution, Labour and Capital*. New York: Autonomedia

Grindstaff, L. (2002). *The Money Shot: Trash, Class, and the Making of TV Talk Shows*. Chicago, IL: University of Chicago Press.

Harcup, T. (2015). *Journalism: Principles and Practice*. London: SAGE Publications.

Hardt, M. (1999). 'Affective Labor', *boundary* 2, 26(2), 89-100.

Hardt, M. & Negri, A. (2000). *Empire*. Cambridge, MA: Harvard University Press.

Hermida, A. (2010). 'Twittering the News: The Emergence of Ambient Journalism', *Journalism practice*, 4(3), 297-308.

Hesmondhalgh, D. & Baker, S. (2013). *Creative Labour: Media Work in Three Cultural Industries*. London: Routledge.

Hill, S. & Lashmar, P. (2013). *Online Journalism: The Essential Guide*. London: SAGE Publications.

Hochschild, A.R. (2012). *The Managed Heart: Commercialization of Human Feeling*. Berkeley, CA: University of California Press (original work published 1983).

James, C. (1989). 'Critic's Notebook; Romanticizing Hollywood's Dream Factory', *The New York Times* (7 November). Retrieved from http://www.nytimes.com/1989/11/07/movies/critic-s-notebook-romanticizing-hollywood-s-dream-factory.html?pagewanted=all.

Jarrett, K. (2015). 'Devaluing Binaries: Marxist Feminism and the Value of Consumer Labour', in E. Fisher & C. Fuchs (eds), *Reconsidering Value and Labour in the Digital Age* (207-223). Basingstoke: Palgrave Macmillan.

Jarvis, J. (2009). 'The Future of News is Entrepreneurial', *Buzzmachine* (1 November). Retrieved from http://buzzmachine.com/2009/11/01/the-future-of-journalism-is-entrepreneurial/.

Lewis, S.C., Holton, A.E. & Coddington, M. (2014). 'Reciprocal Journalism: A Concept of Mutual Exchange between Journalists and Audiences', *Journalism Practice*, 8(2), 229-241.

Marx, K. (1993). *Grundrisse*. London: Penguin (original work published 1858).

Moulier-Boutang, Y. (2012). *Cognitive Capitalism*. Cambridge: Polity.

Nagesh, A. (2016). 'Newsreader Moved to Tears during Report on Syrian Child Pulled from Rubble', *Metro* (19 August). Retrieved from http://metro.co.uk/2016/08/19/newsreader-moved-to-tears-during-report-on-syrian-child-pulled-from-rubble-6077665/.

Örnebring, H. (2010). 'Technology and Journalism-as-Labour: Historical Perspectives', *Journalism*, 11(1), 57-74.

Papacharissi, Z. (2015). 'Toward New Journalism (s) Affective News, Hybridity, and Liminal Spaces', *Journalism studies*, 16(1), 27-40.

Paulussen, S. (2012). 'Technology and the Transformation of News Work: Are Labor Conditions in (Online) Journalism Changing', in Siapera, E. & A. Veglis (eds), *The Handbook of Global Online Journalism* (192-208). Malden, MA: Wiley.

Pavlik, J. (2000). 'The Impact of Technology on Journalism', *Journalism Studies*, 1(2), 229-237.

Pein, C. (2014). 'Amway Journalism', *The Baffler* (28 July). Retrieved from http://www.thebaffler.com/blog/amway-journalism/.

Powdermaker, H. (1951). *Hollywood, the Dream Factory*. London: Secker & Warburg.

Siapera, E. & Iliadi, I. (2015). 'Twitter, Journalism and Affective Labour', *Sur le journalisme*, 4(1), 76-89.

Soronen, A. (2017). 'Emotional Labour in Magazine Work: Suppressing and Evoking Emotions as Part of Project-based Teamwork', *Journalism Practice*, 12(1), 1-18.

Statistic Brain (2017). 'Startup Business Failure Rate By Industry' (5 May). Retrieved from https://www.statisticbrain.com/startup-failure-by-industry/.

Vos, T.P. & Singer, J.B. (2016). 'Media Discourse about Entrepreneurial Journalism: Implications for Journalistic Capital', *Journalism Practice*, *10*(2), 143-159.

Wahl-Jorgensen, K. (2016). 'Emotion and Journalism', in T. Witchge *et al.* (eds), *The SAGE Handbook of Digital Journalism* (128-143). London: SAGE Publications.

Wharton, A.S. (2009). 'The Sociology of Emotional Labor', *Annual review of sociology, 35*, 147-165.

Witschge, T. & Nygren, G. (2009). 'Journalistic Work: A Profession under Pressure?', *Journal of Media Business Studies, 6*(1), 37-59.

21. Affective Qualities of Creative Labour

Zelmarie Cantillon and Sarah Baker

Creative labour is highly individualized, notoriously precarious, and characterized by flexibility, insecurity, and irregularity, along with long hours and low pay. These circumstances increase the likelihood of exploitation. At the same time, creative labour has affective qualities – pleasures as well as pressures. This chapter explores how the working conditions within the creative industries are affectively experienced through three case studies.

Introduction

In the humanities, the 'affective turn' refers to the increasing scholarly interest in emotions, senses, and bodily experiences since the 1990s. In terms of the workplace, the significance of affect has been theorized through concepts such as 'emotional labour' or 'emotion work' (Hochschild, 1983), 'affective labour' (Hardt & Negri, 2000), and 'passionate work' (McRobbie, 2016). Poynter (2002) suggests that such concepts offer 'rich ground for re-examining the relationship between the individual and the objective or structural circumstances in which they find themselves' (*Ibid.*, 248-249).

The literature on affective and emotional labour focuses on the immaterial aspects of contemporary labour processes, which often fall outside what is traditionally recognized as 'work' (Lazzarato, 1996; Gregg,2009). Examples include sociable interactions between workers and colleagues or customers, expressions of care or concern, and the production of cultural, symbolic and artistic works or knowledges (Lazzarato, 1996; Hesmondhalgh & Baker, 2008). In her highly influential work on emotional labour, Arlie Hochschild (1983) suggests that workers must manage their emotions and the emotions of others to meet the expectations of their jobs. Such labour may involve practicing empathy and inducing, enhancing, or suppressing certain feelings (Hochschild, 1983; Grindstaff, 2002). For instance, to offer good service, a worker may need to suppress feelings of exhaustion or stress, perform a personable and cheerful version of the self, and aim to elicit happiness or dispel dissatisfaction among customers. In this sense, affect is integral to the experience of labour.

Although much scholarly work on the affective qualities of labour has examined the service and healthcare industries, there is also a growing body of literature that deals with emotion in media and creative industries. As Hesmondhalgh and Baker (2008) argue, when examining subjective experiences of labour, it is essential to consider the specificities of the sectors in which this labour is taking place. As will become clear throughout this chapter, the creative industries – considered here broadly to include the sectors of advertising and marketing, architecture, crafts, design, media, photography, music, performing and visual arts, IT, and heritage institutions – offer a unique context in which to analyse the nature of contemporary work.

In policy discourse, creative and cultural labour has been frequently valorized as generating economic growth and offering its workers greater affluence, freedom, and opportunities for self-actualization (Hesmondhalgh & Baker, 2008; Arvidsson *et al.*, 2010; Bridgen, 2011; Lee, 2012). However, creative labour is notoriously precarious, characterized by flexibility, insecurity, and irregularity, along with the generally long hours and low pay associated with freelance and contractual work (Gill, 2002; McRobbie, 2002b; Gill & Pratt, 2008; Hesmondhalgh & Baker, 2008, 2010, 2011; Banks & Hesmondhalgh, 2009; Lee, 2012; Phillipov, 2017). In addition to such systemic precarity, creative labour is also highly individualized, with social capital and self-branding – the commodification of the self – being key to one's success (Ursell, 2000; Bridgen, 2011; Phillipov, 2017). These circumstances increase the likelihood of exploitation and a general lack of collective resistance to the conditions thereof, and when internalized, can also lead to neo-liberal forms of self-exploitation (McRobbie, 2002a; Hesmondhalgh & Baker, 2008, 2010; Banks & Hesmondhalgh, 2009; Bridgen, 2011; Lee, 2012).

The central concern of this chapter is how the precarious, individualized working conditions of creative labour are affectively experienced. Drawing on published work by one of the authors, the chapter explores these issues through case studies from three creative industries: the television industry (Hesmondhalgh & Baker, 2008), the music industry (Baker, 2014), and the popular music heritage sector (Baker, 2015, 2017; Long *et al.*, 2017). The findings presented are based on ethnographic fieldwork (interviews and participant observation) on a UK-based television show (in 2007); with musicians in Reykjavík, Iceland (in 2010); and at numerous DIY (do-it-yourself) popular music heritage institutions around the world (from 2010 to 2015). Each case study represents different forms of work, from paid labour to unpaid and volunteer labour, and from media production to media consumption and preservation. We explore the various affective dimensions and subjective experiences of creative labour, attending to the specificity of each industry while simultaneously drawing attention to commonalities between them.

Television production

Production crews on television shows can wield considerable symbolic power, creating cultural products that are disseminated to and consumed by large numbers of people. For example, on the UK-based talent show that was the focus of study, producers have the potential to propel ordinary people to stardom. The researchers and casting team exercise their judgement on applications and auditions, determining which individuals are appealing enough to go forward as contestants, and which will be rejected.

While this power and influence is recognized as one of the perks of creative labour, it also comes with significant pressure. Potential contestants have 'a huge amount to be gained – and lost' (Hesmondhalgh & Baker, 2008, p. 108) – not only in terms of prize money, but also exposure – and are thus often deeply emotionally invested in how well they perform. Rejection, then, can result in anger on the part of contributors (and their friends and family) directed at producers who are perceived as responsible for the decision (even if, in actuality, someone higher up in the production hierarchy is responsible). For instance, junior producers on the show noted that they received emails from parents of contributors proclaiming that they are 'shattering children's dreams' (*Ibid.*, p. 109). To cope with these responses, producers continually work to maintain emotional distance from contributors.

Despite their efforts, however, forming emotional connections with participants is an integral part of the job. Producers must build up a good rapport with contributors and express care for their plight so that they can elicit the desired emotional responses (excitement, nervousness, frustration, sadness, etc.) from them on-camera. Further, as contestants advance throughout the show, workers can become increasingly invested in their success. Having 'discovered' them from the applications and cheered them on through auditions and stage performances, researchers and producers develop a sense of responsibility for whether contestants make it to the live grand final or not. Conversely, if a contestant (or their loved one) has a bad attitude or is difficult to work with, the production team may *not* care about their success or the quality of their performances, thus negatively impacting the programme. Under these circumstances, it becomes crucial for workers to manage their own emotions – particularly feelings of frustration and stress – in order to meet the expectations of their jobs.

As well as the emotional labour necessary for working with contributors, junior members of the production team also reported stress resulting from organizational issues. In particular, the competing visions of the commissioning network and the production company caused anxiety and confusion among workers. The production company wanted the show to have a prime-time television feel on a daytime budget, putting pressure on the production team to cast higher quality acts than would otherwise be expected. At the same time, these acts had to represent a variety of genders, ages, and ethnic backgrounds, as per the commissioning network's guidelines.

Further, the network and production company were often at odds with editorial matters, sometimes leading to last-minute changes to the show being made, causing stress for the production team. Such situations also manifested in tensions between crew members, which is potentially very damaging for an individual in a precarious industry like television – not only is television production a highly collaborative creative process, but maintaining a good reputation and developing professional networks is integral to securing future work. Thus, although relations between the production team were frequently characterized by camaraderie and fun, working relations can also be strained by competitiveness and stress, and the emotional work involved in suppressing negative feelings.

Music industry

As with all creative sectors, labour in the music industry can involve significant pleasures. By working in this industry, individuals passionate about music have the opportunity to hone their craft, work autonomously, achieve recognition, and meet like-minded people. However, as noted earlier, creative work is often precarious, and this can become intensified during times of economic downturn. During the 2008 global financial crisis, Iceland was hit particularly hard and the country's banking sector collapsed. In an effort to raise revenues and create jobs, the government implemented policy aimed at supporting its creative arts industries, including music. In spite of this, Icelandic musicians and industry workers reported increasingly poor working conditions and unfavourable affective experiences.

Iceland's domestic music market is very small, constraining artists' potentials for earning money from shows and album/song sales. Musicians expressed anxiety over the competitiveness for gigs given limited venues and the lack of corporate event opportunities due to the recession. Even if an artist is able to book shows, the pay is considerably less than it was pre-economic collapse, and in many cases, they may be performing for free. These circumstances are especially troublesome for emerging artists, who at the time of being interviewed, believed it is par for the course to perform without pay in order to gain exposure, or to perform in their home country as 'practice' before moving on to the international circuit. This is even more so the case for those artists with unconventional, 'left-field' (Baker, 2014) genres as opposed to Icelandic pop and other commercial styles.

Not only do these conditions adversely impact the diversity and growth of musical arts in Iceland, but they clearly also lead to the normalization of (self-)exploitation. Due to the standard of low (or no) pay for performing, many musicians – including those who are more established – need to have day jobs to survive. The major downside of this, of course, is that it takes time and energy away from developing their creative work. As one musician explained, 'I really just want to play, play, play, play, play', but 'the main problem' getting in the way of this is the need 'to mix the day job and the family life with the musical career'.

Even for those musicians that 'make it', success does not absolve their economic pressures. Breaking into the international market and touring can be very costly, involving frequent air travel (and extra baggage fees for instruments) and hotel stays. Although government funding is available to cover costs of air travel, these grants are competitive and limited in number. Therefore, whether working in the country or overseas, Icelandic musicians face great financial difficulties in sustaining their creative output. Economic pressures are registered affectively, resulting in anxiety and stress.

Nonetheless, musicians tolerate these feelings and poor working conditions because of the pleasurable subjective experiences that their creative labour also entails. For example, in Iceland, it is very common for a musician to work with multiple groups of performers, and those interviewed talked about creative collaborations as being a very rewarding component of their work. When the musician quoted earlier was asked what pleasures help to balance out the pressures of this labour, she explained:

> It's just that I love, it's not a question about doing it, it's something that I need to do, and I feel like doing, every time. I also have really great guys with me, that helps a lot, we meet once a week, just try new songs out, and it's always fun getting together. Every show is just a lot of fun. It never feels like work.

Therefore, much like in television production, despite competitiveness for work, collaboration and camaraderie are important and often highly gratifying aspects of creative labour.

Heritage sector

It is not only the production of creative work that has affective dimensions, but its consumption as well. Music, for instance, can have powerful emotional effects and resonances, and can be significant in shaping individual and collective identities, memories and feelings. It is unsurprising, then, that fans are willing to undertake voluntary, unpaid forms of labour dedicated to celebrating the music that they love. Gregg (2009) explains that, in the context of fan cultures, 'affective labour is used to explain meaningful and productive human activity that does not result in a direct financial profit or exchange value, but rather produces a sense of community, esteem, and/or belonging for those who share a common interest' (*Ibid.*, p. 209).

In music cultures, one such expression of affectively-driven labour is found in heritage institutions devoted to popular music's past. This is particularly evident in DIY heritage institutions – community-based, enthusiast-led, volunteer-run initiatives such as archives, museums, and halls of fame that aim to collect and preserve popular music recordings and other ephemera including clothing, instruments, posters, magazines, and merchandise (see Baker, 2017). Far from being neutral or objective repositories of the past, these DIY institutions are borne out of – and sustained by – care and passion for the genre, musician or locality being documented (Baker, 2015; Long *et al.*, 2017).

DIY heritage institutions are more than just collections of artefacts, and have distinct affective atmospheres (Baker, 2015). Objects housed in these institutions become 'sticky', in Ahmed's (2010) terms, in that they accrue affective associations, cultural and personal value (as opposed to only exchange value), and can elicit happiness, sadness, nostalgia, and so on. Thus, both visitors and staff can have affective engagements with these materials. Indeed, staff may be motivated to work in the institutions by a desire to be in close proximity to the artefacts, which evoke positive feelings and a sense of connectedness to the past. This kind of labour can be very pleasurable, with workers expressing joy in uncovering materials to preserve, curating them in interesting ways, sharing their vernacular knowledge with others, and forming emotional bonds with like-minded colleagues.

At the same time, however, heritage work is also characterized by stress and anxiety. Workers in these DIY institutions are motivated, in part, by a fear that artefacts and historical narratives will be lost and forgotten if they are not properly collected and preserved. As Long *et al.* (2017) suggest, 'anxiety and perhaps urgency is [...] often foundational to the archival impulse' (*Ibid.*, p. 70). These anxieties surround the very existence and ongoing sustainability of the institutions, as well as decisions made on a day-to-day basis about which materials are 'worth' being preserved and which should be discarded.

Considerable pressures also arise from the precarious nature of labour in the DIY heritage sector. Limited resources and a lack of consistent funding threaten the long-term viability of these institutions, which may not be able to retain their physical presence (e.g. if rents are raised) or struggle to secure the staff and skills necessary to perform integral functions (e.g. sorting through donations, opening to the public). Workers are often unpaid volunteers for whom the heritage practice is a 'labour of love' (see Long *et al.*, 2017). Consequently, like the television producers and musicians discussed above, heritage volunteers can have a tendency for self-exploitation, driven by complex feelings of enthusiasm and anxiety.

Conclusion

It is crucial to understand contemporary work beyond just productivity, effectiveness, and economic contribution. Although many nations now have policy initiatives directed at generating new jobs in the cultural and creative industries, little consideration has been given to the subjective experiences of those who fill these roles. As the above case studies demonstrate, creative labour has significant and complex affective dimensions. This work is not only about liaising with talent show contestants, recording music, or sorting through archival material, but also about the feelings bound up in performing these tasks in specific contexts, and how these feelings are managed, expressed, or concealed.

Creative labour cannot be described in binarized ways, as simply offering either pleasure or pressure, freedom or exploitation. Kennedy (2009) captures this well in her critique of the dualism enforced in much literature on new media:

> [...] whether waged or unwaged, new media workers are [portrayed as] either creative and autonomous producers of culture for the digital economy, or they are victims enslaved to the mundane and low-paid elements of knowledge work or the gruelling rhythms of insecure portfolio work. Yet this does not paint a full picture. (*Ibid.*, p. 180)

In actuality, the affective experiences of creative labour are marked by ambivalence. While workers are driven by the enjoyment of pursuing their passion, love for their industry, striving for self-actualization, and achieving recognition, they also face stresses associated with the precariousness of creative industries, arising from intermittent employment, long hours, little (or no) pay, and so forth (Hesmondhalgh & Baker, 2011). Additionally, although creative industries can be the source of camaraderie and valuable networks, they can likewise be alienating, exclusive, and competitive.

This ambivalence is further complicated by the specificities of each industry, each job role, and each individual worker. As our case studies showed, there are differences in the affective experiences of those working in the creative sectors of television, music, and heritage, and the feelings we discuss would also manifest differently in other creative and cultural fields. Pleasures, pressures, and other affects are also experienced in unequal ways, contingent on one's seniority and experience level, as well as factors such as gender, sexuality, race, ethnicity, class, and (dis)ability (see Gill (2002) for an exploration of the gendered inequalities in new media work).

Therefore, it is vital for media students, scholars, policymakers, and practitioners alike to account for these inequalities and particularities, as the affective qualities of creative labour – its pleasures and pressures – raise questions as to the politics of work in the media. That is, how might the pleasurable, 'positive and emancipatory aspects of labour [...] be made more prevalent' in the creative industries, and how might the pressures and 'negative aspects of work [...] be contained, controlled or even eliminated'? (Hesmondhalgh & Baker, 2011, p. 222). Our examples from television production, the music industry, and the heritage sector demonstrate that despite the specificities of each of these creative industries/sectors, the affective experiences of workers, both paid and unpaid, also show a great deal of similarity. Thus, there is a need to consider the politics of media work in conjunction with a focus on experiences of creative labour more broadly.

Further reading
- Case: How pro bloggers, YouTubers, and Instagram influencers affectively experience the working conditions and labour requirements for 'making it' as an online content creator – Duffy (p. 375)
- Context: Five current issues and trends relating to the creative and cultural industries as a result of digitalization and the rise of the global communication giants – Miège (p. 73)
- Contrast: How the affective labour of making media entails using emotions in order to produce emotions in others – Siapera (p. 275)

References

Ahmed, S. (2010). 'Happy Objects', in M. Gregg & G.J. Seigworth (eds), *The Affect Theory Reader* (29-51). Durham, NC: Duke University Press.

Arvidsson, A., Malossi G. & Naro, S. (2010). 'Passionate Work? Labour Conditions in the Milan Fashion Industry', *Journal for Cultural Research*, 14(3), 295-309.

Baker, S. (2014). '"Nobody Expects to be Paid ... Nobody Asks, 'What is the Fee?'": Making a Living from Music in a Time of Economic Crisis – the Icelandic Experience', in L. Marshall & D. Laing (eds), *Popular Music Matters: Essays in Honours of Simon Frith* (31-44). Farnham: Ashgate.

Baker, S. (2015). 'Affective Archiving and Collective Collecting in Do-it-Yourself Popular Music Archives and Museums', in S. Baker (ed.), *Preserving Popular Music Heritage: Do-it-Yourself, Do-it-Together* (46-61). New York: Routledge.

Baker, S. (2017). *Community Custodians of Popular Music's Past: A DIY Approach to Heritage*. New York: Routledge.

Banks, M. & Hesmondhalgh, D. (2009). 'Looking for Work in Creative Industries Policy', *International Journal of Cultural Policy*, 15 (4), 415-430.

Bridgen, L. (2011). 'Emotional Labour and the Pursuit of the Personal Brand: Public Relations Practitioners' Use of Social Media', *Journal of Media Practice*, *12*(1), 61-76.

Gill, R. (2002). 'Cool, Creative and Egalitarian? Exploring Gender in Project-Based New Media Work in Europe', *Information, Communication & Society*, *5*(1), 70-89.

Gill, R. & Pratt, A. (2008). 'In the Social Factory? Immaterial Labour, Precariousness and Cultural Work', *Theory, Culture & Society*, *25*(7-8), 1-30.

Gregg, M. (2009). 'Learning to (Love) Labour: Production Cultures and the Affective Turn', *Communication and Critical/Cultural Studies*, *6*(2), 209-214.

Grindstaff, L. (2002). *The Money Shot: Trash, Class, and the making of TV Talk Shows*. Chicago, IL: The University of Chicago Press.

Hardt, M. & Negri, A. (2000). *Empire*. Cambridge, MA: Harvard University Press.

Hesmondhalgh, D. & Baker, S. (2008). 'Creative Work and Emotional Labour in the Television Industry', *Theory, Culture & Society*, *25*(7-8), 97-118.

Hesmondhalgh, D. & Baker, S. (2010). '"A Very Complicated Version of Freedom": Conditions and Experiences of Creative Labour in Three Cultural Industries', *Poetics*, *38*, 4-20.

Hesmondhalgh, D. & Baker, S. (2011). *Creative Labour: Media Work in Three Cultural Industries*. New York: Taylor and Francis.

Hochschild, A. (1983). *The Managed Heart: Commercialization of Human Feeling*. Berkeley, CA: University of California Press.

Hopper, K.M. & Huxford, J.E. (2015). 'Gathering Emotion: Examining Newspaper Journalists' Engagement in Emotional Labor', *Journal of Media Practice*, *16*(1), 25-41.

Kennedy, H. (2009). 'Going the Extra Mile: Emotional and Commercial Imperatives in New Media Work', *Convergence: The International Journal of Research into New Media Technologies*, *15*(2), 177-196.

Lazzarato, M. (1996). 'Immaterial Labour', in M. Hardt & P. Virno (eds), *Radical Thought in Italy: A Potential Politics* (133-147). Minneapolis, MN: University of Minnesota Press.

Lee, D. (2012). 'The Ethics of Insecurity: Risk, Individualization and Value in British Independent Television Production', *Television & New Media*, *13*(6), 480-497.

Long, P., Baker, S., Istvandity, L. & Collins, J. (2014). 'A Labour of Love: The Affective Archives of Popular Music Culture', *Archives and Records*, *38*(1), 61-79.

McRobbie, A. (2002a). 'Clubs to Companies: Notes on the Decline of Political Culture in Speeded Up Creative Worlds', *Cultural Studies*, *16*(4), 516-531.

McRobbie, A. (2002b). 'From Holloway to Hollywood: Happiness at Work in the New Cultural Economy?', in P. du Gay & M. Pryke (eds), *Cultural Economy: Cultural Analysis and Commercial Life* (97-114). London: SAGE Publications.

McRobbie, A. (2016). *Be Creative: Making a Living in the New Culture Industries*. Cambridge: Polity Press.

Morisawa, T. (2014). 'Managing the Unmanageable: Emotional Labour and Creative Hierarchy in the Japanese Animation Industry', *Ethnography*, *16*(2), 262-284.

Nunn, H. & Biressi, A. (2010). '"A Trust Betrayed": Celebrity and the Work of Emotion', *Celebrity Studies*, *1*(1), 49-64.

Phillipov, M. (2017). *Media and Food Industries: The New Politics of Food*. Basingstoke: Palgrave Macmillan.

Poynter, G. (2002). 'Emotions in the Labour Process", *European Journal of Psychotherapy & Counselling*, *5*(3), 247-261.

Richards, B. & Rees, G. (2011). 'The Management of Emotion in British Journalism', *Media, Culture & Society*, *33*(6), 851-867.

Rowlands, L. & Handy, J. (2012). 'An Addictive Environment: New Zealand Film Production Workers' Subjective Experiences of Project-Based Labour', *Human Relations*, *65*(5), 657-680.

Ursell, G. (2000). 'Television Production: Issues of Exploitation, Commodification and Subjectivity in UK Television Labour Markets', *Media, Culture & Society*, *22*(6), 805-825.

Yeomans, L. (2007). 'Emotion in Public Relations: A Neglected Phenomenon', *Journal of Communication Management*, *11*(3), 212-221.

22.   A Business of One or Nurturing the Craft: Who are You?

Ilana Gershon and Mark Deuze

If you want to be successful as a professional media maker, you have to think of yourself as a 'business of one': always managing, promoting, and performing yourself as a brand. This is a truism throughout all media industries. However, such constant self-branding comes at a cost. This chapter discusses the origin of self-branding and offers an alternative way of finding work in media by focusing on craftsmanship.

Introduction

Especially since the early 2000s, being a professional media maker has meant being conscious of the fact that you have and are a personal brand. Branding yourself has become a ubiquitous task. The reason for this shift may seem obvious: new communicative technologies. Without technologies such as Twitter, Facebook, or earlier predecessors like MySpace, media workers did not have the tools to brand themselves. Yet, suggesting that journalists, advertising creatives, game developers, and all the other professionals across the media industries brand themselves because it is now technologically possible to do so overlooks the history of self-branding as a perceived prerequisite for success in the media industries, and especially bypasses a deeper question: why would anyone think that this was a good idea or a necessary practice in the first place?

Media workers – such as professionals in film and television, advertising, and music – to some extent have always adopted branding tactics for themselves: creating and managing a certain persona, doing the emotional labour necessary in largely informal and reputation-driven working environments to suggest a persona, performing this identity dutifully in order to make it work. The twin developments of precarization of work in the media industries and the rise of digital media have amplified and accelerated the branding trend, often raising the level of self-promotion to stressful levels.

However, branding is not an inevitable practice – it is not even all that measurably effective. In this chapter, we argue that the notion of branding accompanied a shift in how people understand the nature of work and, more specifically, a shift in how people understood what it meant to work for others. People are now expected to view themselves as a business of one (Lane, 2011), seeking to enter into business alliances with others. The employment contract is now seen as a business-to-business contract in which you, as a business, are contracted to provide temporary solutions to another business's market-specific problems (Gershon, 2017). In the case of a professional media maker, this typically means a temporary contract to provide content to a media outlet.

This metaphor, whereby you should think of yourself as a business, was, however, developed to solve a conceptual problem, not a practical problem that actual workplaces face. It was supposed to help bridge the gap between an increasingly dominant philosophy advocated by economists such as Frederick Hayek, Milton Friedman, and others of the Mont Pelerin Society, and how people actually live their lives in the labour market. It may just have been a solution for a conceptual problem, but it has had all sorts of implications for how actual workplaces are run, and how people understand career strategies, including the widespread belief that everyone should have a personal brand.

A business of one

Frederich Hayek (1899-1922) was an Austrian economist who had a conviction: that markets were the best form of spontaneous order for the modern world. Nowadays, many people share this conviction, in part because Hayek and his followers became so influential. But, at the time that Hayek and his circle began to argue for this position, it was a much more controversial and minority ideological position to take. Hayek was responding both to Soviet communism and Fascism, two systems that rely on centralized planning to manage the economy. For Hayek, centralized economic planning was a recipe for disaster. As a basic tenet, he held that human beings are too flawed to be able to plan a complex modern economy. There was no way that a single human being, or even group of human beings, could competently handle the informational complexities of modern economic systems. Given that humans were too limited to be able to plan without imminent disaster, having the market organize large-scale production and distribution was the best alternative available.

At the same time, Hayek understood that markets did not emerge naturally, they are constructed and have tendencies towards monopoly and other business practices that could undercut forming a level playing field. This is the primary reason why governments should exist – government laws and regulations are necessary to ensure that markets function well. Governments should not be providing services to its citizenry such as public transportation or a postal service – Hayek believed these services are most efficiently managed by private interests. Also, governments should not be providing forms of welfare to its citizens, since welfare undercuts how the market allocates value and introduces too much centralized planning. Instead, what governments should focus on, according to Hayek, is organizing markets well and keeping them functioning to promote competition, and thus innovation. Because market competition is the goal, arbitrarily curtailing this competition through tariffs or other nationalist strategies for undercutting a global market was also deeply undesirable. Hayek wanted a truly global market.

This approach to markets and governments, commonly called neo-liberalism by its critics, has become the dominant way in which the global economy is organized. As this theory moved off the page and the blackboard, people who wanted to live according to neo-liberal principles ran into a basic problem. Neo-liberalism implies a specific way of being a capitalist, and not one that everyone agrees with, even if they are committed to capitalism in general. So, as neo-liberalism became more widely accepted, its practitioners had to figure out how to change the infrastructures and the ways of talking about capitalism. To make a neo-liberal approach persuasive, they had to figure out how to live as a neo-liberal. It turns out that there are all sorts of social dilemmas in daily life that are not addressed by saying: 'The market is the best way to organize or determine value.'

True, Hayek understood that he needed to explain what kind of person you had to be in order to engage with the market in the way he wanted. But he never developed a particularly good model for making complicated decisions like deciding who to hire for a job opening, or how to fashion a career over a lifetime. Other economists, like Gary Becker who coined the idea of human capital, had to come up with more concrete ways to understand how people should analyse everyday interactions using a neo-liberal logic. They began to talk about how people need to think about investing in themselves, viewing themselves as an asset whose value only the market could effectively determine. As critics such as Zygmunt Bauman (2007) note, this rationale of 'no consumer unless a commodity' pressures people to think of themselves as a product that needs constant upgrading and development in order to remain current, relevant, and noteworthy for an otherwise unfeeling market. Only when you attract attention and appreciation – for example expressed in a salaried job or paid assignment – can you effectively participate in society. Throughout the second half of the twentieth century, a general consensus emerged that people should indeed view themselves as a business – a bundle of skills, assets, qualities, experiences, and relationships that constantly had to be managed and enhanced.

Workers, especially in the media and the cultural and creative industries, are told to think of themselves as a business in a context in which neo-liberal approaches to businesses have also changed the ways in which a company determines its actual value. Before a neo-liberal perspective became entrenched, companies might be seen as providing a wide variety of benefits to a large number of constituents – to upper management, to employees, to the local community, as well as to shareholders. Many of these benefits were long term. But as the market value began to be seen as the primary and often only way to measure a company's value, increasing the value to shareholders began to be the principle goal for companies. Companies started to focus on quarterly earnings and stock prices as the sole measure of success.

This changed how companies treated employees. To keep stock prices high, companies, for example, had to pay their employees as little as possible. Professional associations such as the National Union of Journalists in the UK and the Media Entertainment & Arts Alliance in Australia have noted that media workers often report they feel more like someone that costs their employer money than a valued employee. Furthermore, under neo-liberal policies companies are increasingly seeking to have as temporary a workforce as their particular business can allow. The less permanent the workforce, the easier it is to expand and contract in response to short-term demands and market fluctuations. Public policies have followed suit, making it easier for companies to fire employees, expanding the various ways in which a company can sub-contract and outsource labour, as well as providing incentives to workers to become self-supporting free agents (or 'entrepreneurs').

The consequences of neo-liberalism

When companies arrange themselves according to Hayek's world view, it relatively quickly leads to precarious work conditions for employees – a process additionally facilitated by a decline in collective organization among (media) workers. What companies need are not workers to whom they have clear obligations to foster long-term relationships through pensions and similar incentives. Instead, they need professionals who work dependably, and in many cases, long, intense hours to finish short-term projects. They want employees who no longer expect long-term commitments from their place of work. This form of precarity means that workers have to figure out how to get contract after contract – a career becomes a string of jobs or contracts.

In practice, media workers have found that this typically means they are constantly searching for a job – that they now have two jobs, the contract they are currently working on and the job of looking for the next contract. But what does looking for the next job actually consist of? In part because it is such a logical extension of the self-as-business metaphor, always looking now involves always branding oneself. This notion of personal branding became popular when Tom Peters, a motivational speaker and management consultant, wrote 'The Brand Called You' for *FastCompany* in 1997, in which he explicitly connected the dots between the self-as-business and branding oneself: 'We are CEOs of our own companies: Me Inc. To be in business today, our most important job is to be head marketer for the brand called You' (Peters, 1997). This take caught on – it certainly captured the emerging neo-liberal spirit of the time.

Now part and parcel of having a career in the media is understood to be regularly crafting your personal brand by (for example) figuring out three or four words that reflect an authentic self (consider for example the space for a bio on a Twitter profile); making sure that all your online and offline interactions are consistent with these terms; spending considerable time managing and interacting through various online profiles (LinkedIn, Twitter, Facebook, and so on); curating what comes up when people (especially prospective employers or clients) Google your name; and so on and so forth. All of this, of course, in addition to creating excellent work and building a reputation among businesses and peers as a desirable hire. If all of this sounds time-consuming, it is. Indeed, for professional media makers these days, the freedom of being able to create work about what you are most interested in, and thus what you are framing as your core brand attributes, comes at the price of no longer having free time.

Now that self-branding is seen as essential for success, this also becomes an avenue for explaining failure that allows media workers to overlook the changes to the labour market – generally attributing a lack of assignments or doing too much underpaid or even non-paid work to a host of factors other than critically reviewing the system as a whole. Self-employed media workers are blaming themselves in a way parallel to what Ofer Sharone says unemployed white-collar Americans do. In his book, *Flawed System/Flawed Self* (2013), Sharone critiques the widespread scholarly belief that Americans are culturally individualistic, and thus prone to see their successes and failures as the result of their own actions, instead of as a result of structural shifts in the labour market. As an example, when an American cannot get a permanent job managing a call centre, he will supposedly claim it is his own fault, not that those jobs were all outsourced to India and the Philippines because of labour costs and government policies.

Sharone notes that when Americans blame themselves, it is not due to cultural blinders on their part, but rather a perfectly reasonable response to how the hiring ritual is structured in the US. He points out that in the US, job seekers are often rejected for an especially nebulous reason – not being a 'cultural fit'. This amorphous term is widely understood as a flexible code for concealing the concrete and often politically charged reasons a hiring committee chooses someone else. While in actuality a hiring manager may have been concerned that a job seeker had spent too little time working at their last couple of jobs, or too much time (both of which tend to be structurally specific issues having to do with those workplaces), the explanation the person will receive for the rejection is the more ambiguous 'not a cultural fit' reason. Or, people are told that networking is the primary way to get a job these days, in part because applicant tracking systems and recruiters screen out so many good candidates. Yet, this advice tends to leave vague what kinds of networking – what activities and what connections – are necessary. People who view themselves as introverted or reluctant to make relationships openly instrumental see their failures to network 'properly' (however ill-defined that may be) as the cause of their unemployment, not employers' poor sorting mechanisms or biases inherent in the top-down system. When given these nebulous explanations enough times, people will start blaming themselves for why they don't have a job.

Media professionals are caught in a similarly ambiguous trap. They are told that in order to succeed, they must work two jobs simultaneously: looking for the next job constantly, that is, self-branding, while also doing the job at hand. At the same time, the job market for self-employed media makers sends out contradictory and ambiguous messages, as opaque for them as 'cultural fit' is for the American job seeker. As a result, they frequently understand failure in terms of personality traits. People who are reluctant to market themselves or not particularly talented at those set of tasks are seen as producing their own career failures.

Freelance media professionals do not tend to suggest that there are structural problems with how the labour market is constructed. Nor do they point out that what makes one good at getting a job is not necessarily what makes one good at doing a job. Instead, they blame themselves for their reluctance to brand themselves, or they blame consumers for not appreciating their art. They might perhaps even blame a specific company or executive for overlooking their talent, but it is rare for them to critique the way professions such as journalism or film and television production are structured. Even if they do, it is generally not considered good form to complain about such arrangements on the job, and the degree of collective organization – which would enable them to act on such grievances – tends to be quite low among media workers.

Passion as a panacea

Job insecurity, self-branding, and passion go hand in hand these days. The emotions you are supposed to feel for your work change when you start seeing yourself as a temporary employee making a career from a long string of jobs. Companies used to try to foster company loyalty in every way they could, since this provided them with a steady bank of workers already familiar with how the company worked. It also meant that the company had people maximally committed to having the company do as well as possible, often with a lot of experience about how the company had done things in the past. But when companies decided to do away with company loyalty, a new emotional connection to work had to be found as a replacement.

While there were a number of possible emotions one could turn to, the general consensus in creative careers such as in the media has been that everyone should feel passion for their work. This is consistently the advice any media professional will give those vying for a spot in their line of work. It seems irrelevant what the job actually is, and whether the job does, in fact, require that someone feels strongly about who they are working for or what kind of work they are expected to do in order to do it well. Since company loyalty is no longer around to guarantee committed workers, passion is now supposed to be the driving force.

Intriguingly, this passion people are supposed to feel is restricted to the tasks at work or to learning certain skills, tracking down leads or becoming better at capturing the most compelling shot. There are many parts of a job that one is never asked to feel passion for, and telling enough, most of these aspects would be the ones that keep you committed to a particular company. So people tend not to express passion for working with particular people (unless that kind of passion is supposed to be performed, such as in 'making of' showreels as part of the promotional campaigns for motion pictures). Media makers also generally do not talk about feeling passion for making the company they work for well-respected among other companies. Instead, they are only supposed to feel passion for the duties of their job role, duties that they could theoretically perform at any media company. Passion is reserved for the tasks that they do (or learn to do) and for the solutions that they might develop for market-specific problems that the company faces. All too often, the market-specific problems that employees talk about being captivated by are problems that a range of companies might face. They are not specific to that particular company. In short, work based on passion is focused on all the tasks that only involve the worker's career trajectory (and narrative thereof), and none of the tasks that solely involve the company's well-being (Gershon, 2017).

Focusing on feeling passion for lucrative tasks makes workers more mobile. When the main reason to work somewhere is because you feel passion, it is all too easy to quit because you have stopped feeling passion. Passion, furthermore, is an exceptionally vague qualifier, and certainly is not necessarily synonymous with either a job well done, or any particular talent or exceptional ability. It is also much harder to develop a substantial critique of the industry you are in if what brings and keeps you at work inside this industry is your own, individual, and intimate passion – you would end up being critical of the very thing that connects most deeply to who you (think you) are. Finally, passion is a rather self-centred focus – if not obsession – more often than not bypassing (caring for) others.

Conclusion: Craftsmanship as an alternative focus

We have been suggesting that there is a price to pay for imagining the labour market as full of businesses – some shaped like people and some shaped like companies – all entering into temporary alliances with each other. Many media makers now work in a situation where they compete with each other to tell their stories rather than in a situation where media companies compete to nurture and support their talent. As a result, the price is more often paid by (and steeper for) media workers in temporary contracts trying to craft a career than by the media companies organizing and benefiting from this temporary labour pool (Deuze, 2007, 2011).

But is there an alternative path that media workers can follow to live more humane lives that doesn't involve the very time-consuming and messy work of starting a revolution or quitting this line of work entirely? We want to suggest here a quieter path towards reform, reviving an older way of understanding what it means to be a worker and its accompanying practices: seeing yourself as a craftsperson instead of a business. Scholars such as Jean Lave, Richard Sennett, and Etienne Wenger have analysed the social practices that make being a craftsperson, including apprentices, a more tolerable way forward (Lave & Wenger, 1991; Sennett, 1998, 2009).

What would thinking of oneself as a craftsperson instead of a business involve? First and foremost, you would see yourself as a maker – someone whose creativity and skill produces texts, images, and objects that can change the world for the better. Doing a task well for its own sake, for the satisfaction of showing mastery, is a very different goal than doing a task solely for profit, and often someone else's profit. As a craftsperson, you are constantly exploring your capacities alongside other people who have different degrees and areas of mastery as well. One editor might be especially good at figuring out how to fashion a catchy phrase, and be able to teach you how to do this better. Another editor might be especially good at knowing what information a reader needs and when to grasp a complex situation. At the same time, as a craftsperson, you are always helping other people become better as well – you are enmeshed in relationships of apprenticeship, co-working, mutual support, and mentoring that make the challenges of working together more valued than the efforts of individually marketing oneself. Part of how you are known as someone who is desirable to work with will be based on how well you tend to your relationships and how well you encourage other people in their pursuits.

Attending to one's reputation, in other words, can be a more social, more ethical, and more nuanced focus than promoting one's brand. The difference lies in the orientation toward the craft or the business. A business reputation is all about performance: not necessarily being good at what you do, but creating and maintaining the image of being good (whatever 'good' may be in the particular context of the project at hand). A craft reputation is about being renowned for the quality of your work and the extent to which you take pleasure from honing your craft (and that of your fellow workers). Being a craftsperson instead of a business also leads more easily to forms of collective organization, whether through unionizing, joining professional associations, or maintaining various networks offline and online. A craft orientation eschews a form of competition that undercuts other media workers in pursuit of work opportunities, it opens up space for collaboration and co-creativity.

There are different ways to understand the work that media makers have to do in order to make it work. Part of this involves not just doing good work, but also being known for doing so. Incessant self-branding is just one route for gaining such recognition, and a deeply problematic one that takes up lots of people's time and without clear cut results. But it takes more than media makers just saying: 'Right, I won't worry about branding myself anymore'. It also means that media companies should consciously decide to retain and nurture talent, rather than just managing to the bottom line. It means valuing other people for the quality of their work and the ethical ways they conduct themselves as colleagues. It involves caring for the (collaborative, co-creative) work and for fellow workers rather than a self-centred focus on finding one's passion.

People participate in making branding seem like an obvious and desirable route at many different moments in the workplace. It is time to cultivate the craft instead.

Further reading
- Case: Three case studies on how the working conditions within the cultural and creative industries are affectively experienced – Cantillon & Baker (p. 287)
- Context: The various new forms of value which circulate in the media industries, resulting from different ways in which media makers and users value media – Bolin (p. 111)
- Contrast: How freelancers in the media industry are collectively working to protect their rights and improve their position – Cohen (p. 235)

References

Bauman, Z. (2007). *Consuming Life*. Cambridge: Polity Press.

Deuze, M. (2007). *Media Work*. Cambridge: Polity Press.

Deuze, M. (ed.) (2011). *Managing Media Work*. London: SAGE Publications.

Gershon, I. (2017). *Down and Out in the New Economy: How People Find (or Don't Find) Work Today*. Chicago, IL: University of Chicago Press.

Lave, J. & Wenger, E. (1991). *Situated Learning*. Cambridge: Cambridge University Press.

Sennett, R. (1998). *The Corrosion of Character: The Personal Consequences of Work in the New Capitalism*. New York: W. W. Norton and Company.

Sennett, R. (2008). *The Craftsman.* New Haven, CT: Yale University Press.

Sharone, O. (2013). *Flawed System/Flawed Self: Job Searching and Unemployment Experiences.* Chicago, IL: University of Chicago Press.

Professions

Music

23. Music in Times of Streaming: Transformation and Debate

Sofia Johansson

Digitalization has had significant consequences for the music industry. It has influenced business models as well as consumption practices, affecting music companies, artists, and fans. This chapter discusses the key issues and debates on music and digitalization, with a focus on questions brought about by the expansion of music streaming services such as Spotify.

Introduction

As record labels, publishing houses, concert promoters, and artists tackle financial and legal uncertainties following digitalization, the internet has become central to music consumption. Well-established shifts in music listening practices include the move from offline to online music listening and the development of file-sharing and communicative activities around music within social media. In recent years, online streaming services have, moreover, contributed to the notion of music as primarily belonging in an online 'cloud' (Wikström, 2013), rather than in personal music collections. Spotify, first launched in Sweden and five other countries in 2008, had over 140 million active users in 61 markets at the end of 2017, with over 30 million songs in its archive. Owning a CD – once considered the height of technological innovation – has become, especially among young people, a nostalgic thing of the past.

Offering constantly available access to vast quantities of music, streaming services can be analysed in relation to their consequences for music artists and the music industry. As a way to deliver cultural commodities, notably music and video, streaming can likewise be approached as a significant development in the media system at large, involving an intertwining of techno-social and economic elements (Vonderau, 2015). Music streaming can also be studied for the way it is integrated into the fabric of social media, with YouTube, for instance, largely based on user-generated content, and the partnership between Spotify and Facebook, effective from the autumn of 2011, an example of commercial dovetailing between two of the main actors in social media and music streaming. The wider shift towards the internet as a main platform for music, equally, opens up investigations into its meanings for listeners. How does cloud-based music listening contribute to engagement in music? How do music fans understand their role in the transforming music and media landscape?

This chapter identifies some of the key issues and scholarly debates on music and digitalization, with a focus on questions brought about by the expansion of music streaming. I start by reviewing long-standing concerns about music and the internet, the subject of intense discussions since the internet became popularized in the mid-1990s. The next section deals with a related analysis of the music industry, variously seen as in desperate free-fall and as revived by new business models. In the last part, I pay attention to questions around digital music consumption, examining research into online fandom and piracy as well as into music streaming as an everyday practice.

Music and the internet: Some key issues

The consequences of digitalization for the music industry, music artists, and listeners have been fervently discussed for over two decades, as a source of both alarm and enthusiasm. During this time, the internet has developed from its complementary role to popular music in the 1990s – as a forum for dedicated music fans, file-sharers, and technological enthusiasts – to a much more crucial position in music consumption and music economies. Today, as pointed out by Nick Prior (2015), the internet should be approached as a 'normal' platform for music listening, part of how many people use and understand music, and intersecting with an everyday life increasingly framed by connected and abundant media use (e.g. Deuze, 2012). Exemplified by a number of key innovations, including the development of the MP3-file and file-sharing programs, the establishment of digital music sales and the expansion of streaming as a system of delivery for media content, this period has seen transitions with lasting impact on the way that music is produced, distributed, and consumed.

Yet, as suggested by Steve Jones (2011, p. 444), the 'real revolution in popular music in regard to the internet' can equally be thought of as related to 'the availability of news, information and discussion about music and musicians'. The study of music and the internet, then, covers a diverse field of research, and interconnects with broader ideas of digitalization as a transformative force (e.g. Katz, 2005; Ayers, 2006; Messaris & Humphreys, 2006).

One over-riding theme in debates about music and the internet concerns the way in which technological development interrelates with production, use and experience of music. Each new music technology, such as the phonograph or the Walkman, has altered the music industry and culture, and so too have digital and online technologies and formats. For example, the MP3 format, allowing compact and easily transferable storage of audio, transformed ways of selling and listening to music (Bull, 2007; Sterne, 2012). Jeremy Wade Morris (2015) uses the term 'the digital music commodity' to describe music accessible through computers or other digital appliances: 'made visible, audible, and tangible through various software interfaces, media players, metadata and hardware devices' (*Ibid.*, p. 3). While related to previous storage forms, like CDs, tapes, and vinyl records, Wade Morris means that the digital music commodity, stripped of non-digital packaging, encompasses specific sonic experiences and understandings of music. Likewise, the shift from the CD to huge archives of online MP3-files and music streams has no doubt changed the way music is stored – and potentially valued. Streaming, in particular, represents a decisive break with music collecting (Marshall, 2014) and is sometimes regarded as contributing to a devaluation of music, with audiences fatigued by endless choice (Vonderau, 2015, pp. 727-729).

While evaluations of the consequences of new music technology may vary, it is clear that it plays an increasingly active role in music use, since the more of this takes place online, the greater the reliance on certain programs and online services for the individual's libraries, playlists, and music preferences. A pressing research question, therefore, concerns how computational and algorithmic processes govern listeners' experiences today (see Snickars, 2016; Beer, 2017).

Another important, and related, issue relates to how the online setting shapes the relationship between the music industry, artists, and listeners. Who is in control of the means of production, when almost anyone seems to be able to make music and distribute it online? The internet has posed a challenge to the music industry in this respect, in part because music artists can more easily spread their work and communicate directly with their audiences via social media (Young & Collins, 2010; Baym, 2012), and because music fans seemingly have gained a greater opportunity to influence artists and the dissemination of music (e.g. Baym, 2007; Bennett, 2011, 2014). While in some sense fitting with ideas of the internet as contributing to the levelling of cultural hierarchies (Jenkins 2006), this development is, however, not clear-cut. Based on an interview study with musicians about their uses of social media, Nancy Baym (2012), for example, shows that while many music artists appreciate the connection with fans offered by social media, this also involves an often time-consuming form of labour and self-promotion that their role previously did not entail.

Rather than understanding social media as simply shifting control from the music industry to artists and fans, a more precise picture is clearly needed. Here, new forms of labour extend to the work carried out by fans, as they perform the role of cultural intermediaries online (Baym & Burnett, 2009), while user data collection is likewise integral to many online music services and platforms (Morris, 2015, pp. 177-181).

The music industry in transformation

Digitalization, then, has had important consequences for the music industry. Not long ago, the music industry was often portrayed as threatened, with popular as well as academic accounts suggesting a purported death of the legacy recording industry and associated stakeholders and businesses. Major music and recording companies were seen as deeply troubled by illegal file-sharing and the circumvention of traditional means of distribution, with falling revenue from physical music sales, the emergence of new intermediaries for music (such as Spotify and Apple Music), and copyright infringement on revenue streams (starting with Napster in the late 1990s). Today, the industry seems to be adapting, with streaming services inspiring new business models, and scholarly analysis of the music industry consequently underlining more complex reconfigurations. For example, a global decline in record sales can be contrasted with a revival of music publishing and revenues from live performances in the digital era (Rogers, 2013).

Descriptions of a unified industry in decline, hence, tend to overlook the diversification in different sectors and markets, with the music industry now involving such a wide range of actors – from promoters to streaming services – that it might be more accurately referred to in plural (see Rogers & Preston, 2016; Nordgård, 2016). It is also important to remember that the new music economies can differ between different parts of the world (see Morrow & Fangjun Li, 2016), something that is easily overlooked as discussions about 'the music industry' often focus on an Anglo-American context, and especially on major US record companies (Marshall, 2013).

While these companies have gone through a notable process of consolidation of ownership, and are continually vying for control over the internet as an arena for music distribution, not least through vigorous copyright battles (e.g. Burkhart, 2014, pp. 396-397; Arditi, 2014), they are joined by streaming services as new major actors in the music industry. Providing a service (access to music) instead of relying on the sale of specific units, the expansion of commercial music streaming services has meant that the physical distribution of music is less important than it used to be (Wikström, 2013; Anderson, 2014). Relying on a process of copying 'bits' of data, as well as on the aggregation of large data sets (see Vonderau, 2015, pp. 717-718), streaming makes music accessible from multiple devices while the songs are not owned by the user and can be removed from the service at any time without notice.

Providing a solution for recording companies grappling with piracy, Spotify emerged as the leading streaming service after setting up deals with the major actors in the music industry. This made them shareholders, with Spotify's business model based on revenue streams to record companies and artists predicated on a pay-per-stream system, and income gained both from subscription and advertising. As highlighted by Rasmus Fleisher and Pelle Snickars (2017, pp. 133-135) it is, however, rather difficult to categorize Spotify, as it pends between definitions of a 'tech' company, merely facilitating the distribution of content, and a media company. Irrespective of whether or not music streaming services should be regarded as part of the music and media industries or as independent tech companies, they can clearly be credited with weakening illegal file-sharing, and appear to contribute to an upward turn for revenues in recorded music while competing with digital music sales (see Rogers & Preston, 2016, pp. 64-65).

Yet, music streaming services have also caused controversy. This includes concerns over their financial viability, as well as whether the transfer of revenue to music artists is fair (Wikström & De Fillippi, 2016, p. 3). It also has to do with worries about a potentially negative impact on smaller artists and independent labels. The argument here is that the pay-per-stream system seems to primarily benefit major and known artists, with the top songs and artists making up a high proportion of the revenue. Even though the tiny amount paid for each song play could add up to a more substantial sum over a longer period, this requires the kind of financial reserves that smaller labels and independent artists may not have (Marshall, 2015, p. 181; Nordgård, 2016).

Another point of contention relates to the role of music streaming services in guiding the listeners' encounter with music, which connects to questions of algorithmic curatorship and the part played by technology in shaping the musical experience (see Kjus, 2016). Far from seeing streaming services as 'just' tech companies, researchers have emphasized how program interfaces, algorithms, and systems for archiving and contextualizing music privileges certain listening modes (e.g. Morris & Powers, 2015; Maasø, 2016), such as providing 'more of the same' based on listeners' previous preferences (see Snickars, 2017; Åker, 2017, p. 101). Analysing a series of 'bot experiments' with different Spotify profiles, Maria Eriksson and Anna Johansson (2017), likewise, draw attention to an overrepresentation of male artists in Spotify's music recommendations as an example of how digital content delivery can also be analysed critically from the point of gender (compare Werner & Johansson, 2016). Such research exemplifies how developments in the industry ultimately interlock with the practices of music consumption, which is the final area to be highlighted in this chapter.

Online music consumption

What people do with music online, and how digital music environments are understood by listeners, can be studied from a range of perspectives. One strand of analysis has focused on music piracy, which became widespread in the 2000s with the launch of Napster in 1999. Given the past pursuit of several controversial lawsuits against individual file-sharers and actors such as Napster and the Pirate Bay (see Gillespie, 2007, pp. 40-50; Andersson & Snickars, 2010), and with major music and media industries involved in ongoing legal actions, the discussion about piracy interlinks with questions of ethics, value, and copyright law (Burkart & Anderson, 2015). Some scholars uncover how file-sharers themselves motivate their practice, finding that it is often connected to ideas of the internet as a supposedly open environment, embedded in beliefs about how culture should be organized and accessed (e.g. Andersson Schwarz, 2014; Beekhuysen *et al.*, 2015).

Less controversial are questions about how music fandom, more generally, is shaped by digital cultures. Fandom can be considered an important sociocultural phenomenon, involving a relatively deep and positive emotional connection with an element of popular culture (see Duffett, 2013, p. 2). It is often regarded as revitalized through digitalization, providing fans with enhanced means to connect to artists and each other online (Pearson, 2010). Studies of online music fans examine how fans form communities around certain artists and music genres, for example looking at how jazz fans organize and express themselves in specific forums (Wall & Dubber, 2010), or how fans of the rock group REM constitute a particular online community (Bennett, 2012).

Likewise, with Web 2.0 allowing for more interactive web technologies, music fandom has been seen not only as producing styles, identity, and communities, but also as a basis for content production relevant to the wider cultural circuit, with fans for instance publicizing and distributing music online (Baym, 2007), or furthering new forms of marketing and financing artists, such as through crowd-funding online (Bennett *et al.*, 2015). An interesting development to consider, too, is the relationship between fans and artists established via social media channels. What, to take one example, does Beyoncé's – currently vastly popular – Instagram account mean for her followers? Should we see this as a smart marketing move to make fans feel closer to an artist, or as a genuine attempt by an artist to foster stronger ties with her fans? Social media have been regarded as having contributed to reducing artists' 'star quality', by encouraging glimpses into their lives behind the scene (Beer, 2008), as well as facilitating feelings of intimacy and friendship with the artists, despite the communicative imbalance characterizing this relationship (Bennett, 2014).

However, not all music listeners are dedicated fans. Online music use can involve more mundane and less engaged forms of listening, just as much as it may entail a devotion to certain genres or artists. In order to understand contemporary meanings of music more broadly, it is important to think about how it is integrated into the routines and contexts of everyday life. Anahid Kassabian (2013) has introduced the notion of 'ubiquitous music' to describe how music available from any digital device and at any time is a formative element of current music cultures (see also Quinones *et al.*, 2015). Although music has been portable through non-digital mobile music devices for a long time, and played extensively in shops, restaurants, and other everyday locations before digitalization (Frith, 2001), contemporary music listening is no doubt characterized by a high degree of ubiquity and fluidity, where, notably, mobile digital media and mobile music applications can play a significant role in personal listening (see Werner, 2017). As showed in a qualitative study of music use, drawing on focus groups with young adults in Stockholm and Moscow (Johansson *et al.*, 2017; Johansson, 2017a, pp. 33-39), online environments can be so central to personal music listening that the internet is indeed experienced as having contributed to a shift in the way music is fundamentally understood. The respondents in this study for example describe music as 'air' or 'breathing', rather than as a particular interest or basis for fandom.

Changes in the overall music landscape therefore point to some new areas of enquiry, where the emergence of streaming services opens up novel research endeavours in terms of the implications of their use. In an in-depth research with users of Spotify and Wimp (now Tidal) in Norway, Anja Nylund Hagen (2015a) examines, based on interviews and diaries with twelve heavy 'streamers' of different ages, how streaming becomes part of everyday life, allowing for a flexible and ultimately user-generated music experience, which seems to facilitate notions of music as a 'taken-for-granted' part of life. Looking at various aspects of streaming on an everyday level, Hagen (2015b) also draws attention to practices around playlist listening, which, despite the fact that users do not physically own the music they listen to, can involve a sense of ownership in the maintenance and compilation of playlists.

Music streaming in conjunction with social media, likewise, can be regarded as contributing to complicate notions of live music (Kjus & Danielsen, 2014) and raise questions about how users understand the sharing of music as part of a wider transformation of public and private communication (Van Dijck, 2013; John, 2017). Here, analyses have underlined selectivity and reflexivity as important facets of online music sharing (Hagen & Lüders, 2016), but have also emphasized how users feel challenged by the pressure to disclose music preferences, and the intensely private nature of some forms of music listening (Johansson, 2017b, pp. 53-58). This is illustrative of the overarching complexities individuals face as their music consumption is increasingly inscribed in online environments promoting the disclosure of music tastes and habits, deserving further analysis in future studies of streaming and how the music and recording industries respond to the digital challenge.

Conclusion

I would like to end this chapter with a gentle note of caution. Having provided a broad overview of literature on music and digitalization, taking a particular interest in music streaming as a significant element of current music cultures, the chapter has foregrounded discussions of novelty and intervention, upheaval and change. However, not all is new. In fact, historical contingencies in how music is produced, performed, and listened to deserve attention too, but are sometimes easy to forget amidst the equal measures of enthusiasm and scepticism surrounding digital music technology. For example, the Walkman, car radio, hand-driven record players, and other analogue technologies have facilitated ubiquitous music for decades. Offline contexts for the discussion, guidance and construction of meaning around music – including fan communities, tape trading networks, and other ways for recording artists to foster relationships with their audiences – also continue to matter. The music industry, likewise, has long been subjected to the introduction of technologies impacting on formats and carriers, with streaming just being the most recent development.

Yet, it is clear that the rise of the internet as a music platform, with streaming currently at its centre, nevertheless has involved significant transformations to forms of music production, distribution, promotion, and consumption – with implications for the very meaning of music as a significant form of communication and as a cultural commodity. As highlighted in this chapter, these changes, moreover, have been the subject of lively debate, relating to overarching ideas of how to understand the relationship between technology and musical value, as well as how to pinpoint the dynamics of convergence. Important questions are being raised both around industry reconfiguration and the emerging practices of music listening. Illustrating the intertwining of technology and cultural experience, such discussion relates to the wider role of digital cultures in contemporary society, with music firmly situated within these cultures.

Further reading
- Case: How streaming music and artist-brand deals encourage an uneven distribution of career opportunities in the music industry – Meier (p. 321)
- Context: How new platforms such as Spotify facilitate and profit from new forms of consumption without creating or producing content – Bilton (p. 99)
- Contrast: An exploration of the rise of the platforms and the powerful role they have in shaping professional media production – Nieborg & Poell (p. 85)

References

Åker, P. (2017). 'Spotify as the Soundtrack to Your Life: Encountering Music in the Customized Archive", in S. Johansson, A. Werner, P. Åker & G. Goldenzweig (eds), *Streaming Music: Practices, Media, Cultures*. London & New York: Routledge.

Andersson, J. & Snickars, P. (eds) (2010). *Efter the Pirate Bay*. Stockholm: Kungliga biblioteket.

Andersson Schwarz, J. (2014). *Online File-Sharing: Innovations in Media Consumption*. London: Routledge.

Arditi, D. (2014). 'iTunes: Breaking Barriers and Building Walls', *Popular Music and Society*, *37*(4), 408-424.

Arditi, D. (2012). *The State of Music: Cultural, Political and Economic Transformations in the Music Industry*. Fairfax, VA: Georg Mason University.

Ayers, M.D. (ed.) (2006). *Cybersounds: Essays on Virtual Music Culture*. New York: Peter Lang.

Baym, N. (2012). 'Fans or Friends? Seeing Social Media Audiences as Musicians Do', *Participations: Journal of Audience and Reception Studies, 9*(2), 286-316.

Baym, N. (2007). 'The New Shape of Online Community: The Example of Swedish Independent Music Fandom', *First Monday*, *12*(8), 1-17.

Baym, N. & Burnett, R. (2009). 'Amateur Experts: International Fan Labor in Swedish Independent Music', *International Journal of Cultural Studies*, *12*(5), 1-17.

Beer, D. (2017). 'The Social Power of Algorithms', *Information, Communication & Society*, *20*(1), 1-13.

Beer, D. (2008). 'Making Friends with Jarvis Cocker: Music Culture in the Context of Web 2.0.', *Cultural Sociology*, *2*(2), 222-241.

Beekhuysen, J., Von Hellens, L. & Nielsen, S.H. (2015). 'Illuminating the Underground: The Reality of Unauthorised File-Sharing', *Information Systems Journal*, *25*(3), 171-192.

Bennet, L., Chin, B. & Jones, B. (eds) (2015). 'Crowdfunding: A New Media & Society Special Issue', *New Media & Society*, *17*(2).

Bennet, L. (2016). 'Singer-Songwriters in the Digital Age: New Trajectories in Connectivity and Participation between Musicians and Fans on Social Media', in K. Williams & J.A. Williams (eds), *The Cambridge Companion to the Singer-Songwriter* (329-340). Cambridge: Cambridge University Press.

Bennett, L. (2014). 'Fan/Celebrity Interactions and Social Media: Connectivity and Engagement in Lady Gaga Fandom', in L. Duits, K. Zwann & S. Reijnders (eds), *The Ashgate Research Companion to Fan Cultures* (109-120). Farnham: Ashgate.

Bennett, L. (2012). 'Music Fandom Online: R.E.M. Fans in Pursuit of the Ultimate First Listen', *New Media & Society*, *14*(5), 748-763.

Bull, M. (2007). *Sound Moves: iPod Culture and Urban Experience*. London: Routledge.

Burkart, P. & Andersson Schwarz, J. (2015). 'Piracy and Social Change: Revisiting Pirate Cultures – Editorial Introduction', *International Journal of Communication*, *9*, 792-797.

Burkart, P. (2014). 'Music in the Cloud and the Digital Sublime', *Popular Music and Society*, *37*(4), 393-407.

Deuze, M. (2012). *Media Life*. Cambridge: Polity Press.

Duffett, M. (2013). *Understanding Fandom: An Introduction to the Study of Media Fan Culture*. London: Bloomsbury.

Frith, S. (2001). 'Music and Everyday Life', *Critical Quarterly*, *44*(1), 35-48.

Eriksson, M. & Johansson, A. (2017). 'Tracking Gendered Streams', *Culture Unbound: Journal of Current Cultural Research*, *9*(2), 163-183.

Fleicher, R. & Snickars, P. (2017). 'Discovering Spotify: A thematic introduction', *Culture Unbound: Journal of Current Cultural Research*, *9*(2), 130-145.

Hagen, A.N. (2015a). *Using Music Streaming Services: Practices, Experiences and the Lifeworld of Musicking*. (PhD thesis). Oslo: University of Oslo.

Hagen, A.N. (2015b). 'The Playlist Experience: Personal Playlists in Music Streaming Services', *Popular Music and Society, 38*(5), 625-645.

Hagen, A.N. & Lüders, M. (2016). 'Social Streaming? Navigating Music as Personal and Social', *Convergence: the International Journal of Research into New Media Technologies*. Advance online publication. https://doi.org/10.1177/1354856516673298.

Gillespie, T. (2007). *Wired Shut: Copyright and the Shape of Digital Culture*. Cambridge, MA: MIT Press.

Jenkins, H. (2006). *Convergence Culture: Where Old and New Media Collide*. New York: New York University Press.

Johansson, S., Werner, A., Åker, P. & Goldenzweig, G. (2017). *Streaming Music: Practices, Media, Cultures*. London & New York: Routledge.

Johansson, S. (2017a). 'Online Music in Everyday Life: Contexts and Practices', in S. Johansson, A. Werner, P. Åker & G. Goldenzwaig (eds), *Streaming Music: Practices, Media, Cultures* (27-43). London & New York: Routledge.

Johansson, S. (2017b). 'Music as Part of Connectivity Culture', in S. Johansson, A.Werner, P. Åker & G. Goldenzwaig (eds), *Streaming Music: Practices, Media, Cultures* (62-78). London & New York: Routledge.

John, N.A. (2017). *The Age of Sharing*. Cambridge: Polity Press.

Jones, S. (2011). 'Music and the Internet', in M. Consalvo & C. Ess (eds), *The Handbook of Internet Studies* (440-451). Malden, MA: Blackwell Publishing.

Kassabian, A. (2013). *Ubiquitous Listening: Affect, Attention and Distributed Subjectivity*. Berkeley, CA: University of California Press.

Katz, M. (2005). *Capturing Sound: How Technology Has Changed Music*. Berkeley, CA: University of California Press.

Kjus, Y. & Danielsen, A. (2014). 'Live Islands in the Seas of Recordings: The Music Experience of Visitors at the Öya Festival', *Popular Music and Society, 37*(5), 660-679.

Kjus, Y. (2016). 'Musical Exploration via Streaming Services: The Norwegian Experience', *Popular Communication: The International Journal of Media and Culture, 14*(3), 127-136.

Maasø, A. (2016). 'Music Streaming, Festivals, and the Eventization of Music', *Popular Music & Society*. Advance online publication. https://doi.org/10.1080/03007766.2016.1231001.

Marshall, L. (2015). '"Let's Keep Music Special: F-ing Spotify": On-Demand Streaming and the Controversy over Artist Royalties', *Creative Industries Journal, 8*(2), 177-189.

Marshall, L. (2014). 'W(h)ither Now? Music Collecting in the Age of the Cloud', in L. Marshal & D. Laing (eds), *Popular Music Matters: Essays in Honour of Simon Frith*. Farnham: Ashgate.

Marshall, L. (2013). *The International Recording Industries*. London & New York: Routledge.

Messaris, P. & Humphreys, L. (eds) (2006). *Digital Media: Transformations in Human Communication*. New York: Peter Lang.

Morris, J.W. (2015). *Selling Digital Music, Formatting Culture*. Oakland, CA: University of California Press.

Morris, J.W. & Powers, D. (2015). 'Control, Curation and Musical Experience in Music Streaming Services', *Creative Industries Journal*, 8(2), 106-122.

Morrow, G. & Li, F. (2016). 'The Chinese Music Industries: Top Down in the Bottom Up age', in P. Wikström & R. De Fillippi (eds), *Business Innovation and Disruption in the Music Industry* (133-152). Cheltenham: Edward Elgar Publishing.

Nordgård, D. (2016). 'Lessons from the World's Most Advanced Market for Music Streaming Services', in P. Wikström & R. De Fillippi (eds), *Business Innovation and Disruption in the Music Industry* (175-190). Cheltenham: Edward Elgar Publishing.

Pearson, R. (2010). 'Fandom in the Digital Era', *Popular Communication: The International Journal of Media and Culture*, 8(1), 84-95.

Prior, N. (2015). 'Beyond Napster: Popular Music and the Normal Internet', in A. Bennett & S. Waksman. *The SAGE Handbook of Popular Music* (493-508). London: SAGE Publications.

Quiñones, M.G., Kassabian, A. & Boschi, E. (2015). *Ubiqitous Musics: The Everyday Sounds that We Don't Always Notice*. Burlington: Ashgate.

Rogers, J. & Preson, P. (2016). 'Crisis and Creative Destruction: New Modes of Appropriation in the Twenty-First Century Music Industry', in P. Wikström & R. De Fillippi (eds), *Business Innovation and Disruption in the Music Industry* (53-72). Cheltenham: Edward Elgar Publishing.

Rogers, J. (2013). *The Death and Life of the Music Industry in the Digital Age*. New York: Bloomsbury Academic.

Snickars, P. (2017). 'More of the Same – on Spotify Radio', *Culture Unbound: Journal of Current Cultural Research*, 9(2), 184-211.

Snickars, P. (2016). 'More Music is Better Music', in P. Wikström & R. De Fillippi (eds), *Business Innovation and Disruption in the Music Industry* (191-210). Cheltenham: Edward Elgar Publishing.

Sterne, J. (2012). *MP3: The Meaning of a Format*. Durham, NC: Duke University Press.

Van Dijck, J. (2013). *The Culture of Connectivity: A Critical History of Social Media*. Oxford: Oxford University Press.

Vonderau, P. (2015). 'The Politics of Content Aggregation', *Television & New Media*, 16(8), 717-733.

Wall, T. & Dubber, A. (2010). 'Experimenting with Fandom, Live Music, and the Internet: Applying Insights from Music Fan Culture to New Media Production', *New Music Research Journal*, 39(2), 159-169.

Werner, A. (2017). 'Phones, Applications, Mobility: Framing Music Use on the Go', in S. Johansson, A. Werner, P. Åker & G. Goldenzweig (eds), *Streaming Music: Practices, Media, Cultures* (145-160). London & New York: Routledge.

Werner, A. & Johansson, S. (2016). 'Experts, Dads and Technology: Gendered Talk about Online Music', *International Journal of Cultural Studies*, 9(2), 177-192.

Wikström, P. & De Fillippi, R. (2016). 'Introduction', in P. Wikström & R. De Fillippi (eds), *Business Innovation and Disruption in the Music Industry*. Cheltenham: Edward Elgar Publishing.

Wikström, P. (2013). *The Music Industry: Music in the Cloud* (2nd ed.). Cambridge: Polity Press.

Young, S. & Collins, S. (2010). 'A View from the Trenches of Music 2.0.', *Popular Music and Society*, *33*(3), 339-355.

24. Popular Music, Streaming, and Promotional Media: Enduring and Emerging Industrial Logics

Leslie M. Meier

The production and consumption of popular music has changed significantly in the digital era, affecting the revenue strategies of the music industries. Focusing on two recent phenomena – streaming music and artist-brand deals – this chapter discusses how these developments encourage an uneven distribution of career opportunities and rewards in the music industries, and elaborates on how the increasingly promotional role of media content means that music is becoming subordinated to marketing.

Introduction

In the digital era, how we learn about and access music has undergone extensive changes, as the dominance of physical albums has been challenged by the rise of new music products and services. Music assumes digital forms (as download, stream, and service), promotional forms (as music licenced to advertisers, branded content, and endorsements), and traditional forms (as CDs, records, compositions, and live performances). While the abundance of music available may make the contemporary music industries appear open and democratic, in order to understand the power relations that govern these industries, we must examine how revenues are generated and profits accrue.

In this chapter, I will focus on two phenomena that, despite in some ways widening access for recording artists, nevertheless encourage an uneven distribution of career opportunities and rewards: streaming, and promotional agreements between artists and brands. In order to delineate changes spurred by both internet-enabled distribution and the expanding influence of promotional media (advertising, marketing, and branding) over the music industries, I will draw on the 'cultural industries' approach to critical political economy as I develop an analysis that builds on trade press and specialist music industry sources.

From selling music to promoting brands

Today, popular music routinely features in and, hence, serves the function of *promotional media*. This term signals something distinct from *music promotion*, which Devon Powers defines as 'the cumulative effect of efforts intended to increase the awareness, presence, longevity, and sale of popular music among the listening public' (Powers, 2013, p. 315). Popular music's use as a tool for lending cultural legitimacy and appeal to brands unrelated to music as such has emerged as a new convention and essential revenue stream under contemporary business models (see Meier, 2017). Though such practices may generate marketing exposure for recording artists, they are not primarily about music promotion. Instead, popular music serves as an instrument for selling goods and services and, even if implicitly, endorsing consumerist values.

The increasingly tight relationship between music and brands is an outgrowth of changing business thinking about how to market and monetize music amid declining record sales and growing consumption of cheap, if not free, digital music. As internet-enabled services prised open major label control over music's distribution, increased competition for traditional revenue sources motivated myriad recording artists and their labels to pursue new business opportunities, including partnering with brands. Licencing music for use in advertising (see Klein, 2009; Taylor, 2012), television, video games, and so on, and various branding, endorsement, and sponsorship arrangements emerged as standard means of generating revenue and marketing exposure, with record companies treating artists as brands that can drive revenues well beyond just singles, albums, and concerts (Meier, 2017). In fact, '[a] record company may have as many as 200 long-term brand partnerships active on behalf of their artists at any point in time' (IFPI, 2016, p.14). Some independent artists cashed in on opportunities to work with brands, even receiving six-figure offers to licence music to advertisers (Klein, 2009, p. 72).

However, as deals between artists and brands became the new 'normal' in the music industries, the payout from music licencing and other promotional agreements to non-star artists dropped dramatically (Meier, 2017, pp. 112-119). Moreover, contractual agreements called '360 deals' – so named for the way they encompass the various forms of income generated by an artist beyond record sales – have enabled record companies to share in the host of revenue streams now tied to artists, be they stars or lesser known artists (*Ibid.*, pp. 74-77; Stahl & Meier, 2012; Marshall, 2013a). Justin Bieber's 360 deal with Universal's Def Jam (Halperin, 2011) means that Universal has various business interests in him, which helps explain why the release of his album *Purpose* reportedly built on the efforts of roughly 1,500 marketing experts (IFPI, 2016, p. 12).

This promotional and commercial view of the recording artist informs how new markets, most recently streaming, are positioned by record companies. Streaming continues to grow in popularity, with Nielsen reporting 133.9 billion on-demand streams in the first quarter of 2017, an increase from 99.1 billion during the same period a year earlier (Christman, 2017). Streaming is just one piece in broader strategies premised on aggregating multiple revenue streams, however (Meier, 2017, pp. 62-68). In order to evaluate the depth of change and the implications of the shift toward artist-brand deals and streaming, we must first understand the music industries' distinctive character as cultural industries.

Music industries as cultural industries: Enduring continuities

Building on the work of Nicholas Garnham (1990), Bernard Miège (1989), Bill Ryan (1991), and others, David Hesmondhalgh (2013) explains how the cultural industries (film, music, broadcasting, and so forth) share a set of common distinctive features. The cultural industries involve considerable *risk*, as it is very difficult to predict audience taste, and entail *high production costs* relative to reproduction costs (Hesmondhalgh, 2013, pp. 27-29). The cost of recording an album can be quite expensive, whereas the cost of pressing and shipping those albums is small by comparison, meaning that profits escalate dramatically once production costs are recouped. Cultural commodities are *semi-public goods*, as they are not destroyed after use, and *commerce* and *creativity* exist in tension, as commercial pressures constrain creativity, yet creativity remains essential to the production of new cultural commodities (*Ibid.*, pp. 28-30).

In response to the risky nature of investments in cultural production, media companies rely on *large catalogues* and *hits* to compensate for commercial failures and generate profits, and promote *stars* and *genres* as marketing categories to lend order to the cultural marketplace (*Ibid.*, pp. 30-32). There is also a strong tendency toward *concentration* and *integration*; the largest companies dominate markets for cultural commodities, and reinforce their might by acquiring or merging with competitors and companies that present strategic advantages, such as enhanced cross-promotional opportunities (*Ibid.*, pp. 30-31). This dynamic is evidenced by the shrinking of the Big Six major record labels to only three (Universal Music Group, Sony Music, and Warner Music Group), and is underscored by the fact that these companies are owned by multinational conglomerates (Vivendi, Sony, and Access Industries, respectively). Companies create 'artificial' scarcity through defending copyrights and managing release schedules, and exercise tight control over distribution and marketing vis-à-vis the considerable autonomy granted to creators (*Ibid.*, pp. 31-33). While a record company will devise the marketing plan, it typically will leave writing music to recording artists (though marketing departments may weigh in on what constitutes a commercially viable sound).

How can these distinctive features and business responses help us understand the contemporary music industries? Four developments are worth highlighting. First, risk has been intensified due to the popularization of (authorized and unauthorized) downloading and streaming, and the attendant decline in album sales. To mitigate this risk, music companies continue to rely on large catalogues (albeit with trimmed rosters), hits, and stars, and also capitalize on new products and services. While recorded music revenues decreased between 2000 and 2016, music publishing revenues grew modestly, branding and sponsorship revenues more than doubled, and merchandising revenues more than tripled (Mulligan, 2017c). Furthermore, music industry expert Mark Mulligan's (2017d) figures suggest that streaming led to growth of US$900 million in recorded music revenue in 2016, accounting for 33 per cent of major label revenue – a number that leapt to 42 per cent in the first quarter of 2017. Significantly, live music reportedly generated 43 per cent of global music revenues in 2016, surpassing the 38 per cent of revenues generated by recorded music – a marked shift from 2000, when 53 per cent of revenue was generated by recorded music and 33 per cent by live music (Mulligan, 2017c). In order to ensure a generous return while managing risk, music companies are offering artists contract terms that 'range from now-standard 360 contracts and joint ventures to new types of licencing arrangements' (Karp, 2017).

The tendency for industry analysts and reporters to cite streaming figures in aggregate, without providing a more detailed breakdown regarding smaller record labels and recording artists, provides only a partial picture of what these developments mean and for whom. Many streaming services employ a pro-rata model when dividing up revenues, under which 'the distribution of revenues [is] based on how many streams a rights-holder's songs constitute from the total number of streams played via the platform' – an approach that benefits rights-holders that receive a high volume of streams (Nordgård, 2016, pp. 182-183). Even 'user-centric' models, under which revenues are distributed in accordance with individual users' listening profiles, have not proven to correct the economic bias toward major labels and stars (*Ibid.*, pp. 183-184). Overall, given low per-stream payouts, individual streams only become substantial revenue generators when accumulated on a massive scale.

Many of the most streamed artists are signed to major record labels, or are star artists signed to independent labels that work with the majors for distribution (e.g. Taylor Swift). For example, in the United States, the top-10 streamed songs in the first quarter of 2017 were all by artists with connections to major labels (Christman, 2017), with 60 per cent of those artists affiliated with Universal – a company that generated 44 per cent of major label streaming revenue in the first quarter of 2017 (Mulligan, 2017b). Characterized by major music company representatives as a 'hit-economy on steroids' (quoted in Nordgård, 2016, p. 182), the streaming economy rewards superstars, with a select few achieving cumulative streams in the billions and corresponding payouts in the millions. As Des Freedman observes of the online media economy more broadly, 'there remains [...] not simply a pattern of monopolistic (and sometimes oligopolistic) markets but an incentive for companies to produce "blockbusters" and an apparent willingness on the part of audiences to consume them' (Freedman, 2016, p. 109).

Contrast this with the case of unsigned and lesser known artists. Paul Resnikoff (2016) of *Digital Music News* was given access to the Spotify royalty statements of an unsigned artist who had achieved over a million streams – an impressive feat that nevertheless only yielded revenues estimated at US$4,955.90. Even in this successful case, little money remains to be divided between bandmates, managers, and so on. For artists signed to record deals, partnering companies would take a cut of such revenues as well (Mulligan, 2017c; Passman, 2015, p. 152).

Exposure to artists via streaming may encourage listeners to attend live performances, with such services serving a promotional function with parallels to radio. Despite gains overall, however, live music remains a source of risk. Impressive revenues in aggregate obscure costs and income for individual artists. Citing the cost of crew, food, accommodation, equipment, and commissions, entertainment attorney Donald Passman (*Ibid.*, p. 404) suggests weekly costs of US$10,000 for a four-person band headlining larger clubs. According to Mulligan (2017c), 'On average, around just 29% of live music revenue makes it back to the artist (after agents, costs etc are factored in) while many artists don't make any money on live until they've reached a certain level of scale. And that's before considering that the top 1% of live artists (many of whom are aging heritage acts) account for 68% of all live revenue.'

The high-risk, high-reward music industries remain highly concentrated, albeit with some new entrants in new markets. Next to the three major labels, the market shares of all independent record companies together add up to less than one third of the total market for recorded music, and the market for streaming services is likewise concentrated. What is distinctive about the streaming sector is that, at the time of writing, '[a]ll the key streaming services are either losing money or are part of a bigger company (which absorbs the losses)' (Mulligan, 2017e). Spotify reportedly lost US$601 million in 2016, despite the fact that the number of users rose to 50 million paid subscribers and 140 million users overall – losses resulting from deals and royalties committed to rights owners (Turner & Shaw, 2017). This dynamic underscores the value now placed on the user base and its connection to projected growth, which complicates valuations of companies limited to revenue generation and profitability. Users and user data function as additional currencies (see Meier & Manzerolle, forthcoming), with services commanding massive user bases wielding considerable corporate power. This helps explain how Spotify's 2018 direct listing on the New York Stock Exchange managed to yield a staggering valuation of roughly US$26 billion (Spangler, 2018).

In the contemporary music industries, integration remains a response to risk, which has been coupled with diversification into the promotional industries (advertising, branding, and marketing). It should be noted that digitalization has encouraged vertical *disintegration* insofar as major record companies have less control over the distribution of music – an area now largely dominated by information technology (IT) companies (Hesmondhalgh, 2013, pp. 203-204). However, we have seen horizontal integration within the music industries (e.g. label mergers) and multisector integration, with companies from outside the traditional music business entering into music sectors, and major music companies extending their reach beyond the music industries proper. For example, digital retailer and cloud computing giant Amazon, which owns a music streaming service, has extended its interests into the ticketing sector and unveiled a concert series that will be exclusive to Amazon Prime members (Mulligan, 2017a), underscoring the close links between the music and IT industries (see Hesmondhalgh & Meier, 2018). Concert promoter Live Nation, which merged with ticketing monopolist Ticketmaster in 2010, purchased a majority share of branding agency GreenLight, enabling that agency to tap into 'a staggering amount of data' (Waddell, 2016). And Sony Music launched its own advertising agency – Arcade Creative Group – in 2008 (Billboard, 2017; Taylor, 2012, p. 225).

The second key development relates to production costs. Despite savings created by digitalization, production costs remain high relative to reproduction costs. The professional studio production still sought by many recording artists remains a 'significant' expense, and 'marketing costs constitute a growing share of the budget as it becomes increasingly difficult to reach and build an audience' (Nordgård, 2016, pp.178-179; see also Marshall, 2013b, pp.582-583). In fact, I suggest that under the 'artist-brand' paradigm, which positions recorded music as just one revenue stream among many, marketing costs ought to be understood *as* production costs: investing in recording artists not only entails developing talent and recording albums, but also managing brand reputation and celebrity-building (see Marshall, 2013b). After all, as Graeme Turner points out, '[a]s the asset appreciates – as the celebrity's fame spreads – so does its earning capacity' (Turner, 2014, p. 37). Today, major record companies reportedly spend more on marketing and promotion for emerging artists – US$200,000-700,000 – than they do for all other activities (compare with US$150,000-500,000 for recording and US$50,000-150,000 for tour support) (IFPI, 2016, p. 6). According to the International Federation of the Phonographic Industry (IFPI), with streaming it can take 'about a third longer, compared to physical and download formats, for a company to recoup its investment in an artist. Consequently, record companies are now funding and supporting sustained marketing campaigns for a longer period of time' (*Ibid.*, p. 11). In this context, IFPI (2017) research suggests that 70 per cent of unsigned artists in the United Kingdom would like to sign a record deal.

Third, the semi-public goods status of recorded music has been amplified. At the most obvious level, amid abundantly accessible digital music, it is apparent that music companies' mechanisms for maintaining artificial scarcity have been wrested open by internet-enabled distribution, despite the continuation of strong copyright regimes. Streaming service experiments with exclusive artist deals and releases of varying durations (e.g. Tidal with Kanye West, Apple Music with Chance the Rapper, Amazon Music with Garth Brooks) (Billboard, 2017) can be interpreted as attempts to restore a type of artificial scarcity. More significantly, we do see a persistence of economies based on scarcity elsewhere: a select set of stars continue to receive a disproportionate share of revenue, audience attention, and interest from brands and streaming services that are seeking promotional deals. As observed by Jonathan Sterne, 'The worldwide proliferation of MP3 files announces the end of the artificial scarcity of recorded music, but it does not guarantee a more just or democratic organization of music. It simply reopens the organization of music – and the infrastructure that supports it – as a social question' (Sterne, 2012, p. 188). The music industries' organization around the production of celebrity marks an intensification of past approaches.

Fourth, the complex relationship between creativity and commerce remains a site of tension. However, in an era marked by escalating marketing influence and close relationships between artists and brands, we are seeing explicitly commercial and promotional considerations shape the creative process in direct ways, as the below section will demonstrate. In an age of branded content, a media environment is taking shape whose raison d'etre is selling.

Music industries as promotional industries: Emerging logics

While the cultural industries share important features, distinctive logics govern particular cultural industries. The music industries, which comprise recording, music publishing, live performance, and now streaming industries, are particularly complex. Miège's influential theorization of the cultural industries identified three key models or logics: the 'logic of the *publishing* of cultural commodities' (e.g. albums, books, and films); the '*flow* logic' (e.g. radio and television); and the 'logic of the *written press*' (Miège, 1989, p. 12; emphasis in original). Most relevant to an examination of the contemporary music industries, which are being shaped by both streaming and 'artist-brand' based business models, are the publishing and flow logics.

Historically, the recording industry abided by a publishing logic, as cultural commodities were sold to end consumers, hits and catalogues were used to mitigate risk and generate profits, and recording artists were remunerated through royalties and fees, not salaries – a system that disproportionately favoured stars (*Ibid.*, pp. 12, 136-137). Radio, which played an important supporting role by encouraging record sales, was governed by a flow logic characterized by: broadcasters providing a continual flow of planned programs (*Ibid.*, p. 138), and, in the case of commercial models, '"creat[ing] an audience", because the financing is entirely assured by means of advertising' (*Ibid.*, p. 12). Potentially productive for understanding the music industries in the streaming age is Jean-Guy Lacroix and Gaëtan Tremblay's 'club logic', which they introduced to conceptualize subscription-based systems such as cable television, which involve financing via 'subscriptions, additional payment for specialized services or pay-per-view, and in many cases, [...] advertising or sponsor revenues' (Lacroix & Tremblay, 1997, p. 64). More recently, Amanda D. Lotz (2017) developed a subscriber model to examine internet-distributed television services such as Netflix, for which advertising plays little role and a logic of curation has displaced that of scheduled programming.

Across the contemporary music industries, we see the coexistence of multiple logics. Fee-based music streaming services could potentially abide by Lotz's subscriber model, under which 'a user pay[s] a fee for access to a collection of cultural goods' that are curated by the service (*Ibid.*, p. 39). However, the significance Lotz places on internet-distributed television's disruption to established linear programming conventions highlights important differences between the television and music industries. While the non-linear experience of much streaming may be distinct from radio, it does not mark a break from listening practices tied to physical albums; audiences have long been able to choose what they want to listen to and when – at least of those albums in their personal libraries. Also, some of the most popular streaming services maintain ties with advertising (e.g. Spotify offers advertising-funded and subscription fee-based systems and Google's YouTube relies on advertising), suggesting that lessons might be learned from the flow model, but the 'problem of product obsolescence' characteristic of radio (immediately after a programme airs, there is need for another) (Miège, 1989, p. 138) does not apply, as entire catalogues are available on demand. Given that some services combine funding methods, perhaps the 'club logic' fits in some cases.

However, one model cannot capture the complex dynamics of the music industries. After all, the embrace of new businesses has not meant the abandonment of traditional revenue streams. Album sales may be on a severe decline, for instance, but it would be premature to strike this still sizeable revenue stream from the balance sheets altogether, meaning the publishing logic is still in force. We can use different models to grapple with specific music industries/sectors and cases.

Overarching power dynamics can be identified, however, which relate to the widespread licencing of music for use by third parties – be it by advertisers and brands or streaming services. This trend heightens the importance of business-to-business (B2B), as distinct from business-to-consumer (B2C), facets of music-related economies. As Garnham famously argued, *'It is cultural distribution, not cultural production, that is the key locus of power and profit'* (Garnham, 1990, pp. 161-162; emphasis in original) – a claim only strengthened by the influence now exercised by streaming services. Furthermore, the mode of finance and, hence, power of the financier produces dependencies and biases toward certain types of content, which are viewed as more commercially viable than others.

As we have seen, the music industries are now reliant on considerable financing from brands, advertisers, and marketers. Jonathan Hardy links 'enhance[d] advertiser influence on (non-advertising) media content' to 'the media entity's dependence on advertising finance', 'corporate level partnerships with marketers and marketing agencies', and 'user support/acceptance of advertising integration', among other factors (Hardy, 2017, p. 24). Given many streaming services' dependence on advertising, record companies' close partnerships with brands and branding firms (and even in-house ventures), and increasing acceptance of a dissolving boundary between advertising and popular music among listeners and recording artists, we see conditions that reinforce marketer power. Interestingly, Miège observed that, despite the centrality of advertisers to the flow logic, 'except in a few rare cases, sponsors stay away from the conception or planning of audiovisual programs, and remain satisfied with promoting their image' (Miège, 1989, p.140). As the below examples illustrate, we are now seeing brands intervene in the creative output.

No longer exclusively interested in simply licencing tracks by recording artists for use in advertisements, branding firms now produce content themselves. Like many similar firms today, GreenLight (mentioned above), a specialist in branded content, sees itself as a content producer, as reflected in company president Dominic Sandifer's statement: 'I think in the best situations we live in a co-creative society now between brands and artists' (quoted in Waddell, 2016). Playing to Live Nation's strengths in putting on spectacular performances, GreenLight arranged a 'collaboration' between Lady Gaga, Intel, and the Grammys, distributing content across digital and social media, and producing a Grammy performance in which Lady Gaga morphed into David Bowie using Intel technology (Waddell, 2016). Branded content of this sort seeks to erase the distinction between media and marketing, entertaining while it promotes (although Intel's role in the performance was advertised through a television commercial).

A promotional 'demo' video for *Over Here* by Rae Sremmurd provides another example. The video is 'Powered by Doritos', and while the branding is subtle (the video primarily features the group performing), as it closes, a handful of tortilla chips and a small Doritos logo appear (Oster, 2016). The point of branded content is to make brand messaging inviting and not something audiences wish to evade or block; excessive branding and egregious product placement are often avoided to prevent upstaging the artist and, hence, the entertainment value of the content.

In keeping with a purportedly 'co-creative' style, Canadian singer, songwriter, and producer The Weeknd signed up as 'creative collaborator and ambassador' for Puma, enabling Puma to combine the brand's 'sport-inspired designs and The Weeknd's street-motivated aesthetics' (press release in Chan, 2016). The Weeknd also 'curated' a fashion line for H&M (H&M, 2017).[1]

We are also seeing star artists being used to promote the adoption of new modes of media delivery. As Turner observes, celebrities serve a key function 'as a *branding* mechanism for media products that has assisted their fluent translation across media formats and systems of delivery' (Turner, 2014, p. 36; emphasis in original). Taylor Swift, who signed a multiyear deal with AT&T that grants the telecommunications company exclusive video content in return, performed at an AT&T/DirecTV-sponsored pre-Super Bowl program designed to support the launch of its content app (Billboard, 2017). Here we see a music celebrity used in efforts to drive up subscriptions to a television streaming service.

Conclusion

This chapter underscores important continuities stemming from the distinctive economics of the cultural industries, but also striking developments during a period of dramatic change. The music industries still economically hinge on hits and stars, with the fragmentation of revenues and increased competition arguably rendering the star system even more central today, producing considerable constraints for new artists. Major label artists with cadres of marketers at their disposal can generate streams in the billions and also garner lucrative branding partnerships. Indeed, the two phenomena I have examined – streaming and artist-brand deals – are deepening previous power asymmetries. Moreover, music is being remodelled in the image of promotional media, as it is being used to push products, lend cool cachet to brands, and deliver persuasive messages.

This increasingly promotional role of media content speaks to wider changes across the cultural industries, which have led Hardy to suggest that '[m]edia and marketing integration is arguably the next phase of convergence, following that of

---

1   Note that the Weeknd later severed ties with H&M in response to the company's troubling release of a hooded sweatshirt and corresponding 'promotional image of a black child dressed in a hoodie reading "coolest monkey in the jungle"' (Beaumont-Thomas, 2018).

mass media, telecommunications, and computing' (Hardy, 2017, p. 21). The character of branded content and related practices is not best understood as the blurring of music and marketing, I suggest, but instead as the subordination of the former to the latter. For those who desire diverse music and artists, the shifts discussed are troubling, because marketer and brand-based modes of finance bring with them biases toward artists and content perceived as promotionally amenable and, hence, commercially viable. Important music that does not conform to the promotional paradigm may not be deemed a worthwhile investment.

Further reading

- Case: Examples of changes in the music industries brought about by digitalization and the expansion of music streaming services – Johansson (p. 309)
- Context: Five current issues and trends relating to the creative and cultural industries as a result of digitalization and the rise of the global communication giants – Miège (p. 73)
- Contrast: How platforms such as Spotify facilitate and profit from new forms of consumption without creating or producing content – Bilton (p. 99)

Acknowledgements: I would like to thank David Hesmondhalgh for his helpful feedback on this chapter. This piece evolved from a plenary talk, titled 'Remodelling Music: The Nexus of the Music, Information Technology, and Promotional Industries', which I gave at the Place of Music conference hosted at Loughborough University in June 2017.

References

Beaumont-Thomas, B. (2018). 'The Weeknd and G-Eazy Cut Ties with H&M over 'Monkey' Hoodie', *Guardian* (10 January). Retrieved from https://www.theguardian.com/music/2018/jan/10/the-weeknd-g-eazy-cancel-partnership-hm-image-monkey-hoodie.

Billboard (2017). 'Billboard's 2017 Branding Power Players List Revealed, Led by Citi's Jennifer Breithaupt', *Billboard* (9 June). Retrieved from http://www.billboard.com/articles/business/7824615/2017-branding-power-players-list-revealed.

Chan, S. (2016). 'The Weeknd Named Puma's New Creative Collaborator and Ambassador', *Hollywood Reporter* (29 September). Retrieved from http://www.hollywoodreporter.com/news/weeknd-named-pumas-new-creative-934008.

Christman, E. (2017). 'Nielsen Music's First-Quarter Numbers: Explosive Growth for Streaming, Not So Much for Vinyl', *Billboard* (6 April). Retrieved from http://www.billboard.com/biz/articles/news/record-labels/7752309/nielsen-musics-first-quarter-numbers-explosive-growth-for.

Freedman, D. (2016). 'The Internet of Capital', in J. Curran, N. Fenton & D. Freedman (eds), *Misunderstanding the internet* (2nd ed.) (85-116). Abingdon: Routledge.

Garnham, N. (1990). *Capitalism and Communication: Global Culture and the Economics of Information*. London: SAGE Publications.

H&M (2017). 'Spring Icons Selected by The Weeknd', *H&M*. Retrieved from http://www2. hm.com/en_gb/life/culture/inside-h-m/searching-for-the-iconic-with-the-weeknd.html.

Halperin, S. (2011). 'Justin Bieber Cover: The Team and Strategy behind Making him a Star', *Hollywood Reporter* (9 February). Retrieved from http://www.hollywoodreporter.com/news/justin-bieber-cover-team-strategy-97658.

Hardy, J. (2017). 'Marketers' Influence on Media: Renewing the Radical Tradition for the Digital Age', in J.F. Hamilton, R. Bodle & E. Korin (eds), *Explorations in Critical Studies of Advertising* (13-27). Abingdon: Routledge.

Hesmondhalgh, D. (2013). *The Cultural Industries* (3rd ed.). London: SAGE Publications.

Hesmondhalgh, D. & Meier, L.M. (2018). 'What the Digitalisation of Music Tells Us about Capitalism, Culture and the Power of the Information Technology Sector', *Information, Communication & Society*, 21(11), 1555-1570.

IFPI (2016). *Investing in Music: The Value of Record Companies*. International Federation of the Phonographic Industry. Retrieved from https://www.riaa.com/wp-content/uploads/2017/01/ifpi-iim-report-2016.pdf.

IFPI (2017). *How Record Labels Invest*. Retrieved from http://www.ifpi.org/how-record-labels-invest.php.

Karp, H. (2017). 'The Wild West of Record Deals: With Industry in Flux, Labels and Artists Shake Things Up', *Billboard* (22 June). Retrieved from http://www.billboard.com/articles/business/7841131/record-deals-changing-new-rules-music-industry.

Klein, B.(2009). *As Heard on TV: Popular Music in Advertising*. Burlington: Ashgate.

Lacroix, J.G. & Tremblay, G. (1997). 'The Institutionalization of Cultural Commodification: Logics and Strategies', *Current Sociology, 45*(4), 39-69.

Lotz, A.D. (2017). *Portals: A Treatise on Internet-Distributed Television*. Ann Arbor, MI: Maize Books.

Marshall, L. (2013a). 'The 360 Deal and the "New" Music Industry', *European Journal of Cultural Studies, 16*(1), 77-99.

Marshall, L. (2013b). 'The Structural Functions of Stardom in the Recording Industry', *Popular Music and Society, 36*(5), 578-596.

Meier, L.M. (2017). *Popular Music as Promotion: Music and Branding in the Digital Age*. Cambridge: Polity.

Meier, L.M., & Manzerolle, V.R. (Forthcoming). 'Rising Tides? Data Capture, Platform Accumulation, and New Monopolies in the Digital Music Economy', *New Media & Society*.

Miège, B. (1989). *The Capitalization of Cultural Production*. New York: International General.

Mulligan, M. (2017a). 'Amazon Prime Live Events, More than Just Gigs for Olds [Weblog post] (9 May). Retrieved from https://musicindustryblog.wordpress.com/2017/05/09/amazon-prime-live-events-more-than-just-gigs-for-olds/.

Mulligan, M. (2017b). 'Announcing MIDiA's State of the Streaming Nation 2 Report [Weblog post] (5 June). Retrieved from https://musicindustryblog.wordpress.com/2017/06/05/announcing-midias-state-of-the-streaming-nation-2-report/.

Mulligan, M. (2017c). 'Do Not Assume We Have Arrived at Our Destination [Weblog post] (15 June). Retrieved from https://musicindustryblog.wordpress.com/2017/06/15/do-not-assume-we-have-arrived-at-our-destination/.

Mulligan, M. (2017d). 'Who's Leading the Streaming Pack?' [Weblog post] (25 May). Retrieved from https://musicindustryblog.wordpress.com/2017/05/25/whos-leading-the-streaming-pack/.

Mulligan, M. (2017e). 'Why Netflix Can Turn a Profit But Spotify Cannot (Yet) [Weblog post] (19 January). Retrieved from https://www.midiaresearch.com/blog/why-netflix-can-turn-a-profit-but-spotify-cannot-yet/.

Nordgård, D. (2016). 'Lessons From the World's Most Advanced Market for Music Streaming Services', in P. Wikström & R. De Fillippi (eds), *Business Innovation and Disruption in the Music Industry* (175-190). Cheltenham: Edward Elgar Publishing.

Oster, E. (2016). 'Multi-Screen Hip-Hop Video Sponsored by Doritos', *Agency Spy/Advertising Age* (24 March). Retrieved from http://www.adweek.com/agencyspy/gsp-launches-interactive-multi-screen-music-video-for-doritos/105180.

Passman, D. (2015). *All You Need to Know About the Music Business* (9th ed.). New York: Simon and Schuster.

Powers, D. (2013). 'Now Hear This: The State of Promotion and Popular Music', in M.P. McAllister & E. West (eds), *The Routledge Companion to Advertising and Promotional Culture* (313-325). Abingdon: Routledge.

Resnikoff, P. (2016). 'My Band has 1,000,000 Spotify Streams. Want to See Our Royalties?', *Digital Music News* (26 May). Retrieved from https://www.digitalmusicnews.com/2016/05/26/band-1-million-spotify-streams-royalties/.

Ryan, B. (1991). *Making Capital from Culture: The Corporate Form of Capitalist Cultural Production*. Berlin: Walter de Gruyter.

Spangler, T. (2018). 'Spotify Stock Pops in IPO Debut, Before Cooling Down to US$26 Billion Market Cap', *Variety* (3 April). Retrieved from http://variety.com/2018/digital/news/spotify-ipo-market-value-1202742246/.

Stahl, M. & Meier, L.M. (2012). 'The Firm Foundation of Organizational Flexibility: The 360 Contract in the Digitalizing Music Industry', *Canadian Journal of Communication, 37* (3), 441-458.

Sterne, J. (2012). *MP3: The Meaning of a Format*. Durham, NC: Duke University Press.

Taylor, T.D. (2012). *The Sounds of Capitalism: Advertising, Music, and the Conquest of Culture*. Chicago, IL: University of Chicago Press.

Turner, G. (2014). *Understanding Celebrity* (2nd ed.). London: SAGE Publications.

Turner, G. & Shaw, L. (2017). 'Spotify's Loss More than Doubles Even as User Growth Surges', *Bloomberg Technology* (15 June). Retrieved from https://www.bloomberg.com/news/articles/2017-06-15/spotify-losses-widen-after-music-site-flags-accounting-errors?cmpid=socialflow-facebook-btechnology&utm_content=btechnology&utm_campaign=socialflow-organic&utm_source=facebook&utm_medium=social.

Waddell, R. (2016). 'GreenLight's Dominic Sandifer on the Future of Music Branding, Live Nation's Acquisition, and How Gaga Turned into Bowie', *Billboard* (10 October). Retrieved from http://www.billboard.com/articles/business/7364633/greenlight-dominic-sandifer-lady-gaga-bowie-live-nation-acquisition-music-branding.

Professions

Television

25. Show Me the Money: How Revenue Strategies Change the Creative Possibilities of Internet-Distributed Television

Amanda D. Lotz

The impact of digitization is not isolated to technological change, but also affects revenue models and financing strategies. This, in turn, influences the programming strategies and content of media. Taking the example of subscriber-funded services HBO and Netflix, this chapter discusses how revenue models and financing strategies shape media content.

Introduction

Digital production technologies have changed practices and possibilities for creatives working in media industries in many ways. But digitization – a process impacting the industries at least since the early 1990s – also introduces profound adjustments to media distribution that have implications for what these industries produce. Capabilities such as personalized, on-demand access are among the affordances of digital technologies that change how viewers/readers/listeners engage with much contemporary media and allow experiences different from previous forms of media making and circulation.

Digitization has also introduced many less obvious adjustments that are related, although not obviously connected to technological change. It also affects revenue models and financing strategies – among many other things – which simultaneously adjust. Changing revenue models and financing strategies matter very much to commercial media production because such adjustments shift definitions of success and alter creative workers' incentive structures, which, in turn, redefine the parameters of the creative goods that can be produced within a commercial mandate. New distributors such as Netflix and Amazon Video are entering legacy industries and adopting different practices to create a more diverse array of industrial norms.

The implications of internet distribution now affect all media industries, but not in precisely the same ways. Those seeking to work in the media industries today must thus understand the practices already in place, as well as those just emerging to most effectively negotiate workplaces and opportunities.

This chapter illustrates how the differences among various revenue models and financing strategies establish various measures of success that encourage different types of creative goods. It draws from the case of television to illustrate how changing revenue models and financing strategies affect creative possibilities – what is and can be produced.

Revenue models

Few media studies textbooks focus on the business aspects of media, so first, some key terms and how they are relevant to media production and media work. A *revenue model* is a central component of a company's business. It encompasses the strategies related to how a good or service generates revenue, or income, for a company. It includes matters such as what is sold, how it is sold, and its pricing strategy. Common revenue models for media include advertiser-funding, transaction payment, subscriber-funding, public funding, and various combinations of these revenue streams.

Many media firms rely on advertising to produce revenue. Such companies create media goods – whether television shows, journalism, or social media feeds – that will attract the attention of audiences that are then sold to advertisers. The most successful advertiser-funded media are those that attract the attention of the most viewers/readers/listeners that advertisers seek to reach.

Other media rely on a revenue model that sells media or access to media, or what is called 'transaction'. French media industries scholar Bernard Miége categorizes media that are sold directly to an audience – such as buying a book, an album, a download, or entrance to a film theater – as 'publishing industries' (Miége, 1989). The key to success for industries that rely on a transaction, or the exchange of money for a media good, is ensuring that the audience that buys these goods matches the scale of the production costs. For example, both big blockbuster films and niche films can be financially successful as long as their production costs match the audience attracted.

Subscription is a revenue model that has become more common since the advent of internet distribution. There are different types of subscription. Those previously common – such as subscribing to a newspaper or magazine – required a small fee from readers, but these media additionally relied heavily on advertiser funding. The affordance of internet distribution that allows more personalized distribution of media without substantial distribution costs has made pure subscriber funding more common. Generally, audiences pay a regular fee for access to a library of goods and services, such as with Netflix and Spotify.

These businesses are successful if they maintain or expand the number of subscribers – those who derive enough value from the service to continue paying a regular fee. This measure of success leads subscriber-funded media to develop different media content than advertiser-supported media. Subscriber-funded media aim not to attract the most viewers/readers/listeners, but to provide content so valued that audiences will pay to access it. This encourages the production of different creative goods than found in advertiser-funded media.

Many media blend revenue streams. Such media include advertising and require some payment from audiences. This has long been the case of newspapers, magazines, and most cable channels. Notably, media with any reliance on advertising tend to be governed by the strategies of advertiser-supported media that prioritize content likely to draw large audiences.

Finally, public funding also supports media. Such funding is commonly derived from taxes or government-levied fees, while viewer/listener donation and corporate underwriting can also fund public service television and radio. Public service media measure success differently from commercial media. Rather than evaluating success in terms of profit earned from advertising or payment from viewers/readers/listeners, public service media often aim to fill the gaps in service left by commercial media. For example, in-depth news coverage, media geared to older audiences, and the representation of non-dominant groups are rarely a priority of advertiser-funded media. Public service media measure success based on metrics developed to evaluate their accomplishment of their stated mission.

In addition to changing revenue streams, new companies reliant on internet distribution are also using different industrial practices to fund the making of media. In comparison with most other industries, media have very high sunk, fixed, or first-copy costs, but very low marginal costs (Caves, 2000). This means that nearly all the considerable costs of making the good – a film, television show, game, album or book – are incurred before the good can earn any income.

Once the good is made, though, it can be sold again and again without incurring new costs. Compare media with the automotive industry. Yes, it is very expensive to design a prototype and then build a new car. But each new car also requires thousands of dollars of material and labour (marginal costs). High first-copy and low marginal costs are defining attributes of media industries that led to the development of particular business strategies.

Media industries developed various practices to cope with the high costs of making media. It is why we see the dominance of a studio system in television and film, big publishers in games, international holding firms in marketing and advertising, or major record labels in music. In other industries, companies seek bank loans to finance new projects. Media projects are notoriously unpredictable and banks lack the expertise to identify those likely to be a good loan investment. Instead, media organizations such as studios, publishers, and record labels function as banks – 'loaning' out money to make new media goods based on their expertise. This money is drawn from the earnings of past successes.

As companies that didn't exist before internet distribution developed – such as Netflix or Spotify – they have adopted different industrial practices related to financing media that have implications for the type of media produced. For example, in the US television industry, studios relied on deficit financing as the dominant practice for funding the production of scripted television series. In this system, production of a television series was the task of a studio and licenced by a network that sought to be the exclusive source of the series for an initial period of time. The licence fee paid by the network only covered about 65 per cent of the production cost. The studio bore the remaining cost (the deficit) in hopes of recouping that deficit by selling the series in domestic syndication or in international markets. The most profitable television shows for studios then, were those that they could sell again and again, while networks measured success in terms of the number of viewers attracted in the first airing.

Other methods of funding production existed. Lower budget programming, and programming that wasn't likely to find additional buyers, such as daily talk shows, were produced without a deficit. Another funding strategy – uncommon in the US but more common elsewhere – is 'cost plus'. In this case, the network agrees to fund the series production for its full cost, plus an agreed upon percentage of profit. In return, the producing studio gives all rights for future sales and earnings to the licencing network. This makes the series much less risky for a studio, but also eliminates the opportunity to earn extraordinary revenue if the series becomes an enormous hit (Doyle, 2016).

Revenue models in practice: HBO

So how does the funding of a television series – whether it is produced for an advertiser versus subscriber funded service or financed by deficit financing versus cost plus scheme – change the content likely to be produced? The programming strategies of US cable channel HBO provide a fitting example.

US scripted television series drew unprecedented accolades for their creativity and accomplishment beginning in the late 1990s. Some important adjustments in industrial practices related to revenue models and financing strategies explain that change in content. The key change was that cable channels began commissioning original scripted series rather than simply buying the second-run licence for shows originally produced for broadcast networks. HBO was one of the first US cable channels to rely on original series as a strategy, and the channel drew considerable attention as the originator of *OZ*, *The Sopranos*, *Sex and the City*, *Six Feet Under*, *The Wire*, and many others. All of these series – in slightly different ways – were shows unlike those that had been produced for US television. To understand how HBO was able to redefine the perceived boundaries of US television, we must consider its revenue model and financing strategy. Also important here is HBO's dual role as the producer (studio) and originating distributor (channel) of these programmes.

First, HBO is a subscriber-funded channel. It does not rely on any advertiser support. As a result, its programme development strategy was focused more on offering subscribers something they valued rather than creating programmes likely to gather the largest audience (Lotz, 2007). The shows HBO developed aren't for everyone. Many feature more violence and sexual explicitness than other US television. They also use more sophisticated narrative techniques and rely on protagonists that are not clearly heroes. Many of these techniques have become typical across US television providers, but were innovative in the US market when HBO introduced them. The distinct attributes of HBO programming were likely to turn some potential audience members away – something advertiser-supported media would avoid. But because HBO was focused on making sure existing subscribers felt it offered something of value, and because its primary goal was attracting more subscribers, HBO recognized the strategic value of creating programming distinctive from what viewers could find on ad-supported channels that required no fee (Lotz, 2018).

Just as the difference in its revenue model encouraged the creation of programming distinct from advertiser-funded channels, HBO also relies on owning its series and a funding practice more like cost plus than deficit financing for most of its original productions (Littleton, 2017). By owning its series, HBO can choose how and where to sell series beyond their initial window, which makes good sense for a subscriber-funded service. If HBO adopted the standard practice and allowed its series to be sold to other distributors, it would sacrifice the value proposition of being the exclusive source for these programmes. In other words, if viewers knew they could see these programmes without paying the subscription fee, it would be much more difficult to encourage subscription. Of course HBO licences its original series in other countries to reach viewers unable to subscribe to the US service. Many of its series also sell well on DVD. Making series available on DVD may discourage some from subscribing, but the transaction revenue from the DVD sales likely compensates.

By owning series HBO is able to control the content produced for its channel over the long term – not just in the first few airings, or the 'first window' in industry terminology. Owning its series also allows HBO to adopt various strategies that help its subscribers derive more value. HBO offered multiple streams of its channels – east and west coast feeds, as well as what it called a 'multiplex' service that featured additional channels such as HBO Comedy, HBO Family, and HBO Latino. The programming for these channels was drawn from the HBO library – so it did not require additional development costs, but provided viewers with more choice from the service before digital video recorders, video on demand, and streaming allowed more viewer control over television schedules. If HBO did not own its programmes, it would have had to negotiate with the studio owning the series to make its series accessible on these services.

HBO also was the first US cable provider to offer much of its library 'on demand' when video on demand (VOD) technology emerged in the early 2000s. Here too, it sought to add value to HBO subscribers by expanding the options of what they could view. A subscriber model means HBO need not care how many people watch at a particular time, so it is not worried about creating more options for viewers or forcing them to watch according to a schedule.

Finally, this revenue and financing strategy enabled HBO to be among the first legacy media companies to provide internet access to its content in the US. The HBO Go service launched in 2010 and was a free additional component for those subscribing to its cable service. The HBO Go library was able to include nearly the entire library of HBO series because the company had self-produced the series and thus retained ownership. The HBO Go service allowed a more expansive library than the VOD service (which was limited by cable operators' capacity) and could be used on computers, tablets, and phones. Eventually HBO launched a standalone internet-distributed service, HBO Now, in the US in 2015 and gradually expanded this service around the world (HBO Nordic) with an international rollout announced for 2018.

Revenue models in practice: Netflix and Amazon Video

Although the case of HBO drawn from the late 1990s may seem pointlessly out of date, this is not at all the case. Internet-distributed, subscriber-funded video services such as Netflix and Amazon Video are following nearly exactly the same strategies two decades later. In fact, starting with the HBO case – one before the arrival of internet-distributed services – makes clear the ways in which internet-distributed services both change and continue practices common in other forms of television distribution. It is not simply technological change that challenges media industries, but changes in economic practices and regulatory considerations as well.

Like HBO, Netflix and Amazon Video are subscriber funded. Both services initially began by licencing second-run content from studios. A key difference between the 1990s version of HBO and these services is that internet distribution provides different affordances than cable distribution. Viewers choose programmes from internet-distributed services because they are interested in the programmes, but also because they offer a distinctive viewing experience. The affordances of internet-distribution allow these services to provide programming on demand and on many different devices.

Just as HBO drew considerable attention with its programmes in the late 1990s, Netflix has achieved similar notoriety since 2013 for its original series, such as *House of Cards* and *Orange is the New Black*, and for providing a distinctive viewing experience that allows viewers to watch all of a season's episodes at a self-determined pace, completely free of a network imposed schedule. This release strategy is possible because of its revenue model. Netflix does not need all, or even many of its subscribers to watch at a certain time. Timeliness is important to advertiser-supported services because many of the sponsored messages are time specific. Advertisers use commercials to drive audiences to a weekend event or evaluate the effectiveness of the advertising based on seeing a change in consumers' purchasing behavior correlated to the advertising spend.

The 'full season drop' also relates to Netflix' use of a practice more like cost plus financing that enables it long, exclusive access to its original series. Since transitioning into a service with global aspirations, Netflix has sought exclusive global control of its programmes for ten years. This illustrates a key difference in the core strategy of subscriber-funded, internet-distributed services. Netflix is building a library, not a schedule. Its key constraint in building that library is budget. In contrast, broadcast and cable channels are constrained by budgets and schedule capacity: adding a new show to the schedule requires removing one from the existing schedule. Libraries are not regulated by timeliness in the manner of schedules. Netflix receives the same benefit from a viewer valuing the service because its library includes *Stranger Things* if that viewer watches it within hours of its release or after it has been in the library for five years. The internet-distributed services also have the advantage of the extensive use data generated from their services. This enables Netflix and other internet-distributed services to understand much more about how and what viewers watch, and to strategically develop programming based on the patterns they observe.

Internet-distributed, subscriber-funded services – and the differences of their industrial practices – encourage the production of different types of programmes than those found on advertiser-supported broadcast and cable channels. Schedule-driven television must fill every hour of every day. It often selects programmes to create blocks of similar programming likely to maintain viewership, and it must cancel a show in order to add a new one. But practices related to building a library and being unconcerned with timeliness encourage and make possible much different programming. Notably, services such as Netflix are also considerably different from advertiser-supported, internet-distributed services such as YouTube (Lotz, 2018).

In these early years of internet-distributed video, there has been a tendency to categorize media based on its distribution technology. This has frequently led to assumptions that Netflix and YouTube are key competitors or operating in the same industry sector. Rather, their different revenue strategies – Netflix' use of subscriber funding versus YouTube's reliance on advertiser funding – make these two companies very different, and their different financing norms likewise illustrate their significant differences.

In this comparison, Netflix operates far more like the legacy television industry in its strategic cultivation and curation of creative goods. YouTube operates very differently. It spends minimally on content creation and operates much more as an open access platform for the distribution of video than a curated service, at least as of 2018. Of course, viewers can use its search and recommendation tools and curated 'channels' to have a more organized experience, but its reliance on advertiser support makes it very different. This comparison illustrates how distribution technology actually tells us much less about the content likely to be available than does the revenue strategy.

Conclusion

This chapter has sought to illustrate how revenue models and financing strategies have meaningful implications for the media content produced. The examples of HBO, Amazon Video, Netflix, and YouTube here illustrate how and why there can be substantial variation within a particular industry. The examples here are also meant to underscore the variation within a particular industry sector.

Media industries developed revenue models and business strategies according to the dynamics of their analog origins. The different affordances of internet distribution change the utility of those strategies. Understanding the behavior of these industries requires understanding how companies operate to better appreciate which are competitors versus those that are in related, but more supplemental, businesses. Appreciating these industrial nuances also aids in understanding the competitive dynamics that make certain types of programming feasible for varied outlets and in evaluating which strategies developed for analog media continue to be effective versus those that are less useful in an environment that includes digital competitors.

Further reading
- Case: The (lack of) innovation of TV production in the UK – Dwyer (p. 347)
- Context: How the business and revenue models in the media industries are changing – Chan-Olmsted & Wang (p. 133)
- Contrast: An exploration of the rise of the platforms and the powerful role they have in shaping professional media production – Nieborg & Poell (p. 85)

References

Caves, R.E. (2000). *Creative Industries: Contracts Between Art and Commerce.* Cambridge, MA: Harvard University Press.

Doyle, G. (2016). 'Television Production, Funding Models and Exploitation of Content', *Icono, 14*(2), 75-96. doi:10.7195/ri14.v14i1.991.

Littleton, C. (2017). 'New Platforms, New Profits', *Variety* (23 March).

Lotz, A.D. (2007). 'If It is Not TV, What is It? The Case of US Subscription Television', in S. Banet-Weiser, C. Chris & A. Freitas (eds), *Cable Visions: Television Beyond Broadcasting* (85-102). New York: New York University Press.

Lotz, A.D. (2018). *We Now Disrupt This Broadcast: How Cable Transformed Television and the Internet Revolutionized It All.* Cambridge, MA: MIT Press.

Miége, B. (1989). *The Capitalization of Cultural Production.* New York: International General.

26. Flexibility, Innovation, and Precarity in the Television Industry

Paul Dwyer

In TV production there has been a worldwide move from a system based on established broadcasters to a system requiring outsourcing to independent production companies. According to the theory of flexible specialization, this would promote flexibility and innovation in TV production. Testing these claims in the UK market – which has a large independent sector and international reputation for innovative reality TV formats – this chapter finds them to be largely false.

Introduction

Recent debates have questioned the extent to which existing theories, particularly Marxist political economy and cultural studies theories, are able to explain changes in media production (see Dwyer, 2015, 2016; Fuchs, 2016; Garnham, 2011, 2016; Murdock & Golding, 2016). This chapter examines one of the most frequently adopted theories of media production, *flexible specialization* (hereafter, FS) (see Storper, 1993; Barnatt & Starkey, 1997; Karlsson & Picard, 2011). It focuses on the way the key concepts of FS theory – innovation and flexibility – have been used by academics, policymakers, practitioners, and industry lobby groups to explain and/or justify the move from vertically integrated broadcasters to a system requiring outsourcing to independent production companies.

This chapter examines the extent to which FS theory provides a good explanation for the trend towards precarity of employment – freelance or casualized work, often with poor terms and conditions – in TV production (Banks *et al.*, 2013). How far can this precarity be said to have been driven by the need to achieve innovation in TV programming through flexible processes of media production? The UK offers a good case study for investigating and understanding trends internationally, as it has a media industry with a prominent role for public broadcasting, a complex production network that is both local and globally networked, and a moderate level of professional organization of media workers.

First, the key policy documents which created the UK independent TV production sector are reviewed to illustrate the way first cost efficiency, and then increasingly flexibility and innovation were advanced as reasons to support the growth of the sector and the accompanying precarity of employment. The underlying theory of FS is then reviewed to identify the proposed relationship between flexibility and innovation and to identify measures with which to test whether the move to independent production has been associated with greater innovation, flexibility, and precarity. The body of the chapter tests these measures against industry data. The chapter concludes that the rise in precarious employment has not been necessitated by a need for flexibility and innovation in TV production. An alternative explanation is briefly sketched, highlighting the potential for alternative theories of media production to challenge the legitimacy of the precarious employment of media workers.

Policy changes

The requirement to legislate for technological changes, principally the availability of new analogue and digital channels, provided policymakers and practitioners with opportunities to support independent TV production. The first policy step, the 1981 *Broadcasting Act*, established a fourth analogue channel and required that this Channel 4 should encourage innovation, educational programmes, and programmes for minority interests by outsourcing all of its non-news production to independents. As Hobson (2008, p. 14) notes, these aims were specifically contrasted to the output of the main commercial channel, ITV. At this stage, therefore, the innovative potential of independent producers was seen as a counter to the homogenizing effects of commercialism and market forces on TV programming. The report of the Peacock Committee (1986) then articulated the case for vertical disintegration and outsourcing proposing that 'the BBC and ITV should be required to increase to not less than 40% the proportion of programmes supplied by independent producers' (*Ibid.*, p. 142). Similar measures have been taken in other countries in the EU and beyond to protect local and national TV and film industries.

The next policy step in the UK, the 1988 *Broadcasting White Paper*, clearly articulated the theoretical relationship between flexibility, efficiency, and innovation and also identified independent production companies, rather than vertically integrated broadcasters, as the means to achieve these aims. The *White Paper* states:

> [...] traditionally, broadcasters in the UK have themselves made the television programmes they have not acquired from abroad. Channel Four broke this mould. The results have exceeded all expectations. Independent producers constitute an important source of originality and talents which must be exploited, and have brought new pressures for efficiency and flexibility in production procedures. [...] the Government has welcomed these developments [and] envisages that independent producers will continue to play a greater part in programme making in the UK (HMSO, 1988, p. 41).

In addition to promoting independents, the policymakers proposed vertical disintegration of the broadcasters – 'a greater separation between the various functions that make up broadcasting and have in the past been carried out by one organisation' (*Ibid.*, p. 41). At this stage, however, the problem identified with the broadcasters' 'excessive degree of vertical integration' (*Ibid.*) was not a lack of product variety but high labour costs in production.

It was after the main cost savings had been achieved (see below) that policy began more explicitly to focus on outsourcing as a means of achieving programming innovation. Policymakers now assumed 'competition in the supply of programmes will tend to provide a better product for audiences' (DCMS, 2005a, p. 86). Vertical disintegration and outsourcing to 'the marketplace of ideas' must inevitably increase innovation; with independent producers as the 'motor of creative change' (House of Lords, 2005, paras 255, 259). In this policy context, the vertically integrated broadcasters had little choice but to accept that outsourcing and internal flexibility are the route to innovation. The BBC voluntarily increased its potential outsourcing quota, claiming this would 'deliver range and diversity [...] across a wide range of output' (DCMS, 2006, p. 41). This logic reached its apogee in July 2014 when the BBC announced the vertical disintegration of all of its in-house production into a commercial subsidiary, creating 'one of the leanest, hungriest, most flexible organisations [...] a production powerhouse that is a beacon for creativity, risk-taking and quality' (Hall, 2014).

Flexible specialization

This policy discourse (implicitly) adopted the key conceptual relationships of FS theory. Although a wide-ranging theory, applied primarily to the manufacturing industry, FS has attracted particular attention in studies of media production. This approach was pioneered by Storper and Christopherson in a series of articles (Storper & Christopherson, 1987; Storper, 1989) arguing that market changes, particularly competition from TV, had forced the Hollywood studios to try to achieve greater product variety. This produced a fundamental transition from vertically integrated, Fordist, studio production to flexible specialization involving outsourcing to independent producers and freelance workers who could provide 'specialized inputs' – skills and techniques unavailable in-house – 'to produce and develop a wide range of products' (Storper, 1989, p. 274). These increases in product variety were deemed 'typical of [...] flexible specialisation' (*Ibid.*, p. 290).

Barnatt and Starkey (1997) applied FS to explain the disintegration of UK television production. For Starkey (2004) 'the ability to reconvene a successful production team in a fluid environment where the majority of workers are essentially "nomadic" is key to firms seeking advantage from innovative programming' (*Ibid.*, p. 266). This results in flexible firms that can potentially integrate diverse knowledge and skills. However, importantly, flexibility is not simply a means of innovation. It is also 'a means to reduce fixed costs [...] as components of the network ceasing to have a function are disbanded rather than becoming a burden on the whole' (Barnatt & Starkey, 1997, p. 273).

The review of policy documents above illustrated that policy makers selected specific elements of FS theory which appeared applicable to media production and helped make their case for a disintegrated and flexibilized media production system. These key propositions of FS theory can be tested against UK TV industry data.

To provide a fair test of the argument, it is important to test only those elements of FS adopted by policymakers and practitioners in the development of UK independent TV production. UK policymakers did not, for example, adopt the FS theorists' claim that vertically integrated organizations produced feature films and TV programmes using routinized mass production principles, which were no more differentiated than the Model T cars rolling off Henry Ford's assembly lines (Storper, 1989). As I have argued elsewhere (see Dwyer, 2015) these claims do not conform to the complex reality of media production, both in the US, the UK, and elsewhere.

However, the policy documents do follow FS in suggesting that broadcasters which outsource production increase innovation by choosing the best ideas from the 'marketplace of ideas', compared to vertically integrated broadcasters which are constrained to choose from ideas and innovations generated internally. The first measure, therefore, is the extent to which outsourcing has resulted in broadcasters selecting the best ideas from across the market.

Secondly, as policymakers adopted the two meanings of flexibility implicit in FS, this generates two measures. First, we would expect to find evidence of independent producers trying to increase innovation through *functional flexibility*, whether through production staff undertaking different roles (such as multitasking) or through accessing specialized inputs in the form of (freelance) workers with specialist skills. We would also expect to find independent firms using casualized labour for *numerical flexibility*, to reduce production costs and so increase profitability and gain competitive advantage over vertically integrated producers employing staff on permanent or long-term contracts.

Finally, both FS theory and policy documents are clear that the driving force of these changes is the need for significantly increased product innovation, so we should expect to find independent producers achieving greater range, diversity and originality in programming than is possible for vertically integrated broadcasters.

The marketplace of ideas

Turning to the first of these measures, there is some evidence that the development of the independent production sector enabled broadcasters, particularly Channel 4, to innovate by choosing from across the marketplace of ideas. When Channel 4 launched in 1982, it opted to work with a very wide range of producers. In 1986, the channel outsourced production to more than 230 independent production companies and by 1990 the number had risen to more than 520 (Ellis, 2013). But in 1993 policymakers required Channel 4 to compete for advertising sales, reducing its protection from the homogenizing commercial influences which had originally been thought fundamental to its potential for innovation and diversity. A new CEO focused on targeting affluent young audiences with programming acquired from US producers. By 2007, the channel was outsourcing to fewer independent producers (around 300) and by 2013 this had fallen to 230 (Mediatique, 2015). More significant than the absolute numbers of producers is the amount of production that is genuinely commissioned from across the market. The data show that between 1998-2003 'Channel 4's profile with the independent sector has undergone a shift [...] by nearly every measure, Channel 4's dependence on large indies has increased' (Mediatique, 2004, p. 18).

British public broadcaster the BBC also had the opportunity to exploit the innovative potential of the marketplace which Channel 4 was increasingly abandoning, when in 2007 the so-called 'Window of Creative Competition' or WOCC took effect: a rule that requires 25 per cent of eligible BBC TV commissions to be open for competition between in-house and independent producers. In 2007, the BBC outsourced programming to 279 producers (*Idem*, 2015, p. 17). However, the BBC largely relied on the same section of the market as Channel 4: 'the BBC's apparent reliance on a limited range of suppliers to deliver the majority of independent programming does not necessarily accord with the plurality of provision desired when the WOCC was introduced' (Turner & Lourenco, 2010, p. 19). Nor did ITV, one of the other major broadcasters, attempt to choose the best ideas from wherever they originated, working with around 70-80 independents. Altogether, from 2008-2013 half of all UK independent TV production was outsourced to large independent producers and another 30 per cent to medium-sized producers (Oliver & Ohlbaum, 2014, p. 6).

The data therefore suggest that the move to outsource production to independents has not, ultimately, resulted in broadcasters seeking innovation by taking the 'best' ideas from across the marketplace. The independent production sector did initially represent a marketplace of ideas – the kind of network FS suggests encourages greater innovation than vertically integrated structures. From 1982-1993, Channel 4 attempted to exploit the innovative potential of this network to the full, working with a large number of often small production companies. But once Channel 4 was required to compete more directly for advertising revenue, it began outsourcing the majority of its content to a much smaller group of large companies. Similarly, when policymakers required the vertically integrated broadcasters to outsource some of their production to independents, they too followed the strategy of working with large independents.

Functional flexibility

The second measure concerns functional flexibility in TV production. The question is how far independents used this flexibility to increase innovation. We would expect small but significant differences between more or less rigid production processes in vertically integrated broadcasters, and flexible production teams, with multitasking and extensive use of freelancers with specialist skills, in the independent productions.

The evidence does support the view of policymakers that in the 1980s, TV production in the vertically integrated broadcasters was unnecessarily inefficient and inflexible to change, as a result of trade union agreements and established working practices. While anecdotal accounts emphasized the extent to which broadcasting unions and their members exploited the system to their own advantage, the original reasons for these rigidities were not simply opportunist. The difficulties of recording and editing video meant that from the 1950s to the 1970s most TV genres (news, soap operas, magazine shows, sitcoms, etc.) were produced live or 'as-live' in a multi-camera studio. Live production established linear dependencies which were inherently less flexible than (for example) recorded (film) production (which was also a key feature of TV schedules). Recording enabled each shot to be created several times, and gave editors the ability to assemble them in a variety of sequences before arriving at the final version. But live, or as-live production required these decisions to be made, and rehearsed, in advance of shooting. Furthermore, prior to the development of digital production technologies, electro-mechanical production equipment was unreliable. When broadcasters had to produce high volumes of live programming, it made practical sense to rely on trusted production routines, with tasks assignment to specialists whose union membership ensured a degree of experience and an understanding of the idiosyncrasies of the equipment (McKinlay & Quinn, 1999).

In addition to underpinning the division of labour, the necessity of maintaining a live broadcast service gave the broadcasting unions considerable power in the labour market. The ability to call a strike and effectively shut down a TV channel, immediately removing a commercial broadcaster's source of income, gave the unions power in negotiating with broadcasters. ITV thus accepted the practice of the 'closed shop', requiring all workers to join the union. Occupational job demarcations, enshrined in national agreements with broadcasters, determined both the minimum number of production staff required on given genres of programming, and the specific tasks they could perform. Production tasks were often strictly controlled by occupational groups; 'An electrician would not touch a sound cable, a sound guy would not touch an electrician's cable or a camera cable, a cameraman would not touch a sound cable or an electrician's cable' (McKinlay & Quinn, 1999, p. 5). Producers had very limited flexibility to adapt production, or use workers with specialist skills, to innovate in programming. Nor was there flexibility to reduce costs by using smaller teams or requiring production staff to multitask. Instead, the agreements enabled production staff regularly to claim overtime payments, or to stand idle ('downtime') during technical breaks in production. The unions were also able to limit management's ability to use new production technologies (first video recording and editing and then non-linear digital systems) to reduce labour costs or increase flexibility in production (Campling, 1995).

By being able to produce, to order, low cost, recorded, non-studio programmes, independent producers enabled broadcasters to reduce their dependence on (unionized) live studio production. Independents also pioneered the introduction of new production technologies and functional flexibility in TV production, particularly the multi-tasking and multi-skilling of production staff. The division between creative/editorial and technical functions was eroded – with creative staff performing technical tasks (shooting and editing their own footage) and vice versa. The next stage was for broadcasters to introduce this model in their own production departments.

However, in recent years, as the independent sector has increasingly focused on producing long running entertainment formats, sometimes based in studios with live audiences, there appears to have been a reduction in functional flexibility and a return to some of the rigidities of series production in the analogue era, albeit now under managerial rather than union control. As a producer pointed out:

[...] very frequently in an indie now the director is brought on after the pre-production work has been largely done, they're brought on just before the shoot. They do the shoot, they take the material into the edit where, because it's a highly-formatted piece, they stay for the first two thirds of the edit and then leave for it to be completed by the series producer and editor. You may only be on contract to that production for eight, ten weeks; you will never see your programme completed. You are absolutely a gun for hire to do a job and the job's not a very creative one (producer interview cited in Turner & Lourenco, 2010, p. 18).

Numerical flexibility

The third measure is numerical flexibility. How far have independent producers used freelance and casual labour to reduce the cost of programme production? During the 1980s, when their main source of income, Channel 4, was outsourcing across the sector, independents faced great uncertainty about future revenue and were unable to employ production staff until they had a project commissioned. There was a clear relationship between the attempt to use the marketplace as a source of innovation, and the need for numerical flexibility (producing greater precarity) in employment of media workers. However, when the BBC and ITV were required to outsource production during the 1990s, they were responding to policymakers advocating the independent model, not as a source of innovation, but as a method of removing the inefficiencies and high costs identified with in-house production. The broadcasters' introduction of flexible organizational structures creating internal markets was intended to reduce costs rather than increase innovation. The BBC's Producer Choice policy, for example, required BBC technical crews and facilities to compete for work against independent companies (Born, 2004). In ITV, between 1985-1995, 'the broadcasting trade unions were decimated [...] the job controls established over almost three decades were obliterated' (McKinley & Quinn, 1999, p. 13).

These initiatives had a huge impact on the employment security of people working for the main broadcasters. Between 1980 and 2016 the BBC shed around 12,500 full time permanent jobs, generating numerical flexibility through using the full-time equivalent of 2,500 freelance and agency workers of (NAO, 2017, p. 7). ITV seems to have hollowed out at the same rate, shedding around 10,000 full time permanent jobs from 1987 to 2017 (Citywire, 2017). The consequence of the move to flexibility is that the independent sector now employs almost as many workers as the rest of the industry combined. However, in the independent sector, 52 per cent of these workers are freelance compared to 36 per cent across cable and satellite channels and 25 per cent across the broadcasters (Skillset, 2015). This adoption of numerical flexibility has been successful in reducing costs (especially of permanent employees) but quickly began to undermine the perception of independents and flexibility as forces for innovation; 'from being considered a progressive force in television [...] with the accent on 'new voices', independent producers have come to be seen by many within the television industry – including some producers themselves – as agents of rationalization' (Davis, 1991, p. 17).

Increased innovation

The final measure is also the most difficult to test against data: how far did the development of the independent sector result in increased innovation in programming? In its early years, Channel 4 acquired a reputation for identifying innovative programmes from independent producers. However, when the channel strategy changed in the mid-1990s, the focus moved from working with innovative independents to importing successful US sitcoms like *Friends* (on Channel 4 from 1995-2004).

A second wave of innovation occurred in the late 1990s, when the independent sector became associated with supplying innovative factual entertainment/reality TV formats to all the main broadcasters, such as internationally successful shows like *Who Wants To Be A Millionaire?* (Celador for ITV, 1998), *Big Brother* (Endemol for Channel 4, 2000), *Pop Idol* (19 Entertainment for ITV, 2001) and *Wife Swap* (RDF Media for Channel 4, 2003). The reality TV format was a genuine innovation, a hybrid form created by combining elements of other genres, particularly documentary, gameshows, and light entertainment. But the success of the format in this period (1998-2003) coincided with a dramatic decline in the factual genres from which the hybrid had been constructed; education (-53%), arts (-23%), current affairs (-22%), and religion (-12%) (Ofcom, 2004, p. 35). Moreover, while the concept of a factual entertainment format was an innovation, the spread of new formats (*Popstars*, *Pop Idol*, *Fame Academy*, *...Got Talent*) was generally based on imitation. The regulator found that, far from providing viewers with innovation and diversity, audiences quickly began to 'resent being repeatedly presented with similar versions of the same format' (*Ibid.*, p. 59).

It will always be hard to be definitive about a measure like innovation. And the data do suggest that independents have been responsible for two periods of innovation, the early period of Channel 4 and the origination of the factual entertainment format. However, in both cases, this was followed by a reversion to a period of reduced diversity or outright imitation. And in the case of the TV format, this imitation has continued since.

Conclusion

This chapter has attempted to test the claims – of policymakers and FS theory – for a relationship between outsourcing, flexibility, and innovation against data from the case of UK TV production. The data show the transformation of the industry from predominantly secure employment to, in the independent sector at least, predominantly freelance work. However, the data do not support a relationship between this long-term trend to precarity of employment and the requirement to use flexibility to increase innovation. In outsourcing to independents, rather than exploiting the innovation advantages of the 'marketplace of ideas', broadcasters quickly reverted to working with a smaller range of trusted independents. Similarly, independents initially developed flexible models of TV production which helped broadcasters overcome the rigidities of existing models. However, in the long run, the divisions between specialist creative/editorial and technical roles have remained fundamentally unchanged and so functional flexibility in TV production is still limited.

The independents were responsible for both innovation and an increase in diversity at Channel 4 in the 1980s. A second period of innovation, from 1998-2003 (roughly from *Millionaire* to *Wife Swap*) coincided with a reduction in diversity across TV genres and increasing imitation in the search for new long-running factual entertainment formats. This, in turn, has enabled managers to reintroduce some rigidities into production in order to reduce costs.

On the basis of the data presented here then, we should reject the claims of FS theory and policy that changes in media production practices and the increase of precarity of employment have been driven by product market pressures requiring continual product innovations and thus a transformation to flexible production systems. While space limitations prevent a full account (see Dwyer, forthcoming), we can briefly sketch the outlines of an alternative theory to help understand and explain these changes and to inform future policymaking.

First, we can note, *contra* FS, that the pressure for vertical disintegration came not from the market but from regulators and the independent producers' own lobbying organizations. Secondly, once policymakers created a secure market for the independent sector, the larger independents began a process of constraining the scope of the 'marketplace of ideas' by acquiring smaller independents. Thirdly, as the major independents have become more focused on searching for the next hit reality format, they have engaged increasingly in product imitation rather than product innovation. In the factual entertainment/reality TV format, the independent sector discovered a product with a potentially highly profitable combination of low cost (using freelance labour) production, high volume content, relative ease of generating new series, and rich potential for international licencing. Initially, the independent companies were unable to exploit the full potential of a hit format. However, after successfully lobbying for further regulatory changes in their favour, in 2003, the independents won sole right to exploit formats internationally. This turned shows like *Who Wants To Be A Millionaire* into continuing, global income streams.

The large independent producers now focus almost exclusively on producing factual/factual entertainment shows; Endemol (64%), All3Media (64%), Zodiak (64%) Shine (90%), and Fremantle (100%) (Oliver & Ohlbaum, 2014, p. 25). The continuing profitability of the independents' format rights attracted the Hollywood majors to acquire UK independent producers – notably 21st Century Fox (Endemol and Shine), NBC Universal (Carnival Films, Monkey Kingdom etc.), Time Warner (Shed), and Discovery/Liberty (All3Media) (Mediatique, 2015, p. 18). In a reversal of the arguments of the 1980s and 1990s, the independent sector has now become a supporter of vertical re-integration, since it enables these global corporations to exercise considerable market power in the UK.

Finally, we can conclude that in the current landscape of the UK independent sector, numerical flexibility is not required to produce innovation or deal with market uncertainty. Instead, it largely reflects the power of these global entertainment companies in the labour market. As the quote from the producer, above, demonstrates, flexibility allows producers to pay production workers for the minimum number of days required. Such cost-reduction measures may be supplemented by exploitative and even unsafe working conditions, as production teams are required to work long hours, on the days they are paid, often being required to accept so-called 'buyout' deals which prevent them claiming overtime payments (Evans & Green, 2017).

This understanding of the major UK independent TV companies, as highly profitable producers of a relatively narrow range of factual/entertainment formats, within the major global entertainment corporations, does not accord with the ideas of flexibility, innovation, and diversity which have dominated the scholarly and policy debate. Instead, it suggests that precarity of employment in the sector is driven not by the need for flexibility and innovation but by shareholder interests in reducing labour costs and increasing profitability.

Further reading
- Case: How the working conditions within TV production are affectively experienced – Cantillon & Baker (p. 287)
- Context: The need for the transformation and innovation of media business models – Villi & Picard (p. 121)
- Contrast: How revenue models and financing strategies of companies such as Netflix have influenced the content of internet-distributed television – Lotz (p. 337)

References

Banks, M. *et al.* (eds) (2013). *Theorizing Cultural Work.* London: Routledge.

Barnatt, C. & Starkey, K. (1997). 'Flexible Specialization and the Reconfiguration of Television Production in the UK', *Technology Analysis & Strategic Management, 9*(3), 271-286.

Born, G. (2004). *Uncertain Vision.* London: Secker and Warburg.

Campling, J. (1995). 'From Rigid to Flexible Employment Practices in UK Commercial Television', *New Zealand Journal of Industrial Relations*, *20*(1).

Citywire. *ITV PLC*. Retrieved from http://citywire.co.uk/money/share-prices-and-performance/share-factsheet.aspx?InstrumentID=79321

DCMS (2005). *Review of the BBC's Royal Charter*. London: DCMS.

DCMS (2006). *A Public Service All: The BBC In The Digital Age*. London: DCMS.

Davis, J. (1991). *TV UK: A Special Report*. Peterborough: Knowledge Research.

Deakin, S. *et al*. (2008). *No 'Third Way' For Economic Organization?* Cambridge: Centre for Business Research, University of Cambridge.

Dwyer, P. (2015). 'Theorizing Media Production: The Poverty of Political Economy', *Media, Culture & Society*, *37*(7), 988-1004.

Dwyer, P. (2016). 'Understanding Media Production: A Rejoinder to Murdock and Golding', *Media, Culture & Society*, *3*(8), 1-4.

Dwyer, P. (forthcoming) *Understanding Media Production: Theory and Practice*. London: Routledge.

Evans, P. & Green, J. (2017). *Eyes Half Shut*. London: BECTU.

Fuchs, C. (2016). 'Against theoretical Thatcherism: a reply to Nicholas Garnham', *Media, Culture & Society*, *38*(2), 301-311.

Garnham, N. (2011). 'The Political Economy of Communication Revisited', in J. Wasko *et al*. (eds), *The Handbook of Political Economy of Communications* (41-61). London: Wiley-Blackwell.

Garnham, N. (2016). 'Review of Fuchs, C. "Digital Labour and Karl Marx"', *Media, Culture & Society*, *38*(2), 294-300.

HMSO (1986). *Report of the Committee on Financing the BBC*. London: HMSO.

HMSO (1988). *Broadcasting in the '90s*. London: HMSO.

Hall, A. (2014). *Compete and Compare*. Retrieved from http://www.bbc.co.uk/mediacentre/speeches/2014/dg-city-university.

Hobson, D. (2008). *Channel 4*. London: IB Tauris.

Karlsson, C. & Picard, R.G. (eds) (2011). *Media Clusters*. Cheltenham: Edward Elgar Publishing.

McKinlay, A. & Quinn, B. (1999). 'Management, Technology and Work in Commercial Broadcasting 1979-98', *New Technology, Work and Employment*, *14*(1), 2-17.

Mediatique (2008). *All Grown Up*. London: Mediatique.

Mediatique (2015). *TV Production Sector Evolution and Impact on* PSBs. London: Mediatique.

Murdock, G. & Golding, P. (2016). 'Political Economy and Media Production: A Reply to Dwyer', *Media, Culture & Society*, *38*(5), 763-769.

NAO (2017). *Managing the BBC's Workforce*. National Audit Office.

Ofcom (2004). *Review of Public Service Television Broadcasting*. Ofcom.

Oliver & Ohlbaum/PACT (2011). *The Role of Terms of Trade*. London: PACT.

Oliver & Ohlbaum (2014). *The Evolution of The TV Content Production Sector*. London: Oliver & Ohlbaum.

Skillset (2016). *2015 Employment Survey: Creative Media Industries.* Skillset.

Starkey, K. (2004). 'Beyond Networks and Hierarchies', in K. Starkey *et al.* (2004). *How Organizations Learn* (2nd ed.). London: Thomson.

Storper, M. (1989). 'The Transition to Flexible Specialisation in the US Film Industry', *Cambridge Journal of Economics, 13*(3), 273-305.

Storper, M. & Christopherson, S. (1987). 'Flexible Specialization and Regional Industrial Agglomerations', *Annals of the Association of American Geographers, 77*(1), 104-117.

Turner, S. & Lourenco, A. (2010). *Competition and Public Service Broadcasting.* Cambridge: Centre for Business Research, University of Cambridge.

Professions

Social Media

27. Creator Management in the Social Media Entertainment Industry

David Craig

Social media entertainment is a rapidly formalizing proto-industry in which creators – influencers, YouTubers, vloggers, gameplayers – play a central role. They use a variety of platforms to engage with global fan communities for commercial and cultural value, and operate outside the traditional structures of legacy media. Creator management takes on many forms. This chapter discusses creator management on three different levels: platforms, intermediaries, and the creators themselves.

Introduction

For little over a decade, we have witnessed the rapid rise of creators, alternatively called content creators, influencers, YouTubers, vloggers, live streamers, gameplayers, KOLS, and *Wang Hong* (in China). Forbes' annual list of the most successful creators extends across multiple content verticals to include 'entertainer' Lily Singh (aka Superwoman II), game player Markiplier, beauty vlogger Michele Phan, and toy unboxer Evan Tube (O'Connor, 2017). These comprise but a small portion of a vast global wave of online cultural producers fostering and blending old and new forms of media entrepreneurialism, management, creative labour, and user practices.

Operating within the proto-industry of social media entertainment, 'creator' has become the industry term to describe social media users harnessing multiple and global-scaling platforms to engage in media entrepreneurialism (Cunningham & Craig, 2019). Creators have emerged natively on and across multiple platforms, fuelled by network effects and diverse technological and commercial affordances, to generate their own media brands. The global social media platform landscape continues to expand and foster new modalities, including text, image, audio, video on demand, and livestreaming. A short list includes first generation platforms, Twitter, Facebook, and YouTube; mobile apps like Instagram, Musical.ly, and Snapchat; and livestreaming platforms including Twitch and YouNow. China's competing *Wang Hong* creator industry fosters an even more competitive platform landscape with more advanced and better integrated commercial features, including Youku, WeChat, and Weibo.

Creator entrepreneurialism has contributed to exponential growth in revenue, albeit difficult to measure in scale and influence. A report on the 'New Creator

Economy' (Shapiro & Aneja, 2018) described 15 million online creators generating revenue off these platforms in the United States alone. Varying industry reports have estimated the total value of the 'influencer economy' from $1 billion US dollars (Mediakix) on Instagram alone to over $50 billion US dollars (Northzone) globally. In China, this industry is even more accelerated, with some creators garnering nearly $50 million US dollars in a year (Tsoi, 2017).

Much like the industry, vital scholarship has rapidly emerged to account for and frame the labour, management, and practices of these creators. A raft of terms have been used to describe these entrepreneurs, including produsers (Bruns, 2008), YouTubers engaging in vernacular creativity (Burgess & Green, 2009), influencers and content creators.

In describing Social Media Entertainment (SME), Cunningham and Craig (2019) place creators centrally within this proto-industry which operates distinct from legacy media. With reference to the American film business, this is industry is Post-Hollywood or PoHo. In their ecological approach, Cunningham and Craig account for the interdependency between the platforms, creators, and intermediary firms and professionals who assist with managing creator brands. In addition to conventional intellectual property (IP) production, creators typically engage in more discursive content creation featuring alternative social media formats and modalities, like vlogging and livestreaming. Content creation is complimented by community interactivity conducted through iterative and typically non-scalable practices of commenting, liking, sharing, sending direct messages, and more, depending on the platform's networking affordance. Across these platforms, creators engage with global communities with similar affinities, interests, identities, and values that can be converted into commercial value. Creators and their associates and platform handlers help manage a portfolio of legacy and new business models, including programmatic advertising, influencer marketing, crowd-funding, virtual goods, e-commerce, performance fees, and media transactions.

This chapter discusses how creator management operates throughout SME across three dimensions: platforms, intermediaries, and creators. *Platforms* manage creators, often through automated programmatic efforts, as reflected by YouTube's partner program, Creator Academy, and Ad Sense features. But the platforms have ceded direct creator management to *intermediaries*, including multi-channel networks, talent representatives, publicists, and influencer agencies. And the *creators* themselves engage in self-management: the diverse practices of creative and production labour, content and platform management, media entrepreneurialism, and community management.

Platform automanagement

Cunningham and Silver (2013) refer to the rise of technology companies, including Google, Apple, and Facebook, as the new 'King Kongs of the online world' threatening a century of Hollywood incumbency. Amongst numerous value propositions and tech services, these tech hegemons have fostered a competitive landscape of streaming video platforms and social media networking platforms with diverse technological, communicative, and commercial affordances. Competing most directly with linear television, Lotz (2017) describes how internet-distributed television portals, including Netflix, Hulu, and Amazon, feature comparable professionally-generated content combined with the emerging logics and related protocols of digital platforms. Alternatively, operating off of Web 2.0 technologies, Facebook, Twitter, and a raft of new social media platforms foster online communities through networking affordances. These platforms are fuelled by the 'logics' of social media (Van Dijck & Poell, 2013), including programmability, popularity, connectivity, and datafication.

YouTube operates liminally, if centrally, in SME by offering a premium streaming video player coupled with social networking capacities through its comment, sharing, and liking features. Although not the first (Vimeo was launched in 2004 and China's Youku debuted six months prior to the launch of YouTube) the platform has dominated the global video streaming market with nearly two billion users. After acquisition by Google, the platform secured the capital to engage in a decade-long array of pivots in value propositions, features, services, and affordances. These reflect intense competitive experimentation designed to compete with legacy television as well as thwart its tech competitors. Informed by what proved to be a protracted quest for monetization and viability over its first decade, YouTube introduced its content management system to eliminate owned IP content along with Google's AdSense technology that automated programmatic advertising across the platform. Alongside repeated changes in algorithms and curation, modest improvements in user interface, and launch of a mobile application, YouTube has morphed into multiple YouTubes: an array of integrated platforms and services including YouTube Premium (subscriptions), YouTube Music (streaming), YouTube Games, and YouTube Live.

Alphabet/Google/YouTube's state of 'permanent beta' conforms with the management strategies of tech culture but has also created ongoing precarity for creators attempting to build and manage sustainable media brands on the platform. Early in 2007, Google offered its creators a revenue-sharing partnership agreement which was invitation-only to premium creators. Over time, the partnership agreement was made available to all users, but has since changed to demand ever-increasing levels of subscriptions, views, and view times. The revenue split has shifted over the decade, primarily to favour the platform and their larger scaling premium creators, especially creators who provide more 'brand safe' advertising opportunities. In addition, YouTube forced creators to join its YouTube Red subscription platform where creators are guaranteed a portion of the subscription fees, albeit with an ever-shifting array of percentages, although the general consensus is that the platform has boosted creator revenue.

These platform-wide initiatives have been less strategic than tactical, often an over-reaction to bad players profiteering off the platform's automated ads and vice versa – like fake news creators, Russian hackers, and Macedonian teenagers. In 2017, the press revelation that YouTube was advertising on extremist and hate group videos contributed to what has become known as the Adpocalypse. As a form of self-regulation, creators were required to use an automated filtering system that categorized their content in generic ways to signal brand safety. The consequence of this taxonomic tyranny was the automatic demonetization of a vast array of creator videos, often tendered without notification or even explanation, even after submitting to a human curated appeals' process. Game players fond of the game *Assassin's Creed* engaging in game play tutorials and commentary were caught up in the platform's onerous and decontextualized filtering system. More troubling, certain minorities and progressive creators were most impacted, including LGBTQ creators whose content was reductively categorized as 'sexual'. Progressive and civic-minded creators like Casey Neistat and Philip DeFranco were deemed 'political'. Although these creators cannot afford to leave the platform and abandon their followers, they have sought out other forms of revenue. In the case of DeFranco, he launched his own interactive website and app (Weiss, 2018).

YouTube's Creator Academy is another example of YouTube's low-touch creator management. The academy is an online DIY trade school, certificates and all, featuring self-help videos designed to teach creators how to self-manage their content, channels, brand deals, and fan communities. Curiously, these creator videos offer less interactivity than a Baby Einstein game or Stanford MOOC while fostering regressive video pedantry set to 1990s muzak. The Academy reflects how YouTube strives to place managerial expertise and responsibility in the hands of the creator, both literally and figuratively, all the while profiting from their efforts. In a break from their aversion to direct interaction with creators, YouTube has hired fleets of talent managers to assist with their premiere creators, while also launching YouTube Spaces around the world offering production facilities and in situ training.

Other SME platforms have followed suit by pursuing their own creator management strategies. Facebook, Twitter, Instagram, and Snapchat introduced their own partnership programs. Instagram has 'creator divisions' dedicated to fostering the growth of their creators, while its parent platform, Facebook, separately launched creator programs. Twitter started numerous features on its platforms, including its livestreaming platform Periscope, nudging creators to generate revenue through programmatic advertising. Twitch's blog is designed like YouTube's creator academy, to teach its streamers and fans how to build their channels. In March 2018, Snapchat hosted its first 'Creator Summit' designed to appeal to their own native creator entrepreneurs who had experienced years of neglect by the platform (Constine, 2018).

The rise and fall of the platform Vine affirms the precarity of platforms, including their challenges with creator management. Acquired by Twitter in 2012 prior to launch, the platform failed to introduce monetization as organically and profitably as other platforms. Its six-second short-form looping video content player placed more demands on brands and advertisers to create unique content than other platforms, even as the platform scaled to 300 million users in record time. However, Vine creators had flourished in loops and followers but were never afforded partnership with the platform's advertising. The 'Viners' protested, even picketed the offices of Vine, and proceeded to leave the platform en masse to other platforms that had launched short video players. Although creator flight was not the only cause, it contributed to the shutting down of the platform literally overnight (Rogers, 2016).

Intermediary (mis)management

As described in the previous section, YouTube and other platforms have gone to great lengths to keep their creator partners at arms' length. Until recently, YouTube deferred direct creator management to a diverse array of outside firms and organizations operating liminally between platforms and creators, as well as legacy media and advertisers. These firms and professionals mostly emulate traditional media management practices, like those engaged by film studios, television network executives, and producers (Albarran, 2008), as well as the representational practices and brokerage skills of talent agents and managers (Roussell, 2015). Media management shares similarities to creative labour (Johnson, Kompare & Santo, 2014), with media management professionals engaging in their own practices of content production, media entrepreneurialism, and datafication. The firms also affirm the practices of strategic media management framed by ongoing technological and industrial disruption (Küng, 2014). As reflected here, some of these intermediaries have proven to be evanescent, rising and falling as a consequence of industrial precarity coupled with creator mismanagement.

YouTube's platform design, which generated user channels coupled with their partner program, contributed to the rise of a set of firms that came to be known as multi-channel networks (MCNs). Certified by YouTube, these outside organizations quickly signed creators to help manage and grow their creator brand in exchange for a portion of their revenue. Operating across diverse content verticals, channel aggregators like Maker Studios, Broadband TV, and Fullscreen signed many as 100,000 creators. Other firms featured smaller lists by focusing on niche categories and content verticals like food (Tastemade), design (Stylehaul), and game play (Machinima). These firms claimed to offer an array of high and low-touch management services, such as proprietary and multi-platform data analytics, branded content and marketing opportunities, traditional media representation, and production training and facilities. In short order, creators would often find that these firms and their management services were over-priced with limited returns on value, often leading to creator flight.

Nonetheless, from 2011-2013, YouTube's multi-million dollar original channel initiatives artificially subsidized these firms. Once the funding disappeared and platforms began to offer competing services, these MCNs either merged, were acquired by legacy media companies, or disappeared. The premiere example is Maker Studios, which was acquired by Disney in 2014 with 55,000 creators, only to be reduced to a sub-brand within Disney's digital division (Spangler, 2017) featuring less than 1000 of their premium creators. By 2018, MCNs all but disappeared from YouTube's directory of certified firms, less than a decade after they first emerged, affirming industrial disruption and managerial precarity. As indicated in the first section, platforms have also assumed some of these management services, venturing in to high-touch management despite their aversion to direct creator interaction.

In addition to MCNs, other classes of firms and professionals have emerged offering diverse creator management services and varying levels of sustainability. Influencer agencies, including divisions of ad agencies, helped negotiate, secure, and manage content branding and influencer marketing deals between creators and advertisers. Social media talent agents, managers, and publicists have emerged, including digital and social media divisions of legacy talent agencies like Creative Artists and United Talent. These firms and representatives have signed creators to '360 talent management deals', the term that agents and managers use to describe a portfolio of business deals and brokerage services (modelled after the popular '360 deal' in the music industry; see Marshall (2012)). These representatives foster talent deals on and across platforms with advertisers, record labels, and book publishers, secure performance fees in traditional media and on live tours, arrange licencing and merchandising deals, and more.

Third-party data firms like Tubular Labs and Social Blade represent yet another type of intermediary assisting with creator management. Offering services previously provided by MCNs, these firms provide multiplatform analytics to help creators, advertisers, intermediary firms, and even legacy media and celebrities optimize their views, subscriptions, and engagement across these platforms.

Creator self-management

Recent scholarship has framed the strategies and practices of creators as extensions of as well as new forms of creative labour (Deuze, 2007), including aspirational labour (Duffy, 2015) and visibility labour (Abidin, 2016). Emphasis has been placed on creators operating on – and therefore managed by – a single platform or working for intermediary firms like agencies. While focusing on creators operating independently and across platforms, Cunningham and Craig (2019) delineate the field between creator labour and intermediary management.

If, as Johnson, Kompare, and Santo (2014) claim, media management may represent creative labour, then the inverse may also be true. Creative labour may be media management, most notably the blurred practices, skills, and strategies of creator labour and entrepreneurialism. These practices are often disorganized, operating outside of the formations of a media firm or organization, particularly as digital and social media practices allow for the collapse of the divisions of production labour. In proposing a differentiated field of study for media management, Deuze and Steward (2011) suggested that scholars consider 'what may be the new networks emerging through the creative industries, not necessarily tied to specific companies, products or places, that define new and evolving constellations of skill sets, practices and beliefs that could provide a road map through the morass of contemporary creative industries' (p. 10).

In this regard, the case could be made that the labour of making media might be better framed as creator management, or rather, self-management. In addition to platform auto-management and intermediary (mis)management, the strategies of creator self-management are vital to the success of their SME brands and are often conducted singularly or with minimal support. As described in the introduction, creator self-management features diverse practices, including content production and circulation, media entrepreneurialism, and community management. These strategies are often derived from user practices and earlier hobbyism before advancing from amateur creation to professionalized commercialization, often through trial and error. As the creator's brand emerges, their self-management practices affirm creator agency and precarity in pursuit of viability and sustainability, often facilitated as well as disrupted by platform and intermediary management.

Creators were once coined content creators as they engaged in what first appeared to be normative practices of media production, albeit digital first. Some creators engage in screenwriting, physical production, and editing that emulate the development and production of scripted and non-scripted media. In addition, however, operating off the networked and technological affordances of platforms, creators have also cultivated new formats, genres, and modalities. In contrast to more scripted fare, this content reflects more discursive and quasi-improvisational content. Vlogging and livestreaming are but two examples that demand alternative practices of content preparation, production, and posting.

These modalities contribute to new verticals or genres of content like game play, DIY tutorials, shopping 'haul' and unboxing, as well as alternative genres of comedy and music, e.g. Zach King's digital illusion videos or Pentatonix a cappella groups that require limited music production. This content represents not only new visual aesthetics but also a certain level of production management, such as multiple camera systems or editing strategies that supplement the information on mobile screens. In addition to video fare, creator production management includes multiple platform modalities, including tweets, photoshopped images, and audio podcasts. These, in turn, give rise to other formats and genres, including memes, gifs, tweet streams, and more.

On any single platform like YouTube, content management by creators may include the curation of playlists and secondary channels that feature alternative content, as well as uploading content onto their subscription platform and advertising-driven site. Creators are practiced in algorithmic and search strategies of content management, like optimizing titles and hashtags. At the same time, creators also engage in content management across platforms customized to their affordances, as described in *Spreadable Media* (Jenkins, Ford & Green, 2013). These skills demand content production and management informed by the affordances of each platform. A ten-minute YouTube video would for instance neither be viable nor recommended for optimal creator benefit as an Instagram story or a Facebook livestreaming session. Content management across platforms also includes scheduling the content at the optimal times for viewing, when fan communities are most likely to watch, like, and share. For English-speaking creators in the Global South, this requires posting content in the middle of the night to secure the attention of Anglo fan communities in more lucrative markets. Cross-platform content management includes such practices as providing links in and under the screen to the creators' other platforms and channels.

Creator self-management incorporates diverse forms of media entrepreneurialism that foster a portfolio of business models and revenue streams. As described in earlier sections, platforms have offered programmatic advertising partnerships that include filtering systems around brand safety. Creators must navigate these systems, in some instance developing strategies to bypass the filters and avoid terms and content that may lead to demonetization. The rise of companion subscription platforms, e.g. YouTube Premium and Facebook Watch, have created new commercial opportunities for creators but additional demands for exclusive content, often featuring more traditional IP formats and genres. These platforms reverse engineer the creator's production management processes, often requiring more professionalization while placing greater demands on the development and production process.

Various platforms have introduced other forms of monetization that creators may profit from but also have to additionally manage. Live streaming platforms like Twitch and YouNow feature virtual goods payments funded through online payment services like bitcoin that allow fans to reward streamers often in exchange for some form of recognition. In China, which features more advanced and better integrated opportunities for creators monetization, female livestreamers can secure millions in Yuan from male online companions.

Secondary platforms have emerged that provide additional business models for creators. Creators use subscription and crowdfunding platforms, which allow their fan communities to subsidize their brands, whether through monthly subscriptions (Patreon) or project-based crowd funding (Kickstarter and IndieGogo). Chinese creators connect their channels with e-commerce and online shopping platforms where they have launched their own Taobao or T-mall stories. Fuelled by China's booming middle class, creators profit from clickthrough links and brand deals on these sites with virtually every product or service they want. As creators generate other forms of content across other platforms, they also pursue new means of monetization. These may include transactional downloads for their music and subscription fees and advertising for their podcasts.

In addition to programmatic advertising and subscriptions, creators have developed the means to generate money on and across platforms. The most lucrative strategy involves influencer marketing deals, also known as branded content deals, with direct payment of fees to promote an advertising brand, product or service. These deals are often secured directly between the brand and the creator, although ad or influencer agencies, agents, and managers, may operate liminally to facilitate the deals and the production. In numerous accounts, the creators dictate the terms for the creation of the campaign, including how they illustrate, use, mention or include links for the product in the video or description across one or more of their channels and platforms.

Creators are rarely interested in pursuing traditional careers in legacy media, where they often lack the professional skills to operate as writer, producer, director or actor. More notably, within existing film and TV production contexts creators would be denied the agency to control their content and appearance, often assuming a persona or character that bears little resemblance to their more authentic content featured in their own creator brand. In limited instances, legacy media present these creators with opportunities and traditional fees. Hannah Hart converted her 'My Drunk Kitchen' YouTube format into her own Food Network cooking show. LGBTQ personality Tyler Oakley has pursued the occasional opportunities as a contestant on *American Race* as well as an award-show and talk show host.

Community management arguably represents the most distinctive practice of creator self-management and reflects common user practices of social networking.

Community management involves reading, liking, sharing, curating, and commenting on and responding to direct messages from their fan community. This creator practice approximates what Baym (2015) describes as 'relational labour' – managing the social and economic relationship between artists and fans through communicative and networked affordances of social media platforms. Community management also represents the least scalable of practices. Depending on the nature of their content and demands placed by their fan community, creators may spend upwards of 50 per cent of their time interacting directly with their community. Whereas creators may secure assistance with production and entrepreneurial management, community management demands direct interactivity.

Conclusion

As described in this chapter, creators operate centrally within the social media entertainment industry. The conditions of creator management extend across platforms, diverse intermediary firms, and the creators themselves. These conditions blur the distinctions between labour, management, entrepreneurialism, and social media user practices, demanding an array of strategies and tactics by creators that are ecological and iterative. Throughout social media entertainment, the practices of creator management are constantly evolving in an effort to manage precarity and create sustainability.

Further reading
- Case: The working conditions and labour requirements for 'making it' as an online content creator – Duffy (p. 375)
- Context: An exploration of the rise of the platforms and the powerful role they play in shaping media production – Nieborg & Poell (p. 85)
- Contrast: How the new platforms facilitate and profit from new forms of consumption without creating or producing content – Bilton (p. 99)

References

Abidin, C. (2016). 'Visibility Labour: Engaging with Influencers' Fashion Brands and #OOTD Advertorial Campaigns on Instagram', *Media International Australia, 161*(1), 86-100.

Albarran, A. (2008). 'Defining Media Management', *International Journal of Media Management, 10*(4), 184-186.

Baym, N. (2015). 'Connect with your Audience! The Relational Labour of Connection', *The Communication Review, 18*(1), 14-22.

Bruns, A. (2008). *Blogs, Wikipedia, Second Life, and Beyond: From Production to Produsage*. New York: Peter Lang.

Burgess, J. & Green, J. (2009). *YouTube*. Cambridge: Polity Press.

Constine, J. (2018). 'Snapchat Hosts First Creators Summit after Years of Neglect' (8 May). Retrieved from https://techcrunch.com/2018/05/08/snapchat-creators-summit/.

Cunningham, S. & Craig, D. (2019). *Social Media Entertainment: The New Intersection of Hollywood and Silicon Valley*. New York: NYU Press.

Cunningham, S. & Silver, J. (2013), *Screen Distribution and the New King Kongs of the Online World*. London: Palgrave MacMillan.

Deuze, M. (2007). *Media Work*. Cambridge: Polity Press.

Deuze, M. & Steward, B. (2011). 'Managing Media Work', in M. Deuze (ed.), *Managing Media Work* (1-11). Thousand Oaks, CA: SAGE Publications.

Duffy, B. (2015a). 'The Romance of Work: Gender and Aspirational Labour in the Digital Culture Industries', *International Journal of Cultural Studies*, 19(4), 441-457.

Jenkins, H., Ford, S. & Green, J. (2013). *Spreadable Media: Creating Value and Meaning in a Networked Culture*. New York: NYU Press.

Johnson, D., Kompare, D. & Santo, A. (eds) (2014). *Making Media Work: Cultures of Management in the Entertainment Industries*. New York: NYU Press.

Küng, L. (2017). *Strategic Management in the Media: From Theory to Practice* (2nd ed.). Thousand Oaks, CA: SAGE Publications.

Lotz, A. (2017). *Portals: A Treatise on Internet-Distributed Television*. Ann Arbor, MI: Michigan Publishing.

Marwick, A. & boyd, d. (2014). 'Networked Privacy: How Teenagers Negotiate Context in Social Media', *New Media & Society*, 16(7), 1051-1067.

Mediakix (2017). 'Instagram Influencer Marketing is a $1 Billion Industry' (3 March). Retrieved from http://mediakix.com/2017/03/instagram-influencer-marketing-industry-size-how-big/#gs.oSu3GGY.

Nilsson, J. & Schadek, W.D. (2018). 'The Influencer Economy is Booming' (30 March). Retrieved from https://northzone.com/influencer-economy-booming/.

O'Connor, C. (2017). 'Forbes Top Influencers: The 30 Social Media Stars of Fashion, Parenting, and Pets (Yes, Pets)', *Forbes* (26 September). Retrieved from https://www.forbes.com/sites/clareoconnor/2017/09/26/forbes-top-influencers-fashion-pets-parenting/#28a547777683.

Postigo, H. (2014). 'Playing for Work Independence as Promise in Gameplay Commentary on YouTube', in J. Bennett & N. Strange (eds), *Media Independence: Working with Freedom or Working for Free?* (202-222). New York and London: Routledge.

Rogers, K. (2016). 'Vine is Closing Down and the Internet Can't Stand It', *The New York Times* (27 October). Retrieved from https://www.nytimes.com/2016/10/28/technology/vine-is-closing-down-and-the-internet-cant-stand-it.html.

Roussel, V. (2015). '"It's Not the Network, It's the Relationship': The Relational Work of Hollywood Talent Agents', in V. Roussel & D. Bielby (eds), *Brokerage and Production in* the *American and French Entertainment Industries: Invisible Hands in Cultural Markets* (103-122). London: Lexington Books.

Senft, T. (2008). *Camgirls: Celebrity & Community in the Age of Social Networks*. New York: Peter Lang.

Shapiro, R. & Aneja, S. (2018). *Unlocking the Gates: America's New Creative Economy*. Retrieved from http://www.recreatecoalition.org/wp-content/uploads/2018/02/ReCreate-Creative-Economy-Study-Report.pdf.

Spangler, T. (2017). 'Disney's Maker Studios Set for Round of Big Layoffs', *Variety* (15 February). Retrieved from http://variety.com/2017/digital/news/maker-2017-layoffs-disney-1201989473/.

Tsoi, G. (2017). '*Wang Hong*. China's online stars making real cash', *BBC News* (1 August). Retrieved from http://www.bbc.com/news/world-asia-china-36802769.

Van Dijck, J. & Poell, T. (2013). 'Understanding Social Media Logic', *Media and Communication*, *1*(1), 2-14.

28. #Dreamjob: The Promises and Perils of a Creative Career in Social Media

Brooke Erin Duffy

Over the last decade, social media have ushered in shiny new career exemplars: pro bloggers, YouTubers, and Instagram influencers. These digitally enabled models of work differ from employment in more traditional media industries. What are the working conditions and labour requirements for 'making it' as an online content creator? This chapter discusses the changing nature of creative work in the social media age.

Introduction

For many teens and college underclassmen, summer provides a welcome respite from the classroom. Some spend the days idly, whereas others pick up seasonal gigs or resume-bolstering office jobs. Yet, in July 2017, a cohort of tech-savvy young people eagerly returned to the classroom to participate in the inaugural SocialStar creator camp. Based in Los Angeles – a city known for the industrial manufacture of status and stardom – the immersive educational camp was hyped as a 'fast track for new and early social media content creators [...][seeking] the best practices for exceptional platforms that result in earning money and viral fame' (socialstarcreatorcamp.com). Over the course of three days and nights, participants received instruction in self-branding, platform monetization, and data analytics, among other splashy topics. First-gen YouTuber Michael Buckley ('What the Buck?'), who figured prominently on the camp agenda, prognosticated that social media training programmes would see a profound uptick in years to come. 'I'm shocked there's not one in every state. This could be very, very huge', he told a *Quartz* reporter (Farokhmanesh, 2017). And, indeed, following the camp's initial run, SocialStar organizers announced their plans to orchestrate similar programmes in Las Vegas, London, and Melbourne.

While the emergence of initiatives like SocialStar raises compelling questions about the valorization of internet celebrity and the ethics of pseudo-educational programmes, they are also telling of the changing nature of work in the digital age. Over the last decade, social media have ushered in shiny new career exemplars: pro bloggers, YouTubers, and Instagram influencers. More telling, still, is the sprawling class of young people who covet success in these proto-professions. A widely cited study of 1,000 children and teens found that more than one-third consider 'YouTuber' their dream job (Weiss, 2017). Though staggering, such findings are perhaps not surprising when social media careers purportedly provide creative autonomy, a flexible schedule, and the glittering promise of fame and fortune.

But to what extent do social media platforms actually enable career success, particularly for aspiring creatives? What are the working conditions and labour requirements for 'making it' as a content creator? And to what extent are these digitally-enabled models of work different from – or similar to – employment in more traditional creative industries? This chapter answers these questions through an analysis of the changing nature of creative work in the social media age. I draw upon dozens of interviews conducted with aspiring and current bloggers, vloggers, and influencers in the US (for more detail, see Duffy, 2017).

The chapter begins by situating the rise of social media work within wider shifts in the creative economy, including the rise of low-cost production and distribution technologies collectively hitched to the promise of digital democratization. I then explore the promises and perils of a career in this field, showing how workers often swap independence and creative license for precarious working conditions and the expectation to always be 'on'. I close by suggesting how new models of work may challenge – or potentially exacerbate – existing inequalities in the creative industries (for an overview, see Conor, Gill, & Taylor, 2015). By tempering some of the glib boosterism of the creative economy, this chapter aims to provide a more nuanced treatment of social media careers.

Creative 'democratization': The case of fashion blogging

The backstory to the kinds of career success promised by bloggers, YouTubers, and Instagrammers is one where digital technologies are ardently celebrated for their potential to upend the power relations that long dominated the cultural industries. In the mid-2000s, as affordable production and distribution technologies were unveiled in rapid succession, techno-enthusiasts celebrated their potential to upset the traditional flow of power from media producers to audiences (Jenkins, 2006; Shirky, 2010). Consumer empowerment was a prevailing refrain, and user-generated content, collaborative communities, and amateur production were upheld as evidence of a radical moment in information and entertainment.

It is against this backdrop that various modes of amateur content creation began to siphon audiences away from mainstream media. Within fashion journalism, an ostensibly new generation of tastemakers surfaced – style journalists like Susie Bubble, Tavi Gevinson, and Bryanboy – all of whom were situated in opposition to the more insular and hierarchical realm of couture fashion (Duffy, 2015; Luvaas,

2016). Media coverage touted the then-burgeoning blogosphere, crediting it as a 'revolution that has turned the fashion world on its head' (Murray, 2011). The terms that framed this so-called revolution were remarkably similar – and unmistakably auspicious: democratic, approachable, authentic, and independent.

With the clarity of hindsight, it seems obvious that these upbeat claims of independence were overstated, particularly as many of these 'new voices' began to garner the attention of the mainstream fashion community. While designers and retailers courted them, their followers grew – some even eager to join their ranks. Today, less than a decade after the genre's emergence, its subcultural trappings have been largely eradicated in the face of super-bloggers and influencers who command seven-figure salaries (McAlone, 2016). Moreover, fashion and lifestyle content continues to migrate from independent channels and Wordpress sites to existing social networks: Facebook, Pinterest, and Instagram. Describing 'the new influencers,' a *Women's Wear Daily* columnist explained how today's style mavens 'aren't just bloggers anymore [...][but] are individuals who, depending on the channel, share and detail much (if not most) of their lives via YouTube, Instagram and increasingly Snapchat' (Strugatz, 2016). A useful framework to understand this movement away from independent sites is through what Helmond (2015) calls the 'platformization of the web', which 'rests on the dual logic of social media platforms' expansion into the rest of the web and, simultaneously, their drive to make external web and app data platform ready' (Nieborg & Poell, 2018).

Burgeoning industries: Commercialization and professionalization

To a large extent, fashion blogs and related Instagram accounts mark a remediation of earlier forms of media, most especially women's fashion magazines (Rocamora, 2014; for a discussion of remediation, see Bolter and Grusin, 2000). At the same time, the progressive transformation of the fashion blogosphere from an indie genre of content creation into a commercial enterprise is not wholly idiosyncratic. Rather, the twin processes of commercialization and professionalization can be discerned across a variety of digital contexts, including music (Morris, 2014), video game commentary (Postigo, 2016), online video (Burgess & Green, 2008), and the more expansive realm of social media entertainment (Cunningham & Craig, 2016; forthcoming). Chronicling the staggering evolution of YouTube over a ten-year span, an *Ars Technica* writer explained, 'As YouTube became more popular and the concept of viral videos became more commonplace, mainstream-type money started flowing onto the platform. That cash trickled down to the creators' (Stoker-Walker, 2017). Featured in this proto-history of YouTube was earlier-mentioned internet personality Michael Buckley, who narrativized his career success as wholly unanticipated. He recalled, 'You start making money, and you think you've tricked the world. 'How did this happen? I was doing this for fun, and for free, and now I have thousands of dollars in my Adsense account. This is crazy. It's nutty' (*Ibid.*).

Accordingly, those outside the social media production circuit often ask with profound incredulity, how do influencers/bloggers/YouTubers make money? A crude answer to this question is by selling (digital) audiences to advertisers. As anyone familiar with the political economies of traditional media can attest, this model has long sustained certain genres of seemingly 'free' media and cultural content (Smythe, 1977; Jhally & Livant, 1986). Today, as advertisers struggle to rise above the din of ubiquitous commercial noise, digital star-personae are enlisted to commodify their social media audiences as they hype branded goods on their blogs, YouTube channels, and Instagram feeds. To brands, these internet personalities are a heaven-sent conduit to reach ad-weary consumers; as influencers, they furnish networked social capital and deliver messages wrapped in a glossy veneer of 'authentic' or 'organic' brand advocacy. In this model of commercial ventriloquism, content creators are remunerated for integrating a product or message into their arsenal of content.

Of course, the particular monetization strategies vary tremendously across platforms: whereas YouTube creators earn income from pre-roll ads, Instagram's commercial offerings range from sponsored posts to revenue-generating apps such as Like to Know It (liketoknowit.com), a service designed to make influencers' content eminently shoppable. In addition to programs that simulate the revenue streams of traditional media – namely drawing audiences and/or advertisers – content creators tend to have diverse portfolios, a nod toward broader shifts in media work toward cross-media proficiencies and multi-skilling (Deuze, 2007; Gill, 2010). Digital content creator Jessie, for instance, explained how 'blogger' is a bit of a misnomer:

> If you see really almost any successful entrepreneur, they don't take that one platform and let that be the end-all, be-all. Because blogging can be a flash in the pan; things keep changing, so who knows how long blogs are going to be here. [...] So it's really about diversifying [beyond the actual blog].

Jessie's efforts to diversify included part-time gigs as a stylist, website writer, TV host, and radio personality. Other full-time content creators, similarly, told me how their pieced-together careers included freelance writing, designing, and lecturing, among others.

The income streams for YouTubers are similarly motley. David Craig, a scholar who has conducted extensive interviews with social media entertainers, describes the disparate funding sources: 'from virtual goods to fan funding to subscriptions on other platforms to e-commerce to live performances, book sales, music sales, film and TV performances,' (Garrova, 2017; see also Cunningham & Craig, forthcoming). The dividends for some social media brand-personae are astonishing; Chiara Ferragni, the fashionista behind The Blonde Salad, reportedly made US$8 million in 2016 (Forbes, 2017). Importantly, though, the attention lavished on Ferragni and other social media success stories conceals the less auspicious realities of a social media career, including the profoundly uneven compensation structure. As one YouTuber noted, 'I wouldn't necessarily encourage [aspiring bloggers] to think, "Oh, great, I'm going to start this site, and it's going to take off and I will have my own business [...] and it will pay the bills", because I think it's a very small percentage that can say that and that become that.' And, indeed, a study published in 2018 pointed at the 'winner-take-all' dimensions of the platform: roughly 85 per cent of viewership goes to just 3 per cent of channels (Bärtl, 2018). Highlighting the barriers to entry, *The Washington Post* noted how YouTube requires channels to have amassed '1,000 subscribers and 4,000 hours of watch time over the past 12 months before they can earn money from ads' (Frankel, 2018).

A similar disparity characterizes other realms of content creation, including Instagram influencers (Duffy, 2017). While some content creators score lucrative contracts with brands, others earn what one informant described as 'next to nothing'. Travel Instagrammer Lauren signalled a troubling 'lack of standardization' within the expansive market for influencers, which means 'it's just every man for himself'. On one hand, certain Instagram stars can garner thousands of dollars for a single post even though brands will never get a return on investment. On the other, brands continue to heavily exploit people. Several of the content creators I interviewed explained how brands sought to leverage their networked reputation – but weren't willing to compensate. In other words, companies expected online personalities to work for free, motivated by the always-deferred promise of exposure.

The realities of social media work

If popular accounts of social media producers are taken at face value, then these content creators get paid just for being themselves (Duffy & Wissinger, 2017). While this narrative dovetails well with the ideal of authenticity endemic to social media culture, the reality is that maintaining a visible presence amid a hyper-competitive landscape requires various kinds of immaterial labour. Long-time blogger Heather, for instance, was quite forthcoming about the difficulty of maintaining a continual queue of content. She recalled, 'I worked harder at this job than any job I've ever had because [...] I was always mining my life for content, so I was *always on*.' Professional Instagrammer Lauren, similarly, described the time and energy she must dedicate to a career that continues to evolve at a breakneck speed. 'I work really hard. I don't have much of a work-life balance at the moment', she confessed, signaling the extent to which the boundary between personal and professional had been rendered indistinct.

Beyond the time-intensive processes of content creation – say, filming a video, writing a post, or editing a photo after a shoot – social media producers felt compelled to devote considerable energy to promoting their work. In other words, they were expected to be hyper-vigilant about their self-branding efforts (Abidin, 2016; Hearn, 2008; Marwick, 2013; Senft, 2013). In addition to 'getting new content', Heather noted, bloggers are 'always, always, always updating every social platform'. Indeed, the content creators I interviewed highlighted the time and effort it took to ensure their content was visible, and some felt this self-marketing orientation had overshadowed the more creative elements of their professions. As Jessie explained to this end, '[Even if] you're the best, if people don't know you're the best it doesn't really matter; you just have to be good enough [...] and well marketed.'

For bloggers, vloggers, and other content creators, a key to being 'well marketed' is investing energy in online relationship-building. Such social practices may take myriad forms: responding to Instagram comments and YouTube queries, utilizing clever strategies to solicit engagement, and contributing to the larger digital community. These activities comprise what Baym (2015) calls relational labour, or the 'regular, ongoing communication with audiences over time to build social relationships that foster paid work' (*Ibid.*, p. 16; see also, Abidin, 2015; Rocamora, forthcoming). As blogger Alissa reasoned:

> I want my readers to know that I'm accessible to [them]. This is part of my job. I chose to be a blogger, so what you think and what you want to see is important, so I have to make sure I'm responding on social media just as much as I'm posting on social media.

In addition to nurturing relationships with digitally networked audiences, social media content creators are also expected to vibrantly contribute to their respective communities. Danielle remarked on the enjoyable, albeit labour intensive, nature of interactions with her fellow bloggers: 'It's incredibly time-consuming, [so] in order for people to find you, you have to be commenting on lots of things, like you have to be very active with it.' The implication is that by commenting on others' content, one will elicit a similar level of engagement on their own. Lifestyle blogger-Instagrammer Ulia explained how a pervasive sense of reciprocity seemed to drive many online interactions; increasingly, she noted, bloggers were placing 'a lot of emphasis [...] into communicating with *other* bloggers.' She described the proliferation of Instagram pods, informal networks of content creators who 'put their picture into a message group, and they ask to comment on the picture so they will have a higher engagement.' She expanded:

> You see a lot of people [and think] 'she has like 5,000 comments [so] she's probably very popular.' But sometimes, it's just because she just sits there and comments on other people in these pods, and they comment back. [....] Because nowadays [many of those commenting] are other bloggers, and they just want comments from you, that's why they comment on your pictures.

Drawing attention to the instrumentality of these community practices is not to suggest that content creators don't benefit from these relational and affective practices in other ways. For as Baym (2015) reminds us, we should not 'understand relationships in labour as inherently either genuine or alienating, empowering or oppressive.' Rather, she continues, 'they are all of these and more, often at the same time' (*Ibid.*, p. 20).

In fact, many of the content creators I interviewed commented on the friendships and other social relations borne by social media. Sophie, for instance, shared, 'I've made really close connections with [other bloggers]. [....] I think a lot of the bloggers will kind of play off of each other and learn from each other and it's really, it's cool to see a positive community.' Meanwhile, Daneen credited her blogging compatriots with helping her navigate the uncertainties of the field. Recalling her early forays into the blogosphere she said: 'Most of my blogging friends are those people who were starting this at the same time I was. And we had no idea what we were doing and we were sort of figuring it out together.'

New hierarchies

Content creators' reflections on the value of audiences and fellow content creators index the role of social capital. After all, amidst a so-called reputation economy, followers, subscribers, hearts and likes are understood as a dominant form of currency (Gandini, 2016). Yet, economic capital also plays a crucial role in structuring social media producers' access and opportunities. Aspiring fashion blogger Alana, for instance, dispelled the common assumption that the blogosphere is a 'free domain'. Instead, she explained, 'You're really spending your money on clothes and your camera equipment, and I know some people hire photographers, [but] I don't have those resources.' The hyper-saturated market of content creators seems to have exacerbated these resource inequalities. She added, 'I'm competing against younger people or people who have been in the industry longer than I have or people who have more money than me.' YouTuber Rachel, similarly, detailed some of the unanticipated costs of working as an independent content creator: website service, cloud storage, paid promotion and – above all – the latest video editing equipment. By contrast, she felt that certain members of the YouTube community have 'family members buying them expensive editing equipment and computers and cameras.'

Of course, technologies of production not only require finances, but also the time to learn to effectively use them. The importance of one's social location came to the fore of popular culture in a 2015 article on 'the hustle of being a beauty blogger.' Writer (and YouTuber) Gaby Dunn chronicled the expectation that content creators purchase the latest cosmetics and makeup tools as well as to produce high-quality videos – a 'demand' placed upon them from both audiences and potential ad partners (Dunn, 2015).

The sprawling market of professionalization resources – including books, online training programmes, conferences, and immersive initiatives like SocialStar – also shores up the boundaries between aspiring content creators from different social classes. These offerings require investments in both time and money; conference registration prices can be especially steep. As Deenie confessed, 'I think it would benefit me if I went to some of these blogger conferences [but they are typically held] during the day, and I can't take off from my day job and pay money [...] they're kind of expensive.' The reserves of social and economic capital that serve as prerequisites for social media careerists is a testament to one of the perils of this buzzy new career field: it is less egalitarian than cheering assertions of digital democratization seem to suggest. Moreover, Dunn's exposition of the labour of beauty vloggers points toward another noteworthy hierarchy in the social media economy, namely pervasive gender divisions. While female content creators dominate fashion, beauty, and parenting, the genres of comedy, tech, and gaming are populated by male voices (Bishop, 2017). Furthermore, women in these highly public spaces are forced to carefully toe what I call 'the line between visibility and vulnerability' as their experiences are shaped by larger patterns of exclusion, surveillance, and misogyny in digital environments.

Conclusion

In the popular imagination, bloggers, vloggers, and YouTubers relish in careers that afford them excitement, flexibility, and above all creative independence. And while these paid content creators must engage in various kinds of immaterial labour as they endeavour to satisfy the gruelling demands of followers and brand 'partners', it is important to note that they enjoy a relatively privileged position. After all, they've found a way to profit – or using the industry euphemism, monetize – their passions. Given the tremendous popularity of these seemingly authentic voices who get paid to do what they love, it's no small wonder that social networking sites are awash with content creators aspiring to emulate their successes. These (mostly) young people represent a pool of aspirational labourers who are willing to engage in various forms of brand-hyping work with the expectation that their efforts will one day be rewarded. In the meantime, they invest time, money, and promotional labour in their digitally enabled dream jobs.

The notion of temporally delayed (or speculative) work is, of course, by no means new within the creative industries: musicians have long performed gigs in hopes of being signed by a label, advertising professionals and agencies routinely produce 'spec creative' to pitch to prospective clients, and unpaid internship activities are structured around an oft-deferred promise of employment. As Hesmondhalgh (2010) reminds, 'In the history of cultural production, only a very few people within any society have taken on the role of cultural producers in return for financial reward' (*Ibid.*, p. 277). What's perhaps different about the current moment in cultural production are the size and scope of these activities – as well as their value to platforms like Instagram and YouTube who benefit from freely provided content, communities, and data.

In closing, it's important to consider some other ways that social media employment mimics the routines and logics of traditional media production, including the characteristic features of long hours, unstable conditions, and the individualization of work – all of which are counterbalanced by a professed love of the work (Gill, 2010; see also, Duffy & Wissinger, 2017; Elefante & Deuze, 2012; McRobbie, 2002). But whereas a previous generation of workers was motivated by what Neff *et al.* (2005) describe as the 'promise of one Big Job being right around the corner' (Ibid., p. 319), today's creative aspirants are roused by the assurance that they're one post away from their #dreamjob.

Further reading

- Case: How creators try to manage their careers within the proto-industry of social media entertainment – Craig (p. 363)
- Context: An exploration of the rise of the platforms and the powerful role they play in shaping media production – Nieborg & Poell (p. 85)
- Contrast: How the affective labour of making media entails using emotions in order to produce emotions in others – Siapera (p. 275)

References

Abidin, C. (2015). 'Communicative Intimacies: Influencers and Perceived Interconnected-
ness', *Ada: A Journal of Gender, New Media, & Technology*, 8. Retrieved from http://
adanewmedia.org/2015/11/issue8-abidin/.

Abidin, C. (2016). 'Visibility Labour: Engaging with Influencers' Fashion Brands and #OOTD
Advertorial Campaigns on Instagram', *Media International Australia*, *161*(1), 86-100.

Bärtl, M. (2018). 'YouTube Channels, Uploads and Views: A Statistical Analysis of the Past 10
Years', *Convergence: The International Journal of Research into New Media Technologies*,
24(1), 16-32.

Baym, N.K. (2015). 'Connect with Your Audience! The Relational Labour of Connection', *The
Communication Review*, *18*(1), 14-22.

Bishop, S. (2017). 'Beauty for Girls, Pranks for Boys – It's the Same Old Gender Stereotypes
for YouTube Stars', *The Conversation* (4 October). Retrieved from: https://theconversation.
com/beauty-for-girls-pranks-for-boys-its-the-same-old-gender-stereotypes-for-youtube-
stars-83927.

Bolter, J. & Grusin, R.A. (2000). *Remediation: Understanding New Media*. Cambridge, MA:
MIT Press.

Burgess, J. & Green, J. (2013). *YouTube: Online Video and Participatory Culture*. Hoboken,
NJ: John Wiley & Sons.

Conor, B., Gill, R. & Taylor, S. (2015). 'Gender and Creative Labour', *The Sociological Review*,
63(S1), 1-22.

Cunningham, S. & Craig, D. (2016). 'Online Entertainment: A New Wave of Media Globalization?', *International Journal of Communication 10*, 5409-5425.

Cunningham, S. & Craig, D. (forthcoming). *Social Media Entertainment*. New York: NYU Press.

Deuze, M. (2007). *Media Work*. Cambridge: Polity Press.

Duffy, B.E. (2017). (*Not*) *Getting Paid to Do What You Love: Gender, Social Media, and Aspirational Work*. New Haven, CT: Yale University Press.

Duffy, B.E. & Wissinger, E. (2017). 'Mythologies of Creative Work in the Social Media Age:
Fun, Free, and 'Just Being Me', *International Journal of Communication*, *11*. http://ijoc.
org/index.php/ijoc/article/view/7322.

Elefante, P.H. & Deuze, M. (2012). 'Media Work, Career Management, and Professional Identity:
Living Labour Precarity', *Northern Lights: Film & Media Studies Yearbook*, *10*(1), 9-24.

Farokhmanesh, M. (2017). 'Take a Trip to Los Angeles New Internet Celebrity Summer
Camp', *The Verge* (20 July). Retrieved from https://www.theverge.com/2017/7/20/15992846/
socialstar-creator-camp-la-teen-internet-celebrity.

Frankel, T. (2018). 'Why Almost No One is Making a Living on YouTube', *The Washington
Post* (2 March). Retrieved from https://www.washingtonpost.com/news/the-switch/
wp/2018/03/02/why-almost-no-one-is-making-a-living-on-youtube/?utm_term=.
a4fod9eeb8c4.

Gandini, A. (2016). 'Digital Work: Self-Branding and Social Capital in the Freelance Knowledge Economy', *Marketing Theory*, *16*(1), 123-141.

Garrova, R. (2018). 'How Do YouTube Stars Make Money?', *Marketplace* (29 March). Retrieved from https://www.marketplace.org/2017/05/29/world/how-youtube-stars-make-living.

Gill, R. (2010). 'Life is a Pitch: Managing the Self in New Media Work', in M. Deuze (ed.), *Managing Media Work* (249-262). London: SAGE Publications.

Gregg, M. (2011). *Work's Intimacy*. Cambridge: Polity Press.

Hearn, A. (2008). '"Meat, Mask, Burden': Probing the Contours of the Branded Self', *Journal of Consumer Culture*, *8*(2), 197-217.

Helmond, A. (2015). 'The Platformization of the Web: Making Web Data Platform Ready', *Social Media+ Society*, *1*(2). https://doi.org/10.1177/2056305115603080.

Hesmondhalgh, D. (2010). 'User-Generated Content, Free Labour and the Cultural Industries', *Ephemera*, *10*(3/4), 267-284.

Jenkins, H. (2006). *Convergence Culture: Where Old and New Media Collide*. New York: New York University Press.

Jhally, S. & Livant, B. (1986). 'Watching as Working: The Valorization of Audience Consciousness', *Journal of Communication*, *36*(3), 124-143.

Luvaas, B. (2016). *Street Style: An Ethnography of Fashion Blogging*. London: Bloomsbury Publishing.

Marwick, A.E. (2013). *Status Update: Celebrity, Publicity, and Branding in the Social Media Age*. New Haven, CT: Yale University Press.

McAlone, N. (2016). 'Meet the YouTube Millionaires', *Business Insider* (9 December). Retrieved from http://www.businessinsider.com/youtube-stars-who-make-the-most-money-in-2016-2016-12.

McRobbie, A. (2002). 'Clubs to Companies: Notes on the Decline of Political Culture in Speeded Up Creative Worlds', *Cultural Studies*, *16*(4), 516-531.

Morris, J.W. (2014). 'Artists as Entrepreneurs, Fans as Workers', *Popular Music and Society*, *37*(3), 273-290.

Murray, A. (2011). 'Fashion Week: The Ordinary People Who Stole the Show', *BBC News*. Retrieved from http://www.bbc.com/news/magazine-14813053.

Neff, G., Wissinger, E. & Zukin, S. (2005). 'Entrepreneurial Labor among Cultural Producers: "Cool" Jobs in "Hot" Industries', *Social Semiotics*, *15*(3), 307-334.

Novak, M. (2016). 'Average Internet Celebrities Make $75,000 Per Instagram Ad and $30,000 Per Paid Tweet', *Gizmodo* (30 August). Retrieved from https://gizmodo.com/average-internet-celebrities-make-75-000-per-instagram-1785956449.

Nieborg, D. B., & Poell, T. (2018). The platformization of cultural production: Theorizing the contingent cultural commodity. New Media & Society, 1461444818769694.

Postigo, H. (2016). 'The Socio-Technical Architecture of Digital Labour: Converting Play into YouTube Money', *New Media & Society*, *18*(2), 332-349.

Rocamora, A. (2012). 'Hypertextuality and Remediation in the Fashion Media: The Case of Fashion Blogs', *Journalism Practice*, 6(1), 92-106.

Rocamora, A. (2018). 'The Labour of Fashion Blogging', in L. Armstrong & F. McDowell (eds), *Fashioning Professionals: Identity and Representation at Work in the Creative Industries*. London: Bloomsbury.

Ross, A. (2013). 'In Search of the Lost Paycheck', in T. Scholz (ed.), *Digital Labour: The Internet as Playground and Factory* (13-32). New York: Routledge.

Shirky, C. (2010). *Cognitive Surplus: Creativity and Generosity in a Connected Age*. New York: Penguin.

Senft, T.M. (2013). 'Micro-Celebrity and the Branded Self', in J. Hartley, J. Burgess & B. Bruns (eds), *A Companion to New Media Dynamics* (346-354). Hoboken, NJ: Wiley-Blackwell.

Smythe, D.W. (1981). 'On the Audience Commodity and Its Work', in M. G. Durham & D. Kellner (eds), *Media and Cultural Studies: Keyworks*. Oxford: Blackwell.

Stokel-Walker, C. (2017). 'More Than a Decade Later, How Do Original YouTube Stars Feel about the Site?', **Arts Technica** (11 November). Retrieved from https://arstechnica.com/features/2017/06/youtube-changed-my-life-a-pair-of-original-videostars-ponder-a-life-lived-online/.

Weiss, G. (2017). 'The Most Desired Career Among Young People is 'YouTuber' (Study)', *Tubefilter* (24 May). Retrieved from http://www.tubefilter.com/2017/05/24/most-desired-career-young-people-youtube.

Professions

Public Relations and Advertising

29. Redefining Advertising in a Changing Media Landscape

Sara Rosengren

Advertising has evolved significantly through the past hundred years, as rapid media developments, changing consumer behaviour, and shifting industry goals have impacted its shape and form. This chapter discusses how to rethink and redefine advertising to better account for contemporary changes in advertising research and practice.

Introduction

Is advertising dead? This question has followed me throughout my years as a marketing scholar. In practice, the question is often posed when new approaches to marketing communication are introduced or growing in popularity. As an illustration, at the turn of the century PR was often said to be replacing advertising (a best-selling book at the time was even titled *The Fall of Advertising, The Rise of PR*). With the growth of social media word-of-mouth was the talk of the town, and lately content marketing has been lauded to take over. In academia, this question has recently gained renewed relevance and interest as the leading academic journal in the field (*Journal of Advertising*) published a special issue on the future of advertising in 2016. The issue comprises many interesting contributions from some of the leading researchers in the field.

In that issue, Micael Dahlen and I tried to predict what the future of advertising might look like. More specifically, we argue that it is more important to understand how advertising is changing than to have it replaced by something 'new'. We therefore set out to provide a working definition of advertising that will be fit for a future where advertising is still alive (Dahlen & Rosengren, 2016a).

Our point of departure was the following: advertising, both as an academic field and as a practice, is undergoing constant change. If we look back in time, advertising has evolved from flyers and magazine ads in print media via radio and tv commercials in broadcast media, to contemporary content marketing and social media campaigns targeting specific individuals and audiences through digital media. As we look to the future of the field, this evolution will most likely continue. This means that advertising can (and will) take different forms and shapes and have other effects than what traditionally has been the case. This is how it has been in the past, and most likely, how it will continue to be in the future. At the moment, the evolution of advertising is driven not only by rapid media development, but also by changing consumer behaviours and increased interest among companies to use advertising to do more than affect customers and sales (*Ibid.*), for example by being a positive change in society or having an internal effect on employees.

The interaction between these three factors is visible in a series of discussions currently in focus within the advertising industry. For example, the increased use of ad blockers (that help consumers screen out advertising in online and mobile media) is a consequence of both media development (i.e. technological advances enabling such behaviours) and consumer reactions to the same (i.e. consumers finding advertising interruptive and disturbing). This development has also had major consequences for both media houses and marketers in how they sell and design advertising (e.g. Rosengren & Dahlen, 2013, 2015). When advertising banners are being avoided, new hybrid formats (i.e. formats combining advertising and editorial content) such as native advertising (i.e. paid content in the shape and form of editorial content) and branded content (i.e., editorial content that is actually paid for) are becoming increasingly important sources of revenue for many media owners.

Another example is that many companies have changed their views on the role that advertising plays in their business. Whereas marketers traditionally have been myopically focused on advertising affecting customers and sales, it is becoming increasingly common that they also discuss and take responsibility for other effects of advertising, such as the role it might have in shaping or reinforcing societal values and stereotypes (e.g. Åkestam, Rosengren & Dahlen, 2017), or how it affects employees (e.g. Rosengren & Bondesson, 2017). As an illustration, the growing interest in social responsibility related to advertising has impacted decisions of who and what to portray in advertising and led many marketers to focus more on how their advertising might influence the everyday life of consumers and on society at large. This clearly shows that the impact of advertising extends beyond just customers and sales, also in the eyes of its practitioners.

In this chapter, I will discuss how to rethink and redefine advertising to better account for contemporary changes in advertising research and advertising practice. In doing so, I will (hopefully) show how defining advertising as 'brand-initiated communications intent on impacting people' (Dahlen & Rosengren, 2016a, p. 334) can help advertising stay relevant as media, consumers, and effects continue to evolve.

A brief history of advertising definitions

Advertising has a long history. While the roots of advertising practice can be traced back thousands of years, the first known definition of advertising is from 1923, when Daniel Starch defined advertising as 'selling in print' (Richards & Curran, 2002; Nan & Faber, 2004). At that time, various formats of print were the predominant medium used by marketers when trying to reach both new and existing customers. Thus, it is not surprising that the initial definition of advertising focused specially on this medium.

Over time, as radio and television grew more popular, the definition of advertising changed to also include these media. More specifically, the term print was replaced by mass media in the definition. In the following decades, different iterations of 'selling through mass media' occurred in different advertising definitions (Nan & Faber, 2004). Summarizing this evolution, Richard and Curran (2002) eventually concluded that the predominant definition of advertising in the late twentieth century was 'paid nonpersonal communication from an identified sponsor, using mass media to persuade or influence an audience' (*Ibid.*, p. 64). They also concluded that this definition was out of tune with contemporary advertising practice in the early 2000s. Based on a survey of advertising experts, Richard and Curran (2002) therefore moved on to update the definition of advertising as a 'paid, mediated form of communication from an identifiable source, designed to persuade the receiver to take some action, now or in the future' (*Ibid.*, p. 74).

In the decade following 2002, the evolution of digital and social media made this definition increasingly out of tune with advertising practice. For example, the growth of digital fora, blogs, and social media platforms made consumer-created messages more visible and impactful. Marketers were increasingly creating advertising campaigns that incentivized or mobilized consumers to act as co-creators. Consequently, advertising researchers increasingly came to explore the impact of customer-created messages. Still, advertising research tended to focus on traditional print and television advertising (Kim *et al.*, 2014). A review of 855 articles published in leading academic advertising journals between 2010 and 2015 showed that only 40 per cent actually researched communications that were within the scope of the Richard and Curran (2002) definition (Dahlen & Rosengren, 2016a).

Based on this observation, a new definition thus seemed called for. Reviewing the existing literature on the evolution of advertising and advertising definitions, Micael Dahlen and I made the following observations:
1. advertising evolves with technology and new media;
2. technology and media evolve, so do consumer behaviours;
3. changing technology and changing consumer behaviours yield new functions and effects of advertising.

Table 1 outlines the implications of these observations in terms of how to rethink and redefine advertising.

Table 1   Three dynamics shaping the evolution of advertising (based on Dahlen & Rosengren, 2016)

Observations	Description	Current examples	Implications for defining advertising
Changing media and formats drive the evolution of advertising	As technology and media evolve, so does advertising	New platforms & hybrid advertising	Not only paid Not only identifiable source
Changing 'consumer' behaviours drive the evolution of advertising	As technology, media, and advertising evolve, so does the consumer	Co-creation & engagement	Not only receiver Not only consumer
Extended effects drive the evolution of advertising	As technology, media, advertising, and consumer behaviour evolve, so does the role of advertising	Advertising effects in context	Not only brand and sales

As highlighted in the table, the implication of these observations is that advertising can no longer be defined as communications in paid channels with identified sources. What is more, consumers are not only receivers of advertising and buyers of advertised products, but engage and co-create content in complex ways. To fully understand contemporary advertising, marketers and researchers need to look beyond the effects on brand and sales. Based on these observations and a survey of advertising academics and professionals, we arrived at a proposed a working definition of advertising as 'brand-initiated communication intent on impacting people' (Dahlen & Rosengren, 2016a, p. 334). Embracing this definition has implications on several levels, ranging from specific content, to overall strategies, and industry organization.

The need for several definitions

Our idea when providing an updated working definition of advertising was 1) to enable a common language for education, research, and practice; and 2) to contribute to broadening the scope and facilitating the development of the discipline. Still, subjecting the updated definition to the same test as the Richard and Curran (2002) definition, it became clear that our definition only captured 56 per cent of the articles published in academic advertising journals. The discrepancy suggests that whereas the proposed working definition captures the practice of advertising, it does not cover the full scope of advertising research. To capture the types of communications studied in contemporary advertising research, we need to extend the definition even further. Only when reformulating and extending the definition of advertising as 'brand-related communication that impacts people' instead of 'brand-initiated communication intent on impacting people' did we capture the full scope of this research stream.

This highlights the difficulties in defining advertising for the future. Whereas the marketing literature traditionally has had clear definitions for different communication disciplines (e.g. advertising being different from public relations, or sales promotions), contemporary advertising practice does no longer adhere to these boundaries. What is more, contemporary advertising practice is increasingly relying on communications created and distributed by others (e.g. communicated though earned rather than bought media). Still, including 'brand-initiated' in the definition means that a restriction is imposed in terms of whether this type of communication is to be characterized as advertising. Marketers typically take the initiative to approach influencers and get them to include brands in their social media posts. These posts are very different from posts that occur without such initiatives. Advertising can thus take shape as created, communicated, and distributed by someone else, but the initiator has to be the brand in order for it to be qualified as advertising. For practical (and legal) purposes, brand initiative thus is a necessary condition for defining advertising.

From a research perspective, however, a wider scope is needed in order to be able to explore potentially new areas and routes of communications that might be initiated by the brand in the future (Dahlen & Rosengren, 2016a). The role of academic advertising research should thus be to explore brand-related communications more broadly. In doing so, it can continuously inform, explore, and challenge the boundaries of advertising. Once we understand such communications better, marketers can take initiatives to ensure desirable impacts on brands, thus making such communications 'brand initiated' in the sense indicated by our updated working definition for advertising.

In a similar vein, I would argue that practitioners working with advertising need to take an interest in all forms of brand-related communications to succeed. First, in addition to crafting advertising that that stimulates brand-related conversations or co-creation, they need to keep an eye out for brand-related conversations that are already out there and come up with ideas on how to make them spread. This will, in turn, impact the content that they create and thus what advertising will be. As an illustration, speaker company Sonos realised that people were posting positive reviews about their products online. However, not enough people were actually finding these reviews. To change this, Sonos launched a (traditional) advertising campaigns with digital and outdoor billboards simply asking consumers to 'Google Sonos', thereby taking the initiative to use those already existing reviews as advertising.

Second, it will impact the scope of advertising and the type of impact sought by marketers and advertising agencies. By opening up to the notion that advertising can impact people, advertising can be used to do more than what has traditionally been the case. Consequently, this will impact the strategies used. As an illustration, Taxi Stockholm, the largest cab company in Stockholm, built a platform around the diversity and language skills of their cab drivers. Under the heading 'Taxi translator' they were able to offer summer visitors to Stockholm a tailored experience in their preferred language. At the same time, showcasing the diversity of their employee-base became a source of internal pride in the company and contributed to societal discourse about the benefits of immigration.

It will also influence the competencies sought by advertising practice. Whereas advertising agencies of the past have been very specialised in crafting a message for a specific media and context, contemporary advertising agencies need to be capable of combining such craft with communications typically performed by PR agencies ('getting things to spread') and/or customers services operations ('understanding what is being said'). This means that the boundaries between different communication agencies are blurring. In fact, many marketers are already demanding this from their agencies. A notable example of this is Spotify. The company has decided to let its social media (customer support) team take charge of digital media campaigns, as the engagement created by their campaigns tends to be a lot higher than the engagement created by their digital and advertising agencies.

Critiques of the working definition(s)

Defining advertising is not an easy task. As illustrated by the work of Richards and Currin (2002), experts tend to hold very different views of what advertising is and how it should be defined. A working definition of advertising as 'brand-initiated communication intent on impacting people' can thus be subject to various critiques and concerns. In the special issue of *Journal of Advertising* five well-known advertising scholars were asked to review and critique this definition (Eisend 2016; Huh 2016; Laczniak 2016; Rust 2016; Stewart 2016). The following three main concerns were raised:

Critique 1: Is there a need for a new definition? Although I argue in favor of the changes in advertising as being part of an evolutionary process, a different perspective would be to say that we are currently experiencing a revolution. The argument made is that advertising (as defined traditionally) can be considered dead (Rust, 2016), declining (Stewart, 2016) or undergoing such radical change that it will no longer be advertising as we know it (Laczniak, 2016). Given these dramatic changes, it is better to let advertising (as we know it) die and allow other forms of communications to take its place. However, given that change is likely to continue, getting rid of advertising in favour of something else would only risk us having to get rid of that something else again in the very near future. As advertising is currently a big business with marketing departments and advertising agencies working systematically in taking initiatives to create communication that impacts people, it seems more fruitful to update and evolve the meaning of the term advertising than to bury it. By getting rid of the technologically based (e.g. print, mass media, mobile, or whichever media dominate the period) denotations in the definition, it helps put focus on what advertising sets out to do (enable brands to impact people). From this perspective, advertising evolves with new technology rather than dies whenever a new medium becomes popular or dominant. Keeping the definition up to date seems to be the most fruitful way forward.

Critique 2: A broad definition of advertising is not desirable. Another concern is that defining advertising too broadly risks diluting the meaning of advertising (e.g., Eisend, 2016; Huh, 2016; Stewart, 2016). If we can't easily categorize advertising, what use do we have for the term? This reasoning seems to have guided many of the past definitions of advertising. By tying advertising to specific media and technologies (e.g. print, paid, mediated, mass media) it becomes easy to identify, but given the high pace of changes in advertising practice and technological context, this identification comes at a risk of quickly being out of tune with the type of communications used by professionals in the industry. If we are to work creatively with advertising, we need a definition that is not too narrow in order to identify new paths and possibilities. Indeed, we argue that a working definition that blurs traditional boundaries and allows for several forms of communication, will both enable and guide the development of current and future advertising. It allows it to reinvent itself, rather than die with changing (and disappearing) technologies, behaviours, and effects. The proposed definition does also provide boundaries. Not everything that is communicated about a brand is advertising.

Critique 3: Does advertising need to be brand-initiated? This critique has several facets. First, there is a discussion about the meaning of a brand (Eisend, 2016; Huh, 2016). 'Brands', in contrast to people and organizations, are not really creatures capable of doing anything (Eisend, 2016). What is more, advertising is a form of communication that is relevant beyond marketing and brands (Huh, 2016). In fact, the term 'brand' is used in the definition due to lack of a better term; using the term 'people' would be too confusing and the term 'organization' would be too limiting (Dahlen & Rosengren, 2016b).

Second, the critique focuses on the increasingly interactive nature of communications. Contemporary consumers not only receive messages about brands, they also create and distribute them. By focusing on brand-initiated communications you might run the risk of missing a big part of what marketers are doing. However, this critique does not consider the fact that the working definition knowingly omits any notion of a sender-receiver relationship to include communications that are created or spread by others than the brand in the definition. The working definition also suggests that even if consumers actively engage in or craft the communication, 'brand-initiated' is needed as a qualifier for the communication to be defined as advertising. This qualifier highlights that not all word of mouth (WOM), publicity, or other forms of communication about a brand (e.g. customer service) are advertising. Thus, the working definition opens up for advertising to take shape as WOM or publicity, but only if a brand has somehow initiated it. To be considered advertising, some agent connected to the brand (e.g., an advertising agency, a marketing department or a fundraising organization) must have initiated it.

Conclusion

It is clear that advertising, both as an academic field and as a practice, is undergoing constant change. Given the constantly changing nature of advertising and the changes we are seeing in media, consumer behaviour, and the impact desired by marketers, it is apparent that any definition of advertising needs to be revisited as advertising continues to evolve. Rather than declaring advertising dead, I argue that a more fruitful way would be to redefine advertising as 'brand-initiated communications intent on impacting people' (Dahlen & Rosengren, 2016a). This allows marketers and creators to think more freely about the different types of media (owned, earned, bought) that can be used to impact people (both customers, employees, and citizens) in several ways (in terms of what they think about the brand, but also about themselves and others).

From a research perspective, however, this definition becomes too restricting. As advertising scholars, we need to involve ourselves in all types of brand-related communications. When we understand different types of communications and their effects, marketers can start taking initiatives to turn them into advertising.

Further reading
- Case: How practitioners view the integration of advertising and public relations – Supa (p. 399)
- Context: The changing business models in the media industry and the importance of media consumer engagement – Chan-Olmsted & Wang (p. 133)
- Contrast: How the increasingly promotional role of media content means that music is becoming subordinated to advertising and marketing – Meier (p. 321)

References

Åkestam, N., Rosengren, S., & Dahlen, M. (2017). 'Think About It – Can Portrayals of Homosexuality in Advertising Prime Consumer-Perceived Social Connectedness and Empathy?', *European Journal of Marketing*, *51*(1), 82-98.

Dahlen, M. & Rosengren, S. (2016a). 'If Advertising Won't Die, What Will It Be? Toward a Working Definition of Advertising', *Journal of Advertising*, *45*(3), 334-345.

Dahlen, M. & Rosengren, S. (2016b). 'Reply to the Comments on "If Advertising Won't Die, What Will It Be? Toward a Working Definition of Advertising"', *Journal of Advertising*, *45*(3), 359-363.

Eisend, M. (2016). 'Comment: Advertising, Communication, and Brands', *Journal of Advertising*, *45*(3), 353-355.

Huh, J. (2016). 'Comment: Advertising Won't Die, But Defining It Will Continue to be Challenging', *Journal of Advertising*, *45*(3), 356-358.

Laczniak, R.N. (2016). 'Comment: Advertising's Domain and Definition', *Journal of Advertising*, *45*(3), 351-352.

Keller, K.L. (2016). 'Unlocking the Power of Integrated Marketing Communications: How Integrated Is Your IMC Program?', *Journal of Advertising*, *45*(3), 286-301.

Nan, X. & Faber, R.J. (2004). 'Advertising Theory: Reconceptualizing the Building Blocks', *Marketing Theory*, *4*(1-2), 7-30.

Richards, J.I. & Curran, C.M. (2002). 'Oracles on "Advertising": Searching for a Definition', *Journal of Advertising*, *31*(2), 62-77.

Rosengren, S. & Bondesson, N. (2017). 'How Organizational Identification Among Retail Employees is Affected by Advertising', *Journal of Retailing and Consumer Services*, *38*, 204-209.

Rosengren, S. & Dahlen, M. (2013). 'Judging a Medium by Its Advertising. Exploring the Effects of Advertising Content on Perceptions of a Media Vehicle', *Journal of Advertising Research*, *53*(1), 61-70.

Rust, R.T. (2016). 'Comment: Is Advertising a Zombie?', *Journal of Advertising*, *45*(3), 346-347.

Schultz, D. (2016). 'The Future of Advertising or Whatever We Are Going to Call It', *Journal of Advertising*, *45*(3), 276-285.

Stewart, D.W. (2016), 'Comment: Speculations on the Future of Advertising Redux', *Journal of Advertising*, *45*(3), 348-350.

30. Perceptions and Realities of the Integration of Advertising and Public Relations

Dustin Supa

The changing nature of the communication landscape and the rise of new message platforms, including social media, has heightened the need for a more integrated approach to advertising and public relations. This chapter examines how practitioners view the integration of advertising and public relations, and provides recommendations for future practitioners on how to maximize efforts towards integration.

Introduction

The integration of advertising and public relations within organizations is not a novel concept. As early as 1904, the University of Pennsylvania's Wharton School of Business was offering a course that taught 'publicity, agency, advertising, forms and correspondence' (Maynard, 1941, p. 383). Early leaders in both advertising and public relations, such as Albert Lasker and Edward Bernays, respectively, were often able to combine the disciplines to best serve their organizations.

Today, the concept of integration can be found extensively in the trade publications, with headlines such as 'Can PR and advertising play nicely together' (Davila, 2012) and '2016 will be the year that PR truly embraces integration and inclusivity' (Barrat, 2016), to the slightly more aggressive 'Integrate or die' (Campbell, 2015). And though these headlines might attempt to convince their readers that the concept is relatively new and at the cutting edge of innovation in providing for clients' communication needs, the truth is that the integration of different disciplines in professional communication has been a topic of conversation for quite a while, and has been executed (both successfully and unsuccessfully) for many years. On the surface, the integration of advertising and public relations may appear to simply be a recycled term for 'integrated marketing communications' (IMC) that was in vogue during the 1970s-1990s. But it has been identified as an unique area (Smith & Place, 2013) and some scholars have suggested that *integrated communication* has replaced IMC (Grunig, 1992).

A substantial amount of scholarly and professional writing has been dedicated to the effectiveness of the integration of advertising and public relations, in various forms, over the past fifty years. However, there has been little empirical research that has examined the perceptions of practitioners in the field with regard to this integration. It is the goal of this chapter to examine those perceptions, based on a series of empirical investigations, and, in turn, to provide readers with an overview of how practitioners view the integration of advertising and public relations. Further, based on this research, recommendations for how future practitioners might maximize efforts towards integration will be proposed.

A long history of practice

Public relations has been defined as a 'management function that establishes and maintains mutually beneficial relationships between an organization and the publics on whom its success or failure depends' (Cutlip, Center, & Broom, 1994, p. 1). And while there are many iterations of the definition of public relations in the public sphere, one key term is omnipresent – that of a relationship.

As a fundamental aspect of the field, relationships between organizations (of all kinds) and their audiences are the primary driver of the work of the public relations professional. These relationships, whether with consumers, investors, the media, employees, etc., are all based around the idea that audiences will have attitudes towards organizations. The goal of the public relations professional is to create, and then maintain, a relationship that is positive; in other words, a relationship where the audience perceives that their voices are heard and that trust is engendered. Successful public relations professionals seek to create highly regarded reputations for their organizations.

The goal of advertising, at least traditionally, has been to establish a different type of relationship with audiences. If we consider that public relations seeks to cultivate an attitudinal relationship, then we might consider that advertising seeks to establish cognitive and behavioral relationships for their organizations. Thus, the goal of advertising is to create awareness and to promote action (in many cases, purchasing a product or service). Advertising can be defined, then as 'information placed in the media by an identified sponsor that pays for the time or space' (*Ibid.*, p. 10).

However, while the two disciplines have traditionally been discreet functions, there has also been an overlap of the fields over time. For example, the advertorial (a paid placement that seeks to create a change in audience attitudes) has long been a tool, used by organizations, which blends the paid space of advertising with traditionally public-relations-oriented messaging. In today's digital world, we would use the term 'sponsored content'.

But sponsored content, while an integration of tools, does not really represent an integration of the fields. Rather, integration is best represented today as an organizational strategy that brings the tools and functions of audience-centred communication together. In other words, those who are in charge of advertising are working with those who are in charge of public relations, and both are working towards common organizational goals, sharing resources (skills, time, and budget), and working together to present messages to audiences that are consistent across multiple platforms. Instead of just using each other, the two fields are basically merged as the voice of an organization.

A leader in public relations, Edward Bernays, wrote early in his career about the advantages of advertising and public relations working together. Bernays advocated for a 'separate but equal' approach, stating:

> The counsel on public relations is not an advertising man but he advocates advertising where that is indicated. Very often he is called in by an advertising agency to supplement its work on behalf of a client. His work and that of the advertising agency do not conflict with or duplicate each other (Bernays, 1928, p. 39).

John Hill, chairman of the board of Hill & Knowlton Public Relations, seemingly agreed with Bernays in terms of maintaining a separation of the two fields, writing in 1958:

> Advertising, in the usual sense, is the use of paid space in newspapers, magazines, or on the air or billboards for the selling of products or services. Public relations, as a function, differs basically in that it is designed, mainly, to promote understanding and public acceptance of an idea or cause. Public relations has many techniques, one of which is the use of the technique of advertising whereby the 'public relations message' can be placed before the desired audiences in exactly the desired phraseology (Hill, 1958, pp. 4-5).

What is clear is that early leaders in the field of public relations recognized advertising as a distinct, and useful, way for organizations to communicate with publics. Clearly, these public relations folks considered advertising to be necessary, though we might infer that they held advertising to be, at best, a tool to be used in conjunction with more strategic efforts.

But recall that these public relations leaders were actually fairly late to the game in terms of integration, as the Wharton School at the University of Pennsylvania was, as early as 1904, teaching a class called 'The Marketing of Products'. Maynard (1941) states the course description was:

> The methods now practiced in the organization and conduct of the selling branch of industrial and mercantile business. The principal subjects in the field are

publicity, agency, advertising, forms and correspondence, credit and collections, and terms of sale (Maynard, 1941, p. 383).

This course was, according to Maynard (1941), a very early introduction to what, nearly seven decades later, would become the concept of *integrated marketing communications*, a concept that would wax and wane in popularity for around thirty years starting in the mid-1970s. In 1974, Bishop released his third edition of a bibliography of research covering the 1964-1972 time frame. There were nearly 300 entries, including articles, books, and dissertations that had at least some aspect of exploring the relationship between advertising and public relations. In the same decade, Kotler and Mindak (1978) questioned whether marketing and public relations should be 'partners or rivals' as they found that both 'normally operate separately, at some loss in overall effectiveness' (*Ibid.*, p. 13). Their research concluded that:

> It may be that the best way to solve a marketing problem would be through public relations activities. It is also possible that the best way to solve a public relations problem might be through the disciplined orientation that marketing provides (*Ibid.*, p. 17).

This type of research further indicated the need for more integration between the fields. However, academics and practitioners were seemingly unable to find common ground. A 1993 report to the Association for Education in Journalism and Mass Communication's advertising and public relations divisions recommended that the fields should seek to integrate their curriculum. Newsom (2009) stated:

> The concept seemed workable, but the plan ran into difficulties at both the professional and academic levels. At the professional level, the economics of advertising and public relations are different. Whereas public relations charges for professional services on a fee as well as an hourly basis [...] advertising billings are based on media placements [...] (Newsom, 1996, p. 475).

The early 1990s was the heyday of scholarly activities surrounding IMC (Miller & Rose, 1994). In particular, many studies were published on how advertising and public relations curricula could best address the concept (Fullerton, McKinnon & Kendrick, 2014; Newsom, 2009), how to best achieve integration in practice (Hartley & Pickton, 1999; Nowak & Phelps, 1994), and the positive perception from clients (Duncan & Everett, 1993). Scholars at the time were hopeful to better inform the practice, though some argued that 'IMC represents a form of marketing imperialism' (Hutton, 1996, p. 155). Many scholars argued that the potential benefits of IMC outweighed the potential negatives (Gonring, 1994; Harris, 1993; Stewart, 1996), leading Gronstedt (1996) to re-emphasize the importance of integration, and to refer to the idea as 'integrated communications' rather than IMC.

This was significant, as research in the late 1990s started to show that while practitioners were still devoting attention to IMC, within some organizations it was potentially limiting the impact of individual practitioners' skill sets (McArthur & Griffin, 1997). In other words, practitioners whose skill sets were outside of traditional marketing were not able to participate as equal members of a team. A public relations professional, for example, who may not have a background in audience analytics or sales projections, might be relegated to only writing press releases – even if that professional had extensive strategy execution experience.

This is not to say that IMC became completely subverted, particularly as some university programmes adopted a version of IMC more closely related to Duncan and Caywood's (1996) ideal – that of a move 'away from the literal integration of major communication functions' and toward an 'expanded concept of audience' (*Ibid.*, pp. 18-19). Smith and Place (2013) state that 'this distinction between IMC and IC has been underrecognized in scholarship' (*Ibid.*, p. 171).

Though IMC has waned in its popularity, there is a substantial body of literature surrounding the fields of advertising and public relations. Much of this work has examined the difference in impact on consumers depending on message type (Hallahan, 1999; Jo, 2004; Michaelson & Stacks, 2007; Supa & Dodd, 2015), how integration works (or doesn't work) in professional communication settings (Kitchen, Kim & Schultz, 2008; Swain, 2004), and the impact of integration on organizational structure and hierarchy (Hallahan, 2007; Smith & Place, 2013). Overall, these studies have found few differences in how audiences perceive messaging in terms of the type of message (either advertising or public relations), and that the relationship between consumers and organizations is not significantly impacted by message type. It stands to reason, then, that integration should be taking place, though a number of studies (Hallahan, 2007; Smith & Place, 2013) indicated that it is not, at least not to the level that provides the organization the greatest benefit.

Some of the challenges researchers have pointed out are the apparent inequities in pay as organizations attempt to adopt integration. For example, marketing executives still tend to earn salaries that are significantly higher than advertising or public relations executives, even in an 'integrated' environment. The research also reveals leadership in integrated organizations tends to be heavily in favour of the marketing perspective, driven by revenue gaining ventures, as opposed to attitudinal or cognitive organizational drivers. Research has also pointed out the challenge for smaller, niche agencies to compete with larger firms that can provide more services, thus leading to greater conglomeration of advertising and public relations agencies.

Advertising and public relations integration: Voices from the practice

Integration within the professional fields of advertising and public relations is a lot like the weather: many people talk, or complain, about it, but very few people seemingly do much about it. The reality of true and full integration is problematic to public relations and advertising professionals, and is often constrained by traditions within each of the areas, difficulties in management and budgets, and the ambiguity surrounding responsibilities for new messaging platforms. A recent series of studies (Supa, 2016; Supa & Berkowitz, 2017) conducted with more than one thousand managers and senior managers in both advertising and public relations (identified public relations n=749, identified advertising n=444) examined the perspectives of those working in the field about integration, primarily focused on the positive and negative aspects of that integration. As a result, we are starting to get a clearer picture of what integration of the fields looks like in the professional workplace.

What we see emerging are three common themes related to the challenges of integration as seen by those in the field. The first common theme that is apparent is the difference of the *goals* of each of the fields. As one advertising professional stated 'Advertising implies running external campaigns and managing media spend for portfolio clients – PR is the external voice of the company. There should be very little overlap between these two fields.' Other advertising professionals disagree, and instead advocate for consistency. An exemplar statement advocating for the fields working together comes from one advertising professional:

> The important thing, I think, is that your organization's PR tactics and advertising tactics *need* to be thought out in advance – they're not separate strategies, they're both relevant (though unequal, in for-profit world) partners in presenting an outward facing snapshot of your brand. Sometimes, one supports the other; other times, one makes up for the other's deficiencies. But in the end, an effective strategy that includes both PR and advertising should achieve a balance that tells your customers – external (purchasers), internal (employees), industry (suppliers and influencers) – who you are and what you stand for. That only gets communicated effectively when advertising and PR are in harmony [...] however imperfect and discordant the messages may sometimes be.

These ideas, however, may be forward-thinking in terms of how practitioners perceive the world around them. While we know that integration is occurring from a management perspective, at least, in terms of overall communication strategy and budgetary concerns, the majority of those 'in the trenches' remain neutral or negative toward the execution of integration. This is likely due, in part, to how messages within organizations filter down to those who are actually doing the work. It is often the case that hierarchy within organizations means that, ultimately, there are a few individuals (sometimes a single person) responsible for the overarching goals and strategies for an organization to communicate, but when it comes to executing those goals, traditional silos of practice take over. One public relations practitioner indicated these silos have a negative impact on the integration of the fields within an organization:

> Unfortunately public relations and advertising are often handled by two different departments or offices and therefore they have two different plans, visions and strategies. It [is] essential for a manager in either one of these fields to have a clear understanding of the organization's business plan and the role their specialty has in moving it forward. All [too] often the two sometimes competing departments that manage PR and advertising do not communicate with one another because of infrastructure in the reporting relationships.

These silos of practice are often created by the *budgetary management* of communication within organizations, which is the second common theme related to the challenge of integrating the fields. This is likely the result, at least to a degree, of the concept of territory in organizations. Organizational budgets are becoming increasingly tight, while at the same time costs are rising for myriad reasons, including labour, materials, shipping, and employee benefit costs. It is no surprise, therefore, that as practitioners think about integration, they quickly think about cost-sharing and downsizing.

A clear disconnect in budgetary concerns are the execution of advertising and public relations message platforms and vehicles. Advertising is, at its core, the paid placement of organizational messages. Public relations, conversely, often relies on the earned placement of messages through influencer and media relations. As such, advertising budgets are often much higher than those in public relations, or are at least perceived to be so. In terms of practice, this often translates to practitioners assuming that advertising budgets should be higher than those in public relations, though in reality, monies used to create and purchase advertisements are often held completely separate from personnel and promotional costs.

Finally, as a third common theme, the professionals in advertising and public relations indicate that there is some confusion over *responsibilities*, particularly with regard to new media platforms and within consumer/audience interactions. When given a list of thirteen tasks commonly associated with either advertising (such as media buying and package design) or public relations (such as publicity and reputation management) or activities that may fall under an integrated organization (such as social media and stakeholder research), Supa (2016) states that 'there is a significant difference between the fields in terms of how they perceive task responsibility among many of the tasks commonly associated with professional communication within an organization'. A large part of this is due to the novelty of new message platforms, including social media, and that these platforms often integrate traditional marketing tactics with directed organization-public relationships, thereby confusing which area should be chiefly responsible.

But this challenge to integration also provides an opportunity to increase the integration of the fields. These changes to the communication landscape also allow that those working in the professions will recognize the changes that are coming to the execution of public relations and advertising. One advertising professional noted that:

> PR is often viewed as the fluffier, less quantifiable cousin of advertising (to the extent that advertising can be measured accurately). Some of that has changed, but there is a strong overlap between, say, SEO and PR. Where does that fit into things from an advertising standpoint along with other channels is a big question that many companies don't ask.

So, at least in some instances, practitioners are recognizing the changing nature of communication, and that those changes may necessitate new ways of doing business, plus the need for cross-trained professionals entering the field. One public relations professional remarked how new platforms were causing new ways of thinking in their organization.

> Advertising and public relations seem to be at odds, as the two disciplines have converged and there is a stepped-up focus on storytelling. The problem is that advertising professionals don't always think of telling the longer-form story, and in some cases, they flat out don't know how to do it. There needs to be less competition and more integration between the two disciplines, as well as an understanding of which discipline takes the lead, depending on the opportunity at hand.

Thus, the challenge moving into the future is for organizations and practitioners to recognize the strengths of traditional advertising and public relations practice, and to integrate those practices in ways that maximize the potential for success in messaging and relating to audiences. The additional challenge, however, is the time it may take for full integration to occur, and what happens in the meantime.

In our current structures (both in practice and education) individuals are often trained in a specific field. In order for integration to be ultimately successful, candidates for positions will need to be trained as integrated communication professionals. The changing nature of communication platforms, in particular the way audiences perceive information, are forcing professional communicators to rethink their approach with regard to audience relationships. Over time, digital natives will become professional communicators and integration will become the norm rather than an exception. The challenge in the interim, though, is moving current structures of professional communication toward integration, and the need to adopt new practices that are most efficient at communicating with audiences.

Conclusion

Public relations and advertising professionals see a commonality in the way that both groups perceive their own roles and the organizations' significance. The ownership of both types of agencies by the same major holding companies has tightened the upper management and financial operation of public relations and advertising. As such, the future of the fields as independent entities is rightfully questioned. Many organizations are moving toward increasing their integration, causing a need for practitioners who are not necessarily specialists or generalists within the broad scope of either advertising or public relations, but practitioners who are both. That is, the future practitioner may have a specialty in either advertising or public relations, but that same person needs to have a strong understanding of how different message platforms and strategies impact audiences.

Without a clear consensus on the role of integration in the advertising and public relations industries, future practitioners have an opportunity that is unique. As Supa (2016) states: 'While there generally seems to be a mutual respect between the professions, as well as an understanding that each field *can* work together to the maximum benefit of the organization, there also seems to be a certain level of territorialism with regard to specific tasks within the organizational communication matrix.' Future practitioners will need to take advantage of these opportunities in order to not only create opportunities for their organizations, but to advance their own careers.

Further reading
- Case: How to rethink and redefine advertising to better account for contemporary changes in the practice of advertising and public relations – Rosengren (p. 389)
- Context: Five current issues and trends relating to the media industries as a result of digitalization and the rise of the global communication giants – Miège (p. 73)
- Contrast: How pro bloggers, YouTubers, and Instagram influencers are used to hype and advertise branded goods on their blogs, channels, and feeds – Duffy (p. 375)

References

Barrat, A. (2016). '2016 Will Be the Year that PR Truly Embraces Integration and Inclusion', *Influence*. Retrieved from http://influence.cipr.co.uk/2016/01/07/2016-will-be-the-year-that-pr-truly-embraces-integration-and-inclusion/.

Bernays, E.L. (1928). *Propaganda*. New York: Liveright.

Bishop, R.L. (1974). *Public Relations: A Comprehensive Bibliography*. Ann Arbor, MI: University of Michigan Press.

Campbell, K. (2015). 'PR, Advertising Execs Say "Integrate or Die"', *Adweek*. Retrieved from http://www.adweek.com/prnewser/pr-advertising-execs-say-integrate-or-die/111221.

Cutlip, S.M., Center, A.H. & Broom, G.M. (1994). *Effective Public Relations*. Upper Saddle River, NJ: Prentice Hall.

Davila, R.J. (2012). 'Can PR and Advertising Play Nicely Together? 5 Tips for Agency Integration', *Public Relations Tactics*. Retrieved from http://www.prsa.org/Intelligence/Tactics/Articles/view/9839/1050/Can_PR_and_advertising_play_nicely_together_5_tips#.VvrStOIrK70.

Gonring, M.P. (1994). 'Putting Integrated Marketing Communications to Work Today', *Public Relations Quarterly, 39*(3), 45-48.

Gronstedt, A. (1996). 'Integrated Communications at America's Leading Total Quality Management Corporations', *Public Relations Review, 22*(1), 25-42.

Grunig, L.A. (1992). 'Power in the Public Relations Department', in J.E. Grunig (ed.) *Excellence in Public Relations and Communication Management* (483-501). Hillsdale NJ: LEA.

Hallahan, K. (1999). 'No, Virginia, It's Not True What They Say about Publicity's Implied Third-Party Endorsement Effect', *Public Relations Review, 25*(3), 331-350.

Hallahan, K. (2007). 'Integrated Communication: Implications for Public Relations beyond Excellence', in E.L. Toth (ed.), *The Future of Excellence in Public Relations and Communication Management*. Mahwah, NJ: LEA.

Harris, T.L. (1993). 'How MPR Adds Value to Integrated Marketing Communications', *Public Relations Quarterly, 38*(2), 5-18.

Hartley, B. & Pickton, D. (1999). 'Integrated Marketing Communications Requires a New Way of Thinking', *Journal of Marketing Communication, 5*(2), 97-106.

Hutton, J.G. (1996) 'Integrated Marketing Communications and the Evolution of Market Thought', *Journal of Business Research, 37*(3), 155-162.

Jo, S. (2004). 'Effect of Content Type on Impact: Editorial vs. Advertising', *Public Relations Review, 30*(4), 603-612.

Kitchen, P.J., Kim, I. & Schultz, D.E. (2008). 'Integrated Marketing Communication: Practice Leads Theory', *Journal of Advertising Research, 48*(4), 531-546.

Maynard, H.H. (1941). 'Marketing Courses Prior to 1910', *Journal of Marketing, 5*(4), 382-384.

McArthur, D.N. & Griffin, T. (1997), 'A Marketing Management View of Integrated Marketing Communications', *Journal of Advertising Research, 37*(5), 19-26.

Michaelson, D. & Stacks, D.W. (2007). 'Exploring the Comparative Communications Effectiveness of Advertising and Public Relations: An Experimental Study of Initial Branding Advantages', *Institute for Public Relations.* Retrieved from http://www.instituteforpr.org/wp-content/uploads/Michaelson_Stacks.pdf.

Miller, D.A. & Rose, P.B. (1994). 'Integrated Communications: A Look at Reality Instead of Theory', *Public Relations Quarterly, 39*(1), 13-16.

Newsom, D. (2009). 'Public Relations and Integrated Communication', in D.W. Stacks & M.B. Salwen (eds), *An Integrated Approach to Communication Theory and Research.* New York: Routledge.

Nowak, G.J. & Phelps, J. (1994). 'Conceptualizing the Integrated Marketing Communication Phenomenon: An Examination of Its Impact on Advertising Practices and Its Implications for Advertising Research', *Journal of Current Issues & Research in Advertising, 16*(1), 49-66.

Smith, B.G. & Place, K.R. (2013). 'Integrating Power? Evaluating Public Relations Influence in an Integrated Communication Structure', *Journal of Public Relations Research, 25*(2), 168-187.

Stewart, D.W. (1996). 'Market-Back Approach to the Design of Integrated Communications Programs: A Change in Paradigm and Focus on Determinants of Success', *Journal of Business Research, 37*(3), 147-153.

Supa, D.W. (2016). 'Do You See What I See? An Examination of Perceptions between Advertising and Public Relations Professionals', *Public Relations Review, 42*(3), 408-417.

Supa, D.W. & Berkovitz, T. (2017). *Professional Perspectives on the Integration of Advertising and Public Relations: A Qualitative Approach to the Relationship between the Fields.* Proceedings of American Academy of Advertising Conference.

Supa, D.W. & Dodd, M.D. (2015). 'Examining the Impact of Advertising vs. Public Relations in Consumer Engagement Initiatives', *PRism 12*(2). Retrieved from http://www.prismjournal.org/fileadmin/12_2/Supa_Dodd.pdf.

Swain, W.N. (2004). 'Perceptions of IMC After a Decade of Development: Who's at the Wheel, and How Can We Measure Success?', *Journal of Advertising Research, 44*(1), 46-65.

Professions

Digital Games

31. Game Production Logics at Work: Convergence and Divergence

Aphra Kerr

The digital games industry has seen some significant changes in the past ten years, marked by the rise of mobile and free to play games. This chapter discusses production and work in the games industry by exploring some of the similarities and differences between digital games and other cultural and creative industries, examining the emergence of new occupational categories, and investigating the persistence of old inequalities.

Introduction

The digital games industry works hard to present itself as significant in revenue terms, and innovative in technological terms. As game researchers start to gather independent data we have a better basis from which to evaluate these claims. Since the early part of this decade a number of industrial and production changes have become evident. As in other media industries, the digital games industry has shifted from the production of material goods to the provision of digital services. Industry data now indicates that digital revenues are exceeding material revenues in some markets – in the American market this trend appeared around 2012. In an industry worth more than $100 billion globally the most rapidly growing segments are online and mobile. More significantly, new business models have emerged – like free to play – and advertising has been growing as a source of revenue (NewZoo, 2016). These shifts have led to new market entrants, including digital distribution companies from outside of the games industry and from different parts of the world. It has also meant that new occupations have been created that either did not exist before, or existed in highly informal ways.

It is tempting to point to these trends as indicating radical technological innovation in the digital games industry. It is all too easy to fall into an uncritical technological determinism – that companies, workers, and players must change in accordance with technological innovation. Yet, histories of media and technology studies more generally would caution against such an approach. My research conducted over roughly two decades on the digital games industry has pointed to some surprising similarities to other media industries and the persistence of certain inequalities in the access to and performance of work in digital games.

This chapter focuses on three aspects of production and work in the digital games industry. Firstly, it explores some of the similarities and differences between the digital games industry and other creative and cultural industries in their production logics. Secondly, it examines the data on work in the games industry and especially the emergence of new occupational categories and the persistence of old inequalities. Finally, we discuss some of the challenges and opportunities that the industry faces.

Understanding the digital games industry

The top-selling games in the last few years include *Call of Duty: World War II* (Activision, 2017), *NBA 2K18* (Take Two, 2017), *The Legend of Zelda: Breath of the Wild* (Nintendo, 2017), and *Clash of Clans* (SuperCell, 2012). Even if you have never heard of these games, it is instructive to note that they are mostly produced in North America and Europe with the exception of Nintendo's Zelda franchise. Just as the industry produces a diverse range of games, they can also be played on a range of technologies: from consoles, computers, and mobile phones to watches. Many digital games are now designed to be 'cross platform' from launch. The starting point for understanding this industry, then, is to appreciate that the market, industrial, and organizational structures are diverse – even if the underlying technologies are all digital. While we have technological convergence, at the same time we have other forms of market and organizational divergence. The GAFA intermediaries (Google, Apple, Facebook, and Amazon) have become significant in terms of digital distribution of social and mobile games in the last decade. They have been joined by Chinese companies like Tencent. The 'legacy' game publishers like Microsoft, Sony, Nintendo, Activision Blizzard, and Electronic Arts have responded by purchasing successful social and mobile game development start-ups and expanding into digital distribution.

A useful way to connect industrial and organizational changes in cultural production to work practices in the digital games industry is the production logics approach. This approach also enables us to compare and contrast the digital games industry to existing creative and cultural industries. The production logics approach has a long lineage, and across the cultural industries a number of different production logics have been identified. Raymond Williams (1974) identified flow as a core characteristic of the production and distribution of television, indicating a constant stream of serialized products. Bernard Miège (1987) subsequently identified five logics across the cultural industries: editorial, flow, press, live entertainment, and electronic information. In an era when digital games were mostly sold on cassettes through retail outlets, he mentions that 'videogame inventors' were part of the electronic information logic but moving towards the editorial logic with salaried workers and royalties.

For Miège, each production logic is based on five characteristics: the economic value chain, the dominant power brokers, the creative workers/professions, the revenue stream, and the overall market structure. While production logics are dependent on the state of technology at a given moment, they do not list technology as a key characteristic. So, for example, in 1989, in Europe, the dominant production logic for broadcasting was the flow logic. Applying the production logics approach we can identify that its economic value chain included television stations as producers and distributors, who were also the dominant power brokers and gatekeepers. The creative workers were mostly full time employees of the television stations, and the dominant revenue streams were indirect via the licence fee. The dominant market structure was mass market. The key challenges in this logic were to build audience loyalty and ensure a continuous stream of content. Scheduling was a key distinguishing feature.

Some minor adjustments to these logics have been made: a club logic was introduced to capture new subscription based content services, and authors argued about the development of an online portal logic (Winseck & Jin, 2011; Miège, 2011). Regardless, the big three of editorial, press, and flow dominated in the cultural industries for years.

How might these five logics relate to digital games? In my first book on the digital games industry, published in 2006, I noted how the production of large console and personal computer games (triple-A games in industry parlance) largely conformed to Miège's editorial logic (Kerr, 2006). Interviews with developers all discussed pitching ideas to publishers, securing a publishing deal to make their game, and receiving royalties after launch. The console segment of the games industry was highly vertically integrated and revenues were based on mass market unit sales. It all sounded very familiar to someone who had studied the broader cultural industries.

Massively multiplayer online games like *World of Warcraft* were significantly different. Development required an industrialized form of production by a diverse team of creative workers, and the subscription services required ongoing content development to keep subscribers challenged and paying. The organization of production was similar to traditional broadcast television or radio – the flow production logic. In the mid-2000s, a nascent market in small games for mobile phones existed, but the market structure was uncertain, the distribution system fragmented, and the available technologies lacked standardization. The task of 'porting' a mobile game to hundreds of mobile handsets was a significant barrier to growth. Few game companies were attracted to the creative and financial challenges of the mobile market. The editorial and flow logics could be identified as dominant production logics in digital games, as elsewhere.

Only ten years later things have evolved significantly. The editorial logic continues to exist in games. MMOGs have evolved in their payment systems but the flow logic contributes to exist. Interestingly, a performance logic has grown strongly in games, and is based around both live eSports and mediated game streaming (Taylor, 2015). Both amateur and professional game players work to make a living in live game play and emerging competition structures modelled on physical sports and broadcast television conventions exist, particularly in the US and in parts of Asia. In addition, new 'club' type services had emerged in the games market with players able to log in to a subscription service and select from a number of contemporary and historical games to play 'in the cloud'. These have been somewhat stymied by the quality of broadband infrastructures in many countries, and thus have been slow to grow. The club logic is sometimes combined with the editorial logic.

Perhaps the most significant shift, however, has been the rise of the Android and Apple digital distribution systems, associated open source tools, and the 'free to play' business model. In my 2017 book on the global games industry, I detail the influence of what can be called a new 'platform' logic, which brings together technological, industrial, creative, and development shifts in the industry (Kerr, 2017). Initially, Facebook was the main distribution platform and social network games were able to work synergistically with the social networking services to promote their games. The emergence of smartphones and the development of alternative digital online retailers with relatively short approval timeframes and standardized hardware and software technologies opened up a new range of creative possibilities for amateurs and professionals. By 2017, indirect forms of revenue had become the norm and 'free to play' had become the dominant business model. Game developers had to rethink elements of their game designs to adapt both to the dominant platforms and to build in-game forms of monetization. Developers were able to access new markets working within this production logic but competition was high and marketing budgets began to grow exponentially.

The central brokers in the platform logic are often technology companies from outside of the games industry and they are capturing a significant share of the economic value created. Companies like Android's Google Play and Apple's App Store take, on average, 30 per cent of upfront or recurring revenues in return for access to their services. Other distribution platforms exist in Asian markets. Nevertheless, the fastest growing segment of the games industry in terms of revenue over the past decade has been mobile games. Companies with less than 50 employees have been making revenues to rival their much larger counterparts. Start-up companies like Zynga from America and Supercell from Finland became overnight successes and targets for acquisition by established Japanese, Chinese, and North American game companies. The Swedish company King, who developed the Candy Crush games, was bought by Activision Blizzard in 2016 for $5.6 billion. Most of their games are free to download and they make their money from advertising and microtransactions (Nieborg, 2015). Later, Tencent bought Supercell for $8.6 billion. Tencent also owns Riot (*League of Legends*) and a share of Activision Blizzard.

Tencent dominates the global games industry in terms of revenues, while Apple, Google, and Facebook have entered the top ten publicly quoted companies by revenue. Blockbusters like *Call of Duty* and *Grand Theft Auto* continue to be made and continue to rival large Hollywood productions in terms of developer team size, marketing budgets, and revenues. They are the most similar in production and work type processes to legacy media industries. At the same time, much of the growth is in companies operating within a platform logic, exploring new business models like free to play, and creating new forms of work. Overall, the production logics in the digital games industry are heterogeneous and a period of rapid divergence and innovation in the late 00s, has now given way to more stable production logics and industrial consolidation.

The passion, precarity, and crunch of game work

National-level employment data is not available in many countries for the games industry because the industry cuts across many pre-existing industrial sectors. This lack of data has not been helped by the development of difficult to classify social, mobile, and associated types of game companies. What data exists is often provided by industry associations or third-party media sites, and is biased towards the Anglophone countries. Over the past five years, and using a network of international researchers and translators, I collated numerous independent reports on employment in the games industry. I established that South Korea, the US, China, and Japan were the largest direct employers globally of game developers, while in Europe the UK, Germany, and Spain were the largest employers. In addition, one cannot ignore that the industry has significant links to hardware production factories in Asia, Eastern Europe, and Central America (Huntemann & Aslinger, 2013). While in this chapter I will focus on content and support workers in game production, it must be noted that workers in these hardware production facilities are also a crucial part of the global games industry.

In content production, we can identify a range of creative professions and a hierarchy in terms of prestige and pay, even if this varies from country to country. Most medium- and large-scale development teams incorporate artists, designers, programmers, engineers, audio specialists, and business and management roles. Data from the US, Canada, and the UK has found that managers, audio specialists, and programmers receive the highest average salaries and that audio and programmers according to one survey were over 90 per cent male (Graft, 2014). By far the lowest paid category in these surveys were quality assurance (QA) testers who were paid less than half what managers are paid and are often on part-time contracts. In addition, in more service orientated production logics we are seeing the formalization of new occupations, including live network operations support and community managers. Companies with transnational online communities may also need public policy specialists.

Full-time contracts are the norm for many in the industry who work for medium- to large-scale companies and the use of freelancers is relatively low – this in contrast to most other media industries. Those in highly sought after job categories can command high salaries, travel visas, and healthcare provisions. Nevertheless, employment can be highly volatile and financial and professional success is based on one's portfolio of completed games, an ability to work in a team, and knowledge of the latest tools. The increasing financialization of the games industry has meant that stock market pressures, company acquisition or poor returns on a game can dictate one's employment status and jeopardize access to bonuses or company stock. Studies in Australia have pointed to the impact of currency fluctuations and the global financial crisis in 2008 on employment in work-for-hire companies (Banks & Cunningham, 2016). The 2016 International Game Development Association's (IGDA) Developer Satisfaction Survey found that respondents had, on average, 2.2 employers in the previous five years – indicating a high level of volatility for permanent employees.

Those at the lower end of the pay scale have less power to negotiate and less protection. A North American qualitative study argued that game testers are 'precarious workers' and pay is kept low due to the high demand for these positions and the perception that this job is a route into the industry (Bulut, 2015). My own research into community managers in the games industry in Ireland found that while these positions demand significant gaming and cultural knowledge, job advertisements rarely give remuneration details – indeed, some interviewees informed me that their employment contracts forbid them from discussing their remuneration (Kerr, 2016). These roles are also subject to significant volatility. Support workers can be dismissed on short notice if player numbers fail to meet expectations. Since 2008, the most significant growth in Ireland has been in small independent companies. Many are graduate start-ups. There has been no Zynga or Supercell. Working for hire, working with transnational virtual teams, and unpaid work are relatively common. The national social welfare system and access to start-up finance has an important role to play in facilitating small-scale game production. The vibrancy of the local community can also play an important support role, as with the demoscene in Scandinavia (Jørgensen, Sandqvist, & Sotamaa, 2015).

Much of what has been researched and written about working conditions in the games industry is dominated by responses to surveys from employees in medium to large sized companies in the UK and North America. The latest surveys point to ongoing issues with time and project management, which contribute to persistent problems with staff retention in a negative feedback loop. Analysis by Mia Consalvo (2011) of the IGDA Quality of Life survey data identified three persistent issues in the industry: a reliance on crunch time to deliver projects, a reliance on passion for games in recruitment, and a problem with staff retention. These findings are in line with the results from my own research. Our analysis of job advertisements for the recruitment of community managers also found that passion was a much sought after requirement. Indeed, in some advertisements it was listed as a required skill. When examined in more detail, passion was found to perform an important role in hailing cultural insiders. It also tended to result in a reinforcement of highly gendered structures in the industry (Kerr & Kelleher, 2015).

As in other media industries, we see the intensification of work and non-standard working hours in the digital games industry. While the average working week in the IGDA (2016) survey was 40-44 hours, there appears to be a normalization of crunch time in some companies with over 60 hours a week reported, and much of this overtime uncompensated. A sizable minority (thirteen per cent) reported working over 70 hours a week during crunch. While many might expect some degree of crunch in the run up to a deadline, it is noteworthy that most of these respondents worked in large companies where one might think there would be more professional processes. Also of concern was that respondents to the survey noted that crunch happened a few times a year. Given this pattern, it is not surprising that the profile of respondents to this survey and, indeed, in the industry more generally tends towards the youthful and inexperienced. These working conditions might also be contributing to another significant ongoing challenge for the industry – their problem retaining staff. Survey after survey in the US, Canada, the UK, and Ireland point to a relatively young industry and a lack of experience across teams in project management.

In all the years that I have been researching the industry the figures on gender diversity in the industry have barely improved. The issue is certainly on the agenda of academics and the industry. The IGDA has a Women in Games special interest group (SIGWIG) and there is a Women in Games international group who for over a decade have run conferences and targeted recruitment initiatives. The trade body for the British games industry UK Interactive Entertainment (UKIE) has a diversity initiative and the focus is on promoting the industry as a great place to work to boys and girls. By 2014, the IGDA Developer Satisfaction survey (n=2,000) indicated that up to 22 per cent of those who responded identified as female, which is low compared to other media industries. The 2016 survey (n=1,186 responses) found that the prototypical game industry worker is a '32-year-old while male with a university degree who lives in North America and who does not have children'

(IGDA, 2016, p. 7). In the latest Creative Skillset (2015) report on employment across the creative industries in the UK the games industry has the lowest proportion of women at nineteen per cent.

The IGDA survey (2016) stated that a significant majority of respondents noted that 'diversity in the workplace' was important, or very important, but the responses on how companies dealt with discrimination were very mixed and ranged from companies having no policies, to those policies not being enforced. Two issues dominated in terms of what respondents felt drove negative perceptions of the industry: working conditions and sexism in game culture, especially #GamerGate.

It is difficult to summarize the range of issues bound up in the #GamerGate controversy and for eloquent accounts see these readings (Mortensen, 2016; Massanari, 2017; Chess & Shaw, 2015). In short, in 2014 the hashtag gamergate started to circulate and become attached to an online and offline campaign of targeting, harassment, and threats aimed at female game designers, academics, and anyone who defended them. Emerging from a critique of ethics in game journalism, and a discourse that the 'gamer' identity no longer existed, it quickly evolved into a loosely organized networked group who used social media to target anyone who critiqued the dominant forms of masculinity often found in games, game culture, and in the industry. Mortensen describes it as a self-organizing 'swarm', and others have highlighted their connections to the alt right in American politics. Of particular note were their attempts to spread misinformation about games research in academia and the work of female and feminist scholars associated with the Digital Games Research Association (DiGRA). Anyone who was critical of the structure and working conditions of the games industry and the lack of diversity in game representations, could become a target. The period caused harm to some game researchers and game developers, but the actions of gamergaters were also defended by some. The 2016 IGDA Quality of Life Survey indicates that gamergate further fuelled negative views of the games industry in the general public in some countries, and highlighted varying approaches to sexism within the industry itself.

Across the games industry we see a variety of creative roles and like in other media industries we see a hierarchy by occupation, gender, and pay, with business and programming roles able to command higher compensation. Even for those with permanent contracts the financialization of the industry has meant that employment is uncertain and rewards are highly varied. Indeed, financial compensation is not necessarily tied to working hours, or to the success of a game, and in these contexts it is perhaps not surprising that the industry finds it difficult to retain experienced staff and those with caring responsibilities. Most workers enter today with a university qualification, but still many have to take an unpaid internship to learn the latest skills. Most enter with significant levels of gaming capital and sufficient social and economic capital to support their 'passion'. These are significant barriers to entry and no doubt reinforce the lack of workplace diversity, especially in core development teams. What is perhaps more surprising is the inability of professional associations and many companies to change existing working conditions and working cultures.

Trends in the global games industry

Some of the key trends in the digital games industry are shared with other media industries. The first issue has to do with the expanded importance of circulation related processes in digital game production. While marketing and publicity are important in an increasingly crowded mediascape, and community managers play a crucial role in service support and governance, I want to highlight another aspect that might be less visible. Of particular note in the platform logic is the impact that 'datafication' of producer/user relationships is having on processes of design in the free to play business model and the platform logic. The second (and related) issue is that the digital games industry is increasingly subject to local and national data, cultural and political policies. These policies are influencing what types of content get made and where. The final issue has to do with the aforementioned lack of diversity in the workforce and the potential influence this is having on future growth.

The most significant and controversial issue in digital games is how best to apply data science to support free to play revenues without undermining the fun of playing games. If the platform production logic was influenced by the affordances of social media in its first iteration, it is more about the role of data in content design in the current iteration. Advertisements for data analysts who understand the game lifecycle abound. The games industry body TIGA in the UK has asked the UK government to put data analysts on their skills shortage list. This trend is not without its detractors as Whitson (2012) notes, and the resistance of game players to 'loot boxes', for example, signals that in-game mechanics that are linked to microtransactions are contentious. Loot boxes are virtual items that players can find or purchase within a game and that given them prizes and advantages in gameplay. However, they may also be considered a form of gambling, and are actively being investigated by regulators in some countries to see if they should be regulated as gambling.

The use of data and game player metrics is having an impact on the creative autonomy of design teams and there is industry discussion of metric driven design. The production of persistent and intermittent digital game services means that new design elements are tested on real world players often by 'soft launching' in a limited number of markets. It also means that player retention is crucial and that both playing and paying players are carefully monitored. Designing fun to play games for the free to play business model requires a careful balance between the quantification of gameplay and the targeted monetization of players.

The status of game companies as data brokers brings new responsibilities in relation to local and regional data and privacy legislation. The General Data Protection Regulation placed new data related responsibilities on all companies holding EU citizen data in mid-2018 and the Children's Online Privacy Protection Act (COPPA) legislation in the US already imposes restrictions in relation to advertising to children. Game companies have been prosecuted in the US for allowing third-party advertising networks to show age and content inappropriate advertising to minors. In addition, game companies who operate transnational services need to conform to other local sensitivities. In China, game companies have to conform to local cultural laws and monitor their game worlds for banned words. Tencent recently introduced additional controls for children in China aged twelve and under in terms of how long they can play mobile games and how much money they can spend. While some well established companies employ staff to attend to the cultural adaptation of the content games to other markets, more recent legislation brings new restrictions on how game companies use player data, attend to user privacy, and control access to their players from third party companies.

Overall, the spatialization of game development has tended not to conform to patterns in other media industries. Game development companies have often located in remote non-capital cities and countries. The relative success of the industry may, however, be contributing to a reshaping of this pattern. National cultural and trade policies aimed at supporting the industry through tax breaks and other non-financial supports have introduced locational competition to the industry. Production tax breaks introduced in France and the UK over the past decade have allowed companies to reduce the costs of labour and production. These policies are based on a 'cultural test'. This means that only game projects that score highly on a list of cultural criteria including, for example, the cultural content and languages offered in the game, links to European cultural heritage, and that locate production in Europe qualify for funding.

Game publishers have been ambivalent as to the desirability of cultural policies which impose restrictions on game content, but, in general, game developers have been much more comfortable being treated as cultural and creative companies (Kerr, 2013). Across the Atlantic generous tax breaks were also introduced in Canada (Quebec, Ontario, British Columbia) and in the US (Georgia, Michigan, Louisiana). Meanwhile, in South Korea, state support is much broader than tax supports and there have been initiatives to promote the playing of games (Jin, 2010). In China, strong state support for indigenous companies and limitations on access to the Chinese market from outside are crucial to understanding the growth of Chinese companies like Tencent (Chung & Fung, 2013).

Some of the European and national funding schemes targeted at the games industry are attempting to support both employment and local content production. They are responding to industry figures, which show that control over the economic value and cultural diversity of games has shifted outside of Europe. The top-ten game companies in revenue terms are all North American or Asian. The top-ten companies are large, and getting larger. In 2013, they accounted for almost 44 per cent of global game revenues. While European game companies are highly successful in creating games and games middleware, they are frequently the target of acquisition. The largest European company by revenue is the French company Ubisoft and it is currently fighting against a takeover from the conglomerate Vivendi. There is a sense that European companies have lost control of key publishing roles in the older production logics, and of key intermediary roles in the newer production logics. If ownership of the key digital marketplaces rests with a small number of non-European companies, how do European companies compete in terms of discoverability? What are the algorithms and rules pushing content towards consumers? In the geopolitics of cultural production regional and national policies are now vying with transnational economic priorities and algorithms.

The final consideration that threatens the growth of the games industry is the lack of workplace diversity and the continuing evidence that some game workplaces and cultures are hostile to females and minorities. Clearly, diversity policies focused on awareness raising and promotion of the industry as a place to work will continue to be insufficient if the industry continues to recruit only those who are immersed in a certain type of gamer culture and continues to tolerate inappropriate game culture and workplace behaviour. In the UK survey, one third of women employed in the industry reported experiencing harassment or bullying. It became a clear issue in my interviews with community managers, and female community managers were careful to mask their gender when responding to players in certain games. In a recent survey that I conducted at gamejams in Ireland, 22 per cent had seen, or experienced, gender based discrimination.

Conclusion

The past decade has seen significant changes in production logics, occupational categories, and the rise and importance of data in the design and circulation of digital games. Over the past decade, the numbers of women who have started to buy and play games, especially social, mobile and online games, has increased exponentially. The number of degree and postgraduate-level courses available in game design and related qualifications in third-level institutions has grown significantly and there is clear demand for these courses. Academic researchers have highlighted workplace and in game representation and harassment issues.

In this context, it is perplexing that the focus of attention from professional industry organizations continues to be on awareness raising about the industry and on its problems recruiting staff. The research that we have to date would indicate that recruitment practices and workplace conditions are contributing to these problems. Staff retention issues are linked to working conditions and the precarity of employment. Still, companies and educational programmes often fail to challenge industry stereotypes, workplace inequalities, and discrimination. Academics need to examine more closely the working culture of the games industry. We need to reflect on gaming education and its role in replicating existing practices. And we need to protect those who are doing the research.

Further reading
- Case: What has changed and what has stayed the same in the global games industry in the past decade – O'Donnell (p. 427)
- Context: An exploration of the rise of the platforms and the powerful role they have in shaping professional media production in the games industry – Nieborg & Poell (p. 85)
- Contrast: How social inequalities in media work arise and what might be done to tackle them – Eikhof & Marsden (p. 223)

References

Banks, J. & Cunningham, S. (2016). 'Games Production in Australia: Adapting to Precariousness', in M. Curtin & K. Sanson (eds), *Precarious Creativity: Global Media, Local Labor* (186-199). University of California Press. Available at https://www.luminosoa.org/site/books/10.1525/luminos.10/

Bulut, E. (2015). 'Playboring in the Tester Pit: The Convergence of Precarity and the Degradation of Fun in Video Game Testing', *Television & New Media*, *16*(3), 240-258. doi: 10.1177/1527476414525241.

Chess, S., & Shaw, A. (2015). 'A Conspiracy of Fishes, or, How We Learned to Stop Worrying About #GamerGate and Embrace Hegemonic Masculinity', *Journal of Broadcasting & Electronic Media*, *59*, 208-220. doi: 10.1080/08838151.2014.999917.

Chung, P., & Fung, A. (2013). 'Internet Development and the Commercialisation of Online Gaming in China', in N. Huntemann & B. Aslinger (eds), *Gaming Globally. Production, Play and Place* (232-250). New York: Palgrave Macmillan.

Consalvo, M. (2011). 'Crunched by Passion. Women Game Developers and Workplace Challenges', in Y.B. Kafai, C. Heeter, J. Denner & J. Y. Sun (eds), *Beyond Barbie and Mortal Kombat. New Perspectives on Gender and Gaming* (177-190). Cambridge, MA: MIT Press.

Creative Skillset (2015). *Employment Survey*. London: Creative Skillset

Graft, K. (2014). 'Transitions. Salary Survey' (22 July). Retrieved from http://www.gamasutra. com/view/news/221533/Game_Developer_Salary_Survey_2014_The_results_are_in.php.

Huntemann, N. & Aslinger, B. (eds) (2013). *Gaming Globally. Production, Play and Place*. New York: Palgrave Macmillan.

IGDA (2016). 'Developer Satisfaction Survey 2016. Summary Report'. Retrieved from http://c. ymcdn.com/sites/www.igda.org/resource/resmgr/files__2016_dss/IGDA_DSS_2016_Summary_Report.pdf.

Jin, D.Y. (2010). *Korea's Online Gaming Empire*. Cambridge, MA: MIT Press.

Jørgensen, K., Sandqvist, U. & Sotamaa, O. (2015). 'From Hobbyists to Entrepreneurs: On the Formation of the Nordic Game Industry', *Convergence: The International Journal of Research into New Media Technologies*. doi: 10.1177/1354856515617853.

Kerr, A. (2006). *The Business and Culture of Digital Games: Gamework/Gameplay*. London: SAGE Publications.

Kerr, A. (2013). 'Space Wars: The Politics of Games Production in Europe', in N. Huntemann & B. Aslinger (eds), *Gaming Globally. Production, Play and Place* (215-231). New York: Palgrave Macmillan.

Kerr, A. (2016). 'Recruitment, Work and Identity in Community Management: Passion, Precarity and Play', in J. Webster & K. Randle (eds), *Virtual Workers and the Global Labour Market* (117-135). New York: Palgrave Macmillan.

Kerr, A. (2017). *Global Games. Production, Circulation and Policy in the Networked Age*. New York: Routledge.

Kerr, A. & Kelleher, J.D. (2015). 'The Recruitment of Passion and Community in the Service of Capital. Community Managers in the Digital Games Industry', *Critical Studies in Media Communication, 32*(3), 177-192. doi: 10.1080/15295036.2015.1045005.

Massanari, A. (2017). '#Gamergate and The Fappening: How Reddit's Algorithm, Governance, and Culture Support Toxic Technocultures', *New Media & Society, 19*(3), 329-346. doi: 10.1177/1461444815608807.

Miège, B. (1987). 'The Logics at Work in the New Cultural Industries', *Media, Culture and Society, 9*(3), 273-289. doi: https://doi.org/10.1177/016344387009003002.

Miège, B. (2011). 'Principal Ongoing Mutations of Cultural and Informational Industries', in D. Winseck & D.Y. Jin (eds), *The Political Economies of Media* (51-65). London: Bloomsbury Academic.

Mortensen, T.E. (2016). 'Anger, Fear, and Games: The Long Event of #GamerGate', *Games and Culture*. doi: 10.1177/1555412016640408.

NewZoo (2016). 'Top 100 Countries by Revenue' (16 March). Retrieved from https://newzoo. com/insights/rankings/top-100-countries-by-game-revenues/.

Nieborg, D.B. (2015). 'Crushing Candy: The Free-to-Play Game in Its Connective Commodity Form', *Social Media + Society, 1*(2). doi: 10.1177/2056305115621932.

Taylor, N. (2015). 'Professional Gaming', in R. Mansell *et al.* (eds), *The International Encyclopedia of Digital Communication and Society*. Malden, MA and Oxford: Wiley Blackwell.

Whitson, J. (2012). *Game Design by Numbers: Instrumental Play and the Quantitative shift in the Digital Game Industry* (PhD thesis). Ottowa: Carleton University.

Winseck, D. & Jin, D.Y. (2011). *The Political Economies of Media. The Transformation of the Global Media Industries*. London: Bloomsbury.

32. Reflections on the Shifts and Swerves of the Global Games Industry

Casey O'Donnell

The games industry is only thirty years old and has already undergone major shifts and changes. Console companies once dominated the field, but the rise of apps and games on smartphones has disrupted the industry. Using an ethnographic study among game developers as a yardstick, this chapter discusses what has changed and what has stayed the same in the global games industry over the years.

Introduction

Since 1988, the Game Developers Conference (GDC) in San Francisco is the largest annual gathering of professional video game developers around the world, focusing on learning, inspiration, and networking. The conference attracts around 12,000 professionals. The event includes an expo, networking events, awards shows such as the Independent Games Festival and the Game Developers Choice Awards, and a variety of tutorials, lectures, and roundtables by industry professionals on game-related topics covering programming, design, audio, production, business and management, and visual arts.

There is something about GDC that serves as an interesting touch point for the ebbs and flows of the videogames industry. Does GDC capture all of the diversity and interesting aspects of the global videogames industry? No, certainly not. While people from around the world attend GDC, it remains very US-centric. There are elements that escape coverage or attention and many developers can't afford to attend. In other cases, aspects are specifically not highlighted by choices made by the event's advisory board. But, there is something important about the pilgrimage that so many game developers make each year to Moscone Center in San Francisco. As such, it continues to serve as an interesting index, or insight, into the various shifts and swells that move the videogames industry.

It is because of this I use GDC as a marker of time's passing in the videogames industry, indeed as an annual event that sort of makes sense. But GDC isn't just about the passage of time. Each year at the event there is something(s) that captivates developers' imaginations and is further brought out into the light. The event proves as an interesting and important metric by which to judge my own work on the games industry. Certainly, while doing fieldwork I often find myself at GDC nodding and thinking about how certain presentations or conversations reveal and explore elements that I have already found salient in my conversations with game developers. GDC captures the pulse of videogame developers.

In 2014, I published *Developer's Dilemma. The Secret World of Videogame Creators* (O'Donnell, 2014a). The book was based on ethnographic material gathered from 2005 through 2008, with a kind of particular attention to games industry news from 2008 to 2012 as I worked on the book. It was intended to be both accessible to a broad audience and simultaneously scholarly, though the structure of the book renders it a little bit strange. The simplest version of that structure is that each 'World' within the book corresponds to a chapter. Worlds are divided into four 'Levels', which correspond to a kind of 'section' within a chapter. Worlds also culminate in 'Boss Fights', which are conclusion sections within each chapter. The organization mimics that of the videogame *Super Mario Bros.*

However, that same structure provided the opportunity for each World to represent what I saw as a collection of broad 'systems' that game development work faces or engages with on a regular basis. Each World deployed its own theoretical construct and examined a different aspect of the intersection of work and broader issues in the games industry. This chapter is based off my visits to the GDC starting with my first conference, which was in 2000 when I first attended. I made my trek up to San Jose (where the event began) from La Jolla where I was working as a game developer. At the time, I was working on an early cross-platform 3D audio sound system for a small game development company. In a rather strange turn of events retrospectively, 2000 was the first year the Independent Game Festival (the competition sponsored by GDC) occurred and Vicarious Visions, the game studio that would eventually become my field site for *Developer's Dilemma*, won an award for best game-technology for their game *Terminus*.

In 2000, GDC didn't have anything like its now very visible 'advocacy' track and the International Game Developers Association (IGDA) had a much bigger presence. The IGDA is a professional association for over 12,000 video and computer game developers worldwide. That isn't to say that the IGDA's presence is less now, rather that its role was different then than it is now. 2000 was the beginning of a games industry epoch that ultimately lasted through 2011. It was the decade of the big bad, too-big-to-fail videogames industry. Then 2011 came. In many respects, I look back at 2011 year as a tipping point in the videogames industry. That was the last year that one might conceptualize 'the industry' as a single living breathing system. It was at GDC in 2011 that I realized how much different the next decade was going to be.

2011 marked the last keynote at GDC put on by a giant console company. Up until this point, usually one or more console companies used the event as an opportunity to make large announcements. In 2011, Satoru Iwata, CEO of Nintendo, was on stage introducing the Nintendo 3DS videogame system. During his presentation Iwata spent a significant amount of time lamenting the rise of $0.99 'apps' and games on smart phones and how it was changing the shape of the games industry. He wasn't wrong. Literally at the same time, across the street in the same conference complex, Steve Jobs, the late CEO of Apple, Inc., was touting the upcoming iPad2 and promoting the rapid rise of app sales on the Apple App Store. 2011 was truly the end of the epoch examined in *Developer's Dilemma*. At the time I asked myself, what does this mean for my book, given that at that moment I was still in the process of writing it.

In this chapter, I examine each World within *Developer's Dilemma* and the 'systems' I examined in the book. In each section, I ask if those same systems remain at work within the games industry or if somehow the passage of time and the ever-energetic pace of the videogames industry have rendered them moot.

The worlds of game development

World 1

World 1 was a somewhat strange chapter in *Developer's Dilemma*. Presented as a tutorial, its overarching argument is that the nature of work has been changing in workplaces typical of the 'new economy', such as in the games industry. I argued that gamework mattered because it told us something about the changing nature of work more generally. I still think that is the case, but I'd expand the argument to be quite simply: game development work matters. Not just because it tells us things more generally about work, but because it matters on its own grounds. Game development is important work because game developers touch so many people's lives through their creations.

Which isn't to say that I don't also believe that the videogames industry and its centres of labour can't tell us important things about work. Game development work remains emblematic of all kinds of new economy work: people from a variety of backgrounds, fields, disciplines coming together to construct massively complicated systems that they then put into full view of the world and hope they work long enough to get people's attention or can be fixed quickly enough that they don't lose people too rapidly. I think the games industry does innovate and push the limits of labour in ways that are critically important. This remains the case. But I think it is also imperative to say that the work/craft of game development is worthy of close scholarly attention.

World 2

The second, more substantive chapter of *Developer's Dilemma* was geared toward systems and why game developers spent so much time thinking about them. I mean this in two respects. Game designers and developers literally construct systems – such as game narratives and storyworlds – that players then interact with. At the same time, developers themselves are often exploring and feeling out systems and technologies – such as game engines and software development kits necessary to publish games for specific hardware environments (game consoles, smartphones) – designed by others. Thus, World 2 made the argument that 'underlying systems matter'. In some respects, the whole point of the book was that 'systems matter'.

Now, you have game developers (and scholars) arguing all the time that systems thinking and the underlying systems within games are as important (or more important) than any other aspect of a game – narrative systems being the one often first mentioned. While I'm not going to agree with one side of that debate or the other, I do believe that game developers are now talking about systems as little tiny gods. This changes what 'matters' for making new kinds of games. It isn't enough to simply make the next 3D-Platforming game or 2D-Puzzle game, but to innovate and come up with new kinds or new configurations of systems that surprise users. More must be done to push the kinds of systems sitting 'under the hood' of a game.

Game developers, unlike data scientists or others that attempt to construct systems that resemble aspects of social life, understand and accept that the systems they make are arbitrary, finite, and situated. Game developers will talk about systems and their discursive power at great length, but they're much more modest about those claims than those in other fields. Yet, at the same time, for a community of people that take very seriously the systems they create, they're not very good at observing the broader games industry and understanding their position in it. They are delightfully good at spotting interesting systems in the wild, but less adept at examining the systems in their own back yards. Game developers continue to not turn this critical gaze back on the games industry itself. It is infrequent at best that game developers level their critique of systems at the games industry itself. While it is much simpler to examine the systems designed by other game developers, the same critical and reflective lens can and should be levelled at the very systems of the games industry, but it rarely is.

World 3

World 3 of the book was about 'experimental systems', and how critically important they are for making games. This included the ability to play with systems and feel them out, and how that connects with the tools that game developers use. In gamework, tools shape the kinds of things that are made and co-construct the possibility space. Tools have to provide insights, but they must also allow for noise. Noise is critical to new discoveries.

The game engine Unity literally haunts the chapter on World 3 in *Developer's Dilemma*. Unity is a cross-platform game engine developed by Unity Technologies. Its initial release was in 2005. It quickly became one of the dominant systems on the market with which both mainstream and independent game developers could develop video games and simulations for computers, consoles, and mobile devices. Yet, when my research for the book was concluding in 2008, Unity only had their first GDC booth. Nowadays, Unity is the default software development kit (SDK) for Nintendo's Wii U video game console platform, while its basic free version is used by millions of developers around the world especially for the development of mobile games. Retrospectively, it makes sense that Unity became such a phenomenon. Rather than attempting to be the biggest, baddest, fastest, most photo-realistic game engine, they took a more subtle approach. Unity was made huge by being the first game engine to take to heart the necessity of the asset pipeline, or how to facilitate and streamline getting things into a game.

At the same time, Unity has as much 'voodoo' associated with it as any other kind of tool (Whitson, 2017). Most developers don't understand its underlying core logics. Nor has enough attention been given to its licence agreements and connections with console manufacturers. However, that is precisely what makes it a compelling and interesting tool. The games industry and even Unity still carries with it all kinds of limitations and barriers on how the tool can be used. Just because a game *can* be made with an engine doesn't mean that a person approaching the tools with no background or history of making games can jump in and make a game. The tools themselves have built-in assumptions about how games can and should be made. These are expressed in the very tools and sub-systems used to create these engines.

World 4

World 4 also discussed tools and interactivity in the workplace, focusing on the disconnect between what people think goes into making games and the actual labour that goes into their production. This is still largely the case. The broader public imagination of what goes into a game is quite limited, not unlike other forms of media work (Deuze, 2007). Games and their production are still viewed rather carelessly. Games are 'easy', when in fact they are quite difficult things to produce. The world around you makes a lot more sense when you recognize it as made by other people and the labour that goes into those things. So, while the tools may have made things more accessible on the one hand, we now get to ignore the fact that making games actually takes some expertise. Which is actually what makes the people involved in the production of games all that much more important.

World 5

Crunch, quality of life, and the concept of 'AutoPlay' dominate World 5, which looks at how all of these systems and the culture of game developers results in the rather chaotic world that game developers find themselves working in. AutoPlay is a term coined by Natasha Schüll in reference to how players of gambling machines (many of which now are much closer to videogames than they are to their mechanical drum-spinning predecessors) can produce a kind of engaged disengagement (Schüll, 2012).

Many theorizations around work/play aren't all that productive. The rhetorical slipperiness of the two terms is used to make the argument, rather than by appealing to the words people use to talk about the playful (perhaps fun or perhaps not) work they perform. Despite our theorizing about work/play, it doesn't really help us understand the kind of brutal crunch that even 'indie' or independent game developers put themselves through in order to ship a game (Lipkin, 2013). Nor does it help us understand the current state of the games industry where mid-sized game studios are closing faster than anyone can really understand. Even successful studios are closed in order for creative directors to pursue new personal endeavors. Moderately successful studios are closed because they don't make enough money.

I have long argued that game developers are the lifeblood of the games industry. Every time a studio closes and a developer is faced with moving or finding a new position at another company, a handful will chose instead to work in another industry. These people embody the tacit knowledge of the craft of game development (Westecott, 2013). When they leave, the broader games industry suffers for it. Whether a developer leaves the industry for a less volatile industry or because they no longer want to work the hours demanded, it is a net loss for the institutional memory of the games industry.

I don't believe this has changed in the least. If anything, the games industry now finds itself at a time and place of even greater precarity. Where once indie game developers had alternative platforms like Kongregate or New Grounds to distribute their work (these platforms haven't gone away by any means), indie game developers now find themselves competing with the 800lb gorillas of the AAA games industry for that featured spot on the front page of the game platform Steam, the Apple App Store or the Google Play Store. World 5 remains a testament to the phrase 'the more things change, the more they stay the same'. But this is really where the developer's dilemma, as in the game theory game, continues to play out. Developers need to find ways to resist some of this continued structure.

World 6

Which leads us to World 6, which was about networks that structure how the games industry functions. On the one hand, it can be argued that independent or 'indie' game developers have much greater access to things like software development kits or tools (such as Unity) that allow them to author games for various platforms. On the other hand, developers and studios are still almost completely dependent on digital distributors – such as Apple and its iOS app store, Google Play, and the Microsoft Store (Vogel, 2014). Game designer Greg Costikyan said it best in his 2014 GDC rant, where he talked about the dire world he saw in 2005 and how it was different and not:

> We're faced now with a scary landscape: Essentially monopolistic distribution channels that have total power over what gets distributed, and what gets attention, with the power to demand whatever portion of the consumer dollar they want. (Costikyan, 2016)

As more and more people have access to the tools and technologies needed to make games and a handful of digital distributors and console manufacturers continue to dominate access to the market (as well as setting up specific constraints on what kind of games they allow), working in the global games industry has become quite precarious. This has spillover effects – even game journalism continues to haemorrhage people. Imagine how many people once worked for the authoritative *Game Developer Magazine* (Staff, 2013) or in other areas of the enthusiast press (Hall, 2014). The games industry is just as impenetrable as it used to be, just in different ways. The precarity of game development work remains largely unchanged. Studios still rise and fall rapidly. The use of contract labour over salaried labour has only risen. The need to get 'featured' on an app store is just as important as what was once a deal with a publisher.

It would be naïve to assume that these kinds of network structures of control have magically disappeared. Indie developers themselves have networks that are structured by their own norms and values. There is a symbiotic relationship between 'indie' game developers and 'the games industry' (Whitson, 2013). Perhaps it even makes more sense to consider them part of the same system, albeit with very different sets of drive mechanisms. These kinds of professional networks structure forms of access.

World 7

World 7 is about the underlying logic that operates at a level above developers and ultimately produces their work environment. It was also about disciplining networks and in particular how those networks in the games and software industries are disciplined with things like copyrights, patents, and other ways to control access. Any time we are talking about 'copy protection', we are not just talking about the rights of companies to earn revenue over the titles and products they develop or publish, we should also be talking about production protection. An example is the birth of Digital Rights Management (DRM) to control access and use of digital products (including games, but also online music and video), such as the Nintendo Entertainment System, with its expensive cartridges and lockout chips. The reality is that part of the motivation to design the 10NES chip for DRM purposes was Nintendo's perception of Americans as a bunch of software pirates, and it was also about controlling the videogame marketplace. We need to reframe conversations about production (O'Donnell, 2011). On the one hand, I understand the need that console manufacturers have for control over a platform's products. On the other hand, I want the ability to play too – both as a developer and as a gamer.

DRM and copyright remain important issues to think about and explore. As players begin streaming their gameplay online in the form of Twitch.TV channels and Let's Play Episodes on YouTube, new questions arise. Game publishers revoke the rights of players to use their content, perhaps with good reason, but the issue remains that we must critically examine these systems (Orland, 2017; Robertson, 2017). DRM and jailbreaking of consoles remains illegal, even though phones and other devices can be modified to allow for personalized or customized software (O'Donnell, 2014b). In a world of convergence culture, where most media industries are increasingly looking at their customers as (potential) co-creators of content, it is strange to see that the early pioneering adventures with this in the games industry – like XNA Express for the Xbox 360 (Microsoft, 2006) or Sony's release of development software for the PS Vita (Donovan, 2008) – have albeit vanished from the world of console games. The walled gardens of videogame consoles have only become more entrenched.

To which some might say, 'Fine, let them have their walls...'. But, that's precisely the point. Those walled gardens are what actually kept the prices of games from falling so dramatically. Most games that are allowed within the walls have already proven their ability to make money. The message remains the same: you must already be established as a game developer to play in these spaces. Just because more open distribution channels remain, that doesn't mean that developers can or necessarily will make money in these spaces. Those game developers that do succeed are those that have already had successes. While some of this can be attributed to experience, talent or other elements, many developers are quick to also point out the importance of serendipity and chance.

World 8

World 8 is a chapter in which I argue that games do something different from other forms of media, and thinking with and through games can be a productive practice. In my own words: 'The game of tug-of-war that we play between systems that restrict as we attempt to muddle through them is an opportunity [...]' (O'Donnell, 2014a, p. 251). Games provide us with an opportunity to approach a topic differently. Games kind of argue with us along the way. We get to ask the question: ' Does the games industry, as a game, suck for those that chose to play it?'

It excites me that the kinds of games that developers are making are different now. The medium is evolving and the developers are trying different things. *Papers Please* would never have been a thing in the 2008 games industry. Games wouldn't be in the strangest places that you now find them, such as: science crowdsourcing games like *Fold.It* and *EteRNA* demonstrate that things have changed in the games industry. These games allow for new forms of public participation in science. I see games and developers doing interesting things: looking out at the world and making sense of it through new lenses. If anything, that's what was missing in 2012. I often quip that *Parable of the Polygons* gets everything right (Bhatia, 2014), while *Battlefield Hardline* gets everything wrong (Walker, 2015).

Game developers not only have the ability to address very real social issues, but they have the desire and the platforms through which to distribute these kinds of experiences. The broader game playing and game making community is at a time and space where making games generates new and interesting conversations. It just took some time and gumption for game developers to get there. To which, I return to Greg Costikyan's rant in 2014:

> Games are good. Games are powerful. The best games are worthy of love, and of passion. We must somehow shape a world in which games that are worthy of love and passion can find their audience. We've had this, for a brief few years; we must not let it go (Costikyan, 2016).

Because, if anything, what has changed is that the games industry has undergone a handful of wakeup calls (Alexander, 2014). It has gotten older and it has diversi-fied. The makeup of both who plays games and who makes games has changed dramatically over the years (Deuze, Martin & Allen, 2007; Shaw, 2011, 2015). Of course that doesn't mean that broader geek culture doesn't have its problems that need to be addressed (Salter & Blodgett, 2017). But that's precisely the point. The industry is growing up and it's going to shake some feathers as developers and the industry find their way.

Conclusion

There is a temptation when studying science, technology or culture (or the intersection of them all) to see only the pace of rapid change. Researchers often move from one game, platform or technology to the next rapidly. It makes sense because the pace of technological development itself is rapid. Yet, one of the things that ethnography can help us understand, in its more methodical and slow pace, is how to recognize the persistence of structure. The old saying is 'The more things change, the more they stay the same.' I think this is precisely what makes texts like *Developer's Dilemma* particularly useful. An ethnography of the videogames industry gives us a sense of the structure of the games industry, not just a descriptive text.

Indeed, the videogames industry changes in rapid and interesting ways, but that doesn't mean that insights from the games industry's past aren't relevant to its future. When an industry is only slightly older than thirty years, its recent past matters even more.

Further reading
- Case: Production logics, working conditions, and inequalities in the global games industry – Kerr (p. 413)
- Context: An exploration of the rise of the platforms and the powerful role they have in shaping professional media production in the games industry – Nieborg & Poell (p. 85)
- Contrast: How the working conditions within the media industries are affectively experienced – Cantillon & Baker (p. 287)

References

Alexander, L. (2014). 'Gamers Don't Have to be Your Audience. "Gamers" are over'. Retrieved from https://www.gamasutra.com/view/news/224400/Gamers_dont_have_to_be_your_audience_Gamers_are_over.php.

Bhatia, A. (2014). 'How Small Biases Lead to a Divided World: An Interactive Exploration of Racial Segregation', *Wired* (12 August). Retrieved from https://www.wired.com/2014/12/empzeal-parable-polygons/.

Bycer, J. (2017). 'The Transparency of Game Development'. Retrieved from http://game-wisdom.com/critical/transparency-game-development.

Chess, S., & Shaw, A. (2015). 'A Conspiracy of Fishes, or, How We Learned to Stop Worrying About #GamerGate and Embrace Hegemonic Masculinity', *Journal of Broadcasting & Electronic Media*, *59*(1), 208-220.

Costikyan, G. (2016). '2014 GDC Rant: We Had a Good 10 Years, But the Walls are Closing In'. Retrieved from http://www.gamasutra.com/blogs/GregCostikyan/20140324/213784/2014_GDC_Rant_We_Had_a_Good_10_Years_But_the_Walls_are_Closing_In.php.

Deuze, M. (2007). *Media Work*. Cambridge: Polity Press.

Deuze, M., Martin, C. B., & Allen, C. (2007). 'The Professional Identity of Gameworkers', *Convergence*, *13*(4), 335-353.

Donovan, M. (2008). 'Become a PlayStation Mobile Publisher for Free'. Retrieved from https://blog.eu.playstation.com/2013/05/08/become-a-playstation-mobile-publisher-for-free/.

Hall, C. (2014). 'Old Gaming Magazines Tell the Awkward Tale of an Industry Growing Up'. Retrieved from https://www.polygon.com/2014/9/29/6867993/egm-electronic-gaming-monthly-history-kunzelman.

Lipkin, N. (2013). 'Examining Indie's Independence: The Meaning of 'Indie' Games, the Politics of Production, and Mainstream Cooptation', *Loading...*, *7*(11), 8-24.

Microsoft (2006). 'Microsoft Invites the World to Create its Own Xbox 360 Console Games for the First Time'. Retrieved from http://www.microsoft.com/presspass/press/2006/aug06/08-13XNAGameStudioPR.mspx.

O'Donnell, C. (2014a). *Developer's Dilemma: The Secret World of Videogame Creators*. Cambridge, MA: MIT Press.

O'Donnell, C. (2014b). 'Mixed Messages: The Ambiguity of the MOD Chip and Pirate Cultural Production for the Nintendo DS', *New Media & Society*, *16*(5), 737-752. doi:10.1177/1461444813489509.

O'Donnell, C. (2011). 'The Nintendo Entertainment System and the 10NES Chip: Carving the Videogames industry in Silicon', *Games and Culture*, *6*(1), 83-100.

Orland, K. (2017). 'FireWatch Dev Uses DMCA Against PewDiePie after Streamed Racial Slur'. Retrieved from https://arstechnica.com/gaming/2017/09/firewatch-dev-uses-dmca-against-pewdiepie-after-streamed-racial-slur/.

Robertson, A. (2017, September 12). 'Why was it so Easy to Weaponize Copyright Against PewDiePie?', *The Verge*. Retrieved from https://www.theverge.com/2017/9/12/16287688/pewdiepie-racism-firewatch-campo-santo-dmca-copyright-ban.

Salter, A. & Blodgett, B. (2017). *Toxic Geek Masculinity in Media: Sexism, Trolling, and Identity Policing*. New York: Palgrave Macmillan.

Shaw, A. (2011). 'Do You Identify as Gamer? Gender, Race, Sexuality and Gamer Identity', *New Media & Society*, *14*, 28-44. http://dx.doi.org/10.1177/1461444811410394.

Shaw, A. (2015). *Gaming at the Edge: Sexuality and Gender at the Margins of Gamer Culture*. Minneapolis, MN: University of Minnesota Press.

Schüll, N. D. (2012). *Addiction by Design: Machine Gambling in Las Vegas*. Princeton, NJ: Princeton University Press.

Staff (2013). 'Game Developer Magazine Closing in July 2013'. Retrieved from https://www.gamasutra.com/view/news/190148/Game_Developer_magazine_closing_in_July_2013.php.

Vogel, J. (2014). 'The Indie Bubble is Popping'. Retrieved from http://jeff-vogel.blogspot.com/2014/05/the-indie-bubble-is-popping.html.

Walker, A. (2015). 'Battlefield Hardline Review: Cop Out'. Retrieved from https://www.pastemagazine.com/articles/2015/03/battlefield-hardline-reviewcop-out.html.

Westecott, E. (2013). 'Independent Game Development as Craft', *Loading...*, 7(11). Retrieved from http://journals.sfu.ca/loading/index.php/loading/article/view/124.

Whitson, J. (2013). 'The "Console Ship is Sinking" and What this Means for Indies', *Loading...*, 7(11). Retrieved from http://journals.sfu.ca/loading/index.php/loading/article/view/125.

Whitson, J. (2017). 'Voodoo Software and Boundary Objects in Game Development: How Developers Collaborate and Conflict with Game Engines and Art Tools', *New Media & Society*, 20(7), 2315-2332. Retrieved from http://journals.sagepub.com/doi/abs/10.1177/1461444817715020.

Professions

Journalism

33. 'It Never Stops': The Implicit Norm of Working Long Hours in Entrepreneurial Journalism

Amanda Brouwers and Tamara Witschge

Journalism is a profession in which many different norms and activities converge. A major influence forms the implicit norm of long working hours, which many journalists consider to be a defining feature of journalism. Combining auto-ethnography with interviews with entrepreneurial journalists worldwide, this chapter discusses how this implicit norm is experienced in the everyday practice of entrepreneurial journalism.

Introduction

In this chapter, we explore the ways in which implicit norms affect the conceptualization of 'work' in entrepreneurial journalism. What it means to work in journalism is not simply a sum of activities conducted by journalists, but is rather formed by an interplay between implicit and explicit norms, definitions, everyday activities, emotions and experiences, to name a few of the elements. Here, we highlight a specific aspect of how understandings about work come into being: implicit norms.

Traditional approaches to researching journalism generally regard journalism from a top-down perspective as a coherent set of practices, in which norms govern routines, and routines direct the characteristics of the output (Witschge & Harbers, 2018). This fails to acknowledge the non-coherent and, at times, arbitrary nature of practices, in which strategic claims and everyday practices interact with each other and are not necessarily aligned. Moreover, it foregoes how implicit norms, routines, and tacit knowing inform practices and self-understandings as much as the codified knowledge that is present in journalism.

We focus in particular on the norm that relates to working hours. We do not speak simply about the actual practices – how many hours entrepreneurial journalists actually work on an average day – but rather about the emotional experience and the discourse that exist around work long hours. Starting from auto-ethnographic data from Amanda Brouwers, who works as a startup journalist as well as a PhD researcher, we explore how the norm of working long hours impacts everyday conceptualizations as well as actual practices of work in entrepreneurial journalism.

Amanda, a classically trained, now entrepreneurial journalist, engages with her struggles with working hours through reflections in her daily audio recordings of her practices, discourses, and emotions. These highlight how implicit norms can be located in affect and embodied knowledge, and how long working hours may become a problematic aspect of entrepreneurial journalism. To explore the way in which the idea of long working hours is naturalized, rejected and/or negotiated, we complement the analysis with interview data with entrepreneurial journalists from various countries to provide insight into the discourse on working hours.

With much discussion in the literature and the professional field about the financial viability of journalism, we would like to highlight here the human factor in discussing the sustainability of practices. Stress levels and burnouts are rising in journalism (Reinardy, 2011). We argue that the discourse on long working hours may not only result in stress and burnout and unpleasant working circumstances – all highly important concerns in themselves – but also result in sub-optimal conditions to push for innovative and quality journalism. As we will show here, the concern is not simply that journalists need more time to research, reflect on, and produce their work. The issue is how the expectation that journalists are always 'on the job' impacts not only the practice and output of journalists, but also the way in which journalism is defined, and shapes the conditions in which journalists work.

In the sections below, we first introduce our methodological perspective on this issue, and then start with experiences that come from the individual auto-ethnographic fieldwork. This is followed by the discourse on working hours as expressed in interviews with entrepreneurial journalists around the world that can help frame and explain Amanda's work experience. Lastly, we reflect on the need to counter implicit norms in our understanding of journalism.

Research on implicit norms

In this chapter, we draw on auto-ethnographic data that detail how it feels to encounter normative conceptions of what journalism is and what it is not, and on discourses on working hours expressed by different entrepreneurial journalists from different countries in qualitative in-depth interviews. The research focuses on something that is not necessarily manifest. Rather than being interested in how many hours a journalist works, we are interested in the norm that is implied or made explicit in discourses on and practices related to working hours and working habits. To gauge such a norm sometimes means to read between the lines, but even this approach to discourse analysis does not necessarily provide insight into how such norms are experienced. The interviews provide us insight into that a norm exists, and allows us to delve into what is considered or represented as 'normal'.

The auto-ethnography allows us to discuss how this norm is experienced in the everyday practice of being a journalist.

We aim to provide in-depth understanding of how journalism as a practice is formed with the rise of what has been called 'entrepreneurial journalism' – which we define here as those forms of journalism where journalists are not only responsible for making but also the selling of their output. The changing nature of the newsroom, and rise of new organizational formats including start-up organizations, flex-working spaces, and home working ask us to explore how ideas about work are taking shape. We use a practice theory approach (Schatzki, 2001) to understand the way in which the norms of this emerging practice of entrepreneurial journalism come into being in the complex interplay between the sayings, on the one hand, (what is said to be 'proper' journalism) and the doings of journalism (the everyday activities), on the other.

What makes entrepreneurial journalism as emerging practice particularly interesting is that it brings together norms from two very disparate domains: entrepreneurship, in which arguably innovation is one of the core defining features (Schumpeter, 1934); and journalism, which has grown into a rather homogenous endeavour that is evaluated from strong normative stances (Deuze & Witschge, 2018) in which tradition is hard to counter. The combination of entrepreneurship and journalism can be questioned for many different reasons, among which most prominently the suggestion that journalism cannot be combined with the drive to make money (Stevenson, 2014). Such discourse on the incompatibility of journalistic and entrepreneurial practices not only foregoes the long history of journalism balancing commercial and public interests (Picard, 2008), but also presents journalism and entrepreneurship as if they are internally consistent practices.

Rather than such reduction of the complexities of entrepreneurial journalism, we need approaches that allow us empirical insight into lived experience in all its inconsistency: showing it is a gloriously messy practice in which many different – and at times opposing – norms and activities are combined (Witschge *et al.*, 2018). We find that journalism and entrepreneurship do not necessarily clash in their norms. They also complement, even reinforce each other with regard to certain norms, including the norm of working long hours: you never stop being an entrepreneur, much like you never stop being a journalist. This is at the core of the discourse of our interviewees, and here we critically investigate how this discourse is naturalized, and how the impact of working long hours is denied or compensated.

To access these discourses on working hours, we draw from interviews with 129 entrepreneurial journalists on four continents in the period 2014-2017. They stem from two different projects that consider start-up culture in comparative perspective: the research project 'Beyond Journalism', led by Mark Deuze and Tamara Witschge, and the project 'Entrepreneurship at Work' led by Tamara Witschge. As part of these projects, interviews have been conducted in different countries with freelance journalists and startup journalists, as well as designers and web developers at the journalistic startups where relevant. These semi-structured interviews were conducted using an interview guide that focused on the everyday practices, routines, and experiences of these journalists in relation to their understanding of journalism and its societal role.

Central to our argument here is that we should not only map the discourses, but also examine how these affect everyday practices. The internalization of implicit norms is very hard to access, as it often takes on the form of 'tacit knowing' (Polanyi, 1966). To provide insight into the integration and impact of the norm, we draw on auto-ethnographic data. Amanda co-founded (in November 2016) and runs PodGront, a podcast start-up in the Netherlands (podgront.nl). Adopting an 'enactive' approach to entrepreneurship (Johannisson, 2009), auto-ethnography provides reflections on and insight into the different components that constitute the practice. This includes reflections on: everyday work activities, professional self-understandings, short- and longer-term aims, emotions (excitement and/or anxiety about the creative and precarious process), personal and professional network relations, and material and economic context.

Living the norm of long working hours: Auto-ethnographic reflection

When I, Amanda, started my PhD in February 2016 – and subsequently my activities as an entrepreneurial journalist – my daily audio-reflections quickly revealed a persistent habit of mine: counting hours. If I didn't work – at least – eight hours per day on academic, entrepreneurial or journalistic activities, I would feel incredibly guilty and would strive to make up for those hours another day. Sitting in my office, I would (and sometimes still will) stay put until eight hours were (or are) over, no matter how unproductive I spent this time. Regardless of several signals my body will send me (fatigue, having trouble to think clearly, tired eyes), I feel I need to make the hours of a full-time week – as if it is my duty or my obligation. Even though I know it will perhaps be more productive to rest body and mind, I cannot stop working.

At such moments, I often feel like I'm in conflict with myself. I can reason very clearly why it would be better to focus on productivity rather than on hours – but there's a persistent feeling of guilt that doesn't seem to be convinced by rational arguments. Rather, it seems to follow a tacit norm that a 'real journalist' works long and hard. How did I get here? Let me go back in time, to my days of learning to be a journalist.

Establishing the norm: Journalism education

'Being a journalist is not a nine-to-five job', our lecturer bellowed at the front of the classroom. As he talked about working long, irregular hours in order to fulfil our public duty as journalists, a feeling of pride swelled up in my stomach. I was more convinced than ever that this was the job for me – and that I was going to prove I could handle the irregular and long hours. The fact that not everybody would be able to work these hours made me feel that I, as a journalist, would be special. That we, as journalists, were a special sort of people. In a sense, the long and irregular hours became a badge of honour, which showed everybody that my job was special.

The feeling of pride re-occurred whenever I told my friends I had to get up at 5 am to start work, or when I had to cover an event during the weekend. It seemed to display the commitment that is characteristic to journalism (Reinardy, 2011). These feelings of pride certainly affected practices. It was not uncommon for students to be at the school's newsroom from opening to closing time whenever there were newsroom assignments. I sometimes stayed in the newsroom, even though my work was finished – I didn't dare to leave before anyone else did. I wonder now what I was afraid of. Judgement of lecturers or classmates? Or that leaving earlier would affect my performance? That I must not be doing well enough if I didn't spend the hours? When I didn't put in long hours, it definitely made me feel insecure, like I wasn't completely doing it – journalism – right.

Maintaining the norm: Professional practices

The exact same practices continued after graduation, when I started working as a freelancer for a local newspaper. My job was to respond to what we would call '112 news' (basically all the news coming from the police or fire department). My shift ran from 6.30 am to 3 pm, and I was expected to stay in the newsroom during that time. I noticed other colleagues often stayed in the newsroom when their shift was over, and sometimes heard colleagues complain about co-workers who left the building the minute their shift was over.

Expressions like 'I'm being paid for forty hours, but of course I work more' or 'Well, I don't mind the long hours, hardly notice them, perhaps because I love this job' were not uncommon.

Especially that last expression always stung and still stings: do I not love my job if I don't (always) work long hours? I always felt slightly guilty when I left after my shift ended – even though my brain was fried and I wasn't going to be able to deliver any more productive work. And if I would leave the minute after my shift was over I would do so announcing I had to be somewhere, as if that justified not working (even) longer hours. Even though I was only paid for a fixed number of hours, and though this made me less insecure leaving after they were done, something kept gnawing at me. I wasn't getting it right: somehow, for me too, even though I couldn't uphold it, making long hours was what defines being a journalist. Not doing so made me feel like less of a journalist.

Becoming an entrepreneur, and having my own business, did not ease this norm. If anything, I felt it even more. Being an entrepreneur means that you have no other rules to live by than your own. You set your own goals, determine your own working routine, and report to no one. Except for that internal voice in your mind, that keeps telling you that you should be working, while you are enjoying a walk with your dog, that tells you that being an entrepreneur means that you work around the clock, driven by a sense of responsibility and intrinsic drive to run the business into great success. Again, the signals of my body kept making me doubt my identity, now not only whether I was a 'real' journalist, but also, whether I was a 'real' entrepreneur. I was not living up to my own mental picture of what an entrepreneurial journalist looked (or felt) like.

'Journalism never stops': Journalists' discourse on working hours

Amanda's experience suggests that she has come to identify the long working hours as an integral part of journalism – it even makes her question the extent that she is a 'real' journalist if she doesn't live up to that norm. Even now, being able to define her own working hours, not being held accountable for her journalistic output by colleagues, editors or publishers, she feels (and it really is a bodily experience) she is doing something wrong. From our interviews, it becomes clear that she is not the only one who considers the working hours as a defining feature of journalism. Our research shows that one of the main places that the norms regarding working hours converge in entrepreneurship and journalism, is that both 'never stop'. Not only is this an important element in explaining the long work hours, it also serves as a powerful trope in justifying and naturalizing them.

Journalism is not something you *do*, it's something that you *are*, and as such you cannot turn it on or off – this is the story our interviewees tell us. A recurring answer to our question on when their day starts and ends: 'I don't ever consider my working day finished'. Even if the freelance and start-up journalists are technically not working, or have left the office, they are still on the job:

> I really don't know what free time is. I mean, I never really since I got into journalism, had free time. Even when I was on vacation, I was always writing, it never stopped. It's not something that you stop doing.

Journalism is not something that you ever stop doing, and though this may sound fatalistic, the interviewees are for the most rather chirpy about it, proud even. They love what they're doing, they can't even help doing what they're doing, or so they claim. As a Dutch journalist working in a freelance collective states: 'the biggest problem is that it's so much fun' – she is not able to say no to assignments because she feels 'so excited' about them. The journalists even question if work is really work. Or as someone working at an Alaskan start-up states: 'I wouldn't really consider it work all the time, because I enjoy it'. Another interviewee states: 'I often don't even see it as work. I even wonder then, how it is that I can write invoices for this'. The founder of an American start-up explains:

> [The other founder] and I both agree with this, if we weren't doing this for a living, this is what we would do in our garage at home. So it's sometimes pleasure and work are one and the same. So I think you might call people like us workaholics because we love what we do, we love working. This is relaxing.

When asked what they do in their free time, they respond that their work is what they do as 'leisure'. But the leisure does come at a cost: almost invariably, the interviewees who work 'all the time' explain how they struggle to juggle work and private lives, and feel the pressure of being always on call, even when they like it – you could even wonder whether this is a trap that they are caught in. Explaining how much they like their work, they are reluctant or apologetic to talk about the pressure it brings – particularly in an industry where there is much talk of layoffs and a financial crisis.

And so, many of the interviewees, after sharing their concerns or worries about the working conditions, will emphasize the 'perks' of the job, the upside of having such a flexible work schedule:

> It's nice to have a flexible schedule so I can, I don't have to think of 'ah, I have to be there at eight', just whatever works for me, I know I have to get everything done. So go as hard as you can without killing yourself and having some fun too, having free time as well.

This focus on the pleasurable nature of their work, the gratitude for being able to do what they do, and the upside of being able to determine one's own schedule all work to neutralize the discourse on working hours. When countering a possibly 'negative' or straining issue in everyday life with stressing how positive their working hours are, the interviewees do justify it for themselves, and normalize such working conditions, making critique harder for others – as Amanda experienced.

Working long hours comes with the job, is the argument; it's part of the business, and in particular the owners of startups that we interviewed present this as unavoidable truth about their work. Here, the discourses on entrepreneurship and journalism converge, as neither ever stop:

> I never am not working in my own head, because this is my personal responsibility, nobody feels it the way I do. [...] All day and all night, every minute of my life I worry about those things. I carry the budget in my head. [...] When you're the owner of a business, that's usually the way it is, other people tell me. You never turn it off.

In particular the statement 'that's usually the way it is' is telling here; this disclaimer normalizes feeling stressed, overworked, or simply experiencing the pressure to work long hours. This is not exclusive to the owners of journalistic organizations, as freelancers and other entrepreneurial journalists also talk about the working hours as a given part of the business:

> It's hard to work all the time. But yeah, that's the nature of the job. [...] It's just how the business is wherever you work. So, I just accept that. [...] Obviously I get frustrated when it's like a Saturday night and I have to work all night. But it's a trade-off.

The interviews show how long working hours are accepted as part of the job, that being a journalist is not something that you can do in a nine-to-five job and that it comes with making long hours. An interesting 'cause' that the interviewees identify in this is technology: being always connected, whether through phone or computer, means you can always (be expected to) work, wherever you are. This is also used to 'explain' how, even when they do have what could be considered 'free' time, they are working:

> And when I cook, I'm photographing my food, and when I'm making projects in the house I'm photographing that, because I do a lot of DIY stuff on my blog, so it's like I'm always putting things on Instagram, tweeting things, always reading the news, calling Alaska news, kind of aggregating it. So I'm always doing that kind of stuff in between the other parts of life. So I can't really quantify it. Journalism is a way of seeing the world and I don't think it's something that's confined to hours.

Being so connected to work, and identifying with work to the degree that they do, a recurring theme for the interviewed journalists is that the only way to not work, is to disconnect from technology. As a freelancer explains: It takes a '350 mile bike race through the mountains' where 'there was no machine' to get away from work. Others too talk about 'getting away from the screen'. One business owner explains that every day he goes to the gym and 'usually I don't bring my phone with me.' With his assistant on 'higher alert' during that time, that is 'probably the only time when I am not doing work'. Another owner explains that her only time off is when she goes fishing, twice a year. She calls it her 'dark time': 'Very far away. Eleven hours driving, there is no electricity, there is no WIFI, it's just peace and quiet'. But even when out in the countryside it's difficult not to see 'stories', to disconnect from being a journalist. But being disconnected from technology does create space:

> So I go hiking, and because I do so much outdoors writing every hike is potentially a story, but I don't think about that... Half the time! Half the time I think about that and then half the time I just go, it's gorgeous out here, look sky, eagle, grass, mountain, no internet following me around. That's probably my biggest saving grace.

It is hard work and takes conscious effort *not* to work. Even when they are not working the interviewees explain they still check their email, the news, think of stories. They talk about how hard it is to ensure that their evenings and weekends are not filled with work. They combine jobs, combine busy family lives with demanding professional lives, and find it difficult to differentiate between what they see as free time and as work time. Focusing on the perks of the job, it is as though the interviewees find it hard to really critique and appreciate the difficulties they are experiencing working the long and fragmented hours that they do.

Conclusion

At a symposium in Groningen (Artistic Research in the North, 2017), anthropologist Tim Ingold stated that one of the greater questions academia seeks to answer is 'how to live'. For journalists, given the prevalent role of and identification with their profession, asking how to live, is asking how to work. Here we aim to uphold our scholarly task by showing how the norm regarding working hours impacts everyday experience. The next step would be to consider, on a larger scale, whom this implicit norm excludes. For Amanda and others to get rid of the guilt when not living up to this norm, we may need to go a step further than merely outlining the ideological work of the implicit norm of working long hours. As Bowker and Star state: 'one person's standard is another's confusion and mess' (quoted in Timmermans, 2015, p. 7).

Raising questions regarding this assumption, we need to ask not only as to how this affects the individual journalists' well-being, but also the sustainability, quality and inclusivity of journalism as a whole. Deuze and Witschge (2018) question whether practicing journalism, in its current precarious form, is increasingly reserved to a privileged few. The findings shared here furthermore show that we need to critically examine the ways of working in journalism: to what extent are the norms excluding not only certain people from practising it, but also privileging certain forms of journalism to arise? If we want the stories told in our societies to add to diversity, equality and reflection, to what extent do we need new types of production practices?

Such change will only come about if journalists are willing to be bold and critically interrogate the assumptions they have built up and keep up as central to journalism. Journalism can be slow, it can be quick; journalists can work long hours or short days; they can love their work, or be instrumental about it. The key question is: how can we build such critical reflection into the production process of journalism? We hope that with this contribution we have inspired readers to observe their own work practices critically and consider to what extent these are informed by lofty ideals, unquestioned assumptions or unhelpful external voices. We believe that moving beyond these will ultimately not only result in a better quality of (work) life, but also increase the diversity of journalism practice and output.

Further reading

- Case: How pro bloggers, YouTubers, and Instagram influencers affectively experience the working conditions and labour requirements for 'making it' as an online content creator – Duffy (p. 375)
- Context: An outline of possible media and culture studies perspectives on startups and entrepreneurship – Werning (p. 207)
- Contrast: A guide to the main skills, competences, and challenges involved in transmedia projects in journalism and beyond – Serrano Tellería (p. 453)

Acknowledgements: This chapter is published as part of the project 'Entrepreneurship at Work' funded by the Netherlands Organization for Scientific Research (NWO, number 276-45-003).

References

Deuze, M. & Witschge, T. (2018). 'Beyond Journalism: Theorizing the Transformation of Journalism', *Journalism*, *19*(2), 165-181.

Ingold, T. (2017). *Art, Science and the Meaning of Research*. Presentation during the symposium 'Artistic Research in the North', (November), Groningen, the Netherlands.

Johannisson, B. (2009). 'Towards a Practice Theory of Entrepreneuring', *Small Business Economics, 36*(2), 135-150.

Picard, R.G. (2008). 'The Challenges of Public Functions and Commercialized Media', in D.A. Graber, D. McQuail & P. Norris (eds), *The Politics of News, the News of Politics* (211-229). Washington, DC: CQ Press.

Polanyi, M. (1966). *The Tacit Dimension.* Chicago, IL: The University of Chicago Press.

Reinardy, S. (2011). 'Newspaper Journalism in Crisis: Burnout on the Rise, Eroding Young Journalists' Career Commitment', *Journalism, 12*(1): 33-50.

Schatzki, T.R. (2001). 'Introduction: Practice Research', in T.R. Schatzki, K. Knorr-Cetina & E. von Savigny (eds), *The Practice Turn in Contemporary Theory* (10-23). London: Routledge.

Schumpeter, J.A. (1934). *Theory of Economic Development.* Cambridge, MA: Harvard University Press.

Stevenson, M. (2014). 'Platforms, Actor-Network Theory and Entrepreneurial Journalism', *Web Cultures.*

Timmermans, S. (2015). 'Introduction: Working with Leigh Star', in G.C. Bowker, S. Timmermans, A.A. Clarke & E. Balka (eds), *Boundary Objects and Beyond: Working with Leigh Star* (1-9). Cambridge, MA: MIT Press.

Witschge, T., Anderson, C.W., Hermida, A. & Domingo, D. (2018). 'Dealing with the Mess (We Made): Unraveling Hybridity, Normativity, and Complexity in Journalism Studies', *Journalism.* https://doi.org/10.1177/1464884918760669.

Witschge, T. & Harbers, F. (2018). 'Journalism as Practice', in: Vos, T. (ed.) *Handbooks of Communication Science: Journalism* (101-119). Berlin: De Gruyter Mouton.

34. Transmedia Production: Key Steps in Creating a Storyworld

Ana Serrano Tellería (with Mirjam Prenger)

Transmedia production is on the rise, as journalists and other media makers are starting to experiment and incorporate different media in the context of converging media industries and digitalization. Based on interviews with a host of academics and media professionals, this chapter offers a basic guide to the main skills, competences, and challenges involved in a transmedia project.

Introduction

One of the key ways in which media firms and professionals can approach the convergence of media production and consumption cultures is through telling stories across multiple media. Transmedia production involves the creation of a storyworld employing different media for different parts of the story, each with their own objectives. It means that each part of the story is developed by employing a specific medium most suitable for that part of the narrative. All parts of the story may share some common pattern that unifies the creation of this narrative universe, and in some cases certain pieces of content may even be repeated throughout.

Transmedia is different from crossmedia (a story that runs across different media), and from multimedia (a story that uses different media). It differs from multimedia and crossmedia in that it creates a world, a universe, where the story is constructed like a puzzle of which each part is independent and can be consumed on its own. The audience plays a fundamental role in this construction, having to navigate the storyworld themselves and in doing so participating in the creation of it. Media production and specifically transmedia production requires in-depth reflection about the ecologies and semiotics of each medium as well as their interconnection. In the economy of attention, choosing the best medium for a story, or for a part of the overall story puzzle, demands both.

Media makers started to experiment and incorporate different media in the context of converging media industries (Pavlick & McIntosh, 2013) and the possibilities engendered by digitalization. Storytelling concepts such as multimedia, crossmedia, and transmedia help to explain the transformations in the production dynamics of the industry (Lee & Yong Jin, 2018). In these processes, the role of the audience has increased at different levels, and across different industries (Tosoni *et al.*, 2017; Witschge *et al.*, 2017). Consumers of media today have become producers, constituting and active role and even life in media (Deuze, 2012; Hepp & Krotz, 2014). As media users become more discerning, demanding and media literate (Ouellette & Gray, 2017), there are greater demands on media makers to produce media that are eminently spreadable (Jenkins, Ford & Green, 2013) and overall embody the ideals of an increasingly participatory culture (Jenkins, Ito & boyd, 2016).

Beyond the creative opportunities of new media storytelling genres, all of this also puts pressure on media professionals to accommodate a variety of dynamic developments: changing audience practices, declining traditional business models, a shift toward digital- (and mobile-) first production processes, the dominant role online social networks and platforms play, the role of data analytics in predicting consumer demand, as well the differences between various media ecologies and technological environments (Serrano Tellería, 2016, 2017, 2018). Thus, in terms of individual traits, skills, and mindsets, the future of work across media industries is envisaged in the form of professionals who (alone or in collaboration) are able to monetize content in innovative ways, connect to their publics in new interactive formats, grasps opportunities, and respond to (and shape) their environment.

One way for makers to grasp the fundamental shifts their industry is going through, is by adopting and experimenting with new ways of telling stories within and across multiple media. In this sense, transmedia narratives form an emerging field, a work in progress with enormous potential. In order to capture the various aspects of transmedia production, I conducted interviews with some key academic and media professionals working in the field of transmedia storytelling, asking them to reflect on the state of the art, the opportunities and challenges, and competencies involved. This chapter provides an overview of their views on the necessary skills and competences needed for transmedia storytelling, the best way to create a storyworld, and the role of audience engagement.

Skills and competences

When it comes to multimedia, crossmedia, and transmedia projects, collaboration is paramount. Kevin Moloney, professor of transmedia storytelling at Ball State University's Center for Emerging Media Design and Development, stresses the importance of teamwork:

> One must assemble contributors with the best skills to accomplish the production. It is very difficult to build an effective transmedia story by oneself, even if it is small. The best work comes from a group of people skilled in writing, photography, video, games, interactive systems, and artefact display.

They have to be good storytellers in their respective disciplines. Miriam Hernanz, responsible for the Spanish RTVE.es Lab, points out that it is essential that there should be all types of sensibilities and skills: the more diverse the team (including a good scriptwriter, developer, director, and so on), the richer the final product. The necessary skills for the media workers involved are: being able to collaborate, knowing the people you are (trying) to work with, and an adaptability to different platforms. The award-winning British online journalist Paul Bradshaw also stresses the need for a critical approach, specific media literacy, and being well-versed in the language of digital culture (including visual design, memes, and so on).

It will be important for future media producers to not only know a range of skills, but to also be quick learners and good problem solvers. As Cindy Royal, professor in the School of Journalism and Mass Communication at Texas State University and founder of the Media Innovation Lab, notes:

> They need to be able to adapt to a dynamic environment, so if software or programming languages change, or if another trend comes on the scene (like virtual reality or bots), they will be able to figure out how to make them useful. They also need to deeply understand the nature of the Internet, web and mobile environments, so they will be able to apply strong judgment when making decisions about which medium to use to tell which parts of the story. They have to be strong communicators, both in words and images, and have strong technical inclination.

What is needed is a basic adaptability in the digital environment that enables you to be flexible in learning any new tool, as well as being creative and taking risks. 'I prefer intuition to systematization', says Agustín Alonso, who develops transmedia fiction projects at RTVE, the Spanish public broadcaster. On the basis of his experience with working on various series, Alonso describes how 'no matter how much you have studied, you always proceed blindly'.

Regarding the group of people or team involved, it is important to have a common idea of what the story is about, to get everyone on the team to share the same vision, and to effectively communicate amongst all the members. For that matter, communication is one of the most important skills, says Helena Bengtsson, who worked as editor for data projects at *The Guardian*. When you have to collaborate with people who work in a totally different way from you, conflict is bound to happen. Bengtsson: 'No matter what kind of project you are trying to do, when there are different competences and skills involved, you need to be open and respectful and above all communicate in order for the project to work.'

The set of skills, competences and levels of cooperation needed for a transmedia production can form an obstacle. According to Ismael Nafría, an independent journalist, writer, editor, consultant, and speaker specialized in digital media, the development of multimedia and transmedia projects continues to be a kind of anomaly in a large number of media firms, which he suggests has mainly to do with a lack of skills and resources.

> Many media consider it an excessive luxury to dedicate energy to this type of work and prefer to employ it on projects that require much less investment and that bring a quicker return. In many cases, this arises from the media having an excessively short-term view, in a complicated business environment where what counts before any other type of strategy is obtaining quick advertising incomes.

Nafría also signals a lack of the necessary digital skills in digital teams. 'This is found especially in the case of narrative projects that include interactivity as an essential component. In many newsrooms there are still no professionals trained in this field, which makes it impossible to develop projects.'

How to create a storyworld

When it comes to actually creating a transmedia storyworld, Howard Rheingold, visiting lecturer in new media at Stanford University and lecturer at UC Berkeley, highlights two elements: the storyboard and critical thinking. The storyboard helps to organize the puzzle, the segments and elements of a story, paying special attention to visuals. Regarding critical thinking, Rheingold and his students have developed (and made available online) an in-depth guide to *Concept Mapping & Mindmapping*. Another recommendation arising from his lessons with students is to experiment and work with lots of different web applications (Tumblr, Instagram, and so on) in order to perceive how these environments function, what their affordances are, and how to deploy these usefully in storytelling projects.

But perhaps the biggest critical skill that a transmedia producer needs is to be able to mentally step back from the project far enough to see the whole of the story unfold in the mind's eye, says Kevin Moloney.

> It is like looking at an impressionist painting – seeing from far away reveals the subject, but when we step close we only see the brush strokes. While managing many individual stories in many forms and on many channels, it can be easy to focus too closely on the smaller pieces or on an innovative technology, and then lose track of the greater whole.

A big challenge is mapping out the plot connections, confirms Alexis Weedon, professor at the Research Institute for Media, Art, and Performance at the University of Bedfordshire. 'You need lots of coffee to keep up your concentration and a large space for mapping out the connections between the storylines.' Based on her experience, Weedon lists the following steps for a transmedia production:

- Identify your story – which could involve playing with adaptations or augmentations of an existing story;
- Evolve the characters – develop and elaborate their background story, invent, role play, create visualizations;
- Think about the genre conventions and how the affordances of the technologies may be used to fulfil them – e.g. mystery/crime/thriller stories contain puzzle elements and hidden clues, so perhaps you can 'hide' them in augmented reality;
- When plotting, think about where you want to put in interaction or audience participation. What do they get from participating? When are they 'hooked' (in terms of payment system/time spent/engagement)?;
- Plot and characters come first, then graphic realization. And music comes last.

Transmedia storytelling is a process, not a format, says Nuno Bernardo, an award-winning and Emmy-nominated Portuguese writer, producer and director. 'Start small and let it grow with the audience. Always have an end goal, plan ahead, step by step, but let the audience interfere and adapt accordingly'. From his experience as a professional and from what he has observed in the results of other projects, a transmedia project is difficult to achieve due to its logistics, economics, and time constraints. It is better to perceive transmedia storytelling as an approach in which there is an ideal to aim for, rather than trying to construct the complete product initially. Bernardo stresses that it is mainly the interaction with the audience that will allow the transmedia project to grow.

Audience engagement

Without an audience, transmedia projects are doomed to fail. The major question is therefore how to engage with the audience. Eva Dominguez, a Spanish digital journalist who has worked on a variety of immersive, interactive digital storytelling projects, stresses that the principle mistake observed in transmedia projects is: ignoring the needs of the audience. With respect to designing a project, she gives priority to understanding and studying the audience, even before the topic is selected.

> Understanding the audience entails asking directly, using direct observation of the users' habits and needs. This accentuates the design process and focuses on the service you are providing to the audience, rather than the end-product.

One shouldn't fall in love with the product but with the essence of the service we are providing.

On the user's experience specifically, Dominguez observes how it is particularly important to recognize how for storytellers as well as media users, augmented reality and virtual reality are emergent fields as narrative platforms. This makes it especially important to think carefully about the role of the user in the process.

Kaeti Hinck leads a visual storytelling team at *The Washington Post*. Before that, she was the design director for the American Institute for Nonprofit News, the director of news technology for the nonprofit news organisation *MinnPost*, and the editor and video producer for *Experience Life Magazine*. From her professional background in visual storytelling, multimedia, 3D, and modelling, Hinck underlines the importance of focusing on the story experiences across different platforms. Flexibility is needed, according to Hinck, as well as a deep understanding of what the audience and the story require. Such an understanding can be based on previous experiences and on experiments. It is important to gather information about users' experiences, and to consider how you are building conversation into a project that lives on various platforms.

She explains that a way to detect a potential project is when the narrative can be easily fragmented, split up into constituent parts. Therefore, main competences and skills of media makers are related to understanding what the overall storytelling looks like and how users would interact with it, the ability to craft sharp narratives, and understanding how to present the core components on different platforms. The constraints and affordances of various media (in combination as well as separately) encourage more creative thinking.

The risks to bear in mind may include losing some of your audience when you split content across platforms, which is why it is important to understand who your audience is when going into any project. Therefore, key steps are centered on identifying the potential readers, on creating a profile of the readers who you create the story for, as well as brainstorming and storyboarding how the project will be presented across platforms. Depending on the project, user research may occur as part of the planning process. Newsrooms can also incorporate A/B testing to see how readers interact with projects after publication.

But as Carlos Alberto Scolari, an Argentinian communication researcher and professor at Pompeu Fabra University in Spain, points out, there is a lack of in-depth studies on user experiences which would enable an efficient strategy to engage audiences. He also places emphasis on incorporating the user from the outset, in some cases even involving them in the narrative project's design. In this respect, Scolari observes that 'professionals continue to think in terms of broadcasting', considering the public only after the fact – as a market to send messages to rather than as potential collaborators. The main challenge is to involve different audiences. Thus, an outstanding skill for the contemporary media maker ought to be the ability to identify and relate target audiences with specific platforms. The process should start with analysing the audience and then planning the objectives and strategies that the technology of the platform allows.

One of the other big challenges for a transmedia creator, according to Christy Dena, an Australian writer-designer-director who has worked on award-winning pervasive games, film, digital and theatre projects, is to understand why their readers or viewers jump from one media platform to the next.

> How do you facilitate that movement? Why would they want to continue with your work from the website to the television, or from the newspaper to the web, or from their phone to their desktop computer? What motivates such movement? Not all give this challenge due thought, because they have weighed their focus onto one end of an audience strategy.

Strategy and design is traditionally directed towards making each media platform a unique point-of-entry that is self-contained. The focus has been on audience *acquisition* rather than *retention*. As Dena explains, the greater challenge is that of keeping your audience across media platforms, retaining them. 'To do this, one needs to understand why our audience would want to stay with the work across the so-called friction of media platforms.'

According to Miriam Hernanz from the Spanish RTVE.es Lab, a key challenge involves identifying which of users' needs can be met most effectively, and then to identify what is the best format in which to expand the story. 'Sometimes, we make the mistake of developing content that is not attractive to users because they have no use for it, but which in our opinion as creators of the story is neat. The greatest challenge is therefore to find a balance between making something attractive and innovative that makes narrative sense, and satisfying the needs of the user.'

Conclusion

Multimedia, crossmedia and transmedia storytelling are creative approaches to a media industry that is in the process of concentrating and converging. It is also a recognition of the fact that for most people, media are used in concert, that is: people use multiple media throughout the day. As media are increasingly digital, always-online, and screen-based, the opportunities increase for stories to travel across media, for different media to interconnect, and for interactivity to be part of the storytelling experience.

From the literature and the interviews one can deduct how these types of stories – whether deploying multimedia, crossmedia or fully fledged transmedia modes of production – are still rare, mainly due to a high degree of complexity, the need for diverse, expensive and often rare skillsets and resources, and a traditional outlook of established media firms toward a single medium (such as a newspaper, magazine, television/radio show, mobile app or website).

According to the experts in the genre from academia and the industry around the world there are five key considerations to take into account regarding transmedia productions:

1. study and understand the audience (both for the story as well as segmented across different media and platforms);
2. put together a team of truly diverse talents and skills, all with a passion for transmedia storytelling;
3. invest in understanding the unique affordances of each medium used in the transmedia experience;
4. always test elements of the story to the overall idea(l) of the storyworld;
5. be ambitious regarding the overall concept (the 'heart' of the story), but start small and build out the storyworld gradually and organically – and keep testing whether (parts of) the story still resonate with the audience.

Further reading

– Case: The changes in the global games industry and its different 'worlds' – O'Donnell (p. 427)
– Context: What media innovations are, what is new about them, and what makes them possible – Krumsvik *et al.* (p. 193)
– Contrast: How audience engagement is the fundamental driver of value creation in media companies' business strategies – Chan-Olmsted & Wang (p. 133)

References

Bradshaw, P. (2018). *The Online Journalism Handbook. Skills to Survive and Thrive in the Digital Age.* London & New York: Routledge.

Dena, C. (2009). *Transmedia Practice: Theorising the Practice of Expressing a Fictional World across Distinct Media and Environments* (PhD Thesis). University of Sydney.

Deuze, M. (2012). *Media Life.* Cambridge: Polity Press.

Hepp, A. & Krotz, F. (2014). *Mediatized Worlds. Culture and Society in a Media Age.* Hampshire: Palgrave Macmillan.

Jenkins, H., Ford, S. & Green, J. (2013). *Spreadable Media. Creating Value and Meaning in a Networked Cultured.* New York: New York University Press.

Jenkins, H., Ito, M. & boyd, d. (2016). *Participatory Culture in a Networked Era.* Cambridge: Polity Press.

Lee, M. & Jin, D.Y. (2018). *Understanding the Business of Global Media in the Digital Age.* New York: Routledge.

Moloney, K.T. (2015). *Future of Story: Transmedia Journalism and National Geographic's Future of Food project.* Retrieved from https://search.proquest.com/docview/1728060951.

Ouellette, L. & Gray, J. (2017). *Keywords for Media Studies.* New York: New York University Press.

Pavlik, J.V. & McIntosh, S. (2013). *Converging Media. A New Introduction to Mass Communication.* New York: Oxford University Press.

Phillips, A. (2012). *A Creator's Guide to Transmedia Storytelling. How to Captivate and Engage Audiences Across Multiple Platforms.* New York: McGrawHill.

Rheingold, H. (2002). *Smart Mobs. The Next Social Revolution. Transforming Cultures and Communities in the Age of Instant Access.* Cambridge: Basic Books, Perseus Book Group.

Rheingold, H. (2012). *Net Smart. How to Thrive Online.* Cambridge, MA: MIT Press Group.

Serrano Tellería, A. (2016). 'Transmedia Journalism: Exploring Genres and Interface Design', *Tripodos, 38.*

Serrano Tellería, A. (2017a). 'Transmedia Journalism within Mobile Devices', in J. Canavilhãs, & C. Rodrigues (eds), *Jornalismo móvel: linguagem, géneros e modelos de negócio* (pp. 547-582). Covilhã: Labcom, UBI.

Serrano Tellería, A. (2017b). 'Innovations in Mobile Interface Design: Affordances and Risks', *EPI, El Profesional de la Información, 26*(2).

Serrano Tellería, A. (2017c). 'Journalism, Transmedia and Design Thinking', *Estudos de Jornalismo, 7.*

Serrano-Tellería, A. (2018). 'Users' management of mobile devices and privacy'. *El profesional de la información, 27*(4), 822-829. https://doi.org/10.3145/epi.2018.jul.11.

Tosoni, S., Carpentier, N., Murru,M.F., Kilborn, R., Kramp, L., Kunelius, R., McNicholas, A. et al. (2017). *Present Scenarios of Media Production and Engagement.* Bremen: Edition Lumière.

Witschge, T. & Deuze, M. (2014) 'Passion, Politics and Play in Journalism Start-Ups'. Paper presented at the conference: *Social Media and the Transformation of Public Space*, University of Amsterdam, June.

Witschge, T., Anderson, C.W., Domingo, D. & Hermida, A. (2017). *The SAGE Handbook of Digital Journalism.* London: SAGE Publications.

Conclusion

35. Making Media: Observations and Futures

Henry Jenkins, Elizabeth Saad Corrêa, Anthony Fung,
and Tanja Bosch

What does the future of making media hold? This is the question that we put to four media scholars and keen observers of media industries and production worldwide. We conducted interviews with them on the basis of key questions and insights gained during the compiling of this book. They provide perspectives from North America (Henry Jenkins), Latin America (Elizabeth Saad Corrêa), Southeast Asia (Anthony Fung), and Africa (Tanja Bosch).

Making media: Production

Q1: Considering the various trends and developments shaping media production, we argue that processes of disruption and consolidation co-exist within the media industries when it comes to media production practices. Organizations and firms can choose to experiment and pioneer to develop new products and services, or opt to double down on existing ways of doing things. What key trends do you observe in this context, and what about this trend makes you hopeful about the prospects for media makers?

ELIZABETH SAAD CORRÊA: The co-existence of disrupting processes and the consolidation of existing ones provides balance to media production, considering the constant IT innovations. It is a trend that is almost mandatory within the media industry. The choice between pioneering or just preserving familiar processes depends on how the organization is engaged in an innovative strategic profile. It also depends on different cultural, social, and economic aspects of each media company. Visual/video storytelling and longform journalism using different visual and graphic resources are evolving trends in the Brazilian media industry. We can find interesting examples, such as *UOL Tab*, with a specialized team working on developing longform stories, and *Nexo Jornal* that uses infographics and data journalism to explore news contextualization.

ANTHONY FUNG: I see four possible prospects. First, digitalization. Digital platforms are now 'the media', a new notion that we haven't seen before. Second, under digitalization, cultural production, curation, distribution, and sharing (as these platforms are all social media or carry the function of social media) may be newer concepts offering new opportunities. Third, there are new profit and business models that do not rely heavily on advertising (meaning reducing the role of economic constraints from advertising), but success in the media becomes more dependent on the media users' flow. Fourth, one has to consider the ever-increasing role of policy and policies under which these platforms survive, as they tend to bypass so-called traditional media laws, licensing, ownership regulations, etc.

HENRY JENKINS: It might be interesting to look at the realm of podcasting in this regard. Podcasting starts out, primarily, as a grassroots media innovation, emerging more or less in parallel with blogging, and embraced by many of the same groups. I first became aware of podcasting when stories hit the news of fan podcasts around Harry Potter – in some cases, produced by high-school students in their basements – reaching half a million listeners. Many cite *Serial* (2014–2016) – coming more than a decade later – as a turning point for podcasting in the United States, as National Public Radio's *This American Life* producers, fully professional, released a podcast that reached 40 million downloads during its initial release schedule, and paved the way for much more extensive professional work in this space.

Today, podcasting is a hybrid media space, involving many different kinds of producers. Public radio professionals continue to play crucial roles. So do professionals for other media sectors – *The New York Times, Slate, Vanity Fair*, and other legacy media publishers have used podcasts to showcase their contributors, cross promote their stories, and reach new audiences through branded content. New producers and distributors, such as Gimlet or Radiotopia, have also bonded together to become recognizable brands in the podcast space via cross promotion. Some figures – comedians in particular – have built a following through other media sectors and use their celebrity to draw attention to their podcasts. Cultural institutions, such as The Smithsonian Institute, see producing podcasts as an extension of their commitment to public outreach and education.

These groups typically dominate the charts of the podcasts with the largest, most concentrated listenership. But there is still a much more varied set of producers – religious organizations, activist groups, educational organizations, fan networks, and amateur creators – who produce podcasts with some substantial following, taking advantage of the low costs of production and ease of distribution that the podcast affords.

So, we can see innovation around the edges still, as diverse kinds of media producers (only some of whom would be considered media professionals) produce and distribute content and then consolidate around core producers and distributors who have reputations based on work in more established media sectors. These producers can command greater attention, have more resources, enjoy the benefits of cross-branding, and so forth. We might also consider how the grassroots podcasts serve as a training and recruiting ground for professional media makers, also testing formats, identifying audiences, etc., and we might think about how professionals in other fields – lawyers, doctors, psychologists, academics – use podcasts not to become media professionals, but as an extension of their own professional agendas.

We can also point to consolidation of distribution platforms, with iTunes, say, being a key entry point for people wanting to listen to podcasts and identify new content. Again, there is space for amateurs to share their work, but there are also gatekeeping functions, where the key distributors can cross-list their podcasts and any new entry starts with a strong competitive advantage over producers who lack that degree of professional clout.

I think it is important to see both sides of the story – grassroots producers don't overwhelm the clout of professionals, but professionals have not foreclosed the possibility of grassroots producers identifying and serving a niche community that would be underserved otherwise. A real strength of podcasting, then, is the diversity of perspectives, including significant representation of minority voices, when compared with the more established radio channels.

TANJA BOSCH: In the African context, web technologies have definitely shaped and transformed many aspects of the media production field. The idea of digital disruption is certainly evident in the emergence of a media production field that is characterized by increasing complexity. While podcasting has not taken off to the extent it has in the Global North, there has been a rise of online radio stations, as well as a trend for mainstream radio stations and news outlets to use social media alongside their traditional offerings, so that news and entertainment is no longer presented in a one-dimensional format. This is exciting, because it means that the gap between audiences and media producers begins to close slowly, increasingly as audiences participate in co-creation production processes via their connected mobile devices.

Q2: 'It is cultural distribution, not cultural production, that is the key locus of power and profit', British media studies scholar Nicholas Garnham wrote in 1990. In this light, in what ways have the new digital intermediaries (Google, Facebook, Spotify, etc.) affected the role, position, and power of media professionals within the media industries?

ANTHONY FUNG: Today, Nicholas Garnham's argument is generally correct. After the recent decades of media conglomeration and dominance, there is now an epoch of media platforms. What is different is that most digital platforms don't produce, they just promote and distribute. Whereas in days gone by media did get involved in cultural productions, nowadays various music platforms (e.g. Spotify), video platforms (e.g. YouTube), or social media sites (e.g. Facebook) control what can be seen or heard in public. The revenue-sharing models (between producers and platforms) further weaken the power of producers. For example, in the music arena, it is always music platforms that create the playlist, decide the rankings, and set the music taste and trends.

HENRY JENKINS: I would break Garnham's claim down into 'profit' and 'power'. There is no question that these new digital intermediaries are the ones who have made the greatest profit from digital media production and distribution. For example, Facebook continues to thrive in a news environment where many traditional publications continue to struggle, in part because Facebook bears none of the cost of newsgathering and satisfies a public of highly motivated news consumers who do not seem to want to pay for the content they consume. So, Facebook has every economic advantage over, say, *The Mercury News*, which used to be a preferred news source for many early netizens, but now seems to be gasping for breath as their ad revenue has dried up.

To think about the issue of 'power', we may need to make the distinction we proposed in *Spreadable Media* (2013) between distribution and circulation. Distribution is top-down and corporate controlled, whereas circulation now takes place in a hybrid economy, shaped by decisions made by an aggregate of social media users who want to shape which content 'spreads' across the net and to what groups. This era of spreadable media has 'power' that can be used constructively or destructively. I don't think Facebook, say, would have chosen to support 'fake news' producers over legacy news producers, but the 'fake news' producers in the last election cycle in the US – many of whom are not journalists but *are*, in some sense, professionals, in that they get paid to write and circulate content – knew how to hit the raw nerves of large networks of people in a deeply divided country and thus had an impact on how many understood the terms of the contest. Whether we understood 'fake news' as the product of a Russian effort at cyberterrorism or simply of black market producers of content designed for networked circulation, we can see these producer/distributors as having exercised real 'power' in US politics.

At the same time, we can see many other kinds of content – from home movies to music videos to internet parodies – getting heightened visibility because its content spreads through various networks. And mass media outlets may amplify that content, moving it from niche consumption to mainstream consumption, as they move it from digital circulation to broadcast distribution. Facebook stands to benefit regardless of what content gets spread, but the issue of media power is much more complex than simply assuming that Facebook, like any traditional media producer, 'controls' what we watch.

TANJA BOSCH: There is no doubt that the new digital intermediaries have had an impact on the role, position, and power of media professionals. The work of professional journalists in particular has been impacted by social media. See for example the growth of social media as a newsgathering tool, its potential to engage with the audience in different ways, and its ability to distribute news. Using Twitter for newsgathering also means that audiences play a larger agenda-setting role. And the immediacy of social media places pressures on journalists to accelerate the traditional news production processes.

Despite the growth of citizen journalism via social media, news organizations still remain central as authorities on news. During the widespread student protests of 2015 to 2017 in South Africa, for example, Twitter was widely used to disseminate news about the protests, and Facebook (and Twitter) were used for discussion on the issues. However, research has shown that the Twitter handles of news organizations remained central as the most retweeted, highlighting the notion that audiences still see these organizations as the most authoritative in news dissemination, despite the rise of citizen journalism.

ELIZABETH SAAD CORRÊA: Digital platforms play an important role as distributors of content for journalism and other media, but we must consider the distribution (and algorithmic) rules of each platform. In deciding to participate in this distribution arena, the media and newsroom production processes have to embed the platform logic that influences the content, title, shape, and format of news, and that could change or increase the routine of media work. For the professional media maker, the need emerges for new skills in storytelling, monitoring audiences, knowing a platform's algorithmic rules, etc.

Beyond these new skills, for the media business as a whole, we have the decision linked to how media brands will be (or will be submitted) under third party distribution and audience controls – something that could affect their power, opinion-maker role, and so on and so forth. In Brazil, the major daily newspaper *Folha de S. Paulo* has decided to stay off Facebook and Twitter since March 2018, and to promote its organic growth on the web. It is a bet (quite successful according to its editors) on the strength of the brand beyond platforms.

Making media: Practices

Q3: A number of scholars point out exploitative labour arrangements within the media industries, and how media professionals tend to internalize the pressures and demands of the working environment (for example, by embracing the ideology of 'creativity' and 'passion' as requirements for the job). How can media professionals break through the precarious cycle and reclaim agency?

TANJA BOSCH: This is a tricky question, as these are perennial issues in the industry. There is a great deal of precarity within the news industry, and in addition to exploitative labour arrangements, there are workplace pressures, including: juniorization of the newsroom (as senior colleagues are phased out, often forced into early retirement), sexual harassment of female journalists, brown envelope journalism (a practice whereby money is offered to journalists to have them produce a positive story or kill a negative story), among others.

Perhaps one way for professional media makers to reclaim agency is not to think of their work as merely a 'job', but to consider their relationship to social and community life, and to take seriously a potential role as civic or public workers, to mirror society to help it see its problems, and to promote forms of agency that highlight solutions. Especially regarding journalism, this role would move the profession beyond simply reporting the news.

HENRY JENKINS: I wish I knew the answer to this question. As a faculty member at the University of Southern California Cinema and Communications Schools, I try to advise students entering the creative industries. The reality is that many, if not most of them, do not make it. The environment is harsh to those trying to break into its ranks, even at a time when there is more American television content being produced, circulated, and consumed than at any other time in history. Those who are not struggling to get in are struggling to keep their jobs, struggling to get their content seen, etc. From top to bottom, precarious conditions shape media work.

That said, I always worry about the implication that 'creativity' and 'passion' are simply ideologies constructed to justify underpaying creative workers. What is the alternative? The kinds of now equally precarious manufacturing jobs, which make no such promise, which used to be emblematic of alienated labour? Creative ambitions are what motivate young people to enter the media sector. Those ambitions may or may not be fulfilled. There are more ways to produce and distribute low budget and independent content (if not necessarily to get paid for it). And the reality is often that they will be asked to sell out their creative control for a paycheck.

ANTHONY FUNG: Hardly any producer can break away from media logic. Such logic is omnipotent and is adopted widely in various global industries. In the name of creative industries, global media (including digital platforms) perpetuate their power and, in certain countries, cultural policy also favours their development.

The economics of these media do not trickle down to all levels of labour. Nowadays, the free labour of fans (and media users generally) participates in the distribution and promotion of cultural products, whereas low-wage labour, such as that done by technicians, drives participation online.

ELIZABETH SAAD CORRÊA: The media industries are increasingly using performance parameters common to other industries. It's okay for the business, considering that the competitiveness is increasing as well, but it's not okay for the professionals involved. Requirements to learn and adopt new skills and abilities now seem to be exclusively in the professional's hands, without any investment of the media business in its main asset. The pressure on performance is real (as we can observe in the Brazilian media) – with pressures due to shortage of time, lack of operational resources, and low wages. These are issues that directly impact the emotional and psychological mood of a media worker.

Autonomy could be an interesting path for the professionals. Produce your own career, be your own boss, work in a cooperative format, engage in (collaborative) entrepreneurship. Although these alternatives also bring pressures and stress, they could give the professional some freedom of choice – an important state of mind for producing quality content, especially in journalism. For example, at the University of Sao Paulo, we are working on a report about Brazilian independent journalism initiatives, listing and analysing 49 new initiatives, with different business models and forms of sustainability.

Q4: One could argue that the ongoing transformation of media industries have also increased the possibilities for creative expression and the agency of media makers. Examples are opportunities for media makers to combine multiple media and engage audiences to collaborate in developing multilayered narratives (e.g. transmedia), and media makers collaborating with communities – especially at a local level – to promote and enhance shared storytelling practices. What do you see as the key promises and pitfalls of such possibilities?

ELIZABETH SAAD CORRÊA: The contemporary media ecology imposes a different working process on professionals, no matter what job or organization. On a positive note, we can say that these new skills could offer the market multi-tasking professionals: people who are more connected to the audience needs, closer to the events and the 'real' world, with a wider comprehension of community sense.

On the other hand, we have lost some specialized abilities built on professional experience, including knowledge of specific issues.

It is also important to consider the different possibilities to engage audiences and to bring their interests and local/hyperlocal knowledge to the mainstream via the legacy media brand. *G1* – the digital journalism platform of the Rede Globo multimedia organization – has developed the app *Na Rua*, where common citizens can make videos about issues and needs of their local community and send it to the G1 newsroom. This is a diversification trend for contemporary newsrooms.

TANJA BOSCH: The opportunities offered by the new media working environment definitely places more pressure on media workers to be generalists rather than specialists. For example, the ordinary journalist, armed with a smartphone or tablet, has to record audio, video, write text, take photographs, and Tweet the story, all at the same time! This is exciting for audiences who are already primed to expect this kind of transmedia content, and there is the potential to attract youth audiences to traditional news content or outlets.

One potential challenge is the possibility that this type of content blurs genres and results in a blurring of the lines between entertainment and hard news. One example of this in the South African context is the growth of tabloid newspapers, which enjoy higher circulation figures compared to mainstream print media, which are on the decline. The tabloid *The Daily Sun*, for example, is South Africa's largest newspaper. Moreover, there has been a critique of the tabloidization of mainstream news outlets as they blur the lines between entertainment and hard news in order to attract larger audiences. These mainstream news outlets have tended to increase a style of reporting that focuses on celebrity news and sensationalism.

ANTHONY FUNG: Creative expression is everywhere with the new global digital platforms. The expression is also not limited to political rights or freedom of speech. I would assume that new media industries include and distribute a combination of different cultural products, from games to news. If there is expression, it could include consumer rights or identity formation, etc. Of course, such expression is still curtailed by the boundaries set by these global media as well as national governments. The point is that, given the omnipotence of digital media across the globe, there is still possibility for creativity in small 'local sites', in a Foucauldian sense.

HENRY JENKINS: Let me focus on transmedia storytelling, since this is where I have done the most work around this topic. We might identify a range of different kinds of creative workers involved in transmedia production. First, we might look at independent artists who are part of the so-called East Coast transmedia movement. Here, we might look at something like the *Lizzie Bennett Diaries*, which translated

Pride and Prejudice into a story told primarily through YouTube videos and social media posts. This was a group of independent artists working with a high degree of creative freedom but with little funding and most had to maintain a day job to support their efforts.

Second, we might point to creative workers in the advertising industry who developed transmedia content as an extension of their efforts to promote the interests of their sponsors. A company like Campfire Media works for a mix of product and content producers, marketing everything from automobiles to cult HBO dramas. They are highly innovative, their reputation allows them to push their sponsors in new directions, and, over time, they develop new strategies for content production and distribution. But, it is still work for hire.

Third, we might look at the major franchises – such as Marvel or *Star Wars* – where the creative professional works at managing a big flagship upon which the fortunes of a major studio may rest. In both of those examples, Disney controls what gets done with the content. There is room for some creative experimentation – this work can be done imaginatively or formulaically, be done well or badly, etc. – and there can be some recognition for the directors, writers, comic artists, game producers, etc., who do work in that space. Certainly, they reach a larger audience than any of the other groups here. But, they also have much more oversight from people higher up the corporate ladder.

So, transmedia producers are working on the cutting edge of contemporary media storytelling, they get to play with the new toys (such as VR or augmented reality), they get to work with some of the most beloved stories and characters, but there is a balance between access to economic resources, including a reliable paycheck, and creative freedom, which reflects the new realities of media work.

Making media: Professions

Q5: There seems to be an ongoing hybridization of practices and careers that make up formerly distinct professions in the media industries. Journalists combine news work with PR gigs, musicians perform to promote brands, product placement and other forms of commercial sponsorship dilute creative work in film, television, and games. Some argue this trend contributes to an ongoing de-professionalization process. What do you see as the key consequence of this trend, or do you see evidence of developments going in another direction?

ELIZABETH SAAD CORRÊA: I understand that we now have communication professionals in the media industry and no longer specific professions – such as a journalist, librarian, PR person, etc. It is a real trend, or more than a trend: it is a concrete reality in the labour market. Maybe we are losing the investigative character of journalists – that curiosity, such narrative skill – but this is an industry change as a whole. I figure that the only way to preserve the intrinsic character of a particular media profession is via the autonomous path.

HENRY JENKINS: I would draw a distinction between specialization and professionalization. At the USC Cinema School, students often enter with hopes of becoming filmmakers. They leave these days with a much better understanding of how to work across media, because even if they have a relatively specialized set of skills – as a cinematographer, say – they are apt to end up working in film, television, perhaps even virtual reality across the course of their career. They will remain media professionals in all of these contexts, but they would be wise not to define their professional identity around a single medium.

Similarly, the lines between production and promotion, between PR, advertising, and community relations, between print, audio, video, and digital journalism, are breaking down, and it is not unusual for someone to work across those various divides across the course of their career, to be collaborating with others from different media sectors, and yes, sometimes working in unimaginable contexts, where a reporter not only writes for print but does a podcast talking about their beat.

Again, I do not see this as de-professionalization so much as a reconfiguration of the categories that organize professional media-making, just as multidisciplinary or interdisciplinary scholarship remains scholarly even if we are now working across established disciplinary boundaries.

ANTHONY FUNG: Such hybridization of practices and careers is common, but this is not something new. Previously, it happened in the music business. This is not about professionalism; it is about a new cultural form shaped by the blurring of the boundaries between consumers and producers. In fact, it returns to a time before modernization and industrialization when most people (e.g. peasants) would consume what they produce. This occasional skipping of the 'middle person' might be the cultural trend to go. That means everyone can be an expert or professional without the need to be 'recognized' by some hegemonic media.

TANJA BOSCH: Hybridization is a trend across multiple industries, not just journalism, and I see it as a change in the way we view 'work' and not necessarily the de-professionalization of any specific industry or discipline. We should probably also consider the possibility that for a journalist to be involved in multiple arenas, there is a chance that this may actually strengthen their work as a journalist, because they have exposure to a much wider range of social life. Without distinct professions in the media production industries, it means that journalists have access to a wider range of skills, which ideally results in a stronger understanding of macro processes. This, on the whole, is potentially very valuable to how they practice everyday journalism and how they see their role in society.

Q6: Media work is a form of emotional labour (in that professionals have to manage and 'produce' their own emotions effectively in order to make it work in the industry) as well as affective labour (as working in the media tends to be seen as a career driven by personal goals and ideals of self-actualization, and emotions are part of making the work meaningful). How does this tension, in your opinion, influence the professional identity of media professionals?

TANJA BOSCH: The tensions between emotional labour and affective labour are constantly at the centre of media work in general, and journalistic practice in particular. In a transitional democracy like South Africa, journalists are at the heart of stories that involve violence and conflict – community protests, xenophobic violence, deep social inequality and poverty, child rape, etc. – placing a hefty emotional burden on reporters that often goes unrecognized. Moreover, the role of journalists is generally still guided by normative notions of the media as a neutral, supposedly 'unfeeling' Fourth Estate, leaving little room for affective labour.

ELIZABETH SAAD CORRÊA: Nowadays, the emotional tensions particular to media work are even more stressful. It is a double pressure: from the organization and from the self. If you don't reinvent yourself at each market change, you will not survive the next innovation wave. This could have implications for the quality of productions, for complex personal issues, for a continuous search for a stable work status, and especially for the professional's self-image, for example when it comes to maintaining a personal brand and potentially losing status vis-a-vis peers in the industry. Looking at independent media initiatives in Brazil, we find that more than 70 per cent of them are businesses of one or two professionals, and they must include, beyond producing news content, skills of business management, IT issues, HR issues, and financial aspects. All these new and additional issues bring a huge dose of tension.

HENRY JENKINS: One of my current PhD students has been discussing the conflicting narratives that film school instructors tell their students about what it takes to make it in the industry. On the one hand, they are asked to 'tell your story', which is where creative differentiation enters the picture. There's some tension about whether that 'story' needs to be defined in relation to the system of genres that currently shape entertainment or whether it might include original and diverse stories reflecting the life experiences of the creative workers. On the other hand, they tell students to 'master your craft', which involves the discipline to work within industry-proscribed norms and to sublimate one's own creative voice to the needs of a collaborative and often corporately controlled project.

My PhD student is interested in the ways minority students often trip over these conflicting messages, since telling their own stories necessarily requires them to push against the norms of the industry, both in terms of telling stories that may not fit established genre conventions and telling stories that may require innovative forms of expression.

I would also identify a third kind of affective labour – the kind Nancy Baym writes about in her book, *Playing to the Crowd: Musicians, Audiences, and the Intimate Work of Connection* (2018). She's interested in the ways that musical performers, almost without regard to genre, are expected to forge strong, emotional connections with their fans through social media, and that this often takes more time than producing their work. This is another kind of emotional labour – one that does not involve managing or exploiting your own emotions, but rather acting as caregivers in maintaining strong social ties with others.

ANTHONY FUNG: The emotive or affective aspect might be the driving forces of media producers (as fans) who have no hopes of seeking reasonable pay from the media. However, affective labour might have real impacts on those real, material labourers, whose positions might be further threatened or exploited by large corporations.

A good example of this is Tencent in China. It has been one of the largest game companies in the world in terms of revenues. Its social platform, Wechat, with 980 million users, is the most popular social network after Facebook, YouTube, and Whatsapp. It also owns the largest digital music platform – the equivalent of Spotify – and one of the most popular online video channels – the equivalent of YouTube – in China. Besides, it is the largest mobile payment service in the world. It has been integrated into the everyday life of Chinese users – and, increasingly, non-Chinese users – in areas such as social media, gaming, music, entertainment, shopping, payment, and investment, becoming the dominant media corporation in Asia.

However, except for video productions like online drama and reality shows, it only circulates digital content and sets the agendas. From national and provincial governments to music producers or private sellers, they all have to rely on the multiple platforms of Tencent to reach their intended audience. While producers are dependent on this global platform company to reach audiences – and hence have been rendered significantly powerless – Tencent continuously expands its span and influence by having large fan communities and audience bases who are connected and networked by virtue of its social media functions. In other words, with such digital platforms the power of producers is curtailed and the affective labour of audience as fans is exploited for its expansion.

Research and Teaching

Q7: Students reading books like Making Media tend to look for qualifications and qualities that future media makers will need in order to survive and succeed in the coming decades. Production scholars are perfectly positioned to give such advice. However, a case can be made that this would diminish the potential for criticism and critique so fundamental to the role of scholarship vis-à-vis the media industries. What is your position on this issue?

ELIZABETH SAAD CORRÊA: I totally agree! I teach at a public state university. I think that because of our 'social status' it is our duty to teach or inspire criticism and reflexive qualities in our students. But these qualities are not valued by the Brazilian media industry. They need professionals who are able to do more 'machine-style' work, rather than someone who is going to question an editor's demands. The industry prefers to hire a young media worker (or even better: get an intern) from a private school that does not have a critical curriculum. This is a very complex question.

TANJA BOSCH: There is a constant tension between teaching production to students who are hoping to enter the job market when they graduate, and fulfilling the academic role of the university to teach media studies, theory, and research methods. Students don't always see the value of the latter, particularly when they are competing for jobs with graduates from technical schools. There is also pressure on academics to be able to provide training on industry-related skills, and to remain skilled in these areas, even though they are not practitioners (many are former practitioners), as well as to conduct research and produce peer-reviewed outputs. This often results in outsourcing such practical teaching to ad hoc staff, which raises issues about the precarity for these adjunct staff members who don't enjoy the same benefits as permanently employed salaried employees. This question also highlights the fact that students increasingly see the university as playing a role in providing a 'service' or a 'product' as opposed to being a space for the creation and formation of intellectual thought.

ANTHONY FUNG: The scholarship of media studies is always a privileged one; that is, scholars act as objective researchers that study the media phenomenon and even offer criticism and critique. It results in scholarship that espouses models of development on the one hand, and research that focus on media influence on the other. While the former neglects the micro-operation of the media political economy (which scholars generally have little or no knowledge of), the study of the influence of media seems still very inconclusive (for example, regarding the study of effects of violence exposure). Now, with these new media and, in particular, digital media in which the audience's participation is strong, active, and technology-savvy (and where many people probably also produce some of the content), scholars of media studies should find it more accessible to study the media production and distribution of these new audiences. However, the large global media (e.g. digital platforms) are still mysterious 'sites' about which media studies offers little knowledge.

The study of media industries and production remains the most under-studied area in Southeast Asia. This does not mean that there is no study on production; it is just that many production studies that focus on media texts, and the logic, mechanism, and intention of media industries and production are too simplified. The black box of media production is seldom explained. For example, in my current research on the film industry in China, how was a film initially conceived and then financed? How do producers, investors, and directors negotiate in order to produce a version that is ready to be censored? How does the censorship take place and what are the points of negotiation? How do the producers and the crew execute the production on the spot? These are concrete media production mechanisms that are seldom explained and elucidated.

Another example is pop music. Media industries might just be a carrier to promote pop music songs and use them, specifically when it comes to streaming platforms (such as Spotify). How pop music taste and content is conceived by the producers and practitioners of those platforms, and how such content can appear prominently on these platforms (while many others are omitted) remains an understudied area.

HENRY JENKINS: As the young ones say these days, let me call B.S. on this last question. For starters, it underestimates the kind of critique that occurs amongst creative workers or amongst fans of media properties. It imagines a world where those who make media are fully indoctrinated into the logic of the system and those who consume media are brainwashed into being compliant consumers. I get how you can fall into these traps if you come from a purely critical perspective, but as someone who moves fluidly across media workplaces and fan conventions alike, I can tell you that I see heated debates about the nature of media work, including considerations of economics, ethics, ideology, and aesthetics, every bit as sophisticated, if not more so, than what I hear from academics. Further, in opting out of participating in those conversations, academics are opting out of potentially influencing the choices that emerge from those conversations. It's pretty damn hard to speak truth to power when you refuse to even talk with anyone who has the power to act upon your concerns. Finally, the reality is that most of us *do* maintain relations with people who work in the media industries – they are called our alumni (at least if we are successful in doing our jobs).

So, what these academics are really saying is that they refuse to provide education in a form that may have long-term use to their students. I think it is far more important to help students understand how to apply the concepts that emerge from our research in the process of their work within and outside creative industries; to help them to develop ethical impulses, including awareness of the choices they make about how to represent diverse groups, be more inclusive in hiring, dealing fairly with their fans, and so forth.

Given the reality that there are not enough academic jobs for us to simply reproduce ourselves through the training of fellow academics, my ideal is to create hybrid creative workers, who combine the critical judgement we foster in the academy with the pragmatic skills they need to survive in the contemporary media workplace. To me, this is simply an extension of our professional commitment to profess – to share knowledge and insights with a public beyond our own academic institutions.

Author Biographies

Sarah Baker is a cultural sociologist and Professor at Griffith University, Australia. Her books include *Community Custodians of Popular Music's Past: A DIY Approach to Heritage* (2017), *Teaching Youth Studies Through Popular Culture* (with Brady Robards, 2014), and *Creative Labour: Media Work in Three Cultural Industries* (with David Hesmondhalgh, 2011).

Chris Bilton teaches management and marketing in the creative and media industries at the Centre for Cultural and Media Policy Studies, University of Warwick, United Kingdom. His research centres on the relationship between creativity and strategy. He is the author of several articles and books, including *Management and Creativity* (2007), 'Uncreativity: The Dark Side of Creativity' (2015), and *The Disappearing Product* (2017). He is currently working on a book on mapping creativities with Stephen Cummings and dt ogilvie.

Göran Bolin is Professor of Media & Communication Studies at Södertörn University, Stockholm, Sweden. His present research interests focus on the relations between media production and consumption, especially in the wake of digitalization and datafication. Bolin has worked in or headed research projects on violence in the media, youth and cultural production, entertainment television and the relation between production practices and textual expressions, media consumption, and the production of value in cultural industries. His publications include *Value and the Media: Cultural Production and Consumption in Digital Markets* (2011), *Media Generations: Experience, Identity and Mediatised Social Change* (2016), and the edited volume *Cultural Technologies. The Shaping of Culture in Media and Society* (2012).

Tanja Bosch is Associate Professor in Media Studies and Production at the Centre for Film and Media Studies, University of Cape Town, South Africa. She teaches and conducts research in social media, democracy, and politics. Her book, *Broadcasting Democracy* (2018), explores the role of local radio in identity production in South Africa. She is currently conducting research on social media and everyday life in South Africa.

Amanda Brouwers is a PhD candidate at the Department of Journalism and Media Studies, University of Groningen, the Netherlands. Her research is part of the Dutch NWO-funded project 'Entrepreneurship at work'. Her project addresses issues such as tacit knowing, lived experiences of failure, and implicit norms in entrepreneurial journalism. She studies these issues through auto-ethnography:

conducting entrepreneurial journalism and reflecting on the experiences gained. The entrepreneurial venture she set up is a podcast production house called PodGront (Podgront.nl). The aim of PodGront is to find a sustainable business model for podcasting in the Netherlands, and subsequently to investigate how audio can be used beyond the forms in which it is used now.

Zelmarie Cantillon is a Research Fellow at Griffith University, Australia. She is Postdoctoral co-editor of *The Routledge Companion to Popular Music History and Heritage* (2018), author of *Resort Spatiality: Reimaging sites of Mass Tourism* (2019), and has published numerous book chapters and journal articles. Her research focuses on spatiality, tourism, and heritage.

Sylvia Chan-Olmsted is the Director of Media Consumer Research at the University of Florida in the United States. She also teaches brand management, consumer and audience analytics, and media management. Her research expertise includes digital/ mobile media consumption, branding, and strategic management in emerging media/communications industries. Her studies involve audience engagement conceptualization/measurement, development and marketing of mobile media content, cross-platform audience behaviour, and branded content. Recipient of over 20 national and international research awards, she holds the Al and Effie Flanagan Professorship at the University of Florida and is the recipient of the 2014 Award of Honor presented by the *Journal of Media Economics* for scholarly contribution to the field.

Nicole S. Cohen is Assistant Professor at the University of Toronto, Canada. She is the author of the award-winning *Writers' Rights: Freelance Journalism in a Digital Age* (2016) and has published many scholarly and popular media articles on issues of work, labour, and collective organizing in media and cultural industries. She is part of the collaborative international research project Cultural Workers Organize (culturalworkersorganize.org), which examines collective responses to precarity and workers' efforts to make media and cultural work equitable.

David Craig is Clinical Associate Professor at the University of Southern California Annenberg School for Communication and Journalism, United States. He teaches graduate courses in legacy and social media industries, management, and practice in the MA of Communication Management programme. His research with Stuart Cunningham into the emerging creator industry will be published by NYU Press in 2019 as *Social Media Entertainment: The New Intersection of Hollywood and Silicon Valley*, followed by a field-setting anthology on creator studies in 2020. Craig is also a veteran Hollywood producer and cable network programming executive. He has supervised production of more than 30 projects that have garnered over 75 Emmy, Golden Globe, and Peabody nominations. He was also appointed a Peabody Fellow in the Peabody Media Center and teaches and conducts research at Shanghai Jiao Tong University at the Institute of Cultural and Creative Studies.

Mark Deuze is Professor of Media Studies at the University of Amsterdam's Faculty of Humanities in the Netherlands. From 2004 to 2013, he worked at Indiana University's Department of Telecommunications in Bloomington, IN, United States. Publications of his work include over 90 papers in academic journals and nine books, including the monographs *Media Work* (2007) and *Media Life* (2012). He is also the bass player and singer of post-grunge band Skinflower.

Brooke Erin Duffy is Assistant Professor in the Department of Communication at Cornell University in the United States. Her research examines the cultures and political economies of social media, with a focus on gender and creative labour. She is the author of (*Not*) *Getting Paid to Do What You Love: Gender, Social Media, and Aspirational Work* (2017) and *Remake, Remodel: Women's Magazines in the Digital Age* (2013). Her research has been published in such journals as *New Media & Society, the International Journal of Communication, Critical Studies in Media Communication, Communication, Culture & Critique, the International Journal of Cultural Studies, Social Media + Society,* and *The Communication Review*. Her popular writing has appeared in *The Atlantic, Times Higher Education Supplement*, and *Quartz*, among others.

Paul Dwyer is Director of Academic Enterprise for University of Westminster's School of Media Art and Design, United Kingdom, and founder and Director of the Creative Enterprise Centre, which seeks to involve creative businesses in education, enable students to work as freelancers while they study, and helps students start-up new creative businesses or gain their first jobs on graduation. He is course leader of the MA International Media Business, a member of Westminster's CAMRI research group, and author of the book *Understanding Media Production: Theory and Practice* (2018). He has worked for independent TV production companies and the BBC, directing and producing drama, documentary, arts and entertainment, current affairs and news programmes (e.g. *Panorama, Rough Justice, Inside Story*). He was Head of Development for Documentary and Specialist Factual, leading a team of producers developing and pitching new formats, series, and films.

Doris Ruth Eikhof is Deputy Director of the CAMEo Research Institute for Cultural and Media Studies and Associate Professor at the School of Business, University of Leicester, United Kingdom. She has worked extensively on work and employment in the cultural industries, focusing in particular on career management, self-entrepreneurship, and workforce diversity and how they interlink, e.g. with cultural organizations' business models and cultural policy. Since 2009, she has led fourteen funded research projects including a large multi-disciplinary, multi-institutional research consortium for the Digital R&D Fund for Arts and Culture in Scotland funded by the AHRC, Nesta, and Creative Scotland. Further contract research included projects for the British Film Institute, Creative Scotland, and various arts organizations. A former HR officer, she has ample experience in working with practitioners and policymakers.

Paulo Faustino is chairman of the International Media Management Academic Association (IMMAA, immaa.org) and is a researcher at the Faculty of Social Sciences and Humanities of Nova University in Lisbon, Portugal, with research activities at the Centre of Tele-Information of Columbia University, United States. He is co-founder of the MA in Communication and Management of Creative Industries and Professor at the Journalism and Sciences Communication Department at Porto University, as well as co-director, with Terry Flew, of the *Journal of Creative Industries and Cultural Studies* (JOCIS).

Terry Flew is Professor of Media and Communication in the Creative Industries Faculty at the Queensland University of Technology, Brisbane, Australia. He is the author of eleven books, including *Understanding Global Media* (2007), *Politics, Media and Democracy in Australia* (2017), *Global Media and National Policies: The Return of the State* (2016), *Media Economics* (2015), *Global Creative Industries* (2013), and *The Creative Industries, Culture and Policy* (2011). He serves as President of the International Communications Association (ICA) in 2019–20, organizing the 69th ICA Annual Conference in Washington DC in 2019.

Anthony Y.H. Fung is Professor in the School of Journalism and Communication at the Chinese University of Hong Kong. He is also a Professor in the School of Art and Communication under The Recruitment Program of Global Experts at Beijing Normal University at Beijing, China. His research interests and teaching focus on popular culture and cultural studies, popular music, gender and youth identity, cultural industries and policy, and digital media studies. He has published widely in international journals, and authored and edited more than 20 Chinese and English books. Among his books are *Youth Cultures in China* (with Jeroen de Kloet, 2016), *Global Game Industries and Cultural Policy* (2016), and *Hong Kong Game Industry, Cultural Policy and East Asian Rivalry* (2018).

Ilana Gershon is the Ruth N. Hall Professor of Anthropology at Indiana University in the United States, and the author of *Down and Out in the New Economy* (2017),

No Family is an Island (2012), and *The Breakup 2.0* (2010). She studies how people use new media to perform complicated social tasks, such as getting a job or ending a romantic relationship. She also edits books of ethnographic fictions, such as *A World of Work: Imagined Manuals for Real Jobs* (2015), which discuss how to be a journalist in Buryat or a professional wrestler in Mexico.

Jennifer Holt is Associate Professor of Film and Media Studies at the University of California, Santa Barbara, United States. She is the author of *Empires of Entertainment* (2011) and co-editor of *Distribution Revolution* (2014), *Connected Viewing* (2013), and *Media Industries: History, Theory, Method* (2009). Her work has appeared in journals and anthologies including *Cinema Journal, Journal of Information Policy*, and *Signal Traffic: Critical Studies of Media Infrastructures*. She is a former Director of the Carsey-Wolf Center's Media Industries Project, and a co-founder of the *Media Industries Journal*.

Henry Jenkins is the Provost Professor of Communication, Journalism, Cinematic Arts and Education at the University of Southern California in the United States. He is the author and/or editor of numerous books on various aspects of media and popular culture, including *Textual Poachers: Television Fans and Participatory Culture* (2nd edition, 2012), *Convergence Culture: Where Old and New Media Collide* (2006), *Spreadable Media: Creating Meaning and Value in a Networked Culture* (with Sam Ford and Joshua Green, 2013), and *By Any Media Necessary: The New Youth Activism* (with Sangita Shresthova, Liana Gamber-Thompson, Neta Kligler-Vilenchik, and Arely Zimmerman, 2016). He is editing a handbook on the civic imagination and writing a book on 'comics and stuff'. He has written for *Technology Review, Computer Games, Salon*, and *The Huffington Post*.

Sofia Johansson is Senior Lecturer in Media Studies at the University of Södertörn in Stockholm, Sweden. Her research interests cover a wide range of phenomena relating to popular culture and media audiences, and she has published widely on topics such as popular journalism, celebrity culture, and online sociality, with a current interest in the everyday contexts and meanings of music streaming and digital music cultures. Among her books are the co-authored *Media Landscapes and Media Cultures* (2016) and *Streaming Music: Practices, Media, Cultures* (2017).

Aphra Kerr is Senior Lecturer and chair of the MA in Sociology (Internet and Society) at Maynooth University in Ireland. She is chair of the Communication Policy & Technology section of the International Association for Media and Communications Research (IAMCR). Current research interests include production, work and diversity in digital games and data politics. Among her publications are

Global Games: Production, Circulation and Policy in the Networked Era (2017) and she was associate editor of *The International Encyclopaedia of Digital Communication and Society* (2015).

Arne H. Krumsvik is Head of Department at the Department of Media and Communications, University of Oslo, and Professor II at Westerdals Oslo School of Arts, Communication and Technology in Oslo, Norway, as well as Affiliated Researcher at the Media Management and Transformation Centre, Jönköping International Business School, Jönköping University, Sweden. He is co-founder of the Centre for Research on Media Innovations at the University of Oslo and the *Journal of Media Innovations*.

David Lee is Lecturer in Cultural Industries and Communication at the University of Leeds, United Kingdom. His research interests include creative labour, media industries, and television studies. He is the author of *Independent Television in the UK: From Cottage Industry to Big Business* (2018), co-author of *Culture, Economy and Politics: The Case of New Labour* (with David Hesmondhalgh, Kate Oakley, and Melissa Nisbett, 2015), and co-editor of *Advancing Media Production Research* (2016). He has published extensively in refereed journals and his research has been funded by the AHRC and the ESRC.

Amanda D. Lotz is Professor of Television and Media Studies at the Queensland University of Technology's School of Communication and the Digital Media Research Centre (DMRC) in Brisbane, Australia. Before that, she worked at the University of Michigan in Ann Arbor, MI, United States, and she is a fellow at the Peabody Media Center. She is the author, co-author, and editor of books that explore television and media industries, including *We Now Disrupt This Broadcast: How Cable Transformed Television and the Internet Revolutionized It All* (2018), *The Television Will Be Revolutionized* (2nd edition, 2014), and *Portals: A Treatise on Internet-Distributed Television* (2017).

Stevie Marsden is a Research Associate at the CAMEo Research Institute for Cultural and Media Studies, University of Leicester, United Kingdom. Her PhD, 'The Saltire Society Literary Awards, A Cultural History: 1936-2015', was completed in 2016 and is the first comprehensive analysis of the Saltire Society Literary Awards, Scotland's oldest series of book awards. She completed her PhD through an Arts and Humanities Collaborative Doctoral Award and worked alongside the Saltire Society in the administration and development of their awards whilst carrying out her research. Her research interests are situated within the literary economy and contemporary publishing culture, specifically literary award culture, judgement culture, and access and inclusivity within the publishing industry.

Leslie M. Meier is Lecturer in Media and Communication at the University of Leeds, United Kingdom. She is the author of *Popular Music as Promotion: Music and Branding in the Digital Age* (2017). Her research interests include the music industries, promotional media, and consumer culture, and the intersections between them.

Bernard Miège is Emeritus Professor of Information and Communication Sciences at Grenoble Alpes University, France, following Stendhal University Grenoble 3, where he has worked since 1973, after having worked as a researcher at the French Ministry of Culture. He assumed various pedagogical, scientific (he was co-founder and director of the GRESEC research laboratory) and administrative responsibilities (he was president of his university). He is the author of 20 books, several of which have been translated into various languages, as well as many articles. His work covers the following areas: the industrialization of culture, information and communications, the mutations of public space, the expansion of ICTS in societies, and the epistemology of information-communication. He continues his activity within the GRESEC research laboratory and also carries out international scientific cooperations.

Stefania Milan is Associate Professor of New Media and Digital Culture at University of Amsterdam, the Netherlands, Associate Professor II of Media Innovation at the University of Oslo, Norway, and a Research Associate at the Tilburg Institute for Law, Technology and Society, Tilburg University, the Netherlands, the Internet Policy Observatory of Annenberg School of Communication, University of Pennsylvania, United States, and the Center for Center for Media, Data and Society, Central European University, Hungary.

Vincent Mosco is Professor Emeritus of Sociology at Queen's University, Canada, where he held the Canada Research Chair in Communication and Society. He is currently Distinguished Professor of Communication, New Media Centre, Fudan University, Shanghai, China. He is the author or editor of 23 books including *The Digital Sublime* (2004), *The Political Economy of Communication* (2009), and *Becoming Digital: Toward a Post-Internet Society* (2017). His *To the Cloud: Big Data in a Turbulent World* (2014) was named a 2014 Outstanding Academic Title by Choice: Current Reviews for Academic Libraries.

Niamh Ní Bhroin is Postdoctoral Research Fellow at the Department of Media and Communications, University of Oslo, Norway. Her project is titled 'Social Media-Innovation: Exploring the empowerment of digital media users'. She is Board Member of the Centre for Research on Media Innovations at the University of Oslo.

David B. Nieborg is Assistant Professor of Media Studies at the University of Toronto in Canada. His work on the political economy of platforms, the military-entertainment complex, and games journalism has been published in academic outlets such as *New Media & Society*, *Social Media + Society*, *Media, Culture & Society*, and the *European Journal for Cultural Studies*. His current research project concerns app studies, which focuses on app economics, app advertising, and political economic methodology.

Eli Noam has been Professor of Economics and Finance at the Columbia Business School at Columbia University, United States, since 1976 and its Garrett Professor of Public Policy and Business Responsibility. He was appointed by the White House to the President's IT Advisory Committee. Noam is Director of the Columbia Institute for Tele-Information, a research centre focusing on management and policy issues in communications, internet, and media. He has published 30 books and over 400 articles in economics journals, law reviews, and interdisciplinary journals, and is a regular columnist for the *Financial Times*. His books include *Media Ownership and Concentration in America* (2009), *Who Own's the World's Media?* (2015), and *Media and Digital Management* (2018).

Casey O'Donnell is Associate Professor in the Department of Media and Information at Michigan State University, United States. His research examines the creative collaborative work of videogame design and development, exploring the cultural and collaborative dynamics that occur in both professional game organizations and formal and informal independent game development communities. His research has spanned game development companies from the United States to India. His first book, *Developer's Dilemma*, was published by MIT Press in 2014. O'Donnell is an active game developer, releasing *Osy* in 2011, *Against the Gradient* in 2012, *GLITcH* in 2013, and *Kerem B'Yavneh* in 2016. His work has been funded by the National Science Foundation and the National Institute of Health.

Penny O'Donnell is Senior Lecturer in International Media and Journalism at the University of Sydney, Australia. Her research interests include work futures in global journalism, comparative media research, and digital transformation of the Australian media landscape. She is a Chief Investigator on the New Beats Project (newbeatsblog.com), an ARC-funded study of the aftermath of job loss and re-employment in Australian journalism. Internationalization of the project now includes case studies on Canada, Indonesia, and the Netherlands. Recent publications from the project have appeared in the scholarly journals *Journalism Studies*, *Journalism*, *Journalism Practice*, and *Australian Journalism Review*.

Alisa Perren is Associate Professor at the Department of Radio-TV-Film at The University of Texas in Austin, United States. She is co-editor of *Media Industries: History, Theory, and Method* (2009), author of *Indie, Inc.: Miramax and the Transformation of Hollywood in the 1990s* (2012), and co-founder as well as former co-managing editor of the journal *Media Industries*. Her book project *The American Comic Book Industry and Hollywood* (2018) is co-authored with Gregory Steirer for BFI's International Screen Industries series.

Robert G. Picard is a Senior Research Fellow at the Reuters Institute for the Study of Journalism at the University of Oxford, United Kingdom, a Fellow of the Royal Society of Arts, and a Fellow at the Information Society Project at Yale University Law School, United States. He was founding editor of the *Journal of Media Business Studies* and the *Journal of Media Economics*.

Thomas Poell is Senior Lecturer in New Media & Digital Culture and Programme Director of the Research Master Media Studies at the University of Amsterdam in the Netherlands. He has published widely on social media and popular protest in Canada, Egypt, Tunisia, India, and China, as well as on the role of these media in the development of new forms of journalism. His co-authored and co-edited books include *Global Cultures of Contestation* (Palgrave/McMillan, 2017), *The Sage Handbook of Social Media* (Sage, 2018), and *The Platform Society* (Oxford University Press, 2018).

Mirjam Prenger is Assistant Professor at the Department of Media Studies at the University of Amsterdam, the Netherlands, and was Programme Director of the Master Journalism and Media there. She researches the history of media innovation and entrepreneurship, as well as the relationship between journalism and public relations, and has authored, co-authored, and edited books on the state of Dutch journalism, self-censorship, and the history of broadcast journalism in the Netherlands. She has a professional background in journalism.

Sara Rosengren is Professor of Business Administration (Marketing) and holder of the ICA Retailers' Chair in Business Administration, especially Retailing, at Stockholm School of Economics, Sweden. Rosengren's research deals with consumer behaviour, marketing communications, and retailing. She is best known for her research on advertising and her research has been published in academic journals such as the *Journal of Advertising*, *Journal of Advertising Research*, and *Journal of Business Research*.

Elizabeth Saad Corrêa is Full Senior Professor and Research Leader at the School of Communication and Arts, University of São Paulo, Brazil. She is the Coordinator

of the COM+ Research Group on Communication, Media and Digital Journalism at the University of São Paulo and the author and editor of several books on journalism and media strategy.

Ana Serrano Tellería is Associate Professor at the Journalism Faculty of the University of Castilla La Mancha in Spain. Her work focuses on media studies, design, multimedia-transmedia, mobile devices, games, and performing arts. She has done postdoctoral work at LabCom.IFP, University of Beira Interior in Portugal, MESO, University of San Andrés in Argentina, and Northwestern University in the United States. Serrano Tellería is the recipient of research grants from various organizations, including the Spanish Confederation of Young Entrepreneurs, the University of the Basque Country, the Brazilian Ministry of Education, the European Union, and the Marcelino Botin Foundation. She is also a theatre teacher, writer, artist, and performer.

Eugenia Siapera is Associate Professor at the School of Communications, Dublin City University, Ireland. She is the Chair of MA Social Media Communications and Deputy Director of the Institute for Future Media and Journalism. She has published several articles and book chapters on topics connected to new media, journalism, and politics. Her book *Understanding New Media* was published with Sage in its second edition in 2018.

Tanja Storsul is Director of the Institute for Social Research, Oslo, Norway, and a member of the Research Board for the Division of Innovation (Research Council of Norway) and the DG Connect Advisory Forum for Horizon 2020. She was the founding Director of the Centre for Research on Media Innovations (CeRMI) at the University of Oslo, and she is considered to be one of the founders of media innovations studies. Her research interests include changing media structures and how new media technologies challenge the media, the media industry, and media policy.

Dustin Supa serves as Senior Associate Dean and as Associate Professor of Public Relations for the College of Communication at Boston University, United States. His research interests include media relations, corporate advocacy, and the integration of public relations as part of the overall organizational communication matrix. His background includes work in agency, not-for-profit, and government public relations.

Nicolas Suzor is Associate Professor at the Queensland University of Technology, Australia, where he researches the regulation of networked society. He is an ARC DECRA Research Fellow in the Law School at QUT in Brisbane, Australia, and a Chief

Investigator of QUT's Digital Media Research Centre. His research examines the governance of the internet and social networks, the peer economy, digital copyright, and knowledge commons. Suzor is also the Legal Lead of the Creative Commons Australia project and the deputy chair of Digital Rights Watch, an Australian non-profit organization whose mission is to ensure that Australian citizens are equipped, empowered, and enabled to uphold their digital rights. Suzor is the recipient of an Australian Research Council DECRA Fellowship (project number DE160101542).

Mikko Villi is Professor of Journalism at the Department of Language and Communication Studies at the University of Jyväskylä, Finland. His work focuses on the contemporary context for journalism, especially new media platforms and social media. Among his interests are also the study of media organizations and media management, thereby connecting the study of organizational communication with journalism and media studies. He has published in a wide variety of academic journals, such as *Journalism Studies*, *Digital Journalism*, and *The International Journal on Media Management*.

Patrick Vonderau is Professor at the Department of Media Studies at Stockholm University, Sweden. His latest book publications as (co-)author and (co-)editor include *Spotify Teardown: Inside the Black Box of Streaming Music* (2018), *Films that Sell: Moving Pictures and Advertising* (2016), *Behind the Screen: Inside European Production Cultures* (2013), *Moving Data: The iPhone and the Future of Media* (2012), *Films that Work: Industrial Film and the Productivity of Media* (2009), and *The YouTube Reader* (2009). He is on the editorial board of the *Media Industries Journal* and *Montage AV*, the leading German-language journal of film and television studies. He co-founded NECS-European Network for Cinema and Media Studies in 2006.

Rang Wang is a doctoral student specialized in Advertising at the University of Florida, United States. Prior to graduate school, she worked as an Account Executive in advertising agencies in Shanghai, China. Her research interests include consumer engagement, branded content, influencer marketing, and brand-consumer relationship. She tries to create a bridge between the academia and the industry.

Stefan Werning is Associate Professor for New Media and Game Studies at Utrecht University, the Netherlands, where he founded the Utrecht Game Lab (2014) and co-coordinates the graduate programme Game Research. He previously held positions as Assistant Professor for Digital Media at the University of Bayreuth (2009–2014) and at the University of Bonn (2004–2006). While completing his PhD thesis, Werning worked in the digital games industry, most notably at Nintendo

of Europe (2007–2009). Since completing a DAAD-funded visiting scholarship at MIT, he has been a fellow of the Convergence Culture Consortium. He is currently finishing a book on cultural implications of game development tools for the Playful Thinking series at MIT Press.

Dwayne R. Winseck is Professor at the School of Journalism and Communication, with a cross-appointment to the Institute of Political Economy, Carleton University, Ottawa, Canada. His research interests include the political economy of media, internet and telecommunications, media history, and media theory. He is also the Director of the Canadian Media Concentration Research Project. His co-authored book with Robert Pike, *Communication and Empire: Media, Markets and Globalization, 1860–1930* (2007), won the Canadian Communication Association's book-of-the-year prize in 2008. He is also co-editor, with Dal Yong Jin, of *Political Economies of the Media* (2011) and several other edited and sole-authored books.

Tamara Witschge is Associate Professor and Rosalind Franklin Fellow at the Faculty of Arts, University of Groningen, the Netherlands. Her research explores the ways in which cultural, technological, economic and social changes are reconfiguring journalism and other cultural industries, with a particular focus on innovation and entrepreneurship. She is co-editor of the *Sage Handbook of Digital Journalism* (2016) and co-author of *Changing Journalism* (2011) and *Beyond Journalism* (2019).

Lawrie Zion is Professor of Journalism at La Trobe University in Melbourne, Australia, and leads the New Beats Project (newbeatsblog.com), which explores the aftermath of journalist jobs losses. He is a former broadcaster and journalist and the writer of the award-winning 2007 documentary *The Sounds of Aus*, which told the story of the Australian accent. His 2017 book *The Weather Obsession* examined how digital media has changed the way we connect to the weather and climate.

Anna Zoellner is Lecturer in Media Industries at the School of Media and Communication at the University of Leeds, United Kingdom, with a professional background in film and television production. Her research interests lie at the intersection of media industries, media production studies, cultural labour research, and television studies, with a methodological interest in ethnography and internationally comparative research. Her work has been published in edited volumes and peer-reviewed journals including *Mass Communication and Society, Journal for the Study of British Cultures,* and the *Journal of Media Practice*. She is co-editor of *Advancing Media Production Research* (2016).